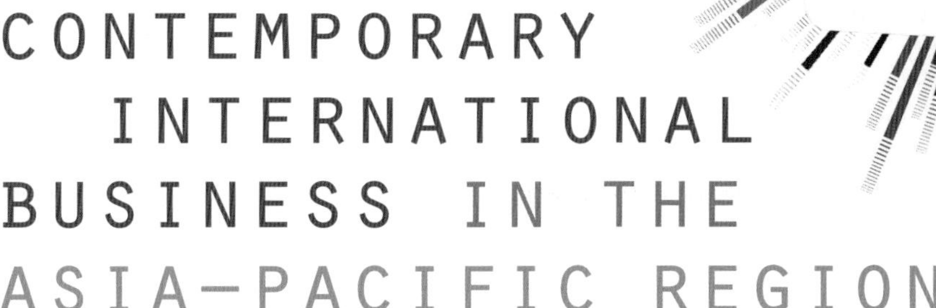

CONTEMPORARY INTERNATIONAL BUSINESS IN THE ASIA–PACIFIC REGION

The increasing dominance of the Asia–Pacific region as a source of international business growth has created a dynamic and complex business environment. For this reason, a sound understanding of regional economies, communities and operational challenges is critical for any international business manager working in a global context.

Presented in a semester-friendly thirteen chapters, with an emphasis on 'doing business in Asia', *Contemporary International Business in the Asia–Pacific Region* addresses topics that are driving international business today. Providing content and research that is accessible to local and international students, this text introduces core business concepts and comprehensively covers a range of key areas, including trade and economic development, dimensions of culture, business planning and strategy development, research and marketing, and employee development in cross-cultural contexts.

Key issues are brought to life by the opening vignettes, as well as numerous regional spotlights and IB masterclass case studies, all of which illustrate the opportunities for and challenges facing Australasian organisations operating across a range of industries. The inclusion of an IB skill builder toolbox supports the development of graduate skills in business report writing and oral communication.

Written by authors with industry experience and academic expertise, *Contemporary International Business in the Asia–Pacific Region* is an essential resource for students of business and management.

Alain Verbeke is Professor of International Business Strategy and holds the McCaig Research Chair in Management at the Haskayne School of Business, University of Calgary.

Robin E. Roberts is an Associate Professor in Agribusiness with the Griffith Asia Institute and an academic with the Griffith Business School, Griffith University.

Deborah Delaney is a Senior Lecturer with the Griffith Asia Institute and an academic with the Griffith Business School, Griffith University.

Peter Zámborský is a Senior Lecturer in the Department of Management and International Business at the University of Auckland.

Peter Enderwick is Professor of International Business in the Department of International Business, Strategy and Entrepreneurship at AUT University.

Swati Nagar is a Lecturer in the Department of International Business, Strategy and Entrepreneurship at AUT University.

CONTEMPORARY INTERNATIONAL BUSINESS IN THE ASIA–PACIFIC REGION

ALAIN VERBEKE, ROBIN E. ROBERTS, DEBORAH DELANEY, PETER ZÁMBORSKÝ, PETER ENDERWICK AND SWATI NAGAR

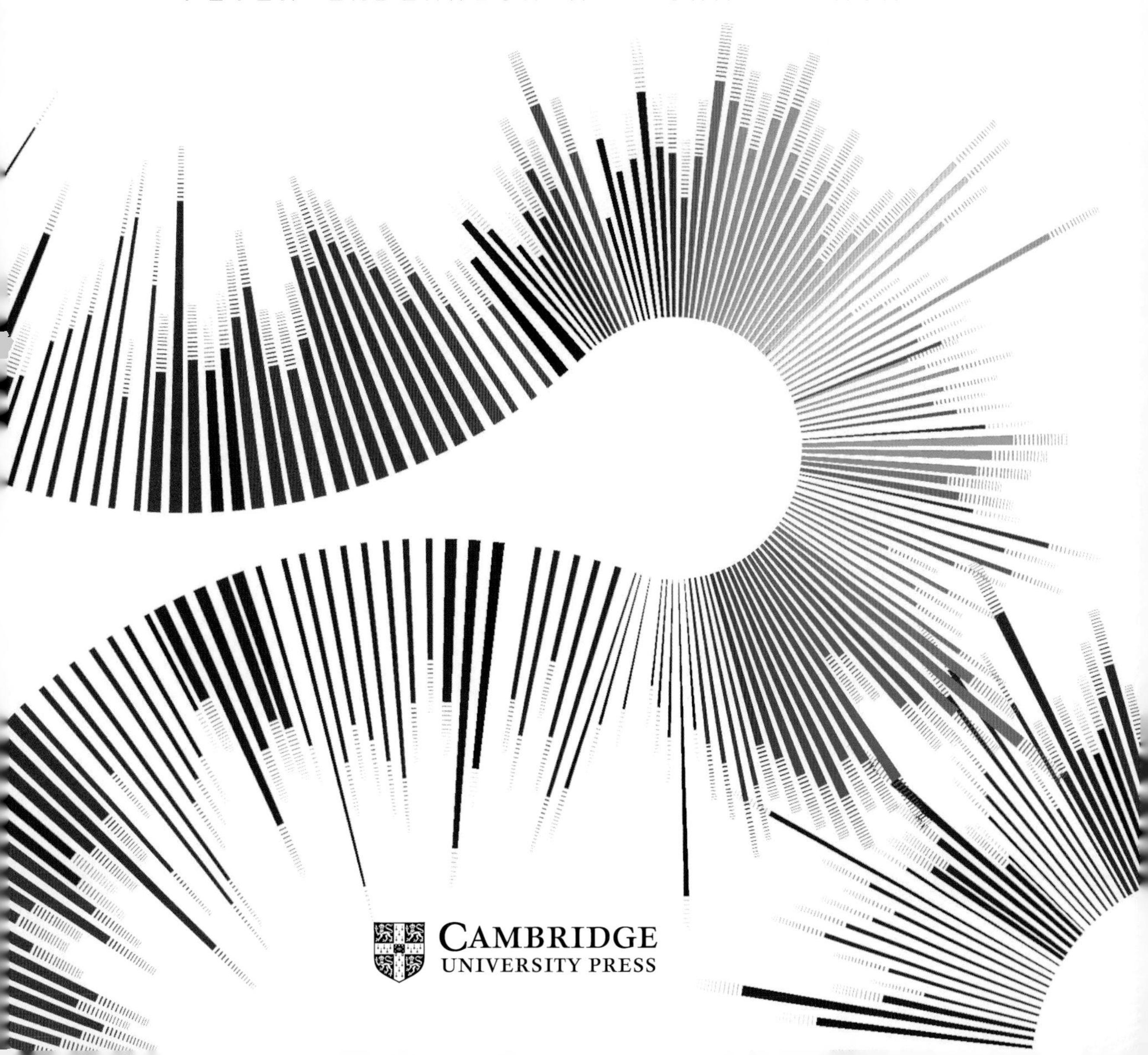

CAMBRIDGE UNIVERSITY PRESS

CAMBRIDGE
UNIVERSITY PRESS

University Printing House, Cambridge CB2 8BS, United Kingdom

One Liberty Plaza, 20th Floor, New York, NY 10006, USA

477 Williamstown Road, Port Melbourne, VIC 3207, Australia

314–321, 3rd Floor, Plot 3, Splendor Forum, Jasola District Centre, New Delhi – 110025, India

79 Anson Road, #06–04/06, Singapore 079906

Cambridge University Press is part of the University of Cambridge.

It furthers the University's mission by disseminating knowledge in the pursuit of education, learning and research at the highest international levels of excellence.

www.cambridge.org
Information on this title: www.cambridge.org/9781108620680

First published 2019

Cover and text designed by Tanya De Silva-McKay, TDSM Design Media
Typeset by Integra Software Services Pvt. Ltd
Printed in Singapore by Markono Print Media Pte Ltd, February 2019

A catalogue record for this publication is available from the British Library

A catalogue record for this book is available from the National Library of Australia

ISBN 978-1-108-62068-0 Paperback

Additional resources for this publication at www.cambridge.edu.au/academic/ibasiapacific

CONTENTS

PART TWO DYNAMICS OF INTERNATIONAL BUSINESS IN THE ASIA-PACIFIC REGION 179

CASE STUDIES

Vignettes

Spotlights

IB masterclasses

SHORTENED FORMS

AANZFTA	ASEAN–Australia–New Zealand Free Trade Agreement
ADB	Asian Development Bank
AEC	ASEAN Economic Community
AFTA	ASEAN Free Trade Agreement
APEC	Asia Pacific Economic Cooperation
APRC	Asia Pacific Research Committee
ASEAN	Association of Southeast Asian Nations
ASX	Australian Securities Exchange
ATO	Australian Tax Office
AWB	Australian Wheat Board
BEM	big emerging market
BOP	balance of payments
BRICS	Brazil, Russia, India, China and South Africa
ChAFTA	China–Australia Free Trade Agreement
CIS	Commonwealth of Independent States
CSR	corporate social responsibility
DFAT	Department of Foreign Affairs and Trade (Australia)
EMNE	emerging market multinational enterprises
EMS	electronics manufacturing services
EU	European Union
FAOSTAT	Food and Agriculture Organization of the United Nations
FDI	foreign direct investment
FMS	flexible manufacturing systems
FSA	firm specific advantage
FTA	free trade agreement
GATT	General Agreement on Trade and Tariffs
GDP	gross domestic product
GRDI	Global Retail Development Index
GST	goods and services tax (Australia)
GVCs	global value chains
HRM	human resource management
IAS	International Accounting Standards
IASB	International Accounting Standards Board
IFRS	International Financial Reporting Standards
IHRM	international human resource management
IMF	International Monetary Fund
IPR	intellectual property rights
JIT	just in time
JVs	joint ventures
KAFTA	Korea–Australia Free Trade Agreement

LAs	locational advantages
M&As	mergers and acquisitions
MAFTA	Malaysia–Australia Free Trade Agreement
MNE	multinational enterprise
OECD	Organization for Economic Co-operation and Development
OPEC	Organization of the Petroleum Exporting Countries
R&D	research and development
ROI	return on investment
ROO	rules of origin
RTAs	regional trade agreements
SME	small- and medium-sized enterprise
TQM	total quality management
TRIPS	Trade-Related Aspects of Intellectual Property Rights
UN	United Nations
UNCTAD	United Nations Conference on Trade and Development
VAT	value added tax (UK)
WB	World Bank
WIPO	World Intellectual Property Organization
WTO	World Trade Organization
WTOI	World Trade Outlook Indicator

ABOUT THE AUTHORS

ALAIN VERBEKE is Professor of International Business Strategy and holds the McCaig Research Chair in Management at the Haskayne School of Business, University of Calgary. He is also the Inaugural Alan M. Rugman Memorial Fellow at the Henley Business School, University of Reading, and a non-resident Senior Research Fellow with the Center for Emerging Market Studies at CEIBS, Shanghai. He serves as the Editor-in-Chief of the *Journal of International Business Studies (JIBS)*, the official journal of the Academy of International Business. He was previously the Director of the MBA program at Solvay Business School, University of Brussels (VUB). He has also been a Visiting Professor at Dalhousie University, the University of Toronto and the Université Catholique de Louvain, as well as an Associate Fellow of Templeton College (University of Oxford). He has been an Academic Associate of the Centre for International Business and Management, Judge Business School, University of Cambridge.

ROBIN E. ROBERTS is an Associate Professor in Agribusiness with the Griffith Asia Institute and an academic with the Griffith Business School. She received her PhD in international business and trade from Griffith University. Robin's expertise is in applied research in the management of global and national consumer brands and products. Her key interests are in mapping export opportunities, value chain research, labelling and packaging, and new product development in the Asia–Pacific region. Robin has proven success in delivering increased business performance through market research, and her understanding and dedicated interest in the South-East Asian region makes her a valuable researcher in the field of international business. Robin took up her current position as an academic with the Griffith Business School, following more than 25 years of industry experience in international trade, commercial research and marketing management with national and international FMCG (fast-moving consumer goods) organisations. Through her industry experience, she has led and collaborated in research teams to successfully launch new products and increase exports for numerous public- and private-sector organisations. Robin is currently involved in a range of international agribusiness research and development projects, and holds a visiting academic position with Shenyang University, China.

DEBORAH DELANEY is a Senior Lecturer with the Griffith Asia Institute and an academic with the Griffith Business School. Following an extensive career as a chartered accountant, she has conducted research in the areas of market and consumer insights and strategies for food products in emerging markets, financial reporting and governance, and in education. Deborah received a PhD from Griffith University in 2010. Through her research, Deborah has established expertise in governance practices with a specific interest in the Asia–Pacific region. Deborah has formal qualifications in financial accounting and is a Fellow of Chartered Accountants Australia and New Zealand. She is currently researching and teaching in the areas of financial reporting and governance, with a focus on the agribusiness sector in Australia and the Asia–Pacific region.

PETER ZÁMBORSKÝ earned his PhD from Brandeis University's International Business School and his master's degree from the London School of Economics. He is a Senior Lecturer in the Department of Management and International Business at the University of Auckland, and an Editorial Review Board member of the International Journal of Emerging Markets. Peter's research focuses on foreign entry mode performance, foreign direct investment spill overs and global innovation. He has published in the areas of international business, management and economics. Peter is the author of two e-textbooks: *International Business and Global Strategy* (bookboon.com) and *Global Strategy: Thriving in a World of Uncertainty* (tophat.com). Prior to his work at the University of Auckland, he was an instructor at Harvard University and worked for the Economist Intelligence Unit in London, United Kingdom.

PETER ENDERWICK is Professor of International Business at AUT University, Auckland, New Zealand. Between 1988 and 2004 he was Professor of International Management at the University of Waikato, Hamilton. He has held visiting positions at the Helsinki School of Economics and Business, Finland, the University of South Australia, Adelaide, Thammasat Business School, Bangkok, and the Centre for International Business, University of Leeds, in the UK. His research interests are emerging markets, global factory systems and transnational crime. He is an editor of *International Business*, Oxford University Press, 2018.

SWATI NAGAR is a Lecturer in the Department of International Business, Strategy and Entrepreneurship, Faculty of Business, Economics and Law at AUT University, New Zealand. Specialising in international business, Swati has over 14 years of academic experience. She currently teaches international business to undergraduate, postgraduate and MBA students at AUT, specialising in business and culture, business in Asia, and international business strategy and management. Swati completed her PhD at AUT in 2015. Her current research interests include the internationalisation of service firms in emerging markets, international construction and labour markets, and outsourcing and corporate governance. She is a member of the Academy of International Business and the Australia and New Zealand International Business Academy.

PREFACE

It is privilege to write this Preface to *Contemporary International Business in the Asia–Pacific Region*. A great team of scholars from Australia and New Zealand, with deep knowledge of managerial practice and academic work in the field, has taken my foundational book, *International Business Strategy*, and transformed it into a pedagogical tool with significant added value for instructors and business students in the Asia–Pacific. This adapted edition is particularly valuable to students enrolled in introductory courses on the international and global business environment.

The book has chapters dedicated to the managerial specificities of the Asia–Pacific region, as well as excellent graduate toolbox resources. The pedagogical approach with introductory vignettes and spotlights in each chapter, some with video links, is particularly useful. The IB masterclass case studies at the end of each chapter are an excellent way to convey advanced knowledge. The usage of eBook tools is also state of the art, and meets the highest business school student expectations.

The main contribution of this text, which is consistent with my original book, is to provide a comprehensive conceptual framework for the managerial understanding of internationally operating firms. Graduates engaged in international business, whether as managers or entrepreneurs, must understand that the global business environment requires more than expertise in functional areas such as finance or marketing. It is important to understand the semi-global or regional environmental parameters that will affect strategic decision-making. Distance still matters when venturing across borders and managing geographically dispersed operations.

I hope that graduates will seize the opportunity provided by this high-quality regional adaptation of my textbook, to equip themselves with the tools needed to respond effectively to the many challenges brought about by the new international business environment. Mastering these tools should ultimately improve international business practice throughout the Asia–Pacific region.

Alain Verbeke
October 2018

PREFACE

Studying international business in the Asia–Pacific region

The objective of this book is to provide a foundation for students regarding the knowledge and skills necessary to develop an understanding of the international business environment in the Asia–Pacific region. The content of this book is designed from the perspective of an international business manager, who is seeking to expand and operate globally, manage risk, and implement a business strategy.

This first chapter introduces the complexities of trade and the issues related to international businesses operating in a global marketplace. The objective of the text is to encourage students to consider beyond the first step of international operations, that of exporting, and consider the amalgamation of factors that underpin successful international operations, including trade, marketing and the integration of strategic business models.

The first studies examining international trade fundamentals and their influence on international business strategy appeared in the early 1980s. The growing economic interdependence between nations, especially the rise of the EU, Japan and the US, drove this focus on understanding international business. Since that time, studies examining the dynamic rise of inter- and intra-regional international business operations of emerging economies in the Asia–Pacific, particularly China and India, have now become a focus for scholars from leading business schools worldwide.

Learning structure for this book

This book is intended to introduce the fundamentals of international business. The content presents the theory and practice of international business to balance conceptual understanding with real-world experience. The planning processes for marketing and operating internationally are complex. The novice international manager will need to understand the broader business environment as it relates to a firm operating globally.

This book presents macro- and micro- environment issues through international business discussions and includes public policy considerations. Part 1 presents the *core concepts* of international business and globalisation. This section describes the operating environment and explores: politics, law and firm specific advantages; economics and the role of regional integration; culture, ethics and the importance of corporate governance; and concludes with international investment theories and practices. Part 2 examines the *dynamics of international business* through market entry and development strategies, and reviews emerging economies in the Asia–Pacific region. Market research stages, including problem recognition, research design and methodology, are stepped through to provide a practical approach to understanding the 'how to' of capturing information needed to inform international business planning and ongoing operations. Part 3 presents the *functional issues* that surround an international business. Foreign currency and international financial management are examined; global markets, sourcing and production are explored; and managing managers in the Asia–Pacific region is discussed. The book concludes with a conversation concerning the ongoing challenges which may affect international business in the Asia–Pacific region. The Appendix

provides an innovative approach by offering a graduate toolbox. Graduates today need a range of skills to connect the knowledge acquired from course work to practical application in the workplace. International business (IB) skill builders are offered as step-by-step and how-to resources to communicate your international business knowledge. This IB skill builder includes guides and frameworks for writing your report and communicating your report.

The overall aim of this text is to provide the academic content required to complete your course, and to inform the next stage of your studies and career with theoretical, policy and strategic characteristics of international business in the Asia–Pacific region.

Robin Roberts
October 2018

ACKNOWLEDGEMENTS

The authors would like to thank Professor Wendy Umberger (University of Adelaide), Dr Peter Ross (Griffith University), the Australian Centre for International Agricultural Research for content contributions in this text, and Pablo Garcia (Director of Xorro Solutions), who provided feedback for the interactive questions for the companion website. We are also grateful to the following academics and industry practitioners who provided thoughtful feedback and helpful suggestions for this text: Professor Leong Liew, Tracey White (Griffith University), Lesley Colvin, Carolyn Burton. Finally, we would like to thank the team at Cambridge University Press for their assistance throughout the preparation of this text.

The authors and Cambridge University Press would like to thank the following for permission to reproduce material in this book.

Text: the Chapter 3 IB masterclass case study is adapted from Ross, P.K. (2014). 'AWB and the Iraqi Oil-for-Food scandal: Just a cost of doing business?'. In Ramburuth, P., Stringer, C. & Serapio, M. (Eds), *Dynamics of International Business, Asia–Pacific Business Cases*. Cambridge University Press: Victoria, Australia, and used by permission of Peter Ross and Cambridge University Press; Spotlight 8.3 is adapted from the research project *RIMS No. 44665 Understanding Vegetable and Broccoli Consumption in Japan*, and used by permission of Griffith University; the Chapter 8 IB masterclass case study is adapted from the research project *RIMS No. 46530 Vietnam Mango Exports to mainland China and Hong Kong*, and used by permission of the University of Adelaide, the Australian Centre for International Agricultural Research and Griffith University; content in Chapter 13 from Khanna, T., Palepu, K.G. & Sinha, J. (2005). Strategies that fit emerging markets. *Harvard Business Review*, 83, 63–76, is © 2006 Harvard Business School Publishing, all rights reserved, and used by permission of HBP.

Figure 3.3, 3.4, 3.5 and **3.6**: courtesy of Silvio Mezzomo, Communications Section, Geoscience Australia. © Commonwealth of Australia (Geoscience Australia) 2019, licensed under CC by 4.0 International Licence, https://creativecommons.org/licenses/by/4.0/; **4.1**: Wikimedia Commons/Chintunglee, Ikea in Tianhe District, Guangzhou, https://commons.wikimedia.org/wiki/File:Ikea_in_Guangzhou_Tianhe.JPG, licensed under CC BY-SA 4.0, https://creativecommons.org/licenses/by-sa/4.0/; **7.1**: © Getty Images/James Leynse/Corbis; **7.6**: by Flikr user Amanda Slater, Jacob's Creek. Vines. Barossa Valley SA, www.flickr.com/photos/pikerslanefarm/3432351656, licensed under CC BY-SA 2.0, https://creativecommons.org/licenses/by-sa/2.0/deed.en; **7.7**: Wikimedia Commons/Land Rover MENA, Jaguar Land Rover press conference, 2014 Paris Motor Show, https://commons.wikimedia.org/wiki/File:Jaguar_Land_Rover_press_conference,_2014_Paris_Motor_Show_07.jpg, licensed under CC BY 2.0, https://creativecommons.org/licenses/by/2.0/deed.en; **9.1**: © Getty Images/ake1150sb; **10.1**: © Getty Images/Fairfax Media, **10.2**: Pixabay/StockSnap; **11.2**: Wikimedia Commons/Diego Delso, Casino Resort MMGM Grand, Macau, https://commons.wikimedia.org/wiki/File:MGM_Grand,_Macao,_2013-08-08,_DD_14.jpg, licensed under CC BY-SA 4.0, https://creativecommons.org/licenses/by-sa/4.0/; **11.4**: © Getty Images/CZQS2000/STS; **11.5**: © Getty Images/Adam Berry.

Image on p. 3: © Getty Images/Photographer is my life; **p. 15**: © Getty Images/AzmanJaka; **p. 21**: © Getty Images/Nikada; **p. 24**: © Getty Images/kosmozoo; **p. 34**: Wikimedia Commons/Norbert Aepli, Switzerland, Geneva Motor Show 2014, retrieved from https://commons.wikimedia.org/wiki/File:2014-03-04_Geneva_Motor_Show_1177.JPG, licensed under CC BY 3.0, https://creativecommons.org/licenses/by/3.0/deed.en; **p. 39**: by Flikr user National Ocean Service, Container Ship, www.flickr.com/photos/usoceangov/5369581593, licensed under CC BY 2.0, https://creativecommons.org/licenses/by/2.0/; **p. 48**: Pxhere **p. 52**: © Getty Images/Maksymka;

p. 57: © Getty Images/d3sign; **p. 74**: by Flikr user dunhilaryu, Starbucks in China, www.flickr.com/photos/dunhillcapina/5513265787, licensed under CC BY 2.0, https://creativecommons.org/licenses/by/2.0/; **p. 85**: Wikimedia Commons/Uvacavmatt at wts wikivoyage; **p. 93**: Pexels/DoDo PHANTHAMALY; **p. 97**: © Getty Images/Narayan Maharjan/NurPhoto; **p. 122**: Wikimedia Commons/Hans Olav Lien, Samsung in SM Aura, Bonifacio Global City, https://commons.wikimedia.org/wiki/File:Samsung_in_SM_Aura,_Bonifacio_Global_City.jpg, licensed under CC BY-SA 3.0, https://creativecommons.org/licenses/by-sa/3.0/deed.en; **p. 128**: Wikimedia Commons/energieexperten, Young palmoil-plantation in East-Malaysia, https://commons.wikimedia.org/wiki/File:Junge_Palmoel-Plantage_in_Ost-Malaysia_Juni_2010_Foto_energie-experten.org.JPG, licensed under CC BY 1.0, https://creativecommons.org/licenses/by/1.0/; **p. 134**: by Flikr user servus, Haze in Kuala Lumpur, https://www.flickr.com/photos/servus/32919747/7, licensed under CC BY-SA 2.0, https://creativecommons.org/licenses/by/2.0/; **p. 141**: © Getty Images/Mick Ryan; **p. 153**: Pixabay/moerschy; **p. 156**: by Flikr user Doug Beckers, Cattle Droving – Upper Dartbrook, Hunter Valley NSW Australia, www.flickr.com/photos/dougbeckers/14594597193, licensed under CC BY-SA 2.0, https://creativecommons.org/licenses/by/2.0/; **p. 159**: Wikimedia Commons/Ogiyoshisan, https://commons.wikimedia.org/wiki/File:Junge_Palmoel-Plantage_in_Ost-Malaysia_Juni_2010_Foto_energie-experten.org.JPG, licensed under CC BY-SA 3.0, https://creativecommons.org/licenses/by-sa/3.0/deed.en; **p. 161**: by Flikr user Steve Jurvetson, www.flickr.com/photos/jurvetson/21359255903, licensed under CC BY-SA 2.0, https://creativecommons.org/licenses/by/2.0/; **p. 175**: Wikimedia Commons/Marc Bryan-Brown, https://commons.wikimedia.org/wiki/File:AIG_Headquarters.jpg, licensed under CC BY-SA 4.0, https://creativecommons.org/licenses/by-sa/4.0/deed.en; **p. 181**: Pexels/ pixabay.com; **p. 186**: © Getty Images/Razvan; **p. 192**: Wikimedia Commons/Dllu, https://commons.wikimedia.org/wiki/File:Self_driving_Uber_prototype_in_San_Francisco.jpg, licensed under CC BY-SA 4.0, https://creativecommons.org/licenses/by-sa/4.0/deed.en; **p. 197**: © Getty Images/lissart; **p. 205**: Wikimedia Commons/Editor182; **p. 211**: by Flickr user Jordan Vuong, Virgin Australia a330-200 short final, www.flickr.com/photos/jordanvuong/8117773852, licensed under CC BY 2.0, https://creativecommons.org/licenses/by/2.0/; **p. 216**: © Getty Images/FangXiaNuo; **p. 223**: © Getty Images/Phillippe Roy; **p. 231**: © Getty Images/Paula Bronstein; **p. 253**: Pexels/pixabay.com; **p. 271**: © Getty Images/Cultura RM Exclusive/Nancy Honey; **p. 280**: © Getty Images/Yuri_Arcurs; **p. 282**: © Getty Images/Yuji Karaki; **p. 300**: © Getty Images/Prasit Rodphan; **p. 315**: © Getty Images/Dilok Klaisataporn; **p. 319**: Wikimedia Commons/Nick-D, The Cloud and Auckland CBD in June 2012, https://commons.wikimedia.org/wiki/File:The_Cloud_and_Auckland_CBD_in_June_2012.jpg, licensed under CC BY-SA 3.0, https://creativecommons.org/licenses/by-sa/3.0/deed.en; **p. 323**: Pixabay/aleksandra-85foto; **p. 331**: © Getty Images/George Build/Pacific Press/LightRocket; **p. 341**: © Getty Images/BJI/Blue Jean Images; **p. 371** and **p. 392**: © Getty Images/Monty Rakusen; **p. 374**: © Getty Images/Hero Images; **p. 377**: © Getty Images/ TVP Inc; **p. 409**: © Getty Images/ROSLAN RAHMAN/AFP; **p. 413**: © Getty Images/FatCamera; **p. 418**: Wikimedia Commons/Eightinc, Nokia Sao Paulo Flagship https://commons.wikimedia.org/wiki/File:Nokia_Sao_Paulo_Flagship.jpg, licensed under CC BY-SA 3.0, https://creativecommons.org/licenses/by-sa/3.0/deed.en; **p. 428**: by Flikr user Oliver Bln, Louis Vuitton, www.flickr.com/photos/63299135@N02/6517140955, licensed under CC BY 2.0, https://creativecommons.org/licenses/by/2.0/; **p. 431** and **439**: © Getty Images/Westend61; **p. 433**: © Getty Images/Image Source; **p. 444**: © Getty Images/Raimon Kataotao/EyeEm.

Every effort has been made to trace and acknowledge copyright. The publisher apologises for any accidental infringement and welcomes information that would redress this situation.

USING YOUR VITALSOURCE EBOOK

Once you have registered your VitalSource access code (see the inside front cover for instructions), you will have access to the enhanced eBook via your VitalSource Bookshelf. The navigation instructions below provide a general overview of the primary features used within this enhanced eBook.

Icons

This icon is used throughout the textbook to indicate the presence of an interactive component in the eBook. A descriptor below indicates the type of content available.

Navigation and search

Move between pages and sections in multiple ways, including via the linked table of contents and the search tool.

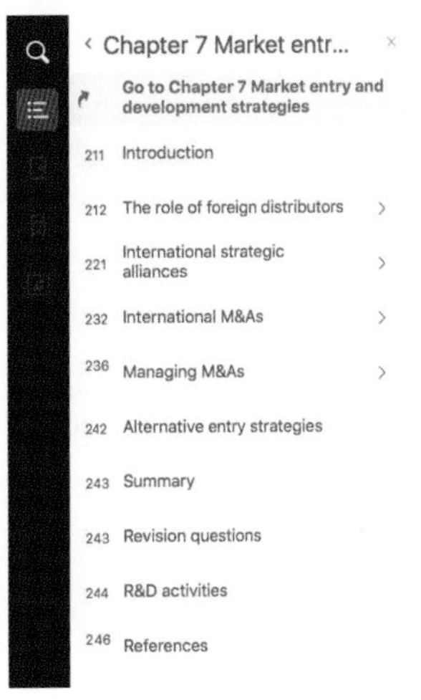

The importance of collabo… change loomed large in the las… sures brought by globalisation… competition. These pressures… Australia operating as an effici… lation creating different haulage and road tran

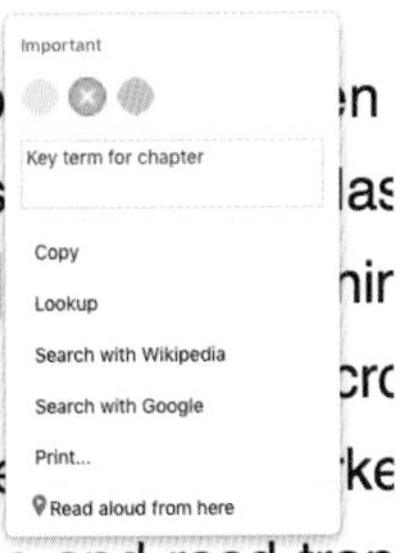

Highlight

Highlight text in your choice of colours with one click. Add notes to highlighted passages.

Key terms

Click on bold terms to display pop-up definitions of key concepts.

marketing as well. For examp…

agent an intermediary that that buys and sells products or services for a commission.

An agent (also known a… seller. The key difference con…

Multiple-choice questions

Open the multiple-choice questions pop-up box, select your choice of correct answers and click 'Check Answers' to assess your results. Note that this box can be moved about the page for you to read text while choosing your responses.

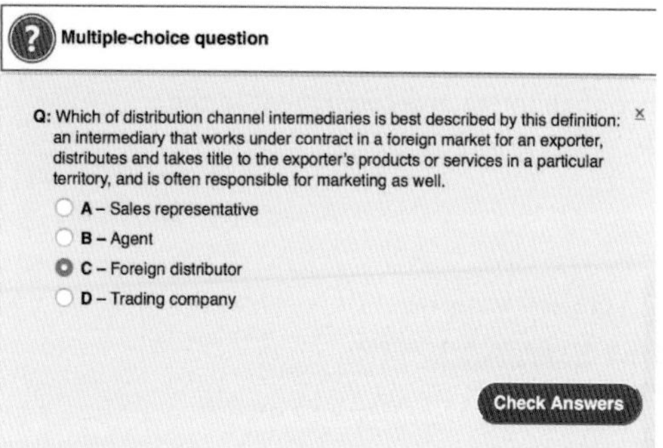

Weblinks

Links to useful websites and resources appear throughout the book to highlight and enhance the topics under discussion.

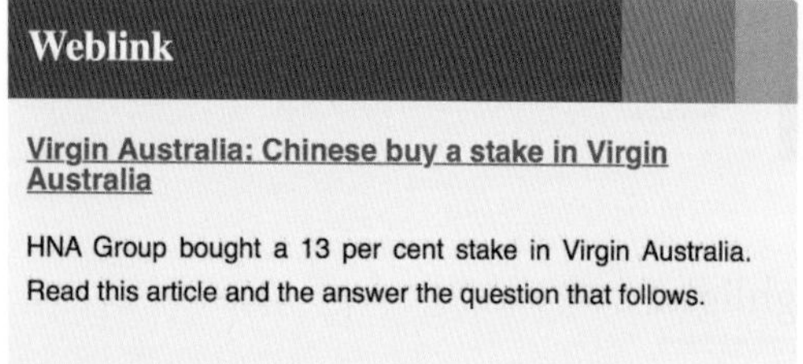

Spotlight questions

Respond to the questions at the end of each Spotlight and use the guided solutions to assess your responses. Note that the solution pop-ups can be moved about the page.

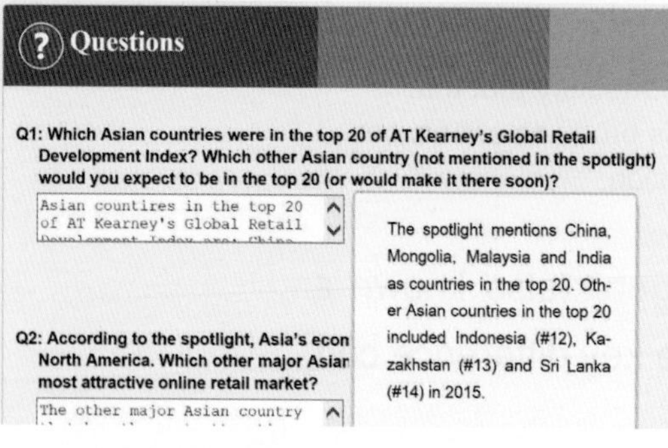

Videos

Informative video links appear throughout the book to highlight and enhance the topics under discussion. Click the icon to access the content.

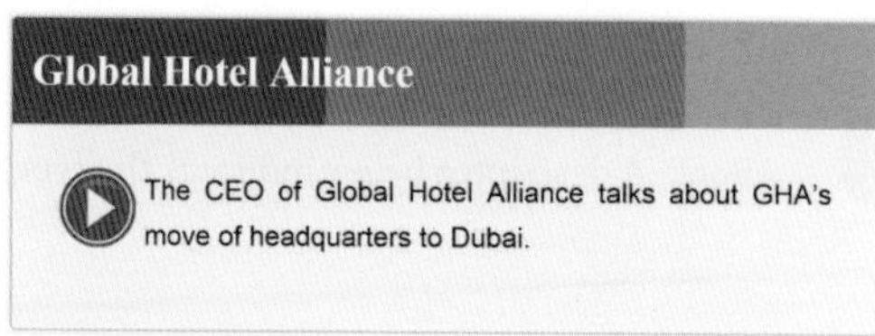

Vignette questions

Read the Vignette, access the resource and then answer the questions that follow. Use the guided solutions to assess your responses. Note that the solution pop-ups can be moved about the page.

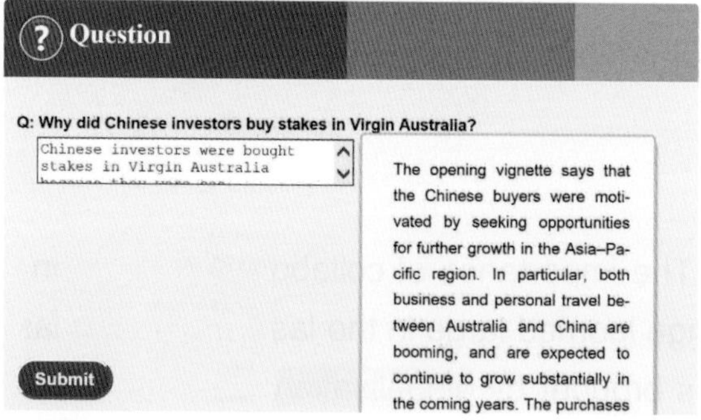

Useful websites

Links to further useful websites can be found at the end of each chapter.

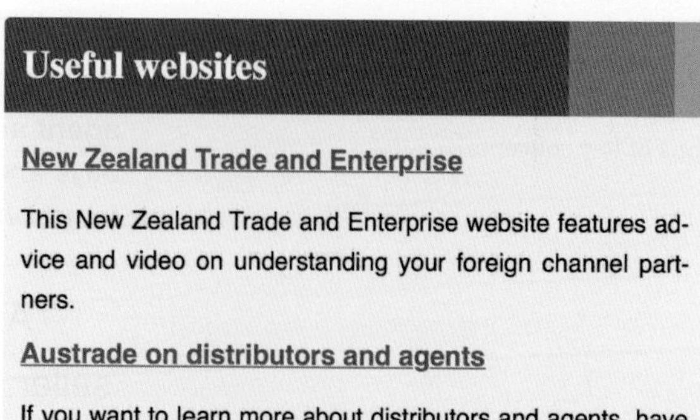

Revision questions

Respond to the revision questions at the end of each chapter and use the guided solutions to assess your responses. Note that the solution pop-ups can be moved about the page.

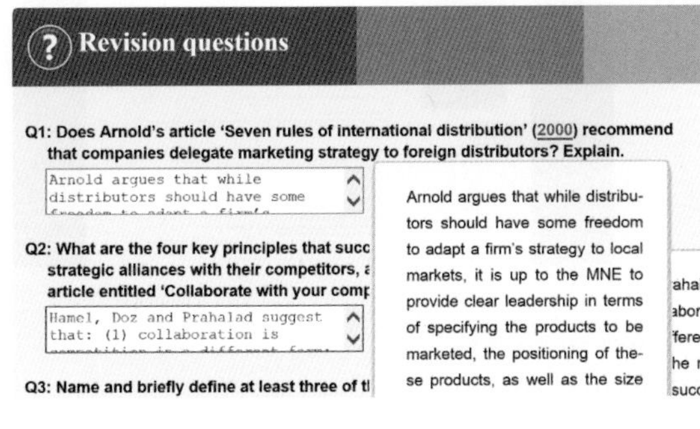

R&D activities

As you complete the R&D activities at the end of each chapter, use the suggested resources and guided responses to direct your investigation. Note that the solution pop-ups can be moved about the page.

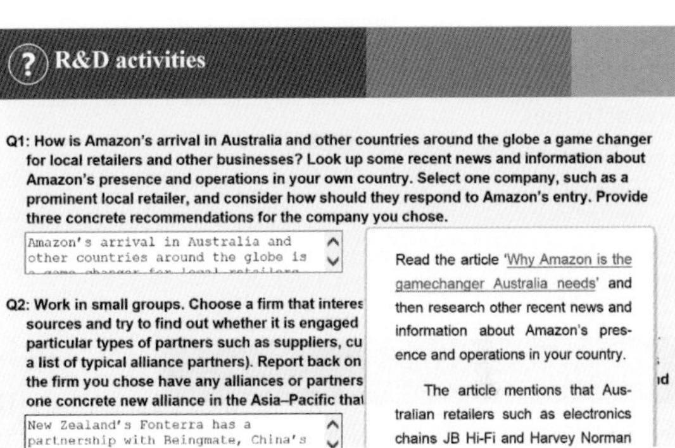

USING THE ONLINE INSTRUCTOR RESOURCES

A variety of resources for instructors are provided on the companion website to this text, at www.cambridge.org/academic/ibasiapacific. These materials are designed to help instructors prepare lectures, tutorials and interactive class activities.

CONTEMPORARY INTERNATIONAL BUSINESS
IN THE ASIA-PACIFIC REGION

Chapter 1 Foundations of international business in the Asia–Pacific

Interactive-case questions

Multiple choice, multiple answer (poll)

1. What were Honda's three key challenges related to manufacturing in the US?
   a. Selecting and training employees
   b. Developing a lean supplier network
   c. Finding an optimal production location
   d. Cultural differences between the US and Japan
   e. Other

Interactive questions

A set of over 70 extra questions is available to instructors. These questions can be modified and loaded into your learning management system to create interactive class activities and facilitate class discussion around core concepts and case studies.

Question types include:

- multiple-choice quizzes
- wordcloud activities
- class polls
- short-answer questions
- ranking questions.

PowerPoint® presentations, including figures from the text

A set of PowerPoint® slides for each chapter provides an outline for weekly lecture presentations and covers key concepts.

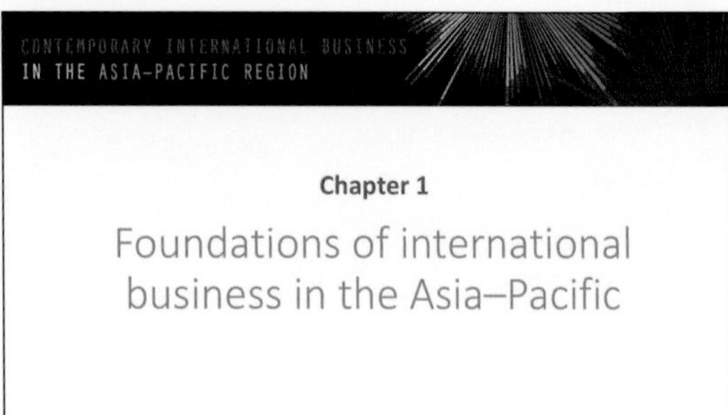

CONTEMPORARY INTERNATIONAL BUSINESS
IN THE ASIA-PACIFIC REGION

Chapter 1 Foundations of international business in the Asia–Pacific

IB masterclass answers: The Honda corporation

1. What specific resources were required to make Honda's proposed international business activities successful in the US?

   Honda's success was dependent on its flexible, skilled workers and loyal, long-time suppliers in Japan. Its key challenges when it began producing in the US were to achieve the same kind of flexibility and productivity from: the US workers who had a very different workplace culture; and the suppliers who either had little experience or the wrong attitude. In turn, the company faced challenges in developing an understanding of these groups. The firm needed to

Instructor toolkits

Answer guide for IB masterclass case studies

An answer guide gives suggested answers to the IB masterclass case study questions.

Stretch materials

Additional online case studies with questions offer further illustrative examples. These can be used to extend class discussion and provide further opportunities for revision.

PART ONE

CORE CONCEPTS

CHAPTER 1

FOUNDATIONS OF INTERNATIONAL BUSINESS IN THE ASIA–PACIFIC

Learning objectives

In reading this chapter, you will learn to:

1. appreciate the term international business and the associated key concepts
2. understand the role of trade in the Asia–Pacific region today
3. recognise the global risks when companies trade internationally
4. understand the growth drivers that are changing international business development.

TODAY'S ASIA: THE GROWTH DRIVER AND CHAMPION

Asia has emerged as a driver of regional growth over the last 25 years, with several Asian countries growing faster than European and US competitors. The People's Republic of China (China) has been the most remarkable, with more than 7.0 per cent growth annually. India, Indonesia and South Korea achieved yearly growth rates of more than 5.1 per cent. Even with a lesser average growth of 3.3 per cent, year on year, Japan's productivity has outpaced North America and Western Europe. The rise of emerging economies in Asia is centre stage globally and aligns with the broader phenomenon of globalisation of markets. Despite political, financial and economic upheavals creating turmoil and uncertainty across the world, the forward-looking prospects for this vibrant region remain positive.

As national economies recovered from the global financial crisis of 2008–09, and the effects of the 2015 share market crash in China, researchers agreed that the Asian region has surfaced as the growth engine for a projected thirty-year period. The Asian Development Bank (ADB) estimated that by 2050 Asia's gross domestic product will exceed 60 per cent of the world's total, making this period in history an 'Asian century' (ADB 2011) While debates on the validity of the Asian century are still on-going, the region's economies continue to perform far better than the world's average. Japan is entering the new era with optimistic productivity and signalling renewed growth. At the same time, ADB data shows that despite huge internal and external challenges, China and India continue to perform as two giant beacons for economic dynamism in Asia and across the globe. South Korea, Taiwan and Thailand are also on track for sustained development with significant improvement in standards of living.

One factor that will contribute to productivity and economic growth is the change in socio-demographic structures within countries. Less attention on societies that have focused on their population as a labour source, and a greater emphasis on skills, training, gender empowerment, augmented process mechanisation and improved use of resources will underpin and shape growth across the region. The competitive advantage for Asian nations is the ability to increase productivity within their own societies. The rate of women participating, for example, is an opportunity for economic and social improvements. Rethinking the definition of work, the nature of work, and the level of engagement an employee has with their employer, are drivers in this change. More particularly, governments in the region will need to restructure and re-engineer their engagement process with private sector organisations, communities and individuals.

VIDEO VIGNETTE QUESTION

Introduction

This first chapter introduces several international business concepts and trends, which will be discussed in detail in subsequent chapters. It starts by examining world trade and investment today. Asia and the Pacific regions are examined with a focus on global reactions, and the role of inter- and intra-regional trade that impact on international business. The chapter concludes by considering international business from a growth perspective, including the influence of regulation changes, human capital and information technology advances.

International business today

The opening vignette illustrates the growing significance of trade and economic development in the Asia–Pacific region for international business managers within the dynamic global-trading environment. This operating context forms the critical background for international business planning and strategy development, which are built on and designed within unique trading environments. The depth of market understanding and the level of preparation undertaken by the international firms largely underpin their achievements and failures. By studying the changing nature of the economies and communities in the Asia–Pacific region, combined with understanding the dynamic nature of the international business operating environment, new graduates will enter a professional situation with the ability to develop a career in a challenging, stimulating and rewarding setting.

This book primarily focuses on the fundamental elements of international business from the perspective of an international business manager. From a conceptual point of view, there is little difference between strategy and implementation of core business functions in either domestic or international environments. However, in an international setting, the dynamic nature of the trading situation is much greater. The operating environment requires interactions with, and an understanding of, regulations, customs and principles, and languages and business operating practices that are disparate from a homogenous national market perspective. The international business manager must acquire several interconnected skills to engage across cultures, participate within and across national borders, and negotiate between home- and host-country business practices.

International business generally comprises all transactions that are devised and implemented within and across multiple countries to satisfy the objectives of individuals and companies. The development of markets on foreign soil may take place in a range of evolving and direct forms, from international engagement with subsidiary firms through to an acquisition, merger or joint venture. A core market-entry strategy, commonly a first step for many firms, is via export and import trading arrangements. Another key entry strategy involves foreign direct investment (FDI), either through the establishment of wholly owned subsidiaries or joint venture arrangements with a foreign partner. Additional ways to engage in international business include licensing, franchising and contract manufacturing. Each method has its own distinct advantages and disadvantages. These will be discussed in more detail in Chapters 7 and 11.

EXPORT AND IMPORT TRADING an import is a product or service brought into one country from another. Imports and exports form the foundation for international trade.

FOREIGN DIRECT INVESTMENT (FDI) an establishment or the expansion of company operations in a foreign country. Like all investments, it assumes a transfer of capital.

While the basic principles of international business remain highly relevant, conducting trade across national borders creates a new set of macro- and micro-environmental factors that must be considered by business managers when they plan to operate abroad. A successful product in one country does not guarantee success in another. The elements of greatest significance to international business managers include laws, regulations, government policies, governance, cultural norms and societal differences. Each of these factors can be enabling or constraining depending on the business context. Key areas of enquiry may vary from sector to sector.

Some frequently asked questions are below.

- How will our ideas transfer into an international market?
- What, if any, product adjustments are required to suit local tastes or conditions?
- Which market-entry method is best to achieve the desired goals?
- Should materials be sourced domestically or abroad?
- What threats do our global competitors pose? How can these be defused?

One organisation that provides insights for international business managers is the World Trade Organization (WTO). The WTO captures statistical information to inform our understanding of trading changes globally through development of trade analytics. The World Trade Outlook Indicator (WTOI), launched in July 2017, provides real-time information to examine the latest trading trends, and to understand how and why global trade is changing.

WEBLINK

The WTOI provides a headline figure to demonstrate performance against trend: a reading of 100 indicates trade growth in line with recent trends, a reading greater than 100 suggests above trend growth, while a reading below 100 indicates below trend growth. The WTOI is updated quarterly.

After examining world merchandise trade at the end of 2016, WTO statistics revealed the lowest recorded growth in volume terms since the financial crisis of 2008, increasing by just 1.3 per cent (WTO 2017a). This was half the level achieved in 2015 and well below the 4.7 per cent average annual growth rate since the early 1980s. The low level of trade growth in 2016 was driven in part by weak world gross domestic product (GDP) growth of 2.3 per cent, down from 2.7 per cent in 2015 and below the 2.8 per cent average annual rate since 1980. Analysis revealed there had also been a decline in recent years in the ratio of trade growth to GDP growth, with a fall of approximately 1:1 in the wake of the financial crisis. This contrasts with international trade growing 1.5 times faster than world GDP on average since 1945. In 2016, for the first time since 2001, the ratio fell below 1.0 to 0.6.

GROSS DOMESTIC PRODUCT (GDP) the total monetary value of goods produced and services provided by a country over a one-year period.

In 2017, the WTOI indicators released for the first half of the year represented good news for the global economy overall (WTO 2018). Global trade received a further boost in 2017 with the implementation of the Trade Facilitation Agreement (TFA). The TFA was facilitated by the WTO and co-sponsored by Australia. It is the first multilateral trade agreement adopted since the creation of the WTO in 1995. More than two-thirds of the WTO member nations have accepted the TFA, the latest being Papua New Guinea in March 2018. The aim of the TFA is to streamline customs procedures and speed up the flow of goods across national borders. The TFA implementation reduces time by up to two days in the export process and a day and half on import practices. This landmark in trade reform relates directly to the cutting of trade costs and barriers globally, and provides the biggest gains to some of the poorest countries in the world, as well as to small- and medium-sized enterprises for which customs processes can be especially onerous. Global trade will be boosted by up to US$1 trillion each year, and the estimated increase to world trade to 2030 is expected to be 2.7 per cent each year (WTO 2018). This agreement facilitates increased international business operations and assists a greater number of countries to trade globally.

MULTIPLE-CHOICE QUESTION

World trade and investment today

Trade is an important engine of economic and social growth, and a mechanism that links markets internationally. Trade was conducted primarily among the nations of Western Europe, North

America and Japan throughout the twentieth century, but as the twenty-first century progresses, it is becoming more evident that the greatest international trade opportunities over the coming decades will be found in the 10 big emerging markets (BEMs); the BEMs have signalled their importance to the future wellbeing of the global community. The BEMs most likely to deliver increased international trade are: Argentina, Brazil, China, India, Indonesia, Mexico, Poland, South Africa, South Korea and Turkey. Other major emerging markets are: Egypt, Iran, Nigeria, Pakistan, Russia, Saudi Arabia, Taiwan and Thailand.

BIG EMERGING MARKETS (BEMs) emerging economies expected to drive international trade; these include: Argentina, Brazil, China, India, Indonesia, Mexico, Poland, South Africa, South Korea and Turkey.

Historic barriers to international trade and investment are breaking down. Politically, national investment policies continue to be geared towards liberalisation, promotion and facilitation of international investment. In 2015 and 2016, 71 measures related to enhancing international trade were implemented globally (Schwab 2017); only 13 measures during this time introduced new restrictions on investment. The emerging economies in Asia have been the most active in the liberalisation of investment across a broad range of industries. The formation of economic groupings is growing and gaining in strength. The G20, Transatlantic Trade and Investment Partnership, Asia–Pacific Economic Cooperation (APEC), Regional Comprehensive Economic Partnership (RCEP) and the BRICS (Brazil, Russia, India, China and South Africa) account for a noteworthy share of global FDI. The objectives of most of these groups include fostering investment-friendly environments to facilitate FDI flows into and within the groups. Results of the 2014 and 2016 World Investment Prospect Surveys undertaken by the United Nations (UN) revealed the emergence and significance of these economic mega-groups, and the related influence on international companies' current and future strategic investment decisions (UNCTAD 2014).

Today, the volume of investments, goods and services crossing national and regional borders each day is greater than the combined total of trade in the second half of the twentieth century. The volume of foreign currency traded every day is more than US$5.1 trillion in transactions, and annual world merchandise exports equates to over US$16 trillion (WTO 2017a). Global trade and world exports are therefore adversely affected by economic downturns, recessions, prices of commodities (such as oil) and volatilities in exchange rates. To note that in *Contemporary International Business in the Asia–Pacific Region*, the US dollar has been used to aggregate and compare global monetary values; in the absence of a single global currency, the use of the US dollar is the acknowledged medium of exchange for international trade and business operations.

Understanding a country's economic position serves as a superior indicator whereby international business managers evaluate economic growth of a country to inform their international business planning. The economic growth rate indicators reveal the capacity of a country's economy to produce goods and services from one period to another. The indicators are presented in nominal or real terms, the latter of which is adjusted for inflation. Aggregated economic growth rates are measured and presented as GDP, and refer to an increase in aggregated productivity. Globally, other than the US, export trade for a number of regions and nations constitutes at least 20 per cent of GDP (see Table 1.1).

Regions with over 40 per cent of GDP represented by export trade include the Middle East and North Africa, and Europe and Central Asia (World Bank 2017). Central Asia is defined as the region of Asia reaching from the Caspian Sea in the west to central China in the east, and from southern Russia in the north to India in the south. Central Asia countries include the five former Soviet republics of Kazakhstan, Kyrgyzstan, Tajikistan, Turkmenistan and Uzbekistan, as well as Afghanistan and part of Iran, China, Mongolia, Pakistan, India and south-western Siberia. The significant role

TABLE 1.1 Export trade as a percentage of regional/national GDP, 1990–2015

Region / Country	1990	2000	2010	2015
Australia	15.14	19.44	19.44	19.80
Canada	25.07	44.24	29.07	**31.58**
China	14.03	21.24	26.27	**21.97**
East Asia & Pacific	21.05	27.52	32.36	**30.47**
Europe & Central Asia	25.48	35.64	38.03	**42.25**
India	6.93	12.77	22.59	19.95
Japan	10.29	10.62	15.04	17.64
Latin America & Caribbean	17.71	19.24	21.88	**20.43**
Middle East & North Africa	29.44	38.95	45.43	**43.26**
North America	10.67	13.71	13.91	14.28
Sub-Saharan Africa	26.68	37.96	31.74	**24.88**
United States of America	9.23	10.66	12.38	12.55
World	**19.56**	**26.24**	**28.90**	**29.49**

Source: World Bank 2017, CC BY 4.0

of this export trade is causally linked to the economic viability of many nations. The process of the move away from a world in which individual countries are relatively independent entities to one where national economies are part of an inclusive, integrated global economic structure is commonly known as globalisation. In globalisation, the barriers to cross-national trade and investment break down, perceived distance shrinks and material culture starts to look similar. The globalisation of business is viewed by much of the world to create and drive economic growth that benefits nations, companies and individuals.

GLOBALISATION an awareness and understanding of, and a response to, global developments and links. A shift towards a more integrated and interdependent world economy.

Globalisation and the international business imperative

A shift towards a more integrated and interdependent world economy would aptly describe globalisation. It is an awareness and understanding of, as well as a response to, global development and its related links; it impacts participants engaged in public, private and not-for-profit sectors. Globalisation more broadly encompasses cultural, economic and societal issues. When considering the term from a business perspective, the narrative speaks to trade, production and ultimately the end market.

Investment and international trade are the most established methods of international business transactions. Investment is the transfer of assets from one country to another; it can also be the acquisition of assets in each country. Assets are identified typically as technology, manufacturing infrastructure, human capital and financial capital, and are referred to as factors of production. International trade is defined as the exchange of merchandise (products) and services across national borders and is conducted via exchanges. These exchanges are usually in the form of exports, imports or sourcing, and may be traded from a home country or second country and received by a third country. Activities like these are known as outbound (exports) and inbound (imports) flows, and include products and services. Products categorised for trading include raw or component products, intermediate products that require further finishing and fully finished products. Two types of investment traded between countries are FDI and portfolio investment. FDI refers to an international business

strategy where an organisation from one country (home) establishes a physical presence in another country (host) to achieve business growth. The FDI assets in the host country may cover plant and equipment, land, labour, technological innovations and capital. This investment strategy may include full or partial ownership of an existing (brownfield) or new (greenfield) enterprise. Portfolio investment is the grouping of assets that focuses on securities from foreign markets rather than domestic ones. An international portfolio is designed to give the organisation exposure to growth in emerging and international markets, and provide diversification. Organisations intentionally plan FDI and international portfolio investments strategically to capitalise in foreign markets.

World trade and investment statistics are central to understanding the wellbeing of our global society. While historically trade has been conducted internationally by nations, businesses and individuals, in the last decade the volume of merchandise trade and trade in commercial services has risen exponentially. The value of merchandise trade and commercial services in 2015 was nearly twice as high as in 2005 (WTO 2016a). Asia, Europe and North America accounted for 88 per cent in total merchandise trade of WTO members over the previous 10 years. The share of developing economies' trade in merchandise exports increased from 33 per cent in 2005 to 42 per cent in 2016. The value of merchandise exports of WTO members totalled US$15.46 trillion in 2016 (WTO 2017a).

DEVELOPING ECONOMIES nations with an underdeveloped industrial base and a low Human Development Index (HDI) relative to other countries.

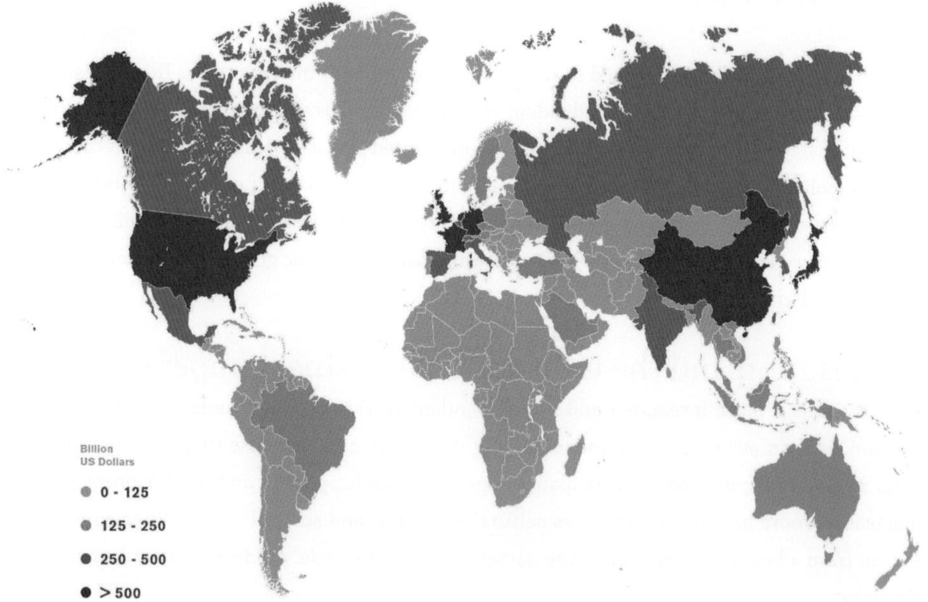

FIGURE 1.1 Economies by size of merchandise trade, 2015
Source: WTO 2016b, p. 14, © World Trade Organization 2018, reproduced with permission.

The sheer volume and value of global trade has guided the shaping of a network of international linkages that connect nations, organisations and people. This network brings together financial markets, technology and livelihood improvements in the process of international trade.

MULTINATIONAL ENTERPRISE (MNE) a company that has facilities and other assets in at least one country other than their home country; typically, an MNE has offices and manufacturing in different countries, usually with a centralised head office.

One institutional driver for the growth in international markets has been the multinational enterprise (MNE). MNEs are businesses that invest and operate in countries around the globe. Many of today's MNEs are truly global with operations, customers and consumers in more than one continent. Both manufacturing and service companies, across a wide spectrum of industries, are engaging in some form of international operation. For example, Vodafone, a UK telecommunications business, has 90 per cent of its assets on foreign soil (Europa EU 2016). Technology is the driving force behind this multinational organisation. Vodafone's technology platform and core competitive advantage connects and propels their international operations strategy, and it connects their business partners, customers and the end consumer. Another example is Nestlé, a registered Swiss organisation; it has 96 per cent of the company's assets and 97 per cent of its employees located abroad, and more than 98 per cent of revenue is generated outside of Switzerland (Nestlé 2018). Other examples of companies with operations spanning multiple continents include: Diageo, a global spirit and beer marketer with over 200 brands; British American Tobacco, headquartered in London and operating in over 40 countries; and the car company Volvo, operating in over 25 countries, and which promotes itself as truly global and proudly Scandinavian (Diageo 2018; British American Tobacco 2018; Volvo 2018).

Ongoing shifts in the macro- and micro-environments create dynamic periods in international business settings. A company's macro-environment contains forces that have the potential to affect the firm's operating practices, which the company has limited control over. Macro-environmental elements include political-legal, economic, sociocultural and technological variables. A company needs to assess these independent variables as part of its international business planning and strategic development to geographically expand its organisation.

Within the macro-environment, trading relationships impact individual markets, and the evidence of national engagement in business activities, linked to export and trade growth, becomes critical. For example, balancing national trade accounts is a priority for most countries, and consequently, a lack of export growth can result in long-term trade deficits. Historically the US ran a surplus economy, however, following the recent export trade recession period, the country is now a world trade debtor. Improved rates of employment signal market strength and, from this view point, importing goods and services drives improvements in local economies, boosts market competitiveness, and delivers variety, all of which are key factors in improving standards of living.

A company's micro-environment contains elements that directly affect business performance and decision making. These elements include competitors, and the channels of distribution for products and services from suppliers through to customers and end consumers. At the micro-environmental level, trading relationships may impact an individual company or industry. Engaging in global markets enables a firm to achieve greater economies of scale by increasing the number of potential customers for the organisation to service. This creates the company's capability to increase its profits and achieve a price-competitive position in its home market, as well as the potential to develop an enhanced understanding of its competitors. Research has shown that international corporations of all sizes and in all industries outperformed companies that have only a domestic focus.

MNEs are central to global innovation patterns and pivotal to global value chains (GVCs), which are at the heart of international trade (UNCTAD 2016). For local companies and economies, MNEs are potential sources to access advances in technology, expertise and best practice, which help support their growth. MNEs, from the perspective of both developing and transitioning economies, may benefit from collaborating with other global conglomerates to achieve a competitive position. However, while globalisation and the expansion of international trade have supporters, there are also critics. Examining the various viewpoints serves to inform our understanding of globalisation and the role of MNEs in international trade.

GLOBAL VALUE CHAINS (GVCs) include all of the people, processes and activities in different parts of the world that each add value to the production of a good or service.

Challenges and opportunities of international trade

International trade has increased over many years with significant benefits flowing to many countries and organisations across the world. International trade aims to deliver services, goods and capital among various countries and regions with limited interference.

International trade accounts for a sizeable part of a country's GDP and is an important source of revenue for a nation. Growth in international trading sectors has been delivered through a range of factors: diversification, opening of new market channels, market differentiation, job creation, GVCs, technology transfer, broader knowledge bases, differences in government regulations, operational flexibility and stronger bargaining power.

- *Diversification:* for many nations, both international trade and traditional industries are core to the country's competitive advantage. MNEs that reside in their home countries can leverage differences and take advantage of opportunities between countries that do not exist for firms operating purely in a domestic market. As the level of international diversification increases, the potential opportunities for an MNE also increase (Thomas & Eden 2004, p. 94).
- *Opening of new market channels:* foreign investors can help create new export opportunities to host countries by opening reciprocal markets in their home countries. For example, in Australia, many recent Chinese investments in the iron ore sector have included 'offtake agreements' that guarantee future sales in China to secondary companies developing new mines.
- *Market differentiation*: organisations can target differences in tastes, demands and income levels to achieve business growth and enhanced economic benefits. MNEs can shift sales from low-income to high-income markets, generating higher profits from the firm's resources. This is known as market-seeking FDI. Likewise, as products become obsolete in high-income markets, MNEs can shift sales towards low-income markets, extending the life of an obsolete product line (Thomas & Eden 2004, pp. 93–4).
- *Job creation*: MNEs introduce products and services to a country, which leads to employment gains. In the process of FDI, businesses are built and expanded, and jobs are created as capital is put to productive use regardless of the source. Workers also benefit since exporting companies of all sizes typically pay significantly higher wages than non-exporters. For example, in 2016, the Australian dairy producer Bega purchased the Australian icon Vegemite from US food giant Mondelez International. Media outlets heralded the news that Vegemite was once again in Australian hands. Few consumers were aware it had been more than 80 years since Vegemite had been fully Australian-owned and that Vegemite continued to be produced in Australian factories by Australian workers with Australian ingredients, regardless of the business ownership (Ciobo 2017).
- *GVCs*: international business has triggered a global re-orientation in production and supply strategies. Between 1995 and 2016 most developed and developing countries significantly increased their contributions to GVC development, resulting in a geographically more diverse manufacturing base (OECD 2016). Lower trade costs and improved communications technology have fostered this development. Gains are achieved either by horizontally integrating FDI (producing the same product lines in two or more countries) or vertically integrating FDI (where products are not made in a single country but stages of production are spread across multiple economies). GVCs are common across Asia, specifically in automotive, textile and electronics industries. South-East Asian economies have increased significantly the share of imported components in their exports. A leading example is Cambodia, an emerging economy that has increased its vertical specialisation by 24 per cent between 1995 and 2011, demonstrating how quickly integration into regional supply chains can occur

(WTO 2015). The growing importance of GVCs has been authenticated by the WTO through the introduction of value chain data in their standard reporting profile from 2014.

- *Technology transfer:* MNEs undertake most of the private research for technology development. Engaging in investment with these corporations allows an economy to access the technologies that they hold. For example, Australia's clean energy industry is an emerging area where foreign investment is proving to be beneficial.
- *Broader knowledge bases:* MNEs with business units in more than one country draw on the established knowledge base from their foreign affiliates to improve products and processes, which generates worldwide organisational learning throughout their network (Thomas & Eden 2004, p. 95). For example, the Boeing corporation, recognising Australia's high skills base and research for development expertise, has invested US$1 billion in the Australian market in recent years (Austrade 2018). This investment created 1200 new jobs, drove collaborative technological advances with leading national institutions, and assisted Australian engineering and machining companies to diversify and win new export markets. Over 1000 Australian small- and medium-sized enterprises are accessing Boeing's global supply chain.
- *Differences in government regulations:* investment shunting can be used to shift production to locations with lower taxes, higher subsidies or easier regulations. MNEs set up financial affiliates in tax havens or move investments to avoid restrictive tariffs and anti-dumping duties (Thomas & Eden 2004, p. 95).
- *Operational flexibility:* MNEs take advantage of multiple locations to respond flexibly to changes in the external operating environment. International diversification of a firm's operating markets and production locations may cushion the MNE from exchange rate shocks that are region specific (Thomas & Eden 2004, p. 95); for example, the 2014 Russian financial crisis, the Brazilian economic crisis of 2014–2017 and the 2015 Chinese stock market crash.
- *Increased bargaining power:* large MNEs have more bargaining power relative to location-bound entities, such as governments and domestic firms, due their ability to move assets quickly between countries (Thomas & Eden 2004, p. 95). This is evidenced in the textile industry with the movement of apparel manufacturing hubs from India and Bangladesh to Vietnam and Cambodia in recent years.

Despite the recent recessions and financial crises, financial organisations anticipate that international trade and global economic growth in the next two decades will be faster than in the last 20 years (WTO 2017a). This growth will occur within the trading environments of emerging economies where per capita income is predicted to increase from 2.5 per cent to 3.3 per cent. The global real GDP rate was 2.4 per cent in 2016 and expected to grow to 2.6 per cent by the end of 2017, and forecast to reach 2.9 per cent in 2018–19. While world trade volumes are significant and used as predictors in the international business environment, trade flows and composition of trade are much more dynamic than statistics can show.

Composition of trade and trade flows

The composition of international trade has transformed in recent decades. Prior to 1960, the primary industries sector was the core of a country's global trading strategy. The period from 1960 to the 1990s saw the rise of trading in manufactured goods. Trade in merchandise exports has fluctuated over the last 20 years. A range of crises impacted international trade between 1995 and 2001, including Mexico's monetary crisis (1995–2001), the Asian financial crisis of 1997, and the bursting of the dotcom bubble in 2001. The latter two factors resulted in negative growth for merchandise

trade in 1998 and 2001 (WTO 2016a). The 2008 global financial crisis, triggered by the US lending crisis, led to a worldwide recession between 2008 and 2011, which resulted in international export trade declining by 12 per cent. China's admission to the WTO in December 2001 paved the way for the country's economic rise and significant contribution to increasing world trade outputs from 2002 to 2008. Trade merchandise statistics rebounded in early 2010; however, from 2011 onwards, the European debt crisis and intensifying geo-political tensions have contributed to a slowing of world trade growth (WTO 2016a). The Chinese stock market crash in 2015 further challenged global trade. The weakening outlook for China's growth put pressure on emerging economies, especially those who depended on Chinese trade for industrial and commodity products. Europe's recovery has remained tenuous and export dependent. The US is proving to be more robust, with an economy less in debt and consumers sourcing local product in contrast to the levels of global shopping demonstrated in the 1990s and 2000s.

The average share of exports and imports of merchandise and commercial services in world GDP in value terms increased significantly from 20 per cent in 1995 to 30 per cent in 2014 (WTO 2016a). Undoubtedly, today's GDP is highly influenced by international trade. From a historical viewpoint, the US has relied on Europe for both markets and sources of supply. As more nations open their markets, this pattern has shifted. In 2014, 20.2 per cent of US exports were sold within the Asia region, followed by Europe at 15.2 per cent. From a source of supply perspective, the US has the greatest reliance on Asia, sourcing 18.1 per cent of its goods from the region in contrast to 7.9 per cent from Europe.

While the manufacturing sector remains a significant player in world trade, it is the services industry, including firms in consulting, software, insurance and education, that continue to make gains globally. The value of merchandise trade and the value of trade in commercial services was nearly twice as high in 2015 as it was in 2005 (WTO 2016a). Data from WTO (2015) shows that merchandise exports from WTO members totalled US$18.0 trillion in 2014, and the top 10 traders in merchandise trade accounted for over 50.5 per cent of global total trade. Exports of commercial services from WTO members reached US$4.9 trillion in 2014. Global trade in commercial services increased by 8 per cent on average annually over the last two decades, recording particularly strong double-digit growth from 2002 to 2008. The 10 leading traders in global commercial services represented more than half of the world's total trade in commercial services in 2014.

Individual services categories, such as financial services and computer and information services, have often outpaced the average upsurge (see Figure 1.2). Driven by rapid technological progress, the communications sector, telecommunications, has recorded remarkable growth since 2000 (WTO, 2015).

Participation in world trade by developing economies in commercial services continues to rise, reaching 34 per cent of global exports in 2014 (WTO 2015). In the last 10 years these countries have progressively expanded their share of services trade with the increase due mostly to developing economies in Asia, which accounted for 22.4 per cent of world export of services trade in 2014. Asia's share of world imports of commercial services has expanded even more rapidly, largely due to China's booming services imports and other developing economies' demand for services (WTO 2015). International trade in commercial services has been less volatile than merchandise trade in the last 20 years, indicating a greater resilience of the services sector to global macro-economic disruptions (WTO 2016a).

Merchandise exports and import trends continue to change globally and reveal shifts in regional trading. In terms of value, world exports and imports have increased exponentially (see Tables 1.2 and 1.3). China overtook Japan as the leading exporter in Asia in 2004, three years after entry into the WTO. China surpassed the US and Germany in 2016 to become the leading export nation globally.

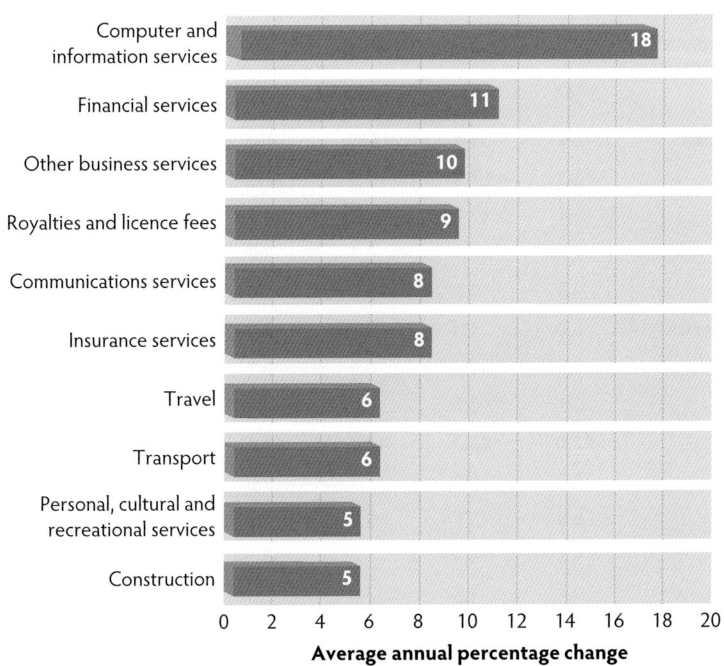

FIGURE 1.2 Growth of world exports of commercial services, main sectors, 1995–2014

Source: WTO 2015, p. 20, © World Trade Organization 2018, reproduced with permission

TABLE 1.2 World merchandise exports, 1963–2016

	1963	1973	1983	1993	2003	2016
World value (US$ billion)	**157**	**579**	**1838**	**3688**	**7380**	**15 464**
North America	**19.9**	**17.3**	**16.8**	**17.9**	**15.8**	**14.3**
United States	14.3	12.2	11.2	12.6	9.8	9.4
Canada	4.3	4.6	4.2	3.9	3.7	2.5
Mexico	0.6	0.4	1.4	1.4	2.2	2.4
South and Central America	**6.4**	**4.3**	**4.5**	**3.0**	**3.0**	**3.3**
Brazil	0.9	1.1	1.2	1.0	1.0	1.2
Chile	0.3	0.2	0.2	0.2	0.3	0.4
Europe	**47.8**	**50.9**	**43.5**	**45.3**	**45.9**	**38.4**
Germany	9.3	11.7	9.2	10.3	10.2	8.7
Netherlands	3.6	4.7	3.5	3.8	4.0	3.7
France	5.2	6.3	5.2	6.0	5.3	3.2
United Kingdom	7.8	5.1	5.0	4.9	4.1	2.6
Commonwealth of Independent States (CIS)	**–**	**–**	**–**	**1.7**	**2.6**	**2.7**
Africa	**5.7**	**4.8**	**4.5**	**2.5**	**2.4**	**2.2**
South Africa	1.5	1.0	1.0	0.7	0.5	0.5
Middle East	**3.2**	**4.1**	**6.7**	**3.5**	**4.1**	**5.0**
Asia	**12.5**	**14.9**	**19.1**	**26.0**	**26.1**	**34.0**
China	1.3	1.0	1.2	2.5	5.9	13.6
Japan	3.5	6.4	8.0	9.8	6.4	4.2
India	1.0	0.5	0.5	0.6	0.8	1.7
Australia and New Zealand	2.4	2.1	1.4	1.4	1.2	1.4
Six East Asian traders	2.5	3.6	5.8	9.6	9.6	9.9

Source: WTO 2017b, p. 100, © World Trade Organization 2018, reproduced with permission

TABLE 1.3 World merchandise imports, 1963–2016

	1963	1973	1983	1993	2003	2016
World value (US$ billion)	**164**	**594**	**1883**	**3805**	**7696**	**15 799**
North America	**16.1**	**17.2**	**18.5**	**21.3**	**22.4**	**19.4**
United States	11.4	12.4	14.3	15.9	16.9	14.3
Canada	3.9	4.2	3.4	3.7	3.2	2.6
Mexico	0.8	0.6	0.7	1.8	2.3	2.5
South and Central America	**6.0**	**4.4**	**3.9**	**3.3**	**2.5**	**3.4**
Brazil	0.9	1.2	0.9	0.7	0.7	0.9
Chile	0.4	0.2	0.2	0.3	0.3	0.4
Europe	**52.0**	**53.3**	**44.1**	**44.5**	**45.0**	**37.5**
Germany	8.0	9.2	8.1	9.0	7.9	6.7
United Kingdom	8.5	6.5	5.3	5.5	5.2	4.0
France	5.3	6.4	5.6	5.7	5.2	3.6
Netherlands	4.4	4.8	3.3	3.3	3.4	3.2
Commonwealth of Independent States (CIS)	**–**	**–**	**–**	**1.5**	**1.7**	**2.1**
Africa	**5.2**	**3.9**	**4.6**	**2.6**	**2.2**	**3.2**
South Africa	1.1	0.9	0.8	0.5	0.5	0.6
Middle East	**2.3**	**2.7**	**6.2**	**3.3**	**2.8**	**4.2**
Asia	**14.1**	**14.9**	**18.5**	**23.5**	**23.5**	**30.3**
China	0.9	0.9	1.1	2.7	5.4	10.0
Japan	4.1	6.5	6.7	6.4	5.0	3.8
India	1.5	0.5	0.7	0.6	0.9	2.3
Australia and New Zealand	2.2	1.6	1.4	1.5	1.4	1.4
Six East Asian traders	3.2	3.9	6.1	10.2	8.6	8.9

Source: WTO 2017b, p. 101, © World Trade Organization 2018, reproduced with permission

Noticeably, percentage shares of export trade by the US, the EU and Japan have continued to decline (WTO 2017a). This trading capacity is largely being taken up by China and other developing economies including India, Mexico and other East Asian nations. Exports from developing countries have continued to increase in value terms, although the share of total exports has decreased over the period 1993 to 2016. In Asia, over 50 per cent of total exports are commercially traded within the region (WTO 2015).

DEVELOPED ECONOMIES
nations that have a highly developed and stable economy, advanced technological infrastructure relative to other less industrialised nations and a very high per capita income.

Imports by China and India have surged while import levels in developed economies have stagnated. The US, however, remains the leading merchandise importer. The top four importing nations in 2015, China, the US, Germany and Japan, accounted for more than one-third of world import trade while the top three countries accounted for more than one-quarter (WTO 2016a).

Today's international trading environment has increased the level of interdependence required among nations. With the composition of trade and trade flows, inward and outward, the changing interdependence between nations and their reliance on one another is not static. Apart from trade interactions, global economies are profoundly affected by the influences of FDI, portfolio investment and the daily flow of currency in markets. For domestic firms, participating in international markets has become an imperative to avoid loss in home markets because of increasing foreign competition. Firms entering international business markets on the global stage require the critical success factors of innovation, creativity, flexibility and speed to achieve success.

MULTIPLE-CHOICE QUESTIONS

SPOTLIGHT 1.1

Asian century: engaging our neighbours and developing a capable workforce

Following a review of the Australian education curriculum in 2014, Asian studies have become an increasingly important part of the academic, social and personal development of all young Australians. Five-year-old students who started school in 2014 will enter their adult lives at a time when China and India are projected to be the world's leading economies. In 2014, Australia's Federal Trade Minister, Andrew Robb, argued that with an escalating middle class of Asia, the region would be the world's largest consumer of goods and services by 2019. The future of students in Australia will be shaped by the dynamics of global mobility, including trade, technology and youth cultures that will largely be driven by advances in Asia.

Between 2000 and 2010, the number of children born in Australia to migrant parents doubled, with 42 per cent of those migrants arriving from Asia. Hinduism and Buddhism are Australia's fastest growing religions. The Asia Education Foundation (2014) contends that Australia's engagement with Asia in terms of trade, investment, education, tourism, immigration and humanitarian assistance is growing at a rate faster than our engagement with the remainder of the world

combined. This has created a strong level of agreement among educators, communities, businesses and government agencies that growing the Australian economy and building regional relationships requires an 'Asia capable Australia'. Consequently, Australians who can speak Asian languages, understand cultural contexts and navigate local networks will have an advantage. The Australian Government believes that training adults in the workplace environment is not enough and that capacity building needs to commence at the school level. The 'National Strategy to Develop an Asia Capable Workforce', a partnership between the Australian Government and the business sector, advises that 'the next generation must enter the workforce with intercultural capability and knowledge of Asia'.

Source: Asia Education Foundation 2014

SPOTLIGHT QUESTIONS

QUESTIONS

1. What opportunities would a dedicated national Asia capable employment strategy deliver for young graduates seeking to enter the international business environment?
2. What challenges might be encountered by governments, private sector and communities from a dedicated Asia-focused education strategy within our school curriculums?

Asia and the Pacific: trade position today

The success of the economic development in Asia has been extraordinary, even in the face of severe regional challenges. Despite setbacks, such as the 2011 Great East Japan Earthquake, the 2012 China floods, Cyclone Haiyan in the Philippines, the India floods of 2013 and the 2015 Nepal earthquake, the economic transformation of Asia remains strong. The large developing economies of China and India continue to thrive and build the prominence of the Asia–Pacific region on the global stage. Specifically, Asia has accounted for more than half of the world's economic growth since 2001, and its current contribution to the increase in global GDP is more than that of the US (WTO 2017a). The Asia–Pacific continues to input more than any other region to the recovery of global trade, despite the financial crisis of 2008–2009.

In 2015, the Asian region took the lead in global merchandise exports with a value of US$5.96 trillion, followed by Europe at US$ 3.72 trillion and North America with US$ 2.3 trillion. China overtook Japan as the leading Asian country exporter in 2004; it surpassed the US in 2007 and Germany in 2009 to officially become the world's leading exporter (WTO 2016a). Export orders and container shipping data, in relation to China, produced strong figures in early 2017, but trade growth has not proceeded at the same rapid rate of previous periods.

Asia continues to attract the attention of MNEs. This has been evidenced by the region receiving the largest volume of FDI inflows globally (see Figure 1.3). However, a major proportion of the Asia-bound FDI inflows are into relatively high-income or large economies within the region (UNCTAD 2017). In 2015, the four largest recipients, Hong Kong, China, Singapore and India, received more than three-quarters of total inflows to Asia. In the same vein, inward FDI into other developing Asian economies, such as Indonesia and Vietnam, while smaller in comparison, is still greater than the levels being invested in comparative developing and transitional nations, for example, in Africa.

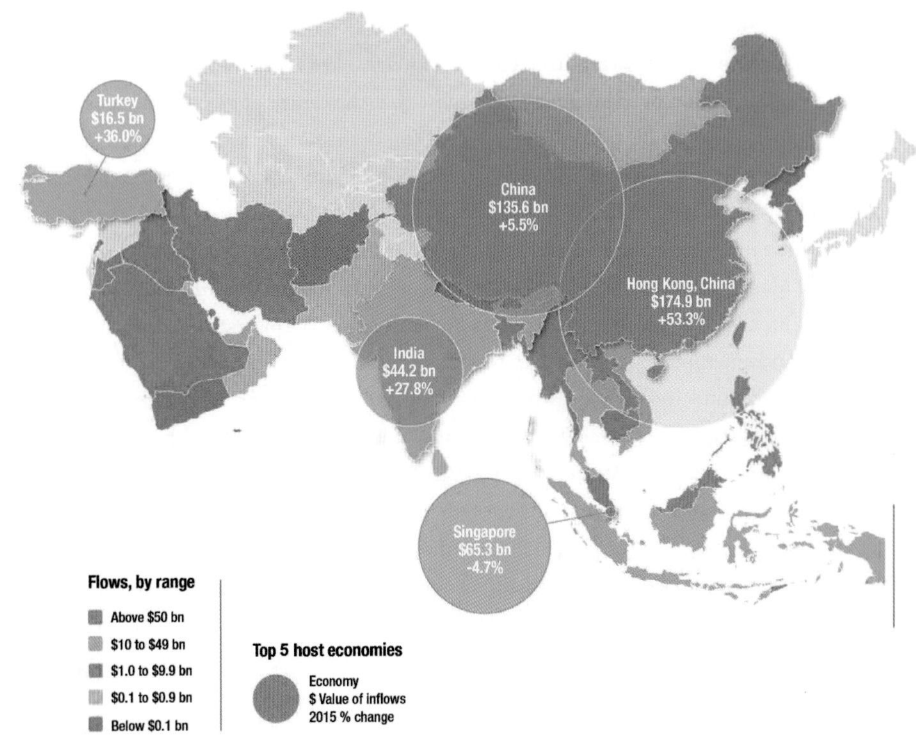

FIGURE 1.3 Top five FDI flows, 2015
Source: UNCTAD 2016, p. 43

In 2015, in Asia, over half of the region's total exports (52 per cent) were sold intra-regionally. Due to close linkages and interdependencies within Asia, the fast-paced rise of China's economy has been an instrumental factor in integrating the economies in the broader Asia–Pacific region. Intra-regional trade has increased rapidly from a low level to the point where Asia has now become China's most important trading region globally.

Economic growth in China has been linked to changes in three factors: capital, labour and productivity. With the increase in all three factors for many years, growth rates have been exceptional in China. Investment reached a staggering ceiling of 49 per cent of GDP in 2012. In that same period, the working age of the population peaked and manufacturing was spurred on by technological advancements that resulted in greater productivity. However, by 2015, the combination of factors that widened the gap between China and other regional developed nations began to contract, suggesting lower productivity growth rates.

Recent statistics explain this slowdown in China. In 2016, total national debt had climbed to approximately 250 per cent of GDP, up 100 percentage points since 2009 (World Bank 2016). Through the global financial crisis, China's debt provided a safety net but not without a substantial repayment burden. During this time China had a record high level of unsold homes, with much of the credit flowing to property developers. The real estate sector, which previously accounted for some 15 per cent of economic growth, faced outright contraction and new property starts fell by nearly one-fifth in the first two months of 2015, compared with the same period the previous year

(S.R. 2015). The suddenness of China's current slowdown looks more cyclical than structural; after all, a period of adjustment following after a period of heightened economic growth is natural.

Therefore, it is not an overstatement to suggest that the centre of global economic power has shifted from the US and the EU to the Asian region, despite the noted market corrections. The Asian region faces challenges because, on the one hand, as commodity prices weaken, financial markets continue to be volatile and exchange rates fluctuate; however, on the other hand, the region also has opportunities such as investment, manufacturing and trade which continue to strengthen. The International Monetary Fund (IMF) (2015) estimated global economic growth would achieve 3.6 per cent in 2018, up from 3.4 per cent in 2017 and 3.1 per cent in 2016, despite a deep uncertainty in trade growth and emerging economies witnessing a declining growth trend.

The rising economic powerhouses of China and India are driving these trends, and rapidly changing the world economic order. China, Japan and India contributed 62.4 per cent of the regional GDP in 2016, with strong projected growth by end of 2018 (IMF 2017). Figures for 2016 revealed challenges to growth for the three nations over the period 2015 to 2016. China's growth slowed to 6.1 per cent in 2016, from 6.3 per cent in 2015 and was predicted to achieve 5.5 per cent by the end of 2020. Japan is on course to attain modest economic expansion in 2017 through to 2020 in line with the government's plan to continue to manage the significant debt burden. The first quarter of 2017 delivered an annualised 2.3 per cent in GDP growth, with a modest 1.7 per cent growth by 2020, spurred on by increased international trade over the next period.

In contrast, the Indian national economy delivered an increase of 7.6 per cent GDP growth in the period 2015–16, and advanced estimates forecast an increase to 7.3 per cent for the 2017–18 period, which is expected to grow to 7.5 per cent in 2019–20 (IMF 2017; World Bank 2017). India has emerged as the fastest-growing major economy and safe haven for long-term growth due to its planned economic expansion. India's industrial sector, comprising mining, manufacturing, electricity and construction, is a driver behind the growth. In accordance with advanced estimates, national income for the year 2016 recorded a growth rate of 9.5 per cent for the manufacturing sector. Growth in the manufacturing sector was led by higher production outputs in areas such as furniture, clothing, automobiles, semitrailers, chemical products, nuclear fuel and petroleum products. Government initiatives within the sector, including Invest India, e-biz Mission Mode Project and Make India, under the country's e-governance plan, are being lauded as the framework for this success. The Make India initiative was launched to focus on transforming India into a global hub of manufacturing, and was expected to boost entrepreneurship in manufacturing, service and infrastructure sectors. The economic reports auger well for the country and the region at large.

Regional challenges and changes

The WTO estimates that over 4.48 billion people live in the Asia–Pacific region, representing over 59.9 per cent of the world's population, and this figure continues to grow (WTO 2016a). Nearly half (49.5 per cent) of this population lives in capital cities and urban areas. Economic growth, although slowed from 2015 onwards, is being driven by political changes and a range of socio-economic factors that keep the positive momentum for the region moving forward. Privatisation and deregulation will continue to have an impact in the financial, energy and transport sectors in the region.

The complexity of the Asia–Pacific region's diversity presents as both an opportunity and a challenge. Apart from cultural differences, the Asia–Pacific's 49 economies can be classified into seven high-income developed economies; 11 fast growing, converging economies; and 31 slow or modest growth aspiring economies (ADB 2011). Businesses strive to adopt varying strategies to achieve success in different markets. Despite intra-regional differences, organisations in the private sector and public sector in Asian countries all have one business priority in common: powering the growth engine.

PRIVATE SECTOR
the part of an economy that is not under state or national control.

PUBLIC SECTOR
the part of an economy that is controlled by a state or nation.

One transformational change evidenced throughout the past decade has been the development of mainland China as a source destination market. The focus for businesses looking at the Asia–Pacific region has clearly shifted from seeing an extensive labour pool for manufacturing to a target market with an affluent emerging middle class. The approach is no longer about benefiting from low-cost sourcing, but to tap into the world's strongest growth market. Additionally, Chinese companies are proactively pursuing mergers and acquisitions in developed countries thereby making China one of the largest FDI investors into other developed countries (UNCTAD 2017). The Chinese multinational Haier organisation is an example of this. The firm's acquisition of the US company, GE Appliances, positioned Haier as the largest home appliance manufacturers globally. Another example is the Chinese privately owned Wanda Group, which purchased several large assets in the entertainment industry. The company acquired AMC Theatres in 2012 and then purchased Legendary Entertainment for US$3.5 billion in January 2016. Announcements revealed the subsequent purchase of US Carmike Cinemas, making Wanda the largest market operator for entertainment in China and the US.

Other economies in the region are seeking to establish bilateral or multilateral agreements to facilitate trade growth. The Australian Government has negotiated and finalised three major bilateral trade deals with China, Japan and South Korea in recent years. In 2017, the Australian Tourism and Trade Minister, Steven Ciobo, believed these deals placed Australia in a strong position to feed the demand for goods and services in these booming Asian economies (Ciobo 2017). For small exporters, this has meant new markets and new opportunities. Flametree Wines is an example of an Australian firm benefiting from the demand that Australian produce, including wine and cheese, is experiencing in mainland China. Chinese consumer sentiments recognise the quality of Australian produce and the preferential tariffs deliver the competitive edge. This competitive advantage also extends to the key markets of South Korea and Japan where Australia is equally placed to achieve wins. Australian beef exporters are benefiting from lower tariffs (27.5 per cent), in comparison with international competitors such as the US (38.5 per cent), and from better market access points.

There is a range of considerations critical to success in undertaking international business and establishing ongoing trade relationships across the Asia–Pacific region. These include culture, language, ethnicity, debt and socio-economic elements.

Culture is a key element in international business, particularly when operating within Asia. Cultural expectations or nuances, if misunderstood or unanticipated, can significantly weaken and lessen opportunities in foreign markets. Cultural variables may act as barriers or opportunities and thus are a major factor in shaping business strategies. Cultural mistakes may easily become costly for organisations. Missed opportunities, embarrassment, loss of customers, legal action and tarnished reputations are all potential consequences of a failure to consider cultural differences in the global market.

Critical for firms is to recognise and understand how culture affects business across the core areas of communication, etiquette and organisational hierarchy. The firm that does not take the time to make itself aware of these differences runs the risk of launching an international venture that may fail at any number of points. With the rise of globalisation set to continue, cross-cultural teams

are becoming an imperative for international businesses. There is a multiplicity of ethnic groups in the Asia–Pacific region. Diversity presents through culture, religion, economics, geography and history. Such diversity shapes the political practices and as a consequence can interrupt the process of economic-led approaches to regional integration (Pimoljinda 2013). It is important for international businesses to understand the nuances between regions either building from direct experience or harnessing the knowledge of trusted partners to ensure well-informed approaches. Success of a product in one region of Asia does not guarantee success in another.

Since the pattern of financial crises over the last decade, credit-to-GDP ratios have risen across much of the Asia–Pacific region and in some economies there has been a sharp increase. In the markets of South Korea, Malaysia and Thailand, household borrowing has increased rapidly. Across Chinese households, businesses and local governments have all increased their borrowings. The risks of credit build-up have been mitigated by sustained income growth and supportive financial conditions. This credit, supplied through domestic banks, cross-border lending and non-bank financial institutions, has aided finance consumption, real estate activity and equity prices, which has helped lift GDP growth (IMF 2015).

Sustaining and augmenting growth for the medium- and long-term in Asian countries is crucial for several reasons, particularly in relation to living standards. Despite the rapid economic growth in the region in the decades prior to the financial crises and the resilience of Asian economies during the environmental disasters, developing nations across Asia still exhibit high levels of poverty, and lag far behind developed nations in terms of quality of life and workforce progression. The region remains home to two-thirds of the world's poor.

POVERTY
the state of being extremely poor and having little or no money, goods or means of support.

Asia's growth performance has been assisted by socio-demographic developments, and the movement of labour and capital from low- to high-productivity sectors. The Asia–Pacific region is the fastest ageing globally and already accounts for more than 211 million people aged over 65 years (World Bank 2016). Forecasts by the Chinese government propose that by 2050, more than 100 million fewer people aged between 15 to 24 years (or 43 per cent less) will enter the workforce than in 2010; and those aged 70 to 74 years will comprise the largest cohort in any five-year age grouping. Most South-East Asian countries face a similar outlook, with the population profiles of Thailand and Vietnam tracking the same as China (Callick 2015). To address this challenge, countries including South Korea, Japan and China, are looking to invest in improving workforce skills through lifelong learning and steps to attract younger migrants. However, immigration may not be the most appropriate solution to address labour shortages, particularly in enormous markets like China, where the current population already stands at over 1.3 billion.

The extent to which the Asia–Pacific region meets accelerating expectations or needs of their ageing populations presents significant social and political challenges. While the populations within the region reveal a sharp divide between those with wealth and those in poverty, rising economic growth has brought about an emerging middle class. The middle class in Asia is expected to grow from 500 million currently to over 3 billion by the year 2030 (Statista 2018), generating demand which, in turn, creates employment opportunities. This is creating a shift to higher productivity within several sectors. Significantly, roles for women in the workforce have been transformed as part of this process. A greater number of women in the labour force will lead to an increase in dual-income households, which further increases demand and drives economic growth. There are now unprecedented opportunities for companies, industries and governments to enter the international business environment across the Asia–Pacific region.

MULTIPLE-CHOICE QUESTIONS

SPOTLIGHT 1.2

Inside Asia: changing times

The Asia–Pacific hotel revenue management landscape continues to change and advance. Leading hotel technology firms contend there has been a paradigm shift in adopting a more open pricing methodology versus the more basic revenue practices. Not all countries are embracing new revenue management practices at the same rate. In some markets, revenue management departments remain focused on administrative tasks of updating rates and reservations, and making rate changes based on daily or seasonal occupancies. In globalised markets like Bangkok, Singapore and Hong Kong, revenue management teams have become more strategic, future orientated and proactive, rather than simply being reactive and tactical.

Revenue management teams play a more critical strategic role in international hotel chains with many reporting directly to the general manager rather than sales and marketing heads. A strong academic background with economic and commerce studies has become a key selection criterion in recruiting multidisciplinary teams. As revenue management and distribution becomes increasingly complex, hiring graduates with statistics, information technology and science qualifications will enable teams to stay ahead of the curve.

There are limited barriers to entry in the hotel industry and competition is increasing. The proliferation of new hotel rooms as well as fresh players like Airbnb entering the market, particularly in key Asian cities such as Bangkok, Beijing and Shanghai, means revenue management disciplines are continuously being challenged. Projecting forward five years, revenue management practices are expected to be increasingly more strategic than tactical in nature. There will be a greater focus by hotel management in terms of cost-of-guest-acquisition versus the financial value a guest places

on their choice of booking channel. As technology evolves, hotels are expected to further embrace open pricing, and management will need to engage actively in implementing room occupancy strategies at a faster pace.

SPOTLIGHT QUESTIONS

QUESTIONS

1. What factors do you think are driving the need for hotel revenue strategies to have a greater focus on the guest?
2. Consider why you believe the key Asian cities of Bangkok, Beijing and Shanghai have been the hotspots for new international businesses entering the hotel market.

Global risks and international business

International businesses operate in dynamic environments which present a range of opportunities and challenges in which risk is a key consideration. Identifying risk is an essential part of international business planning. Therefore, identifying what is risk, understanding what drives risk and how to manage risk in international business environment is critical.

The annual World Economic Forum engages with key global experts and opinion leaders. Over 700 of the experts in the World Economic Forum's multi-stakeholder community participate in a yearly study, the Global Risks Perception Survey. The terms 'global risk' and 'global trend' have been defined by the World Economic Forum: global risk is 'an uncertain event or condition that if it occurs can cause significant negative impact for ... countries or industries within the next 10 years'; global trend is 'a long-term pattern that is currently taking place and that could contribute to amplifying global risks and/or altering the relationship between them' (World Economic Forum 2016p. 11). The outputs from the survey highlight the ways in which global risks are evolving and may impact over the next 10 years.

The results from the 2016 report revealed that risks previously identified in past surveys were now becoming evident in new and unanticipated ways that harm markets, organisations and societies (World Economic Forum 2016). The respondents are from business, universities, institutes, communities and the public sector from a range of countries, across a range of age groups and with varying areas of expertise. The survey asks the respondents to rate 29 risks in the categories of economy, environment, geopolitics, society and technology over a 10-year period by identifying their likelihood of occurrence and resulting impact. Over the last three years from 2016, the top five most impactful risks were: failure of climate change mitigation and adaptation (leading the list), weapons of mass destruction, water catastrophes, large-scale involuntary migration and severe energy price shocks.

The risk rated most likely to occur was large-scale involuntary migration, followed by interstate conflict with regional consequences, environmental risks of extreme weather events, failure of climate change mitigation and adaptation, and major natural catastrophes. Understanding and recognising global risks for international business organisations and their trading partners remains a serious issue due to the combined impact and likelihood of economic risk including fiscal crises in key economies that results in high structural unemployment or underemployment (World Economic Forum 2016). Profound social instability and cyber-attacks were also identified as issues of concern.

The 2016 survey results concluded with a discussion regarding the impact that a Fourth Industrial Revolution could place on an economy or a society and highlighted the necessity to protect future benefits.

FOURTH INDUSTRIAL REVOLUTION a range of new technologies that are blending the physical, digital and biological worlds, impacting all disciplines, economies and industries, and stimulating ideas about what it means to be human.

International businesses must also consider cascading risks. Three risks are very apparent (World Economic Forum 2016). First, the potential for climate change to aggravate water crises increases the probability for further conflicts and increased forced migration. A stronger water governance platform to adapt to climate change, and adjust for the growing population and economic development may be implemented by national governments. Second, the risk of not addressing the global refugee crisis, cascades risk into areas of national security, anti-immigration sentiments, burdens on public finances and other humanitarian obligations. A focus on building resilience through policy implementation at a country level may have consequences for international businesses. Third, organisations failing to fully understand how the transition in the Fourth Industrial Revolution influences trading opportunities and operations at a time of slow-moving economic growth will increase their exposure to risk.

The risks of highest concern for engaging in international business and trade over the next decade related to being prepared to deal with risk and developing a level of resilience. Two main economic risks for doing business globally have been identified: employment (unemployment and underemployment) and the response to energy price shocks. Economic risks including fiscal crises, asset bubbles and energy prices are of most concern to the EU, while the US is focused on cyber-related risks and attacks. Central Asia identifies fiscal crises, unemployment, unmanageable inflation and interstate conflict as chief areas of concern. East Asia and the Pacific target environmental risks, energy prices and asset bubbles as their primary risks. Challenges South Asia identifies include fiscal crises, unemployment and the failure of national governance.

Suggestions as to what international firms can do are based around connectivity as the formula for managing risk (World Economic Forum 2016). Well-developed planning, monitoring and evaluation of risk – including strategic risk and risk management methodologies, supported by high quality data, analysis and information – are required. This means placing the risk management strategy in the heart of organisational planning. One such method is scenario planning, where the 'what if' strategy identifies the degree of impact of an event and the measurement of the probability of the event affecting the firm. This decision to include and engage in scenario planning starts at the executive level of the organisation. One such firm who focuses on this type of planning is Zurich Insurance, which delivers the risk management approach of scenario planning to their clients.

International firms, operating within regions and across multiple countries, need to create a culture of risk awareness within the business and through development of strategic risk management plans. When global risks impact the business, the success or failure of the organisation can be felt particularly at the operational level through the firm's physical assets, supply chains, distribution and employees. Organisations must plan to manage immediate risks, and need to create continuing stability by implementing a deliberate framework to protect and provide resilience against global risks for the company. International business managers look at risk holistically to prepare for the breadth and depth of challenges that arise in this Fourth Industrial Revolution era.

MULTIPLE-CHOICE QUESTION

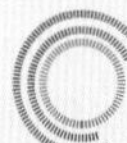

SPOTLIGHT 1.3

Outlook for South-East Asia, China and India

According to the Organization for Economic Co-operation and Development (OECD) (2016), growth in emerging economies in Asia is expected to remain robust with an average of 6.2 per cent per annum between 2016 and 2020. India's growth is anticipated to accelerate to one of the highest rates in the region because of increased government focus and investment, particularly in relation to public infrastructure development, and private investment motivated by business environment improvements. This expansion will offset the continued moderation of China's growth rate. The ASEAN-5 nations of the Philippines, Vietnam, Cambodia, Laos and Myanmar will produce a projected 5.2 per cent growth over the same period. Private consumption is predicted to be a large driver of growth due to higher wages and improved benefits for public sector employees in comparison to the previous decade.

To sustain growth momentum, the region will need to cope with potential domestic and external risks. First, the slowdown in China's economy will continue to impact the collective region as export demand and FDI flows decline. Second, monetary tightening in the US, while mild, is expected to have implications for the region. Those countries with more developed financial markets will be less likely impacted than those with less-developed markets. Third, the slowing trend in productivity growth across emerging economies in Asia since the global financial crisis needs to be addressed. One suggestion is that regional ties need to be enhanced beyond the ASEAN group by addressing issues and developing policies to augment international trade, private sector development, renewable energy and green growth in the region.

Overall, improvement is required in the implementation of development plans in emerging Asian economies for the region to remain competitive and benefit from opportunities presented by deeper regional cooperation and integration with the wider global economy.

QUESTIONS

1. Consider 'improvement is required in the implementation of development plans in emerging Asian economies' and discuss what these plans may relate to in this statement.
2. What recent regional ties have been established by ASEAN and Australia?

SPOTLIGHT QUESTIONS

International business development: growth drivers

Change in regional communities is accelerating as the Asia–Pacific region becomes the driver of global economic growth. The 'made in Asia, consumed in the West' development model that has been entrenched over a number of decades is giving way to economic growth that is more inclusive and sustainable (Heyzer 2011). As a region, the Asia–Pacific is associated with myriad business opportunities. Increasing wealth, a rising middle class and new customer segments all form part of the ever-changing landscape. While developing Asia has rebounded strongly from global financial crises, the region faces the medium- and long-term challenge of maintaining growth beyond these events (Park & Park 2010).

Park and Park (2010) suggest that many elements that contributed to the region's superior long-run performance in the pre-crisis period will remain valid for post-crisis success. However, some of the factors that influenced the previous economic success in Asia 'will be less relevant today, because the region's very success has transformed it from a low-income, capital-deficient region to a middle-income capital-abundant region' (p. 22). The key forces that will help unlock and drive future growth are regulation, human capital, and innovation and technology.

Regulation

Across the Asia–Pacific region, countries are reviewing their approach to regulation and management. National governments are starting to synchronise their efforts across borders as they introduce new risk-based frameworks. Regulatory impacts present challenges and opportunities, including:

- robust regulatory frameworks positively support industry but increase the cost of compliance
- convergence of regulations make markets attractive for foreign investments
- consumers benefit from innovative ideas and solutions
- a healthier competitive marketplace with better managed companies benefits from lower capital requirements.

The ownership of wealth in the Asia–Pacific is generally highly concentrated, which contributes to the acceleration and agility of domestic business and the economy. The less robust financial regulation system in Asia, for example, presents corruption risks and legal compliance issues for foreign companies. With no single regulator, different trading centres and diverse currency rates, Asia–Pacific nations promote export growth by keeping their currencies low. Economic zones in China and India operate under their own set of regulations, rather than a national one. MNEs that enter this environment must manage unfamiliar trading environments. Business-to-business contracts may not comply with overarching trade practices regulations as bribery to hasten or ease up processes may be involved from either side (Chavey 2015).

Ritchie (2008) states that 'global economy boundaries have been muted in the past few years with the advent of the internet'. Each country has created laws or regulatory requirements for the different industries. Treaties have been established between countries, under international law, to provide an agreement on subjects. When a company is operating globally, this is compounded by the individual requirements of each country in which they have a presence.

For all organisations – national or international, private, public or non-profit – governance plays a significant role in creating oversight, accountability and information security. For international companies, more vigilance is required at the global level to keep abreast of the regulatory climate and, Ritchie proposes, more stringent regulations are on the horizon from many countries. For example, prosecution of data theft is becoming prevalent in the digital age. Developing a framework that allows agile compliance to these future requirements is a critical success factor in not only enabling sustained growth and entry into new markets, but also in the protection of business assets in a time where organised crime, terrorism and other groups have found a very lucrative business in capturing and re-selling critical information (Ritchie 2008).

With increasing protectionism towards the domestic economy, particularly in South Korea, China and Japan, government regulations are being put in place in the private sector to drive domestic economic growth. Such regulations place pressure on MNEs to incorporate domestic interests in their local partnerships. For example, the South Korean government has heavily regulated foreign investments and favours domestic industrial conglomerates. It has therefore become a requirement for foreign firms to create partnerships with domestic enterprises in South Korea at the cost of losing total control of management (Chavey 2015).

Conversely, deregulation can provide opportunities. Deregulation of the airline industry resulted in air transport costs being significantly reduced, leading to intense competition and increased access for a larger number of consumers. In the Asia–Pacific region, up to a dozen different airlines compete on a single route. This decreased level of regulation creates incentive for innovation in customer service standards. As regulations in other key regions including the US and the EU have a wider impact around the world, regulatory oversight continues to develop towards global standards.

Human capital

The planned management of education, migration and employment training strategies for the new age workforce will underpin the future development of the region (Salze-Lozac'h 2015). Human capital issues are now widely recognised as being critical to international business sustainability, competitiveness and success, and firmly feature at the top of most corporate agendas. International migration is a growing phenomenon and is a key component of the globalisation process. The United Nations (2013) estimates that in 2010, there were some 214 million international migrants worldwide, representing 3 per cent of the global population, and that there is as much international migration between less-developed nations as there is from less-developed nations to more developed countries.

Estimates by the International Labour Organization (Salze-Lozac'h 2015) show that there are over 30 million guest workers in the Asia–Pacific region, a number that is only expected to increase. The economic contributions of Asia's migrant workers are significant, providing 'skills, labour power and services in their host countries, as well as financial remittances, skills and knowledge once they return to their countries of origin'. Women constitute 42 per cent of these guest workers as the gender profile of migrant population shifts. Salze-Lozac'h (2015) suggests that 'harnessing the full economic potential of women in the economy is a powerful way to promote economic growth and reduce poverty' with United Nations estimates showing that the Asia–Pacific economy could grow by US$89 billion annually if women were fully integrated into the workforce.

International migration is a positive force for development, both in countries of origin and in countries of destination (Ocampo 2006). Large migration flows can be attributed to a diverse range of reasons. A primary rationale is that highly skilled migrants are valued for bringing a diversity of skills, talents and cultural understanding to workplaces that design and produce goods for the global market. They are also respected for their willingness to manage risk (proven through the risk of their mobility) and for entrepreneurial aptitude (United Nations 2013). Improved education levels influence migration flows; for example, India and China are now producing more engineering and computing students per capita than the US. Changes in the demographic profile of some countries, such as an ageing population, create the need to attract migrant workers to service market demand.

Over the next 40 years one of the most significant demographic trends for economies in the Asia–Pacific will be the ageing population. Approximately 1.2 billion people will be aged over 60 years with some 200 million people placed in the new cohort of 'very old', aged over 75 years (Heyzer 2011). There will be opportunities to increase the rate of participation in the workforce for those aged over 60 years. Consequently, the nature of work and the kind of support needed for older workers are new areas that need to be explored. There is potential for web-based technologies to improve engagement in the workforce.

In the dynamic growth environment of the Asia–Pacific region, a firm's ability to harness opportunities presented by an emerging customer base, is highly dependent on developing and engaging workers with key capabilities. Competition for talent and leadership is intensifying at all levels of international organisations, a key challenge for business is to retain talent (Deloitte 2015). Organisations need to develop a company culture and core values that inspire employees to stay and proactively contribute to the overall success of the firm.

Innovation and technology

Innovation and technological capacity remain instrumental to enhancing productivity in international business sectors and are a key market differentiator. The promotion of innovation to improve quality and enhance value is critical for businesses operating in the Asia–Pacific to remain competitive. Technology is one of the drivers for success in international trade and will accelerate the development of economies.

Technological progress in transportation has significantly reduced the perceived distance between different regions of the world, and has increased safety and reliability measures. Globally, nations and organisations are interconnected more than ever before with the ability to trade and distribute products and services in a time-sensitive environment. Transport, logistics and distribution infrastructure is of strategic importance to governments. This is being accelerated by public and private partnership agreements to facilitate trade within and between nations. For example, infrastructure upgrades estimated at US$7 trillion are planned for South-East Asia, while China has focused on building a high-speed railway to Singapore and on a dedicated strategy, 'One belt, one road', to connect with Europe (Salze-Lozac'h 2015).

Improvements in communications technology is facilitating the way people interact and reducing the time needed to perform business activities. The influence of mobile phones has grown more

significant in recent years. In less than five years, the number of mobile telephone subscriptions in the Asia–Pacific region more than doubled, rising from around 1.08 billion to 2.53 billion over that period. In East Asia, for example, 83 per cent of people living in rural areas have a mobile phone (Heyzer 2011). The cost of mobile phones has reduced considerably with intense competition from domestic mobile phone providers rivalling international telcos.

Internet use, captured by penetration rates, in the Asia–Pacific has soared, creating a new wave of 'e-empowered' citizens. An increasing number of businesses and consumers are gaining access to digital devices and platforms. This is creating technology improvement, lowering of entry costs and opening opportunities for innovative entrepreneurs with limited asset, technical or investment capacities. The way in which the Asia–Pacific does business is being transformed by the emergence of ecommerce, e-banking, mobile technologies, software tools and technologies across a range of sectors, including retail, health, agriculture and financial services (Salze-Lozac'h 2015).

Ecommerce has helped to reduce trade costs as innovative technology, improved internet access, and electronic pay and delivery systems have created a new ecommerce distribution channel. Given the constraints on gathering data concerning international ecommerce transactions, it is not possible to accurately measure the size of this market using official sources, however, private sector estimates indicate that the Asia–Pacific region is the largest ecommerce market (WTO 2015). Ecommerce will become an important source of job creation across all age cohorts in the workforce.

Summary

This first chapter opened with a study that illustrated the growing significance of international business and economic development for managers operating in the Asia–Pacific region, and set the scene for the remainder of the book.

Learning objective 1: Appreciate the term international business and the associated key concepts.

International business primarily involves all transactions that are devised and implemented within and across multiple countries to satisfy the objectives of organisations. Development of markets on foreign countries may take place in a range of forms, some evolving and some direct, from international engagement with subsidiary firms or through acquisition, merger or joint venture. A core market entry strategy commonly used as a first step for many firms is via export–import trading arrangements.

Learning objective 2: Understand the role of trade in the Asia–Pacific region today.

The rise of markets in the Asia–Pacific region has been extraordinary, even in the face of severe regional challenges. The large developing economies of China and India continue to thrive and build the prominence of the Asia–Pacific region on the global stage. Specifically, Asia accounts for more than half of the world's economic growth. Asia continues to input more than any other region to the recovery of global trade despite the financial crises of the last two decades. The Asia–Pacific continues to attract multinational enterprises. The largest recipients of FDI in the region are Hong Kong, China, Singapore and India.

Learning objective 3: Recognise the global risks when companies trade internationally.

Participants in international business environments compete for world market share and in realising investment opportunities. Trade is the important engine of economic and social growth and a mechanism that links markets internationally. While trade was conducted through the twentieth century primarily among the nations of Western Europe, North America and Japan, it is becoming evident in future decades the greatest international opportunities will be found in the 10 BEMs, signalling their importance to the future wellbeing of the global community.

Learning objective 4: Understand the growth drivers that are changing international business development.

The international trading environment has increased the level of engagement by domestic firms in foreign markets. For domestic firms, participating in international markets has become an imperative to avoid loss in home markets as a result of increasing foreign competition. Managing an international business is different from managing a domestic business and is more challenging due to a variety of reasons, including country differences, the greater intensity of competition, increased likelihood of intervention by governments (home and host), and the added complexity of conducting transactions in different currencies. Firms entering global markets require the critical success factors of innovation, creativity, flexibility and speed to achieve success.

USEFUL WEBSITES

REVISION QUESTIONS

Revision questions

1. Why is it important for students to understand international business? What are the elements of international business that are of greatest interest to international managers?
2. Provide an overview of how trade flows and the composition of trade have changed since the mid-twentieth century. Consider the key economic regions of the EU, the US or the Asia–Pacific and the role they have played.
3. Why is the twenty-first century being labelled as the 'Asian century'? What are some of the critical hurdles to overcome to ensure success in conducting business in Asia?
4. What workforce challenges are Asia–Pacific businesses currently facing? What changes in workforce participation rates will present the greatest opportunities in the region? Why?
5. What is the suggested approach for managing risk in international markets?

R&D ACTIVITIES

R&D activities

1. What is RCEP? Explain the advantages and disadvantages of this arrangement.
2. You are a new graduate for an MNE and your manager has asked you to use data obtained from the WTO at www.wto.org to determine the following information:
   a. List the top ten countries for global import and export trade for merchandise and commercial services.
   b. Identify the trading nations that are the top five fastest growing over the last five years.
   c. List the top five trading partners of ASEAN. How has this changed since 2000?
   d. Describe the change in terms of composition of trade for ASEAN nations since 2000.
3. GVCs have been an important driver of the expansion in international trade across the Asia–Pacific region in the last decade. With China and India set to be the two largest economies globally, you have been charged to present a case supporting why a firm should use GVCs to advance its international business dealings.
4. Using information available on the World Economic Forum website (www.weforum.org), prepare a presentation discussing why the Scandinavian countries of Norway, Sweden and Denmark are ranked highly in the Global Energy Architecture Performance Report. Consider and discuss the steps required by Asia–Pacific economies to advance their energy sustainability position in the Global Energy Architecture Performance Index (GEAPI).

IB MASTERCLASS

The Honda corporation: international business strategy

Overview

For the Japanese car manufacturer Honda, the domestic and international environments in the early 1970s brought tremendous challenges to its export strategy, which previously were based on mass production in Japan. Honda sought to develop extensive production capabilities in international markets, especially the US. However, Honda had two business concerns about using foreign facilities: whether Japanese cost levels could be met, and whether the quality level characteristic of Japanese-built cars could be retained.

The early 1970s

Internationally, Honda confronted three major environmental changes in the early 1970s: the rising value of the yen against the US dollar, new US regulations on tailpipe emissions and the first global oil crisis. Although the rising yen threatened Honda's traditional export strategy, the other two factors, together with the success of its small, fuel-efficient Civic model in Japan and the US, provided a window of opportunity for Honda to expand manufacturing into the US.

The rising value of the yen in 1971 increased the costs of exporting cars to the US, Honda's largest overseas market. The first oil crisis of 1973 negatively affected Honda's domestic operations as rising oil prices significantly increased the company's manufacturing costs. Conversely, consumer demand for more fuel-efficient cars to counteract the costs of soaring oil prices increased significantly.

In 1970, the US Congress passed the Clean Air Act imposing stricter requirements on tailpipe emissions. However, the US automakers had not been able to reach a consensus regarding the appropriate technology to meet such requirements. Both the first oil crisis and the Clean Air Act pushed the demand for fuel-efficient cars, which became the market niche US automakers had not been able to occupy. Honda viewed the US regulations as a welcome opportunity to catch up. This was reflected in the words of Honda's President, Soichiro Honda, '[T]his allows latecomers like us to line up at the same starting line as our rivals' (Honda 2005).

In 1972, Honda released its Civic car model in the Japanese market. This Civic was equipped with the CVCC (controlled vortex combustion chamber) engine, which met the US emissions standards. The CVCC engine permitted the regulated burning of a very lean fuel mixture without the catalytic converter or exhaust recirculation required by most other engines. In Japan, the Civic model won the Car of the Year Award for three consecutive years from 1973; in the US, it beat all other competitors in a fuel economy test for four consecutive years from 1974.

The challenge

The popularity of the Civic model in the US suggested support for an increase in Honda car imports to the US, but such an increase may have provoked the US government to impose import restrictions. This potential risk, together with the rising yen and the first oil crisis, led Honda to consider establishing a motorcycle manufacturing operation in the US. For this purpose, Kiyoshi Kawashima, Honda's President, requested a feasibility study in 1974. This study expressed doubts about the potential for achieving the required quality levels in US-based motorcycle production. The study further suggested a Honda factory would not be profitable if it manufactured only motorcycles. For these reasons, Kawashima decided not to build a manufacturing base in the US at that time.

The concept of a manufacturing base in the US resurfaced with the continuing high demand for the Civic model in Japan and in the US. To address this demand, Honda's Suzuka and Saitama factories had been operating at full capacity. Given the plausible expectation of further growth in market share, Honda had the option to expand its domestic factories. Kawashima did not choose that option, saying, 'Since it [Honda's auto business] is a budding business, we shouldn't assume we're ready to charge into competition with the other Japanese manufacturers, either in terms of sales or capital. So, rather than compete domestically to no avail, I would like to use this opportunity to take a chance in America, the world's largest market. I would like to build a motorcycle factory and eventually an automobile factory in the United States' (Honda 2005). Masami Suzuki, the Managing Director in charge of oversea manufacturing, was assigned the responsibility for a new feasibility study and relocated to the US in January 1976.

The second feasibility review

Suzuki first discussed the plan with the American managers at American Honda Motor Company. These managers expressed scepticism about achieving comparable quality standards by manufacturing in the US. They based their doubt on their own experiences with what they regarded as the intrinsic problems of contemporary American-made cars. For Suzuki, these discussions still left the quality issue unanswered.

In the spring of 1976, Lee Iacocca, President of Ford Motor Company, offered Suzuki the chance to investigate the American way of auto manufacturing. In conjunction with Suzuki's negotiations to sell CVCC engines to Ford, Iacocca invited Suzuki to tour the most highly rated plant at Ford. The tour gave Suzuki a detailed look at the knockdown system characteristic of American auto manufacturing. In this system the main car assemblies were shipped via railroad from Detroit, Michigan, to the Ford plant where multiple various small volume production methods were used to manufacture cars. Compared with the American system, Honda's manufacturing methods used much less presswork, more integrated welding processes thereby delivering improved real-cost performance.

Suzuki came out of the tour convinced that car quality depended primarily on the management system and that Honda would be able to produce high-quality cars in the US by applying its existing management principles. At that stage, Honda began searching for an appropriate US location for its plant, which required a site of 100 to 200 acres, with easy access to railroad transport and a pool of highly skilled labour.

In 1976, Honda commissioned an American consulting firm to search for an optimal location, and in 1977 it hired a research institute to analyse labour market conditions. Based on the resultant research, Suzuki and his colleagues visited more than 50 sites in Ohio but to no avail. Before excluding an Ohio location, Suzuki visited the state governor and the chief of Ohio's Economic Development Bureau in July 1977, leading to the selection of the location in Marysville, Ohio.

Manufacturing motorcycles in the US

Honda of America Manufacturing (HAM) was established in 1978. Its business objective was to manufacture motorcycles first and cars later, once enough manufacturing existed. HAM's top priority, to manufacture high quality products, was dependent on two key factors: capable employees to build the cars, and reliable suppliers to provide the parts and raw materials.

Challenge 1

The first challenge involved selecting and training employees. A selection committee, led by HAM's Executive Vice President and Manager of General Affairs, recruited 50 people out of more than 3000 applicants. They were hired not because of their experience or knowledge in motorcycle manufacturing but because of their passion for their work. Honda believed it would be easier to transfer the company's work philosophy to this type of employee.

In 1979, Japanese engineers commenced training workers at HAM, and HAM's American managers were sent to Japan to study Honda's manufacturing processes. In September of that year HAM began to manufacture the CR250 R motocross bike. After the workers gained enough experience, the production of the Gold Wing GL1000, a more sophisticated model, was transferred to HAM in April 1980.

Challenge 2

Developing a lean supplier network in the US was the next step. Honda had its supplier groups in Japan but only a few of them agreed to follow Honda and build plants in the US. To supplement those suppliers, Honda needed to develop a supplier network in the US from only three sources: suppliers of motorcycle parts (who had to be willing to eventually make auto parts); other small suppliers in Ohio and surrounding states, who had to learn the Honda standards of quality, cost and timely delivery; and large suppliers who also served other automakers, especially the US Big Three (General Motors, Ford and Chrysler).

Honda decided to focus on the first two groups as it considered managerial attitudes were more important than technical expertise. The first two groups appeared more willing to respond to Honda's expectations despite facing challenges in terms of technical and organisational skills. The third group, with superior capabilities, was not as responsive to Honda's requirements as the other two.

To upgrade the expertise of the selected suppliers, Honda became actively involved in their operations, from examining manufacturing processes to developing quality circles and hiring new managers. The core of such supplier development activities later became a programme called 'BP', which stood for Best Position, Best Practice, Best Process and Best Performance. With the BP program, Honda sent out teams of specialists to its suppliers to help them improve to the required performance level. HAM expanded its supplier network from a handful of local suppliers in the early 1980s to 320 North American suppliers by 1994. In that year more than 80 per cent of its parts were purchased locally (Fitzgerald 1995).

Manufacturing cars in the US

In January 1980, Honda announced its plan to manufacture cars in the US, with the construction of the necessary facilities to start in December 1980. The prime focus of this new operation was still to build high-quality products. To achieve this objective, Honda sent some 300 experts and veteran associates from its Sayama plant in Japan to the US. Additionally, many experienced workers involved in motorcycle production at HAM were transferred to the new auto plant. HAM's first Accord car model rolled off the production line on 1 November 1982 with the promised high level of quality (Honda 2005).

Since that time, HAM has become Honda's largest manufacturing plant, producing cars not only for the US but also for Japan and other countries. At the end of 2016, Honda was the largest foreign-based company in the US motor vehicle industry, with nearly 12 300 employees in manufacturing facilities, and over 6100 across affiliates. Additional people were employed at Honda's non-manufacturing facilities (Ohio Development Services Agency 2016, p. 40). In the aftermath of the 2008 global financial crisis, favourable exchange rates and lower labour costs signalled a revival of the American automotive sector from 2012 onwards. In that same year

Honda announced intentions to invest US$218 million and expand its Ohio-based operations (Boudette 2012). As at 2016 there are Honda plants in East Liberty, Greensburg, Lincoln, and Maryville.

Honda today

Honda's successful entry into the US is largely credited to the company's planned strategy and managerial expertise, giving rise to the term the Honda effect' (Pascale 1996). Several researchers have argued that the company's management approach in reacting strategically to new challenges was what facilitated the success in the problematic US market. Honda now operates globally in Asia, Oceania, Europe, the Middle East, Africa, China, South and North America, and Japan.

Honda continues to establish itself in unfamiliar industries and markets. In 2012, the company took further steps towards achieving Soichiro Honda's 'long-standing dreams to advance human mobility' (Fujino 2012). Honda reached the final stages of Federal Aviation Administration certification for its Honda Jet fleet. HondaJet applies just-in-time inventory principles to manufacture 80 jets per year, a figure almost double the industry average (Dawson 2012; Kim 2012).

The overarching Honda Company principal continues to guide corporate decisions and aligns the international affiliate and subsidiary business ventures: 'Maintaining a global viewpoint, we are dedicated to supplying products of the highest quality, yet at a reasonable price for worldwide customer satisfaction' (Honda 2018).

The five management values are embedded across and within Honda's business activities:

1. Proceed always with ambition and youthfulness.
2. Respect sound theory, develop fresh ideas, and make the most effective use of time.
3. Enjoy your work and encourage open communications.
4. Strive constantly for a harmonious flow of work.
5. Be ever mindful of the value of research and endeavour (Honda 2018).

The Honda organisation operates within a framework that underpins the basis for their business operations, and how their products and services add value to lives of their customers.

Refer to https://global.honda for further interesting reading on the history and journey of Honda.

QUESTIONS

1. What specific resources were required to make Honda's proposed international business activities successful in the US?
2. Which value-added activities in which foreign locations permitted Honda to expand internationally?
3. What were the main costs and benefits of using complementary resources of external stakeholders in the US to fill resource gaps?

References

Asia Education Foundation (2014). AEF submission to the Australian curriculum review. Retrieved from www.asiaeducation.edu.au/research-and-policy/australian-curriculum-review/aef-submission

Asian Development Bank (2011). Asia 2050: Realizing the Asian century. Retrieved from www.adb.org/publications/asia-2050-realizing-asian-century

Austrade (2018). Boeing opens largest R&D lab outside US in Australia. Retrieved from www.austrade.gov.au/Local-Sites/India/News/Boeing-opens-largest-RandD-lab-outside-US-in-Australia

Boudette, N. (2012). New US car plants signal renewal for manufacturing. *Wall Street Journal*, B.3, 26 January.

British American Tobacco (2018). BAT website. Retrieved from www.bat.com

Callick, R. (2015). Challenges ahead as Asia–Pacific ages rapidly: World Bank. *The Australian*. Retrieved from www.theaustralian.com.au/business/opinion/rowan-callick/challenges-ahead-as---ages-rapidly-world-bank/news-story/9bed54af94fbd6605064037020d4428d

Chavey, A. (2015). Five challenges American companies face in Asia. Retrieved from http://globalriskinsights.com/2015/06/five-challenges-american-companies-face-in-asia

Ciobo, S. (2017). The importance of Asia in the twenty-first century. Speech. New York: Australia America Association. Retrieved from http://trademinister.gov.au/speeches/Pages/2017/sc_sp_170123.aspx

Dawson, C. (2012). Why Honda says it can fly (and GM won't). *Wall Street Journal*, 30 January.

Deloitte (2015). *Human Capital Trends 2015: Leading in the New World of Work*. Dublin: Deloitte.

Diageo (2018). Where we operate. Retrieved from www.diageo.com/en/our-business/where-we-operate/global

Europa EU (2017). Europe's Digital Progress Report 2017: United Kingdom. Retrieved from https://ec.europa.eu/digital-single-market/en/news/europes-digital-progress-report-2017

Fitzgerald, K.R. (1995). For superb supplier development – Honda wins! *Purchasing*, 119, 32–9.

Fujino, M. (2012). *HondaJet*. Speech made in 2012.

Heyzer, N. (2011). Digital Asia–Pacific in the twenty-first century. *UN Chronicle*, 48, 3.

Honda (2005). Company information. Retrieved from https://global.honda/about

——— (2018). Honda corporate profile. Retrieved from http://world.honda.com/profile/philosophy

International Monetary Fund (2015). Asia and Pacific: Stabilizing and outperforming other regions, *Regional Economic Outlook*.

——— (2017). IMF website. Retrieved from www.imf.org

Kim, C.-R. (2012). Honda out to shake up market with 1st biz jet next year. Reuters, 31 January.

Nestlé (2018). About us: Nestlé worldwide. Retrieved from www.nestle.com/aboutus/globalpresence

Ocampo, J.A. (2006). International Migration and Development. United Nations. Retrieved from www.un.org/esa/population/migration/turin/Turin_Statements/OCAMPO.pdf

OECD (2016). Economic outlook for Southeast Asia, China and India: Enhancing regional ties. Retrieved from www.oecd.org/dev/asia-pacific/SAEO2016_Overview%20with%20cover%20light.pdf

Ohio Development Services Agency (2016). The Ohio Motor Vehicle Report, December 2016. Retrieved from https://development.ohio.gov/files/research/B1002.pdf

Park, D. & Park, J. (2010). *Drivers of developing Asia's growth: Past and future*. ADB Economics Working Paper Series No: 235. Philippines: ADB. Retrieved from www.adb.org/sites/default/files/publication/28279/economics-wp235.pdf

Pascale, R. (1996). The Honda effect. *California Management Review*, 38(4),80–91.

Pimoljinda, T. (2013). *Ethno-cultural Diversity: A Challenging Parameter for ASEAN Regional Integration*. Paris: Atlantis Press. doi:10.2991/icpm.2013.11

Ritchie, J. (2008). Global security challenges. Retrieved from www.scmagazine.com/global-security-challenges/article/554408

S.R. (2015). 'The Economist' explains why China's economy is slowing. *The Economist*, 15 May. Retrieved from www.economist.com/the-economist-explains/2015/03/11/why-chinas-economy-is-slowing.

Salze-Lozac'h, V. (2015). Trends that will shape Asia's economic future (Part 2). The Asian Foundation. Retrieved from http://asiafoundation.org/2015/02/11/trends-that-will-shape-asias-economic-future-part-2/

Schwab, K. (2016). *The Impact of the Fourth Industrial Revolution: What Everybody Should Know*. Geneva: World Economic Forum.

——— (2017). *Global Competitiveness Report 2017–2018*. Geneva: World Economic Forum.

Statista (2018). Forecast of the global middle class population from 2015 to 2030, by region (in millions). Retrieved from www.statista.com/statistics/255591/forecast-on-the-worldwide-middle-class-population-by-region

Thomas, D.E. & Eden, L. (2004). What is the Shape of the Multinationality-Performance Relationship? *Multinational Business Review*, 12(1), 89–110, https://doi.org/10.1108/1525383X200400005.

UNCTAD (2014). *World Investment Prospects Survey 2014–2016*, New York and Geneva.

——— (2016). World Investment Report 2016: Investor Nationality: Policy Challenges. Retrieved from http://unctad.org/en/PublicationsLibrary/wir2016_en.pdf

——— (2017). UNCTAD website. Retrieved from http://unctad.org/en/Pages/Home.aspx

United Nations (2013). UN system task team on the post-2015 UN development agenda: Migration and human mobility. Retrieved from www.un.org/millenniumgoals/pdf/Think%20Pieces/13_migration.pdf

Volvo (2018). Volvo website. Retrieved from www.volvocars.com

World Bank (2016). World Bank: Stable growth outlook for East Asia & Pacific in 2016–18. Retrieved from www.worldbank.org/en/news/press-release/2016/10/04/world-bank-stable-growth-outlook-for-east-asia-pacific-in-2016-18

——— (2017). World Bank open data. Retrieved from http://data.worldbank.org

World Economic Forum (2016). The Global Risks Report 2016, 11th edn. Geneva: World Economic Forum. Retrieved from www3.weforum.org/docs/GRR/WEF_GRR16.pdf

World Trade Organization (WTO) (2015). *International trade statistics 2015*. Geneva: World Trade Organization. Retrieved from www.wto.org/english/res_e/statis_e/its2015_e/its2015_e.pdf

——— (2016a). *World Trade Statistical Review 2016*. Geneva: World Trade Organization.

——— (2016b). Trends in world trade: Looking back over the past ten years. In: *World Trade World Trade Statistical Review 2016*, Chapter II, pp. 9–15.

——— (2017a). *World Trade Outlook Indicator*. Geneva: World Trade Organization. Retrieved from www.wto.org/english/res_e/statis_e/wtoi_e.htm

——— (2017b). *World Trade Statistical Review 2017*, Geneva: World Trade Organization. Retrieved from www.wto.org/english/res_e/statis_e/wts2017_e/wts2017_e.pdf

——— (2018). *Trade facilitation fact sheet*. Retrieved from www.wto.org/english/tratop_e/tradfa_e/tf_factsheet_e.htm

CHAPTER 2

DRIVERS AND CHALLENGES OF INTERNATIONALISING FIRMS

Learning objectives

In reading this chapter, you will learn to:

1. understand the reasons why firms internationalise
2. examine the role of firm-specific advantages in the internationalisation of firms
3. identify the role of home-country advantages for firms seeking to internationalise
4. analyse and understand the effects of host-country differences and policy implications in Asia–Pacific economies and firms
5. recognise the role international relations plays and identify international legal frameworks.

THE COMPREHENSIVE AND PROGRESSIVE AGREEMENT FOR A TRANS-PACIFIC PARTNERSHIP

Globalisation is a result of market intervention combined with favourable government policy. Continual reduction of trade barriers and tariffs has allowed the free flow of goods and services between economies, which has led to greater economic integration. Multilateral and regional free trade agreements have played a vital role in facilitating greater economic interaction between economies. The most recent example of such an agreement is the Comprehensive and Progressive Agreement for Trans-Pacific Partnership (CPTPP), formerly known as TPP. The CPTPP is a proposed trade pact between 11 nations: New Zealand, Australia, Brunei Darussalam, Canada, Chile, Japan, Malaysia, Mexico, Peru, Singapore and Vietnam. The key goals of the agreement are to:

- enhance trade and investment flows among partner nations
- promote innovation, economic growth and development, and support the creation and retention of jobs

- increase productivity and competitiveness
- raise the standards of living
- promote good governance and transparency (Gracie 2016; New Zealand Foreign Affairs & Trade 2015).

The CPTPP proposes to improve international labour standards; for example, the agreement will require participating nations to protect the interests of their labour by giving more freedom to industries to form unions as well as prohibit the exploitation of both adult and child labour. The agreement will also ensure that the local industries offer a minimum wage and decent working conditions to the workforce.

The CPTPP plans to introduce better environmental protection standards. In addition, it aims to eliminate or reduce tariff and non-tariff barriers substantially across all trade in goods and services, and investment to create new opportunities for businesses, workers and consumers alike (Greenfield & White 2017; Young 2018a). The agreement also intends to promote innovation, productivity and competitiveness by encouraging the development of the digital and technical expertise among industries of participating nations. Finally, the CPTPP is intended to act as a platform for regional integration and it is designed to include additional economies across the Asia–Pacific region (Vaswani 2016; Young 2018b).

Once put into action, the CPTPP will be the largest economic partnership created and it will have an important bearing on the global economy. The partnership is also the only agreement that brings together developed and developing nations (Vaswani 2016).

Upon the withdrawal of the US, after Trump's election, China has expressed its interest to join this trade pact (Miyazaki & Westbrook 2016; Zhou 2015). The Chinese government was once concerned about losing its influence in the region because of the CPTPP, but now views the pact as a mechanism to further strengthen its influence in the Asia–Pacific region (Greenfield & White 2017). The potential economic impact of China's involvement with the agreement is dependent on several factors, but most importantly will be influenced by the extent of economic cooperation among China and current CPTPP member nations.

VIDEO VIGNETTE QUESTIONS

Introduction

This chapter has five specific learning objectives. First, the chapter starts with a discussion on key international business theories that analyse the main motives behind the internationalisation of firms. Among other factors, the nature of firm-specific advantages (FSAs) influences the internationalisation of a firm. The ownership of specific advantages also assists in the dissemination and the assessment of distinct corporate profiles, which enables a firm to develop a competitive advantage, especially when it operates in a foreign market. Accordingly, the second objective of the chapter is to outline how resources, such as capital and human resource, assist in the development of FSAs. Following this, the chapter's third objective examines the role of factor and demand conditions, supporting industry, firm strategy and government in determining the nature of national and international competitiveness of a firm. Given that location advantages of a host country play a critical role in influencing inward foreign investments, it is important to understand the nature of the host-country's institutional environment and the influence it has on MNEs operating in each market. The fourth objective of the chapter consequently examines how factors such as political and institutional risk, protectionism, corruption, bureaucracy and intellectual property can impact an MNE's operations in a host country. The chapter concludes with the fifth objective, which is a discussion on the different legal considerations that an MNE must bear in mind when considering operations in a foreign market.

FIRM-SPECIFIC ADVANTAGE (FSA) the distinct resource base available to the firm, critical to achieving its success in the marketplace. FSAs usually comprise of propriety advantages, often related to a firm's intangible assets, that enable it to compete against other firms.

Internationalisation theories of firms

There is a vast amount of research that explains different facets of firm internationalisation. Traditional explanations of international firm behaviour are rooted in economics and often use frameworks to explain the process of internationalisation from an asset exploitation perspective. Indeed, the ability of the firm to succeed in an international setting is determined by its firm-specific advantages and resources. Also, the nature and pace of the firm's internationalisation is often influenced by the location of the foreign market (its geographic and psychic distance), nature of the industry, external environmental variables (its institutional environment) as well as firm-specific factors (such as its level of international experience). These factors play a vital role in determining the strategies that a firm deploys to effectively overcome barriers that may stem from a lack of market knowledge, international experience, and geographic and psychic distance from foreign markets.

The Uppsala model, the eclectic paradigm, resource-based view (RBV) and Mathews' LLL model are key theories of company internationalisation. They offer comprehensive explanations on how firm-specific advantages and resources determine a firm's ability to internationalise, and their concepts assist the business in attaining a competitive advantage, especially in an international context.

Process theory: Uppsala model

The Uppsala model (1975) explains the nature of the internationalisation process of a firm. Researchers in the department of business studies at Uppsala University conducted a study collecting data from a database of Swedish-owned subsidiaries operating abroad. According to their research, firms first internationalise with ad hoc exporting, and subsequently formalise their presence in a foreign market through deals with intermediaries (often agents), who represent the firm's business interests in the foreign market. As sales grow, the firm replaces the intermediaries with their own sales organisation and, as growth continues, the firm may begin to manufacture in the foreign market to overcome trade barriers. The researchers labelled this dimension of the internationalisation pattern 'the establishment chain' (see Figure 2.1).

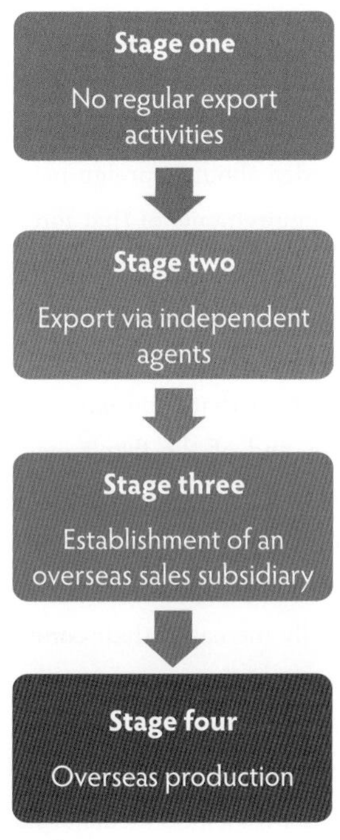

FIGURE 2.1 The establishment chain
Source: Adapted from Johanson & Vahlne 1977

Another feature of the pattern, according to the model, is that internationalisation frequently starts in markets that are close to the home country in terms of 'psychic distance.' Psychic distance is used to explain the market and institutional-factor differences between the home and host country, which may affect a foreign firm's operations. Psychic distance is often correlated with the geographic distance between home and host markets – the larger the geographic distance, the more distinct the differences are between the two markets, such as cultural, political and economic variances (Andersen 1993; Carlson 1975).

HOME COUNTRY
the domestic market where the headquarters of a firm are located.

HOST COUNTRY
the foreign market where a firm may invest or set up operations.

The Uppsala model states that firms progressively consider markets further away, especially in terms of psychic distance. This approach originally stems from the liability of foreignness. The liability of foreignness explains how a firm can use an FSA to offset a liability in a foreign market. It is assumed that the greater the psychic distance between the home and host country, the larger the liability of foreignness. Initially, the Uppsala model presented a fundamental understanding of market complexities that helped explain the difficulties that firms face when internationalising.

LIABILITY OF FOREIGNNESS
the challenges a foreign firm faces when compared with local firms, which is possibly reflected in its lower survival rate.

However, subsequent research by Johanson & Vahlne (2009) on international marketing and purchasing in business markets changed the model to encompass a business network view. This change is based on business network research and has two aspects. First, the revised model states that markets are 'networks of relationships in which firms are linked to each other in various complex and, to a considerable extent, invisible patterns' (p. 1411). Second, relationships offer the potential for learning, building trust and commitment in a foreign market. Both these aspects are relevant for small- and medium-sized enterprises (SMEs) as these firms often lack the necessary experience

and knowledge of operating in foreign markets. Therefore, networking becomes a primary source of information gathering in an international context.

This assumes that developing knowledge is fundamental to a firm's internationalisation, the knowledge that is developed from experience of operating in a foreign market. Knowledge can be developed through networking and relationships with other firms, potential partners and stakeholders in a foreign market. The revised model also emphasises that firms change through experiential learning. As firms gather knowledge about a foreign market, they are likely to change their operational strategies to best suit the requirements of that foreign market. As a firm builds knowledge through experience of operating in a foreign market, that body of knowledge then influences its entry strategies, level of commitment (to the market, potential partners or project) and the ability to take risks.

In addition, the Uppsala model suggests that experiential learning results in a 'gradually more differentiated view of foreign markets, and of the firm's own capabilities' (Johanson & Vahlne 2009, p. 1415). This point is supported by a study conducted by Górska (2013). The author used the Uppsala model to understand the internationalisation of Polish advertising agencies into China. The findings of the study partially confirm the Uppsala model. According to the study, 26 of the 32 agencies that were interviewed, gradually increased their commitment to the Chinese market. As early entrants in China, the firms increased their commitments in the market as they developed their experiential knowledge. For example, internationally renowned advertising agency Saatchi & Saatchi followed the gradual establishment path proposed by the Uppsala model. The firm entered the market by establishing a relationship with a local media broker and set up a representative office in Guangzhou. After operating in the market for two years, the firm eventually established its own branch offices in the region. It was also noted that some of the firms skipped steps of the establishment chain as they had a smaller psychic distance to the Chinese market. The findings of this study are a good illustration of how important the extensions of the original Uppsala model are for understanding the differing patterns of internationalisation.

The eclectic paradigm

The eclectic paradigm was first proposed by Dunning in 1977. It has proven to be an extremely useful framework that helps understand the operations of multinational enterprises (MNEs). The framework proposes three factors that might encourage a firm to undertake international operations: ownership advantages (O), locational advantages (L) and internalisation advantages (I). The eclectic paradigm is therefore also known as the OLI framework.

According to the framework, a firm's ability to compete is determined by its ownership advantages in relation to its major competitors, which it uses by moving its production facilities to overseas sites that are attractive due to the advantages of the location. According to Dunning (1980), there are two types of competitive advantages. The first type of competitive advantage is related to the ownership of unique intangible assets, such as firm-specific technology or a human resource. The second type of competitive advantage is determined by the ownership of complementary assets, such as the ability to innovate.

These advantages and their use are assumed to increase the wealth-creating capacity of a firm and hence the value of its assets. Assuming that condition one, ownership advantage (O), is satisfied, the extent to which a firm perceives it to be in its best interests to add value to its O, rather than sell those advantages, or the firm's right to use independent foreign firms, is an internalisation advantage (I). In other words, internalisation advantages arise when a firm retains control over its networks of assets, both intangible and complementary.

If condition one and two (i.e. O and I) are satisfied, the extent to which the international interests of the firm are served by creating, accessing or utilising its O and I in a foreign market determines the locational advantages (L) of that foreign market. Locational advantages are relative advantages that a host country offers in comparison to a firm's home country. These relative advantages indicate why a firm would choose to expand in that market. Countries would normally seek foreign direct investment (FDI) as a means of improving their locational advantages through linkages due to MNE activity in their country.

There are four primary reasons for a firm to internationalise its operations. According to Dunning & Lundan (2008), a firm seeks to internationalise its operations:

a. *to source resources from a foreign market (resource-seeking FDI).* This is where the firms are motivated to invest abroad to acquire and specific resources of a higher quality at a lower cost than could be obtained in their home country. There are three main types of resource-seeking firms: firms that seek physical resources (such as minerals and raw materials), firms that seek skilled or unskilled labour, and firms that seek to acquire technological ability, management or organisational skills.
b. *to expand its business to new markets (market-seeking FDI).* This is where the firms invest in a country or region to supply goods or services to that given market or adjacent countries. Market-seeking FDI may be undertaken to sustain or protect existing markets or to exploit or promote new markets. Another important reason for market-seeking investment is that a firm may consider it necessary as part of its global production strategy, which makes it necessary for the firm to have a physical presence in leading markets that are served by its competitors.
c. *to improve its economies of scale and reduce risk (efficiency-seeking FDI).* The motivation for efficiency-seeking FDI is to rationalise the structure of an established resource-based market in such a way that the investing firm can gain from the common governance of geographically dispersed activities.
d. *to acquire assets from firms in foreign markets (strategic-asset seeking FDI).* This is where firms engage in FDI by acquiring the assets of other foreign firms to promote their long-term strategic objectives, especially those related to sustaining or advancing their global competitiveness. The investing firms may include both established MNEs and first-time foreign direct investors seeking to further their business interests in a foreign market.

The eclectic paradigm states that the importance of and the conformation between each of the OLI advantages can be context specific. In other words, the importance of the OLI advantages may vary across distinct types of value-added activities or industries, countries or geography, and between firms. For example, the country-specific ownership advantages of New Zealand civil construction firms will be different to those from civil construction firms from, say, the US or Italy. Also, the extent of market failure experienced by a firm in a foreign market is likely to be dependent on the types of products or services it tends to offer, as well as the nature of the industry that the firm operates in. Finally, the relationship with the comparative locational advantages of foreign markets may be regarded differently by different firms depending on the strategies that the firm wishes to pursue in those markets. The comparative locational advantage of Taiwan and Thailand as a production base, for example, may be considered differently by Toyota than by Honda (Cantwell & Narula 2003, 2010). The OLI framework helps understand the role that ownership advantages play in influencing a firm's internationalisation.

Resource-based view

Like the eclectic paradigm, the RBV (first proposed in 1986) concentrates on the ownership advantages of a firm. The RBV is an established theoretical framework that explains the relationship between a firm's resources and its ability to develop competitive advantage. The RBV states that the source of competitive advantage for a firm is ownership of, or access to, a bundle of resources that are both immobile or imperfectly mobile and heterogeneous in nature (Barney 1986, 1991, 1996). Resources are considered immobile in two cases:

a. if the resources of a given firm are distinctive in nature
b. if the intellectual property rights of resources are heterogeneous in nature.

To develop and sustain a competitive advantage, a firm's resources must have the following attributes:

a. A firm's resources are *valuable*, that is, they can allow the firm to exploit opportunities or neutralise threats.
b. A firm's resources are *rare* among the firm's current and potential competitors.
c. A firm's resources are *inimitable* so that they cannot easily be replicated by other firms.
d. A firm's resources are *non-substitutable* by alternative strategically equivalent resource.

The theory also emphasis that resources and capabilities, either complementary or unique, are vital for a firm. In other words, a firm's ownership advantages can help a firm make strategic choices when operating in an international market and can therefore influence the performance of the firm in that location. The value and amount of resources can further assist a firm devise its strategies to expand its operations in a foreign market. Therefore, the theory assumes that limitations in resource availability may restrict the strategic options available to the firm considering international expansion. Although this is true for any firm, it is particularly relevant for SMEs and emerging market firms because often they lack enough resources to successfully operate in a foreign market. SMEs and emerging market firms either need to have enough resources to internationalise, or the firms should be able to source resources from strategic partnerships in a foreign market.

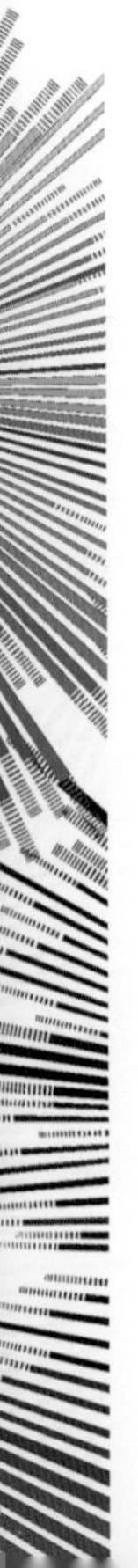

While the RBV has been revised to incorporate the network perspective, the theory only partially addresses the possibility of a firm being able to source necessary resources by developing strategic alliances or networks. This aspect is particularly important when examining the internationalisation of SMEs and emerging market firms. The competitive advantage of SMEs and emerging market firms, especially in an international context, cannot be based on their static resources as these firms often form alliances when internationalising and may acquire new resources as a result of those alliances (Buckley et al. 2007; Connor 2002). Also, compared to large firms, SMEs and emerging market firms tend to have far fewer managerial and financial resources that may be required to build vital competitive (ownership) advantages to succeed in a foreign market. This means that SMEs and emerging market firms are often not in a position to make the investments needed to develop and exploit ownership advantages in a foreign market compared to larger firms (Deng 2007).

Hence, although RBV serves as a useful theory to analyse how specific resources help a firm in developing sustained competitive advantage, it is important to note that the theory cannot be applied to examine the internationalisation of SMEs and emerging market firms.

Mathews' LLL model

Mathews' LLL model (the LLL stands for linkage, leverage and learning) was first proposed in 2002 and is seen as complementary to the eclectic paradigm. The LLL model, also a strategic framework, is based on the idea that the internationalisation of firms is not necessarily founded on the possession of ownership advantages, but rather on a firm's ability to leverage its capability in organisational learning. One of the main differences between the LLL model and the traditional theories of internationalisation, such as the eclectic paradigm and RBV, is that these approaches reflect the experiences of firms based largely in either Europe or the US, and are based on firms that are relatively large and established in an international context. Also the focus of the traditional theories discussed earlier is to analyse the barriers that may affect the entry of a firm in a foreign market (Stoian 2013).

By contrast, the LLL model discusses how such barriers may be overcome. Although the model mainly analyses the internationalisation of firms from emerging markets, it is also applicable to SMEs because they may not possess enough resources and market knowledge when considering international operations, given their size. SMEs may build strategic partnerships with potential foreign counterparts, which gives them access to the resources and market knowledge that they lack (Stoian 2013).

The LLL model analyses how newcomer firms can challenge large, established MNEs in the global economy. The LLL model is based on the philosophy that firms internationalise not to exploit resources but in the pursuit of resources. The model discusses the process of internationalisation of firms, classified either as latecomers or newcomers, that pursue international expansion in search of untapped resources and assets compared to other established and large incumbents. The considerations that apply to firms that contemplate international expansion in the pursuit of resources, not otherwise available in their domestic market, are quite different from those that apply to firms that consider international expansion to exploit existing resources (Mathews 2002, 2006a). Latecomer and newcomer firms often regard the world economy as an integrated web of inter-firm connections from the outset of their international operations. This aspect can be responsible for driving novel approaches to and patterns of internationalisation, which may not be acknowledged in traditional theories of internationalisation.

The LLL model states that strategies based on networking and leveraging from those connections 'are most likely to succeed in this interlinked global economy [and] are precisely those likely to be pursued by firms which lack substantial prior resource bases' while internationalising (Mathews 2002, 2006a, p. 9). In other words, firms that are late entrants in a foreign market are most likely to pursue strategies that are based on networking and building strategic relationships with partner firms in foreign markets. This approach to internationalisation is most often observed in the case of SMEs and emerging market firms. International expansion through strategies 'based on linkage, leverage and learning (accomplished through repeated applications of linkage and leverage) provides a point of contrast with some of the dominant frameworks' used (Mathews 2006a, p. 9).

Linkage

Linkage is an outward-oriented concept. It refers to the ways in which the firm may extend its influence into new markets or new businesses. In an international setting it refers to the capacity of the firm to extend into new cross-border activities via inter-firm relations (Mathews 2002). The denser these inter-firm connections, the more opportunities there are for the firm to be drawn via such linkages into the international economy. A critical point to note here is that latecomer and newcomer firms are not always reliant on their own advantages, but on the advantages which can be acquired externally. Hence, a global orientation becomes a source of competitive advantage since the opportunities through which these firms can expand are likely to be found in international markets rather than in their domestic environment (Mathews 2002).

Accordingly, internationalisation becomes a necessity for the latecomer or newcomer firm. An outward orientation is often riskier and has higher uncertainties compared to a more conservative inward focus (Mathews 2002). A firm seeking to acquire resources and complementary assets in a foreign market must overcome problems of market intelligence and uncertainty concerning the quality of knowledge potentially available to the firm (Mathews 2002, 2006a). SMEs must find ways to offset these risks. Thus, joint ventures (JVs), strategic alliances or other forms of collaborative partnerships are options that emerge as a means of entering a foreign market. These linkages help a firm develop relationships with their potential partners. The relationships are seen by aspiring firms as principal vehicles for reducing risks involved in international expansion (Mathews 2006a). Networks, or linkages, therefore can be created with the aim of acquiring resources from potential partners. Linkages also can help SMEs reduce the level of risk and uncertainties that arise due to lack of market knowledge.

Leverage

If the resources of a firm are lacking, then their leverage from external sources is the obvious way to proceed (Prahalad & Hamel 1990). The concept of resource leverage best describes the strategies used by the latecomer and SMEs. The concept was first introduced by Prahalad and Hamel (1990) and is since used as a means of explaining how incumbents keep up with new developments. The concept suggests that firms often create alliances to 'identify and secure access to the resources needed to keep diversifying their product portfolio' (Mathews 2006b, p. 323). The same idea underpins the strategy of the latecomer firm or SMEs (Prahalad & Hamel 1990; Mathews 2006b). SMEs and emerging market firms may often lack resources to succeed in an international market. Hence, to successfully operate in an international setting, latecomer firms and SMEs often seek to establish alliances with local firms in a foreign market. Through linkage, the latecomer firm or a SME can 'tap its links with more advanced firms to acquire [market] knowledge, technology, and market access – things that would otherwise be beyond the firm's limited resources' (Mathews 2006b, p. 314). The capacity to secure more from a relationship than the firm puts in, is termed as leverage (Mathews 2002, 2006b). Thus, by creating effective linkages, latecomers and SMEs can leverage necessary resources and expertise from their partner firms. Such leverage is particularly important for the latecomer firm or SME as it allows these firms to build competitive advantages critical to succeed in an international market.

The Indian-owned Mittal Steel Company is a classic example of a latecomer firm that used its international connections with incumbents to successfully leverage resources, such as technology. This strategy was particularly used by the firm to enter more mature markets like Europe and the US. To successfully enter and operate in these countries, the company acquired former state-owned steel plants and built a global network of interconnected mini-steel mills. These acquisitions gave the firm an access to DRI (Direct Reduced Iron) technology that it previously lacked (Mathews 2006a). Because of this, the firm was able to attract international customers and gain a competitive advantage in the global market. By establishing an integrated management system, the firm was also able to leverage requisite resources and information needed to succeed in both Europe and the US. Thus, the firm's global network helped it to not only access resources but also to build an international presence.

Similarly, in the case of service firms, linkages play an important role in helping a firm enter a foreign market, and in assisting its access to necessary resources and knowledge to succeed in that market. Tata Consultancy Services (TCS) is an Indian-based IT services, consulting and business-solutions firm. TCS offers a consulting-led, integrated portfolio of IT, business process outsourcing (BPO), infrastructure, engineering and assurance services to a global consumer base. The firm is a part of the Tata group, India's largest industrial conglomerate, and has operations in over 46 countries (Tata 2018). As an emerging market firm, TCS was a late entrant in the international arena. The international expansion of TCS in the last two decades is a result of strategic acquisitions and joint ventures. The firm, for example, entered Australia by acquiring a Sydney-based financial network services firm in 2005 (Verbeke 2013). Because of this take over, TCS was able to gain knowledge about IT solutions and services required to serve the needs of international financial institutions, and it secured access to a global customer base. The acquisition helped TCS strengthen its position in the Australian banking, financial and insurance sector. Similarly, by acquiring the Chile – based ComiCrom, TCS set up its operations in Latin America. ComiCrom was a BPO that did not have the expertise to provide banking and telecommunication services, while TCS lacked the market knowledge required to operate in the region (Verbeke 2013). The acquisition helped TCS gain market knowledge and ComiCrom the technical capabilities required to service the clients in the market.

The internationalisation strategy of firms like Mittal Steel and TCS indicate that leverage helps a firm's integration in the global supply chain by creating and making use of connections to further their business interests in foreign markets.

Learning

Learning is the 'enhancement of capabilities that results from repeated application of linkage and leverage strategies' (Mathews 2002). In other words, 'repeated application of linkage and leverage processes may result in the firm learning to perform more effectively' in an international setting (Mathews 2006a, p. 20). Learning is essential for any firm to adapt, improve and innovate to survive, especially in a foreign market. Also, through learning, firms better understand routine processes, practices and techniques, which help them customise their operational strategies in foreign markets. SMEs and emerging market firms tend to follow incumbents closely as it assists them in identifying the strategies adopted by incumbents in a foreign market, and helps them avoid the mistakes made by incumbents while operating in that market. This is termed experiential learning. A firm acquires tacit knowledge through experience of operating in a given foreign market. This experience and subsequent knowledge may not only influence a firm's commitment to that market, but also help the firm identify resources that are most likely to have a positive impact on the internationalisation of that firm.

Linkage, leverage and learning thus help explain why SMEs and emerging market firms go to such lengths to develop strategic partnerships that may help them succeed in a foreign market. The concept of linkage, leverage and learning holds relevance for this study for two reasons. First, it helps understand how firms without necessary resources internationalise. Second, it discusses the importance of local partnerships where firms may lack a permanent presence or the market knowledge required to operate in a foreign market.

SPOTLIGHT 2.1

Dr. Reddy's international expansion

This spotlight highlights the importance of internationalisation and the strategies used by Dr. Reddy's Laboratories, which have made it a leading global pharma success.

Established in 1984, Dr. Reddy's Laboratories (DRL) is a leading global pharmaceutical firm offering a wide range of products, including active pharmaceutical ingredients, generics, and biosimilar and differentiated formulations. The firm has operations in Europe, the US, Russia and the Commonwealth of Independent States (CIS); it generates 80 per cent of its revenues internationally.

Stiff domestic competition and import tariffs were the two main reasons that forced DRL to consider opportunities beyond its domestic market, India. The internationalisation process of DRL is typical of an emerging market firm. To gather market knowledge and technical expertise, the firm undertook a series of acquisitions in Mexico, the US, the United Kingdom and, more recently, the Netherlands. In addition to acquisitions, the firm has also sought international partnerships to help expand its global presence. The acquisitions and strategic partnerships have allowed the firm to leverage local talent and technologies to create unique cutting-edge products and services to a global consumer base. The firm today operates in five main international markets (Australia, the US, the UK, Germany and Russia) and six secondary international markets (Canada, China, Romania, South Africa, Spain and New Zealand) (Centre of Management Research 2012). Operations in a select few markets has allowed the firm to develop a niche, especially in the areas of biosimilars, cardiovascular, neurology and pain or palliative drugs, and anti-diabetic drugs. Firms like DRL internationalise with the intent to further their business interests, but also because they see it as an important mechanism to acquire resources and technical know-how.

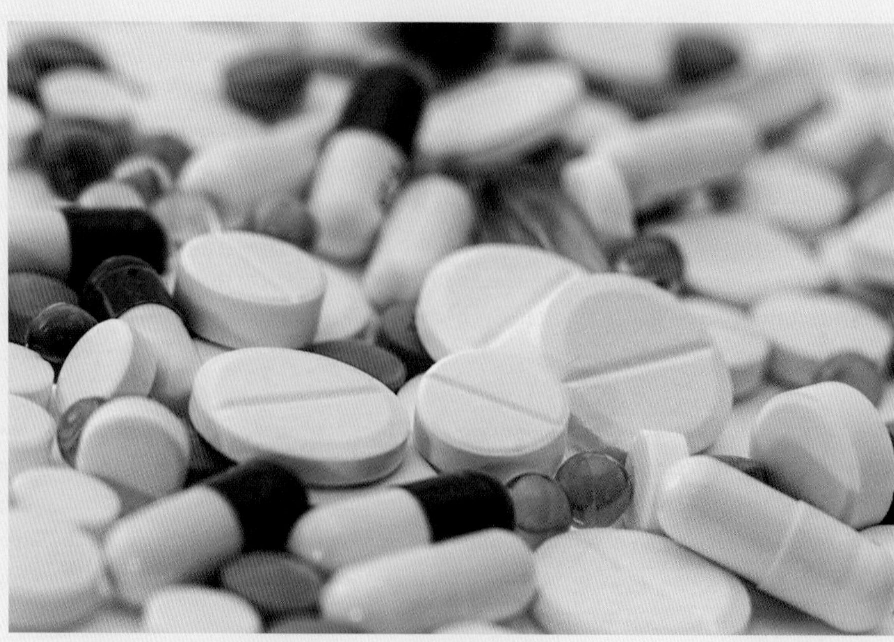

In terms of its domestic market, DRL was the first pharmaceutical firm in India that created direct links with the end user to provide comprehensive customer service and to inform patients of any upcoming products. The success of DRL in both emerging and developed economies can also be attributed to its diverse product offerings. (Bhadoria et al. 2016). In emerging markets, for example, generic drugs are sold under various branded names, whereas the firm uses its DRL brand to market and sell its products in the developed markets. A focus on research and development (R&D), the right marketing efforts, and the philosophy that healthcare must be widely accessible and affordable, has made DRL a global name in the pharmaceutical sector. Despite its success, DRL constantly deals with the issue of attaining legitimisation in its international markets. For example, the ban imposed by the US Food and Drug Administration (FDA) on products made at DRL's Mexico unit for violation of manufacturing practices has recently put the firm's image as a quality drug maker in disrepute. The ban has also affected the firm's revenues from the US market (Palmer 2017). Further, a series of accidents at the firm's Indian manufacturing facilities of late, have brought its safety practices under question. The above points indicate that, although emerging market firms like DRL attain success, these firms also have to constantly grapple with a unique set of challenges when operating internationally (Dey 2015).

QUESTIONS

VIDEO SPOTLIGHT QUESTIONS

1. Discuss the importance of internationalisation for emerging market firms like Dr. Reddy's.
2. Refer to the article: 'India's Dr. Reddy's hit by FDA warning, shares fall 15 percent' (Siddiqui 2015) and outline the key challenges that emerging market firms are likely to face when considering foreign markets.

FSAs and internationalisation

A firm's ability to compete in an international context, among other factors, is determined by its FSAs. FSAs are 'a firm's capacity to deploy resources, usually in combination, using organisational processes and routines, to create desired capabilities' (Amit & Schoemaker 1993). FSAs are therefore, exclusive or privileged possession of country-specific or firm-specific assets, which gives the firm proprietary advantage.

FSAs: tangible and intangible assets

Firm-specific assets can be tangible or intangible in nature. Tangible assets are assets that have a physical form. Firms are likely to display tangible assets in the way of niche capabilities or specialisation such as machinery and equipment, and technical expertise. This follows from the intangible nature of advantages, which tend to embody the firm's name, reputation and experience, and human resource skills. The level of specialisation facilitates the diffusion and evaluation of distinct corporate profiles. Firms that have a strong reputation are considered to have a competitive edge when considering international operations. A firm tends to gain recognition when it demonstrates the ability, technical know-how and experience to overcome challenges that may emerge when internationalising. Reputation also helps a firm market itself through its past successes; it also creates goodwill which can play a critical role, especially in relation to international operations.

The importance of resources, innovation, research and development

A firm's resources play a significant role in influencing its ability to develop firm-specific capabilities. Resources are firm-specific assets, knowledge, organisational processes and attributes that firms use to select, develop and devise their capabilities. According to Prahalad & Hamel (1990), core capabilities or FSAs are developed through a combination of multiple resources and skills that allow a firm to distinguish its product or service offerings in a given market. The nature of the core competencies allows the firm to develop a competitive advantage. Thus, it can be stated that resources strengthen a firm's performance (Conner & Prahalad 1996). Among other assets, a firm's human and financial resources play a vital role in determining the nature of its core competencies.

Human resources

Knowledge in a firm is based on the expertise (technical skills and education) and work experience (both domestic and international) of its personnel. Knowledge of personnel becomes particularly relevant for firms considering international operations. This is because operating in a foreign market requires staff that understand the dynamics of operating in an international setting. Also, firms operating in an international environment often require continuous intervention, rather than management by exception, as the business process of a firm, especially in an international setting which comprises highly complex interrelated tasks that require the acquisition and co-ordination of different categories of human resource skills (Chetty & Campbell-Hunt 2003). Therefore, firms seeking to internationalise often strive to create value through their selection, development and use of appropriate human capital (Dowling et al. 2013). Beca Group Limited, a leading New Zealand-based engineering consultancy (see Spotlight 2.2), is an example of a firm that has achieved international success because of its ability to attract and retain the right talent. With over three thousand staff working across 20 offices in the Asia–Pacific region, the firm has a diverse employee base. This diversity allows Beca to draw on a range of skills that have helped the firm better understand and deliver customised engineering solutions to a wide range of international clients. Also, to retain talent, the firm has developed an ownership scheme that encourages staff to invest by purchasing a stake in the firm. This strategy has been central to developing an effective incentive system where the employees across different subsidiaries are an integral asset to the firm. This in turn has created a culture where the employees see the firm as a local entity. This example indicates that the quality of human resources plays a critical role in the international success of a firm. It also suggests that firms need to effectively engage with their employees to develop core competencies which may help it succeed in an international setting.

Financial resources

The ability of a firm to attract capital is crucial when operating in an international environment. In developed countries, capital markets are sufficiently well developed and deep for financing potential prospects. However, capital markets in Asia–Pacific economies such as China and India, often lack enough financial depth. This is perhaps because historically these economies had severe investment restrictions in place, which made it difficult for them to attract foreign investments. This aspect may significantly limit the ability of foreign firms to obtain capital that may be required to undertake work in such markets. Also, access to debt capital in many Asia–Pacific emerging economies is largely controlled, and the banking sector acts in consent with the government to support political initiatives and national priorities. Such restrictions may affect foreign firms considering operations in these economies because the state may prioritise funding to domestic firms compared to foreign ones. Also, relatively weak governance in several emerging economies in the Asia–Pacific, especially makes it difficult for foreign firms to access local funding. Access to capital is vital for any firm, but becomes particularly critical for firms considering international operations as it determines the ability of the firm to respond to opportunities in a given foreign market. Firms, therefore, rely on local connections and networks to overcome financial impediments, and they complement such inflows through the formation of an internal capital market to support their operations in a foreign market.

Innovation, research and development

There is an increasing significance for firms to augment their existing assets by undertaking R&D activities and establishing R&D facilities in international markets. Indeed, with increasing technological complexity, firms today have a strong incentive to develop their technological capabilities. In doing so, firms upgrade their existing product or service offerings as well as enable new product development. Further, intense competition in the domestic and international context has meant that firms often need to pursue knowledge and capabilities beyond their home markets. The main intention here is to acquire, develop and enhance technological erudition in contemporary product markets to achieve competitive advantage domestically as well as internationally. Internationalisation of R&D activities allows a firm to develop technological proficiencies through dispersed geographical locations. Internationalisation of R&D activities also helps a firm improve its innovation performance, which is critical to sustain its competitive advantage internationally (Kafouros et al. 2008).

The role of FSAs in the internationalisation of a firm

Succeeding in international markets requires strong intrinsic capability. Firms therefore build FSAs to adapt, integrate and renew their resources in response to changing environments or markets. Examples such as Beca (see Spotlight 2.2) indicate that firms attain competitive advantage internationally by offering customised solutions for their clients. The expertise the firms offer and the tailored products or services allows them to build a powerful reputation in foreign markets. In addition, firms considering international operations must invest in R&D, which assists in developing customised products or services that suit the requirements of the foreign markets. Hence identifying a differentiator is paramount to the success of firms especially in an international setting.

However, as evident from Mathews' LLL model, firms may not necessarily possess resources when internationalising. This is particularly true in the case of SMEs and latecomer firms that internationalise in the pursuit of resources rather than to exploit them. These types of firms often depend on networks to secure the resources they require to successfully operate in a foreign market. Networks (linkages) are developed with the aim of procuring resources from potential partners, and can also help SMEs and latecomer firms better manage uncertainties that may arise due to a lack of market knowledge.

SPOTLIGHT 2.2

The growth of Beca in the Asia–Pacific

This spotlight highlights how FSA can enhance a firm's competitiveness in an international context.

New Zealand-based Beca is one of the largest civil construction and engineering consultancies in the Asia–Pacific region. Operating for over 90 years, the firm has an established presence in New Zealand and internationally. As well as numerous engineering consultancy services, Beca offers services in architecture, transport infrastructure and cost management, land information, earthquake engineering, transport infrastructure, water treatment and energy solutions. The firm has extensive international operations spanning markets in Australasia, Asia, the Middle East and Eastern Europe. Beca has three main hubs: New Zealand, Australia and Asia. The firm has operated in Asia for more than four decades, and has a wealth of knowledge and experience of operating in the region. Given its technical expertise, especially in seismic engineering and design, the firm enjoys a formidable reputation in Asia. The development of the Pacific Plaza, a landmark in Jakarta, is a classic example of FSAs that New Zealand civil construction and engineering firms bring to the international market. Beca provided mechanical, electrical and structural engineering services, working alongside a design team of international architects from Smallwood Reynolds Stewart and local architects and engineers. Being a 'complex three-tower structure in a seismically active area, Beca's seismic design expertise was a major factor in developing successful structural solutions early in the design process' (Beca 2007).

VIDEO SPOTLIGHT QUESTIONS

QUESTIONS

1. Outline the FSAs of the Beca Group.
2. How have FSAs helped Beca in developing an international presence?

Home-country advantages and internationalisation

The way in which firms create and sustain competitive advantage in domestic and global environment is strongly determined by the nature of the home-country advantages.

The nature of home-country advantages

Firms gain a competitive advantage in an industry when their home base allows and supports the accumulation of resources; this can lead to the development of specialist skills and capabilities by the firms. Bangladesh, for example, is seen today as a leading destination for apparel manufacturing. Employing nearly 50 per cent of the nation's population, the apparel sector is a vital contributor to the economy of Bangladesh (Seddiqe & Basak 2014). Abundant labour and resultant cheaper cost of production are the key reasons that have seen the country develop a global reputation as a leading garment and textile manufacturer. Similarly, Japanese car manufacturers, such as Nissan and Suzuki, have gained global recognition for their expertise in car design and fuel efficiency. The question, therefore, is why do different countries develop an international competitive advantage in an industry? This is best explained by Michael Porter (1990a, 1990b) who developed the 'diamond model' to explain how and why nations are able to create and sustain a competitive advantage in a particular industry.

Determinants of national and international competitiveness

Considering the key determinants that allow the country to develop national and international competitiveness is important. According to Porter's diamond model (1990a, 1990b) there are four distinct determinants that contribute to the competitiveness of a country:

1. factor conditions
2. demand conditions
3. supporting and related industries
4. firm strategy, structure and domestic competition.

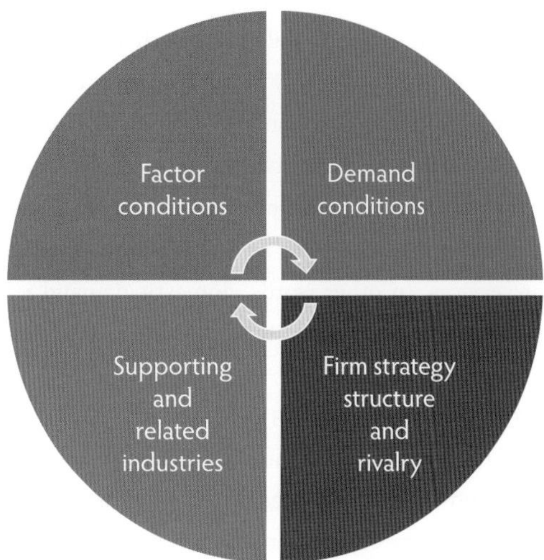

FIGURE 2.2 The diamond model
Source: Adapted from Porter 1990a, 1990b

Factor conditions

The first determinant in Porter's diamond model is factor conditions. Each country possesses a variety of factors of production. Factors of production are the inputs necessary to operate and compete in an industry. The basic factors of production include the following: human resource (labour), capital, natural resources and infrastructure. The model states that these resources provide the necessary building blocks of value creation and productive activities. However, it is also argued that advanced factors, such as knowledge and human capital alone, may not institute a competitive advantage in knowledge and technology-intensive industries, especially in today's information-based global economy. In such industries, nations and firms can create a source of competitive advantage by investing the development of sophisticated technology, innovation and effective utilisation of limited resources. The success of Korean firms, such as Samsung and LG, are prime examples of firms that have achieved a competitive advantage in industries where cost advantages are minimal, and where effective utilisation of existing resources have played a critical role in their international success.

Demand conditions

The second determinant of Porter's diamond model highlights a country's demand conditions. The influence of demand patterns on a nation's competitive advantage are determined by the nature of the needs of the home buyers. In fact, the composition of home demand shapes how firms perceive, interpret and respond to consumer needs. Nations and firms gain competitive advantage where home consumers demand certain types of products or services; this pressures local firms to innovate and develop sophisticated capabilities to better respond to their needs. An example of this is the rapid growth of mobile or m-commerce in India. Among other applications, the demand for mobile banking has seen a steady increase in the Indian market. With initiatives such as the Immediate Payment Service (IPS) and developments by the Reserve Bank of India, mobile banking services have increased manifold; approximately 12 per cent of the 143 million mobile phone internet subscribers use banking services on their mobile phones (Behl et al. 2016). This demand has seen an advancement in the operating systems of mobile phones and mobile technology like 3G and 4G, which are today offered by several Indian mobile firms such as Bharati Airtel, Tata and Reliance. It has also brought a significant change in the way of working for providers of mobile banking services such as IDBI and State Bank of India (Behl et al. 2016; Pandiya & Gupta 2015). This illustrates that as demand conditions in the domestic market become more sophisticated, domestic firms are more inclined to upgrade their production capabilities, with an intent to offer superior quality goods or services. A sophisticated home market serves as a pull factor, where firms benefit for producing world-class products or services. In other words, domestic demand may require firms to further refine their capabilities and as a result contribute to the national competitiveness.

Supporting and related industries

The third determinant of the Porter's diamond model are the supporting and related industries that provide components and support services to the final producers. The presence of sophisticated supplier and related industry clusters are essential in assisting firms to develop advanced capabilities that help them compete in the domestic, as well as the international, markets. Some of Japan's most dominant automobile firms, for example, owe their success to process and technology expertise as well as an often-disregarded factor – their relationships with the supporting and related industries. Over the past two decades, many Japanese automobile firms have turned these relationships into a strategic tool for constant innovation and the reduction of production costs. Toyota serves as a good example to illustrate this. Despite its recent issues in quality, research conducted by Aoki and Lennerfors (2013) states that Toyota has benefited tremendously from its network within the supporting and related industries. The firm has managed to develop a more open, global and cost-conscious relationship with its suppliers, which has fostered greater collaboration and support. This has allowed Toyota to further refine its operational processes, and better learn and respond to its customers' demands. This demonstrates that supporting and related industries can generate positive externalities, both in terms of knowledge spill overs and transactional efficiencies for firms operating in a given industry.

Firm strategy, structure and domestic competition

The final determinant of Porter's diamond model examines a firm's strategy, structure and the extent of domestic competition. The home-country environment greatly influences the way in which firms are created, organised and managed. It also determines the extent of domestic competition that may exist in each industry. Domestic competition or rivalry play a critical role in influencing the competitiveness of firms. The presence of strong local competition is a strong impetus for the firms to develop and improve their existing capabilities. Domestic competition, for example, may force firms to lower their costs and upgrade or improve their product or service offerings to compete more effectively in each industry. Also, the presence of such competition allows firms to further augment their technical expertise and innovate new processes. Competitiveness of firms results from a conjunction of management practices and business policy, which enables a country to develop a national competitive advantage in an industry.

The New Zealand marine industry is one such example. The thriving New Zealand marine industry includes three sub-sectors: recreational boats, commercial vessels and the marine defence industry. Of the three sub-sectors, the recreational boat sub-sector has garnered a global reputation for customised manufacturing, and with an estimated turnover of NZ$1.6 billion, the market is a significant contributor to the national economy. Approximately 884 firms operate in this sub-sector, making it one of the most competitive in the New Zealand marine industry (Murray 2009). Intense domestic competition has meant that New Zealand recreational boat builders have developed niche capabilities in superyacht building, repair and refit services, and boating equipment manufacturing (Tupou 2017). This focus has enabled firms in this sub-sector to offer high-quality customised boat building and marine services to the domestic and international markets. This illustrates that domestic competition can foster the development of a reputation for quality, and can lead to international and domestic competitiveness.

Porter's diamond model illustrates how the four determinants, discussed in this section, affect the competitiveness of the nation and its firms. In addition to the four country-level determinants, it is also important to consider the impact of firm-level and individual-level determinants on a nation's competitiveness. Finally, Porter also discusses the notion of clusters, an addition to the original diamond framework. According to Porter (1998) the competitive advantage of a nation's industry is not only determined by a single determinant, rather it is a result of integrated vertical and horizontal relationships within and across the firms and industry. The concept of clusters emphasises the importance of linkages, and spill overs of information and technology across firms and industry, both within national and international borders (Sölvell 2015).

Role of government

The government plays a vital role in influencing a nation's competitiveness. Indeed, a government's policies can affect a nation's economic activity by way of trade flows, and the nature of inward and outward investments. Government policies can act as catalyst to promote the development of a nation's firms and industries. The Japanese government provides a good illustration of this. Over the past four decades, the Japanese government has undertaken a series of policy initiatives that have seen the development of pioneering technology, especially in the automobile and electronic industry. The Japanese government, for example, rolled out projects and established systems to reward the quality, innovation and development of technical capabilities. This, and a host of other policies, has helped Japanese firms earn national as well as global recognition for their technical and innovative expertise.

Equally, a government can deter the development of industry and its firms in each nation. The retail sector is good example to support this point. Productivity in the Japanese retail sector is low, perhaps because large-scale stores are essentially prohibited from operating in Japan. This is particularly so in the case of food-retailing, where the market is dominated by independent domestic players. Domestic retail conglomerates in Japan, for example, operate multiple chains and do not necessarily compete with other domestic rivals. Also, laws such as the large-scale retail location law, impose social and environmental criteria. The aim of laws like these is to limit the entry of large-scale retailers (McKinsey Global Institute 2000). The executives of the local dominant firms also represent domestic interests on various approval committees, which makes it difficult for new local and foreign firms to enter the Japanese retail sector.

The examples discussed in this section highlight the role of the government in facilitating or hindering the development of firms and industry within a nation.

SPOTLIGHT 2.3

The importance of home-country advantages and the internationalisation of Fonterra in the Asia–Pacific

This spotlight highlights the role of home-country advantages in the internationalisation of a firm.

Home-country advantages have a key role in the internationalisation of domestic firms. New Zealand firms are a prime example of firms that have successfully capitalised their home-country advantages to build a global presence. The New Zealand dairy industry, for instance, is one of the most efficient dairy producers in the world. With an established infrastructure, this industry enjoys a low-cost, low-input pasture-based production, which is well known to attract a skilled workforce and to continually invest in maintaining its world-class research and development facilities.

Fonterra, owned by 10 500 farmers, is New Zealand's largest cooperative. With exports to over 140 countries, the cooperative generates 25 per cent of New Zealand's exports, and accounts for approximately 7 per cent of the country's GDP. The cooperative has successfully capitalised on its home-country advantages to build a global consumer base and is renowned for its premium dairy products. Fonterra operates across Australasia, Africa, Asia, the Middle East and Latin America, Fonterra Brands, the consumer products division of Fonterra, is responsible for the production, distribution, marketing and sales of its ready-to-use dairy products. Of the various regions that Fonterra enjoys a presence, Asia, is one of the most important regions for Fonterra Brands.

A combination of a growing affluent young population and increasing interest in high-end dairy products has meant a burgeoning demand for Fonterra's products in markets like China, Indonesia and Vietnam. Recognising this need, Fonterra Brands has developed specialised brands to better meet the tastes and preferences of Asian consumers. Infant formula Anmum and Anmum Materna are examples of products that are specially developed to meet the demands of young Asian mothers. Incorporating the clean, green image that New Zealand food and beverage products enjoy, Fonterra Brands has been able to successfully market its products to a wide range of consumers within the region. Also, the ability to develop innovative and speciality dairy products to address varied consumer needs, has enabled Fonterra Brands to develop an excellent product and service reputation, which has played a critical role in building a strong presence in Asia.

In addition to resources, innovation is the key ingredient to Fonterra's international success. For example, the firm owns one of the largest dairy research facilities in the world, including a leading dairy pilot plant. With R&D centres in Australia, Germany, the US and Singapore, Fonterra's product development and innovation is an integral part of the firm's philosophy. Consistent investments in R&D have allowed the firm to develop world-class nutritional solutions that address a variety of consumer needs. One project is the Anlene range, which is especially formulated for adults to help maintain optimal bone health and strength – bone decay is a major international health issue. With investments of over US$40 million, the R&D team at Fonterra responded to this need by combining bone-strengthening nutrients such as calcium, protein, zinc, and magnesium with nutritionally rich milk proteins. Initial product trials in Asia showed women that consumed the Anlene range benefited from a lower rate of bone loss. This highlights the importance of resources and innovation, and the role these factors play in a firm's international success (Asia Foundation 2011; Penn 2017).

VIDEOS
SPOTLIGHT
QUESTIONS

QUESTIONS

1. Outline the role of home-country advantages in the internationalisation of firms.
2. How has Fonterra Brands developed a strong presence in Asia?

The host country and the MNE

There are numerous host-country advantages for MNEs such as market-seeking FDI, resource-seeking FDI, strategic-asset seeking FDI and efficiency-seeking FDI.

Market-seeking FDI

Market-seeking FDI is perhaps the most common form of FDI. Here MNEs aim to capitalise on their ownership advantages such as brand image, marketing expertise and innovation. They also want to take advantage of supply and distribution networks by seeking to operate in large foreign markets. There is certainly a positive relationship between outward FDI and the market size of the host country. This is particularly true for MNEs wanting to establish a presence in many economies within the Asia–Pacific region. Given the pace of economic development and growth experienced by a number of those economies, many MNEs have sought to enter markets with the intention of benefitting from the opportunities that the markets provide. For example, Ikea, the world's largest furniture retailer, has rapidly expanded in Asia in recent years; it now has stores in China, India, Singapore, Thailand and Malaysia. Recognising the opportunities offered by markets in Asia, the firm intends to boost its sales by 50 per cent in the Asian region over the next four years (Magnusson & Molin 2016).

Resource-seeking FDI

This is where MNEs aim at access or control of the natural resources that are available in a host economy. This type of FDI is generally undertaken by MNEs in the heavy manufacturing or mining industries. For example, even though India is primarily a service-driven economy, there are examples of Indian MNEs that have acquired other international firms to access other nations' resources and sustain their firm's growth. The acquisition of the US General Chemicals by Tata Chemicals in 2008 and Corus by Tata Steel in 2006 serve as good examples of resource-seeking FDI (Buckley et al. 2012).

Strategic-asset seeking FDI

When undertaking strategic-asset seeking FDI, the MNE aims to acquire strategic assets such as brands, high technology and scarce skills. Foreign acquisitions are normally undertaken with the intent of acquiring requisite knowledge and technology to complement a firm's existing firm-specific capabilities. Acer, for example, is a firm that used acquisitions and alliances to leverage key resources to succeed internationally. The firm began its internationalisation in the late 1980s through large acquisitions which nearly led the company to bankruptcy. It then regrouped and pursued an incremental strategy of expansion through partnerships with local firms in its target markets, which led to its global expansion (Mathews 2006a). These linkages allowed the firm to develop an innovative cellular organisational structure, which meant that the firm was able to gather local market knowledge that was required to successfully operate in several international markets.

Efficiency-seeking FDI

The main intention of efficiency seeking is to benefit from a variety of resources, cultural and institutional provisions, demand patterns, economic policies and market structures by concentrating production in a limited number of locations to supply multiple markets (Dunning 1980). An abundance of low-cost labour and favourable economic policies are the two factors that have made economies in emerging Asia (for example China, Indonesia and Cambodia) attractive destinations for MNEs seeking to outsource their production to achieve greater economies of scale.

The host country and the institutional environment

In addition to the motives discussed in the above section, the locational advantage of a host country is also determined by the level of political stability that country has, as well as the development of the host country's industrial, financial, technological, transport and institutional infrastructure.

A host-country government has a significant influence on the political, institutional and legal policies, which may impact an MNE's operations. That government will, for example, have a bearing on labour laws, and it will determine the nature of polices that influence trade and investment, exchange controls, taxation and capital policies, price controls and intellectual property rights. However, increasing pressure for global integration, heightened competition for inward FDI, and a need for economic growth and development, will strongly encourage a host-country government's cooperation with MNEs (Marinova 2014).

From the perspective of an MNE, the growing pressure to lower the cost of production and achieve greater economies of scale have meant increased foreign investments in locations that offer a favourable environment to relocate their operations.

To make the domestic environment more favourable and attract foreign investments, host-country governments, especially in the Asia–Pacific region, offer a wide range of incentives to MNEs. These incentives may include grants and investment allowances, subsidies for infrastructure development, tax breaks, exemptions on imports and funding. In some cases, government regulations, import control or strategic trade policy may prompt MNEs to relocate their investments to foreign markets. This is particularly true for emerging economies in the Asia–Pacific as the governments of these countries have created Special Economic Zones (SEZs) with the intention of attracting foreign investment. Among other incentives, the Government of India, for example, provides an exemption of 100 per cent on income tax for export income from SEZ units for the first five years, an exemption of 50 per cent for the next five years, and an exemption of 50 per cent of the ploughed-back export profit for the following five years. The government also allows external commercial borrowing by SEZ units of up to US$500 million in a year, without any restriction through recognised banking channels (Government of India 2009). Incentives like this make these markets an attractive destination for MNEs to invest.

Although a host country may offer an attractive investment climate, not all sectors and firms may benefit from a relaxed policy regime. For example, to attract foreign investments, the Chinese government undertook major economic reforms to relax its investment policies in the 1980s and 1990s. However, the impact of these reforms is largely limited to China's manufacturing sector. The Chinese government has placed prohibitions on foreign ownership in domestic air and maritime transport services, and a full prohibition on foreign investment in postal and domestic express services. Limitations on foreign ownership also apply in basic telecommunications services and in 'value-added telecommunications services', which include a number of ICT services (OECD 2017). Although China undertook important reforms in 2016, most service sectors remain subject to screening, with FDI approval being conditioned on the proof of net economic benefits to the Chinese economy. The Chinese government also applies labour-market tests for the movement of intra-corporate labour market movements, whereby the hiring of foreigners requires a demonstration of special needs and a lack of suitable domestic candidates (OECD 2017). This demonstrates that the attractiveness of the FDI incentives offered by the host-country government varies with the nature of sector and market orientation.

The contribution to the host country: legitimacy and good corporate citizenship

One of the main objectives of an MNE in the host country is to attain legitimacy where the MNE is seen as a part of the domestic environment. To achieve this, the MNE must be viewed as an entity that contributes significantly to the local economy. In doing so, the MNE can attain greater access to local markets and create alliances that help it overcome any regulatory obstacles. McDonald's is a good example of an MNE that contributes to the host-country economy. McDonald's Australia, for example, is committed to supporting local producers and manufacturers; approximately 94 per cent of the produce and packaging needs for the business are sourced from local Australian producers and manufacturers (McDonald's 2018). Developing relationships with local firms and contributing to the local economy is an example of good corporate citizenship; it has helped McDonald's create a positive brand image in its host country, Australia.

Good corporate citizenship is also important where MNEs operate in countries that have a poor regulatory environment. The Rana Plaza collapse in Bangladesh brought the world's attention to worker safety issues and the human cost of cheap fast fashion (Westervelt 2015). The incident resulted in the death of 1134 workers and injured hundreds of other people. The collapse of the plaza was due to oversights and poor construction. In the aftermath of the incident, Primark, an Irish fashion retailer, was one of the first MNEs to set up a compensation fund – Rana Plaza Donors Trust Fund – for the victims of the disaster (Robinson 2013). The firm also urged other global brands including H&M, Mango, the Gap and Walmart, among others, to contribute to the fund. Primark also played an active role in addressing worker safety issues in Bangladesh by working with government agencies and non-governmental organisations to draft guidelines and strategies for improving the working conditions in the garment industry. The actions of Primark earned the company praise by the government and the consumers in Bangladesh as well as its primary markets in the UK and Europe (Robinson 2013). This highlights the role that MNEs can play in improving the working conditions of the workers in countries with a poor regulatory environment.

The challenges of operating in the host country

For sustainable competitive advantage in the host country, an MNE should also consider market-based factors that are beyond its control. The strategic performance of an MNE is greatly affected by the environment in which it operates and the influence of external market factors is a primary determinant of performance. However, uncertainties are an inherent part of a foreign market environment since the MNE has little control over external market factors. Uncertainties are heavily influenced by politics, policies of the government, institutions, macroeconomic conditions and cultural distance. Hence the following section addresses political risk, institutional environment, cultural distance and the liability of foreignness.

Political risk

The impact of political risk on MNEs has been long recognised in international business. Political risk is not only concerned with political instability, but also encompasses the impact of uncertainties that may arise due to an unstable economic and regulatory environment, as well as changes in investment conditions. In other words, political risk in the host country reflects ambiguity over the continuation of current political conditions and economic environment, which are critical to the survival and profitability of an MNE's operations in that country. MNEs are more vulnerable to changes in their host country compared to domestic firms because MNEs often lack the experience and knowledge of operating in the area. Additionally, MNEs are likely to commit large investments in the host country, which makes them more susceptible to risk. Political risk also constricts the decision-making ability of MNEs and can put them at a competitive disadvantage in the host country. An environment of high political risk may therefore restrain MNEs from making investments in their host country.

The general body of international business literature divides political risk into three categories.

The first type of political risk is in terms of government or sovereign action. This type of political risk considers government interference and the consequences of such action on the operations of the MNEs.

The second type of political risk may occur in the form of political events or restrictions imposed at a specific industry or firms. Examples of political events may include changes in government or civil unrest that may create uncertainty in the host country. Restrictions on the MNEs may typically include expropriation, constraints on remittance of profits, inequitable taxation policy and competition. In extreme cases of expropriation, the MNE may be forced to divest its assets in the host country as the host-country government may nationalise or transfer ownership of assets from MNEs to domestic firms or the state (Gilpin 1987). Also, changes in investment policies may reduce the ability of the MNE to own assets in the host country; for example, in the 1970s, as a policy requirement, MNEs operating in India were given a certain amount of time to complete the 'Indianisation' process, which was to develop operations that focused solely on functioning within the Indian market. The government also made it mandatory for foreign investors to retain 60 per cent of earnings in the Indian market. This was done with the intention of constraining MNEs from remitting revenue back to their home country (Buckley et al. 2012).

Finally, the third type of political risk is operational in nature where MNEs may find it difficult to anticipate the changes in the business environment. Changes in the host-country business environment may constitute a risk, especially if the change affects the operations or investments of the MNE in that country.

Most governments today have a favourable view on foreign investments, but the level of political risk is still considerable in many countries. This is particularly true in the Asia–Pacific context. Although, emerging economies in the Asia–Pacific region are fast-growing and offer numerous opportunities for MNEs, many of these markets are still structurally volatile as they continue to transition to more developed states (Enderwick 2007). Hence, it is important that an MNE considers the extent of political risk before pursing operations in a host country.

Institutional environment

Institutions are specialised intermediaries that support and facilitate transactions between buyers and sellers. Examples of such arbitrators include agencies that can verify the credibility of the products and the services sold or rendered by the firm in each market. These may include auditing agencies and third-party certification agencies.

Credit ratings and consumer reports serve as good indicators of the credit worthiness of the firms that operate in a chosen market (Khanna & Palepu 1997). In addition, organisations and transaction facilitators, such as the banks, labour unions and platforms such as Amazon or eBay, play a vital role in ensuring smooth operations in a given market. These intermediaries are central for facilitating business transactions in a market. The absence of such mediators may create high levels of risk and uncertainty as it becomes easier for firms and supporting organisations to engage in corrupt practices or embezzlement if the market is lacking in governance, transparent reporting, and efficient judicial and legal systems (Gao et al. 2017; Khanna & Palepu 1997, 1999).

The institutional environment has an important influence on the firm's strategies as conformity with the local institutional environment helps the MNEs achieve legitimacy in their host countries. However, undeveloped or volatile institutions can lead to the misallocation of resources and competitive disadvantages. Markets that have an absence of intermediaries can create an unstable environment for the firms to effectively engage in productive transactions; markets such as these are often termed as emerging, developing or underdeveloped economies.

Given that several economies in the Asia–Pacific region are emerging or developing, MNEs need to give careful consideration when pursuing opportunities in the region. Among other factors, an undeveloped institutional environment is reflected in high levels of protectionism, corruption and bribery, extensive bureaucracy and lack of intellectual property rights (Gao et al. 2017).

Protectionism

Elevated levels of protectionism can have an adverse effect on an MNE's competitiveness in the host country. Protectionism can occur due to over-regulated markets, unfair competition from highly protected state-owned enterprises and market protectionist policies. Despite firm-specific competitive advantages such as access to financial and human resources, innovation and technological expertise, continued protectionism can put MNEs at a disadvantage in the host country. The dairy industry in India is an example of this. By introducing high sanitary requirements, arbitrary export certificate requirements and restrictive maximum residue levels, the Indian government has played a key role in prohibiting dairy imports entering the country. In addition, the current import duty on milk and milk products ranges from 40 to 60 per cent. This has meant that many international dairy producers, including New Zealand and the US, have been effectively blocked from entering the Indian market (Independent Press 2013). The government's intention here is to protect the domestic dairy industry and support local farmers to help them build their competitiveness.

Corruption

Dealing with bribery and corruption has always been a challenge for MNEs, especially when considering operations in the Asia–Pacific. Corruption occurs when firms, both domestic and foreign, need to make ad hoc payments to accomplish their business and political objectives. Bribery and corruption risks are particularly high when firms are required to obtain contracts or licenses to conduct business. Corruption can create blockages or halts to business, and the absence of appropriate regulations that prohibit corrupt behaviour can lead to higher costs of doing business. This can be particularly challenging for MNEs to deal with since many foreign firms do not have the requisite knowledge of how to best operate in that kind of setting. Therefore, MNEs must develop strategies to operate in these kinds of environments; engaging in corrupt practices is risky and can be damaging to the MNE's reputation.

The recent scandal of Samsung highlights the impact dubious practices can have on a firm. Lee Jae-Yong, business magnet and Vice Chairman of the Samsung Group, was recently charged with bribery in a national scandal, which also saw the impeachment of the former South Korean president Park Geun-hye. Lee was accused of offering US$36 million in bribes and donations to four not-for-profit entities that were run by Choi Soon-sil (a friend of Park Geun-hye) in return for political favour. The money was offered to Choi Soon-sil to secure government support for the contentious merger of two Samsung affiliates that would strengthen Lee's control over the conglomerate. The wide-ranging scandal highlighted the nature of collusive relationships between senior politicians and family-owned conglomerates, commonly known as *chaebols* (BBC 2017). The scandal caused widespread anger and outrage, with a mounting public pressure on the South Korean courts to deliver a guilty verdict. Past South Korean business figures, who had committed similar crimes, had received light sentences, which fuelled the public's criticism that *chaebol* leaders are treated with unwarranted leniency by the justice system. Though the firm's fortunes were unaffected, the verdict did have a significant impact on Samsung, one of South Korea's biggest and most well-known companies; domestic consumers increasingly lost confidence in one of their country's most iconic brands (Stone et al. 2017).

Bureaucracy

Bureaucracy is an inherent feature of many markets in the Asia–Pacific region. Extensive red tape increases the cost of doing business because of the additional paperwork and approvals that are needed. Meeting the requirements of the central government and local councils can delay operations of MNEs in a host country, and it can also create uncertainty and impede an MNE's long-term planning (Tan & Chintakanada 2016).

Bureaucracy is often associated with a lack of transparency in a host country, which constrains time and financial resources. For example, infrastructure projects in most markets in the Asia–Pacific region is often known to be bureaucratic; the legalities often associated with such projects can be complex to understand. Also, dissimilarities in legalities between state and central governments in markets such as, for instance, China, India Indonesia and Vietnam, can be challenging to deal with, especially if the MNEs have no prior experience of operating in such settings.

Intellectual property

The protection of intellectual property is a major concerns for MNEs seeking to operate in the emerging markets within the Asia–Pacific region. This is because the threat of piracy and the lack of protection of intellectual property in such settings are well known. The key issues that MNEs face lie with copyrights, patents, trademarks and technology transfer. Despite this, intellectual property protection remains an afterthought for many MNEs wanting to tap into these markets for production or research and development purposes. Government regulations, and patency and copyright protection laws are not stringent; they tend to be loosely defined, which makes their implementation problematic and the ability to protect critical information and the property of MNEs operating in those markets difficult. As a result, there is a significant risk of a breach occurring in intellectual property.

An example of this is seen in the case of Novartis, a global leader in innovative pharmaceuticals, generics, vaccines and healthcare products, which has well-established operations in India. The case revolves around a patent application filed by Novartis for its anti-cancer drug Glivec in 2005. The company was refused the patent by the Indian patent office in January 2006 because the Indian office felt that the drug was not inventive enough to merit a patent under the 2005 Indian law (Kannan 2013). In response to this, Novartis approached the Madras High Court in Chennai in May 2006, challenging two distinct elements of the decision (Kannan 2013). First, the firm challenged the grounds on which the Indian patent office, led by the Patent Controller, had rejected the patent. Second, the firm also challenged the reliability of the patent system in India as the decision not only contravened with Trade-Related Aspects of Intellectual Property Rights (TRIPS) as governed by the World Trade Organization (WTO), but also the Indian Constitution, (article 14, within the patent protection law), which ensures equality before the law. The firm pursued legal action against the Indian government, subsequent to its decision to decline the patent for Glivec, in January 2007 (Kannan 2013). Novartis stated that they had pursued the action to challenge the establishment of additional hurdles to patentability in India that discourages both breakthrough and incremental innovation. Novartis, which has patented Glivec in 36 countries worldwide, stated that it wanted clarification on the Indian law as the company wanted to ensure that it gets adequate patent protection for any drugs it plans to offer in India in the future. Novartis also suggested that the company was not challenging any provisions of the Indian patent law that are currently in place, but was concerned with safeguarding Novartis' intellectual property. Novartis lost the case in 2013, seven years after the case was first filed (Kannan 2013).

This example shows that although a government does have laws to protect the intellectual property of a firm, those laws may not always be observed. The gaps in the provisions and the system make it difficult for MNEs to protect their intellectual property. The protection of the intellectual property is important for any firm since significant investments are made to maintain a competitive advantage in an industry and market. As innovation and R&D is the core to any business model, MNEs may find operating in such markets challenging.

The distance between the host and home country

A prominent distance framework suggested by Ghemawat (2001) is the CAGE (Cultural, Administrative, Geographical and Economic) distance framework. Cultural and administrative distance is perhaps the most crucial factor for MNEs. Cultural distance is attributed to the way people interact with each other, companies, and institutions, religion, language and cultural norms (Ghemawat 2001). Differences between two countries can deter trade and investment between them. Cultural similarities help in reducing transactions costs and the risks of entering a foreign market due to comparable business laws, customs, ways of doing business and possibly familial links. In other words, cultural similarity reduces the psychic distance between countries.

Any firm that seeks to operate in an international environment, particularly, in the Asia–Pacific region, faces the liability of foreignness in that market. This concept was first introduced by Hymer. According to Hymer (1976) a key factor shaping the internationalisation of the firm is the liability of foreignness, which increases with the distance between the home and host countries. The Uppsala model further explains this concept. According to the Uppsala model, any firm that seeks to operate in a foreign market faces the barrier of foreignness in that market. The liability of this foreignness is the extra costs incurred by a firm once it enters a foreign market that the local firms would not incur. These costs may be investing, operating, and managing in the foreign country's institutional environment. The outlays mainly occur due to a lack of familiarity with: the local business environment, such as with suppliers, buyers, competitors and distributors; cultural differences, which incur adaptation costs; geographical distances, which create transport and communication costs; and the institutional environment, such as legal, regulatory, political, sociocultural and economic requirements (Johanson & Wiedersheim-Paul 1975). Although MNEs that have strong FSAs can use those advantages to offset these types of costs, a direct consequence of these types of additional costs can result in a competitive disadvantage for a foreign firm.

The liability of foreignness is perceived to be determined by the geographic and cultural distance between countries. In other words, an MNE would potentially perform better in foreign markets that are closer to its home market, in terms of geography and cultural similarities. In situations where the firm considers internationalisation through equity modes (for example FDI), the firm will only build local knowledge once it has established a presence in that foreign market (Gulati 1999). Hence, it can be assumed that the liability of foreignness will be substantial, especially in the initial stages of the operations. Additionally, if an MNE seeks to enter a market that has greater physic distance, normally it would take its other foreign operations as a stepping stone to the new market. Gradual resource commitment and planned geographic expansion can help reduce foreign market unfamiliarity substantially prior to the establishment of an MNE's operations.

This is evident in the study conducted by Petersen and Pedersen (2002). The study analysed the liabilities of foreignness perceived by businesses in Denmark, Sweden and New Zealand. These three countries are relatively small in terms of their population and market size. Due to their limited home markets, most firms in these countries are forced to engage in international operations at an early stage of their development. The profiles of the firms analysed from Denmark (n = 201) and Sweden (n = 176), for instance, were remarkably similar in terms of size and level of internationalisation. However, the firms differed in their levels of international experience. For instance, Swedish firms (30.3 years) and the Danish firms (20.9 years) typically had longer export experience as against New Zealand firms. According to the study, the firms from New Zealand (n = 117) had less international experience (16.1 years) and operated in fewer countries. The study also suggests that the ability of firms to adapt to their host-country's environment is expected to be highly correlated with the international experience of the firms. In other words, the more the firms are exposed to foreign markets, the greater the international experience, and the greater the ability is to adapt to new markets. This certainly holds true for MNEs considering opportunities in the Asia–Pacific region, where the liabilities of foreignness, especially in the emerging markets, are high. Structural uncertainties in the industrial and institutional environments in these locations can make it challenging for MNEs to control external instabilities when they operate in the Asia–Pacific region.

Political, social or economic ties between home and host country can become a source of competitive advantage for MNEs. These country-specific linkages can translate into FSAs when they affect the motivations and internationalisation strategies of MNEs pursuing opportunities in markets where their home country enjoys a favourable relationship with the host-country government. For example, a bilateral treaty or an association with an international organisation may aid the development of trade and investment relationships among member nations, which in turn helps MNEs in developing linkages to establish their operations within member countries. MNEs increasingly

BILATERAL TREATY an agreement between two countries.

MULTIPLE-CHOICE QUESTION

utilise such country linkages as a tool to develop firm-level linkages that help them overcome the various challenges discussed in this section.

The legal environment and international relations

INTERNATIONAL RELATIONS are concerned with the political and economic relations between two or more nations.

The legal environment and international relations play influential roles in what drives and what challenges a firm's internationalisation.

International legal systems

The legal system plays a significant role in influencing the operations of a firm in each country since the legal system provides a framework of rules and norms of conduct that dictate, limit or permit specified relationships among people and firms that operate in that context. There are three main international legal systems: common law, civil law and theocratic law.

Common law

Common law, which originated in England, is based on case law created in the legal system. A distinct feature of the common law system is that judicial decisions are grounded on the precedents provided by past cases. In other words, a common law system relies on the past cases heard in the court as a source of law rather than statutes of law created by a government. Also, the rulings of a judge plays a key role in the common law system. This is because the system allows discretion in interpreting the law depending on the characteristics of an individual case rather than basing the decision on a given law (Kaske 2002). Examples of countries that follow the common law system include New Zealand, the UK, Australia, Hong Kong and India. Business and legal contracts in a common law system tend to be detailed and lengthy.

Civil law

Civil law, also referred to as codified law, is a legal system that is based on specific laws and regulations stated by the legislation of a given country. Laws that are enacted by the government and the state legislatures are referred to as statutes, whereas laws that are enacted by the lower levels of government (for example local councils) are referred to as codes. The aim of this legal system is to provide statutes and codes which are comprehensive and precise. The statutes and codes are based on principles that are universally applicable, rather than on specific laws like in the common law system. Therefore, civil law is less flexible in comparison to common law. The difference between the two legal systems means that business and legal contracts under the civil law system tend to be concise (Kaske 2002; Prevot 2016). Examples of countries that follow the civil law system include France, Germany, Russia, Latin America, China, Taiwan and South Korea.

Theocratic law

Theocratic law is based on religious teachings as described in religious scriptures. Sharia or Islamic law is one of the most widely practised religious legal systems in the world. Based on the Koran, this legal system is informed by the religious texts and interpretation of the holy book of Islam. Unlike other legal systems, Islamic law evaluates social and business decisions on morality rather than commercial or personal interests. Islamic law is mainly observed in the Middle East, Indonesia and Afghanistan. The practice of Islamic law may differ between nations that follow this legal system.

Both Saudi Arabia and UAE, for example, follow the Islamic legal system. However the establishment of civil law and criminal courts has led to diminishing role of Islamic law in UAE, while Saudi Arabia still observes the traditional theocratic law (Kaske 2002). MNEs operating in countries governed by this legal system must consider the practices that are deemed appropriate by the religion followed in that context. For example, MNEs that specialise in the food and beverage industry, must comply with halal requirements when marketing their products to consumers in the Middle East.

Implementation of law

MNEs operating in the Asia–Pacific region, especially in emerging markets, often have issues with the enforcement of law to protect their commercial interests. Achieving effective conflict resolution, for example, can be particularly challenging in countries where contracts are only viewed as a formal document that is subject to change as required. Verbal contracts and interpersonal trustworthiness are considered more important than written contracts in the Chinese business environment, for instance, as there is a lack of formal rules and regulations there to dictate the legalities of doing business in that setting (Hubbard et al. 2012; Prevot 2016, Ruru et al. 2016). Further, the fragmented nature of the judicial systems in the emerging markets makes it difficult for litigants in countries such as China, India, Vietnam and Indonesia to claim damages or enforce action to protect their intellectual or commercial interests.

Legal risks in the host country

The stability of the legal environment dictates the level of foreign investments in the host country. MNEs that decide to invest in markets with uncertain legal environments must develop capabilities and willingness to engage with the governments to better manage risks that may arise because of government intervention. Host-country government intervention may include policies such as constraints on foreign equity ownership, non-adherence to or a lack of intellectual property protection laws, profit remittance laws, and laws related to marketing and distribution.

Constraints on foreign equity ownership

An MNE's ability to own its assets and investments can be restricted by the laws in a host country. A host-country government may introduce laws that restrict an MNE's ability to wholly own its operations. Such laws may impact the effectiveness and efficiency of the MNE in that setting. Until early 2016, the Indian government prohibited 100 per cent FDI in bricks-and-mortar retailing, claiming it would put small domestic retailers at an economic disadvantage. However, to boost the competitiveness of its retail industry, the government introduced reforms in March 2016. Among other changes, foreign retailers are allowed up to 51 per cent FDI in multi-brand retail and 100 per cent, which went up from 51 per cent, in single-brand retail (IBEF 2018). The government also intends to allow 100 per cent FDI in the ecommerce space, subject to the condition that the products sold online must be manufactured in India. These polices have resulted in increased participation from foreign and domestic players alike. With the aim to gain from the liberalised regime, leading global retail chains such as Walmart, GAP and Tesco, for example, are increasingly establishing wholly owned offices or managed sourcing-and-buying offices in India (IBEF 2018). This demonstrates how laws can affect an MNE's ability to successfully operate in a foreign market.

Profit remittance

The ability of an MNE to remit profits back to their home country is governed by host-country laws. Due to the wide variety of regulatory policies undertaken by individual nations, remittance policy is an important consideration for investors and can substantially impact the ability of a host country to attract investment. Compared to other countries in the Association of Southeast Asian Nations (ASEAN) group, Indonesia, is more prohibitive towards MNEs. For example, MNEs operating in Indonesia must provide Bank Indonesia with a record of all profit transfers to their home country or any other foreign location, including the amount transferred in Indonesian rupiah (IDR) (Dezan Shira & Associates 2016). Such restrictions not only limit the ability of an MNE to repatriate profits back to its headquarters, but can also stop them from making investments in such markets.

Marketing and distribution

Host-country laws can dictate the marketing and distribution strategies used by MNEs to advertise, promote, and distribute their products and services. For example, New Zealand laws restrict MNEs in advertising and promoting cigarettes and tobacco-related products. The key government agency involved, Ministry of Health, is responsible for the development of the main policies, services and operational aspects of tobacco control in New Zealand. In addition to current restrictions on advertising and promotion placed by the ministry, tobacco-standardised packaging is part of the New Zealand government's comprehensive tobacco-control program (Ministry of Health NZ 2016). From March 2018, for example, tobacco packets sold in New Zealand are a standard dark brownish green colour. There are enlarged photos and health warnings to cover at least 75 per cent of the front of the tobacco packets and all tobacco company marketing imagery has been removed (Ministry of Health NZ 2018). Although tobacco manufacturers such as British American Tobacco will be allowed to print a brand name and variant on their tobacco products, the regulations will standardise how the packet looks, where the restrictions will be placed on the pack, and the type of font size and colour that will be used (Jones 2016). Such restrictions can certainly impact the ability of the MNEs to market their brands and consequently their profitability.

Lobbying

LOBBYING
a firm-level strategic action aimed at changing policy proposals to benefit firms and/or industries to further their commercial interests.

Lobbying is defined as a firm-level strategic action aimed at changing policy proposals to benefit firms and industries, and to increase their value in the long run. Corporate lobbying may be inspired by market power and firm size or due to pressure from industry peers. Cost and benefit factors might also drive MNEs into lobbying. There is an invariable connection between lobbying and litigation as successful lobbying may influence a change in laws and regulatory policies.

The 2010 employment dispute between the New Zealand actors' union (NZ Actors' Equity), the Australian actors' guild (the Media Entertainment and Arts Alliance) and the producers of *The Hobbit* is an illustration of the lobbying power of MNEs. The issue revolved around use of non-unionised actors in the production of *The Hobbit*. The dispute commenced when the International Federation of Actors issued an order prohibiting actors from New Zealand, Australia, the US and Canada from working on the film as the producers were offering non-union contracts with no minimum payments and conditions of work (Conor 2015). Compared to the US, Australia and New Zealand have had long-standing legislative frameworks in place to ensure that workers in film are not covered under collective bargaining agreements (Kelly 2011; Conor 2015). This meant that. depending on where the production was based, New Zealand and Australian actors would be not covered by the collective

union agreement at all filming locations. Also, working conditions, payment of a minimum wage and other benefits would vary between filming locations. In light of increasing protests and the possibility of moving the production from New Zealand, the New Zealand government worked with Warner Brothers to change the New Zealand *Employment Relations Act (2000)* (Conor 2015). The amending legislation, the Employment Relations (Film Production Work) Amendment Bill, was introduced as part of a deal between the Government and Warner Brothers to keep *The Hobbit* film production in New Zealand. The bill, termed the 'Hobbit Law', changed the terms and conditions of employment for the film industry workers in New Zealand (Conor 2015). The new legislation created a default category in the Employment Relations Act by categorising all film production workers as independent contractors, which would mean that Warner Brothers would not be legally obliged to offer employment agreements or contracts to the actors and the production staff.

This is an example of an effective lobbying strategy used by an MNE to keep a workplace, an industry and a labour market union-free and unregulated, resulting in reduced worker protection.

Treaties

Treaties or agreements are mechanisms to create international cooperation. Although nations do pursue some goals in isolation, international cooperation on matters of economic integration and regional security can provide an opportunity to effectively achieve national aims. Treaties can exist between two nations in a bilateral agreement or between more than two nations in a multilateral agreement. There is no standard procedure or process prescribed in international law for the formation of a treaty. However, the formulation of a treaty is generally dependent on the intention and agreement of the nations that are party to it. Nations become part of an international treaty when they are an original signatory or they join an existing treaty. International treaties may also be called agreements, pacts, conventions, protocols, covenants, acts, memorandums of understanding and statutes.

MULTILATERAL AGREEMENT an agreement between three or more countries.

TREATY an agreement of achieving international cooperation on matters of trade politics and security.

Over the last few decades, the political relations among nations have become increasingly complex, which has increased the need to strengthen and promote international law, and the rule of law at national and international levels. The Treaty of Amity and Cooperation in Southeast Asia (TAC), signed at the first ASEAN summit, is an example of a treaty that was established with the intent to protect territorial integrity, sovereignty and cooperation. The aim of this treaty is to promote political cooperation and security dialogue among ASEAN members. In addition to TAC, ASEAN has also signed a treaty to create a nuclear-free zone. The South-East Asian Nuclear-Free Zone Treaty was originally signed on 27 November 1971 (ASEAN 2018). However, due to the unfavourable political environment in the region at the time, the formal proposal for the establishment of this treaty was put forward for discussions in the mid-1980s. After a decade of negotiations among the ASEAN members, the treaty was signed by the 10-member nations in Bangkok in December 1995. According to the treaty, ASEAN members are not allowed to develop, manufacture, use and test nuclear weapons. Also the member nations are not allowed to dispose of any radioactive material or wastes on land, sea and atmosphere in the ASEAN territory (NTI 2018).

In addition to political interests, countries also sign treaties to facilitate trade and investment. Trade and investment treaties or agreements impose the obligation of national treatment. This means that participating countries cannot discriminate between imported versus domestically produced goods, or between domestic and foreign investment. Many trade and investment treaties also have a most-favoured nation clause that entitles the signatory nations to favourable investment policies. As an example, the New Zealand and South Korea Trade Agreement (signed in December 2015) facilitates the easy flow of goods and services between the two nations. As well as removing trade barriers, the agreement has also allowed for more cooperation in the areas of agriculture, education, trade facilitation, science and technology, and media (New Zealand Foreign Affairs & Trade 2015). The agreement enables New Zealand and Korean firms to have open, competitive and non-discriminatory access to government contracting opportunities. Further, the two countries have an understanding to maintain competition laws against anti-competitive behaviour.

There are two international organisations that govern patent protection – the WTO and the World Intellectual Property Organization (WIPO). The TRIPS agreement, governed by the WTO, imposes an obligation on member countries to provide patent protection for inventions in all fields of technology; similarly, WIPO is an independent agency that monitors intellectual property rights. The organisation works with individuals and firms from around the world to offer services in patent protection, trademarks, industrial designs, appellations of origin and domain names. WIPO administers 26 international intellectual property treaties. Of the various regional treaties, the Regional Bureau for Asia and the Pacific is responsible for providing legal and technical assistance to 38 countries in the Asia–Pacific region. This bureau supports member states in strengthening their IP systems and strategies through providing them with development and institutional capability building programs (Miller 2015; WIPO 2018).

Other legal aspects to consider from a home-country perspective

There are several international acts that monitor fraudulent practices that may be undertaken by firms when operating across borders. One piece of legislation that is often referred to and enacted is the Foreign Corrupt Practices Act. This is a US act that criminalises any offer, or authorisation of any offer, of payment, or payment of anything of value, to foreign officials or business alliances, with the intent of furthering or protecting commercial interests in a host country (US Department of Justice 2018). The act is applicable to US corporations and citizens, as well as MNEs that trade in the US securities market. As an example, the US-based snack-maker, Mondelez International, was charged US$13 million by the Securities and Exchange Commission, the US market regulator, for bribing Indian government officials and top state politicians to obtain licenses and approvals for a chocolate factory in India (Narayanan 2017).

Corporate transparency and disclosures

Most nations document good practices of corporate governance in their country codes. These codes outline the level of transparency needed in financial and non-financial disclosures, as well as the nature of the compliance that is required to meet legal and regulatory requirements (Berg & Holtbrügge 2001). Corporate transparency refers to the disclosure of firm-specific information to various external stakeholders of the firm and is an integral part of corporate governance practices (Madhani 2015). MNEs often face additional complexities and challenges in maintaining good corporate governance and disclosure practices due to the diversity of rules, regulations and stakeholder expectations between the home and the host country (El-Gazzar et.al 1999; Madhani 2015).

International accounting standards

International Accounting Standards (IAS) are accounting standards that are applicable to MNEs operating in a variety of foreign markets but are not necessarily recognised by all countries. This means that the adherence of IAS is not always monitored. As a firm expands internationally, the firm may be required to disclose their financial statements to their key stakeholders. To keep with the host-country legalities, a firm may need to prepare financial statements that are comparable to local statements (El-Gazzar et.al 1999). Also, in the absence of a universally acceptable set of accounting standards, an MNE might have to produce multiple financial statements to comply with the accounting standard laws prevalent in its host country, which could be a very costly and time-consuming process (El-Gazzar et.al 1999).

Summary

Learning objective 1: Understand the reasons why firms internationalise.

Four theories that identify why and how firms internationalise were discussed, namely: the Uppsala model, the eclectic paradigm (also known as the OLI framework), the RBV theory, and Mathews' LLL model. The Uppsala model outlines the nature and pace of a firm's internationalisation. In the case of the eclectic paradigm and the RBV, it is assumed that the firm builds capabilities and resources in its domestic market prior to its internationalisation. This, however, may not always be the so. According to the LLL model, firms may internationalise in pursuit of resources so their internationalisation strategy is driven by building networks that help them acquire the resources necessary for operating in a foreign market.

Learning objective 2: Examine the role of FSAs in the internationalisation of firms.

The discussion highlighted that resources like personnel and finance are perhaps the most critical assets for a firm. In addition to these resources, the level of innovation and R&D also influence the nature of FSAs. Firm-specific assets facilitate the diffusion and the evaluation of distinct corporate profiles, which enables firms to develop a competitive advantage in a foreign market.

Learning objective 3: Identify the role of home-country advantages for firms seeking to internationalise.

The chapter outlines how home-country advantages – such as factor conditions, demand conditions, supporting and related industries, firm strategy, structure and domestic competition, and the role of the government – are all responsible for determining the nature of national and international competitiveness in a firm's internationalisation.

Learning objective 4: Analyse and understand the effects of host-country differences and policy implications in Asia–Pacific economies and firms.

The locational advantages of the host country are a critical factor in influencing inward foreign investments. In addition, the nature of the host country's institutional environment can greatly influence or deter MNEs from operating in that market. Factors like political and institutional risk, protectionism, corruption, bureaucracy and safeguarding intellectual property can all impact an MNE's operations in each host country. Cultural and administrative distance between the home and host country were also addressed. As most countries in the Asia–Pacific are emerging markets, their legal, political and institutional environments influence firms' activities in those markets.

Learning objective 5: Recognise the role international relations plays and identify international legal frameworks.

Three legal systems were outlined in this chapter: common law, civil law and theocratic law. Legal risks such as constraints on foreign equity, profit remittance, marketing and distribution, and lobbying influence MNE activity within the host country. The importance of treaties and their ability to facilitate international economic and political cooperation was also discussed. Finally, the chapter presented legal considerations for an MNE from a home-country perspective, and the importance of the IAS and corporate governance.

USEFUL WEBSITES

Revision questions

REVISION QUESTIONS

1. Outline the key internationalisation theories discussed in the chapter.
2. Discuss the key determinants that define a nation's competitiveness.
3. Explain the location advantages and the several types of FDI.
4. What are the main challenges that MNEs encounter when operating in the host country?
5. Outline the legal risks in the host country.

R&D activities

1. Watch the video 'ASEAN automotive: huge potential' (www.youtube.com/watch?v=iiSpVV_wHe0) and identify the locational advantages of the ASEAN economies for the outsourcing of the automotive production.
2. Visit the survey results of the Corruption Perceptions Index 2016 by Transparency International (www.transparency.org/news/feature/corruption_perceptions_index_2016) and identify the relation between corruption and inequality.
3. Read the articles 'Top multinationals pay almost no tax in New Zealand' (www.nzherald.co.nz/business/news/article.cfm?c_id=3&objectid=11607336) and 'Labour plans crackdown on multinational tax avoidance to help fund spending plans' (www.stuff.co.nz/business/industries/94817709/labour-plans-crackdown-on-multinational-tax-avoidance-to-help-fund-spending-plans) and discuss the main points on the issue of tax avoidance as stated in the articles and video.
4. View the video 'Asia's airline wars: The great profit squeeze in the sky' (https://asia.nikkei.com/Spotlight/Cover-Story/Asia-s-airline-wars-The-great-profit-squeeze-in-the-sky) and discuss the main points on the opportunities and challenges for regional and international air carriers.

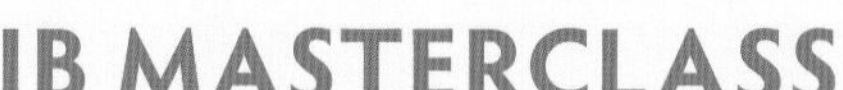

Starbucks an unlikely failure: challenges of operating in the Asia–Pacific region

This case illustrates how failure to understand consumer taste and compete with a strong local coffee culture led to the closure of Starbucks in Australia. It addresses the inability of Starbucks to successfully develop competitive strategies and a business model that would have helped it better understand and operate in the Australian market.

Background

Operating over 25 000 stores, the company today has a presence across 64 countries. From its humble beginnings in 1971, the company undertook rapid expansion in its domestic market, the US, in the 1990s and had approximately 140 stores across the US in 2000 (Delaney 2008). By early 2008 the company claimed to open seven stores worldwide every day. The successful international expansion of the company has made it one of the most recognised brands in the world.

Today, Starbucks is the largest coffeehouse chain worldwide and its brand value can be seen to rival McDonald's, one of the most famous restaurant chains. In 2016, Starbucks revenue reached a company record of US$21.32 billion dollars (Brook 2016).

Internationalisation: a focus on the Asia–Pacific region

The Asia–Pacific region has been particularly important to the international success of the company. The region has offered Starbucks new prospects for growth considering increasing competitive pressures in the more mature and traditional speciality coffee markets of North America and Western Europe.

The company's expansion into the Asia–Pacific started with its first coffee shop in Tokyo, Japan, in October 1995 (Patterson et al. 2010). After its success in Tokyo, the company expanded its presence in the region by entering the Chinese market in 1999. Today, China and Japan are the company's best performing international markets, with 2382 and 1288 stores respectively (Statista 2016).

Compared to Japan, market size and growing consumer desire for Western brands, have made China the fastest-growing market for the company. As an example, revenue from its China and Asia–Pacific stores rose 13 per cent to US$768.9 million in the quarter ended April 2017 (Statista 2016). Growing at its current rate, CEO Howard Schultz aims to more than double the number of locations and stores in China by 2021, making it a bigger market than the US (Ramakrishnan 2017; Patton 2016; Statista, 2016). An affluent emerging middle class of Chinese urbanities favour Starbucks for its experience, ambience and service. Also, Starbucks has customised its offerings by introducing drinks (for example the Osmanthus & Cherry White Chocolate Flavoured Mocha, or the Teavana Peach Delight Iced Shaken Tea and food (for example, mini pastries and mooncake) to better cater local tastes and preferences in China (Ramakrishnan 2017).

Success in the Chinese market has not come without challenges. Over the last decade, the company has faced numerous issues in China, including extensive local competition and

copyright infringement (for example, the Xing bake case in 2006) (Dickie 2006). However, the ability to adapt its marketing and operational strategy has allowed the company to build a strong presence in China.

The Australian coffee market

Valued at over US$4.3 billion, the Australian café and speciality coffee shop industry is dominated by a large number of local independent players (MarketLine 2016). For example, 95 per cent of all cafés are owner-operated, with only five per cent of the market controlled by coffee chains such as Gloria Jeans, McCafé, Dunkin Donuts, 7-Eleven and Coffee Club (Euromonitor International 2017a).

The Australian appreciation for coffee is clearly reflected in the consumption of the drink – on average, Australians consume 25 tonnes of coffee every year (Euromonitor International 2017a). Apart from being among the highest consumers of instant coffee, Australian consumers also have a keen taste for speciality local coffee. For example, in 2016, Australians spent AUD$219 million at local speciality coffee shops, of which AUD$107 million was spent at independent speciality coffee shops (Euromonitor International 2017b). This is a stark contrast to just AUD$40 million that were spent at coffee chain outlets, which is 8 per cent below the previous year (Euromonitor International 2017b). This suggests that unlike the emerging markets of the Asia–Pacific, Australia has a mature and sophisticated café culture.

Starbucks entered Australia in 2000 by establishing wholly owned subsidiaries: Starbucks Capital Asset Leasing Company, LLC and Starbucks Coffee Company (Australia) Private Limited. The company then undertook rapid expansion in Australia.

Starbucks identified an opportunity to serve a burgeoning Australian middle class that had a keen taste for the café culture. In a market that was already dominated by local cafés, Starbucks opened its first store in Sydney. By 2004, the company owned and operated 80 stores across major metropolitans in Australia (Patterson et al. 2010). However, the coffee shop locations were in areas that were well-catered by local cafés, which made it difficult for Starbucks to attract and retain consumers. Five years after setting up operations, as the company struggled to break even, Howard Schultz realised there was a level of antagonism from Australian consumers towards Starbucks (Patterson et al. 2010). This was probably because the consumers felt that the company's approach and philosophy did not meet the expectations of the Australian palate (Mercer 2008).

Eight years after Starbucks first launched its operations in Australia, it closed over two-thirds of its outlets (Lee 2004). More recently, Starbucks has continued to lose ground in the Australian market amidst declining sales and intense competition (SBS 2014). In comparison, its competitors have fared well to meet consumer needs. The fast-food giant McDonald's, for instance, has 750 McCafé outlets in Australia and recorded US$4 billion in sales in 2016 (Brook 2016). To broaden its market, McDonald's also plans to open a hipster café called 'The Corner' in Sydney. Convenience store chain, 7-Eleven, owned by the Withers and Barlow Group, is also doing thriving business with its AUD$1 coffee. With 600 stores across the country, the company has experienced a 30 per cent growth in sales in the 2016–17 period alone. The Coffee Club, Australia's largest home-grown café group, has over 300 stores and is seen as a dominant player in the Australian café retail sector (Brook 2016).

Failed Australian operations: the key issues

Poor marketing combined with little market research meant that Starbucks failed to understand and market their brand to the Australian consumer. Among other things, the company did not appreciate that an overpriced US product would not suit Australian taste. A homogenous marketing approach did not work in the company's favour (Wong 2014). Indeed, when evaluating the international success of Starbucks, it becomes apparent that the company has only done well in markets where there has not traditionally been a coffee-drinking culture (for example, Japan, Thailand, Indonesia and China). Given the strong establishment of the local Australian coffee culture, the core product of coffee was not seen as any different from a good local café (Wong 2014). Therefore, the company's point of differentiation had to be in its supplementary value-added services, namely its ambience, service and brand. However, Australians did not consider this worth paying a premium price.

Coffee is not viewed as a luxury item in Australia, rather it is positioned as an affordable beverage, which is a part of a daily routine for many consumers. The company's premium price strategy therefore made it difficult to attract and retain customers. Further a strong sense of buying from and supporting local café vendors is part of the Australian coffee experience; an aspect of customer experience that the company failed to grasp (Patterson et al. 2010). While Starbucks made changes to its menu in other international markets, this was not the case in Australia. Rather, the focus was on offering a standardised US experience to consumers, but those consumers were after a more customised product and service offering (Wong & Berfield 2013).

The other issue related to the closure of many of the company's stores was its rapid growth in the Australian market. Adapting its US business model to Australia, the company undertook swift expansion by opening a cluster of stores in major cities across the country (New Zealand Herald 2008). However, this approach led to market saturation with stores cannibalising each other to survive. Being too common and commercial also meant that the uniqueness of the 'Starbucks experience' soon wore off (Hurst 2014; Wong 2014). As a late entrant, Starbucks faced extensive competition and the company struggled to attain a strong foothold in the Australian café retail sector.

The company also failed to communicate its brand. In a market dominated by consumers loyal to their local coffee retailers, advertising and promotion was crucial for Starbucks. However, their lack of advertising and effective marketing meant that the consumers failed to make a personal connection to the brand (Brook 2016).

Lastly, the business model used by the company did not work in its best interests. Unlike other markets, Starbucks owned and controlled all the stores in Australia (Brook 2016; Heffernan 2015). This meant that company continued to make huge investments to keep the stores operational, but with little return. The thought that size and strength of their brand would be enough to attract the discerning Australian consumer was also a major issue. Starbucks' focus on global domination, rather than catering to the tastes of the local market proved, to be a fatal error for the company (Wong & Berfield 2013).

Lessons learnt from the Starbucks experience

There are three lessons that can be learnt from the Starbucks experience in Australia. First, the company did not understand the importance of following a 'global' strategy. This is where a company seeks to customise their offerings to better understand and deliver customer value. In fact, most successful global brands are known to extensively customise their product and service offerings to meet the localised demands of the customers in a host country, something that Starbucks did not address.

Second, the company did not undertake market research prior to entering the Australian market. Starbucks assumed that the 'American experience' would be a major pull factor to attract consumers. While this strategy has worked in Asian markets, this was not the case in Australia. Further, there was no point of differentiation for the Australian market; a standardised approach failed to gain much attention from Australian consumers.

Finally, a premium strategy to cover operational costs meant that the company struggled to remain financially viable and incurred huge losses as a result. More recently, Starbucks has sold its rights to Withers and Barlow Group, Australia's largest business group, with the aim to re-launch its operations in Australia; Starbucks currently has 41 stores in Australia.

QUESTIONS

1. Outline the key characteristics of the Australian coffee market.
2. How and why has Starbucks succeeded in some of the emerging Asia–Pacific markets?
3. Discuss the main reasons behind Starbuck's failure in Australia.

VIDEO

References

Amit, R. & Schoemaker, P.J.H. (1993). Strategic assets and organisational rent. *Strategic Management Journal*, 14(1), 32–46.

Andersen, O. (1993). On the internationalisation process of firms: a critical analysis. *Journal of International Business Studies*, *24*(2), 209–31.

Aoki, K. & Lennerfors, T.T. (2013). The new improved Keiretsu. *Harvard Business Review*, 91(9), 109–13.

ASEAN (2018). Treaty of amity and cooperation in Southeast Asia Indonesia, 24 February 1976. Retrieved from http://asean.org/treaty-amity-cooperation-southeast-asia-indonesia-24-february-1976

Asia Foundation (2011). Fonterra: innovation. Retrieved from http://asia-knowledge.tki.org.nz/Business-case-studies/Case-study-5-Fonterra/Innovation

Barney, J. (1986). Strategic factor markets: expectations, luck, and business strategy. *Management Science*, 32(10), 1231–41.

——— (1991). Firm resources and competitive advantage. *Journal of Management*, 17(1), 99–120.

——— (1996). *Gaining and Sustaining Competitive Advantage*. Ohio: Wesley Publishing.

BBC (2017). Samsung Heir Lee Jae-yong jailed for corruption. *BBC News*, 25 August. Retrieved from www.bbc.com/news/business-41033568

Beca. (2007). Pacific Place Jakarta. Retrieved from www.beca.com/what-we-do/projects/buildings

Behl, A., Singh, M. & Venkatesh, V.G. (2016). Enablers and barriers of mobile banking opportunities in rural India: A strategic analysis. *International Journal of Business Excellence*, 10(2), 209–39.

Berg, N. & Holtbrügge, D. (2001). Public affairs management activities of German multinational corporations. *Journal of Business Ethics*, 30(1), 105–19.

Bhadoria, B., Goyal, A., Kumra, G. & Rajpal, J. (2016). Reshaping an emerging market giant. McKinsey&Company, March. Retrieved from www.mckinsey.com/industries/pharmaceuticals-and-medical-products/our-insights/reshaping-an-emerging-market-giant

Brook, B. (2016). Starbucks coffee is quietly expanding in Australia after humiliating retreat eight years ago. News.com, 30 September. Retrieved from www.news.com.au/finance/business/retail/starbucks-coffee-is-quietly-expanding-in-australia-after-humiliating-retreat-eight-years-ago/news-story/b7f136c4d78f24aaa600a3822b1e31b4

Buckley, P.J., Clegg, L.J., Cross, A.R., Liu, X., Voss, H. & Zheng, P. (2007). The determinants of Chinese outward foreign direct investment. *Journal of International Business Studies*, 38(4), 499–518.

Buckley, P.J., Forsans, N. & Munjal, S. (2012). Host–home country linkages and host–home country specific advantages as determinants of foreign acquisitions by Indian firms. *International Business Review*, 21(5), 878–90.

Cantwell, J. & Narula, R. (eds) (2003). *International Business and the Eclectic Paradigm*. London: Routledge.

——— (2010). The eclectic paradigm in the global economy. *International Journal of the Economics of Business*, 8(2), 155–72.

Carlson, S. (1975). *How Foreign is Foreign Trade? A Problem in International Business Research*. Uppsala: Uppsala University Press.

Centre of Management Research (2012). *Dr. Reddy's Laboratories: Growing Pains*. Retrieved from www.icmrindia.org/casestudies/catalogue/Business%20Strategy/BSTR403.htm

Chetty, S. & Campbell-Hunt, C. (2003). Paths to internationalisation among small- to medium-sized firms: A global versus regional approach. *European Journal of Marketing*, 37(5), 796–820.

Conner, K.R. & Prahalad, C.K. (1996). A resource based theory of the firm: Knowledge versus opportunism. *Organizational Science*, 7(5), 477–501.

Connor, T. (2002). The resource-based view of strategy and its value to practising managers. *Strategic Change*, 11(6), 307–16.

Conor, B. (2015) 'The Hobbit' law: precarity and market citizenship in cultural production. *Asia Pacific Journal of Arts and Cultural Management*, 12(1), 25–36.

Delaney, B. (2008). Starbucks to go. *The Guardian*, 31 July. Retrieved from www.theguardian.com/commentisfree/2008/jul/30/australia.starbucks.

Deng, P. (2007). Investing for strategic resources and its rationale: the case of outward FDI from Chinese companies. *Business Horizons*, 50(1), 71–81.

Dey, S. (2015). Dr. Reddy's get US FDA warning letter for quality issues. *The Times of India*, 6 November. Retrieved from https://timesofindia.indiatimes.com/business/india-business/Dr-Reddys-get-US-FDA-warning-letter-for-quality-issues-in-3-Indian-facilities/articleshow/49692533.cms

Dezan Shira and Associates (2016). Remitting profits in ASEAN – Part 2: Thailand and Indonesia. ASEAN Briefing, 11 March. Retrieved from www.aseanbriefing.com/news/2016/03/11/remitting-profits-in-asean-part-2.html

Dickie, M. (2006). Starbucks wins case against Chinese copycat. *Financial Times*, 3 January. Retrieved from www.ft.com/content/89ca5d4a-7bb1-11da-ab8e-0000779e2340

Dowling, P., Festing, M. & Engle, A. (2013). *International Human Resource Management*, 6th edn. London: Cengage.

Dunning, J.H. (1980). Toward an eclectic theory of international production: some empirical tests. *Journal of International Business Studies*, 11(1), 9–31.

Dunning, J.H. & Lundan, S. (2008). *Multinational Enterprises and the Global Economy*. Cheltenham: Edward Elgar.

El-Gazzar, S., Finn, P. & Jacob, R. (1999). An empirical investigation of multinational firms' compliance with international accounting standards. *The International Journal of Accounting*, 34(2), 239–48.

Enderwick, P. (2007). *Understanding Emerging Markets*. London: Routledge.

Euromonitor International. (2017a). *Cafes and Bars in Australia*. Sydney: Euromonitor International.

——— (2017b). *Coffee in Australia*. Sydney: Euromonitor International.

Gao, C., Jones, G., Zuzul, T. & Khanna, T. (2017). Overcoming institutional voids: a reputation-based view of long run survival. Working paper. Boston: Harvard Business School.

Ghemawat, P. (2001). Distance still matters: the hard reality of global expansion. *Harvard Business Review*, 79(8), 137–47.

Gilpin, R. (1987). *The Political Economy of International Relations*. New Jersey Princeton University Press.

Górska, M. (2013). Does the Uppsala internationalisation model explain the internationalisation process of professional business service firms? Conference Paper presented at CBU International Conference on Integration and Innovation in Science and Education, Prague, Czech Republic, July.

Government of India (2009). Facilities and incentives. Retrieved from http://sezindia.nic.in/cms/facilities-and-incentives.php

Gracie, C. (2016). US leaving TPP: A great news day for China. *BBC News*, 22 November. Retrieved from www.bbc.com/news/world-asia-china-38060980

Greenfield, C. & White, S. (2017). After US exit, Asian nations try to save TPP trade deal. Reuters, 24 January. Retrieved from www.reuters.com/article/us-usa-trump-asia-idUSKBN15800V

Gulati, R. (1999). Network location and learning: the influence of network resources and firm capabilities on alliance formation. *Strategic Management Journal*, 20(5), 397–420.

Heffernan, M. (2015). Booming coffee market moves into consolidation phase. *The Sydney Morning Herald*, 28 March. Retrieved from www.smh.com.au/business/retail/booming-coffee-market-moves-into-consolidation-phase-20150317-1m1g1p.html

Hubbard, J., Thomas, C. & Varnham, S. (2012). *Principles of Law: New Zealand Business Students*. Wellington: Pearson.

Hurst, P. (2014). This is why Australians hate Starbucks. Munchies, 4 November. Retrieved from https://munchies.vice.com/en_us/article/4xb9gd/this-is-why-australians-hate-starbucks

Hymer, S.H. (1976). *The International Operations of National Firms: A Study of Foreign Direct Investment*. Cambridge: The MIT Press.

IBEF (2018). Indian Retail Industry Analysis. India Brand Equity Foundation, September. Retrieved from www.ibef.org/industry/indian-retail-industry-analysis-presentation

Independent Press. (2013). India adopting protectionist measures in agri, dairy sectors. *The Economic Times*, 14 March. Retrieved from http://economictimes.indiatimes.com/news/economy/foreign-trade/india-adopting-protectionist-measures-in-agri-dairy-sectors/articleshow/18969295.cms

Johanson, J. & Vahlne, J.E. (1977). The internationalisation process of the firm – a model of knowledge development and increasing foreign market commitments. *Journal of International Business Studies*, 8(1), 23–32.

——— (2009). The Uppsala internationalisation process model revisited: from liability of foreignness to liability of outsidership. *Journal of International Business Studies*, 40, 1411–31.

Johanson, J. & Wiedersheim-Paul, F. (1975). The internationalisation of the firm – four Swedish cases. *Journal of Management Studies*, 12(3), 305–23.

Jones, N. (2016). Plain packaging for tobacco likely to be in place early next year. *New Zealand Herald*, 31 May. Retrieved from www.nzherald.co.nz/nz/news/article.cfm?c_id=1&objectid=11648047

Kafouros, M.I., Buckley, P.J., Sharp, J.A., & Wang, C. (2008). The role of internationalisation in explaining innovation performance. *Technovation*, 28(1–2), 63–74.

Kannan, S. (2013). Novartis: India rejects patent plea for cancer drug Glivec. Delhi: BBC.

Kaske, T. (2002). The co-existence of common law systems and civil law systems in modern society: A comparison between the legal systems of New Zealand and Germany. *Canterbury Law Review*, (8), 395–424

Kelly, H. (2011). 'The Hobbit' dispute. *New Zealand Journal of Employment Relations*, 36(3), 30–3.

Khanna, T. & Palepu, K. (1997). Why focused strategies may be wrong for emerging countries. *Harvard Business Review*, 75, 41–51.

——— (1999). Policy shocks, market intermediaries and corporate strategy: Evidence from Chile and India. *Journal of Economics and Management Strategy*, 8(2), 271–310.

Lee, J. (2004). Starbucks adds shop closures to the experience. *The Sydney Morning Herald*, 26 August. Retrieved from www.smh.com.au/articles/2004/08/25/1093246617341.html?oneclick=true

Madhani, P. (2015). MNC subsidiaries vs domestic firms. *SCMS Journal of Indian Management*, 12(1), 5–24.

Magnusson, N. & Molin, A. (2016). Ikea targets China, India expansion to meet sales growth aim. Bloomberg, 13 Sept 2016. Retrieved from www.bloomberg.com/news/articles/2016-09-13/ikea-sales-rise-7-1-as-it-prepares-first-india-serbia-stores

Marinova, S. (2014). *Institutional Impacts on Firm Internationalisation*. London: Palgrave Macmillan.

MarketLine (2016). *RTD Tea and Coffee in Australia*. Sydney: MarketLine.

Mathews, J.A. (2002). *Dragon Multinational: A New Model for Global Growth*. New York: Oxford University Press.

——— (2006a). Dragon multinationals: new players in 21st century globalisation. *Asia Pacific Journal of Management*, 23, 5–27.

——— (2006b). Catch-up strategies and the latecomer effect in industrial development. *New Political Economy*, 11(3), 313–35, DOI:10.1080/13563460600840142

McDonald's (2018). Meet the suppliers. Retrieved from https://mcdonalds.co.nz/about-maccas/our-supply-chain

McKinsey Global Institute (2000). Why the Japanese economy is not growing: retail sector. McKinsey Global Institute, July. Retrieved from www.mckinsey.com/global-themes/asia-pacific/why-the-japanese-economy-is-not-growing/japanese-retail-sector

Mercer, P. (2008). Shunned Starbucks in Aussie exit. *BBC News*, 4 August. Retrieved from http://news.bbc.co.uk/2/hi/business/7540480.stm

Miller, T.B. (2015). *Current International Treaties*, Vol. 6. New York: Routledge.

Ministry of Health NZ (2016). *Standardised Tobacco Products and Packaging Draft Regulations.* Wellington: Ministry of Health. Retrieved from www.health.govt.nz/system/files/documents/publications/standardised-tobacco-products-packaging-draft-regulations-consultation-may16_1.pdf

——— (2018). *Tobacco Standardised Packaging*. Retrieved from www.health.govt.nz/our-work/preventative-health-wellness/tobacco-control/plain-packaging

Miyazaki, A. & Westbrook, T. (2016). Trump sinks Asia trade pact, opening the way for China to lead. Reuters, 22 November. Retrieved from www.reuters.com/article/us-usa-trump-tpp/trump-sinks-asia-trade-pact-opening-the-way-for-china-to-lead-idUSKBN13H0OT

Murray, C. (2009). *Industry Snapshot for the Auckland Region: The Marine Sector*. Auckland: Auckland Regional Council. Retrieved from http://knowledgeauckland.org.nz/assets/publications/Industry_snapshot_for_the_Auckland_region_The_marine_sector.pdf

Narayanan, D. (2017). Mondelez to pay $13 million to settle India FCPA violation charges. *The Economic Times*, 9 January. Retrieved from http://economictimes.indiatimes.com/industry/cons-products/food/mondelez-to-pay-13-million-to-settle-india-fcpa-violation-charges/articleshow/56422345.cms

New Zealand Foreign Affairs & Trade (2015). NZ–Korea Free Trade Agreement. Retrieved from www.mfat.govt.nz/en/trade/free-trade-agreements/free-trade-agreements-in-force/nz-korea-free-trade-agreement

New Zealand Herald (2008). Starbucks to shut 61 Australian stores. *The New Zealand Herald*, 29 July. Retrieved from www.smh.com.au/business/starbucks-to-close-61-australian-outlets-20080729-3mkm.html

NTI (2018). South-East Asian Nuclear Weapon Free Zone Treaty (Bangkok Treaty). NTI, 30 April. Retrieved from www.nti.org/learn/treaties-and-regimes/southeast-asian-nuclear-weapon-free-zone-seanwfz-treaty-bangkok-treaty

OECD (2017). China Policy Brief: OECD, March. Retrieved from www.oecd.org/china/china-investment-fostering-foreign-direct-investment-in-services-sectors.pdf

Palmer, E. (2017). Manufacturing issues whack Dr. Reddy's FY 2017 sales in US. FiercePharma, 15 May. Retrieved from www.fiercepharma.com/manufacturing/manufacturing-issues-whack-dr-reddy-s-fy-2017-sales-u-s

Pandiya, S. & Gupta, S. (2015). A study of changing pattern and demand for mobile banking services in India. *Global Journal of Enterprise Information System*, 7(1), 16–27.

Patterson, P., Scott. J. & Uncles, M. (2010). How the local competition defeated a global brand: The case of Starbucks. *Australasian Marketing Journal*, 18(1), 41–7.

Patton, L. (2016). Starbucks plans to double number of locations in China by 2021. Bloomberg, 19 October. Retrieved from www.bloomberg.com/news/articles/2016-10-19/starbucks-plans-to-double-number-of-locations-in-china-by-2021

Penn, J. (2017). Innovative the path to the future. *New Zealand Herald*, 20 July. Retrieved from www.nzherald.co.nz/business/news/article.cfm?c_id=3&objectid=11891762

Petersen, B. & Pedersen, T. (2002). Coping with liability of foreignness: Different learning engagements of entrant firms. *Journal of International Management*, 8(3), 339–50.

Porter, M. (1990a). The competitive advantage of nations. *Harvard Business Review*, 68(2), 73–93.

——— (1990b). *Competitive Advantage of Nations*. New York: The Free Press.

——— (1998) Clusters and new economics of competition. *Harvard Business Review*, 76(6), 77–90.

Prahalad, C.K. & Hamel, G. (1990). The core competence of the corporation. *Harvard Business Review*, 68(3), 79–91.

Prevot, C. (2016). The taking of evidence in international commercial arbitration: A compromise between common law and civil law. *Dispute Resolution Journal*, 70(2), 73–96.

Ramakrishnan, S. (2017). Starbucks is paying $1.3 billion for 1300 stores in China. *Business Insider*, 27 July. Retrieved from www.businessinsider.com/starbucks-is-paying-13-billion-for-1300-stores-in-china-2017-7?IR=T

Robinson, D. (2013). Primark increases compensation to Rana Plaza factory victims in Bangladesh. *Financial Times*, 24 October. Retrieved from www.ft.com/content/3548c5b0-3cb3-11e3-86ef-00144feab7de

Ruru, J., Scott, P. & Webb, D. (2016). *The New Zealand Legal System: Structures and Processes*. Wellington: Lexis Nexis.

SBS (2014). *Why Starbucks just can't crack the Australian market*. SBS, 2 June. Retrieved from www.sbs.com.au/news/thefeed/story/why-starbucks-just-cant-crack-australian-market

Seddiqe, M.M.I.S. & Basak, A. (2014). Importance of human resource management and the competitive advantage: a case analysis on basis of the textile industry of Bangladesh. *Global Journal of Management and Business Research: Administration and Management*, 14(9), 1–7.

Siddiqui, Z. (2015). India's Dr Reddy's hit by FDA warning, shares fall 15 percent. Reuters, 6 November. Retrieved from www.reuters.com/article/us-dr-reddys-fda-warning/indias-dr-reddys-hit-by-fda-warning-shares-fall-15-percent-idUSKCN0SV0FA20151106

Sölvell, Ö. (2015). The competitive advantage of nations 25 years – opening up new perspectives on competitiveness. *Competitiveness Review*, 25(5), 471–81.

Statista (2016). Number of Starbucks stores in China from 2005 to 2017. Retrieved from www.statista.com/statistics/277795/number-of-starbucks-stores-in-china

Stoian, C. (2013) Extending Dunning's investment development path: The role of home country institutional determinants in explaining outward foreign direct investment. *International Business Review*, 22(3), 615–37.

Stone, B., Kim, S. & King, I. (2017). Summer of Samsung: a corruption scandal, a political firestorm – and a record profit. Bloomberg, 27 July. Retrieved from www.bloomberg.com/news/features/2017-07-27/summer-of-samsung-a-corruption-scandal-a-political-firestorm-and-a-record-profit

Tan, B.R. & Chintakananda, A. (2016). The effects of home country political and legal institutions on firms' geographic diversification performance *Global Strategy Journal*, 6, 105–23.

Tata (2018). Tata Consultancy Services. Retrieved from www.tata.com/company/profile/Tata-Consultancy-Services

Tupou, L. (2017). America's cup win to spark boat building boom. *Radio New Zealand*, 28 June. Retrieved from www.radionz.co.nz/news/national/334051/america-s-cup-win-to-spark-boat-building-boom

US Department of Justice (2018). Foreign Corrupt Practices Act. Retrieved from www.justice.gov/criminal-fraud/foreign-corrupt-practices-act

Vaswani, K. (2016). Asia's winners and losers from Trump's TPP dump. China: BBC.

Verbeke. A. (2013). *International Business Strategy: Rethinking the Foundations of Global Corporate Success*. Cambridge: Cambridge University Press.

Westervelt, A. (2015). Two years after Rana Plaza, have conditions improved in Bangladesh's factories? *The Guardian*, 25 April. Retrieved from www.theguardian.com/sustainable-business/2015/apr/24/bangladesh-factories-building-collapse-garment-dhaka-rana-plaza-brands-hm-gap-workers-construction

Wong, V. (2014). Starbucks has an Australia problem. Bloomberg, 28 May. Retrieved from www.bloomberg.com/news/articles/2014-05-27/starbucks-has-an-australia-problem

Wong, V. & Berfield, S. (2013). For Starbucks, coffee is so 1990s. *Bloomberg Businessweek*, (4353), 30–1.

World Intellectual Property Organisation (2018). Regional Bureau for Asia and the Pacific. Retrieved from www.wipo.int/about-wipo/en/activities_by_unit/units/aspac/index.html

Young, A. (2018a). Jacinda Ardern hails breakthrough in revised TPP, Canada agrees to stay in. *New Zealand Herald*, 24 January. Retrieved from www.nzherald.co.nz/business/news/article.cfm?c_id=3&objectid=11981117

——— (2018b) Revised TPP on track to be signed by 11 countries in March. *New Zealand Herald*, 24 January Retrieved from www.nzherald.co.nz/business/news/article.cfm?c_id=3&objectid=11980912

Zhou, S. (2015). The TPP Risks making U.S.-China Relations Worse. China: Aljazeera.

CHAPTER 3

ECONOMICS AND THE ROLE OF REGIONAL INTEGRATION

Learning objectives

In reading this chapter, you will learn to:

1. appreciate the historical growth of regional economic integration
2. recognise the types of economic integration among regions and between nations
3. comprehend the costs and benefits of integrated arrangements
4. explore the economic integration that has emerged in the Asia–Pacific
5. consider the strategic challenges that economic integration poses for international business firms.

THE ASIA–PACIFIC: AN ECONOMIC UPDATE

The global economic environment and individual country vulnerabilities pose risks to the Asia–Pacific region's prospects for economic growth. The risks include protectionist attitudes in several developed economies, collective high levels of national debt and rapid credit expansion, and rising US exchange rates. Addressing and managing these risks is the challenge. Policy makers in the region are focused on cautiously controlling macroeconomic levels and safeguarding fiscal balances for the longer term. Regional growth, in the short term, is being boosted by strong demand from domestic countries with a combination of public and private investments. The economic role of exports in the Asia–Pacific will be important, as trade with emerging markets and developing nations improves.

China's economic growth and the broader regional outlook are expected to remain positive over the coming years. The key drivers will be domestic demand, global economic recovery and the steady increase in commodity prices (World Bank 2017). Robust domestic demand will shape and benefit commodity exporters. Increased commodity prices will boost national incomes and open the doors for greater bank financing and fiscal expansion.

In the immediate term, Asia–Pacific policy managers are prioritising measures that will counteract global risks threatening the availability and price of external finance and export development. The growth of credit accessibility in regional countries such as Vietnam, the Philippines and Laos reveals the importance of reinforcing regulations and increasing the supervision of financial flows.

East Asia has advanced regional integration by promoting ongoing initiatives aimed at reducing barriers to labour mobility and increasing cross-border trade flows within the ASEAN group. Future economic growth prospects for the region may lie on a more sustainable path through improved pollution management linked to increased agriculture productivity.

WEBLINK
VIGNETTE
QUESTION

Introduction

In this chapter, we discuss the regional integration that has taken place globally and its role as a catalyst in driving economic growth, with a focus on the Asia–Pacific region. We begin with a broad overview of the historical growth of regional economic integration and regional trade agreements (RTAs). The types of economic integration, and the distinguishing features among regions and countries are also explained. Issues related to the costs and benefits of integrated arrangements are presented, and integration in the Asia–Pacific region, including Asia–Pacific Economic Cooperation (APEC) and the Association of Southeast Asian Nations (ASEAN), that has emerged in the last 30 years, is discussed. The chapter concludes with a summary of the strategic challenges that integration presents for international businesses.

REGIONAL TRADE AGREEMENTS (RTAs) reciprocal preferential trade agreements between two or more countries created for partners to obtain economic benefit, ensure increased market access, improve bargaining strength and promote regional domestic industries.

ASIA–PACIFIC ECONOMIC COOPERATION (APEC) a forum established in 1989 that aims to secure free and open trade and investment among 21 member countries in the Asia–Pacific.

ASSOCIATION OF SOUTHEAST ASIAN NATIONS (ASEAN) established in 1967 to promote political and economic cooperation. It includes the countries of Brunei, Cambodia, Indonesia, Laos, Malaysia, Myanmar, the Philippines, Singapore, Thailand and Vietnam.

The growth of regional economic integration

The benefits of trade agreements have been highlighted in the first two chapters. The underlying premise of a successful trade agreement is to provide participating nations with a measure of independence and a level of mutually agreed control. In recent history, nations have secured and strengthened their trading relationships by establishing regional trading blocs. Such trading blocs have allowed the movement of goods, services, capital and labour between nations. These arrangements have intersected and interacted, creating a global trading landscape.

TRADE PROTECTIONISM
a form of government policy that limits unfair competition for domestic industries from foreign industries. Countries use a variety of strategies to protect their domestic industries. One way is to impose tariffs that place high levels of tax on imports to create a competitive advantage for domestic products and services.

Though past trends have been towards more openness and greater integration in international trade agreements, and away from trade protectionism, advancements in economic integration have not been straight forward, and there have been significant setbacks and difficulties along the way. Economic integration should be viewed as a scaled range. At one end of the scale, the utopian global economy would be all countries sharing a common currency and with factors of production, goods and services able to freely flow among countries. At the opposite end of the scale are closed economies, seeking to be autonomous and self-supporting. The current status of global economic integration lies mostly within the middle point of this scale and is the main topic of this chapter.

From empires to international agreements

In the eighteenth century, a major shift emerged in international trade, spurred on by a rapid rise in the economic power and leadership of the open-trade promoter, the United Kingdom (UK). In cities such as London, Manchester and Glasgow, industrialists contended that the country's restrictive trade polices encouraged other nations to exclude British exports from their markets. The British industry's view point was that competitiveness could be achieved by reducing the cost of labour to aid exports and lowering the country's high agricultural import barriers. These regulatory barriers were known as the Corn Laws. From the mid-1800s the British government reduced import duties with a few countries and began developing several structured agreements. In 1860, the Cobden–Chevalier Treaty between the UK and France was signed, which was a significant historical point in time because reciprocal reduction of tariffs between the two nations was introduced for the first time. The arrangement was designed to improve political relations and strengthen economic ties, spurring on a wave of European nation agreements. It is an early demonstration of competitive trade liberalisation. This early treaty, alongside the expansion of unilateral trade liberalisation, became the start of regional integration that foreshadowed the proliferation of trade agreements that took place a century later.

The continuing evolution of regional trade integration was halted in the early 1900s by World War I (1914–18). Post-war recovery was sluggish, reflecting slow economic growth, a lack of global economic leadership by the isolationist US and the long-term damage sustained by the UK. History shows the recession of 1929 moved into the Great Depression of the 1930s due to fiscal and monetary policy errors by governments around the world. This situation was made worse by some nations trying to shield themselves and reverting to protectionist trade strategies, which resulted in record high unemployment and preferential trading arrangements. An example is the Dutch–Scandinavian Economic Pact of 1930, which was designed to coordinate tariff policies and promote trade between the Netherlands, Denmark, Sweden and Norway. Between 1933 and 1936, Germany created its own restrictive trade arrangements as a drive for its economic independence. And Japan developed the Greater East Asia Co-Prosperity Sphere from 1936 to 1945, with a focus on providing a trading autonomy in the region against the West.

The foundation and movement for regional integration came after World War II (1939–45), and even more so in the late 1950s, with the emergence of Europe and the US as the dominant trading regions. At this time, the Asia–Pacific region was a trading partner with Europe and the US. In 1967, the ASEAN alliance was formed (Indonesia, Malaysia, the Philippines, Singapore and Thailand), and by the 1970s, the Asia–Pacific region had emerged as a new regional trading bloc and rest of the world became increasingly fragmented. In the 1980s, the South-East and East-Asian areas started recording growth in intra-Asia regional trade.

By the 1990s, the Mercosur (Argentina, Paraguay, Uruguay and Brazil) trading bloc had formed between South American nations. The EU had had increased membership across most of Europe and was the most significant economic integration of the period. In 1993, the Maastricht Treaty allowed the four freedoms of regional integration in Europe: the movement of goods, services, people and money. The informal American block of the US, Canada and Mexico was officially formalised by the countries agreeing to form the North American Free Trade Agreement (NAFTA).

From the emergence of the GATT (General Agreement on Trade and Tariffs) in 1948 and the formation of the World Trade Organization (WTO) in 1995, regional trading agreements have increased appreciably (see Figure 3.1). Regional trading activities and agreements have intensified across and within all world regions. As at June 2017, the number of agreements in force notified to the WTO reached 445. The historical increase in the overall number of agreements in force or inactive was reported at 665 since GATT's inception in 1948. The continued evolution of trading agreements is complex and sophisticated, with a few nations seeking bilateral, regional and multilateral agreements to coexist in the framework of a global trade architecture.

WORLD TRADE ORGANIZATION (WTO) facilitates the rules of trade and oversees the flow of trade between nations, with the aim of liberalising trade under rules agreed to by member countries for reciprocal benefits.

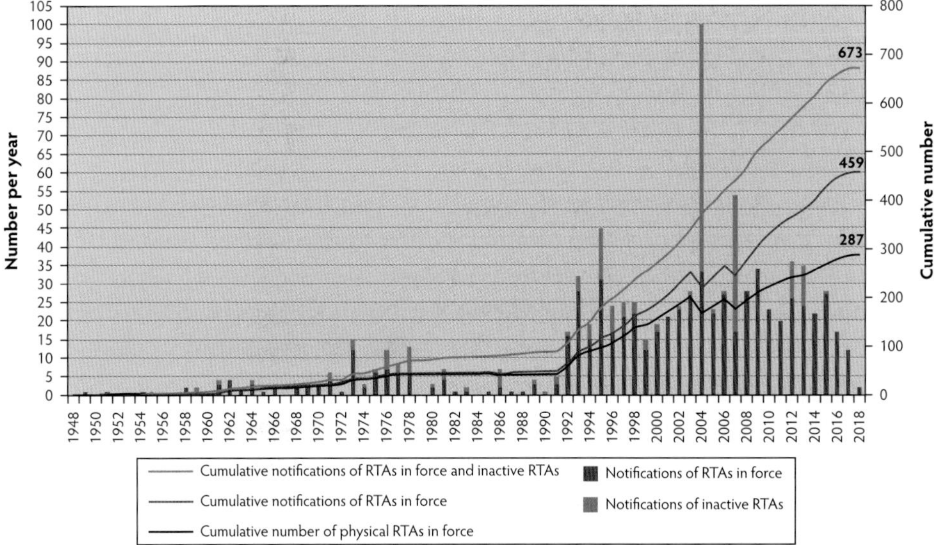

FIGURE 3.1 Evolution of RTAs in the world, 1948–2018

Note: Notifications of RTAs: goods, services and accessions to an RTA are counted separately. Physical RTAs: goods, services and accessions to an RTA are counted together. The cumulative lines show the number of notifications or physical RTAs that were in force for a given year.

Source: WTO 2018, © World Trade Organization 2018, reproduced with permission.

Types of economic integration

RTAs are a major, and perhaps irreversible, feature of today's multilateral trading system that facilitates economic integration. Multilateral trading systems involve groups of member countries within a geographical region (usually contiguous) that agree on common trading policies with the rest of the world in terms of tariffs and market access, and preferential treatment for members. Agreements may be made between two countries (bilateral) or several countries (multilateral). Among market regions, the orientation of such arrangements may vary depending on the degree of cooperation between participating nations, but the core objective of ensuring the economic growth and benefit of member countries remains universal. WTO members, who are increasingly seeing these arrangements as valuable tools in their trade policies, are embracing these agreements. There are four primary forms of economic integration that range from a very loose association to a complete economic integration; these forms are: the free trade area, the customs union, the common market and the economic union (see Figure 3.2.)

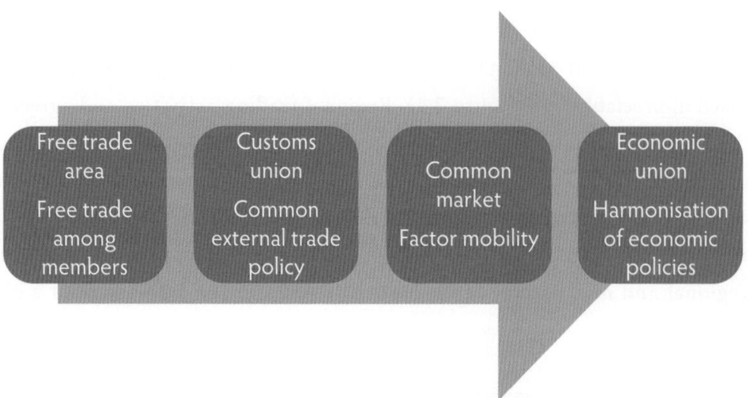

FIGURE 3.2 Forms of RTA that accelerate economic integration

FREE TRADE AREA
a geographic area where all barriers to trade among member countries are removed to allow goods to be landed, stored, handled, manufactured or reconfigured, and re-exported with no taxes for member countries. It is a trade bloc that comprises of member countries who have signed a free trade agreement (FTA).

RULES OF ORIGIN (ROO)
a specific criterion related to determining where a product is made and is a main feature of contemporary free trade area agreements.

The free trade area

The free trade area is the least restrictive and loosest form of economic integration among nations; it is a trade bloc that comprises of member countries who have signed a free trade agreement (FTA). All barriers to trade among member countries are removed with goods and services freely traded among member countries. No tariffs, quotas or other trade barriers are applied to member countries. The most notable feature of a free trade area is that each member country maintains its own individual trading policies with non-member countries.

One of the main features of contemporary free trade area agreements is the criterion for rules of origin (ROO). ROO criteria are used to determine where a product is made. It can be challenging to determine where a product is made with the advent of worldwide outsourcing for raw materials and manufacturing because the assembly of the product may be scattered across the globe to achieve economies of scale and scope. FTAs often have ROOs embedded in their arrangements, and they are explicit about the content thresholds and the interpretation of the inclusion. Members in a free trade area typically have different tariffs on their imports from non-members; it is then necessary to have rules of origin, which are designed to prevent trade deflection or the re-routing of imports from non-members through members that have lower tariffs. These agreements differ in terms of the approved operating parameters. In some instances, agreements are formed only for certain classes of goods and services, such as agriculture products; this approach is generally confined to developing countries. In contrast, other trading agreements, between developed and developing countries that go beyond the WTO regulatory framework, include provisions on investment, competition, intellectual property rights, environment and labour.

FTAs are the most common category of regional trading arrangements, accounting for over half of all agreements (in force) notified to the WTO. Bilateral trade agreements are easier to negotiate as they are between two countries, and account for over three-quarters of trade agreements signed and in negotiation. However, multilateral trade agreements, between three or more countries at once, usually have important geographical considerations so can be more complicated. While bilateral and multilateral trading arrangements vary, they all exist to create a more stable and transparent trading and investment environment. Free trade areas are not immune to upheaval from political leadership change. With the inauguration of Donald Trump as President of the US in 2017, the country made significant economic changes and shuffled trading arrangements in line with the political leadership strategies of the new president. Given the dynamic nature of the global political climate, several countries have expressed less interest in free trade pacts, either bilateral or multilateral, and are more interested in home-country protectionist policies.

In addition to free trade zones, Special Economic Zones (SEZs) are now being established in key trading regions to attract and facilitate trade expansion. For example, the SEZ areas in mainland China were created to promote rapid economic growth. Four SEZs were first established in 1980 by Chinese leader Deng Xiaoping and included three small cities in Guangdong province, Shenzhen, Zhuhai and Shantou, and in Fujian province in the port area of Xiamen. The Chinese government stimulates their economic agenda in these areas by providing tax and business incentives to attract foreign investment and technology. Foreign investors are given the ability to develop their own infrastructure without the approval of the central government. As at 2018, important progress has been made in shifting a little-known farmland called Xiong'an New Area, near Beijing, into a high-tech innovation hub. Plans are in progress for this area to be a centre for new business and universities, and it will encapsulate a state-of-the-art transport infrastructure. Like Shenzhen, it is expected Xiong'an New Area will offer trade and investment opportunities.

The customs union

The customs union takes a step further in the economic integration process. As in the free trade area, goods and services are freely traded among members who agree to apply external tariffs to imports from the rest of the world. That is, members enter a FTA and apply a common external tariff (CET) schedule to imports from non-members. A customs union is considered a greater degree of integration than a free trade area; generally, it requires more coordination and a greater loss of autonomy. Customs unions require a high level of collaboration, especially related to government policy planning and implementation, to achieve successful outcomes. They are not without disadvantages. In the customs union environment, members are not free to negotiate individual trade deals. Therefore, if a member country needs to protect a declining or infant industry, it cannot do so through imposing its own tariff.

CUSTOMS UNION
a formal agreement among trading countries where trade barriers are removed for members and a common trade policy is agreed with respect to non-members.

Geographical considerations have traditionally been a major factor in the formation of customs unions. The oldest functional customs union is the Southern African Customs Union (SACU) established in 1910, and the most successful example of economic integration in Africa. Today, the union comprises Botswana, Lesotho, Swaziland and Namibia. One element that has contributed to the union's success has been the design of the CET that supports the agreement. There has been several political disputes over time relating to the use and allocation of the collected duties (CET funds) between the countries. These disagreements have been concerned whether the collected revenues should be treated as community property or as income accruing to each member country. The SACU commission established a regional secretariat to ensure the smooth operations of the union and the distribution of the CET funds.

A more recent example of a functioning customs union is the formation of the Australia–New Zealand Closer Economic Relations Trade Agreement (ANZCERTA) first commenced in 1983. This agreement forms the foundation for expanded economic and trade relations between the two countries. The agreement includes over 80 government-to-government bilateral treaties, protocols and other provisions covering trade, movement of people, investment, aviation, business law coordination, mutual recognitions of goods and professions, taxation, healthcare, social security, superannuation portability, food standards and government procurement. The trade goals between Australia and New Zealand have largely been met. In 2006, the two countries began planning a single economic market (SEM) approach to closer economic integration. The SEM aims to harmonise the two countries to facilitate business, investors and consumers to operate across the Tasman Sea in a unified regulatory setting (DFAT, 2016).

The common market

COMMON MARKET
is a free trade agreement that allows mobility of factors of production, including labour, capital and technology.

FACTORS OF PRODUCTION
all inputs in the production process: capital, labour, land and technology.

FACTOR MOBILITY
the ability to freely move factors of production across borders.

As cooperation increases among member countries of a custom union, the next level of economic integration is the formation of a common market. This level of integration has the same features as a customs union, with no barriers to trade among members and a common set of external tariffs on non-members. What moves this next phase along the economic integration continuum is the allowance of a free flow of factors of production among members. The factors of production are defined as labour, capital and technology. Principally, the common market allows for the abolition of restrictions on immigration, expatriation and cross-border investment. The importance of factor mobility in this setting is fundamental to delivering and sustaining economic growth. Factor mobility delivers the productivity that is achieved from the freedom to employ capital, labour, and technology effectively and efficiently.

The members of a common market commit to cooperate cohesively when planning monetary, fiscal and employment policies. Members fundamentally all seek to achieve aggregated productivity, but the distribution of economic benefits cannot always be shared evenly among all participating countries. The inherent challenges of a common market model have meant less uptake in many areas of the world, including parts of the Asia–Pacific and Central America. Today's EU had its foundations in the Treaty of Rome, signed by France, West Germany, Italy, the Netherlands, Belgium and Luxembourg in 1956, to form the European Economic Community, which was also known as the Common Market, and provided the free movement of labour and capital among member nations. The EU is now one of the largest trading unions in the world and represents over 15 per cent of total world trade (European Commission 2017).

The economic union

An economic union is a group of countries that are united by a central political body, that coordinates common economic, foreign and social policy, and that share judicial collaboration. A series of subsequent treaties, and the expansion from 6 member countries to 22, continued to develop the European Economic Community until 1992 when the Treaty of Maastricht formerly created the European Union in 1994. The Maastricht Treaty has been expanded by the treaties of Amsterdam (1997), Nice (2001) and Lisbon (2007). With the introduction of the Euro, a single common currency, in 1999 for its members, with the exception of Denmark, the EU has achieved the next level of economic integration, the formation of an economic union (see Figure 3.3).

ECONOMIC UNION
a union among trading countries that has the characteristics of a common market as well as provisions for the harmonisation of monetary policies, taxation and government spending.

An economic union requires the harmonisation of economic policies, both monetary and fiscal, taxation regulations and government spending programs, in addition to the free movement of goods, services and production factors, a common external tariff and a common currency. In the formation of an economic union, nations are required to surrender a significant degree of their national sovereignty to the overarching supranational authority institution. For example, member countries have representatives in the European Union Parliament and associated regulatory bodies such as the European Central Bank. Member countries however remain politically independent within their own nations.

The key characteristics for each level of economic integration are quite separate and distinguishable (see Table 3.1). The *free trade area* removes tariffs and quotas among members. The *customs union* removes tariffs and quotas, and additionally agrees upon and applies a common external tariff on imports from non-members. A *common market* removes tariffs and quotas on members, agrees common external tariffs for imports from non-members, and allows mobility for factors of production (labour, capital and technology). An *economic union* among trading countries has the characteristics of a common market, and harmonises monetary policies, taxation, government spending and uses a common currency.

TABLE 3.1 Key characteristics of forms of economic integration

Stage of economic integration	Removal of tariffs and quotas among members	Common tariff and quota system for non-members	Allows mobility for factors of production	Harmonisation of monetary policies, taxation and government outlays
Free trade area	✔	✘	✘	✘
Customs union	✔	✔	✘	✘
Common market	✔	✔	✔	✘
Economic union	✔	✔	✔	✔

Economic integration and the processes for its development are complex. Depending on the agreement, the challenges relate to the level of integration and differing laws, and are compounded by issues related to investment, movement of capital, intellectual property and market competitive landscapes.

MULTIPLE-CHOICE QUESTION

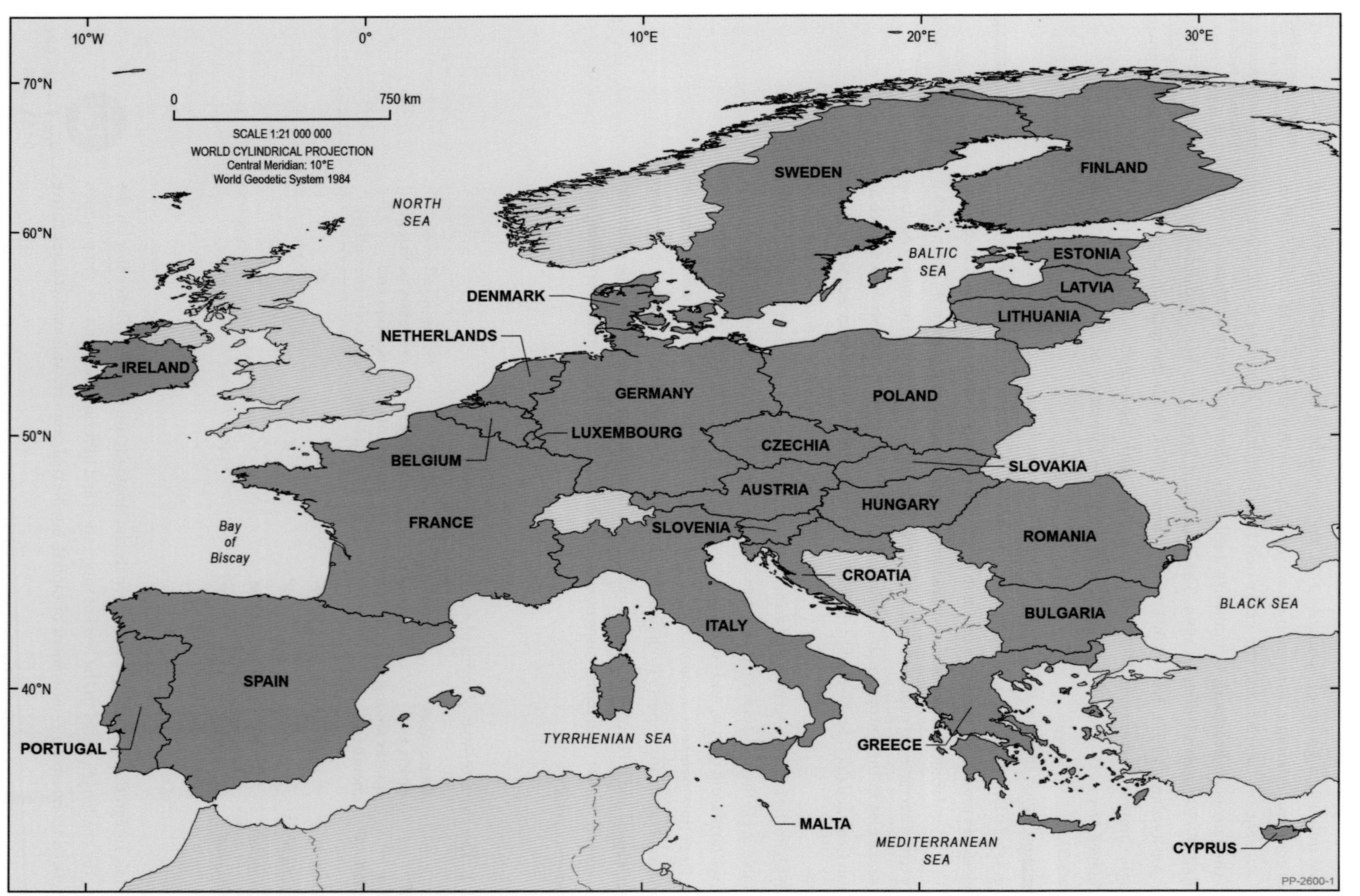

FIGURE 3.3 The European Union member countries

SPOTLIGHT 3.1

Asian Development Bank

Established in the early 1960s, the Asian Development Bank (ADB) is a major promoter of economic growth and cooperation in the Asia–Pacific region and contributes to the advancement of developing countries in one of the poorest regions in the world. In collaboration with member nations, independent specialists and other financial institutions, the ADB has a focus on supporting development across five infrastructure areas. These areas are key enablers for economic progress in the region, and include energy, information and communication technology, transport, urban development and water supply.

The fundamental objective of the bank is to stimulate economic and financial cooperation among members. The Asia–Pacific region is the most populous and fastest-growing region in the world. The bank provides financial support through loans for member countries engaged in projects linked to the bank's core objectives. The aim is squarely focused on an Asia–Pacific free from poverty, and the facilitation of programs that improve the quality of life for people and communities in the region. The ADB pays special attention to the needs of smaller or less-developed countries, and prioritises subregional, regional and national projects that contribute to the harmonious economic growth of the region as a whole.

Source: Asian Development Bank 2018

QUESTIONS

1. Review the ADB website (www.adb.org) and identify and explain the five key areas of focus for the bank.
2. Explain why the mission of the ADB to reduce poverty is so important.

SPOTLIGHT QUESTIONS

The costs and benefits of integrated arrangements

The abundance and complexity of economic integration presents nations with opportunities and challenges. The advancement of free trade fosters trade liberalisation and enables developing countries to participate in world trade, yet the development of these complex networks raises issues due to the differing laws, intellectual property rights and the competitive landscape. There is a range of issues linked to the costs and benefits of economic integration: the creation and disruption that happens with integration, economies of scale and competition, reduction of import rates, higher factors of productivity, and nationalistic versus regionalist sentiments.

Integration drivers, trade creation and trade diversion

Economic integration is motivated by a variety of factors, including economic, political and security considerations. In some instances, they enable a deeper integration of economies than is possible through the WTO. Economic integration contributes to commercial and industrial growth, with an outcome of economic progress delivering improvements in living standards and higher tax revenues for member nations. The four main drivers for a nation to pursue integration are: stronger defensive and political position, market scale growth, development of external FDI, and economies of scale and improved productivity.

Stronger defensive and political position

For smaller nations, trading agreements are a defensive necessity, while larger countries turn to them for strategic alliances. This was one of the motives for the original formation of the EU, post-World War II. The initial period was linked to the defensive relationships within Europe, particularly against the political and military might of the Union of Soviet Socialist Republics (USSR). In more recent years, this stance is a counterbalance to the economic influences of the US. The formation of such alliances allows nations to gain greater bargaining power globally. Generally, nations are more powerful when they cooperate rather than operating as individual nations.

Market scale growth

Preferential trade agreements enable favoured access to larger, more developed markets. Developing countries may well be willing to commit to signing agreements with developed countries to secure access to their vast markets. In this situation, the agreements perform a *dual locking* function by locking out competition and locking in investment. Through integration, the scale of the market place for nations and businesses is increased within the trading bloc. Vietnam's membership of ASEAN, for example, provides Vietnamese businesses simpler access to a market of approximately 640 million consumers. When the multilateral agreement between ASEAN, Australian and New Zealand (AANZFTA) is finalised, firms and consumers within the trading bloc will gain access to a greater selection of products and services.

Development of external FDI

Integration for some economies is a vehicle for securing FDI, particularly for those countries with lower labour costs. The attraction for firms to be part of an economic bloc is that the manufacturing facilities they build within the bloc will receive preferential treatment. The Tata Group of companies from India has invested heavily in the EU. By establishing regional hubs for Tata Consultancy Services, the firm has been able to conduct substantial operations in the Netherlands, France and Hungry.

Economies of scale and improved productivity

An expanding market size within a trading bloc provides firms from member countries with an ability to increase the efficiencies and scale of production, manufacturing, and marketing of goods and services. The concertina effect is that firms then develop the capabilities and capacity to compete and trade more effectively outside the bloc. Ultimately, efficient use of resources should lead to lower costs of production and lower prices for consumers.

The previous sections illustrate that when trade barriers between two or more nations are removed, nations and their industries can boost an efficient use of resources. A range of circumstances have been identified in which FTAs facilitate this process to create trade and decrease trade diversion.

- Countries that only minimally engage each other should not generally enter into an FTA as minimal trade leads to increased trade diversion.
- The external barriers to trade should be low.
- FTA member nations should be geographically close to reduce distribution and transport costs.
- Member nations should have complimentary economic structures.

Regional integration can drive change and innovation, and the process of achieving multiple RTAS can lead to nations becoming better negotiators (Crawford & Fiorentino 2005). Those opposed to integration point out that the benefits of regional integration are determined by the extent of trade creation, rather than trade diversion. RTAs will only benefit the world if the amount of trade created exceeds the amount it diverts. Another potential trade-distorting outcome from the increase in FTAs is the additional cost of administration and enforcement of the rules that govern such agreements. These costs of engaging in international business operations in some regions increase risk and reduce overall productivity.

Increased competition and economies of scale

Relaxed trade parameters open access to larger markets that were formerly protected from foreign competition. Larger markets lead to more intense international competition, which may result in a lower level of monopoly in the production of certain goods and services, as well as act as a stimulant for innovation. The outcome is greater efficiency and lower prices for consumers. Competition may lead to the rationalisation of production and the closure of inefficient factories or companies. This creates a net positive outcome as it leads to overall greater productivity (Kritzinger-van Niekerk 2000). In the Asia–Pacific, an export-led growth strategy steered many economies out of the recent financial crises. Exports enabled Asian producers to 'overcome the limitations of small domestic markets' and impelled them to 'become more efficient in order to compete successfully in highly competitive foreign markets' (Park & Park 2010, p. 3).

Some industries require large-scale production to obtain economies of scale. The steel and automotive industries are key examples. In small, trade-protected countries, these industries may simply not be economically viable. However, the establishment of a trading bloc enables access to a significantly increased market size that can validate large-scale production and in turn generate per-unit cost reductions due to the internal economies of scale achieved.

Reduced import prices

Import prices can be significantly impacted because of RTAs. Many small countries will impose an import duty or tariff on specific goods, typically to protect home market industries. Noticeably, the price of imported goods will be higher for the end consumer as sellers increase their prices to cover the cost of the tariff. In many cases, such price increases result in lower demand for these imported goods.

However, a different scenario exists in relation to RTAs. Should a bloc of countries impose a duty or tariff, the fall in demand for imported goods will be much more substantial and may force the exporting country to reduce their prices. Through exercising the greater market power of the bloc relative to that single country, the potential of lower prices for imports may result in an improved trade position for bloc members. Such trade gains are offset by a deteriorating trade position for the exporting country. Unlike the win–win situation resulting from free trade, the scenario involving a trade bloc is sometimes win–lose.

Higher factor productivity

The impact of factor mobility on economic growth cannot be underestimated. When factors of production are freely mobile, then the capital, labour and technology can be employed in the most productive way. It allows businesses to shift labour and capital resources to areas of higher productivity, resulting in better returns and increased overall wealth for the bloc countries. The free movement of labour can contribute significantly to the knowledge economy due the prominent level of cross-cultural communications required. As people move, so too do their ideas, skills and cultural traits, leading to more cross-cultural understanding.

Regional integration and trading agreements do not guarantee that each country in a bloc will benefit from factor mobility. Poorer countries may be disadvantaged in two ways. First, they may lose critical investment capital to a richer country where opportunities are perceived to be more profitable. Second, they may lose their most skilled and talented workers when they are given increased freedom to seek out better opportunities. Such a practice is nowadays commonly referred to as the 'brain drain phenomenon'. Poorer less-developed countries may be adversely impacted by factor mobility. Many of the more developed countries fear that companies may close their national operations in favour of starting up business in member countries where operating costs, like wages, are lower.

Nationalism versus regionalism

Regional trading blocs are increasingly shaping the pattern of world trade, an occurrence often referred to as regionalism. Regional trade liberalisation delivers three fundamental benefits:

- allows member countries more economic and political bargaining power in international negotiations
- expands and creates market opportunities for member countries
- helps in developing intra-company and inter-government trade movements.

Those opposed to regional agreements criticise these advantages as being contrary to the aims of the WTO and further weaken its multilateral approach to dealing with the issues of international trade. There is also an assumption that trade diversion harms non-member countries and the benefits of trade creation are not significant enough to offset such diversion. Supporters argue that the WTO permits these agreements on the provision that there is not an increase to current barriers imposed on excluded countries. Many countries, including Australia, have embarked on bilateral or regional FTAs as these offer more rapid gains than the WTO can deliver. In addition, supporters suggest regionalism is a positive step in an increasingly global marketplace. The downside is that regional agreements create a web of complex rules, which make trading environments extremely complicated.

Despite the current proliferation of RTAs in force, there is an increasing trend towards nationalism. Nationalism is a major impediment to regional integration with countries averse to relinquishing a measure of their autonomy. For example, companies like Facebook are banned in China, partially in preference for national social networks and also due to government regulation over internet content. Nationalism has the potential to make the global political landscape hostile towards international business (Hult International Business School 2017).

Economic integration will not make everyone happy, despite promises of benefits from the free flow of people, goods, services and capital. Even developed countries, such as the US and the EU's wealthier nations, have their concerns, fearing a potential outflow of jobs as companies shift their operations to less prosperous regions with lower wages or fewer governmental controls. Economic theories suggest, however, that opening economies to free trade and investment is a positive-sum game, in which all participating countries stand to gain. Because of such considerable advantages, regional trade groupings are likely to not only remain a key component of the international business landscape but also expand through the inclusion of more countries.

MULTIPLE-CHOICE QUESTION

SPOTLIGHT 3.2

What is enabling economic growth?

Asia–Pacific nations are now digitally engaged. Digital technologies and the internet are influential enablers for regional markets, and contribute significantly to boosting economic growth. Digital infrastructure contributes to opening new channels of business and enhances productivity to deliver the economic development. The digital tools support governments, industries, businesses

SMALL- AND MEDIUM-SIZED ENTERPRISES (SMEs)
small and generally independent firms that employ less than a given number of employees (in the case of Australia, this is usually less than 200 employees).

and consumers. In the government sector, digital technology aids the development of smart cities, supports civil infrastructure, drives the development process forward, and supports economic and social policy agendas. Industries and businesses use digital expertise to boost trade in the region through increased access and connectivity for small- and medium-sized enterprises (SMEs). Consumers and communities use digital technology to be more mobile, socially connected and networked. Ultimately, well implemented digital technologies are a powerful enabler for the Asia–Pacific region.

SPOTLIGHT QUESTIONS

QUESTIONS

1. What role does the internet and digital technology play for international business development?
2. What are the two benefits digital technology brings for consumers?

Economic integration in the Asia–Pacific region

The Asia–Pacific region, with its 'dynamic economy and rich cultural diversity, is growing rapidly in significance and is set to play a critical and important role in the world as the twenty-first century unfolds' (OECD/The Bob Hawke Prime Ministerial Centre 2005, p. 3). For many observers of the world economy, this century 'will belong to the Asia–Pacific region' and 'the sheer dynamism of its peoples and its huge economic and technological potential do indeed bode well for the future' (p. 5). Economic integration development in the Asia–Pacific region is unique. In terms of economic and political distance, the member countries are considered distant from each other, especially when compared to the EU and the Americas.

The Asia–Pacific's interest in regional integration has risen sharply for logical reasons. In recent times, most of the trade growth for countries within the region has come from intra-Asian trade. Having a collective understanding and policies has strengthened regional ties, and become a necessity in achieving continued economic growth. Although interdependence has increased in recent times, there is room for further progress. A key factor in contributing to the success lies in the 'capacity and willingness of the region's countries to cooperate with one another across a wide range of activities' (OECD/The Bob Hawke Prime Ministerial 2005, p. 3) and 'the pace towards greater interchange may now be gathering speed, as countries in the region show growing interest in, and place greater emphasis on, more formal cooperation' (p. 5).

Intra- and inter-regional economic integration has been, and continues to be, a key development strategy for Asia–Pacific nations. Inter-regional integration played a substantive role over the past century for the region. In the past few decades, however, intra-regional integration has played an increasing role with exports now accounting for more than half (54 per cent) of all Asia–Pacific trade, compared to 46 per cent in 2002. The share of intra-regional FDI inflows to total FDI inflows in the Asia–Pacific also increased to around 52 per cent in 2014, compared to around 35 per cent in 2001. Many Asia–Pacific nations have leveraged GVCs as the vehicle for trade, in particular trade in components. Their participation in GVCs expanded significantly from the mid-1990s to now. The outlook for the Asia–Pacific is that domestic demand will continue to play a strong role in economic growth, and that established arrangements in the region such as ASEAN will continue to drive growth.

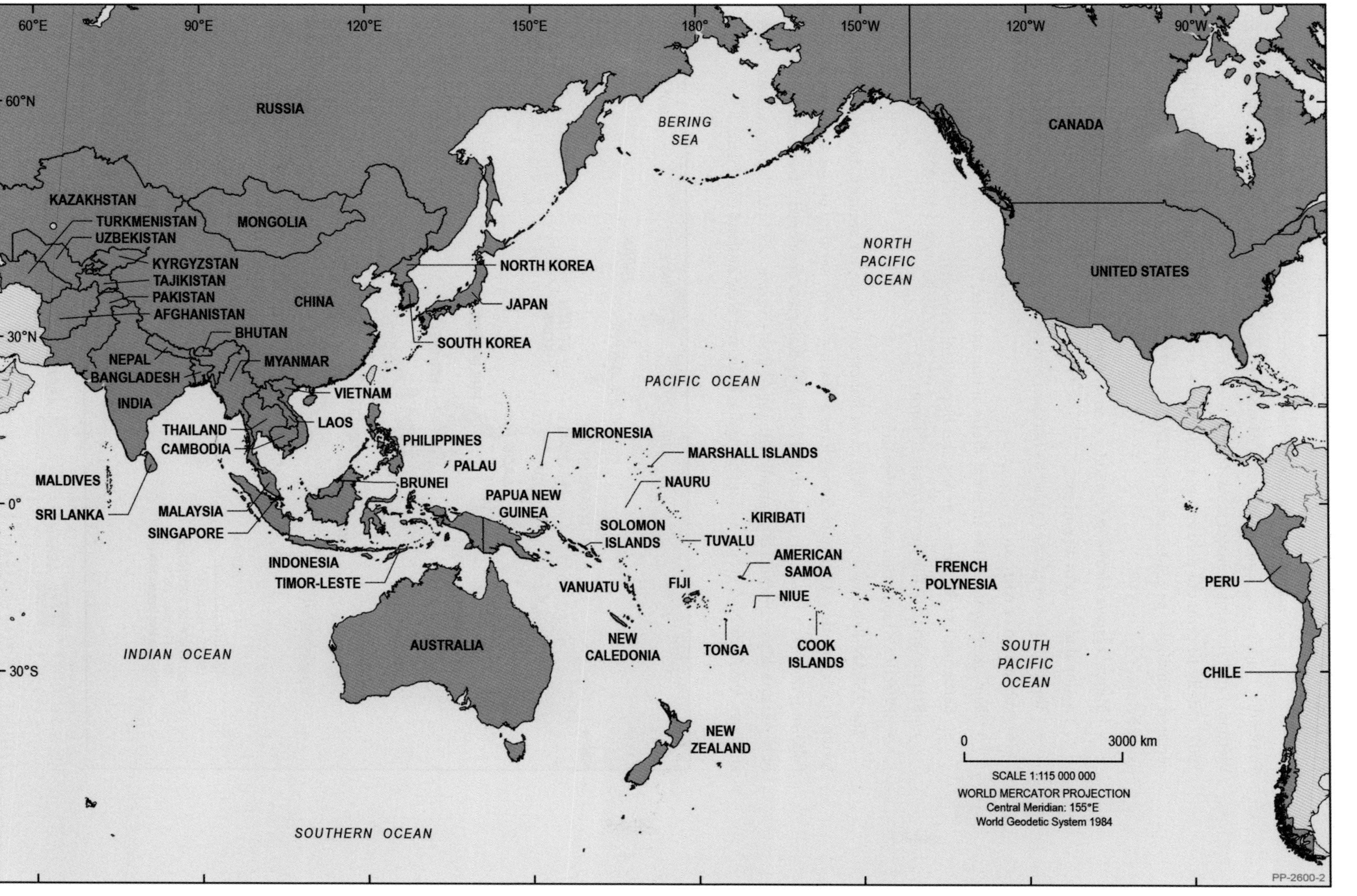

FIGURE 3.4 Map of the Asia–Pacific

ASEAN

There are over 628 million people across the 10-member ASEAN states, comprising of Brunei, Cambodia, Indonesia, Laos, Malaysia, Myanmar, the Philippines, Singapore, Thailand and Vietnam, and forming a major Asia–Pacific economic bloc. The association was established in 1967, chiefly to promote political and economic cooperation, and regional stability. The ASEAN declared principles, as contained in the TAC of 1976, are the foundation of the group and are listed below.

- Mutual respect for the independence, sovereignty, equality, territorial integrity, and national identity of all nations.
- The right of every State to lead its national existence free from external interference, subversion or coercion.
- Non-interference in the internal affairs of one another.
- Settlement of differences or disputes by peaceful manner.
- Renunciation of the threat or use of force.
- Effective cooperation among themselves.

The ASEAN Regional Forum (ARF) is an important forum for security dialogue in Asia. The forum draws together 27 members that have a bearing on the security of the Asia–Pacific region. Following the Asian financial crisis of 1997–98, the dialogues developed a framework for 'ASEAN Plus' relationships, commencing initially with the ASEAN+3 group of China, Japan and South Korea, and later, the ASEAN+6 group, adding Australia, India and New Zealand (see Figure 3.5).

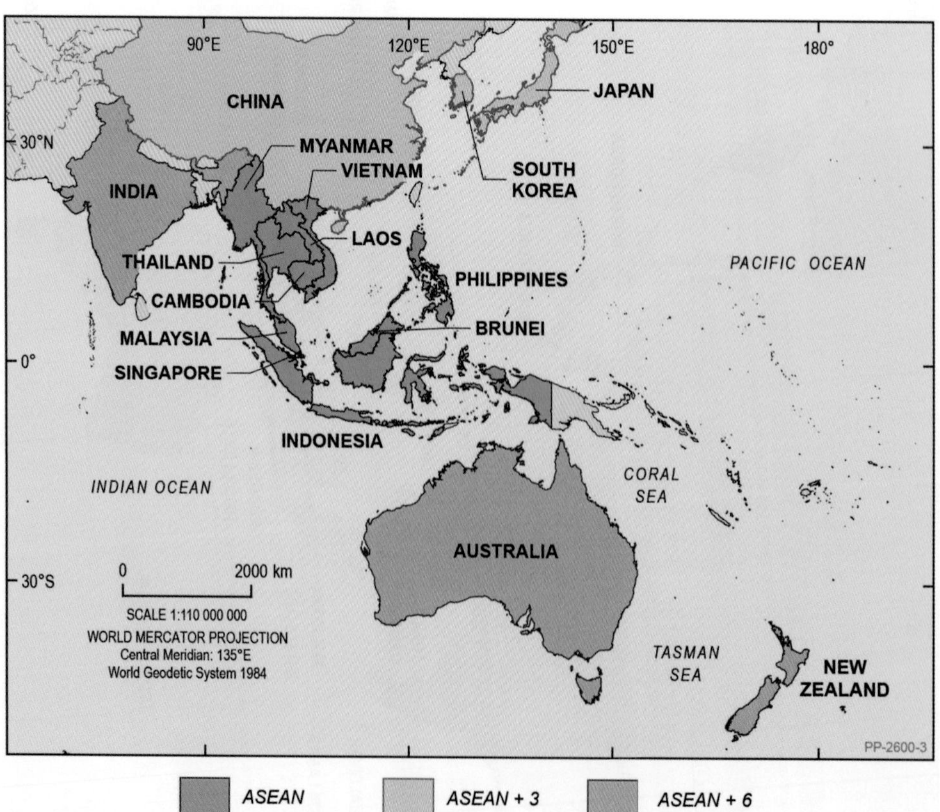

FIGURE 3.5 MAP of ASEAN, showing ASEAN countries, ASEAN +3, ASEAN +6

The ASEAN Free Trade Agreement (AFTA) was signed in 1992 and has succeeded in reducing tariffs of up to 5 per cent among member countries. However, the formation of the ASEAN Economic Community (AEC) in 2015 was a key milestone in the regional economic integration agenda. This specific community offers opportunities in the form of a large market valued at US$2.6 trillion. In 2017, the AEC was cooperatively the third-largest economy in Asia and the sixth largest in the world. The AEC opens the opportunity for ASEAN member states to develop through trade and investment, and to capitalise on the demand generated by other Asian economies.

The outlook towards 2030 is encouraging. ASEAN members have a unique opportunity to capitalise on the rise of the Indian and Chinese domestic markets as intra-regional economic interdependence intensifies. Goods and services that cater to local consumption have significant opportunity in both huge economies, which are home to a vast middle class that is continuing to grow. Recent forecasts predict that by 2030 more than 1.2 billion people in China (85 per cent of the population) and 1 billion people in India (70 per cent of the population) will have achieved medium or high income status (Capannelli 2014). This has significant impact on consumption patterns as well as rapid increases in demand for energy and food. Beyond their ability in manufacturing, ASEAN economies have a fantastic opportunity to increase their energy and food exports, and play an increasingly strategic role in the region.

In 2016, the combined GDP of ASEAN states rose 4.8 per cent to $2.55 trillion, representing 3.4 per cent of world share. ASEAN is the third fastest-growing Asian economy after China and India. In this context, the economies of ASEAN are showing strong macro-economic fundamentals and robust economic growth. This region has a comparatively large, and still young, internal market, with a rapidly expanding middle class of over 200 million people, representing one of the major strengths of the association. Member nations are strategically located in the heart of Asia, and connected to China and India through sea and overland trade routes. The association has abundant natural resources including oil, gas, hydropower, minerals, a large biodiversity, and an extensive agricultural base (Capannelli 2014).

Intra-ASEAN trade in 2016 represented 23.5 per cent of total trade and the largest market for the group. China holds the position as ASEAN's top external trading partner (16 per cent), followed by the EU (10.5 per cent), Japan (10 per cent) and the US (9.4 per cent) (ASEAN 2017). Closer collaboration is vital for ASEAN member nations to profit from buyer–supplier agreements in complex production and distribution systems. They can also benefit from the technology transfer facilitated by FTAs and interrelated economies such as China, Japan and South Korea, which continue to invest in maintaining leadership in many product and process technologies and expanding-production capabilities. ASEAN has been 'an integral part of Asia's ongoing socio-political and economic transformation, and remains an example for other regional groups of how carefully crafted cooperation can benefit all members – even if extremely diverse in size, geography, culture, income level and resource endowment' (ADBI 2014, p. ix).

The bringing together of large and small powers, provides a catalyst and stimulates regional benefits (ADBI 2014, p. 189). 'ASEAN is expected to become a single market by 2020, 'with a free flow of goods, services and investment, a freer flow of capital, equitable economic development, and reduced poverty and socio-economic' development (Dean & Wignaraja 2007, p. 9).

APEC's development and history

Proposed by Australia, APEC was formed in 1989 with the broad mission of achieving greater prosperity for people in the region by promoting balanced, inclusive, sustainable, innovative and secure growth, and by accelerating regional economic integration. With 21 members, the APEC region is home to over 2.8 billion people (39 per cent of world population) (see Figure 3.6). Figures by APEC

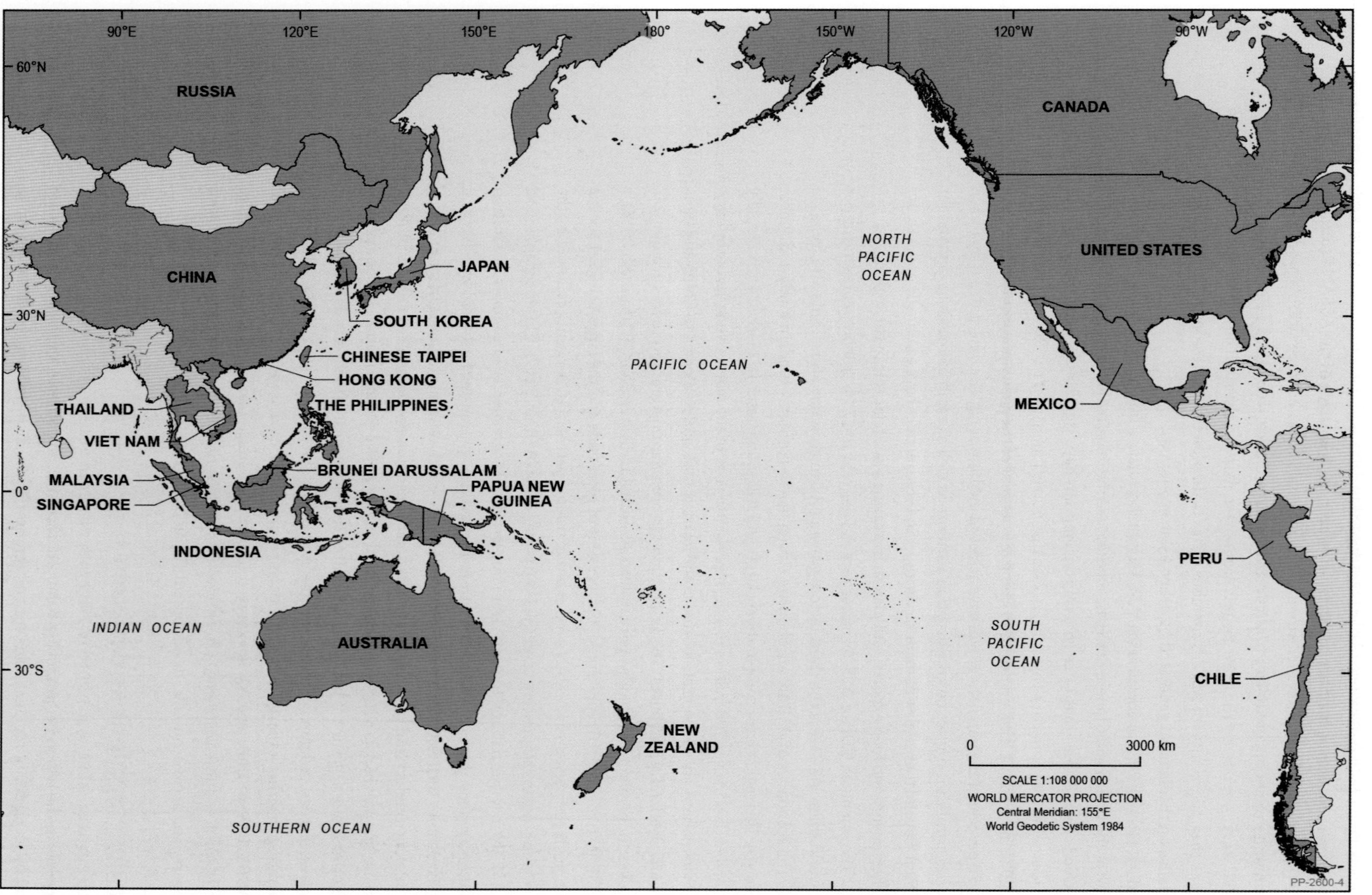

FIGURE 3.6 Map of APEC countries

(2018) show that the US and China accounted for 39 per cent of the world's total nominal GDP in 2015. Economic growth has soared in the region, with trade in merchandise goods and commercial services reaching US$20 trillion in 2015, which was almost half (48 per cent) of the world's total trade. China, Japan and the US accounted for 29 per cent of global trade (APEC 2018).

APEC has been more than just an economic forum; it has facilitated regional integration, which is essential to promoting trade and economic growth in the area. In a trade-driven region, with the world's largest pool of savings, the most advanced technologies and the fastest-growing markets, APEC has become a dynamic engine of economic growth.

The number of FTAs signed by APEC members continues to increase. As at 2016, APEC members had signed a total of 165 FTAs, with 156 still in force. Of the FTAs signed, 64 were signed with at least one other APEC member, with 62 still in force (see Figure 3.7).

APEC member countries ensure that goods, services, investment and people move easily across borders. Member economies facilitate this trade through faster customs procedures at borders, more

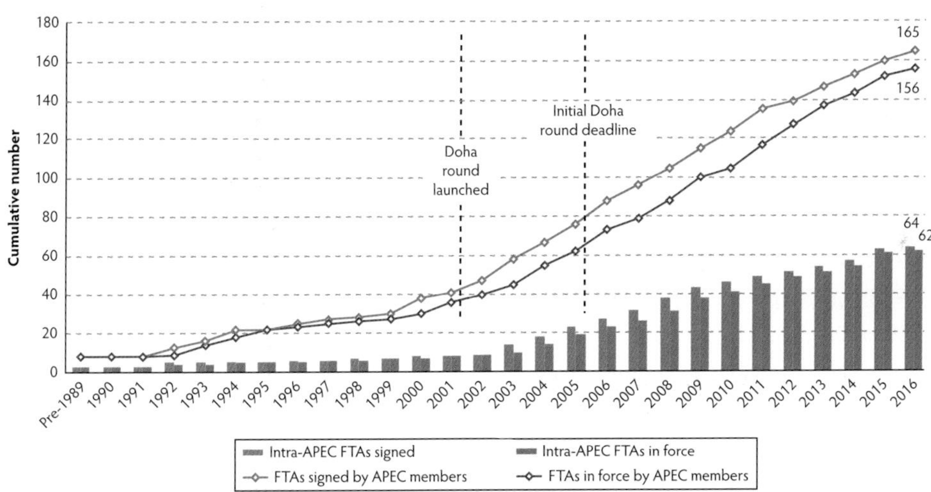

FIGURE 3.7 FTAs in APEC (cumulative), pre-1989–2016

Source: APEC Secretariat, APEC Policy Support Unit 2017, p. 17, reproduced with permission of ASEAN

favourable business climates behind the border, and aligning regulations and standards across the region (APEC Secretariat 2017). It is important to note that there are no binding commitments between APEC members. Any decisions or agreements are undertaken on a voluntary basis. It is likely that APEC's role will continue to be important in realising sustained growth among its members. The short-term future goals continue to be trade liberalisation, and trade facilitation by harmonising standards and building human capacities to realise the ambitions.

Implications for Asia–Pacific markets

Although the Asia–Pacific region is the world's fastest growing, the elimination, or at least the significant reduction, of poverty and starvation will critically depend on the ability of the region to integrate and develop successfully. The region is home to nearly half of the world's poorest people, rendering poverty a key issue to be addressed. According to the World Bank (2016), an estimated

766 million people in the Asia–Pacific survive on less than the poverty line of US$1.90 per day, with approximately 33 per cent living in South Asia and 9 per cent in East Asia and the Pacific.

MULTIPLE-CHOICE QUESTION

Businesses are increasingly looking to emerging markets for sources of growth and competitive advantage. These developing parts of the world have outpaced the developed countries in economic growth in the first decade of the twenty-first century. The implications for Asia–Pacific markets are significant.

The emergence of FTAs in the Asia–Pacific region

RTAs traditionally occur between 'natural' trading partners, which are geographically connected countries with well-established trading patterns. Notable examples of this are Australia and New Zealand. Most nations sign their first RTA with one or several neighbouring or regional partners, however, 'once a country has exhausted its strictly regional prospects, it may begin to look further afield for preferential partners' (Crawford & Fiorentino 2005, p. 5).

Australia and New Zealand's FTA policies aim to maximise the economic benefits that flow into each country from the cooperation of these agreements. Both countries cite multiple benefits of being a party to FTAs (single or multilateral) as:

- free flow of trade creates stronger trading ties
- removal of tariff and non-tariff barriers contributes to improving investment support, increased cooperation, and enhancing intellectual property and ecommerce development
- productivity increases through access to cheaper inputs, introduction of modern technologies and innovation
- adoption of ROO and broader acceptance of product and quality standards
- enhanced market competitiveness
- improved trading opportunities that contribute to sustainable economic growth for all.

Australia's recent FTAs have further strengthened integration within the Asia–Pacific region, and complement Australia's existing FTAs with Thailand, Singapore and ASEAN. In 2012, an FTA was signed with Malaysia (the Malaysia–Australia Free Trade Agreement, known as MAFTA); in 2014 agreements were concluded with South Korea (the Korea–Australia Free Trade Agreement, known as KAFTA) and with Japan (the Japan–Australia Economic Partnership Agreement, known as JAEPA); and in December 2015, after 10 years of negotiations, the trading agreement with Australia's largest trading partner, China, was signed (the China–Australia Free Trade Agreement; ChAFTA). ChAFTA in particular was an historic agreement that will support ongoing economic growth, employment opportunities and improvements in living standards.

The implementation of ChAFTA has created an unprecedented mindset change in Australian politics. Australia's relationship with China is well understood to be its most important economic partnership (Turnbull 2015). Nonetheless, Australia has a long history of being hesitant about foreign investment, even though Australia is a country that is resource rich and capital poor. Generally, reform involves winners and losers. With the ChAFTA agreement, however, the winners, remarkably, outweigh the losers. China is known as the world's single largest market, and Australia has few barriers to foreign trade and investment. Therefore, the committed relationship with China is a big net gain and the size of this win is limited only by the extent of engagement initiated by Australian businesses (Turnbull 2015). These agreements are opening opportunities for Australian goods and services in dynamic Asian markets, which are home to in excess of 2 billion consumers (DFAT, 2017).

For any government, FTAs are an ongoing process of negotiation, development and maintenance. Regional integration in the Asia–Pacific may be needed to maintain leverage and balance against the other two principal trading blocs of the EU and NAFTA.

Other regional economic cooperation

APEC connects East Asia with the Americas and ASEAN connects the nations of South Asia, with Australia and New Zealand also being well connected with the region through a series of FTAs. Apart from these economic groupings and initiatives, regional economic integration has also taken place between and within other parts of the Asia–Pacific region. On the Indian subcontinent, the seven nations of India, Pakistan, Bangladesh, Sri Lanka, Nepal, Bhutan and the Maldives have launched the South Asian Association for Regional Cooperation (SAARC) in 1985. While often hampered by political unrest, cooperation has been achieved in the relatively non-controversial areas of agriculture and regional development. The US and South Korea formed an agreement to trade in 2007 (United States–Korea Free Trade Agreement, known as KORUS) and this was labelled as the biggest agreement signed by US since NAFTA. Politically, the agreement has provided the US with a significant presence in the Asia region to counterbalance the growing influence of China. Economic partnership has provided for duty-free movement of goods and outlined areas of potential conflict. The agreement rolled back tariffs on most goods between the two countries in the last decade.

SPOTLIGHT 3.3

ASEAN economic integration: challenges and opportunities

According to an ADB study, ASEAN economies will continue to face dynamic times through to 2030. The introduction of deep structural reforms in domestic markets and continued efforts toward regional economic integration will assist ASEAN nations to head in the direction of tripling per capita incomes between now and 2030. The objective is to raise the quality of life for Asia–Pacific communities to levels enjoyed by members of the OECD. Without appropriate supporting policies, ASEAN economies will face negative consequences. GDP growth may be subdued to an average of only 3.2 per cent per year over the next 20 years. Several countries may reach an income ceiling if they fail to invest in and upgrade education standards, and R&D pipelines. This situation is further intensified by challenges from climate change, increasing natural disasters, and escalating political friction within and among nations.

The global volatility of natural resource prices, combined with the unclear economic recovery of the eurozone and the US, and China's wavering growth rates provide challenges for ASEAN region to reach the 2030 targets. There are several considerations ASEAN member countries need to consider, including the ongoing support for a borderless community that allows individual nations' GDP levels to expand more rapidly by achieving economies of scale, the rise of industrial hubs, and the wider economic integration with the remainder of the world.

Source: Asian Development Bank Institute 2014

QUESTIONS

1. When was ASEAN established and who are the member countries?
2. What is the motto of ASEAN?

SPOTLIGHT QUESTIONS

Understanding the impact of regional integration on MNEs

Economic integration will not please everyone, despite promises of huge benefits from the free flow of goods, services and capital. However, regional economic integration creates opportunities and challenges for the international business manager. Overall, international businesses have benefited from regional trade arrangements by having more consistent criteria for investment and trade as well as reduced barriers for their entry into various markets. An international manager generally approaches decisions regarding the choice of market entry from four considerations:

- assessing the range and impact of changes resulting from integration
- developing strategies to relate to such changes
- re-organising to take advantage of the changes
- lobbying for favourable trading terms.

The changing competitive landscape

Regional economic integration has intensified over the last few decades. Larger markets are formed by design and create increased business opportunities. With larger markets and fewer trade barriers, competition also increases. The changes in the competitive landscape which result from regional integration can be intense. First, the deregulation of trade forces monopolies to exploit scale opportunities, drive innovation, strive for efficiencies and transform themselves into competitive industries. This often leads to favourable outcomes for the home nation. Second, the competitive landscape continues to evolve based on the technological advancement that has come with increasing globalisation. To navigate effectively, and build and maintain competitive advantage, strategic flexibility in operational planning is required. This includes:

- employing strategic leadership
- building core competencies within the international business
- focusing on and developing human capital within the international business team
- effectively using new manufacturing and information technologies
- implementing new organisational structures and developing internal culture.

The emerging regional trading landscape requires firms to reinvent their organisational structure and leadership team to achieve a market winning position. Human resource capability and development for international businesses will be discussed in further detail in Chapter 12.

Strategic planning and company authority

There are a few factors that impact a company's ability to pursue international business strategies. Understanding the external environment in relation to culture and ethics, international relations and the political stage, as well as the economic differences across the various regional markets, is fundamental to international expansion and success.

A considerable amount of international business activities are conducted regionally in the first instance rather than on a global level. There are only a small number of truly global firms. These firms present with a balanced distribution of sales and assets worldwide, especially in the three dominant markets of NAFTA, the EU and the Asia–Pacific. For 500 of the world's largest MNEs, the clear majority have a strong home-region orientation, with over three-quarters of their sales from within that area. This means that many of the world's largest firms are not global but regionally based in terms of breadth and depth of their market coverage. The observed dominance of the home region in sales and assets has important implications for a business' strategy. The observation that most MNEs have a significant percentage of their sales in their home region is also not limited to Europe and North America; it is an increasingly relevant factor in the future for the Asia–Pacific as well. When engaging in strategic decision making for international markets, senior executives within a regionally diversified firm will focus their attention on the businesses within the geographic area that represents the majority of revenue and assets. This area of the business is typically the firm's main source of cash flow, and where talent and knowledge generation capabilities are required to enable future expansion and growth.

International business managers must develop a strategic response to the dynamic operating environment to maintain a sustainable long-term competitive advantage. They need to determine whether to adopt a standardised or adaptation approach to their products. Companies which already have a presence in an integrated market may look to fill gaps in their portfolios through acquisitions or alliances to expand a regional presence, rather than just a national presence. In industries, such as automobiles, mobile telephony and retailing, integration may lead to industries being 'dominated by two or three giants, leaving room only for niche players' (Czinkota & Ronkainen 2012, p. 125). Those with currently weak positioning or no presence at all will have to create alliances with established firms for market entry and development. Too much adaptation will lead to excessive costs. Too much attention to scale and scope will prevent access to location advantages in host environments. Too much focus on exploiting national differences will lead to vulnerable supply chains and severe coordination problems.

Finally, when operating in integrated markets, organisational structures must indicate where the authority for decision making and control rests. A business may choose a decentralised work system where regional subsidiaries are granted a high degree of autonomy, or a centralised work system where decision making is concentrated at the corporate headquarters in the firm's home country.

Summary

Learning objective 1: Appreciate the historical growth of regional economic integration.

The Cobden–Chevalier Treaty signed in 1860 between the UK and France became the start of regional integration that foreshadowed the proliferation of trade agreements that took place post-World War II. Following on from the emergence of the GATT in 1948, through to the formation of the WTO in 1995 and up to the present day, the movement for regional trading accelerated with key trading blocs being established, including ASEAN, Mercosur, EU, APEC and NAFTA. RTAs have intensified across and within global regions, and play a critical role in the international business landscape. The most successful example of economic integration is the EU, which has succeeded in eliminating most of the barriers to the free flow of goods, services and factors of production, as well as establishing the Euro as a strong common currency among most of its member nations.

Learning objective 2: Recognise the types of economic integration among regions and between nations.

Regional economic integration involves agreements made between countries that allow goods, services and factors of production to flow more freely across borders. Agreements may be made between two countries (bilateral) or several countries (multilateral). The level of integration determines how weak or strong such links are. Economic integration may take one of four primary forms, including the free trade area, the customs union, the common market and the economic union. Free trade areas are the most common form of integration, accounting for over half of all enforced agreements notified to the WTO.

Learning objective 3: Comprehend the costs and benefits of integrated arrangements.

The benefits derived from economic integration include larger and consequently more competitive marketplaces, which can lead to economies of scale and drive innovation. Trade creation, improved trading terms, a reduction of monopoly power, greater factory productivity, and enhancements in cross-cultural understanding can also be achieved. However, a few disadvantages also exist. Most notably, economic integration may work to the detriment of non-members by creating trade diversion. There is also no guarantee that all members of a regional trade agreement will share in the gains from integration.

Learning objective 4: Explore the economic integration that has emerged in the Asia–Pacific.

The Asia–Pacific region, with its lively economy and great cultural diversity, is growing in significance. Inter-regional economic integration has been, and continues to be, a fundamental development strategy for Asia–Pacific countries. In recent times, intra-regional integration has becoming increasingly important. The Asia–Pacific, with its proliferation of free trade agreements, has become one of the most dynamic and integrated regions in the world, with ASEAN playing a strong catalyst role. Some 147 FTAs involving an Asia–Pacific economy are in operation as of July 2017.

Learning objective 5: Consider the strategic challenges that economic integration poses for international business firms.

The international business manager needs to analyse the increasingly complex effects of regional agreements to determine how economic integration affects trade and investment decisions.

Economic integration, by design, forms larger markets creating more potential trading opportunities; it creates a larger market and fewer trade barriers, but entails increased competition. Businesses must first choose where authority for decision making and control rests – a decentralised work system where regional subsidiaries are granted a high degree of autonomy or a centralised work system where decision making is concentrated at the head office in the firm's home country. Firms also need to determine whether to take a standardisation or adaptation approach to their products. Too much adaptation will lead to excessive costs. Too much attention to scale and scope will prevent access to location advantages in host environments. Too much focus on exploiting national differences will lead to vulnerable supply chains and severe coordination problems.

USEFUL WEBSITES

Revision questions

REVISION QUESTIONS

1. What is the difference between a free trade area and a customs union? Explain why the free trade area is a more popular form of economic integration.
2. What are two ways that regional economic integration can help international firms?
3. Describe why the EU is considered a highly integrated economic cooperative agreement.
4. Are economic trading blocs a solid foundation or are they stumbling blocks as far as global free trade is concerned? Prepare arguments for and against.
5. Provide a broad overview of ASEAN and the importance of the association in the region and globally.

R&D activities

R&D ACTIVITIES

1. Select an SME with headquarters in Australia or New Zealand. Investigate how the firm is involved in international trade, either in the sourcing of supplies or in the marketing of finished products or services. How might this company take further advantage of the ongoing shifts in the international business environment and regional integration? Discuss past activities and future opportunities for your SME.
2. Export and import services is an increasingly important sector throughout the world. Using data from the ASEAN website (https://asean.org) and the *ASEAN Services Report 2017*, discuss the services sector's contribution to ASEAN's GDP and how this has changed since 2000. Explain the initiatives that individual ASEAN members are undertaking to enhance their services sector as well as their engagement with non-ASEAN members in various FTAs involving services.
3. In 2016, 766 million people lived below the poverty line of US$1.90 per day, with 33 per cent living in South Asia and 9 per cent living in East Asia and the Pacific. The WB has accepted the goal of reducing this figure of extremely poor to less than 3 per cent by 2030. Using articles from the WB and the WTO, found on their respective websites, explain the role that regional economic integration could play in achieving these ambitious goals.
4. 'Quality growth and human development' is the theme guiding APEC's initiatives and growth strategies. Using information from the APEC website (www.apec.org) discuss the key strategies that place social and individual progress at the centre of this effort, and the role that economic integration plays.

IB MASTERCLASS

The cost of regional integration – when it all goes wrong: the Australian Wheat Board scandal

Overview

In 2005, the Australian Government initiated an inquiry, subsequently known as the Cole Inquiry, into certain Australian firms in relation to the United Nations (UN) Oil-for-Food programme (OFFP). This inquiry investigated what was to become Australia's biggest international corruption scandal, comprising AU$300 million in kickbacks to the Saddam Hussein-led Iraqi government by the Australian Wheat Board (AWB). The lack of regulatory oversight and economic mismanagement may have been causal factors in the corruption that resulted when the UN-administered OFFP was introduced in Iraq and opportunistically facilitated by the AWB.

Background

In 1990, Iraq, with Saddam Hussein as President, invaded neighbouring Kuwait. Following the invasion, the UN Security Council voted for economic sanctions against Iraq (Harris 2007). These sanctions prohibited UN members from trading with Iraq and included an embargo on the purchase of Iraqi oil, the country's main source of export revenue. The aim was to apply economic and political pressure on the Iraqi government to remove its forces from Kuwait. These sanctions failed to induce Saddam Hussein to withdraw his forces, resulting in the first Gulf War.

The UN endorsed a military action, Operation Desert Storm, in which the US led a coalition force to liberate Kuwait in 1991. Because of the successful military action, the Iraqi government was required to open the country to UN weapons inspectors. This included the inspection of sites suspected of being linked to the development of weapons of mass destruction (WMDs) by the UN Security Council Resolution 687 (Fisher 2004). The responsibility of finding weapons, including WMDs, was given to the UN Monitoring, Verification and Inspection Commission, and the International Atomic Energy Agency.

Following the war, the UN Security Council renewed and maintained the economic sanctions due to the Iraqi government's apparent failure to fully comply with UN Resolution 687. Much of the pressure to maintain this approach came from the US government. The problem with implementing wide-ranging sanctions is that they are typically a blunt economic instrument, negatively impacting the most vulnerable. While sanctions aim to change a country's behaviour, the influential and the elite within the targeted country often find ways to avoid the sanctions or simply use their power base to appropriate a bigger percentage of a shrinking economy. For example, Saddam Hussein continued to build palaces and his family maintained an opulent lifestyle, despite the economic sanctions reducing much of the population to poverty.

The UN strategy to help address the humanitarian problems in Iraq was through the creation of the OFFP, where limited amounts of Iraqi oil could be exported for defined essential goods, such as food products and medicines. The UN passed an initial resolution for the support strategy in early 1992 but the Iraqi government rejected the terms and the final agreement was not made until 1996. The UN made a significant concession whereby the Iraqi government, not the UN, would have the final decision on who could buy its oil and which firms could supply humanitarian goods

(Holmes 2006). This allowed Saddam Hussein and the Iraqi government to exert a great influence over the OFFP process. In line with this agreement the Iraqi government refused to approve any OFFP purchase of wheat from the US because of their continued support of the sanctions.

The OFFP agreement stipulated that all monies received under the program were to be paid into a UN escrow account, which in turn would monitor the receipt and disbursement of all funds. Between December 1996 and 2003, Iraqi oil worth US$64 billion was sold under the auspices of the OFFP, with only US$34 billion spent on humanitarian goods and $18 billion spent on reparations (Volcker, Goldstone & Pieth 2005; Harris 2007).

The actors and their actions

The AWB was an entity of the Australian Government before being privatised in 1999. The AWB was the beneficiary of the Australian Government's 'single-desk' policy, which gave the AWB the power to veto any firm's application for a licence to export wheat from Australia (Aulich & Botterill 2007). This gave the AWB a virtual monopoly on all wheat exports from the country. The logic behind the single-desk policy was to improve AWB's bargaining power. Australia is one of the world's largest wheat exporters and selling all wheat exports through one source gave AWB, and by extension, Australian wheat farmers, more power to negotiate deals in a competitive global market. The single-desk policy had broad widespread support from Australian wheat farmers and the National Party, a rural based political party that was a junior member of the ruling conservative Liberal–National Coalition that governed Australia from 1996 to 2007.

The AWB gained a reputation for aggressively courting markets, which was in part related to the power gained from its monopoly status in Australia. Auchlich and Botterill (2007) argued that following privatisation, the government regulatory oversight of AWB's export activities was relatively weak. The Australian Government had sold wheat to Iraq for more than 50 years and Iraq had developed into one of Australia's, and therefore the AWB's, biggest trading partners. Australian hard wheat was well suited to making Iraqi bread, and Iraq itself did not have the arable land available to grow its own requirements (Holmes 2006). The AWB therefore actively tendered for wheat sales to Iraq under the UN OFFP, with the support of the Australian Government. Further, as outlined above, under the OFFP terms agreed by the UN in 1996, the Iraqi government was able to prohibit wheat imports from the US and eliminate one of Australia's major trade competitors. In 2002, the year before the OFFP finished, Australia exported AU$800 million worth of wheat to Iraq, and by 2005 the Iraqi wheat market represented around 10 per cent of the AWB's entire wheat exports for that year (Tucker 2006). This was a significant and lucrative market for the AWB and the Australian Government.

The deal: Australian wheat exports to Iraq

Over time, the AWB's success in Iraq raised concerns with a number of major wheat-producing countries. The Canadian government and wheat farming representatives lodged claims with UN personnel regarding rumours of kickbacks being paid by an Australian firm to the Iraqi government (Volcker, Golstone & Pieth 2005). However, the UN did not initiate any large-scale investigation at the time. Australia was considered to have solid democratic and transparent institutions, significant regional trading ties and generally low levels of corruption (www.transparency.org). The idea that a large, long-established, previously government-owned organisation could be engaging in high-level illicit activity appeared to have been unthinkable to UN officials at the time (Holmes 2006).

It would take the UN-led inquiry into the OFFP in 2004 to 2005, led by Paul Volcker, and the Australian Government's Cole Inquiry of 2005, to uncover the level of corruption. The contractual mismanagement by the AWB began in 1999. During this year, two AWB representatives visited Iraq and were told that the price of wheat would need to include the trucking fee of US$12 per tonne on all wheat sold to Iraq (Cole 2006a). The Iraqi government officials explained that this money was required to transport the grain from the port to the various inland regions of Iraq. This trucking fee would be added to the overall price that the Iraqi government was paying for the wheat, therefore the AWB would not lose any money from the deal. This meant that AWB would receive an extra US$12 per tonne for the wheat, but this extra US$12 would then be paid back to a transport firm nominated by the Iraqi government.

Given that the US$12 per tonne was well above actual transport cost, this was, in effect, a kickback to the Iraqi government. Although this payment, in US dollars to a company nominated by the Iraqi government was in direct contravention of the UN sanctions, AWB inserted a clause in its contract advising that 'discharge costs will be a maximum of US$12 … and should be paid by sellers to nominated maritime agents in Iraq.' (Holmes 2006). In July 1999, the AWB submitted the contract to DFAT for its scrutiny, and DFAT then forwarded the contract on to the UN for approval (Holmes 2006). In the event, neither DFAT nor the UN identified or queried this clause.

UN sanctions did not allow the AWB to pay the transport fee directly into any Iraqi financial institution, so the Iraqi government asked the AWB to pay the money to a Jordanian trucking company, Alia Transportation. During the Cole Inquiry, it emerged that this firm was 49 per cent owned by the Iraqi Ministry of Transport, and the monies for 'transport fees' that it received were later transferred to the Iraqi government (Holmes 2006). Between 1999 and 2003, the AWB entered into 26 contracts under the OFFP, but neither the fact nor the amount of the payment for transport fees made to Alia Transportation was shown on any of the 26 contracts (Cole 2006b, p. 9). During this period, the transport fees also increased from US$12 to US$50 per tonne (Holmes 2006).

The UN-led Volcker Inquiry

Rumours concerning the corruption of the OFFP had been circulating for some years, but it was not until the defeat of Saddam Hussein's forces in the Second Gulf War of 2003 that significant amounts of evidence emerged from Iraqi government files and archives. Following the discovery of this evidence, the then UN Secretary-General, Kofi Annan, initiated an inquiry into the administration and workings of the OFFP, chaired by Paul Volcker. The Volcker Inquiry discovered that while the OFFP improved the lives of ordinary people, the process had been systematically corrupted. The inquiry estimated that more than 2200 foreign firms had paid prices and kickbacks to the Iraqi government (Harris 2007). Of all the firms linked to illicit payments and the OFFP, the organisation found to have paid the highest amount of corrupt payments to the Iraqi government was the AWB. The Volcker Inquiry estimated that between 1999 and 2003, the AWB paid US$221 million (approximately AU$300 million) in illicit payments, accounting for 14 per cent of all the illegal funds paid to Saddam Hussein's regime under the OFFP.

The Australian-led Cole Inquiry

Following public pressure, in 2005 the Australian Government initiated an inquiry into the activities of Australian firms in relation to the OFFP. The inquiry focused on the activities and the role of the AWB, and was presided over by Commissioner Terence Cole. The inquiry called many witnesses, including senior AWB management, and, in its published findings, suggested that the AWB knew that its payments of transport fees to Alia Transportation contravened UN rules (Cole 2006a, 2006b). The inquiry report further claimed that the AWB management had engaged in a pattern of deliberate obfuscation to the hide the true nature of the transport fee payments from UN officials (Cole 2006a, 2006b). The then Prime Minister, John Howard, the Minister for Foreign Affairs, Alexander Downer, and the Minister for Trade, Mark Vaile, were all called to give evidence. None of the ministers where charged or resigned.

The aftermath

The negative publicity surrounding the AWB's activities led to the newly formed Iraq government placing a ban on Australian wheat imports in 2006. Following extensive lobbying from the Australian Government, the Iraqi government subsequently agreed to receive limited imports of Australian wheat, provided they were not supplied by AWB (Pash 2006). The findings of the Cole Inquiry led the Australian Government to suspend AWB's veto power over Australian wheat exports and the government subsequently approved export applications from alternative firms; the veto power was transferred to the Federal Minister for Agriculture, Fisheries and Forestry (Minder 2006). The AWB was restructured and the single-desk policy was abandoned.

The OFFP scandal embarrassed and arguably reduced the credibility of the UN. The sheer size of the corruption unearthed by the Volcker Inquiry and the Cole Inquiry, and the apparent ease by which the OFFP was manipulated by Saddam Hussein's regime, seriously questioned the UN and the Australian Government's business and governance processes. This case highlights that firms and international businesses, and by extension international business managers, are faced with commercial choices, and that short-term gains may not always accord with the best long-term interests of international trade.

Source: Adapted from Ross 2014

QUESTIONS

1. A review of the transparency international website (www.transparency.org) suggests Australia is not considered to be corrupt. What do you think went wrong in the AWB case?
2. In your opinion, which of the following institutions listed were chiefly responsible for AWB's behaviour? Give reasons for your answer.
   - Australian Government
   - the UN
   - AWB management
   - Iraqi government.
3. Considering the opportunistic trading situation that was presented to AWB, with the major competitor (the US) restricted from trading wheat with Iraq, do you think the Australian Government should have paid closer attention? Given the value and volume of the trade, do you think this has left a question mark over Australia's trading image globally?

References

APEC (2018). Achievements and benefits. Retrieved from www.apec.org/About-Us/About-APEC/Achievements%20and%20Benefits

APEC Secretariat (2017). APEC outcomes and outlook 2016/2017. APEC, February. Retrieved from http://publications.apec.org/Publications/2017/02/APEC-Outcomes-and-Outlook-20162017

APEC Secretariat, APEC Policy Support Unit (2017). APEC in charts 2017. APEC, November. Retrieved from http://publications.apec.org/Publications/2016/11/APEC-in-Charts-2016

ASEAN (2017). ASEAN economic integration brief. ASEAN, 30 June. Retrieved from http://asean.org/storage/2017/06/ASEANEconomicIntegrationBrief_No.01_30Jun2017.pdf

Asian Development Bank (2018). Our Work. Retrieved from www.adb.org/about/our-work

Asian Development Bank Institute (2014). *ASEAN 2030* Toward a Borderless Economic Community. Tokyo: Asian Development Bank Institute. Retrieved from www.adb.org/sites/default/files/publication/159312/adbi-asean-2030-borderless-economic-community.pdf

Aulich, C. & Botterill, L. (2007). *A very peculiar privatisation: the end of the statutory Australian Wheat Board*, Proceedings of the Australasian Political Studies Association Conference, Melbourne.

Capannelli, G. (2014). *The ASEAN Economy in the Regional Context: Opportunities, Challenges, and Policy Options*. ADB working paper series on regional economic integration, No. 145. Manila: Asian Development Bank. Retrieved from http://hdl.handle.net/11540/2271

Cole, T. (2006a). *Report of the Inquiry into Certain Australian Companies in Relation to the UN Oil-for-Food Programme*, vol. 1. Canberra: Commonwealth of Australia.

——— (2006b). *Report of the Inquiry into Certain Australian Companies in Relation to the UN Oil-for-Food Programme*, vol. 4. Canberra: Commonwealth of Australia.

Crawford, J.-F. & Fiorentino, R.V. (2005). The Changing Landscape of Regional Trade Agreements. Geneva: World Trade Organization. Retrieved from www.wto.org/english/res_e/booksp_e/discussion_papers8_e.pdf

Czinkota, M.R. & Ronkainen, I.A. (2012). *International Marketing*, 10th edn. Mason: Cengage.

Dean, M.K. & Wignaraja, G. (2007). ASEAN+3 or ASEAN+6: Which Way Forward. Paper presented at the Conference on Multilateralising Regionalism, 10–12 September, Geneva: Asian Development Bank Institute. Retrieved from www.wto.org/english/tratop_e/region_e/con_sep07_e/kawai_wignaraja_e.pdf

Department of Foreign Affairs and Trade (DFAT) (2016). Australia–New Zealand closer economic relations trade agreement. Retrieved from http://dfat.gov.au/trade/agreements/in-force/anzcerta/Pages/australia-new-zealand-closer-economic-relations-trade-agreement.aspx

——— (2017). ASEAN–Australia–New Zealand Free Trade Agreement. Retrieved from http://dfat.gov.au/trade/agreements/aanzfta/pages/asean-australia-new-zealand-free-trade-agreement.aspx

European Commission (2017). Taxation and customs union – unique in the world. Retrieved from https://ec.europa.eu/taxation_customs/facts-figures/eu-customs-union-unique-world_en

Fisher, W. (2004). Iraq, in L. Dean, ed., *The Middle East and North Africa*, 50th edn. London: Taylor & Francis, pp. 443–522.

Harris, H. (2007). Through public inquiry: Oil-for-food, the Volcker and Cole inquiries, and Australian wheat exports to Iraq. *Business and Society Review*, 112(2), 215–26.

Holmes, J. (2006). Cash crop (Parts 1 and 2). *Four Corners*, ABC TV, 10 April (Part 1), 17 April (Part 2). Retrieved from http://abc.net.au/4corners/ontent/2006/20060417_awb/video.htm

Hult International Business School (2017). The 11 biggest challenges of international business in 2017. Hult. Retrieved from www.hult.edu/news/international-business-challenges

Kritzinger-van Niekerk, L. (2000). Regional integration: concepts, advantages, disadvantages and lessons of experience. Working paper. South Africa: World Bank. Retrieved from http://siteresources.worldbank.org/EXTAFRREGINICOO/Resources/Kritzinger.pdf

Minder, R. (2006). Canberra grants permits to grain exporters, *Financial Times*, 23 December, p. 6.

OECD/The Bob Hawke Prime Ministerial Centre at the University of South Australia (2005). *Regional Integration in the Asia Pacific: Issues and Prospects*. Paris: OCED Publishing. Retrieved from https://doi.org/10.1787/9789264009172-en

Organization for Economic Co-operation and Development (2005). Glossary of Statistical Terms. OECD. Retrieved from https://stats.oecd.org/glossary/detail.asp?ID=3123

Park, D. & Park, J. (2010). *Drivers of developing Asia's growth: Past and future*. ADB Economics Working Paper Series No: 235. Philippines: ADB. Retrieved from www.adb.org/sites/default/files/publication/28279/economics-wp235.pdf

Pash, R. (2006). Iraq to buy $134 m of wheat. *The Age*, 30 March. Retrieved from www.theage.com.au/news/national/iraq-to-buy-134m-of-wheat/2006/03/29/1143441216087.html

Ross, P.K. (2014). AWB and the Iraqi oil-for-food scandal: just a cost of doing business? in P. Ramburuth, C. Stringer and M. Serapio, eds, *Dynamics of International Business, Asia–Pacific Business Cases*, Melbourne: Cambridge University Press, pp. 3–13.

Tucker, S. (2006). Canberra fury as Iraq suspends wheat deal. *Financial Times*, 14 February, p. 9.

Turnbull, M. (2015). ChAFTA and rebalancing of Chinese and Australian economies: Speech to Australia–China Business Forum. Malcolm Turnbull website. Retrieved from www.malcolmturnbull.com.au/media/China-Business-Week

Volcker, P., Goldstone, R. & Pieth, M. (2005). *Independent Inquiry Committee into the United Nations Oil-for-Food Programme*, Vol. 1. New York: United Nations.

World Bank (2016). Stable growth outlook for East Asia and Pacific in 2016–18. World Bank, 4 October. Retrieved from www.worldbank.org/en/news/press-release/2016/10/04/world-bank-stable-growth-outlook-for-east-asia-pacific-in-2016-18

——— (2017). World Bank open data. Retrieved from http://data.worldbank.org

World Trade Organization (WTO) (2018). Regional trade agreements: Facts and figures. WTO. Retrieved from www.wto.org/english/tratop_e/region_e/regfac_e.htm

CHAPTER 4

CULTURE, ETHICS AND CORPORATE GOVERNANCE

Learning objectives

In reading this chapter, you will learn to:

1. appreciate the role of culture and its effect on international business
2. understand ethics in international business
3. examine the concept of corporate governance, guidelines and practice
4. analyse the role of sustainability and corporate social responsibility in an international context
5. understand the interactions between ethics, corporate governance and corporate social responsibility.

IKEA IN CHINA

Ikea, a global company known for its low-price and innovative furniture designs, entered the Chinese market in 1998, opening its first shop in Shanghai as part of a JV. It now has over 25 stores in China and is looking to move into other parts of Asia, including India and Vietnam. Ikea understood that Chinese living areas are small, and the market required functional solutions. The company learnt that emerging economies are not ready for environmentally friendly practices and they don't like the do-it-yourself concept that Ikea is famous for. In addition, although Ikea is globally branded as low-price, the products were a high price in the Chinese market. Ikea's marketing strategy includes using a product catalogue. In China, this provided opportunities for competitors to copy their products and offer them at cheaper prices. Ikea identified that, to build long-term customer relationships and value, it must think globally but act locally; a country's culture must be considered in a marketing strategy. Ikea adapted to the challenges by changing its target market to customers with higher incomes by using Chinese social media and micro-blogging. Ikea also built several factories in China and sourced local materials to reduce the high import taxes, cut costs and assist with technological developments. By paying due respect to the Chinese culture in product, price, place and promotion, Ikea adapted its marketing strategy to appeal to local customers while maintaining its global corporate culture. This resulted in Ikea's success in China.

Source: Chu, Girdhar & Sood 2013

WEBLINKS
VIGNETTE QUESTIONS

FIGURE 4.1 Ikea opens its first store in Shandong Province, China, on 21 August 2017

Introduction

The management of international companies and businesses control an increasingly large share of world resources and so they affect the lives of all people. A company's decisions affect the economic prosperity of the people involved with that company, such as shareholders, employees, suppliers, contractors and other associated businesses. However, a company's decisions also have a wider impact because they affect global financial markets, the environment and local economies. In recent years, the impact of poor decision making has had serious ramifications worldwide; for example, the global financial crisis, corporate collapses and environmental disasters were largely the result of poor decision making in companies. These instances of poor management have highlighted the need for good corporate governance, an understanding of ethical conduct, and a consideration of environmental and sustainability issues in international business. To appreciate the overarching importance of good corporate governance, we need to first examine the effect of culture.

Understanding culture in international business

As international trade has grown in importance to companies, culture been recognised as a factor that influences international trade and governance. Businesses are increasingly operating on a global scale, irrespective of their size, partly due to the technological and transportation advances that allow communication and the timely flow of goods and services between stakeholders. Today, it is as quick and easy to discuss a business matter with a person on the other side of the world as it is with someone next door. Therefore, it is important to understand the behaviours, attitudes and values that contribute to the cultural differences among trading partners, and how these effect business management.

STAKEHOLDERS
the individuals or groups that an organisation impacts or that influence the organisation in the management of its business operations.

VALUES
judgements about what is important in life, which form standards for behaviour.

CULTURE
the ideas, customs, and social behaviours that are learned and shared by a group of people or society.

NATIONAL CULTURE
the set of norms, behaviours, beliefs and customs that exist within the population of a sovereign nation.

But what is culture? Culture is one of the most complicated words in the English language and so it is difficult to define. Williams uses the word culture 'to designate the entire way of life, activities, beliefs and customs of people, groups or society'(1976, p. 80). It can be seen as the 'collective programming of the mind distinguishing the members of one group or category of people from others' (Hofstede 2011, p. 3). In the context of international business, culture could be defined as a learned, shared, compelling, interrelated set of symbols, the meaning of which provides solutions to problems that a business must solve if it is to survive (Terpstra & David 1985).

Hofstede, and his fellow researchers, developed six dimensions of national culture that distinguish one country's culture from another. The dimensions observe: how a society examines inequalities among its people; whether individualism or collectivism is preferred; what ideas there are about masculinity versus femininity; the degree to which a society feels comfortable with uncertainty and ambiguity; how a society deals with the challenges of the present and the future; and whether a society is indulgent or suppressant in the gratification of needs.

As this research implies, culture and national culture does not just include how a society lives, but also encompasses how people behave towards each other, what their attitudes and feelings are, as well as which customs and communication styles they have accepted for common use.

Context and interactions

Socialisation is the term that refers to the process of learning what is accepted as appropriate behaviour for a member of a smaller group within society. Every person within society learns the habits, attitudes, values and beliefs of the group that it is born into. This is the way in which society passes its culture from one generation to the next. Acculturation is the process through which a person or group from one culture adopts the practices and beliefs of another culture, while maintaining their own cultural characteristics. This process is especially important in international business operations and for people who live in other countries for extended periods of time such as expatriates.

HIGH-CONTEXT CULTURE
a culture where behavioural nuances strongly influence communication of information. Non-verbal messaging is considered important in fostering congenial relationships.

LOW-CONTEXT CULTURE
a culture where verbal communication and clarity of spoken words is important.

Societies are referred to as either high-context culture, where many aspects of cultural behaviour are not made explicit because members know what to do (for example, how to act with your family at an expensive restaurant or in a religious meeting); or low-context culture, where people have many shorter-term connections, often for a particular reason (for example, how to act at a supermarket chain, playing a game of sport with clear rules or being at an airport). Countries such as China, Africa, Japan and Greece are regarded as high-context cultures, where the context is equally as important as what is said, while Germany, Switzerland, Scandinavia, the US and northern Europe are regarded as low-context cultures where a collective understanding of context is assumed. It should be noted that, within a country, there may be both contexts depending on the situation.

Most companies have an organisational culture that distinguishes them from other companies. This is a stated and shared set of beliefs, attitudes and modes of behaviour. In the international business environment, organisational culture can support employees whose native culture differs from the culture of the country that they are working in. Professional culture also has a role to play in international business as it supports employees that share the same profession and hence the same professional code of ethics and beliefs (for example, lawyers, accountants and engineers all have benchmarks and standards for conducting business professionally in their fields). National culture considers a country's culture, whereas organisational culture is focused on the shared set of beliefs, attitudes and modes of behaviours of a specific organisation.

ORGANISATIONAL CULTURE
the pattern of shared values and beliefs that govern how employees behave within an organisation.

ETHICS
the standards of conduct based on moral principles and values that govern the behaviour of people and businesses in society.

Why culture matters in international business

Multinational and cross-cultural teams are becoming more common. These types of teams have an increasingly diverse knowledge base and bring new ways to problem solve that are advantageous to businesses. Culture can affect international business in multiple ways. It impacts how a business communicates with its employees and with its international trading partners, and it shapes product development and promotion, how to negotiate and structure contracts, and, in fact, all aspects of doing business globally.

The Euro Disney Resort opening in Paris in the early 1990s illustrates the importance of understanding the host country's culture when operating a business internationally. The US-based Disney made a number of cultural mistakes, including supplying plastic cutlery for food in a country that prides itself on its culinary experiences, and not providing kennels and other support services for a nation where it is common to travel with pets. In addition, product support was only available in English, and Disney promoted the use of the 'Disney dollar' rather than an equivalent 'Disney euro'. It also failed to offer wine with meals.

Similarly, cultural problems can arise within organisations in a home country through a business' lack of understanding of the diversity of its employees. For example, in the Australian workforce, approximately 17 per cent of employees identify as East Asian, but the companies they work for encourage them to adapt to Western culture. Issues that arise from not recognising the diverse cultures include: the fast-paced and dynamic nature of the Western conversation style, which can make group meetings difficult for some not culturally used to that style of communication; if there is a lack of context in communication, the gap can create confusion for some people from East Asian cultures that have a high-context culture; and the value that Western culture places on the individual is different to cultures such as Japan and China, where acting in the interest of the group is considered more culturally appropriate (Szkudlarek 2017).

Key dimensions of culture

To understand culture, some general measures have been developed to describe the cultural aspects of a group of people. Characteristics common to all cultures, and so useful as a basis of comparison, include: language, education, religion and belief systems.

Language

Language refers to verbal and non-verbal communication. Therefore, learning a language also requires learning the behaviours of a society and its culture. This is because messages are communicated not just through words but also through non-verbal cues such as eye contact, gestures and

postures, as well as the tone and character of voice. In an international business setting, cross-cultural communication is nuanced because meaning goes beyond simple word recognition and this non-verbal context can potentially cause problems.

Ensuring that a translation from one language to another truly represents the meaning of what is being communicated is essential in international business. Therefore, the translation of business content to a new market needs to be undertaken in a multilingual and multicultural context. This means that the translator must have a knowledge of the country and its culture, because this is as important as knowledge of the language itself. There are many examples of translations of advertisements from English to other languages that have failed. For example, KFC's slogan 'finger-lickin' good' translates in Chinese to 'we'll eat your fingers off'; Pepsi's slogan 'come alive with Pepsi' translates in Chinese to 'Pepsi bring your ancestors back from the dead'; and Coco-Cola translates in Chinese to 'female horse stuffed with wax' or 'bite the wax tadpole' depending on the dialect. Similarly, when Procter & Gamble began selling Pampers nappies in Japan, it used an image of a stork delivering a baby on its packaging. When the product failed to sell as predicted, market research found that the reason could be the confusion the Japanese market had with the stork image used, since babies are brought to parents on giant floating peaches in Japanese folklore.

In many Asian countries, time is seen as flexible, with people coming late to meetings or not coming at all. In China, punctuality is seen as a sign of respect and sincerity, however in India, Malaysia and Thailand, lengthy waiting times are normal and business meetings rarely commence on time. In many cases, as in big Asian cities such as Jakarta in Indonesia, the traffic congestion is bad and travel times can vary, which makes it difficult to plan timing. Notably, Asian businesses are making an effort to conduct business in a punctual and timely manner when negotiating business with developed nations, since punctuality is important to developed nations and in establishing a long-term relationship with them.

Another non-verbal consideration is personal space. East Asians, for example, like wider personal space, whereas Western and South-East Asians prefer to stand close to people when they talk. In Western countries, it is acceptable for a male manager to make direct eye contact with and shake hands with a female colleague, whereas in most Asian countries, this would be considered unacceptable. Additionally, Asian business managers prefer to negotiate business transactions with people they know on a personal level and with whom they have a trusting relationship. This leads to business deals being committed to with a handshake rather than a formal contract

Education

Globalisation has resulted in the comparison of education systems between countries. A Learning Curve Data Bank, developed by the Economist Intelligence Unit, ranked each country's performance in education in 2014; included in the top 20 were: South Korea (1st place), Japan (2nd place), Singapore (3rd place), Hong Kong (4th place) and Australia (15th place) (Pearson 2014). The ranking systems of educational outcomes generally measure literacy, numeracy and educational attainment. However, for each country, the inputs to education, such as funding, school choice, number of years in school and pupil–teacher ratios, can vary greatly, and are culturally specific.

The cultural context in which education occurs is an important consideration. Culture plays a key part in the behaviour of the students, and the role and position of the teacher. Finland, for example, is noted for giving its teachers a high status. Asia tends to have a collective culture, where people belong to groups that look after them in exchange for their loyalty to the group; whereas people in most Western countries look after themselves and their immediate family. The role of females in a culture also has a bearing on educational achievements such as completing schooling and going to university. In countries such as China and Japan, so-called masculine values dominate, and there is a focus on success and achievement for males; feminine values are seen as consensus-seeking and caring, and females are less likely to take leadership roles (Wursten & Jacobs 2013). In addition, when Asian students come to Western universities, they often find it difficult to adapt to the so-called normal behaviours of students in that country. Therefore, in educating students for work in international businesses, it is important for them to understand the context and culture of their schooling, and to make the most of their international experience to translate it to business practice.

Research has shown education is correlated to income levels and living standards. In introducing new products, or the set-up of a new business venture, international business managers must consider the market and education level of the area. For example, there is little chance of success when introducing sophisticated expensive technology to a market with a prominent level of illiteracy. Education levels also affect other areas of a business, such as the ability to recruit and train local staff. In recent years, MNEs have sent local staff to the home country for training. Additionally, as labour is cheaper in countries such as India, many MNEs are outsourcing their routine operational tasks such as call centres and data input. The Asian demand for a Western university education has increased dramatically and provides evidence that Asian nations value the international experience; they see the benefit of learning about other cultures.

Religion and belief systems

Religion can be described as a set of beliefs relating to the cause, nature and purpose of existence. It generally includes devotional and ritual practices, and a moral code relating to human affairs (BBC 2014). Most cultures are based on religious beliefs, which are reflected in the values, attitudes and behaviours of the culture; similar beliefs in different cultures can provide a basis for understanding between countries. The most dominant religions around the world are Christianity, Islam, Hinduism, Buddhism, Sikhism and Judaism; however, ancient Chinese religions and ethical philosophies, such as Confucianism and Taoism, inform much of Chinese cultural attitudes today.

Religion can have a significant influence on international business so companies must be knowledgeable of and sensitive to the religious beliefs of individuals they do business with and their international markets. A sincere respect for another culture's customs is necessary, otherwise business relationships may be strained and cultural misunderstandings can occur which will negatively impact the business.

Even though most developed nations have a dominant religion, they tend to have residents from many different countries so religious tolerance is practised; there is usually a separation of state and church in these nations. Many countries, however, have legal systems, social behaviours and cultural norms that are all heavily influenced by religion. An example of this is a predominantly Islamic country, which prohibits the sale or consumption of alcohol, gambling, immodest behaviour, and the lending and borrowing of money which requires interest repayments. These kinds of laws are in line with Islamic beliefs on moderation, discipline and morality. However, it does mean that international businesses that sell alcohol or engage in any of these types of activities are affected. For instance, these types of laws mean that dress requirements are needed in businesses like hotels and resorts, and for the advertising and marketing of products. Financial institutions also need to be

aware of the types of services they can offer because some actions may be illegal. An understanding of the basics of a country's religion is, therefore, essential to doing business in that country.

Culture shock

Culture shock refers to the disorientation people feel when they move to an unfamiliar culture for an extended period. When managers in MNEs move to another country, they may experience this phenomenon, irrespective of the level of orientation training they have received. Organisational culture shock, where the person is disorientated by the culture of the new business unit, can also occur; this can be due to a person's inability to adapt, but it can also be due to the MNE's communication with the manager being unrealistic or inadequate. The manager may then experience negative emotions manifesting in resentment, hostility, bitterness and physical illness. This can have undesirable effects on the MNE too because the manager is likely to be less productive, influence colleagues in ways that damage the business, or perhaps leave their job. Outside the organisational culture, expatriate communities have developed in many areas of the world, and are a useful source of information and interaction with people from the employee's home country.

MULTIPLE-CHOICE QUESTION

SPOTLIGHT 4.1

Samsung's organisational culture

Samsung Electronics, the world's largest maker of smartphones and memory chips, recently announced that it aims to reform its internal culture. The company plans to move away from a top-down culture towards a working environment that has open dialogue and fosters innovation. The stimulus for this change has come from a decline in smartphone profits and a lack of innovative new businesses to drive growth. The reputation of Samsung was damaged in 2016 when the Galaxy Note 7 smartphone was recalled because of a battery malfunction that caused it to overheat and explode;

and, in the same year, some of Samsung's top-load washing machines were recalled because the lids unexpected flew off at higher spin-cycle speeds.

Samsung is re-evaluating all aspects of its operations including marketing, design and engineering, as well as leadership and culture. Samsung built its brand by being first to market with the newest technologies; for example, they released smart watches the year before Apple released its Apple Watch. Samsung has said, 'If we don't change, we don't survive', which shows its willingness to change organisational culture and to ensure that products are fully tested before being released into markets. Samsung stated that changes include flexible working hours, updates to dress-code requirements, less pressure for employees to attend after-work drinks (part of Korean corporate life), more training for employees, simplifying reporting procedures, and reducing unnecessary internal meetings.

Sources: Kovach 2016; Lee 2016

QUESTIONS

SPOTLIGHT QUESTIONS

1. Discuss the initiatives that Samsung is putting in place to improve its culture. How successful do you think they will be? Provide evidence to support your answer.
2. Apple's organisational culture states that it facilitates rapid innovation and a culture of secrecy to protect its intellectual property. Compare this to Samsung's culture. What issues might arise because of the culture in each company's home culture?

Ethics in international business

Business and professional ethics has been widely discussed, especially in the wake of the global financial crisis and the resultant corporate collapses. As companies continue to expand their markets to trade globally, understanding what ethics means and its importance in business around the world is essential. Governments in all countries provide laws and regulations, and put in place processes to ensure that businesses comply with those laws. Managers in global organisations need to be aware that politics, levels of economic development and culture differ among countries, and may affect what is ethical practices in a country.

Ethical beliefs shape the way we live – what we do, what we make and the world we shape through our choices (The Ethics Centre 2018). In business, the fundamental ethical principles are considered to be objectivity, integrity. honesty, competency and due care. Some have suggested that ethics include specific and universal values such as 'honesty, integrity, promise keeping, fidelity, fairness, caring, respect, responsible citizenship, excellence and accountability' (Josephson 1992) Simply stated, however, ethics can be seen as moral principles that govern a person's behaviour. Personal ethics will influence the business decisions that a person makes. People also have different levels of moral development and ethical courage.

Ethical issues

There are common ethical issues that arise in international business, often due to the differences in how societies operate in different countries. These issues include global sourcing, intellectual property, employment standards and conditions,, the environment, political regimes, bribery and corruption.

CORRUPTION
the exercise of power in a dishonest or fraudulent manner for private or business gain.

The violation of intellectual property rights (IPR) has become a major issue for companies. The OECD defines intellectual property as the 'assignment of property rights through patents, copyright and trademarks' (OECD 2002). IPR provide exclusive rights to use that property for a specified period, thereby restricting imitation and duplication. IPRs are designed to encourage R&D in new products and processes, and provide a competitive advantage for companies and individuals that engage in innovation. Patents, plant breeder's rights and other intellectual property rights, increasingly protect agricultural biotechnology. Some examples of IPRs include: a patent over Gardasil, an anti-cervical cancer drug; a trademark of the name Qantas, an Australian-based airline; plant breeder's rights over broccolini, a variety of vegetable; copyright over *Game of Thrones*, a TV series; and trade secrets regarding the Coca-Cola formula.

The protection of IPRs is limited to the countries where the proprietary asset is registered, which means the laws of one country may not offer the asset global protection. This has led to the counterfeiting of products, such as what has occurred for the brands Prada, Billabong and Chanel, as well as pirating of movies and software, and other property. In the 1986–94 Uruguay Round of trade talks, the TRIPS agreement was introduced to provide WTO member countries with IPR protection. TRIPS requires all WTO members to establish minimum standards of legal protection and enforcement for specified IPRs. Due to their different social and economic structures, as well as technological and scientific capabilities, developing nations have highlighted the need for different standards of IPR protection agriculture and health issues. For example, India and China may benefit from higher standards than other less developed countries. This is because India and China are committed to the protection of IPR to safeguard innovations from being copied. They recognise that intellectual property is a company's biggest asset and generates the most maximum economic benefit. Therefore, in these fast-growing economies, protecting IPR is necessary to ensure the local companies thrive, and the MNEs continue to develop products and invest.

Ethical philosophies and their application

Several philosophies, theories and approaches to ethical behaviour have been proposed and adopted by businesses as ethical decision-making approaches. Ethical theories are often divided into three broad categories: those concerned with the ethical consequences of the action (utilitarian approach); those concerned with the intentions of the person making an ethical decision about an action (the rights approach and the justice approach); and those concerned with the overall ethical status of the individual or agent rather than the action and its effects (the legitimacy theory).

The utilitarian approach

The utilitarian approach views the moral worth of actions and practices through their consequences. (Beauchamp, Bowie & Arnold 2004). Decisions are ethical when the social benefits outweigh the costs of pursuing that action; that is, ethical decisions are those that result in the highest benefit for most people. There are downsides to this approach to business ethics. Often, measuring the costs and risks of a course of action against what appears to be a less risky course of action in the short term, may later become a considerable risk in the long term. In addition, this approach ignores the minority for the benefit of the majority and hence fails to consider issues such as social justice, where the individual may be disadvantaged.

The rights approach

The rights approach to ethics sees the best ethical action as that which protects the rights of those affected by the action. It is derived from Kantian ethics; Immanuel Kant was an influential German philosopher (1724–1804). The rights approach is to behave 'in such a way that you treat humanity, whether in your own person or in the person of another, always at the same time as an end and not simply as a means to an end' (Bowie 2017). This theory was the underlying motivation for the Universal Declaration of Human Rights adopted by the UN in 1948, following the end of World War II. The agreement holds that every individual should enjoy universal human rights, irrespective of where they live or the culture of the country in which they reside. Article 23 of the Declaration reads: 'Everyone has the right to work, to free choice of employment, to just and favourable conditions of work ... to equal pay for equal work ... and to form and to join trade unions for the protection of [personal] interests'.

HUMAN RIGHTS basic rights that belong to each person. They are based on dignity, equality and mutual respect regardless of nationality, religion or beliefs.

The justice approach

The US philosopher John Rawls argued that ethical principles are those that are chosen by free and rational people (Rawls 2009). He sees fairness as a precursor for a just action and argues for individual human rights in society. Rawls believes that a country can achieve justice where decisions are made with complete impartiality. To reflect impartiality, Rawls coins the term 'veil of ignorance', which means that people are ignorant of all personal characteristics of another, such as nationality, gender, intelligence and social class. Under these conditions, Rawls says, agreement would be reached regarding basic human rights. He further states that once this agreement is reached, inequality is allowed if it benefits society as a whole. An example of this would be that an MNE can earn greater revenue so long as it promotes economic growth and pays workers in foreign countries the same as home-country workers, thereby benefiting the least-advantaged members of society.

Legitimacy theory

Legitimacy theory has been used to understand corporate activities in relation to social and environmental issues. A social contract describes how a business interacts with society to survive into the future (Gray et al. 1995). The theory argues that a company can only continue to operate where that society believes that it is operating with a value system similar to the society's own (Gray et al. 1996). Friedman, in discussing social responsibility, states that 'there is one and only one social responsibility of business – to use its resources and engage in activities designed to increase its profits so long as it stays within the rules of the game, which is to say, [it] engages in open and free competition without deception or fraud' (1962). The values of society have changed since Friedman's time when the only expectation of companies was to make a profit. Businesses are now required to consider social and environmental issues rising from their activities.

Codes of ethics

Ethical decision making in the global environment is more complex for international business managers as they must balance ethics, culture and social responsibility while complying with the laws and regulations across multiple countries. Therefore, building an organisational culture that actively promotes ethical behaviour is essential for MNEs. Many MNEs have a code of ethics as part of their policies that reflects the ethical standards of that organisation. For example, the Kellogg Company has a global code of ethics titled 'Living our values'. In the code's introduction, former CEO, John Bryant, states: 'Our continued success and reputation depends upon each of us living our values and acting ethically, responsibly and in compliance with the law. Our global code of ethics ... represents the culture we've built and the commitment we've made to continue earning the trust of those who love our brands.'(Kellogg's 2018, p. 3). The global code of conduct of the Kraft Heinz Company 'addresses every aspect of our business, sets high standards for conducting business in a legal and ethical manner and is the foundation of our corporate policies and procedures' (Kraft Heinz 2018). It is available in 17 languages, including Chinese, Indonesian, Korean, Hindi and Japanese.

After an MNE has set up a code of conduct, it is essential that managers and other employees comply with the code and report concerns in the manner set down in the policy document. This policy generally will also set down principles for dealing with suppliers; for example, Kraft Heinz Company states that it aims to 'ensure consistency across our operations with regards to upholding uniformly high standards of quality and service. The principles also require compliance with local labour and environmental laws' (Kraft Heinz 2018). Whistleblowing is a method of reporting an organisation for illegal, immoral and unethical behaviour by an employee after the company fails to address the ethical issues raised by the employee. The employee can be a current or former worker and can report unresolved issues to an outside regulatory or media body to ensure the company addresses the matter.

WHISTLEBLOWING when a member of an organisation discloses to an outside party the organisation's illegal, immoral or illegitimate practices.

All over the world financial services regulators are taking steps to impose stringent obligations on the reporting of suspicious and large-sum transactions by financial institutions. This has been a major focus in China in recent times, because insurance agents, brokers, consumer finance and loan companies, and financial institutions like banks are now subject to anti-money laundering obligations as part of reforms to tighten the Chinese regulation on illicit activities (Norton Rose Fulbright 2017).

China has embarked on a program of reform to provide regulated entities more autonomy in conducting businesses, while increasing the risks of non-compliance. Such measures send a clear message to financial institutions that they are to act in an ethical, anti-corrupt and professional manner. Since companies in China are largely owned by government agencies, and international businesses operating in China are often JVs, the government is largely responsible for establishing the code of conduct that is expected.

Ethical dilemmas

Ethical behaviour is often considered to be 'the right thing to do', which extends to the requirement of following the laws of a country. A company or person with a reputation for ethical behaviour usually enjoys an excellent corporate or personal image, and that can result in improved ethical performance. For example, the business' performance is enhanced by the attraction of ethical employees to the business based on the company's ethical reputation, and that, in turn, increases the perception of high ethical values of the company to its global trading partners and foreign governments. An ethical dilemma arises when there is a choice between two or more justifiable options, but none of which resolves the situation in an ethically acceptable fashion.

ETHICAL DILEMMA a situation that arises when there is a choice to make between two or more options, but all approaches to resolve the problem do not meet ethical standards.

Ethical standards vary among countries and are often influenced by the culture of a country. The opportunities for Australian companies in South-East Asian markets may present obstacles because of the cultural differences between the Australia and South-East Asian countries. Although corrupt practices are usually illegal, they may nevertheless be prevalent in the region. The 2013 Rana Plaza collapse in Bangladesh illustrates that corrupt practices have broad implications on human rights and human lives. Kim reports that the building, which housed over 3000 female garment workers, 'collapsed due to corrupt practices complemented by the lack of regulations and oversight in the construction of the building' (2015). Other countries in Asia, such as Singapore and increasingly China, have 'moved towards increased transparency in the private sector' where 'the issue of corruption is not culturally defined nor inherent' (Kim 2015). Companies that operate globally should understand the country they seek to operate in and put a good governance structure in place.

Establishing an ethical culture and framework for decision making is important, but ethical dilemmas can still arise because there is no clear or obvious solution to the ethical issue. Often, MNEs find using an ethical decision-making model helpful because it helps to identify the issues and clarify different thought processes when the business makes a decision. For example, Langenderfer and Rockness (1990) developed a seven-step ethical decision-making model that was adopted by the American Accounting Association (AAA). The seven steps are: inputs – (1) facts and (2) ethical issues; guidelines – (3) norms, (4) principles, (5) values and alternative courses of action; risk/assurance – (6) best course of action and consequences of each course of action; outputs – (7) decision. The importance of leadership, and an organisational culture that promotes and rewards people who engage in ethical behaviour will encourage ethical decision making in complex situations.

SPOTLIGHT 4.2

Nestlé's ethical issues

Nestlé is one of the largest food and beverage companies in the world but suffers from a poor reputation when it comes to ethical issues. Five of the most talked about ethical issues relate to:

1. *Infant formula*: Nestlé has been accused by the Changing Markets Foundation of 'violating ethical marketing codes and manipulating customers with misleading nutritional claims about its baby milk formulas'. A report by the Changing Markets Foundation found that 'Nestlé marketed its infant milk formulas as "closest to", "inspired by" and "following the example of" human breastmilk' in several countries, despite a prohibition by the World Health Organization (Nelson 2018).
2. *Child slavery*: in 2012, the Fair Labor Association accused Nestlé of violating its own labour laws. It is claimed that the company supports child slavery by refusing to tighten controls on the companies they buy from (Hawksley 2012).
3. *Organised labour and unions*: there are claims that workers who attempt to organise into unions in Nestlé facilities have been threatened with the termination of their employment and physically intimidated. Nestlé has a history of locating production facilities in countries with lax labour laws.
4. *Palm oil*: In 2010, Greenpeace engaged in a fight with Nestlé regarding its use of palm oil in its products. Palm oil is associated with rainforest clearing and habitat destruction, and Nestlé was accused of using suppliers known for clear-cutting without government permits. Concern was also expressed relating to greenhouse emissions.

5. *Water bottling*: Nestlé bottles water in desert regions of California that are subject to water usage restrictions. Researchers claim that excessive groundwater usage has resulted in a rise in the oceans sea level (Smith 2015).

SPOTLIGHT QUESTIONS
MULTIPLE-CHOICE QUESTION

QUESTIONS

1. Investigate the ethical issues surrounding Nestlé. It is claimed that they have a history of unethical behaviour. If this is so, why are they still operating and so profitable?
2. How do Nestlé's actions affect nations in the Asian region? In which countries did each of the five scandals noted in Spotlight 4.2 occur?

Corporate governance, guidelines and practice

CORPORATE GOVERNANCE
the mechanisms by which corporations are managed, directed and controlled to ensure that management is held accountable for its actions.

Corporate governance has become a widely discussed concept in recent times, largely because of concerns over the management or MNEs and corporate misconduct globally. The Australian Institute of Company Directors defines corporate governance as 'a broad-ranging term' that among other things 'encompasses the rules, relationships, policies, systems and processes whereby authority within organisations is exercised and maintained' (2018). Organisational governance is formed by numerous internal factors, such as a company's constitution or its policies, and external factors, such as a country's laws, regulations and community expectations (Australian Institute of Company Directors 2018).

Sir Adrian Cadbury, in the Global Corporate Governance Forum held by the WB states:

> Corporate governance is concerned with holding the balance between economic and social goals, and between individual and communal goals. The corporate governance frame-

work is there to encourage the efficient use of resources and equally to require accountability for the stewardship of those resources. The aim is to align as nearly as possible the interests of individuals, corporations and society. (Iskander & Chamlou, 2000, vi)

The need for corporate governance arises because of the separation of the management of the organisation from those who contribute the resources for the business to operate; some examples of resource contributors are shareholders and investors.

Corporate governance, therefore, relates to organisations of all sizes and in all sectors; including for-profit businesses and non-profit organisations.

Some examples of the problems that occur with management of organisations are listed below.

1. The use of resources of the company to benefit the management of the company personally. For example, Parmalat SpA, a family-run farm in Northern Italy, was founded in 1961 and grew into one of the largest dairy and food companies in Italy, eventually becoming a multinational conglomerate with 214 subsidiaries in 48 different countries in 2003. It appears that when the company's financial performance started to decline in 1990, Parmalat executives 'used a wide range of unethical techniques' to commit fraud (Rimkus 2016). Rimkus reports that Parmalat 'inflated revenues by creating fake transactions through a double-billing scheme. They used receivables from these fake sales as collateral to borrow more money from banks. They created fake assets thereby inflating reported assets. In some cases, they took on legitimate debt that they hid from investors. Parmalat also worked with investment bankers to engage in financial engineering that misrepresented debt and equity on the financial statements, and colluded with auditors and bankers to finance the fraud indefinitely (Rimkus 2016).
2. Actions are taken by management that stakeholders and society may consider undesirable. For example, the recent case of Volkswagen's emissions sandal, was partly caused by the decline in profits after the global financial crisis. The management strategy employed put pressure to increase sales in the US, which meant that engineers had to design cars that could pass the exacting US emissions testing and pollution regulations. To do this, a group of the company's engineers installed software in cars exported to the US to cheat on the tests (Lynch & Santos 2016).
3. Remuneration for directors and key management personnel may not be aligned to their actual performance. This issue is discussed worldwide, with greater differences in linking pay to performance noted in Asian practices when compared to other countries (Mercer 2014).

Current guidelines and practices

The OECD principles of corporate governance was originally issued in 1999, and updated in 2004 and 2015; they are general principles of corporate governance to be applied in all countries. The OECD principles were considered necessary because many countries did not have guidelines in place, and a benchmark was needed to assess and improve corporate governance globally. They have been used by the WB for the review of more than 60 countries worldwide (OECD 2015). The six core OECD principles are:

1. ensuring the basis for an effective corporate governance framework
2. the rights and equitable treatment of shareholders and key ownership functions
3. institutional investors, stock markets, and other intermediaries
4. the role of stakeholders

5. disclosure and transparency
6. the responsibilities of the board.

In Australia, the *Corporate Governance Principles and Guideline* were issued by the Australian Securities Exchange (ASX) in 2007, with amendments in 2010. Listed companies are expected to comply with these principles and recommendations. If they fail to comply, they are expected to explain why they did not. The eight principles listed in the ASX are:

1. lay solid foundations for management and oversight
2. structure the board to add value
3. promote ethical and responsible decision-making
4. safeguard integrity in financial reporting
5. make timely and balanced disclosure
6. respect the rights of shareholders
7. recognise and manage risk
8. remunerate fairly and responsible (ASX, 2010, pp. 10–12).

Systems of corporate governance vary between countries; there are two broad approaches: a market-based system and a relationship-based system. A market-based, or shareholder system of governance, is driven by competition and market forces, and is used in the US, the UK, Australia and New Zealand. Market-based systems are present where there is widespread equity ownership of companies by individuals and institutional investors, and good governance is needed to attract investor funds.

A relationship-based system of governance is based on close and constructive relationships between insiders, known as stakeholders; this system is used in Germany, France and other European nations, as well as Asian countries such as Japan and China. This system is characterised by restricted share ownership, with many large companies being family-controlled. There is reliance on bank funding, with banks also being shareholders in some cases. Asian countries have a considerable concentration of ownership of companies and dominant shareholders by a family or the state. The systems for enforcement of rules and regulations vary considerably throughout the Asian region. The cultural diversity characterised by different political and legal structures, and social traditions has led to differences in corporate governance policy and practices. As a result, many countries in the Asian region, legislated practices have been adopted rather than relying on the substance of good corporate governance.

MULTIPLE-CHOICE QUESTION

The role of sustainability and corporate social responsibility

SUSTAINABILITY the patterns of development that meet the needs of the present without harming the ability of future generations to meet their needs.

Sustainability issues are having an increasing influence on business decision making and the social and environmental performance of organisations worldwide. The General Assembly of the UN noted sustainable development as a key area of concern in the Brundtland Report, 'Our Common Future', commissioned in 1987. Sustainable development was defined in this report as 'development that meets the needs of the present without compromising the ability of future generations to meet their own needs' (United Nations World Commission on Environment and Development 1987). The focus of this definition relates to economic, environmental and social development, and considers both inter- and intra-generational equity. Intergenerational equity takes the long-term focus that consumption of resources today should not affect future generations, while intra-generational equity takes a short-term view relating to the ability to meet current needs of the population. Sustainable development is a global initiative involving governments, organisations and companies, and requires them to consider how their management decisions affect the economy, environment and society.

Increasingly, sustainability has become important to organisational stakeholders. For example, customers are interested in recyclable packaging, employees are interested in equity issues and community groups, and governments are interested in environmental issues such as carbon emissions. Stakeholders play an important role in ensuring that organisations address sustainable development issues. This was demonstrated in 2018 when a Qantas Boeing Dreamliner 787–9 took the world's first biofuel flight between the US and Australia. The flight was powered by a blended fuel of converted mustard seeds, resulting in 7 per cent fewer emissions, and aligned to customers' increasing expectations for sustainable aviation.

The significance of corporate social responsibility

Corporate social responsibility (CSR) refers to good citizenship by the firm; in other words, its obligations to society, particularly when society is affected by the firm's strategies and practices (Vachani & Smith 2004). When expanding abroad, MNEs are expected to act as good local citizens in all the locations where they are active. In fact, profitable business models can go together with good citizenship and produce positive CSR outcomes.

CORPORATE SOCIAL RESPONSIBILITY (CSR)
the management and operation of a business' activities is done in a manner that meets or exceeds the ethical, legal, business and societal expectations of their stakeholders. CSR refers to good corporate citizenship.

According to the Hewlett-Packard Company (HP), its international citizenship efforts are based on a simple framework: 'strong ethics and appropriately transparent governance form the platform of integrity on which all our policies and decisions must be based' (Dunn & Yamashita 2003, p. 53). HP focuses its practise of CSR in three areas: privacy, environment and e-inclusion. In terms of privacy, HP advocates international data protection for its consumers. The area of environment is demonstrated by the company designing its products to minimise their ecological impact. Lastly, by focusing on e-inclusion, HP uses technology to improve people's access to social and economic opportunities (Dunn & Yamashita 2003, p. 53).

HP's citizenship efforts are closely aligned with its business strategy. The company establishes clear strategic objectives for each social issue that is addressed, and attempts to apply sound business practices to each project. HP utilised seven such practices in its i-community initiative in Kuppam, India (Dunn & Yamashita 2003). These are outlined below.

1. *Unearthing customer needs.* HP's technology business operations demand the ability to 'divine the needs of their customers by probing at underlying problems and transferring that understanding to the innovation process' (Dunn & Yamashita 2003, p. 50). In the technology industry, products are rarely developed simply by asking customers what they want. Instead, customer problems must be uncovered (often with some effort) and technological solutions then developed to solve those problems. HP reports that most community development initiatives do not approach the problem with this type of underlying needs analysis. In addressing social challenges, HP invests in a needs-finding process that takes the form of an iterative cycle. This resource recombination process, which HP refers to as its 'living lab methodology', involves uncovering a need and quickly developing a prototype solution. The prototype solution is then deployed on a limited basis, which allows for observation and solution modification. After modification, the cycle is started over again.
2. *Citizenship efforts by fielding a diversely talented team.* MNEs often entrust community development initiatives to individuals with a background in philanthropy or development.

Drawing on its business experience, HP sees the benefit of complementing those philanthropic and development skills with a broader range of knowledge, including line-management knowledge, expertise in government affairs, and a rich understanding of culture. In other words, citizenship efforts cannot be effective and perhaps even translate into FSAs without involvement of (human and other) resources that are the core of the firm's more conventional FSAs.

3. *Adopt a systems approach*. A systems approach does not attempt to optimise individual parts, but instead views these parts in a broader context and aims to optimise the whole. In HP's case, this approach suggests that development initiatives should do much more than provide technology. 'Community leaders must advocate for the solution, trusted individuals within the community must lend their reputations to the effort, Kuppam businesses must get involved, and other technology companies must integrate their technology into the solution' (Dunn & Yamashita 2003, p. 51). This third business practice shows the complexity involved in HP's efforts to combine its extant FSAs in technology with resources in the local environment.
4. *The creation of a leading platform*. In the ICT industry, the concept of leading platform refers to a standardised, generally accepted configuration of hardware, as well as a specific operating system and other software, which allows the functioning of computers and computerised devices (for example, personal digital assistants and cell phones). This can then be linked to other hardware or software. Working with all the partners involved, HP provides the main ICT infrastructure (both hardware and software), to which each partner can then add its own technologies and applications. HP's partners are thus able to add value by building upon their own distinctive strengths.
5. *Building an ecosystem of partners*. HP recognises that most sustainable communities have many different stakeholders with a vested interest in a long-term solution. Therefore, HP brings together government, local leadership, business people, healthcare professionals, NGOs, informal networks within the community, and local and international technology partners. While it is not easy to align these interests in the short term, HP believes that the long-term alignment of strong interests from all these parties is the best path to sustainable solutions. The alignment of interests offers protection from hazards associated with each partner's bounded reliability. In short, HP does not attempt to drive all the value creation itself, but instead tries to create a healthy ecosystem of partners, all dedicated to solving problems and bringing their complementary resources to the initiative.
6. *Community development initiatives is simply to set a deadline for the project*. HP has found that deadlines create a sense of urgency, which keeps all participants in the partnership focused. Deadlines move the initiative to the action phase and encourage participants to find common ground quickly. Setting a deadline indicating the end of the MNE's active involvement also focuses the project on becoming self-sustaining after the MNE's direct involvement has ceased.
7. *Solving, stitching and scaling*. This practice, derived from HP's experience in taking new products to market, initially customises a solution for a single customer. This focus eliminates the bounded rationality challenge of trying to figure out all the possible forms the solution will eventually take. The single customer solution is also known as the lighthouse account because of its ability to point other customers towards the firm. Building upon

> such experiences with single customers, managers can then begin to stitch a collection of solutions into a total solution that can be scaled (Dunn & Yamashita 2003, p. 52).

Within HP's three CSR areas of privacy, the environment and e-inclusion, the company centred its efforts in Kuppam on e-inclusion. E-inclusion means using technology to reduce economic and social divides. In this program 'the company creates public–private partnerships to accelerate economic development through the application of technology while simultaneously opening new markets and developing new products and services' (Dunn & Yamashita 2003, p. 48). One tangible expression of this community initiative is the Kuppam information centre, which allows people to make phone calls, photocopies and faxes, and offers computers with access to the HP-built i-community portal. The centre not only offers the infrastructure for micro-enterprise development, but it is also itself owned by locals selected by an NGO. This ownership structure fits well with HP's 'ecosystem of partners' approach to community development. Kuppam's i-community now includes five community information centres, where students, teachers and parents can develop skills to access information via the internet.

For the MNE manager, the business value of the project is the template or routine from which the project was developed. In this case, the template consists of four key phases of project development. The first phase, lasting approximately five months, is the 'quick start'. This phase attempts to establish credibility and momentum by achieving a few quick successes. Other elements in this phase include visioning exercises and the gaining of high-level alignment with partners in the public and private sectors. The second phase, lasting approximately eight months, is the 'ramp up'. This phase is characterised by gathering resources for prototyping, evaluating solutions and training stakeholders so they can take ownership of the initiative. The key to the ramp-up phase is bringing the ecosystem of international and local partners into a true coalition. Third, running from the beginning of the second to the middle of the third year of the initiative is the 'consolidation' phase. In this phase, HP evaluates the intellectual property generated to date, helps local partners decide which solutions to deploy and stops sub-projects unlikely to reach their goals. Fourth, overlapping with the consolidation phase is the 'transition' phase, which runs from the beginning of the second year to the end of the third year. Here, community leaders are identified, and power and knowledge are transferred to local participants (Dunn & Yamashita 2003, p. 50).

The benefits of the Kuppam initiative have extended to other communities. For example, HP transferred the lessons learned from the Kuppam i-community project and applied these to a project that tested new technology by providing portable solar-powered digital photography hardware to women entrepreneurs. These women were able to utilise the technological infrastructure to develop a solid business model. This approach gave them the confidence to seek a line of credit from a co-op bank, and the extra income offered the means to provide education for their children.

HP realised that its earlier philanthropic donations, though generating results, were actually sub-optimal, and that much more could be accomplished if doing good and doing well could be made mutually reinforcing (Dunn & Yamashita 2003, p. 54). The benefits of the Kuppam initiative for HP have included market growth, leadership training and technological development. HP emphasises that projects such as Kuppam are not about short-term profits but about the opportunity to achieve long-term growth and, in the process, improve the human condition in regions where the firm does business. Through the process, HP has also gained knowledge and contacts within new markets, and

these benefits have made HP a stronger competitor in those markets. These citizenship initiatives also help HP develop international leaders. In fact, the firm reports that more can be learned from living labs like Kuppam in three years than from virtually any leadership development programme or graduate course: 'Indeed, though it wasn't among the primary goals of the i-community, teaching leaders new ways to lead may be one of the largest competitive benefits of the initiative. Ultimately, it's the knowledge that these leaders and their teams gain in places like Kuppam that will allow HP to become a stronger competitor.' (Dunn & Yamashita 2003, p. 53)

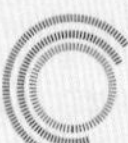

SPOTLIGHT 4.3

Environmental disasters

There have been several environmental disasters caused by corporate irresponsibility. These have had a disastrous effect on the local communities involved and will take many generations to overcome. The cases noted here all have something in common: an MNE operating in a developing area of the Asian region.

Bhopal, India, 1984

An accident at the Union Carbide India Ltd pesticide plant released a highly toxic gas, methyl isocyanate, and other poisonous gases. More than 600 000 people were exposed to the gas cloud, with the government reporting an estimated 15 000 deaths over the years. The toxic material is still present with many of those exposed to the gas in 1984 giving birth to physically and mentally disabled children later in their lives.

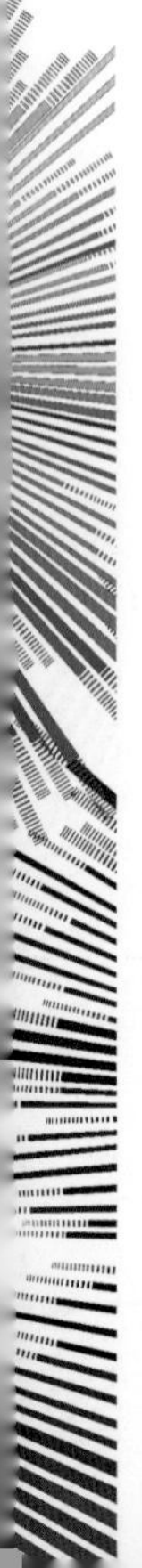

Ok Tedi mine waste, 1984–2013

Approximately 2 billion tonnes of untreated mine waste were discharged into the Ok Tedi River from the Ok Tedi open-pit mine, due to the collapse of the tailings dam system in 1984 and a lack of a suitable waste retention facility. The mine waste was deposited along the bank of the Ok Tedi and Fly Rivers, destroying downstream villages, agriculture and fishing, as well as killing large tracts of forest. Experts have predicted that it will take 300 years to clean up the toxic contamination.

South-East Asian Haze, 2016

A smog outbreak caused by fires was attributed to illegal slash-and-burn practices to remove vegetation by companies and individuals. The land clearing, to make way for palm oil and pulpwood plantations, is on carbon-rich peat land. The smog has reportedly caused 90 000 deaths in Indonesia, 6500 deaths in Malaysia and 2200 deaths in Singapore.

Sources: Agence France-Presse 2016; Cochrane 2015; Lal 2017; Mineral Policy Centre 1999; Taylor 2014

QUESTIONS

SPOTLIGHT QUESTIONS

1. Do the corporations involved in these environmental disasters have a responsibility to ensure their business practices don't cause harm to society and the environment?
2. Have these environmental disasters affected the nature and importance of CSR reporting? In what ways?

Corporate environmental sustainability

Environmental management is playing an increasingly important role in broader CSR approaches by MNEs. Recent concerns over global warming have put the environment at the forefront of consumer and non-governmental organisation (NGO) advocacy efforts. MNEs are particularly scrutinised for their environmental footprint by a variety of stakeholders, as these firms tend to dominate pollution-intensive sectors, such as the oil and gas, chemical, energy utility and automotive industries. The development of the Kyoto Protocol and the Paris Agreement, were the result of the general rise of public concern over global warming climate change issues, and the arguments being offered in favour of environmental regulations that improve resource productivity (Porter & van der Linde 1995).

THE KYOTO PROTOCOL

The Kyoto Protocol was finally negotiated and concluded at the third meeting of the United Nations Framework Convention on Climate Change (UNFCCC), Conference of Parties (COP-3) in December 1997 in Kyoto, Japan. The Kyoto Protocol entered into force on 16 February 2005. Australia signed the Kyoto Protocol on 24 April 1998, but did not ratify it until 12 December 2007, following the election of the ALP government. To date, 182 parties have ratified the Kyoto Protocol.

The object and purpose of the Kyoto Protocol

The Kyoto Protocol serves to meet the UNFCCC's objective of reducing human-induced greenhouses gases (GHGs) to address climate change, guided by the UNFCCC's key principles of precaution, intergenerational equity, sustainable development, and common but differentiated responsibilities and respective capabilities.

Source: Parliament of Australia 2018

THE PARIS AGREEMENT

The Paris Agreement, also known as the Paris Climate Accord or Paris Climate Agreement, is an agreement within the United Nations Framework Convention on Climate Change (UNFCCC). The agreement deals with greenhouse gas emissions mitigation, adaptation and finance starting from the year 2020. 'To reach these ambitious goals, appropriate financial flows, a new technology framework and an enhanced capacity building framework will be put in place, thus supporting action by developing countries and the most vulnerable countries, in line with their own national objectives' (United Nations Climate Change 2018).

Senior MNE managers can be guided in their approach to the sustainability opportunities in a heterogeneous international marketplace by distinguishing among three types of economies: developed, emerging and surviving, each with its own sustainability challenges (Hart & Milstein 2003, p. 26).

First, the *developed* or consumer markets represent an economy of one billion wealthy customers, and are characterised by advanced infrastructure for rapid manufacturing and distribution. In these markets, managers should seek to reduce the firm's ecological footprint by reinventing products and processes. Developed markets at present contain many mature technologies and product systems that tend to leave a very large environmental footprint, associated with enormous resource waste and environmental spill overs. These mature systems and technologies also provide diminishing performance gains from large investments in technology, and thus are ripe for replacement by radical new technologies. For example, the automobile industry shows signs of a mature technology reaching its limits, as such components as metalworking and the internal combustion engine are, according to the authors, inherently inefficient. The industry is susceptible to creative destruction via radical technologies that will greatly improve resource use. These radical technologies may include fuel cells, ultralight bodies and new drive trains (Dunn & Yamashita 2003, p. 27).

The authors also point to the chemical industry as another example of a mature industry susceptible to radical innovations. According to the authors, even the generalised adoption of so-called best practices such as the 'responsible care' program, an expression of self-regulation by the industry, made mandatory by the Chemical Manufacturers Association, does not cut it: simply having the entire industry adopt prevailing best practices (including principles and codes related to preventing pollution, engaging in proactive environmental behaviour and involving the firm in the community) ultimately does not serve global sustainability goals at the societal level. The latter would require drastic reductions in the levels of resources used and negative impacts on the environment. However, the good news is that some firms such as DuPont are trying to move away from being large-volume producers of chemicals with a large ecological footprint, towards becoming high value-added producers of information services and 'green' products, thereby shedding their most resource and pollution-intensive activities.

Second, the *emerging* economies, with roughly two billion people, mainly have customers who can meet their basic needs but have minimal purchasing power. Here, MNE managers must avoid a major imbalance between the expanding demand for products, fuelled by population growth, urbanisation and industrialisation, and the limited physical capacity of these countries to provide the necessary infrastructure, and institutional context for efficient supply and disposal. MNEs should avoid simply transferring conventional practices or technologies from rich economies to emerging ones, because these markets' ecological, infrastructural and institutional systems simply cannot sustain these practices and technologies. In the environmental sphere, it is suggested that managers should explicitly assess the sustainability of perceived opportunities, because the presence of fragile ecosystems, combined with infrastructural and institutional voids (for example, in health and safety regulations) could otherwise lead to particularly negative outcomes. Here, key issues are whether the existing ecosystems can sustain rapid industry growth and whether leapfrog technologies (such as the generalised use of mobile telephone systems, without the presence of a conventional, fixed line infrastructure) can be deployed to avoid non-sustainability (Locke & Romis 2007, p. 28). Essentially, managers operating in emerging economies must develop the ability to meet rapidly growing demand without repeating the wasteful and outdated practices prevailing in developed markets.

Third and finally, *survival* economies, with three billion potential customers, are largely rural. Most individuals have unmet basic needs. These markets have minimal or non-existent infrastructure. MNE managers should recognise the opportunity presented by this massive consumer group. In line with the idea of recombining resources and deploying FSA bundles to match the location advantages of a given market, it is suggested that managers should apply state-of-the-art technology in fundamentally new ways to meet the basic needs of customers in survival economies. More specifically, conventional infrastructure that meets basic needs in developed economies, such as a large, grid-based energy supply system, may well be infeasible to develop, thus providing unparalleled opportunities for deploying more decentralised systems, building upon solar power, wind and hydro energy as credible and economically viable alternatives.

Managers must be aware of which industries and products are vulnerable to creative destruction. As noted above, these are the industries and products for which large investments in technical development yield only small gains in performance. Entrepreneurs who can introduce radical new technologies that generate significant performance gains will sow creative destruction and experience tremendous success.

Implicit in linking environmental management with competitive strategies is the alignment of firm-level and societal interests. Porter and van der Linde had the important insight that environmental stewardship can be achieved through higher resource productivity, which in turn increases the competitiveness of the firm in their classic *Harvard Business Review* article (Porter & van der Linde 1995). Thus, the concept of resource productivity brings the profit-seeking interests of the firm into alignment with society's interest in environmental sustainability.

Interactions between culture, ethics, corporate governance and CSR

International business managers need to have factual and interpretive knowledge of the culture of the host country, and with the companies they are developing relationships with there. In addition, managers must understand the governance structures of that country to ensure that they operate within the established societal framework. A knowledge of ethics and ethical decision making will assist the manager in making the right decisions, and maintaining the company's position as a good corporate citizen. International business managers should undertake the following steps to ensure they undertake best practice.

1. Determine the meaning of corporate citizenship in each country where you operate and across all the firm's international operations.
2. Assess each CSR initiative in terms of its joint contribution to 'doing well' and 'doing good', and evaluate the longer-term business opportunities that CSR activities can create for the firm in host countries.
3. Improve working conditions and labour standards at your factories and your suppliers' by effectively implementing CSR activities.
4. Rethink your pricing decisions by trading off profit maximisation against fulfilling obligations to society.
5. Align your CSR activities to your host-country business objectives, and the host-country socio-economic and institutional context.

By following these steps, international business managers, and the companies they represent, will be able to act in a manner consistent with the legal, ethical, commercial and socially responsible expectations of stakeholders, and the country in which their business is conducted.

Summary

Learning objective 1: Appreciate the role of culture and its effect on international business.

Companies must consider cultural differences and nuances of different countries when they conduct their business internationally. Language, education and religion all influence culture, and the way that business is transacted in a country. Managers in MNEs should ensure that when they do international business, they understand and are sensitive towards the cultural differences they find in the host country.

Learning objective 2: Understand ethics in international business.

Maintaining ethics in international business practice means understanding the rules, policies and culture of a company, as well as the country the business operates in, and balancing these with the expectations of stakeholders of that company. Fundamental principles of ethics in business are: objectivity, integrity. honesty, competency and due care. People have different levels of moral development and ethical courage that will influence their decision making in a situation. Using a decision-making philosophy and a model will assist international business managers in identifying issues and clarifying thoughts to make ethical business decisions.

Learning objective 3: Examine the concept of corporate governance, guidelines and practice.

Corporate governance relates to corporate conduct. It encompasses internal and external factors, and community expectation that ensure a company conducts itself appropriately. Corporate governance should encourage the efficient use of resources, accountability for those resources and a closer alignment of all stakeholders' interests. The need for corporate governance arises because owners and investors are distinct from a large company's management, and so the management must be held to account for its actions. The OECD issued six core principles of corporate governance that are widely used as a framework for reporting throughout the world. There are two main systems of corporate governance used (market-based and relationship-based) driven by the relationship between stakeholders in a company in each country.

Learning objective 4: Analyse the role of sustainability and CSR in an international context.

CSR refers to a firm's obligations to society, particularly when society is affected by the firm's business activities and decisions. MNEs are expected to act as good local citizens in all the locations where they are active. Once considered merely a philanthropic option, good corporate citizenship is now increasingly imposed by the new economic reality of powerful NGOs, grassroots consumer networks and rapid international information dissemination. In addition, environmental sustainability is increasingly being noted as of key importance as part of CSR. While good citizenship can be viewed as the equivalent of a cost increase, it can also be an opportunity to develop FSAs and to improve performance.

Learning objective 5: Understand the interactions between ethics, corporate governance and CSR.

International business managers need to have factual and interpretive knowledge of the culture of the companies they develop relationships with and the country they operate in. In addition, managers must understand the governance structures of that country to ensure that they operate within the societal structure established. A knowledge of ethics and ethical decision making assists the manager in making

USEFUL WEBSITES

the right decisions and maintaining the company's position as a good corporate citizen. The manager and the company represented will thereby act in a manner consistent with the legal, ethical, commercial and social expectations of their stakeholders and the country in which business is conducted.

REVISION QUESTIONS

Revision questions

1. What is culture? Explain how culture is an important consideration in international business. What attributes should a regional manager of an international company have to ensure the successful management of clients and employees from diverse regions?
2. Should companies care about ethical behaviour? Does it really make any difference to company performance?
3. What is whistleblowing? How and why has this evolved since the global financial crisis? Explain the importance of whistleblower protection.
4. In some countries, such as the US, corporate governance practices are enshrined in legislation, whereas in other countries guidelines have been introduced. Should governments legislate, or should companies be permitted to self-regulate, thereby choosing their own corporate governance structures? Provide examples of countries that legislate, and countries that self-regulate.
5. CSR has meant companies have to disclose to their stakeholders any social and environmental issues that affect the company and its profitability. Explain, using examples, what is meant by a social reporting measure and an environmental reporting measure. How would these affect a company's profitability?

R&D ACTIVITIES

R&D activities

1. In 2014, the General Court of the European Union (in *Case T-286/09 Intel vs Commission*) upheld the 2009 decision by the European Commission to fine US chipmaker Intel €1.06 billion for anti-competitive practices. 'When large companies abuse their dominance of the market, it causes direct harm to consumers. The court's ruling issued a strong reminder that such behaviour is illegal and unacceptable,' said BEUC director-general Monique Goyens (Foo 2014). BEUC is a European consumer lobby group. With reference to the Intel case:
   a. Discuss the comments made by Monique Goyens regarding abuse by companies of their dominance in the market.
   b. Identify Intel's stakeholders and discuss the nature of the interest they have in Intel. How will they be affected by this decision?
   c. Do competition laws stifle a company's ability to be competitive?
   d. Explain the corporate governance implications of this behaviour for Intel's board of directors.
2. D&R Carpet Gallery is based in Brisbane, Australia and imports rugs for retail sales from China, Thailand and India. Its aim is to deliver sustainable, high-quality products and solutions that customers demand. These rugs are woven in several villages around the world and, due to the intricacy of the weaving, often require children to weave. In many cases D&R are the sole customer for the rugs that are created. The directors of D&R believe they are supporting communities to preserve a craft that will be handed down and will sustain the villages.

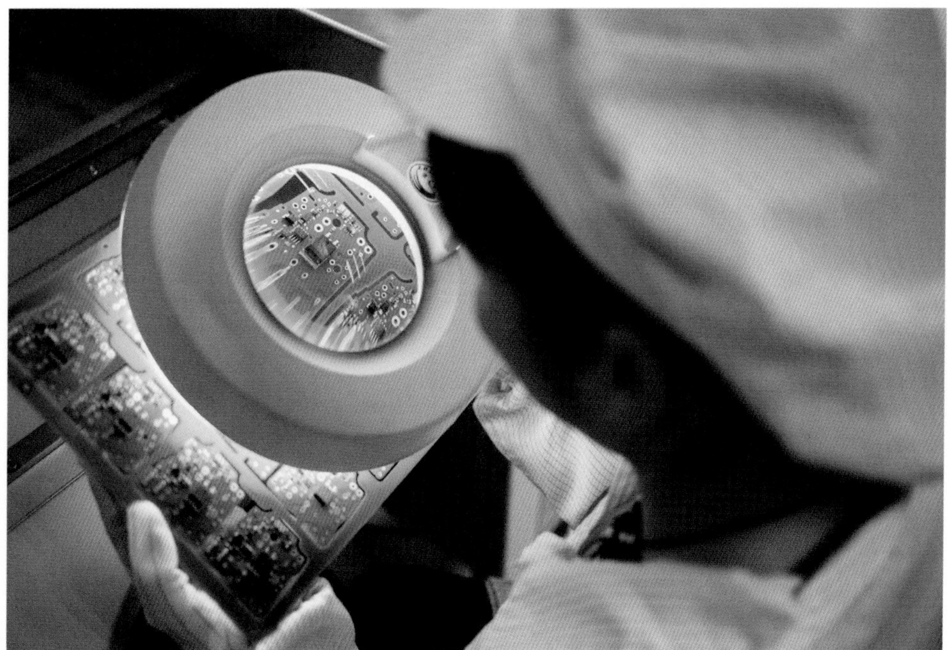

Due to the success of the company, media attention has been drawn to D&R's rug suppliers. A television report describes how adults and children work long shifts in poor conditions, and claims that this has led to poor eyesight and the children not attending school. The examples used in the media report are not associated with D&R but have reflected badly on them.

   a. What are the issues facing D&R considering the poor publicity?
   b. What steps might they take to overcome this problem?
   c. Investigate other companies that have sourced products in a similar way. What were the economic consequences for the suppliers? What did they do to overcome real or perceived negativity?

3. Visit multinational company websites from two different industries. Compare their statements on corporate governance. What do you consider their strengths and weaknesses to be?
4. In October 2017, fraud charges were brought against Rio Tinto by the US Securities and Exchange Commission (SEC) arising from their investment in Mozambique. Investigate this claim and discuss its legal, reporting, ethical and CSR aspects and the legal cases. What are the penalties for each of these areas of responsibility?
5. KFC has become the most popular brand of fast food in China but it's nothing like the US brand. Compare KFC in China and the US. Why was it necessary to make them different? You might like to consider:
   a. size of stores, population and geographical locations
   b. food offerings
   c. what the Chinese stores offer the consumers that's special
   d. who goes to KFC.

IB MASTERCLASS

Sweatshop wars: Nike and its opponents in the 1990s

In the 1990s, US-based Nike, Inc., the largest athletic shoe company in the world, was accused by labour and human rights activists of operating sweatshops in Indonesia, Vietnam and China. Nike initially viewed such accusations as public relations problems, but finally changed its defensive tactics to a more proactive approach after serious damage was inflicted to its reputation in the late 1990s.

In the new millennium, Nike has tried to distance itself from its tainted image associated with worker exploitation, by monitoring its contractors more closely, integrating its supply chain through lean manufacturing and pushing for consistent global standards in the apparel industry. In 1998 Nike founder Phil Knight publicly committed to changing the company's practices; it appeared that this has occurred.

However, the company's practices of worker exploitation might be occurring again. On 29 July 2017, a day of protests was organised by the United Students Against Sweatshops (USAS) claiming that Nike workers in a factory in Hansae, Vietnam, suffered wage theft and verbal abuse, and laboured in temperatures more than the legal limit of 90 degrees Fahrenheit (32.2°C). USAS accused Nike of cutting jobs in the Hansae factory and cutting production in Honduras because of a strong union presence in those locations. There have also been claims that the Worker Rights Consortium (WRC) was denied the right to inspect Nike factories and to conduct independent monitoring of them. Like Nike did in 1990s, the company has provided explanations for their actions and denies any wrongdoing.

History and Nike's business model

Nike started as a venture in 1964 between Phil Knight, an undergraduate and athlete at the University of Oregon, and Bill Bowerman, his track coach at the same university. They identified a need for high-quality running shoes at a time when Adidas and Puma dominated the US market. Phil Knight went on to do his MBA at Stanford, where he realised that he could combine inexpensive Japanese labour and American distributors to sell cheap but high-quality track shoes in the US, thereby ending the European dominance of the market. In 1964, Knight and Bowerman founded the Blue Ribbon Sports Company, which was renamed Nike in 1971.

Nike's business model had three major components. First, Nike would outsource all manufacturing to low-cost areas in the world. The money thus saved would be invested in the two other components of the business model: R&D of innovative new products on the upstream side, and marketing to promote these products on the downstream side. In its marketing, Nike went beyond conventional celebrity endorsements and named Nike shoes after famous athletes such as Michael Jordan and Tiger Woods. These celebrities further strengthened Nike's image.

This business model worked very well. In the early 1980s, Nike became the leading athletic shoe company in the US. In 1991, Nike became the first sports company to surpass yearly sales of US$3 billion. During this time, Nike shifted its contract manufacturing locations, first from Japan to South Korea and Taiwan, and then later to Indonesia, Vietnam and China, always taking advantage of the cheapest labour in the new emerging economies.

Labour rights in Indonesia and Nike's initial response to criticisms

By 1990, Indonesia had become a key location for Nike. Labour costs in Indonesia were only 4 per cent of those prevailing in the US. Moreover, Indonesia had a population of 180 million, with a high unemployment rate and weak employment legislation. To Nike, that meant millions of people willing to work for low wages. Six of Nike's contract manufacturers were in Indonesia, together employing around 24 000 workers and producing 8 per cent of Nike's global output.

In the late 1980s and early 1990s, Indonesia started to experience labour unrest. The number of strikes reported by the Indonesian government rose from 19 in 1989 to 122 in 1991, and Indonesian newspapers also documented some labour abuses by Indonesian factories. An NGO called the Asian-American Free Labor Institute (AAFLI) produced a report on working conditions at Indonesian factories in 1991, based on research by Jeff Ballinger, a labour activist assigned to be the Indonesian branch leader of the AAFLI in 1988.

Ballinger found that his criticism of Indonesia in general did not draw worldwide attention to labour rights abuses in Indonesia. The criticism lacked focus, and it was unclear what sympathetic people in developed countries could do to help the situation. Then, Nike emerged as the perfect target for Ballinger: Nike contractors paid their workers less than US$1 a day; Nike contractors hired children in Indonesia; and moral outrage could be capitalised upon to tarnish Nike's brand names and image. Applying the more focused 'one country–one company' strategy, Ballinger started to publish reports and distribute newsletters specifically about labour issues at Nike's contractors in Indonesia.

In January 1992, because of criticism from activists like Ballinger, the Indonesian government increased the minimum daily wage to IDR Rp2500 (US$1.24). Nike was aware of the labour conditions at its Indonesian contractors, but it believed that such issues were its contractors' responsibility, as Nike did not own any manufacturing facilities itself. Firm in its stance, Nike did draft a code of conduct in 1992, addressing issues of child labour, forced labour, compensation, benefits, hours of work or overtime, environment, safety and health.

Until that point, criticism of Nike's Indonesian operations came almost exclusively from Indonesia itself.

Criticism spreads to the US: Nike's hot seat

However, it didn't take long before Nike was criticised in the US media too. In 1992, *Harper's Magazine* published an article by Ballinger, famously demonstrating that it would take an Indonesian factory worker 44 492 years to earn Michael Jordan's endorsement fee at Nike (Ballinger 1992, pp. 46–7). In the same year, a prominent newspaper in Oregon (Nike's home state) also published articles criticising Nike's Indonesian operations. In 1993, a CBS report revealed that Indonesian workers at a Nike contractor's factory were paid only 19 cents an hour, and that women employees could only leave their onsite dormitory on Sundays and with written management permission.

Such criticism drew national attention, but Nike's stance was still firm. Nike argued that it had provided job opportunities and contributed to local economic development. Phil Knight, Nike's CEO, dismissed any criticism, stating 'I'm proud of our activities' (Baker 1992, A1). He argued that, taken in context, Nike was benefiting Indonesia: 'A country like Indonesia is converting from farm labour to semiskilled – an industrial transition that has occurred throughout history. There's no question in my mind that we're giving these people hope' (Katz 1993, p. 64).

Further, Nike responded to the above criticism by hiring Ernst & Young, the accounting and consulting firm, to audit Nike's foreign factories, but the objectivity of the auditing was questioned by activists.

In the next several years, criticism directed towards Nike continued to rise. In April 1996, Kathie Lee Gifford, a popular daytime talk show host at CBS, had learnt from human rights activists that a line of Walmart clothing endorsed by her had been manufactured by child labour in Honduras. She soon apologised on national television, spurring a wave of media coverage on labour issues in developing countries associated with other Western companies. In July 1996, *Life* magazine published an article about child labour at Nike's contractors in Pakistan. Then, on 17 October 1996, CBS News ran a *48 Hours* program focusing on Nike's shoe manufacturing plants in Vietnam, reporting low wages, physical violence inflicted on employees and sexual abuses of several women workers. The program informed US viewers that temporary workers were paid only 20 cents an hour. On 14 March 1997, Reuters reported physical abuses of workers at Nike contractors' factories in Vietnam. Consequently, because of such widespread negative news coverage, Nike gradually emerged as a symbol of worker exploitation.

Such news coverage also drew the attention of political leaders to look for legislative solutions. In 1996, Robert Reich, the US labour secretary, launched a campaign to 'eradicate sweatshops from the American garment industry and erase the word entirely from the American lexicon' (Smotrova 1996, p. 4). Even President Clinton convened a presidential task force on sweatshops and called for industry leaders to develop acceptable labour standards in foreign factories (Bernstein 1998).

To quell the above criticisms, Nike tried to build credibility in two main ways. First, Nike established a Labour Practices Department in October 1996 and a Corporate Responsibility Department in 1998, to deal formally with worker issues in its supply chain. Second, in 1997, Nike hired Andrew Young, a former UN ambassador and civil rights leader, to review Nike's Far Eastern factories. However, Andrew Young's conclusion from his 10-day visit to China, Vietnam and Indonesia that Nike was doing a good job was publicly challenged at the time and later shown to be flawed (Herbert 1997; Nguyen 1997).

Changing to managing responsibility

Pressures continued to rise. In May 1997, Doonesbury, the popular comic strip, focused several times on Nike's labour issues. Millions of readers read the strip, making hurling stones at Nike so popular that a media critic commented, 'It's sort of like getting in Jay Leno's monologue. It means your perceived flaws have reached a critical mass, and everyone feels free to pick on you' (Mannings 1997). Later in 1997, an internal report prepared for Nike by Ernst & Young was made public by the Transnational Resource and Action Center. The report found that workers at a Nike factory in Vietnam worked in unsafe conditions, were forced to work 65 hours a week and were paid only US$10 a week.

Around this time, Nike realised that it had made a big mistake. Phil Knight noted in 1998 that, 'The Nike product has become synonymous with slave wages, forced overtime and arbitrary abuse' (Cushman Jr 1998, p. 5). Nike's sales, financial performance and stock prices slumped in 1998 because of its tarnished image, its failure to follow shifting consumer preferences and the Asian financial crisis.

On 13 May 1998, Nike finally bowed to 'pressure from critics who have tried to turn its famous shoe brand into a synonym for exploitation' (Cushman Jr 1998, p. 5). Nike promised to allow human rights activists and independent auditors to investigate the working conditions in Nike contractors' factories in Asia, and to increase the minimum age for new hires at shoe factories to 18, and the minimum age for new hires at other factories to 16.

Nike did not address the below-subsistence wage issue, one of the key human rights problems in Nike's overseas factories. Nike paid workers in China and Vietnam less than US$2 a day and workers in Indonesia less than US$1 a day, much lower than the US$3 a day required to reach adequate living standards. However, Nike's promises did elicit positive comments from several organisations.

By 2000, the anti-sweatshop movement's efforts had forced several Western firms to improve working conditions. Knight noted that the movement's efforts 'probably speeded up some things that we might have done anyway ... Basically, the workers in footwear factories, not just our factories, are better off today than two years ago' (Greenhouse 2000). In 2001, Nike released its first Corporate Responsibility Report, with one section dealing with its labour practices to explain how it monitored child labour and legal minimum wages at contractor factories (Nike 2001).

Hard to be responsible: Adjusting Nike's business model

Although Nike started to audit its approximately 900 suppliers in the late 1990s, the suppliers' failure to respect Nike's labour codes continued to be reported by the media. For example, the NGO Global Alliance uncovered a string of problems including verbal abuse and forced overtime after the Alliance surveyed 4450 workers at nine Indonesian Nike factories (Akst 2001, pp. 3–4). In May 2001, a BBC documentary revealed that Nike and GAP contractors in Cambodia had broken their own strict anti-sweatshop codes of conduct (Kenyon 2000).

The frustrated Nike CEO convened a team to figure out why Nike was not able to implement its own codes of conduct. The team, led by Nike's vice president for corporate responsibility, Maria Eitel, concluded that it was partially Nike's business model that counteracted its efforts to improve working conditions at its suppliers.

The problematic component of Nike's business model was the effort to minimise costs in its supply chain through outsourcing. Nike's procurement teams chose suppliers based on price, quality and delivery times, and the core goal was to search for lower prices. Such a business model both encouraged Nike to switch to low-cost suppliers whenever possible, and pushed Nike's contractors to push costs down to extremely low levels to win Nike's orders. Moreover, the prevailing trade agreement in the apparel industry, the Multifiber Arrangement (MFA), set country-based import quotas for the US market. Thus, Nike had to search for spare quotas, hindering efforts to establish long-term relationships with suppliers. Finally, Nike managed inventory tightly. Whenever forecasting errors occurred, suppliers were pushed to meet delivery deadlines, thereby increasing the use of overtime in their factories (Zadek 2004).

Nike's analysis suggested that it would have to change its business model to accommodate the new goal of improving worker conditions. After the MFA expired on 1 January 2005, Nike started to move towards lean manufacturing (in other words, a seamless supply chain, from purchasing inputs to serving the customer, with a focus on waste reduction, consistent quality and reliability), and towards establishing more stable relationships with its suppliers. Nike hoped that these changes would help its suppliers implement its code of conduct.

In its corporate responsibility report in 2004, Nike used a full section to explain its approach to labour conditions in contract factories (Nike 2004). As compared with the narrow first report from 2001, this second report in 2004 described a more detailed monitoring process, with compliance rating criteria to assess a factory's compliance on a wide variety of issues. Moreover, Nike started to build strategic relationships with manufacturers for a more integrated supply chain. Nike realised that its influence on suppliers was dependent on the relationships it had with each subcontractor. These relationships varied substantially between shoe and apparel suppliers. The company's contracts with shoe suppliers were typically long term and allowed Nike to have more influence on processes. Contracts with apparel suppliers were shorter term, which made it more difficult for Nike to influence behaviour. Finally, in 2005, a group of Nike factories opened their doors to research teams from MIT's Sloan School to identify the root causes of problems, as Nike had found that monitoring could identify only problems, not underlying causes and much less solutions. The report stated that in spite of 'significant efforts and investments by Nike ... workplace conditions in almost 80 per cent of its suppliers have either remained the same or worsened over time' (Nike 2004). The solution for Nike was to implement lean manufacturing to provide more on the job training and organisation. Nike hoped that the additional training would make suppliers more concerned about keeping their skilled employees and ultimately motivate managers to provide better work environments for their employees.

Collective responsibility: Nike won't go it alone

Nike was afraid that adopting responsible practices could bring competitive disadvantage, if its competitors in the industry did not act accordingly. Therefore, since the late 1990s, Nike had been involved in creating mandatory global standards in the industry. It joined multi-stakeholder organisations such as the Fair Labor Association (FLA) and the Global Compact (an initiative by UN Secretary-General Kofi Annan) to harmonise global compliance standards. Nike substantially improved its CSR practices, but it made sure it did not have to do so alone.

What happened in Indonesia?

In the new millennium, the shoe business has partially moved out of Indonesia to China and Vietnam. After Nike terminated its relationship with the Doson factory (a 7000-employee factory where most of the workers were unionised), Indonesia accounted for only 24 per cent of Nike footwear production in 2011, a big drop from 38 per cent in 1996. However, Nike still employed, through its suppliers, 120 000 people in Indonesia, and it made the (disputed) claim that it had decided to terminate its business with the Doson factory not because of unionisation, government regulations or wages in Indonesia, but because of the factory's overall unsatisfactory performance as compared with other factories (Dhume & Tkacik 2002, A.12).

Nike continues to manufacture shoes in 43 other Indonesian factories but still struggles to maintain optimal labour practices (*Wall Street Journal* 2012). A lawsuit was settled in January 2012 on overtime pay that was not distributed to employees in a factory over a two-year period. Nike agreed to pay US$1 million to cover payments and set up stronger grievance procedures to avoid repetition.

In 2011, contract plants in Vietnam, China, Indonesia and India produced 39 per cent, 33 per cent, 24 per cent and 2 per cent of Nike brand footwear, respectively (Nike 2012, p. 5). Some commentators claim that labour leaders misread competitive conditions faced by Indonesian companies, and that these leaders actually jeopardised jobs in Indonesia (Mapes 2002, A.1). Opinions differ as to whether the new labour environment – fewer jobs, but with better working conditions – is better for Indonesians.

Public movement pressures Nike

Although Nike is now strongly focused on CSR, it continues to face pressure from the public. In 2009, Nike ended a contract with a factory in Honduras. Unfortunately, severance pay and unemployment benefits were not provided by the subcontractor. It did not take long for university students in the US to pressure Nike to accept responsibility in this matter. The University of Wisconsin-Madison ended its contract with Nike and Cornell University threatened to follow suit if something wasn't done. Although Nike reaffirmed that this was not the firm's responsibility, the company adopted a different approach than before and provided support to the subcontractor's employees. By July of 2009, Nike had set up a US$1.54 million worker relief fund for the affected employees, a measure reinforcing the suggestion that Nike had learned from its mistakes (Murphy 2010, pp. 3–4).

An ongoing process

More than a decade after Nike decided to change its CSR practices, the public's perception of the company has also changed, but the firm continues to face challenges.

Shifting the majority of its production to China and Vietnam has created a new environment of labour conditions for Nike to manage. With the added attention from the 2008 Beijing Summer Olympics, Nike was keen to exhibit transparent supply-chain management in China. China is now one of Nike's largest supplier countries, which has made the evolution of CSR compliance statistics in that country very important in determining the progress of Nike's initiatives. The results so far have been somewhat disappointing, though not unexpected. Nike stated in this context that 'corporate responsibility is a relatively new, rapidly evolving business practice in China. Adoption and understanding vary widely' (*Wall Street Journal* 2008). Non-compliance occurs mainly due to false documentation, unpaid wages, lack of grievance processes and usage of underage workers.

To combat non-compliance, Nike has developed two methods to monitor Chinese factories. The first method, 'management audit verification', involves verifying the conditions associated with the individual employee, including hours worked, wage, benefits and complaints. The second method, 'environment, safety and health audits', monitors the conditions within the given factory (Economist Intelligence Unit Limited, 2008). Results from these tests revealed that Chinese factories, when compared to other international factories, often had poorer grievance systems, overtime tracking, and fire safety and health. Nike has suggested that improving the labour conditions in China is a priority, but government laws and regulations create obstacles. It has been argued that discrepancies between Chinese labour laws and guidelines set by the International Labour Organization create unfavourable conditions for Chinese workers (Mitchell 2008, p. 3).

Nike's companywide CSR team consists of 140 people aiming to implement better practices in all aspects of Nike's businesses (*The Economist* 2012, p. 73). Nike's 2011 corporate responsibility report outlined the progress and challenges the firm continues to face. Unfortunately, Nike saw a decrease in the percentage of factories given an 'A' rating, down from 6 per cent in 2010 to just 4 per cent in 2011. Additionally, 'B' factories increased from 33 per cent in 2010 to 45 per cent in 2011. This prompted a strong message to all suppliers from Hannah Jones, VP of sustainable business and innovation, stating: 'We will be moving away from companies that are not committed to putting workers and sustainability at the heart of their growth agendas.' (Townsend 2012). The report outlined the goal that all suppliers must meet Nike's standards by 2020.

CEO Mark Parker is proud of how far Nike has come, but realises that CSR is 'a never-ending challenge' (Levenson 2008).

Sources: Bain 2017; Everatt & Slaughter 1999; Hendry & Fujikawa 2000; Nisen 2013; Spar 2002; Spar & La Mure 2003; Zadek 2004

QUESTIONS

1. What are Nike's FDI motivations in Japan, Taiwan, Indonesia and Vietnam? What are the locational advantages of these countries in the context of Nike's business?
2. Nike tried to revise its business model to integrate its supply chain. How did Nike's earlier business model affect its contractors' behaviour? To what extent do you think the changes to Nike's business model will improve contractors' compliance with Nike's codes of conduct? Could there be any drawback because of such business model changes?
3. Provide an update on Nike's responses to human rights complaints, using materials available online.

References

Agence France-Presse (2016). Haze from Indonesian fires may have killed more than 100 000 people – study. *The Guardian*, 19 September. Retrieved from www.theguardian.com/world/2016/sep/19/haze-indonesia-forest-fires-killed-100000-people-harvard-study

Akst, D. (2001). Nike in Indonesia, through a different lens. *New York Times*, 3.4.

ASX (2010) *Corporate Governance Principles and Recommendations with 2010 Amendments*, 2nd edn. Sydney: ASX Corporate Governance Council. Retrieved from www.asx.com.au/documents/asx-compliance/cg_principles_recommendations_with_2010_amendments.pdf

Australian Institute of Company Directors (2018). What is corporate governance? Australian Institute of Company Directors' website. Retrieved from http://aicd.companydirectors.com.au/resources/all-sectors/what-is-corporate-governance

Bain, N. (2017) Nike is facing a new wave of anti-sweatshop protests. Quartz, 1 August. Retrieved from https://qz.com/1042298/nike-is-facing-a-new-wave-of-anti-sweatshop-protests

Baker, N. (1992). The hidden hand of Nike series: Nike's world power & profits. *Portland Oregonian*, 9 August, A1

Ballinger, J. (1992). The new free-trade heel. *Harper's Magazine*, 285, August, 46–7.

BBC (2014). Religions. BBC. Retrieved from www.bbc.co.uk/religion/religions

Beauchamp, T.L., Bowie, N.E. & Arnold, D.G., eds (2004). *Ethical Theory and Business*. London: Pearson.

Bernstein, A. (1998). A floor under foreign factories? *Business Week*, 2 November, 126–30.

Bowie, N.E. (2017). *Business ethics: A Kantian perspective*. Cambridge: Cambridge University Press.

Chu, V., Girdhar, A. & Sood, R. (2013) Couching tiger tames the dragon. *Business Today*, 21 July. Retrieved from www.businesstoday.in/magazine/lbs-case-study/how-ikea-adapted-its-strategies-to-expand-in-china/story/196322.html

Cochrane, L. (2015). Ok Tedi Mining confirms wall collapse at massive open-cut mine in PNG, denies link to shutdown. *ABC News*, 24 August. Retrieved from www.abc.net.au/news/2015-08-24/ok-tedi-mining-confirms-wall-collapse-at-massive-open-cut-mine/6721504

Cushman, J.H., Jr (1998). Nike pledges to end child labor and apply U.S. rules abroad. *New York Times*, 13 May, 5.

Dhume, S. & Tkacik, M. (2002). Footwear is fleeing Indonesia – output drop by Nike, others has implications for key export model. *Wall Street Journal* (Eastern edition) 9 September, A.12.

Dunn, D. & Yamashita, K. (2003). Microcapitalism and the megacorporation. *Harvard Business Review*, 81, 47–54.

The Economist (2012). When the job inspector calls, working conditions in factories. *The Economist*, 402 (8778), 73.

The Economist Intelligence Unit Limited (2008). Just doing it. *Business China,* 31 March.

The Ethics Centre (2018). What is ethics? Retrieved from www.ethics.org.au/about/what-is-ethics.

Everatt, D. & Slaughter, K. (1999). Nike Inc.: developing an effective public relations strategy. Richard Ivey School of Business Case 9A99C034.

Foo, Y.C. (2014). Intel loses court challenge against $1.4 billion EU fine. Reuters, 12 June. Retrieved from https://uk.reuters.com/article/us-intel-court-eu-idUSKBN0EN0M120140612

Friedman, M. (1962). *Capitalism and Freedom*. Chicago: University of Chicago Press.

Gray, R., Kouhy, R. & Lavers, S. (1995). Corporate social and environmental reporting: a review of the literature and a longitudinal study of UK disclosure. *Accounting, Auditing & Accountability Journal*, 8(2), 47–77.

Gray, R., Owen, D. & Adams, C. (1996). *Accounting & Accountability: Changes and Challenges in Corporate Social and Environmental Reporting*. New York: Prentice Hall.

Greenhouse, S. (2000). Anti-sweatshop movement is achieving gains overseas. *New York Times*, 26 January.

Hart, S.L. & Milstein, M.B. (2003). Creating sustainable value. *Academy of Management Executive*, 17(2), 56–69.

Hawksley, H. (2012). Nestle 'failing' on child labour abuse, says FLA report. *BBC News*, 29 June. Retrieved from www.bbc.com/news/world-africa-18644870

Hendry, J. & Fujikawa, T. (2000). Nike in Asia – Just do it. The University of Cambridge Case 300–069–1.

Herbert, B. (1997). Mr. Young gets it wrong. *New York Times*, 27 June, A.29.

Hofstede, G. (2011). Dimensionalizing cultures: The Hofstede model in context. *Online Readings in Psychology and Culture*, 12 (1). https://doi.org/10.9707/2307-0919.1014

Iskander, M.R. & Chamlou, N. (2000). *Corporate Governance: A Framework for Implementation – Overview*. Washington: the World Bank Group. Retrieved from http://documents.worldbank.org/curated/en/831651468781818619/pdf/30446.pdf

Josephson, M.W. (1992). The Need for Ethics Education in Accounting, in S. Albrecht, ed., *Ethical Issues in the Practice of Accounting*, Ohio: Southwestern Publishing, pp. 1–20.

Katz, D. (1993). Triumph of the swoosh. *Sports Illustrated*, 16 August, 64.

Kellogg's (2018). Living our founder's values: Kellogg Company's global code of ethics. Retrieved from http://crreport.kelloggcompany.com/living-our-values

Kenyon, P. (2000). Gap and Nike: no sweat? *BBC News,* 15 October. Retrieved from http://news.bbc.co.uk/2/hi/programmes/panorama/archive/970385.stm

Kim, J. (2015). Ethical risks in doing business in the region. Australian Institute of International Affairs, 13 November. Retrieved from www.internationalaffairs.org.au/news-item/ethical-risks-in-doing-business-in-the-region

Kovach, S. (2016). Samsung's culture needs to change if it wants to survive. *Business Insider Australia*, 6 November. Retrieved from www.businessinsider.com.au/samsung-reaction-to-note-7-recall-2016-11?r=US&IR=T

Kraft Heinz (2018). Ethics and Compliance. KraftHeinz website. Retrieved from www.kraftheinzcompany.com/index.html

Langenderfer, H.Q. & Rockness, J.W. (1990). *Ethics in the Accounting Curriculum: Cases and Readings*. Florida: American Accounting Association.

Lal, N. (2017). Bhopal gas tragedy still haunts India. *The Diplomat*, 19 April. Retrieved from http://thediplomat.com/2017/04/bhopal-gas-tragedy-still-haunts-india

Lee, S.Y. (2016). World's biggest start-up? Samsung Electronics to reform corporate culture. Reuters, 24 March. Retrieved from www.reuters.com/article/us-samsung-elec-culture-idUSKCN0WQ0CP

Levenson, E. (2008). Citizen Nike. *Fortune*, 158(10), 165–170.

Locke, R. M. & Romis, M. (2007). Improving work conditions in a global supply chain. *Sloan Management Review* 48, 54–62.

Lynch, L.J. & Santos, C. (2016). VW emissions and the three factors that drive ethical breakdown. Darden Ideas to Action, 17 October. Retrieved from https://ideas.darden.virginia.edu/2016/10/vw-emissions-and-the-3-factors-that-drive-ethical-breakdown

Mannings, J. (1997). Doonesbury could put legs on Nike controversy. *The Oregonian*, 25 May.

Mapes, T. (2002). Newly aggressive labor groups pressure companies in Indonesia. *Wall Street Journal* (Eastern edition) 14 August.

Mercer (2014). Executive compensation in Asia – best practices in a dynamic environment. Mercer. Retrieved from www.mercer.com/content/dam/mercer/attachments/asia-pacific/asia/Mercer_Executive_Compensation_in_Asia_Best_Practices_10525A-HC.pdf

Mineral Policy Centre (1999). One of world's worst mine disasters gets worse – BHP admits massive environmental damage at Ok Tedi mine in Papua New Guinea, says mine should never have opened. Mining Watch Canada, 11 August. Retrieved from https://miningwatch.ca/news/1999/8/11/one-worlds-worst-mine-disasters-gets-worse-bhp-admits-massive-environmental-damage-ok

Mitchell, T. (2008). Nike sees 'gaps' in China labour law. *Financial Times*, 10 March, 3.

Murphy, E. (2010). Nike finally just does it. *Dollars and Sense,* 290, September–October, 3–4.

Nelson, A. (2018). Nestlé under fire for marketing claims on baby milk formulas. *The Guardian*, 2 February. Retrieved from https://amp.theguardian.com/business/2018/feb/01/nestle-under-fire-for-marketing-claims-on-baby-milk-formulas

Nguyen, T. (1997). Report on Nike work force glossed over issues. *New York Times*, 30 June.

Nike (2001). Corporate Responsibility Report 2001. Oregon: Nike.

——— (2004). Corporate Responsibility Report 2004. Oregon: Nike.

——— (2012). 2011 Annual Report. Oregon: Nike.

Nisen, M. (2013). Why the Bangladesh factory collapse would never have happened to Nike. *Business Insider Australia*, 10 May. Retrieved from www.businessinsider.com.au/how-nike-solved-its-sweatshop-problem-2013-5

Norton Rose Fulbright (2017) Business Ethics and anti-corruption: Asia Pacific Insights – Issue 12. Norton Rose Fulbright, August. Retrieved from www.nortonrosefulbright.com/knowledge/publications/155378/business-ethics-and-anti-corruption-asia-pacific-insights-issue-12

OECD (2002). Glossary of statistical terms. OECD. Retrieved from https://stats.oecd.org/glossary/detail.asp?ID=3236

——— (2015). G20/OECD Principles of Corporate Governance. Paris: OECD Publishing. http://dx.doi.org/10.1787/9789264236882-en

Parliament of Australia (2018). The Kyoto Protocol. Parliament of Australia. Retrieved from www.aph.gov.au/About_Parliament/Parliamentary_Departments/Parliamentary_Library/Browse_by_Topic/ClimateChangeold/governance/international/theKyoto

Pearson (2014). Index – Which countries have the best schools? Pearson. Retrieved from http://thelearningcurve.pearson.com/index/index-ranking

Porter, M.E & van der Linde, C. (1995). Toward a New Conception of the Environment-Competitiveness Relationship. *The Journal of Economic Perspectives*, 9(4), 97–118.

Rawls, J. (2009). *A theory of justice*: Revised edition. Boston: Harvard University Press.

Rimkus, R. (2016). Parmalat. CFA Institute, 29 November. Retrieved from www.econcrises.org/2016/11/29/parmalat

Smith, S.E. (2015). Five shocking scandals that prove it's time to boycott Nestlé. The Daily Dot, 15 May. Retrieved from www.dailydot.com/via/nestle-california-bottled-water

Smotrova, O. (1996). US takes up arms against sweatshops. *Financial Times*, 15 July, 4.

Spar, D.L. (2002). Hitting the wall: Nike and international labor practices. Harvard Business School case 9–700–047.

Spar, D.L. & La Mure, L.T. (2003). The power of activism: assessing the impact of NGOs on global business. *California Management Review*, 45, 78–101.

Szkudlarek, B. (2017). Four cultural clashed that are holding East Asian employees back. The Conversation, 6 March. Retrieved from http://theconversation.com/four-cultural-clashes-that-are-holding-east-asian-employees-back-72661

Taylor, A. (2014). Bhopal: The world's worst industrial disaster, 30 years later. The Atlantic, 2 December. Retrieved from www.theatlantic.com/photo/2014/12/bhopal-the-worlds-worst-industrial-disaster-30-years-later/100864

Terpstra, V. & David, K.H. (1985). *The Cultural Environment of International Business*. Ohio: Southwestern Publishing.

Townsend, M. (2012). Nike raises factory labor and sustainability standards. Bloomberg, 3 May. Retrieved from www.bloomberg.com/news/articles/2012-05-03/nike-raises-factory-labor-and-sustainability-standards

United Nations Climate Change (2018). The Paris Agreement. United Nations Climate Change. Retrieved from https://unfccc.int/process/the-paris-agreement/the-paris-agreement

United Nations World Commission on Environment and Development (1987). *Our Common Future – The Brundlandt Report*. Oxford: University of Oxford Press.

Vachani, S. & Smith, N.C. (2004). Socially responsible pricing: lessons from the pricing of AIDS drugs in developing countries. *California Management Review*, 47, 118.

Wall Street Journal (2008). Nike report cites continuing problems in China. *Wall Street Journal* (Eastern edition) 15 March.

——— (2012). Nike contractor to pay workers for overtime. *Wall Street Journal*, 12 January.

Williams, R. (1976). Developments in the Sociology of Culture Volume. *Sociology*, 10(3), 497–506. https://doi.org/10.1177/003803857601000306.

Wursten, H. & Jacobs, C. (2013). The impact of culture on education: can we introduce best practices in education across countries? ITIM International.

Zadek, S. (2004). The path to corporate responsibility. *Harvard Business Review*, 82, 125–32.

CHAPTER 5

INTERNATIONAL INVESTMENT

Learning objectives

In reading this chapter, you will learn to:

1. examine the theories related to international investment
2. consider FDI into ASEAN
3. understand how countries measure international economic transactions through the balance of payments
4. appreciate how economic crises impact the balance of payments.

DOES THE US RELY TOO MUCH ON CHINA FOR ITS FINANCE?

When Nobel Prize-winning economist Joseph Stiglitz wrote the article 'The Chinese century' for *Vanity Fair* in 2014, he raised many social, political and economic questions. First, he described his concern over China's ownership of US government debt. Second, Stiglitz suggested how the trade deficit, or the shortfall in US imports over exports, needs to be financed. The US current account deficit with China has increased as a function of the trade deficit and the returns earned on China's investment in the US. This causes the US financial account to continue deteriorating with no major improvement in sight. The reliance on China as the world's largest economic power has caused some apprehension, especially considering China financing the US debt. Carl Tannenbaum, who served as the head of the Federal Reserve's Risk Group in Washington, warns that China having a financial crisis is the biggest risk to the world economy (Tannenbaum 2017). This is despite the recent decrease in China's relevant ownership of US government debt.

China's growth has created a new destination for capital and it is a source of finance for the rest of the world. One area of exponential growth for China is the amount of inbound and outbound FDI. UNCTAD reported that FDI inflows grew from US$40 715 million in the year 2000 to US$135 610 million in 2015, and outflows increased from US$916 in 2000 to US$127 560 million in the same period (UNCTAD n.d.). This creates opportunities for MNEs in China since the Chinese economy is growing at a pace that is twice that of developed economies. However, investors and governments need to understand the multitude of implications regarding China's trade surplus and the possible impact of a sudden decrease in its financial account.

WEBLINKS
VIGNETTE QUESTION

Introduction

International investment represents part of the globalisation and integration of economies in developed, developing and emerging regions. It represents the direct investment flow of investment funds across foreign borders and was originally considered as a way of bypassing a country's trade restrictions. Today, FDI and international trade operate together in a company's international trade strategy. This area of MNE financing can be technical and complex so this chapter first examines theories relating to international investment, particularly in the ASEAN region. It then examines the balance of payments (BOP) as the key measure of a country's international economic transactions and financing considerations. Finally, the chapter discusses major economic crises in relation to the BOPs to understand the reasons why international investment can go wrong.

Transferable FSAs

The MNE creates value and satisfies stakeholder needs by operating across national borders. When crossing its home country border to create value in a host country, the MNE is, almost by definition, at a disadvantage compared to firms from the host country, because the host country's local firms possess a knowledge base that is more appropriately matched to its local stakeholder requirements. Further, the MNE incurs additional costs of doing business abroad because of the cultural, economic, institutional and spatial distance between the home- and host-country environments.

MNE managers often find it difficult to anticipate the liability of foreignness resulting from the cultural and institutional differences with their home-country environments, even though these may be reduced over time as the firm learns and gains increased legitimacy in the host country. Stephen Hymer wrote about the additional costs of doing business abroad back in 1976, and the concept has since received considerable attention by international business scholars (Hymer 1976; Eden & Miller 2004). Obviously, MNEs can reduce the liability of foreignness by forging alliances, such as JVs, with local partners in host countries.

To overcome the additional costs of doing business abroad, the MNE must have proprietary internal strengths, such as technological, marketing or administrative knowledge of, for instance, governance-related issues. In principle, the MNE can transfer, deploy and exploit these FSAs successfully across borders. Non-location-bound FSAs can be embodied in final products; for example, when the MNE exports goods and services that are valued highly by host-country customers. Alternatively, when faced with natural or government-imposed trade barriers, the MNE may transfer some FSAs abroad directly as intermediate products.

The paradox of an internationally transferable FSA is the following: if the FSA consists of easily codifiable knowledge, then it can be cheaply transferred, and effectively deployed and exploited abroad, but it can also be easily imitated by other firms. In other words, if the FSA can be articulated explicitly, like in a handbook or blueprint, the costs of the FSA's transfer, deployment and exploitation may be relatively low, but the potential value of that may also be relatively low if competitors can easily imitate what the MNE is best at doing.

In contrast, MNEs face great difficulty transferring, deploying and exploiting FSAs that consist of tacit knowledge. Tacit knowledge is difficult to transfer, deploy and exploit abroad because it cannot be fully replicated through simple communication channels, such as technical manuals. Employing tacit knowledge requires person-to-person communication and is necessarily associated with sending human resources abroad, building up experience over time, learning by doing and so on. If the tacit knowledge is collective knowledge, embedded in a team of individuals rather than a single person, it may be necessary to re-embed this knowledge in a foreign team. Though it is expensive and time-consuming to transfer, deploy and exploit tacit knowledge across borders, the benefit to the MNE is that this knowledge is also difficult to imitate. Therefore, tacit knowledge is often a key source of competitive advantage when doing business abroad.

Perhaps the most important bundle of tacit knowledge is contained in the MNE's administrative heritage: the key routines developed by the firm since its inception. The vision of the founder and the firm's set of external circumstances is often what determines an MNE's heritage ('this is the way we do things in this company'). At a general level, and when looking at the early history of large numbers of MNEs, we can distinguish among four archetypes of administrative heritage, each associated with a specific routine of international FSA transfer.

The main types of MNEs

The first archetype is the *centralised exporter*. This is when a home-country-managed firm builds on a tradition of selling products internationally, out of a limited number of (scale-efficient) facilities in the home country, and with only minor, usually customer-oriented, value-creating activities abroad. Standardised products manufactured at home embody the firm's FSAs (themselves developed based on a favourable home-country environment, including local clustering) and make the exporting firm successful in international markets. The foreign subsidiaries act largely as facilitators of efficient home-country production. Multinational activities occur primarily in the downstream end of the value chain, and are related to marketing, distribution and related logistics operations.

The second archetype of administrative heritage is the *international projector*. This firm builds on a tradition of transferring its proprietary knowledge developed in the home country to foreign subsidiaries, which are essentially clones of the home operations. Many US MNEs fit this model, as they expand internationally based on a large and sophisticated home-country market, as well as proprietary technology and unique management practices. Knowledge-based FSAs developed in the home country are transferred to subsidiaries in host countries. The international projector MNE seeks international expansion by projecting its home-country recipes of success abroad. To the extent that international projection requires the systematic and continuous transfer of tacit knowledge to multiple locations (particularly when the product offering contains a large service component), this firm relies on an extensive cadre of professional managers, who can act as expatriates or repositories and transfer agents of the home country's success recipes.

The third archetype of administrative heritage is the *international coordinator*. This centrally managed firm's international success does not build primarily on home-country FSAs embodied in products exported internationally (as was the case with the centralised exporter), it also does not simply transfer FSAs to foreign subsidiaries to replicate home-country success (as was the case with the international projector). The international coordinator builds on a tradition of managing international operations, both upstream and downstream, through a tightly controlled but still flexible logistics function. International operations are specialised in specific value-added activities and form vertical value chains across borders. The MNE's key FSAs are in efficiently linking these geographically dispersed operations through seamless logistics. Many large MNEs in natural resources industries fit this archetype. They search for relevant resources internationally, manufacture in the most cost-efficient locations, and sell their products wherever there is demand for them.

The fourth and final archetype of administrative heritage is the *multi-centred MNE*. This firm's international success does not build primarily on knowledge-based FSAs developed in the home country. The multi-centred MNE consists of a set of entrepreneurial subsidiaries abroad, which are key to knowledge-based FSA development. National responsiveness is the foundation of the international strategy. The non-location-bound FSAs that hold these firms together are minimal: common financial governance, and the identity and specific business interests of the founders or main owners (typically entrepreneurial families or financial investors). Ultimately, the multi-centred MNE should be viewed as a portfolio of largely independent businesses.

Although these four archetypes probably describe the bulk of most large MNEs, especially the *Fortune 500* ones, there are other types. For example, in the late nineteenth century, several mainly British and Dutch freestanding companies were set up abroad. Another MNE that does not fit one of the four archetypes includes many firms in the emerging economy MNEs. These firms typically derive their strengths from building on generally available resources in their home country, such as low-cost labour, and various forms of government support, such as access to capital, usage of the government international trade and investment apparatus, and so on; they thrive on recombining whatever FSAs they may possess with resources accessed abroad. However, irrespective of the form of MNE, the commonality among all types is the transfer of at least some FSAs across borders.

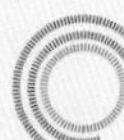

SPOTLIGHT 5.1

Who owns Australian agriculture?

Agricultural investments and exports are quickly growing with the urbanisation of Asian countries. David Irvine AO, chairman of the Foreign Investment Review board, has advised that 13.6 per cent of Australian agricultural land had some form of foreign ownership (Irvine 2017). He said that in 2015–16, foreign investment in agriculture had increased by 80 per cent over the previous year to AUD$4.6 billion dollars. A report by KPMG and Sydney University in 2017 has advised that Chinese investments in agriculture were AUD$1.2 billion in 2016, which is a tripling of Chinese investment in 2015 (KPMG and University of Sydney 2017). Chinese investment in agricultural land is includes the purchase of the S. Kidman and Co., a pastoral company which owns 1.3 per cent of Australia's total land area. The cattle herd is expected to increase to 20 000 head after an AUD$19 million investment in capital improvements. The acquisition was made by a JV of Hancock Prospecting and Shanghai CRED Real Estate Stock Co. Ltd.

Bloomberg reported that Shanghai CRED Real Estate made other purchases in 2016, including Yukka Munga Station and Elizabeth Station through its Australian operating arm Shanghai Zenneth (2016). These kinds of investments appear to be strategic, especially in regard to a report by the ANZ bank, which estimates that the rural sector will export an extra AUD$0.7 to $1.7 trillion by 2050 (Efrat 2016). The increase in demand for Australian agricultural exports will also attract further investment from MNEs, who would expect rural commodity prices to lift.

QUESTIONS

1. Why would a Chinese MNE want to invest in Australian agriculture?
2. By which archetype would these investments be categorised?

WEBLINKS
SPOTLIGHT QUESTIONS

The advantages of location

The MNE's economic success does not occur in a spatially homogeneous environment: location matters. Specifically, many firms are successful internationally because they take advantage of a favourable local environment. Location advantages represent the full set of strengths characterising a specific location, and useable by firms operating in that location.

Locational strengths should always be assessed relative to the useable strengths of other locations. Such strengths are really stocks of resources accessible to firms operating locally, and not accessible, or less so, to firms lacking local operations. Location advantages are often instrumental to the type of FSAs that can be developed by locally operating firms relative to firms operating elsewhere. For example, abundant natural resources may help the creation of successful firms in the natural resource industry. A superior educational system – another location advantage – will support firms that build on sophisticated human resource skills. For similar reasons, the presence of a demanding and sophisticated local market for specific products will likely foster local innovation in the relevant industry.

Location advantages do not confer an equal strength to all locally operating firms vis-à-vis firms operating elsewhere. Rather, the more effective and efficient use of location advantages by some firms – usually the combination of these location advantages with specific proprietary resources – may confer to them an additional FSA over other locally operating firms. This may explain why only a few firms from world-renowned domestic industries, such as the French perfume industry, have been able to grow internationally.

Location advantages can vary widely in their geographical scope. In some cases, a location advantage accrues to all firms operating in a country; for instance, if the government has created a favourable tax regime for specific economic activities, or general business incentives for skill upgrading of human resources. In some cases, location advantages accrue only to firms operating in part of a country. Economic clusters, for example, are usually located in only part of a country. The physical locations of the firms that constitute the heart of the cluster determine the cluster boundaries. In other cases, location advantages reach across country borders. The creation of cross-border location advantages is one of the key purposes of most regional trading and investment agreements, intended at least partly to confer a location advantage to insiders at the expense of outsiders.

Common MNE motivations to invest abroad

Why would an MNE want to engage in FDI in a host country? The answer is that an MNE should engage in FDI only if the host country confers a location advantage relative to the home country. In each case, the value proposition of the foreign activity must be more attractive than alternative value propositions at home. We can distinguish among four motivations to perform activities in a host country rather than at home. (To note that the four motivations included here have been well documented in the international business literature; see Dunning 1992, for example.)

The first motivation, *natural resource seeking*, entails the search for physical, financial or human resources in host countries. These resources are, in principle, not proprietary, and their availability in host countries (which constitutes the location advantage of those countries) means that investment abroad leads to higher value creation than investment at home. A precondition to such investment is that the host-country institutional environment allows foreign MNEs to access these resources.

The second motivation, *market seeking*, reflects the search for customers in host countries. Firms are market seeking when they conclude that deploying productive activities and selling in the foreign market confers higher value to the firm than engaging in alternative investment projects at home. The host-country location advantage is the presence of customers willing and able to purchase the firm's products. Note that market seeking is not the same as mere exporting: market seeking involves business activities in the host country, based on resource bundles transferred there over which the MNE retains strategic control.

The third motivation for an MNE to invest abroad, *strategic resource seeking,* is the desire to gain access to advanced resources in the sphere of upstream knowledge, downstream knowledge, administrative knowledge or reputational resources. These resources, which constitute the host-country location advantages, are in principle not generally accessible, in contrast to the resources sought with natural resource seeking and market seeking. Therefore, this type of FDI typically involves taking over other companies, engaging in alliance activity or becoming an insider in foreign knowledge clusters. The underlying reasons to engage in strategic resource seeking typically include the goal to become an established industry player in a set of strategically important knowledge development centres or output markets.

Finally, *efficiency seeking* is a firm's desire to capitalise on environmental changes that make specific locations in the MNE's international network of operations more attractive than before for the consolidation or concentration of specific activities. Such environmental changes may include technological breakthroughs allowing greater scale economies; an increased industry focus on innovation, triggering higher required R&D investments; customer-induced, shorter product cycles; and the reduction of trade and investment barriers through regional agreements such as NAFTA and the EU. Here, the location advantages of the various relevant countries may change relative to each other, making one more attractive than another and, therefore, more likely to receive new FDI. (To note an MNE, in principle, could restructure its existing network of affiliates and engage in rationalisation investments without the prior occurrence of substantial environmental change but, in practice, such environmental change is usually the key driver of restructuring.)

MULTIPLE-CHOICE QUESTION

SPOTLIGHT 5.2

H&M's operations and experience in Asia

Retail outlets have been benefitting from cheap imports from Asia. Asian low wages and the host governments' willingness to invest in infrastructure has created opportunities for many MNEs. Hennes & Mauritz (H&M) is one such retail company, which now has a global footprint.

The company's 2016 annual report advised that H&M had operations in 64 markets and that China was the fifth-largest of these markets, where it employed an average of 10 224 people (H&M 2016). The company reported four Hong Kong-based and three China-based subsidiaries. A major benefit of H&M's operations in Asia is the sourcing of low-cost production from local suppliers. This can cause problems for the company, however, because H&M can be criticised for the actions of its suppliers. An example of this was the reported rioting in a factory in Myanmar, owned by a Chinese-based company, over the working conditions for its employees (Butler 2016). This factory is one of 40 that H&M deals with in Myanmar; the relationship has been suspended because of the incident. To resolve these kinds of problems, H&M has been working with its suppliers to maintain a fair living wage. Although the progress on this seems to be lagging in Myanmar and in other South-East Asian economies; a report from the International Labour Organization has advised that 738 000 Myanmar garment workers usually work 51.6 hours per week, similar to workers in Cambodia, Laos, Vietnam and Pakistan. The average daily wage in the Myanmar garment industry is US$3.40 for an eight-hour day (Huynh 2016). This type of reporting on daily wages can be a public relation nightmare for an MNE operating in the area, however, there is evidence that some companies like H&M are trying to instigate change.

QUESTIONS

1. What benefits would H&M realise from outsourcing the manufacture of their garments?
2. Name some problems that this approach can cause for H&M.

WEBLINKS
SPOTLIGHT QUESTIONS

Implications of FDI strategy for MNE performance

International business managers must reflect on the MNE's strengths, relative to rival companies, and the MNE's ability to match its distinct resource base, with the challenges and opportunities found in the international environment, thereby creating value and satisfying shareholder needs.

The question then arises whether an international expansion program is likely to improve MNE performance. A vast international business literature attempts to answer the question whether international expansion and the related increase of international diversification (for example, the share of foreign investment to total investment, foreign sales to total sales or foreign production to total production) is likely to have positive effects on the MNE's return and risk. The answer is that it depends on several factors.

First, at the project level, the MNE should compare the expected net present value per invested monetary unit in foreign expansion with that of domestic expansion, considering a variety of risk factors. MNEs should undertake foreign expansion projects only if these make more economic sense than domestic projects. MNEs should expand internationally until, at the margin, the next domestic and foreign expansion projects are equally attractive.

Second, the international transfer of FSAs, whether embodied in final products (leading to scale economies), intermediate products such as R&D and marketing knowledge (leading to scope economies, as benefits are gained from transferring and sharing valuable knowledge across borders) or coordinating skills (leading to benefits of exploiting national differences), is not costless. In most cases, even internationally transferable FSAs need to be complemented by additional, location-bound FSAs in host countries. In more general terms, even with a strong recombination capability (entailing entrepreneurial dynamism, available excess resources and access to untapped resources in host environments), international success requires substantial investments, learning and legitimacy creation over time.

Third, even if the necessary investments in location-bound knowledge have been made, and both learning and legitimacy-building have occurred in host nations, the MNE's growth will not necessarily lead to improved economic performance. Substantial adaptation to host-country environments will increase the costs of internal governance. Central headquarters, faced with increased bounded rationality and bounded reliability problems, will find it more difficult to select particular investment trajectories and to choose among alternative international expansion patterns, each favouring specific subunits in the organisation located in different countries.

Expanding internationally can have important effects on the firm in terms of where and how it creates value. However, the keys to successful international business strategy – and thus the MNE's performance – are its FSAs relative to rivals, and its effectiveness and efficiency in deploying and augmenting these FSAs across borders (Verbeke & Zaman Forootan 2012).

SPOTLIGHT 5.3

Tesla's operations in China

China has increasingly become strategically important to MNEs as it continues to become more urbanised. This is true for Tesla, which is arguably the world's most innovative company, with revenue increasing from US$318.5 million in 2015 to US$1065 million in 2016 (Tesla Annual Report 2017). These figures are compared to an increase in total revenues from US$4000 million in 2015 to US$7000 million in 2016 (Cendrowski 2017; Lambert 2017b). China accounted for over 14 per cent of Tesla's revenues through 2016 and appears to be increasing its total share. Tesla's footprint in China accounts for nearly 12 per cent of the MNE's total property plant and equipment as at the end of the 2016 calendar year. Fortune International reported that JL Warren Capital, a leading equity research firm focused on Chinese companies, advised that Tesla sales had increased 350 per cent in the first three months of 2017 compared to the first three months of 2016 (Cendrowski 2017). This increase is extraordinary and highlights the vast potential a market like China can create for MNEs.

International trade works both ways; China's electric vehicle manufacturer BYD Motors has advised the US cable network CNBC that it is expanding its US sales, with the completion of their Lancaster production facility (Shaffer 2017). BYD achieved 100 000 unit sales compared to Tesla's 76 000 in 2016. The growth of the electric car as an alternative to the fuel-driven automobiles has brought new players to the market, to compete alongside the traditional General Motors, Toyota, Mercedes and so on. There has been reports that Apple has been working with a Chinese partner to develop an electric car battery (Lambert 2017a; Rivera 2017). Like in every industry, multinational trade enables MNEs to access large markets for their products; however, it also brings greater competition from corporations that have large balance sheets. Tesla appears to be winning this battle and increasing its sales, although any decrease in relative quality will quickly diminish any comparative advantages that the company may have.

QUESTIONS

SPOTLIGHT QUESTIONS

1. Which archetype could Tesla operations in China be categorised?
2. What would be the main motivation for Tesla's movement into China?

International business strategy takeaway messages

The above analysis suggests that international business managers should answer the following seven basic questions in international strategy formation.

1. What is our distinct resource base, including elements of our administrative heritage, that provides internationally transferable FSAs?
2. Which value-added activities in which foreign location(s) will permit us to exploit and augment our distinct resource base to the fullest?
3. What are the expected costs and difficulties we will face when transferring this distinct resource base?
4. What specific resource recombination (associated with each alternative foreign entry and operating mode) will be required to make the proposed international value-added activities successful?
5. Do we have the required resource recombination capability in-house?
6. What are the costs and benefits of using complementary resources of external actors to fill resource gaps?
7. What are the main bounded rationality and bounded reliability problems we will face when extending the geographic scope of our firm's activities, given the changed boundaries of the firm, the changed linkages with outside stakeholders and the changes in our internal functioning?

FDI into ASEAN

The recent trends in FDI flows by groups of economies are presented in Figure 5.1. In 2016, FDI flows were lower than in previous periods by approximately 2 per cent globally due to low economic growth and the perception by MNE's of significant policy risks. The performance of ASEAN nations differed in attracting FDI with five receiving more FDI (including Vietnam, Cambodia and Myanmar); two

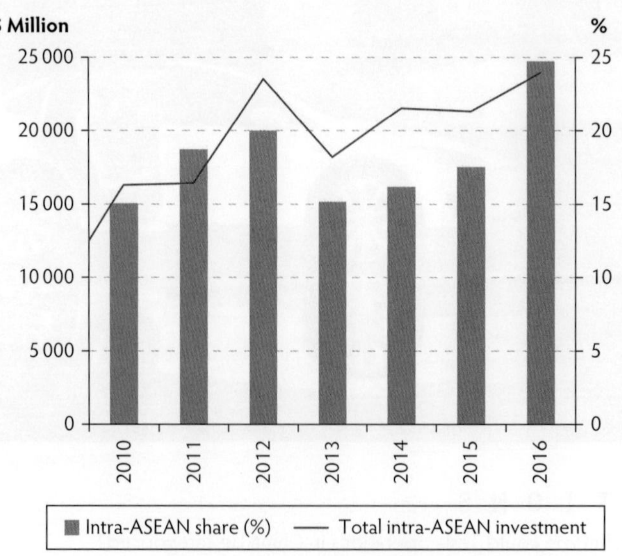

FIGURE 5.1 Intra-ASEAN investment flows, 2010–16 (millions of dollars)

Source: ASEAN Secretariat 2016, reproduced with permission of the Association of Southeast Asian Nations (ASEAN)

remained constant and three declined (ASEAN, 2016). FDI inflows were noted in the manufacturing sector, with continued investment expansion in MNE and equity capital financing. The level of inter-regional investment continues as the largest source of FDI flows underscores the increase in inter-regional connectedness.

In 2017, developing Asian countries noted FDI flows reducing for the first time in five years by 14 per cent to US$443 billion, but FDI remains the most popular method of finance in developing countries. An improved economic outlook for major Asian economies is expected to see an increase in FDI inflows as countries such as China and Indonesia review their policies to attract FDI, and other Asian countries strengthen their position in their production networks.

Foreign and ASEAN companies are undertaking or planning to extend their footprint in South-East Asia because of the improved economic and investment performance of the region, and the recent measures taken to facilitate and support FDI. Regional interconnection is highlighted through the establishment of regional headquarters and production hubs, and regional production networks. At present, investors view South-East Asia as a promising region for FDI and the continued investment in the ASEAN member countries will support the economic development of the region.

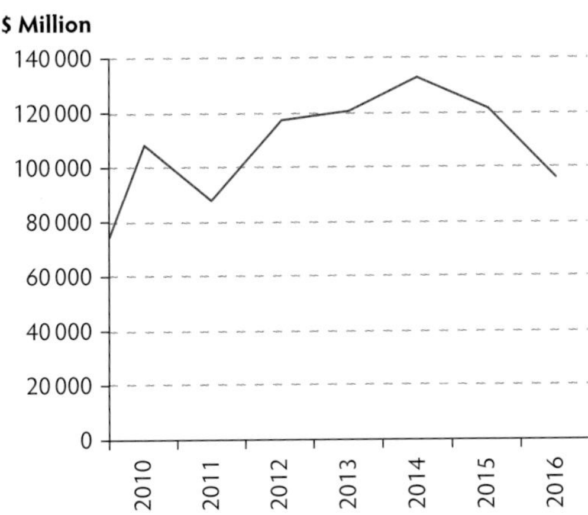

FIGURE 5.2 FDI flows in ASEAN countries, 2010–16 (millions of dollars)
Source: ASEAN Secretariat 2016, reproduced with permission of ASEAN

The role of government in FDI

The underlying goal of FDI is the maximisation of shareholder wealth; that is, business decisions and investments are made with the goal of making the business owners wealthier. Government agencies and state-owned enterprises (SOEs) make up an important segment of shareholders in many emerging and developing countries in the Asian region; for example, in Singapore there is Neptune Orient Lines (shipping), DBS Bank (development finance), Keppel Corporation and Jurong Shipyard; and in China there is Sinopec Group, China National Petroleum Corporation and State Grid Corporation of China. SOEs are also known as government corporations, government business enterprises, public enterprises and public sector units among other names. They are important as shareholders but also as large consumers of goods and services, including technology, office furniture, motor vehicles, and legal, accounting and consulting services sourced from local and foreign companies. In addition, SOEs influence the purchasing and contracting of privately-owned companies; for example, the Indian government undertakes public housing works by contracting to private companies. SOEs are now a global force, with most large SOEs engaged in international trade; the top eight countries with the highest SOE shares are China, UAE, Russia, Indonesia, Malaysia, Saudi Arabia, India and Brazil, which account for 20 per cent of world trade; China's SOEs accounted for 10 per cent of world merchandise exports in 2010 and has now become the world's largest goods (Kowalski et al. 2013; Eckart 2016).

A few centrally planned economies, such as Cambodia, China, Laos and Vietnam, have moved from having largely state-owned industries to promoting privatisation primarily to attract FDI. Privatisation is a country's government divesting its ownership and operation of a business by transferring it to a private company. This gives opportunities for foreign companies to enter transition economies; the foreign companies bring cultural influences and add, through sale proceeds, hard currency foreign reserves that can be used to reduce sovereign debt. The reform process is different for each country and is largely dependent on where the country started out; for example, if the country had a long period of communism, whether the political regime is stable, or the degree of industrialisation versus agricultural in the country's economy, will each affect the reformation process differently.

In contrast to the experience in Eastern European countries, Asian countries enjoy a more favourable transitioning from SOEs to free trade. This has been aided by important reforms introduced in agricultural land use and ownership, and in financial markets. In Vietnam, for example, reforms in the agriculture sector allowed farmers to sell production at free market prices; later they were permitted to open their own sales outlets. In China, reform occurred gradually in both the agricultural and financial sectors to ensure the stabilisation of inflation that occurred in response to the changes of opening the market. Agricultural reforms granted medium term leases for farming land and permitted farmers to sell more produce than the amount required to be given to the state. In the early 1990s two stock exchanges, the Shanghai Stock Exchange (SSE) and the Shenzhen Stock Exchange (SZSE), were established to provide a market place for the sale of SOEs. In 2017, the SSE and SZSE have over 3100 companies listed, and are among the largest stock exchanges globally in terms of capitalisation. The stock exchanges play a fundamental role in raising corporate capital for business investments and projects, and they facilitate private corporate ownership for SOEs. There are two classes of shares traded on the two Chinese stock exchanges. A-shares are shares of mainland China-based companies and are quoted in Chinese renminbi. While historically these shares were only available to mainland China citizens, since 2003 A-shares can now be traded by selected foreign institutions through the Qualified Foreign Institutional Investor scheme (QFII). B-shares are available for trade by both domestic and foreign investors, but as they are quoted in foreign currencies such as the US dollar and are generally difficult for Chinese investors to access. Although foreigners can now invest on the two Chinese stock exchanges, there is a limit of 20 per cent on the repatriation of funds per month to foreign countries. So, despite China's attempts to be seen as an advanced global economy, the restrictions on foreign investors are viewed as major limitations in China's development.

Nevertheless, SOEs continue to provide governments with an instrument for societal and public value creation; they are a vehicle for working with other stakeholders to achieve those goals. In the present-day economy, it is increasingly important for the SOE to be actively owned and managed, and to avoid competing unfairly in markets where the private sector can deliver the goods and services that people want more efficiently and effectively (PWC 2015). For soon-to-be privatised SOEs, the government involved should consider how to extract the most value for the country; the motivation to retain state ownership will change as economic conditions also alter. Air New Zealand, for example, was privatised in 1989 but renationalised in 2001. Commentators suggest that the New Zealand government wanted to rescue the failing airline because it thought that ensuring there was a national airline to support the New Zealand tourism industry was important. This move has paid-off since Air New Zealand is now ranked highly; it was the top airline in 2014 and its number of international arrivals increased by 51 per cent between 2000 and 2013 (PWC 2015, p. 17).

International transactions and the balance of payments

The balance of payments (BOP) is a record of a country's transactions with the rest of the world over a period of time. BOP is presented using the principles and format of double-entry bookkeeping. The BOP of home countries and host countries is important to a range of stakeholders, including managers, investors and governments because it affects and is affected by macroeconomic variables; for example, exchange rates, interest rates and gross domestic product. There are three overarching reasons why BOP is important.

BALANCE OF PAYMENTS (BOP) the record of all of a country's economic transactions between one country and the rest of the world for a given period.

1. The BOP provides detailed information relating to the demand for and supply of a country's currency; therefore, is an indicator of the country's foreign exchange rate. For example, if Australia imports more than it exports, then the supply of Australian dollars is likely to exceed the demand in the foreign market and that situation will force a depreciation of the Australian dollar. As a result, firms trading with or investing in Australia may experience foreign exchange gains or losses. This situation may also trigger the introduction or removal of foreign exchange controls.
2. The BOP can indicate the country's potential as a trading partner for other countries. If a country has a BOP deficit, it may impose measures to restrict imports and control cash disbursement, such as dividends, interest, license fees and royalties, to foreign firms and investors. Conversely, where a country has a BOP surplus, the country would encourage imports and investments by foreign firms and loosen its cash controls.
3. The BOP can indicate the international competitiveness of a country because it signals the international trade performance of the country.

Some real-life examples of international transactions included on the BOP of each trading country include:

- Chinese Oppo invested in a manufacturing facility in India to produce smartphones
- Chinese Huawei provided operational and consulting services and equipment in telecommunications globally, including to the US, France, India and Turkey
- Malaysian Petronas invested in Gladstone LNG Australia in 2010 and paid dividends back to the parent company
- The BOP provides a systematic method for classifying the exceptionally large number of international transactions that occur each year.

CURRENT ACCOUNT an account in the BOP that records all international economic transactions involving the income or payment for the import and export of goods and services.

CAPITAL ACCOUNT the record of all international economic transactions relating to the transfers of financial assets, and the acquisition and disposal of non-financial assets.

FINANCIAL ACCOUNT the record of all international economic transactions relating to direct investments, portfolio investments and other asset investments.

NET ERRORS AND OMISSION ACCOUNT the resulting net credit or net debit balance that results when all actual BOP entries are collated and finalised.

OFFICIAL RESERVE ACCOUNT the record of foreign currencies and securities held by the government generally in its central bank. It is a subdivision of the capital account. It is used to balance the payments; that is, it will decrease when there is a net deficit and increase when there is a net surplus on the BOP.

DOUBLE-ENTRY BOOKKEEPING the recording of financial transactions in which every transaction has equal and opposite effects on at least two different accounts. This keeps the accounting equation Assets = Liabilities plus owners' equity in balance.

INTERNATIONAL MONETARY FUND (IMF) an organisation of 189 countries working to develop global monetary cooperation, secure financial stability and facilitate international trade.

Accounting for BOP

The BOP is made up of three primary sub-accounts: the current account, the capital account and the financial account. There are two additional sub-accounts to consider, the net errors and omissions account and the official reserve account. The BOP must always balance, but a sub-account of the BOP may be imbalanced. In measuring international economic activity, shareholders need to recognise that the BOP tracks cash movements over the period. In addition, although double-entry bookkeeping is employed, occasionally errors and omissions occur in practice as entries are recorded in the sub-accounts independently.

BOP current account

The BOP current account includes the export and import of goods and services; that is, it records international transactions which result in cash inflows or cash outflows. In 2017, countries such as Australia, UAE, Singapore and Germany maintained a trade surplus, whereas countries with a trade deficit included Vietnam, Hong Kong, the US and the UK. A deficit on the current account indicates that a country imports more than it exports, and this imbalance must be financed by borrowing from foreign entities or by redrawing its accumulated foreign wealth. A current account deficit, therefore, indicates a reduction in the country's net foreign wealth.

The current account is divided into four categories: merchandise trade, services trade, factor income and transfers.

1. *Merchandise trade*: this represents payments and receipts for exports and imports of goods; for example, coal, LNG, electronics, smartphones and cars. The trade balance represents the net merchandise export of a country; that is, if there is a deficit the country relies on imports of goods.
2. *Services trade*: this represents payments and receipts for exports and imports of services; for example, financial and legal services, engineering consulting, royalties, insurance premiums and tourist expenditure. The rapid advancement in information technology has resulted in new types of tradable services. For instance, many Australian accounting practices outsource data entry to the Philippines, in which case, Australia has imported an accounting service from Philippines.
3. *Factor income*: this represents payments and receipts associated with investments made in prior periods such as dividends, interest and other income from foreign investments, as well as salaries paid to non-resident employees.
4. *Transfers*: this represents one-way payments and receipts; for example, foreign aid, reparations, gifts and grants from one country to another.

BOP capital and financial accounts

The capital and financial accounts record all international transactions of financial assets. The capital account shows transfers across country borders of non-produced non-financial assets; for example, patents, licenses and trademarks, and capital or financial asset transfers by residents who move to a foreign country. The capital account category was recently separated from the financial account by the International Monetary Fund (IMF) with capital account items being relatively minor in magnitude when compared with the financial account.

The financial account is divided into three payment categories: direct investment, portfolio investment and other capital investment.

FDI can be seen as the allocation of resource bundles – such as combinations of physical, financial, human, knowledge and reputational resources – by an MNE in a host country. The resource bundles are so the MNE can performing business activities and retain strategic control. The direct investment component of the financial account measures the balance of capital paid to invest in fixed assets in foreign countries to conduct business operations while retaining control over the assets.

Portfolio investment represents the net balance of capital flows that involve the long-term financial assets but do not result in the transfer of control.

Other capital investment consists of other short- and long-term capital investments, including currency transactions, trade credits, trade credits, and debtor and creditor transfers relating to foreign trade.

BOP net errors and omission account

The recording of receipts and payments relating to international transactions is undertaken at separate times, in various places and using different methods. Although most merchandise trade-related transactions can be recorded with a degree of accuracy, cross-border electronic transactions relating to financial movements are more difficult to monitor. As a result, a balancing item is always presented on the BOP as a net error or omission.

BOP official reserves account

The official reserves account represents the total reserves held by a country's official monetary authority and is used to balance the payments from year to year. It includes official reserve assets, such as major currencies used in international trade and financial transactions, gold and special drawing rights (SDRs). In 2014, the Chinese government's foreign exchange reserves were the largest in the world but, by 2017, they slipped to their lowest point in six years. This is primarily due to Chinese investors making investments in other foreign countries and the Chinese government drawing down on reserves to stop the effect of the outflow on the value of their currency, the yuan. The depletion of the reserves, and the depreciation of the yuan against the US dollar, are indicators of a weakening financial system, which has resulted in government intervention through the tightening of controls on the payment of cross-border funds and a changing of the formula for setting the daily yuan price. This example illustrates the significance of government intervention in the setting of the exchange rate; that is, whether a country has a fixed exchange rate or a floating exchange rate system.

Where a fixed exchange rate regime exists, the government of the country officially sets the exchange rate for its currency. Where a floating exchange rate is used, the exchange rate is set by the foreign exchange market based on supply and demand for a currency compared with another countries currency. The official monetary authority may trade in local currency to adjust the floating exchange rate, for instance if there is a volatile market, or intervene indirectly by adjusting the interest rates to impact the flow of investor funds. Countries with a floating exchange rate regime include the G7 nations (Canada, France, Germany, Italy, Japan, the UK and the US), the Philippines, Australia, Thailand and Indonesia.

MULTIPLE-CHOICE QUESTION

FIXED EXCHANGE RATE
an exchange rate regime where the value of a currency is set relative to the value of another single currency, a basket of currencies or another measure of value, such as gold at a specified rate. It is often referred to as a pegged exchange rate.

FLOATING EXCHANGE RATE
an exchange rate regime where the value of a currency naturally responds to the supply and demand for currencies in the foreign exchange market. The current price is set by the foreign exchange market based on supply and demand for a currency compared with other currencies.

Economic crises and the impact on BOP

Foreign currency is required by an extensive range of stakeholders, including: companies, for the payment of imports and the receipts from exports; investors, for investments in currencies, bonds, shares and other financial instruments; and currency traders, visitors and expatriate workers. The BOP is based on the premise that the exchange rate is derived from the balancing of the net flows of foreign exchange from the current account with the net flows of foreign exchange from the capital and financial account. This approach can be used to analyse international economic conditions and to assess international economic relationships.

There have been several financial crises throughout history, including the Latin American debt crisis in 1982; the Asian crisis in 1997; and the global financial crisis in 2008. In 2017, the UK voted to leave the EU and this caused great concern in terms of the economic ramifications. By examining these cases, it can be seen that, although there are many similarities in their causes, each crisis has unique characteristics from which we can gain insights.

The Latin American debt crisis

The Latin American debt crisis originated in the early 1980s when countries such as Brazil, Argentina, Mexico and more than 20 other developing countries that had borrowed enormous amounts of money from international lenders, including the WB and private lenders, were not able to repay their debts. The purpose of the funding was to enhance economic stability and reduce poverty through a program of infrastructure development and industrialisation. The economies of these Latin American countries were buoyant in the early 1970s and oil rich nations believed that lending to the governments of these countries (so that they had a sovereign debt) represented a safe investment. At its peak, the WB estimated that debt levels in many Latin American countries exceeded 53.6 per cent of their GDP, with interest payments making up 22.3 per cent of export income; it noted that debt levels had been growing at approximately 20 per cent per year (Dillinger 1997). Bank borrowings were generally made in US dollars and on a floating-rate basis.

The source of the crisis can be found in the world economic recession and the dramatic increase in the world's oil price. High oil prices were associated with increases in inflation and unemployment, and a tightening of monetary policy leading to increased real interest rates in most developed nations. The global recession affected the economies of the Latin American nations and the higher interest rates became unaffordable, thus making it impossible for these nations to service their debt obligations. The sharp decline in international reserves forced the Mexican government to devalue their currency, the peso, and hence increase the amount of US dollars owed to international lenders (Pastor 1989). The Mexican government ran out of funds to pay its debts and other nations in the region soon found themselves in a similar situation.

There are several underlying causes of the crisis. The lending process, known as petrodollar recycling, began with the OPEC cartel increasing the oil price, resulting in them having a large amount of US dollars that needed to be invested. In many cases these petrodollars were invested in less-developed countries (LDCs). Investments in LDCs were enticing due to economies of scale – one large loan could be made rather than many small loans to domestic investors and developers; the loans offered a high yield at floating interest rates; and there was a notion that a sovereign government was guaranteed as a country cannot go bankrupt (Ewert 1988).

The Latin American debt crisis was effectively managed out of catastrophe through refinancing arrangements brokered by the US Treasury and the IMF.

The Asian financial crisis

The Asian financial crisis began in mid-1997 when the government in Thailand decided to no longer peg their domestic currency (the baht) to the US dollar. Following this, many of their Asian neighbours followed suit by allowing their currencies to float, which resulted in stock market declines, reduced import revenues, and created widespread economic turbulence in the Asian region and in other nations, including Russia, Japan, Europe and the US. Until this time, Thailand had experienced a period of economic expansion that attracted international interest in the country through capital inflows, as well as a supply of products and services. High spending and low savings fuelled Thai domestic price bubbles, particularly in real estate and products, which resulted in higher interest rates. Since the Thai baht had been linked to the US dollar, it was protected from depreciation because of these inflationary factors and international investors found Thailand to be an attractive place to invest. Unlike the Latin American Debt crisis, which was exposed to risk via sovereign governments, the Asian financial crisis was primarily due to the local banks and investors.

There were numerous interwoven causes of the Asian financial crisis. There was a large capital inflow into the domestic banking sector and Thailand was welcoming of these funds to support the growth of the country. However, the amount of inflow of funds was greater that the banks could utilise in high quality loans. As a result, the banks made riskier loans, lending to developers based on past performance rather than on basis of sound business plans. Poor investment choices were made by the banks partly because of the close interrelationships that existed between financial and commercial institutions, and weak corporate governance regimes. Simultaneously, developers and other companies were borrowing large amounts to grow the economy, and the Thai government was borrowing to fund an infrastructure development plan. Although initially the oversupply of funds put downward pressure on interest rates, the growing demand soon pushed interest rates higher and borrowing became awfully expensive. This situation made Thailand susceptible to foreign investors losing confidence in its economy and Thailand became vulnerable to losing a large outflow of funds. At this time, the US dollar strengthened against European and Japanese currencies, making imports from these countries cheaper. Products from Thailand and the Asian regions were not as competitively priced. In July 2017, foreign investors began to recognise the weakness in the baht and began to sell their baht in exchange for US dollars, which put downward pressure on the Thai domestic currency. The Thai government detached the baht from the US dollar to stop the decline, but the decline continued and dropped more than 20 per cent in a five-week period.

A rescue package was put together by the IMF and other countries, including Japan. The bailout package at the time of US$8billion was second only to the US$50 billion bailout package given to Mexico during the Latin American debt crisis, and it was subject to the criticism that funding was misallocated due to corruption in Thailand. Although the crisis began in Thailand, it spread rapidly to other Asian countries and then worldwide. The contagion of the monetary and financial crisis spread from one country to another due to the integration of national economies. Most South-East Asian countries were experiencing similarly high growth to Thailand, with large loans being made to high-risk ventures. However, the decline in demand for products from Thailand was similarly experienced by other nations in the region; the integrated trading activities affected the reciprocal demand for South-East Asian products. Further, when foreign investors recognised the crisis in Thailand, they realised that it could happen in other South-East Asian countries with similar economic conditions, and so foreign investors began to withdrew funds.

In addition, foreign investors also reconsidered their international investments outside of Asia where they believed similar effects could occur. Russia was particularly singled out, and the withdrew of funds there caused a massive devaluation in the rouble. The Hong Kong stock market dropped markedly, and interest rates were increased to stop funds leaving the country. Japan was affected by a decline in exports to the region and it had subsidiaries in many South-East Asian countries that were affected by the downturn in local economic conditions. Latin American countries were affected by the reduced demand for exports from its region because of the increased demand for cheap Asian product. European and US companies were similarly affected by the change in trade patterns, and losses were experienced because of loan exposure and reduced returns from subsidiaries that were set up in Asian countries.

The Asian financial crisis of the late 1990s provides an interesting insight into the effects of internationalisation and the interwoven markets that it creates. Because of the crisis, much needed financial and government reforms were implemented in Asian countries. Although the currency collapse and resultant BOP difficulties were the visible cause of the Asian crisis, the underlying issues related to corporate governance, financial management and banking stability played a major part as well. Investors in South-East Asia had largely provided funds to local banks and, despite this, it was largely believed that the government would come to the aid of these private businesses if they were to experience financial difficulty. Additionally, the close interrelationships between businesses, financial institutions and the governments meant that the interests of other groups, such as creditors, employees and small shareholders, were not considered. Further, the banking sector lacked the regulations and structure that had become the industry standard throughout the world. Although it is 20 years since the Asian financial crisis, commentators have suggested the possibility of a second one. In early 2016, China encouraged its Asian neighbours to reduce domestic interest rates. In Japan, this resulted in negative interest rates and forced the increasing borrowing of funds on global equity markets. The Japanese yen increased in value, which resulted in increased costs of exports, thereby weakening the economy.

Government interventions – such as import tariffs, subsidies, and trade barriers – to mitigate these crises, will affect trade and FDI, which could impact a company's profitability.

The global financial crisis

From late 2007, the US economy experienced a severe financial crisis that led to a global recession officially lasting over three-and-a-half years in the US; globally the recovery has been slow, with world economies remaining fragile to this day. On 14 September 2008, Lehman Brothers, a major US investment bank with a global footprint, filed for bankruptcy sparking a major crisis of confidence in global financial markets. Stock prices plummeted around the world and unemployment rose markedly. The crisis caused the collapse of securities markets worldwide and was the worst recession since 1929.

The global economic downturn began as a credit crunch in the US, where property prices had escalated dramatically because they were funded by easy-to-get mortgage loans. There were several factors that contributed to the credit crunch in the US.

First, the repeal of the Glass–Steagall Act in 1999 resulted in restrictions on affiliations between investment and commercial banks being lifted. Additionally, banking institutions were permitted to undertake a larger range of activities, including insurance underwriting and stock market dealing activities. Consequently, funds from the previously tightly-regulated money market became available to customers who would previously been ineligible.

Second, several large economies, including Japan, China, Korea and OPEC members, had current account surpluses generated through the export of consumer goods and, in the case of OPEC, from the sale of petroleum to the world. This allowed economies to invest and lend substantial amounts to the US to earn income in the form of interest. Further, vast sums were being held in US dollars, which resulted in an elevated level of liquidity. The large amounts of ready funds were a key factor in keeping interest rates low. This low interest rate environment, and the lowering of credit standards by many US banks and mortgage lenders, created the means for many customers to afford mortgage financing for first homes and to trade-up to better ones. The subsequent excess demand for homes pushed prices up and created a property bubble. In addition, many homeowners withdrew equity from their homes to use for the purchase of consumer goods, many of which were imported from foreign markets thereby contributing to a US current account deficit.

As noted, many the mortgage loans made were to customers who would not previously have qualified for loans under a strict credit regime; these customers would not have been able to afford mortgage repayments at a higher interest rate. These loans are referred to as subprime mortgages. Subprime mortgages were generally not held by the originating bank, but instead they were packaged into mortgage-backed securities, and sold as investments on the open market to domestic and foreign banks and financiers. The US Federal Reserve began tightening monetary policy in 2004 so interest rates began to rise. The demand for credit slowed and house price stagnated before declining; subprime borrowers began to default, leading to the erosion of the capital base of banks and lending institutions globally. In the period following, consumer purchasing reduced dramatically and hence those businesses who relied on the credit market were severely impacted. For example, in the automotive industry, US production by Toyota was reduced by 40 per cent in 2009 due to a 60 per cent drop in exports in 2008; car sales in France reduced by 16 per cent and in Spain they reduced by approximately 60 per cent (Kirkup 2011).

The global economy is now showing signs of recovery from the recession, with jobs growth returning to pre-2007 levels and the stock market remaining strong. The global financial crisis was created through the availability of easy credit, and consumers and financial institutions taking on too much risk. This easy money funded an upward spiral of property prices and stock market values. The consistent current account deficits that marked the US economy indicated that it was living on money borrowed from foreign creditors and had failed to self-regulate the excess. The factors leading to the global financial crisis are like those discussed in earlier financial collapses and countries need to learn the lessons from this experience.

The European debt crisis

The EU comprises of 27 member nations that all must agree to any actions taken. In the past decade, five EU member nations – Spain, Greece, Ireland, Portugal and Italy – have experienced economic crises, resulting in their difficulty in meeting their financial commitments. The European debt crisis is of continuing concern for stakeholders in the financial affairs of these countries. Recent political events have caused social unrest, and poor economic management and the inability of leaders to make the tough decisions required to ensure economic improvement are indicators of instability in the region.

Since 2015, a rising number of unauthorised refugees have arrived in the EU, giving rise to the European migrant crisis. This has caused political unrest and economic consequences for the European nations the migrants have entered. In France, President Emmanuel Macron was elected on the promise of pro-business reforms, illustrated the mood of the country to reshape the political landscape and move away from mainstream political parties. In 2016, the UK voted to withdraw from the EU (Brexit is the popular term for this move) and in 2017, voters returned a hung parliament. The change in political climate appears to reflect the discontent of voters with the current economic, social and financial changes in the EU.

Countries continue to implement economic reforms to reduce public debt and manage monetary policy, while dealing with a social crisis and political turmoil. Global stakeholders, with interests in the EU, continue to express their concerns the economic and financial issues being experienced in the region.

Summary

Learning objective 1: Examine the theories related to international investment.

International investment is part of a trading company's strategy. Not only does a company buy and sell goods locally but they increasingly trade with consumers, businesses and governments in foreign countries. As a result, a company may decide that there is a competitive advantage to be gained, for instance by manufacturing goods or in setting up a regional production and distribution hub in another country. The movement of investment funds represents FDI in a foreign country, and facilitates the operation of an international business environment by financing resources, production, skills, technology and infrastructure

Learning objective 2: Consider FDI into ASEAN.

The forecast for economic growth in ASEAN continues to be positive making the region attractive for FDI. FDI is usually comes in the form of equity capital to finance investment projects; MNEs invest in all areas of an international economy, including manufacturing, finance and infrastructure. ASEAN companies also make investments in the region and contribute positively to its interconnectedness.

Learning objective 3: Understand how countries measure international economic transactions through the BOP.

The BOP records a country's international trading, borrowing and lending through three accounts: current account, capital and financial account, and reserves accounts. The sum of the balances of these three accounts must always equal zero, otherwise, to cover any shortfall, a country must either borrow more than it lends on the international market or use its reserves. The BOP can be seen as the bank account of a business, with the current account being the statement of income and expenditure, and the capital and financial accounts showing borrowing and lending. Therefore, the BOP explains the level of a country's imports versus its exports and, where there is a deficit (imports > exports), the capital and financial account shows how much the country borrowed from international markets to pay for the shortfall.

Learning objective 4: Appreciate how economic crises impact the BOP.

The business environment today is a dynamic market place with businesses being intertwined regionally and globally. Economic crises in one industry, country or region have an immediate impact on other industries and countries (for instance, by changes in interest rates, commodity prices and exchange rates). Government interventions resulting from these crises, include import tariffs, subsidies and trade barriers; these measures may impact a business's profitability because of their effect on the country's trade and FDI. The key features of almost every economic crisis in recent times have been excessive borrowing by consumers, businesses and governments, enticed by lowering of credit standards and low interest rates.

REVISION QUESTIONS

Revision questions

1. What are the four archetypes of administrative heritage? Discuss the importance of each.
2. When an MNE's reason for investing abroad is strategic resource seeking, what does this refer to?
3. What sparked a major crisis in confidence in global financial markets in 2008 and what was its affect?
4. Define FDI.
5. Explain what is meant by a current account deficit. Why is this so important in relation to FDI?

R&D ACTIVITIES

R&D activities

1. Find an MNE online which has just set up in a foreign country and explain why this country was chosen by the board.
2. Review Apple's operations in China. Why have Apple undertaken this strategy?
3. Refer to the Spotlight 5.3. Explain Tesla's distinct resource base that provides it with international transferable FSAs. Include a discussion on economies of scale, R&D, marketing knowledge and coordinating skills.

IB MASTERCLASS

Globalisation of finance: AIG Corporation

The collapse America International Group (AIG), a giant insurance company founded in China and headquartered in New York, the US, was a pivotal event in the global financial crisis. Today AIG offers insurance, pension plans, asset management and financial services in over 130 companies. The near-collapse of AIG came about in September 2008 during the global financial crisis and its ramifications were felt globally. The globalisation of finance has forced an examination of the roles of MNEs, banks, governments, the IMF and the WB, as well as the development of strategies to limit the effects of contagion in the global community.

Background

AIG was established in 1919 in Shanghai, China, as a general insurance agency. With business growing rapidly, it expanded into life insurance and opened branches throughout South-East Asia, including Malaysia, Indonesia, and the Philippines as well as in the US and Latin America. By the 1980s AIG offered a wide range of specialised products, including political risk, energy, transportation and shipping. In 1992, AIG was granted a foreign insurance license to operate in China – the first such license to be given.

Issues faced

AIG continued its worldwide expansion strategy throughout the remainder of the 1900s and early 2000s. In 2004, AIG reached a settlement with SEC and the Justice Department, relating to regulatory contraventions and investigations into the sale of non-traditional insurance products. In 2005, a fraud investigation resulted in the termination of the CEO and Chairman, Maurice R. Greenberg, with the payment of large fines and criminal charges for several senior executives.

The investigation resulted in the restatement of financial statements encompassing periods from 2000 to 2003 due to accounting errors.

During this time, AIG expanded into the credit default insurance market, taking on billions of dollars of risk associated with mortgages and using collateral on deposits to purchase the mortgage-backed securities. Although it insured the derivatives, AIG failed to purchase re-insurance against that risk.

The global financial crisis

In 2008, all major credit rating agencies downgraded AIG to below an AA- credit rating. Due to the provisions in AIG's agreement, the calls for collateral on its credit default swaps kicked in and AIG experienced an unprecedented call on its assets. Additionally, AIG experienced massive losses from taking its collateral and investing in high-yield, high-risk assets, including those backed by subprime home loans.

Because of the losses experienced by AIG and its falling stock price, the US federal government bailed out the company and took control of its business. AIG went through a period of rationalisation of its business through the sale of a few its businesses worldwide, while also defending several damages claims against the company.

Today

By the end of 2012, AIG had paid back the US government all monies owed, and again began on a growth path raising funds from domestic and international investors to use for expansion and acquisitions.

QUESTIONS

1. Throughout its history, AIG has been involved in global trade and expansion. What were the institutional voids relating to its expansion into China?
2. Was AIG capable of meeting its resource requirements in-house or did they need to outsource in the period from the global financial crisis to 2012? What are the costs and benefits of using external parties to fill the resource gap? How has this changed in AIG's current business operations?
3. AIG has had a long and interesting history. Explain the impact of the collapse of AIG on its stakeholders, including shareholders, other lenders, the US government, and its global subsidiaries and trading partners. How did these events impact on the BOP in the US and other stakeholder countries?

References

ASEAN Secretariat (2016). *ASEAN Investment Report 2016: Foreign Direct Investment and MSME Linkages*. September. Jakarta: ASEAN Secretariat.

Butler, S. (2016). H&M factories in Myanmar employed 14-year-old workers. *The Guardian*. Retrieved from www.theguardian.com/business/2016/aug/21/hm-factories-myanmar-employed-14-year-old-workers

Cendrowski, S. (2017). Tesla started 2017 with a sales boom in China [Press release]. *Fortune*, 2 May. Retrieved from http://fortune.com/2017/05/02/teslas-china-sales-boom-will-start-in-2017

Dillinger, W. (1997). Brazil's state debt crisis: lessons learned. The World Bank. Retrieved from http://documents.worldbank.org/curated/en/981201468743800265/Brazils-state-debt-crisis-lessons-learned

Dunning, J. (1992). *Multinational Enterprises and the Global Economy*. Reading: Addison-Wesley.

Eckart, J. (2016). Eight things you need to know about China's economy. World Economic Forum, 23 June. Retrieved from www.weforum.org/agenda/2016/06/8-facts-about-chinas-economy

Eden, L. & Miller, S.R. (2004). Distance matters: liability of foreignness, institutional distance and ownership strategy, in M.A. Hitt and J.L.C. Cheng (eds), *The Evolving Theory of the Multinational Firm: Advances in International Management*, Amsterdam: Elsevier.

Efrat, Z. (2016). What Asia's food boom means for Australia. Bluenotes, 7 October. Retrieved from https://bluenotes.anz.com/posts/2016/10/what-asia-s-food-boom-means-for-australia

Ewert, K. (1988). The international debt crisis. Foundation for Economic Education. Retrieved from https://fee.org/articles/the-international-debt-crisis/

H&M (2016). Annual Report 2016. Retrieved from https://about.hm.com/content/dam/hmgroup/groupsite/documents/masterlanguage/Annual%20Report/Annual%20Report%202016.pdf

Huynh, P. (2016). Employment and wages Myanmar's nascent garment sector. Asia–Pacific Garment Footwear Sector. Research note. Regional Office for Asia and the Pacific. Issue 6, November. Retrieved from www.ilo.org/wcmsp5/groups/public/–asia/–ro-bangkok/documents/publication/wcms_535188.pdf

Hymer, S. (1976). Doctoral dissertation. The International Operations of National Firms: A Study of Direct Foreign Investment. Cambridge: MIT Press.

Irvine, D. (2017). Agribusiness Outlook: Investment, Innovation and Growth. Retrieved from http://firb.gov.au/2017/07/ceda-keynote-address

Kirkup, J. (2011). World facing worst financial crisis in history, Bank of England Governor says. *The Telegraph*, 6 October. Retrieved from www.telegraph.co.uk/finance/financialcrisis/8812260/World-facing-worst-financial-crisis-in-history-Bank-of-England-Governor-says.html

Kowalski, P., Büge, M., Sztajerowska, M. & Egeland, M. (2013), State-owned enterprises: trade effects and policy implications. OECD Trade Policy Papers, No. 147. Paris: OECD.

KPMG and University of Sydney (2017). Demystifying Chinese investment in Australia, June. Retrieved from https://assets.kpmg.com/content/dam/kpmg/au/pdf/2018/demystifying-chinese-investment-in-australia-june-2018.pdf

Lambert, F. (2017a). Apple is reportedly working on electric car batteries with China's biggest battery maker. Retrieved from https://9to5mac.com/2017/07/20/apple-electric-car-batteries-china-battery-maker

——— (2017b). Tesla (TSLA) announces Q4 and 2016 earnings result: Beats on revenue, miss on earnings and model 3 on track for July. Retrieved from https://electrek.co/2017/02/22/tesla-tsla-q4-financial-results

Pastor, M., Jr (1989). Latin America, the debt crisis and the International Monetary Fund. *Latin American Perspectives*, 16(1), 79–110.

PWC (2015). State-owned enterprises catalysts for public value creation? PWC. Retrieved from www.pwc.com/gx/en/psrc/publications/assets/pwc-state-owned-enterprise-psrc.pdf

Rivera, D. (2017). Apple working on electric car battery: Yicai [Press release]. Investopedia, 21 July. Retrieved from www.investopedia.com/news/apple-working-electric-car-battery-yicai/?utm_campaign=quote-bloomberg&utm_source=bloomberg&utm_medium=referral&utm_term=fb-capture&utm_content=/&lgl=rira-baseline-vertical

Shaffer, L. (2017). Watch out, Tesla: This Warren Buffett-backed Chinese electric vehicle maker plans US expansion [Press release]. CNBC, 18 July. Retrieved from www.cnbc.com/2017/07/18/tesla-faces-rival-as-chinas-warren-buffett-backed-byd-plans-us-expansion.html

Stiglitz, J. (2014). The Chinese century. *Vanity Fair*, 4 December. Retrieved from www.vanityfair.com/news/2015/01/china-worlds-largest-economy

Tannenbaum, C. (2017). Why Asia should fear a Chinese hard landing. Barron's, 29 May. Retrieved from www.barrons.com/articles/why-asia-should-fear-a-chinese-hard-landing-1496104645

Tesla Annual Report (2017). Tesla. Retrieved from http://ir.tesla.com/secfiling.cfm?filingid=1564590–17-3118&cik=1318605

United Nations Conference on Trade and Development (UNCTAD) (n.d.). General Profile – China. UNCTADSTAT. Retrieved from http://unctadstat.unctad.org/CountryProfile/GeneralProfile/en-GB/156/index.html

Verbeke, A. & Zaman Forootan, M. (2012). How good are Multinationality-Performance (M-P) empirical studies?, *Global Strategy Journal*, 2(4).

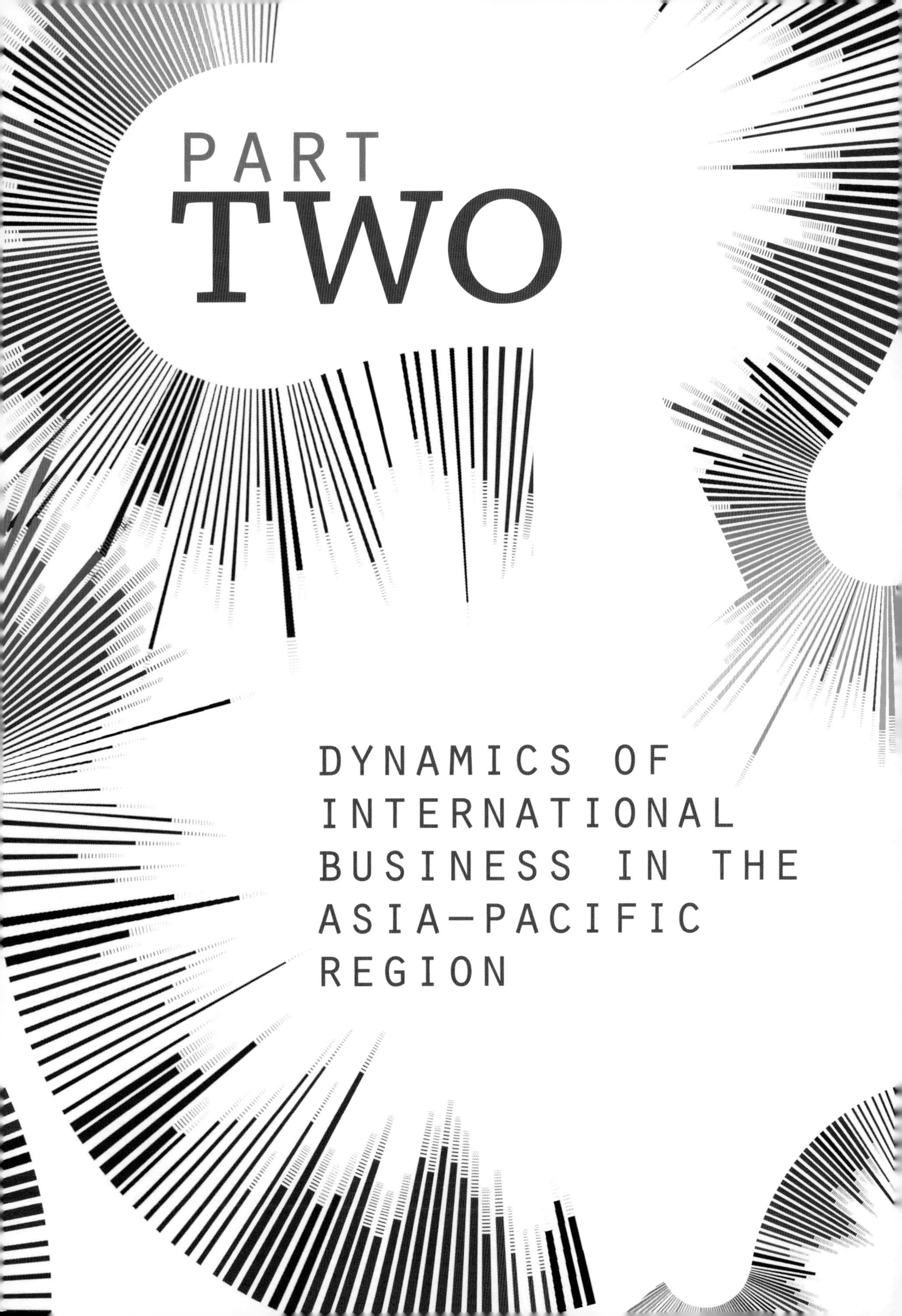

PART TWO

DYNAMICS OF INTERNATIONAL BUSINESS IN THE ASIA–PACIFIC REGION

CHAPTER 6

EMERGING ECONOMIES

Learning objectives

In reading this chapter, you will learn to:

1. understand the distinctive characteristics of emerging economies, and what distinguishes them from developed and other developing economies
2. describe the opportunities and challenges that MNEs face when operating in emerging Asia–Pacific economies
3. examine the implications of institutional differences in emerging Asia–Pacific economies and possible strategic responses to these
4. describe and explain the nature of GVCs in emerging Asia–Pacific economies, and the role of local firms within these
5. understand the competitive implications of the rise of Asia–Pacific emerging MNEs.

CHINA'S DOMINATION OF SOLAR POWER

The rise of emerging economies since 1989 has been a fundamental development in the global economy. Emerging and developing economies now account for almost 60 per cent of global GDP, up from just under half only a decade ago. Between 1980 and 2011, they raised their share in world exports from 34 per cent to 47 per cent and their share in world imports from 29 per cent to 42 per cent. Much of this increase was because of robust growth in several Asian emerging economies.

Less well understood is the rapid pace at which emerging economies, such as China, have moved up value chains, shifting their focus from labour-intensive commodities, like clothing, footwear, toys and sporting goods, towards sophisticated electronics products and emerging technologies, including solar and wind power.

China's position in the solar-power industry is illustrative of the country's technological and competitive aspirations. China now dominates the world solar industry with two-thirds of global production capacity and half of its installed capacity. It expanded solar-power production capacity by a factor of more than 10 between 2007 to 2012, and is now home to 6 of the 10 leading solar-panel producers in the world, including the two top firms. The technological sophistication of China's solar panels now matches that of Europe, the US and South Korea.

China's solar-panel producers have prospered through massive government support, despite facing trade restrictions. Public support comes in the form of low-cost loans from state banks that finance R&D and cover ongoing company losses, as well as the provision of subsidised land for new factory investments. The US and Europe imposed trade restrictions in 2012, and again in 2013, in retaliation for the Chinese government subsidies, and a belief that panels were being dumped in overseas markets. In response, Chinese firms have pushed down prices and moved some building outside of China to Malaysia and Vietnam, which has enabled them to avoid the import limits. Solar-panel prices have fallen by 90 per cent over the past decade and took a sharp dip in 2016 when the Chinese authorities announced that they would slash subsidies paid to homeowners. Solar-panel producers cut their prices by more than a quarter, driving many competitors in the US and Europe out of business.

In China's preliminary stages of development, it attracted low technology labour-intensive industries, such as clothing and footwear sectors, that were no longer competitive in the more developed economies. But this is no longer the case and China is now targeting sectors that are in their embryonic stages, competing directly with the most advanced economies.

WEBLINK
VIGNETTE QUESTION

Source: Bradsher 2017

Introduction

In this chapter we consider the benefits and challenges of doing business with emerging markets, particularly those within the Asia–Pacific region. Over the past half century, several emerging markets have grown strongly, and have significantly increased their global shares of production, trade and investment. The larger emerging markets, particularly China and India, now play a central role in the strategy of MNEs enterprises (Enderwick 2009). We begin by considering what defines an emerging market, and the distinctive characteristics that make them both attractive and challenging for international business.

The remainder of this chapter examines Asia–Pacific emerging economies in more detail. First, the discussion considers why MNEs are attracted to these economies and the diverse motives that determine their investments. Then, some of the distinctive challenges that a business faces when operating in an emerging economy are outlined. This is followed by a discussion of some of the ways in which outsider firms can be successful in emerging markets and how they might overcome the considerable challenges they are likely to face. At this point the discussion turns to an important feature of global production, which is its increasing fragmentation and dispersion into GVCs and the role that Asia–Pacific emerging economies play in these chains. The participation of local firms as partners and suppliers has provided them with opportunities to upgrade their competitiveness and in several cases these firms have themselves internationalised. The strategies of emerging market multinationals (EMNEs) are then examined. The final section offers a brief summary and concluding comments.

EMERGING MARKET MULTINATIONALS (EMNEs) multinational enterprises that originate from emerging markets.

The nature of economies in the Asia–Pacific region

A defining characteristic of the Asia–Pacific region is its considerable diversity. This diversity is apparent in terms of economics, politics, culture and climate. The degree of diversity across the Asia–Pacific region is greater than that found in other major regional groupings such as Europe or North America. The range of conditions make the Asia–Pacific region an attractive one for international businesses seeking natural resources, large and growing markets, lower-cost labour or specific skills. In economic terms, the Asia–Pacific region includes a number of wealthy, highly developed economies, such as Japan, Australia, New Zealand and Singapore, rapidly developing economies, including China and India, as well as some of the poorest nations such as Cambodia and Laos. There are also considerable differences in economic specialisation, with some economies enjoying huge levels of natural resources (Australia and Indonesia, for example), others have a comparative advantage in agriculture (Thailand, New Zealand and Malaysia), while some economies have plentiful supplies of relatively low-cost labour (China and Vietnam for instance). Economies, such as India and Taiwan, offer specialist skills in areas such as software, pharmaceuticals and manufacturing. It is not surprising, then, that several of the world's leading emerging economies, most notably China and India, are found within the Asia–Pacific region.

Emerging economies, a subgroup of developing economies, are those that show distinct signs of potentially transitioning from a developing to a developed status because of their rapid economic growth and structural transformation. Emerging economies are playing an increasingly significant role in the global economy; they are central to the massive economic transformations that have occurred since the 1980s, popularly characterised as 'globalisation'. Our focus will be on those emerging economies situated within the Asia–Pacific region, particularly China and India (refer to Engardio 2007).

The distinctive characteristics of emerging economies

What is meant by an emerging economy? If we describe countries by their level of economic development, typically measured by income per capita, we can draw a broad distinction between three groups: advanced or developed economies, which are typically members of the OECD group;

developing economies such as those with lower levels of income; and the least developed or poorest economies in the world. Most countries strive for higher levels of wealth, usually achieved through economic growth. The fastest rates of economic growth are generally found within the middle group, developing countries. This is mainly because the wealthiest countries have already enjoyed the rapid economic gains that result from the shift from agriculture to manufacturing or services (urbanisation), and from investments in healthcare, education and innovation. Many of the very poorest countries are unable to achieve this upgrading because low levels of education and poor health lead to weak productivity and income levels that preclude the savings necessary to finance economic advancement. The opportunities for rapid economic development are highest among the middle-income countries where such savings and subsequent investment are feasible.

However, developing economies do not enjoy equal opportunity for advancement. This is apparent if we examine the number of countries that have made the transition from developing to developed status. Within the Asia–Pacific region and over the past 70 or so years, we can count Japan, Singapore and South Korea as clearly achieving this step. We might also include Taiwan and Hong Kong. But even with a broad categorisation, this number is small, which suggests that there may be certain features or characteristics that a developing country must possess if it is to 'emerge' from developing, and aspire to a developed economic standing.

The most fundamental of these features is stability. An economy is not attractive to investors if it is characterised by economic, political or social instability. Further, an emerging economy needs to engage with the rest of the world; there are no recorded cases of countries that have achieved a high level of development through a strategy of autarky, effectively isolating themselves from other nations. Engagement with other economies brings opportunities for trade, for sales in new markets, for the movement of people, and exposure to innovative technologies and ideas. In essence, economic engagement facilitates greater specialisation, which underpins productivity, generates higher incomes and creates the ability to achieve sustainable levels of economic growth.

AUTARKY
a strategy of economic independence or self-sufficiency.

Emerging economies can be defined as a subgroup of developing economies achieving a rate of long-term growth and development that brings positive structural change and contributes to its future growth. Such economies would display several distinct characteristics.

First, they would have achieved political and economic stability. This was something that China achieved with the fall of Mao and the new economic strategy of Deng Xiaoping in the 1980s. Similarly, Vietnam attained stability and began to experience sustained growth following the economic reforms (Doi Moi) introduced in 1986.

Second, we would see these economies as outward focused and involved in the global economy. China is often referred to the 'world's workshop' and in a noticeably brief period has become the world's leading trading nation. It is playing an increasingly significant role in the global economy, in many ways emulating the US in the mid-twentieth century. Its recent One Belt, One Road initiative will impact more than 65 countries, many of which have been marginalised in the current globalisation wave. Similarly, since India began to reform its heavily protectionist economic policies in the 1990s it has enjoyed unprecedented growth rates that have lifted millions from poverty.

PROTECTIONIST ECONOMIC POLICIES
government policies that restrict trade with the aim of limiting competition faced by domestic industries.

A third distinguishing feature of emerging economies is that they should exhibit higher-than-average growth rates. These rates indicate a sharp upward trajectory that other developing economies cannot achieve. China, for example, enjoyed an average growth rate of almost 10 per cent over the period 1978–2008. Over the period 1980 to 2008, it increased its share of global GDP from 5.2 per cent to 17.5 per cent.

EMERGING ECONOMY
a country enjoying an above average economic growth rate and experiencing structural change in progressing towards advanced economic development.

ECONOMIC INSTITUTIONS
institutions in society that support economic activity and security through the provision of market facilitating services.

Fourth, such rates of growth bring structural change to an economy, which again differentiates emerging economies. Structural change manifests itself in a number of ways including growing specialisation (China specialises in manufacturing and assembly, whereas India specialises in service activities), rising urbanisation, a growing middle class of consumers enjoying strong discretionary spending, and the increasing sophistication of economic institutions. These features are plain in the emerging economies of the Asia–Pacific region. The level of urbanisation in China has increased from 26 per cent in 1990 to 56 per cent in 2015. China's consumer spending increased by almost 400 per cent between 2006 and 2016, while comparable spending in India, although starting from a lower level, increased fivefold over the same period.

China and India are clearly emerging economies in the Asia–Pacific region. Because of their huge populations they are often referred to as large emerging markets and form part of the widely-discussed BRICS group (Stuenkel 2015). Because of their size, the changes experienced by these economies have major implications for the rest of the world economy as the opening vignette illustrates.

It is important to understand that emerging economies, within the Asia–Pacific region or more broadly, are not a homogeneous group. They vary significantly in terms of their structures (China focuses on manufacturing and India on services, but Russia and Brazil are resource-based economies), in their economic performance (with China being the strongest performer in recent decades), their political orientation (China is communist, whereas India is the world's largest democracy), and in terms of their business structures, reliance on markets, and the degree of government involvement.

MULTIPLE-CHOICE QUESTION

Furthermore, the characteristics described are revealing, but also disguise a great deal. For example, the high rate of growth that emerging economies enjoy are not always stable. Volatility in emerging markets can affect returns on investment and is higher than in developed economies (Enderwick 2007). The benefits of economic growth are not shared equally. In China, the coastal regions closest to Hong Kong have been the driver of growth, with much slower growth rate experienced in the north and far west of China. Similarly, urban income levels are much higher than those in the countryside, contributing to ongoing internal migration and urbanisation. Similar inequalities are also evident in India (Das & Das 2013). Business decisions need to be based on finely graded information when considering opportunities in any emerging economy.

Conducting business in emerging Asia–Pacific economies

The richness and diversity of Asia–Pacific emerging economies suggest that MNEs are attracted to these countries for numerous reasons, which is supported by a wide range of evidence (Urata, Yue & Kimura 2006). However, there are four broad motives: accessing new markets; taking advantage of lower-cost conditions; creating learning opportunities; and using reverse innovation.

New markets

The first motive for entering an emerging economy is to pursue sales. Emerging markets often appear particularly attractive to Western MNEs who may find their home and regional markets saturated or subject to high levels of competition. The size, rapid development, and dynamism of emerging economies offers new opportunities for the sale of products and services. Consumers in emerging markets may be more willing to try new products, could display lower levels of brand commitment than in more established markets and are more likely to be first-time buyers for products such as motor vehicles. For example, the number of cars per 1000 people in Australia in 2015 was 764, and in New Zealand 712, but just 128 in China and 18 in India. This means that car companies are primarily seeking replacement sales in the more developed markets, while looking for opportunities to target new, often first-time buyers, in emerging economies. Indeed, first-time buyers make up about two-thirds of the Chinese car market. China's car market has been the world's largest since 2008 and is forecast to increase tenfold between 2005 and 2030.

Consumers in emerging markets are increasingly brand conscious and are likely to base their purchase decisions on what they perceive as value for money. However, it would be a mistake to think that sales are easy to achieve in many emerging markets. Often competition is high; for example, there are more than 70 vehicle brands competing in China, and the challenges of distribution and advertising can be considerable. Nevertheless, for many MNEs, emerging markets such as China and India play a central role in their global business strategies (Enderwick 2009).

SPOTLIGHT 6.1

Breaking into China's movie market

In 2012, China overtook Japan to become the world's second largest film market, surpassed only by the US. Hollywood depends on overseas markets for around half of its total revenue so access to the Chinese market is critical. Unfortunately, penetrating the Chinese market is not straightforward: it is highly protected by a raft of government measures.

The Chinese authorities are anxious to protect their national and cultural values from what they see as potentially dangerous Hollywood content. In fact, Hollywood films were banned in China between 1949 and 1994. Following the lifting of the ban, China imposed an import quota on US-made movies allowing just 10 per year between 1994 and 2001, rising to 20 after 2001. In a breakthrough agreement in 2012, China increased its annual quota to 34.

Other restrictions are in place. For example, the distribution of foreign films in China is monopolised by two groups: China Film Group, which is a subsidiary of China's State Administration of Radio, Film and Television (SARFT), the film regulatory body; and Huaxia, a state-owned enterprise that also contributes to SARFT. As well as import and distribution restrictions, China also uses politically motivated black-out periods, typically one to three months, during which foreign films cannot be shown. Black outs provide an advantage to domestic movies by ensuring they get the greatest exposure during holiday periods and the summer months. The authorities also limit the success of US movies by forcing shared opening times. This effectively pits two or more potential blockbusters directly against each other, limiting their revenue prospects.

In these more liberal times, the Chinese authorities impose a complex regulatory framework to protect the market share of domestic film producers. Policy is implemented by SARFT, which reviews and regulates all movies shown in China. Censorship is of considerable importance in China because the country does not operate a ratings system, commonplace in many other countries. In 2008, SARFT issued a list of guidelines setting out what was not acceptable in foreign films. The list

included, among other things, 'disparaging the image of the people's army', 'murder, violence, terror, ghosts and the supernatural', and 'showing excessive drinking, smoking, and other bad habits' (HKTDC 2008).

Even though these guidelines were quite explicit, they have not been enforced in a consistent way. Indeed, if they were enforced, almost any Hollywood movie could be excluded! However, it appears that censors are more pragmatic than they might first appear and compromise is often possible. Hollywood studios have adopted several strategies to increase their likelihood of acceptance. Some studios rely on past experience and consultants to predict what might or might not be acceptable. Selective enforcement of the rules and the possibility of pre-release editing mean that appeal and negotiation is a reality. Others have moved towards China-friendly fantasies (like *Kung Fu Panda*) and have avoided sensitive subject matter. Some studios have adopted a strategy of co-production in China, involving local stars or locations. In part, Hollywood has been able to avoid the barriers because it is not just economically powerful, but also politically connected. Although, the international experience of the Chinese film industry does suggest that there is room for negotiation in the movie business.

Source: Cieply & Barnes 2013; O'Connor & Armstrong 2015

QUESTIONS

SPOTLIGHT QUESTIONS

1. Given the difficulties of ensuring that foreign movies are shown in China, why are Hollywood producers so keen on the Chinese market?
2. Many would characterise the challenges of entering the movie market in China as less of a risk and more of an uncertainty. If this is true, what can be done by the US to reduce the level of uncertainty faced by Hollywood?

Low-cost production locations

A second key motive for involvement in emerging Asia–Pacific markets is a result of their comparatively low-cost structures and the availability of key resources such as labour. A plentiful supply of labour, often internal migratory workers moving from the countryside to the cities, has held wage costs down, despite the massive growth in employment. The result has been explosive growth in productive capacity in Asia–Pacific emerging economies. For example, China, which has focused on manufacturing, has seen its share of global manufacturing value increase from 7 per cent in 2004 to 24 per cent in 2014, while the shares of the US, Japan, and Germany have all declined. India has emerged as a highly favoured location for a variety of business services ranging from call centres to bio-testing and advanced analytics. The low-cost environment in both these economies is encouraging inward investment from MNEs establishing plants for local production and sales as well as for export. Emerging market-based firms are also benefitting from the low costs; they are developing as contract suppliers and international sellers in their own right.

The diversity of the Asia–Pacific region also encourages the implementation of regional value chains. For example, a firm using the resources and capabilities offered by Greater China (mainland China, Hong Kong and Taiwan) has access to plentiful natural resources and low-cost labour (in mainland China), specialist manufacturing skills (Taiwan), as well as world-class finance, logistics, and communications (in Hong Kong).

The cost savings offered by the less-developed ASEAN nations are, in particular, attracting labour-intensive manufacturing. For example, the manufacture of false eyelashes is concentrated in Purbalingga in central Java, Indonesia, where a cluster of some 100 000 workers, 90 per cent of whom are women, labour to make false lashes for lucrative Western markets. Pay rates are low with the typical worker receiving compensation equal to just 1.3 per cent of the retail price (Chamberlain 2013).

While low-labour costs appear highly attractive, the actual savings firms enjoy may not be as sizeable as expected. This is because productivity levels can also be low and managing operations in distant locations, such as China and India, can add to control and coordination costs. Lengthy supply chains also create difficulties in monitoring and maintaining quality levels, and may reduce an MNE's flexibility when responding to market changes. Therefore, it is relevant for firms to consider 'landed costs' that provide a more accurate assessment of actual cost savings when products are brought to final markets. However, despite these difficulties, many technologically standardised and labour-intensive products, such as clothing, footwear, consumer electronics, toys and sports goods as well as business processes, such as IT call centres and payroll, are now sourced predominantly from emerging markets in the Asia–Pacific region.

MULTIPLE-CHOICE QUESTION

Learning opportunities

A third motive for doing business in emerging Asia–Pacific economies lies in the opportunities for learning. While this is not usually a primary driver for entering these markets, the learning benefits can be considerable.

Asia–Pacific economies display a diversity of characteristics, often quite distinct from Western markets, and companies can exploit huge learning opportunities when they operate in novel institutional settings and business systems. Distinctive features of emerging markets are their high rates of growth and the evolution of market structures as new competitors appear. This rapid development provides significant learning prospects for managers who are more familiar with relatively stable market structures and competitive pressures in developed markets. Such dynamism increases the significance of issues such as market entry timing and appropriate market positioning.

MARKET ENTRY TIMING
the decision as to when to enter a market in comparison to competitors.

MARKET POSITIONING
efforts to influence buyer perceptions of the positioning in a market of a product or brand relative to a competitor's offerings. The objective is to define a unique and competitively advantageous position in the mind of the consumer.

In addition, the behaviour of consumers, suppliers, competitors and government officials can also differ. Consumers in emerging markets seek value for money, but may be more willing to sample the latest brands and offerings. A wide range of suppliers exist in these markets, and identifying and developing them may add to a buyer's competitiveness. Cooperation in the areas of technology, design and distribution can provide valuable lessons in product and market adaptation. Levels of competition in emerging markets are often higher than many new entrants anticipate, and the diverse types of competitor encountered can be enlightening. Western firms may find themselves facing state-owned and supported firms (common in China), sizeable family-dominated firms (in India), large diverse corporations (widespread in Japan and Korea), as well as myriad small and highly adaptive competitors (characteristic of Taiwan, Malaysia and Thailand, for example). The opening vignette illustrated the significant role that the state can play in an emerging economy. In addition, of course, the considerable attractions of Asia–Pacific economies draw in major competitors from many parts of the world. As a result, competitive tactics may seem novel, including practices such as pervasive government support and protection, discrimination based on ownership nationality, cross-subsidisation and predatory pricing, which are usually not common in the home markets of many investors.

CROSS-SUBSIDISATION
a strategy of supporting a product using profits generated by another product.

PREDATORY PRICING
the pricing of goods or services at such a low level that other firms cannot compete and are driven from the market.

There are also opportunities to learn new skills in the management of government relations. Many Asia–Pacific economies are characterised by prominent levels of government involvement, with officials often favouring local firms. This may be observed in countries such as China, South Korea, and Singapore, for instance, where state direction of business is prevalent. Our earlier discussion of the Chinese solar-panel industry is an example. The transparency and robustness of institutions governing labour and capital markets, the protection of intellectual property rights, and the safeguarding of consumer interests, may not be comparable to those found in more developed and established economies. Differing levels and forms of corruption add to challenges and the need to understand alternative business systems.

QUALITY FADE
a gradual and deliberate reduction in the quality of a good or service with the intention of increasing profit margins.

Emerging markets offer business systems that bring challenges that many Western managers may never have encountered before. An example is the widespread counterfeiting of products and how to respond to the damage that such products can do to brand reputation. Similarly, avoiding quality fade as suppliers seek to cut costs to increase their margins, requires levels of monitoring and intervention that many managers may have never had to assume. However, careful observation of these markets can be revealing. A few countries in the region have skipped development stages that once seemed inevitable; for example, going straight to the adoption of mobile phones and bypassing landlines, or moving from bicycles to cars, but omitting motorcycles, as the primary mode of transport. Equally, countries such as China are at the leading edge in technologies, including wind and solar power, and offer valuable lessons to the rest of the world. India has pioneered novel low-cost solutions in areas such as lighting, communication devices, computers and the world's cheapest car, the Tata Nano.

Reverse innovation

A final motive for engaging with emerging markets is the opportunity to undertake reverse innovation. To understand reverse innovation, it is helpful to first understand more conventional innovation diffusion. Traditionally, the majority of product and process innovations originated in the most developed economies and, after reaching market maturity, were sometimes transferred to less-developed economies. The rationale for this was that wealthy markets contained consumers both willing and able to buy the most innovative products. Over time, as product prices fall, incomes will rise in emerging economies and knowledge of new products spreads so that demand in these markets begins to emerge. Reverse innovation posits the opposite process. Here, because of unique needs, certain types of product or processes may be initiated in an emerging market, and then found to have appeal in more wealthy markets. This process has been described as 'trickling up' in contrast to the conventional view of 'trickle down'.

REVERSE INNOVATION
also known as trickle-up innovation; describes innovations that are first developed and applied in developing economies, and then transferred to more developed economies.

There are several reasons why MNEs might innovate products in emerging markets. First, as already indicated, these markets may have unique needs and, with lower average income levels, the existing offerings may fail to fully meet demand. If anticipated demand is large enough, firms may invest to create products more suited to local conditions. These might then appeal to certain segments of more developed economies (Govindarajan & Trimble 2012). An example is the Nokia 105 mobile phone. This is a basic model that appealed to less-developed markets because of its low cost, but it has also become adopted as a second phone by consumers in wealthier markets that already possess a smart phone. It is also a phone that many parents in developed countries have provided to their children.

Reverse innovation is also encouraged by the lower costs of undertaking R&D in emerging markets. Salaries for engineers and scientists are much lower in these markets so a wider range of innovations can be pursued. Companies that use reverse innovation include Microsoft and General Electric (GE). GE introduced a low-cost baby warmer, the Lullaby, for use in medical facilities in developing countries. Because it excluded some of the features of its more expensive Giraffe Shuttle, the product aimed at developed markets, the Lullaby was a lower-cost option that has also appealed to hospitals in developed economies experiencing budgetary pressures. This type of thinking has become widely established in a number of emerging economies, for example in India, where it is known as jugaad innovation, thinking outside the box in frugal and flexible ways.

JUGAAD INNOVATION
a process of innovation that emphasises lower costs through the reduction of complexity.

The challenges of doing business in emerging Asia–Pacific economies

The previous section summarised the key motivations for doing business in emerging Asia–Pacific economies. However, potential investors within the region need to balance these attractions again the considerable challenges they are likely to face in emerging markets.

Understanding risks

The first challenge is the likely level of risk that is encountered. Of course, all markets are risky; there is no guarantee that products or services will sell or that an acceptable level of profit can be made. But, in the case of emerging markets, MNEs face risks that go beyond these commercial considerations. This is partly because of the dynamism of emerging markets.

These kinds of markets are likely to be 'emerging' from one set of conditions to another, perhaps from being communist and planned (like China or Vietnam) or from operating behind high levels of protectionist barriers (such as India or Malaysia). Take the case of China. It is an economy undergoing several transitions – from planned to market, from agricultural to industrial, from rural to urban, all simultaneously, and all at an unprecedented pace. What this means for business is that a risk premium is likely to be incurred. Risks in emerging markets are higher because of the dynamic rate of change, the volatility, policy instability, and the lack of well-established market-supporting institutions that provide stability and predictability. This does not mean that the risks in these markets are unacceptable, rather that managers need to understand and compensate for them. It is too easy to be seduced by the numbers associated with emerging markets – their population, economic growth rates, demand for products and services. Attractive as such opportunities might appear to be, they are rarely easy to exploit.

RISK PREMIUM
the return in excess of the risk-free rate of return an investment is expected to yield.

Overcoming informational deficiencies

The limited availability of information, so necessary in making sound business decisions, adds to the risk of investing in emerging markets. Problems can result from the lack of information, its poor quality, timelessness or that insiders enjoy privileged access. There are several ways of increasing the quality of information, such as private collection, using multiple sources or developing local partnerships, but all these add to costs. Commercial information on cost structures, suppliers, customers and so on may be difficult to obtain when businesses are privately held or highly centralised, or where good management practice favours intuition. Differences in accounting practices and conventions also create difficulties, particularly when pursuing acquisitions or partnerships. One implication of this is the tendency to observe imitative behaviours, when firms tend to follow similar strategies, perhaps because they believe that an early mover has informational advantages.

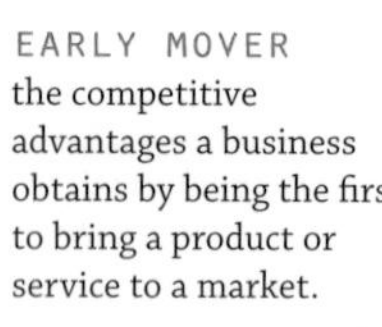
EARLY MOVER
the competitive advantages a business obtains by being the first to bring a product or service to a market.

Inequality

Development in emerging economies is an uneven process, which creates a challenge because most attractive business opportunities are likely to be found in the more prosperous cities or regions. This highlights the dangers of relying on aggregated data measuring factors, such as income levels or consumer spending, in a rapidly evolving emerging economy. The sheer size of large emerging markets like India and China means that most firms are realistic about focusing their efforts into specific cities or regions. The growth rates between regions vary significantly. Within India, the average urban income in 2012 was 440 per cent higher than rural incomes that averaged less than half the national average. Urban income growth averaged 9.8 per cent per annum over the period 2002–12, which was 50 per cent higher than the rural income growth. These differences were reflected at the state level, with some regions such as Gujarat, Punjab and Tamil Nadu performing strongly, while others such as Bihar, Uttar Pradesh, and Jharkhand experienced much slower growth rates. These poorer performing states tended to be more rural and to suffer from a range of problems, including law and order, infrastructure and poor administration. Research suggests that India's high performing states and cities will account for more than half of all incremental economic growth between 2012 and 2025 (McKinsey & Company 2014). The implication for business is clear: granular analysis suggests that there is a strong correlation between urbanisation and rates of economic growth, and it is the metropolitan centres that offer the most lucrative opportunities.

We see a similar picture when looking at China. Historically, growth was centred on the major cities of Beijing and Shanghai, and the southern coastal centres that provided strong links to the rest of the world. Not surprisingly, these are the areas of highest income in China. Like India, there is a significant rural–urban income disparity, with the major centres enjoying income levels some three times above those of the poorer regions such as Guizhou, Yunnan and Gansu. Innovative activity is also heavily concentrated in the tier-one cities and most prosperous regions. However, the Chinese authorities are pursuing a rebalancing of the economy, with a greater domestic focus while, at the same time, rising costs are driving many firms inland. The result is modest growth convergence with some tier-three cities of the north and west expected to experience the strongest rates of economic growth in the future. Such changes highlight the dynamism of emerging economies and the challenges of breaking into areas with less-developed infrastructure.

TIER-ONE CITIES (CHINA)
the big four cities of Beijing, Shanghai, Guangzhou, and Shenzhen.

TIER-THREE CITIES (CHINA)
primarily the open coastal cities, high income cities, and cities experiencing significant economic development, such as Hangzhou and Chongqing.

Levels and forms of competition

Competition is often a challenge in emerging Asia–Pacific economies, and one that many multinational investors underrate. Levels of competition may be high because domestic firms, perhaps recently freed from the constrictions of state ownership or planning, have moved aggressively to take advantage of strongly growing markets. Domestic firms are actively seeking to improve their competitiveness, investing in R&D and marketing skills, for example. Similarly, a few international businesses moved early to establish a distinct market position. Consider the Volkswagen (VW) Group which began operations in China through a JV in 1984. This gave it an opportunity to create a strong brand and although many new competitors, both foreign and domestic, have now entered the vehicle market, the VW Group still has a leading market position producing 5 of the 10 best-selling cars in China.

The type of competitors that Western firms face may also differ from those they normally encounter. Long histories of state planning and involvement have created powerful business groups, some still state-owned, with other large, diversified family conglomerates under the control of favoured elites (Amsden 1992; Wade 1990). Such firms are widespread in countries such as India, Thailand, Malaysia and South Korea. They may compete in ways that Western firms find unusual. State-owned firms may enjoy protected monopoly positions or preferential access to fast growing and lucrative new sectors. They may be granted access to low-cost funds, in some cases even being exempted from repaying such loans (refer to the opening vignette). In the same way, governments in India, South Korea and Taiwan have used proven and successful entrepreneurs to spearhead industrial development, creating large diversified conglomerates such as Tata in India or the LG group in South Korea. Both types of firm are likely to enjoy advantages not available to Western MNEs. They may receive information from officials regarding future plans or policies providing advantageous opportunities, or they may benefit from high levels of protection where competing imports or inward investment are restricted. They may also enjoy 'patient capital' where returns on investment or loans may be deferred and profit maximisation requirements may be relaxed in favour of goals such as growth or market share. More generally, they are likely to possess advantages of familiarity in understanding consumers, suppliers and government officials, advantages that outsider firms have to create over time. It is important for multinational managers to examine carefully the level and types of competitors they are likely to face in an emerging market.

SPOTLIGHT 6.2

Uber pulls out of China

Despite rapid growth and success in numerous markets, Uber, the innovative ride-sharing service, has run into problems in China. In entering China, Uber faced fierce competition from local rival Didi Chuxing. Because of the fierce competition, both companies were incurring heavy costs; Uber spending US$1 billion a year. In August 2016, Uber swapped its branding, operations and data for a 20 per cent stake in Didi.

Uber has experienced significant challenges in the past. These have ranged from protests by taxi drivers in London, Jakarta and Rio to legal challenges against its apps in France and Germany. London Transport has even decided not to renew Uber's operating license because of ongoing concerns with CSR, and the company's failure to properly vet drivers and investigate serious complaints.

While the decision to pull out of China seems inconsistent with Uber's plans for global domination, it offers several benefits. Pulling out of China releases funds that Uber can then use to further its investments in self-driving cars, on developing its UberEATS food-delivery service, building its own mapping service and on expansion in other markets. Of interest to Uber is the rapidly developing Indian market. While there is a strong local competitor, Ola, the market is not characterised by the sturdy state-supported firms that are common in China.

A second benefit is that the threat to Uber from possible alliances between Didi Chuxing and rivals, such as Lyft in the US, Ola in India and Grab in several parts of South-East Asia, is much reduced when the two companies enjoy cross-holdings.

Third, the tie-up between Uber and Didi Chuxing signals the strength of the so-called 'gig economy' and the immense opportunities for further disruption. Indeed, analysts take the view that these companies are no longer focusing on the taxi industry, rather they want

to disrupt the huge revenue enjoyed by the automobile industry and its model of private ownership of vehicles.

A seemingly unstoppable Uber seems to have met its match in China, however.

Source: Davies 2016

QUESTIONS

SPOTLIGHT QUESTIONS

1. Research the Chinese firm Didi Chuxing and discuss what you see as its competitive strengths. How are these strengths related to the nature of the Chinese economy?
2. Why does Uber believe that entry into the Indian market will be easier than the Chinese market?

Understanding institutional and market weaknesses

Challenges arise when doing business in emerging markets because of weaknesses, sometimes even failures, in markets and institutions. Market failure refers to situations where markets do not operate efficiently or effectively. They create management challenges by adding to transaction costs and to uncertainty, and they require innovative business responses. Such failures can occur in several distinct markets such as labour, product, and technology markets. Labour market failures result from inefficiencies in mobility, adjustment and quality of workers. China, for example, has restrictions on the movement of labour, particularly between its provinces. India, in operating a massive informal labour market alongside a smaller and more formal one, limits the movement of workers between industries and organisations. Regulations limit layoffs and the management of industrial disputes in both countries.

MARKET FAILURE
a situation where free markets fail to allocate resources efficiently. Such failure may prompt government intervention to remedy the perceived malfunction.

TRANSACTION COSTS
the costs associated with the exchange of goods or services; they are incurred in overcoming market imperfections.

Governments intervene within product markets to restrict ownership of key industries; in many cases, governments retain state ownership. India restricts the rights of production of a wide range of products to small- and medium-sized enterprises, while both India and China impose price controls and production quotas. Intellectual property protection is imperative in the emerging Asia–Pacific markets. Counterfeiting and piracy are prevalent in the region, and can mean revenue losses and costly brand damage. Pressure to remove trading and investment restrictions may be the most effective way to reduce these market weaknesses.

Efficient markets require the foundation of sound market-supporting institutions. Institutions set the rules for exchange within a society. They provide both the incentives and restrictions on interactions, whether they are social, political or economic. Examples of formal institutions include the rule of law, property rights protection, financial markets and government bureaucracies. Formal institutions tend to mirror the informal institutions of a society, such as its beliefs, norms and traditions.

When formal institutions are weak or absent, informal institutions play a greater role. They facilitate the exchange of ideas and knowledge through social relationships that encourage economic exchange by increasing levels of trust and information sharing. Firms devise strategies to overcome such failures in extreme cases, where formal institutions are absent or 'void' (Khanna & Palepu 2010). For example, in the absence of reliable capital markets, conglomerate firms may pool funds and operate a shadow internal capital market.

INTERNAL CAPITAL MARKET
a capital allocation process whereby funds are collected across a company's various divisions and the dispersion decisions are made by a central authority.

Managing in distinctive business systems

The distinct institutional, economic and social features of emerging Asia–Pacific economies means that international managers face significant challenges in learning to do business effectively in these contexts.

The key difference is the greater reliance in emerging economies on personal relationships. Such relationships are often used to compensate for a lack of trust, or the absence of reliable market processes. In China these relationships are termed *guanxi* and individuals make considerable investments in the creation and development of these networks. Chinese business people seek to do business with those they know and trust, in effect, personal trust displaces reliance on impartial legal and contractual institutions. While China and other emerging markets are strengthening their institutional frameworks, enabling greater reliance on market exchange, the importance of personal relationships is likely to persist. This is because such relationships extend beyond commerce into political and social links. Similarly, the creation of these networks, often developed through schools, universities and military service, give locals a significant advantage over outsiders entering their economies and so are unlikely to be surrendered lightly. The implication of the importance of personal relationships is clear: doing business in many emerging Asia–Pacific economies may require a requisite period of establishing trust and building a positive relationship with other parties.

Corruption

One element of heavy reliance on personal relationships is the danger that they could contribute to corruption. The cultures of many Asian economies do not clearly distinguish between gift giving and favours. The maintenance of personal networks could easily cross the line of what is seen as acceptable behaviour for people from other cultures. Corruption, which is the abuse of public office for private gain, is damaging because it adds uncertainty, distorts investment decisions and may impose heavy costs on the public sector. The widespread practice of corruption also encourages illegal activities more generally.

The institutional and administrative structures of many emerging economies contribute to corruption. Pervasive government intervention in economic development provides the opportunities through cumbersome regulations and price setting to extract illicit payments. The delegation of decision-making powers to bureaucrats, particularly when their actions are not closely monitored, places them in a position to demand payments. Measures of corruption show that there is a considerable problem within the developing economies of the Asia–Pacific region. In 2016, China and India were both rated by Transparency International as 40 out of 100, where 100 indicates a completely corruption-free state. Equally concerning is that other potentially emerging economies, including Vietnam, Cambodia, Indonesia, Thailand, Laos and the Philippines, were rated as even more corrupt. Pervasive corruption in the region creates significant challenges for MNEs, especially those based in home countries that have implemented strict regulations of improper payments.

Competing in Asia–Pacific emerging economies

The decision to do business in an emerging economy should not be based on a simple comparison of the expected benefits and challenges; it may be possible to overcome, at least in part, some of the perceived challenges and costs. In fact, this is the role of an effective competitive strategy. A competitive strategy seeks to identify the determinants of success and to ensure a focus on them. Western firms formulating a sound strategy in Asia–Pacific markets may enjoy a significant advantage over local firms. This is because the very high rates of growth experienced in these markets has enabled local firms to prosper, in many cases without the need to develop detailed strategies. Firms that have been suppliers to Western buyers, for example, tend to emphasise operational efficiency rather than market penetration, meaning that a multinational entrant able to implement an effective strategy could enjoy a strong competitive edge.

If we consider the distinctive characteristics of the Asia–Pacific emerging markets outlined, a few strategic responses likely to help in overcoming the challenges can be identified.

Rapid growth and change

Rapidly growing markets offer significant opportunities but also necessitate an appropriate strategic posture. Market dynamism highlights the need for effective environmental scanning so that opportunities can be identified or anticipated. Resources need to be carefully managed as they may need to be swiftly redeployed. This applies across a value chain so investing firms must work closely with suppliers and partners. The necessity for flexibility is strong. Location and sourcing decisions can change quickly because rapid growth affects cost structures, market attractiveness, and regional supply chains. China's experience is illustrative. As costs have risen rapidly in the coastal regions, producers have moved inland and to smaller urban centres. Some firms have even moved operations away from China or considered dual sourcing from lower-cost locations such as Cambodia or Vietnam. Market dynamism endorses the need for, and likely benefits of, developing a sound strategy in the face of rapid change, offering a competitive benefit to multinationals who plan carefully.

Overcoming institutional differences

The institutional configuration of an economy affects an MNE's business organisation and strategy. Competing in an economy characterised by institutional weaknesses or voids requires understanding of how such features manifest themselves, and how they influence an operating strategy. Where the rule of law and market institutions fail to provide a reliable foundation for the use of contracts, competitors will develop substitute mechanisms. Firms can restrict business to those with which they have well-developed ties and therefore trust. Social sanctions, including reputation, replace contractual enforcement.

INSTITUTIONAL FAILURE a situation where market facilitating institutions are either absent, or not functioning effectively, raising transaction costs.

Local firms may internalise their supply chains, diversifying horizontally and vertically, to ensure that suppliers come under shared ownership. This creates an opportunity for multinational outsiders since it means that there may be a pool of independent suppliers or contractors they can approach. The lack of consumer protection in emerging markets offers an opportunity to trusted international brands. In recent years, the scandal-ridden Chinese dairy industry has enabled international brands from Australia and New Zealand to capitalise on their strong positive country of origin effect, and enjoy a premium for infant formula products. Strategies for addressing weak intellectual property protection include modifying products to eliminate leading edge technologies, fragmenting supply relationships to ensure that no single partner has access to the entire technology (Gooris & Peeters 2016), or accelerating technological change and product updates so that technologies rapidly become obsolete and copying less attractive. The latter is a strategy that Apple has pursued for several years. This suggests that there are a range of strategic responses that should be considered when operating in business systems that are distinct from those of the home country of investors.

INTERNALISE to conduct transactions within the confines of a corporation rather than in the open market.

Managing government involvement

As we have noted, many emerging Asia–Pacific economies have high levels of government involvement in economic affairs. This provides opportunities and challenges for MNEs entering these markets. Opportunities exist when governments provide tax and other incentives to attract or develop certain types of activities such as R&D or management functions. Because they often possess leading edge technologies or capabilities, MNEs can be specifically welcomed for the resources they bring. Where the government is less trusting, there are a few things that investors can do to increase their legitimacy and acceptance.

Use of local partner organisations

One way to increase legitimacy and acceptance is by forming partnerships with local firms. This has the advantages of providing access to local networks, attracting additional resources, and creating a close relationship likely to facilitate the transfer of knowledge and skills to the local firm.

Overcoming liability of foreignness

A second strategy is to make a very substantial investment as a way of indicating commitment to an economy. Some firms even spread their investments over several separate locations to create the impression of a more sizeable presence. While such a strategy increases risk exposure, it emphasises economic contribution. This type of integrative strategy is most appropriate if an MNE is entering for market seeking purposes and plans to be in the market for a significant time. Governments are more likely to favour investors who are willing to share technology and to continually upgrade, contributing to positive economic development.

Competing directly against a state-owned business or challenging government policy is likely to be a dangerous strategy. In some cases, particularly for very powerful firms, it may be possible to influence government policy. In the case of India, Walmart has argued that allowing entry of multiple product retailers would contribute to the creation of a nation-wide chilled supply chain, badly needed in a country that sees around 40 per cent of its food crops wasted. The Indian government needs to consider this in light of the possible loss of many small Indian retailers, who would otherwise struggle to compete against the behemoth that is Walmart.

Competing for customers and overcoming the liabilities of foreignness that MNEs face in emerging markets also needs to be considered. New entrants must recognise that emerging market consumers are increasingly knowledgeable and discerning; emerging markets are not willing to accept obsolete technologies and product designs that have reached the end of their life cycles in developed markets. Rather, they are increasingly global consumers – they are well informed about choice, able to search widely, expect value for money and want a high level of service. These are the very skills that many MNEs possess and can deploy effectively (see the IB masterclass case study). Therefore, such a strategy is also the best way for an MNE to respond to competitors: to provide differentiated products and services that offer value to buyers reflected in premium prices and returns.

Our discussion highlights several management implications. First, the diversity of the Asia–Pacific region means that a single business model or strategy is unlikely to bring success. Markets such as Japan and South Korea are quite different to the developing ASEAN economies, which, in turn, are radically different to Australia and New Zealand. The region requires the development of different strategies for different segments. Similarly, the required competencies differ across countries. As the closing case shows, the technological knowledge and the premium product features that work in the most developed markets are of little value when trying to penetrate an emerging market such as India.

Second, there are budding areas of social concern in business that advanced international MNEs are better able to address than their emerging market competitors. An example is growing consumer awareness about the sustainability and ethical content of products. The ability to display a socially responsible and transparent supply chain may become a powerful competitive advantage as incomes and consumer awareness rise in emerging markets (see Spotlight 6.3).

SPOTLIGHT 6.3

The mining of mica

Mica is a naturally occurring mineral used in a range of consumer products, including electronics, cosmetics and car paints. It is valuable because of its innate ability to refract and reflect light giving a shimmery appearance to finishes. While mica is produced in a few locations – China, Europe and the US – a quarter of global production is mined in Jharkhand and Bihar, two of the poorest states in India. More than half of India's production is exported as pearlescent pigments.

Production of mica in India has been linked to the widespread use of child labour in illegal mining operations. Children as young as 10 are reported as working in the industry, with some estimates suggesting as many as 20 000 underage workers may be involved. Such employment is illegal in India, and exposes children to skin diseases, respiratory infections and injury. Production from illegal mines enters global supply chains after it is sold to local traders who pass it on to exporters. It can then be incorporated into the supply systems of major MNEs such as BMW, L'Oréal, Procter & Gamble, and PPG Paints.

While the Indian authorities claim they are regulating much of the industry, the extent of illegal mining appears to be considerable. For example, official Indian figures suggest that exports of mica in 2013 were around 128 000 tonnes, some six times larger than official production at 19 000 tonnes. The difference is presumably the result of illegal mining using low-cost, child labour.

Interesting issues arise from this situation. First, to what extent are affluent consumers aware of how their product choices, such as specifying a new car with a metallic paint finish, affect child and illegal labour? Would greater awareness affect their purchasing behaviour? Second, how can multinational brands protect their integrity and reputation when sourcing what is effectively a non-differentiated mineral commodity? Can they rely on their suppliers to ensure transparent supply chains? Third, from a policy perspective, how should such a problem be tackled? Blaming poor and often illiterate parents for allowing their children to work seems unlikely to have much effect; forcing intermediate buyers to ensure the integrity of their purchases in a sector where 85 per cent of production appears to be illegal also does not seem likely to succeed. Finally, are multinational sellers likely to assume responsibility for the extraction and sale of first-stage inputs that occur across markets, often many thousands of miles from their final production operations?

Sources: Bengsten & Kelly 2016; Chandran 2016

SPOTLIGHT QUESTIONS

QUESTIONS

1. Why is it important for consumers to be aware of the true costs of producing the products they demand and consume?
2. Is tackling illegal mining the responsibility for multinational producers or Indian authorities?

GVCs in Asia–Pacific emerging economies

One of the most important ways in which the emerging Asia–Pacific economies are linked into the global economy is through their participation in GVCs. In the early 1980s, researchers began to identify important changes in the ways in which production systems were being organised. There was a clear move towards more globally dispersed, but hierarchically organised, production systems. Several activities, initially production in standardised sectors such as footwear, clothing and textiles, were being relocated to emerging economies, several of which were within Asia.

GVC thinking was important in conceptualising sets of inter-firm transactions that provided the nodes in a value chain organised internationally but linked from concept to customer. A few GVC studies gave the basis for moving beyond strategy at the level of the firm to offering a framework for studying the creation, differentiation and sharing of value at the industry level. This conceptualisation emphasised two key dimensions: location and governance of transactions. Locational dispersion increased as trade barriers fell, communication and control costs decreased, more countries sought to integrate into the global economy, and transport innovations such as containerisation were adopted. Widening spatial choice favoured emerging markets because of their locational advantages, including their low-cost labour, specialist skills and rapidly developing markets. Governance of transactions refers to how activities are managed. The basic choice for companies is to: undertake activities themselves, sometimes termed internalisation; and buy from others, either though arms-length market transactions or some form of relational supply arrangement, often referred to externalisation or outsourcing (see Chapter 11).

ARMS-LENGTH MARKET TRANSACTIONS business transactions in which the buyer and seller act independently and with no interest in the other's benefit.

EXTERNALISATION the contracting out of a business process or task to an outside provider.

This focus on GVCs helped to highlight several key elements of contemporary production systems, especially geographic dispersion, value adding, the institutional context and governance choices. However, in practice, it was governance that received the bulk of research attention (Gereffi, Humphrey & Sturgeon 2005). GVC thinking helped elucidate the nature of contemporary global production systems. It shifted the emphasis from trade flows to cross-border production systems and their integration. In addition, the focus on networks and local clusters of expertise has encouraged analysis of hybrid forms of governance (those between the extremes of market and hierarchy).

From GVCs to global factories

While providing several valuable insights, the GVC approach has been criticised on a few grounds. One relates to understanding governance. The GVC perspective sees contractual arrangements as being imposed by the buying firm and the terms of the arrangement reflecting the relative bargaining power. This is likely to be a complex, negotiated and contested process. A second concern is how value is shared. The GVC view is that value is likely to be extracted from weaker partners in the chain, while an economic perspective would suggest sources of competitive advantage, skills in overcoming market failure, and knowledge in the coordination of business functions as more likely sources of returns. The chain approach is also weak on predicting locational choice and the evolution of network relationships.

Further development of these ideas has provided a model termed the 'global factory' (Buckley 2011). This conceptualisation extends chain theorising in a few ways. First, the global factory perceives the focal firm (the firm driving and integrating the supply chain) as more than simply a buyer; its key role is in coordinating cross-border transactions. This suggests that the choice of governance mode is prompted not simply by cost minimisation but by a set of strategic considerations incorporating cost, quality, and flexibility. Second, the focus on coordination highlights the critical role of information flows within the global factory, a factor given scant attention in the chain literature. The global factory model distinguishes goods flows (that may be externalised) and information flows (that are generally internalised). Emphasising management, and not simply the governance of transactions, enables the global factory model to effectively combine the local and global contexts of production.

Global factory thinking also adopts a more comprehensive view of value capture along chains. Rather than thinking of value simply as revenue or profit, the global factory is also concerned with flexibility and the creation of resilience. This implies that local suppliers may be selected not simply because of their cost performance, but because they may offer other advantages, such as flexible production systems or rapid deployment of resources. This suggests that value capture is more than a zero-sum game; rather value in its various forms (cost, quality, flexibility or contribution to innovation) may be sought by the focal firm. The reality is that MNEs are at the very centre of GVCs and account for around four-fifths of world trade (UNCTAD 2013).

MULTIPLE-CHOICE QUESTION

Opportunities for local firms to participate in GVCs

A leading policy concern in emerging markets is how to increase the participation of local firms in global production systems. From a global factory perspective, a focal firm seeks the services of local suppliers when this generates competitive advantages. Such advantages arise from, for example, access to lower costs, network relationships, local market knowledge and specialist skills. Over time, the continuing appeal of local firms will necessitate their upgrading in areas such as quality, technological capability and flexibility. There is a belief that inward investment into emerging markets can play a key role in such upgrading and in raising the attractiveness of local suppliers. The relationship is described in the concept of the *investment development path* (Dunning & Narula 1996). This framework posits that inward investment into a country can have a positive effect on the competitiveness of local firms. This occurs through two primary effects: direct and indirect. A direct positive impact can arise if the foreign investor forms a partnership with the local firm. The direct relationship facilitates the exchange of technology and skills. Indirectly, spill over effects can encourage competitive upgrading of local firms. Spill overs take a few forms including competitive effects (increased competition stimulates the local firm to upgrade in response), demonstration effects (exposure to new ideas from observation of the investing firm) and labour turnover (when a former employee of the multinational investor moves to a local firm, for example). Over time, if conditions enable enough upgrading and the creation of competitive advantages, local firms may themselves become multinational investors (see the following section). Inward investment has been an important stimulus to the development of domestic firms in the Asia–Pacific region, particularly in the case of China (Graham & Wada 2001).

The rise of Asia–Pacific EMNEs

The rapid development of several emerging Asia–Pacific economies has resulted in rising levels of outward investment from these countries. In 2015, developing country MNEs from Asia became the largest outward investing bloc responsible for almost a third of the total. Not surprisingly, China and India are the largest international investors, but other economies in the region are also major sources, including Hong Kong (China), South Korea, Malaysia, Singapore and Taiwan (UNCTAD 2015).

Much of this investment from emerging markets takes the form of cross-border mergers and acquisitions, and more than two-thirds is targeted towards other developing economies. In many cases, this intra-regional investment increases regional integration to strengthen regional value chains. The data also reveals that a powerful motive for mergers and acquisitions by EMNEs is the acquisition of assets such as brand names and technology from developed-economy MNEs. In recent years, this asset-seeking motive has accounted for about half of all acquisitions by EMNEs (UNCTAD 2015).

Explaining the rise of EMNEs

The rise in outward investment from emerging markets has led to international business theory being questioned, particularly regarding theories of firm internationalisation. The existing theories were based largely on the internationalisation experiences of MNEs originating from developed markets, such as in the US, Japan and Europe, during the 1970s and 1980s when the world economy was less competitive and globally integrated (Johanson & Vahlne 1977; Dunning 1988). These theories were based on an assumption that MNEs can compete successfully in overseas markets because they possess FSAs. The traditional theories describe how these advantages serve to offset the disadvantages or liability of foreignness that international firms face in overseas markets, where the local competitors enjoy strong advantages of incumbency through political connections or better knowledge of the local operating conditions. The type of advantage that traditional MNEs possess share certain characteristics: they must be unique to the firm, difficult to imitate and internationally transferable. Research highlights that typical advantages are a result of superior technology, strong brands and marketing capability, and management skills. While it may be relatively straightforward for firms in developed economies to invest in creating such advantages in their home markets prior to international involvement, this may be more difficult for EMNEs; that is, firms based in volatile and rapidly evolving, emerging markets.

This has led to various attempts to address the challenges for internationalisation theory (Cuervo-Cazurra & Ramamurti 2015). Several approaches have been proposed. One is to revisit process models such as those of the Uppsala School (Johanson & Vahlne 2009) and to apply them to the processes displayed by emerging market EMNEs (Meyer 2015). A second approach is to extend the concept of the FSAs to consider potential emerging market home-based sources of advantage, such as unique institutional characteristics (Buckley et al. 2007) or the role of government (Wang et al. 2012). Other ideas have built on the asset-seeking motives of EMNEs, suggesting that they internationalise through a springboard process to catch-up with more established MNEs (Luo & Tung 2007). Perhaps the most ambitious endeavour to provide a focused explanation is that of Mathews (2006).

MULTIPLE-CHOICE QUESTION

The strategy and structure of EMNEs

Mathews (2006) provides a comprehensive analysis of the strategy of EMNEs while developing an alternative conceptual framework of their internationalisation processes. He argues that the internationalisation of EMNEs is occurring in distinct ways, partly because they are late comers to the global economy and must catch-up, but also because, for them, internationalisation is less of a choice and more of a competitive necessity. The pressure to internationalise is especially strong because past liberalisation of emerging markets means that EMNEs are now subject to high levels of competition from outsider firms, and are strongly linked into international trade and production systems.

Mathew's framework is built around three Ls: linkage, leverage and learning (refer Chapter 2). Linkages are the starting point and explain how resource-constrained EMNEs build competitive advantage. This is achieved by tapping into the assets and capabilities of more established MNEs. Linkages can take a variety of forms ranging from trade links, through joint alliances, to shared ownership in partnerships or subsidiaries. An interesting point to note here is that EMNEs are assumed to have a global or international focus from a very early stage and this underpins their ability to identify suitable partner organisations. Without such a focus, emerging market firms would be unable to attract the resources or skills required to internationalise.

Linkages compensate for the lack of FSAs within emerging market firms. Partner organisations contribute towards finances, knowledge and in underwriting risk. The most widely sought resources include technological know-how, marketing proficiency and managerial understanding. Such resources typically complement those already possessed by the firm, ensuring there is an adequate level of absorptive capacity (Cohen & Levinthal 1990), the requisite level of capability within the EMNE to assimilate and utilise new skills and knowledge, particularly those sought from outside organisations.

ABSORPTIVE CAPACITY
the ability of a firm to recognise, assimilate and apply new information.

Leverage, the second element of the framework, implies making the best use of limited resources as well as offering something to attract potential linkage partners. Asia–Pacific EMNEs can draw on their diverse resource base to offer incentives for potential partner firms pursuing the motives outlined in market seeking (new markets), resource seeking (low-cost production locations), opportunities for learning and reverse innovation.

The third L, learning, explains how the EMNE strengthens its competitive advantages, through exposure to new ideas and their repeated application, to improve processes, practices and, eventually, productivity. Of value to the budding EMNE is knowledge of quality-production practices, market entry and development, and the management of international operations.

There are several EMNEs including Haier, Lenovo, and Tata that have broadly followed the pattern of internationalisation described by Mathews. Similarly, we can see how such firms can utilise their home-country locational advantages to facilitate internationalisation. If we consider Indian firms, for example, research suggests that because of high growth and once protected markets, such firms often possess adequate finance but may lack strong technological knowledge. Indian firms can supplement the latter though through the use of targeted acquisitions (Buckley et al. 2016). In addition, they can draw on India's cost advantages in labour, design, equipment and even raw materials. Further, Indian firms are likely to have a sound understanding of marketing products towards the 'bottom of the pyramid' – the segments that are present in many other markets around the world (Pralahad & Hart 2002).

Summary

Learning objective 1: Understand the distinctive characteristics of emerging economies, and what distinguishes them from developed and other developing economies.

This chapter has discussed emerging economies within the Asia–Pacific region; those economies achieving high rates of growth and development, and aspiring to reach a developed-economy status. Emerging economies are distinguished from other developing economies by their ability to achieve above average rates of growth and modernisation. Because of their size and rapid growth, emerging economies are playing an increasingly important role in the global economy.

Learning objective 2: Describe the opportunities and challenges that MNEs face when operating in emerging Asia–Pacific economies.

Emerging Asia–Pacific economies are attractive to MNEs as they offer new markets, low-cost production sites, and exposure to novel business practices and structures. However, they also present significant business challenges that investors must overcome. These challenges result from high levels of uncertainty and volatility, uneven development, institutional and cultural differences, high levels of competition, and novel business practices.

Learning objective 3: Examine the implications of institutional differences in emerging Asia–Pacific economies and possible strategic responses to these.

Particularly challenging for many Western firms are the differences in business systems found within the Asian region, often characterised by greater levels of government involvement, less sophisticated or absent markets and market-supporting institutions, and a marked reliance on personal relationships in business. Asian businesses have developed effective responses to market and institutional voids, ranging from family and conglomerate business forms, internal capital markets, alliances with state-owned and directed businesses, and the cultivation of political connections. Western firms seeking to compete in the Asia–Pacific region need to be aware of these unique strategy formats.

Learning objective 4: Describe and explain the nature of GVCs in emerging Asia–Pacific economies, and the role of local firms within these.

The Asia–Pacific region is central to many of the key industry GVCs, with China especially playing a major role as a central node for sectors ranging from electronics to clothing. Analysis of a region's business through the perspective of GVCs clarifies the nature of supply chains, the availability of potential supply-chain partners, the role that local firms play, and the distribution of value globally. Many Western MNEs are anxious to create or tap into such chains, and host-country governments are eager to move up value chain systems. There is increasing collaboration along such chains, which is an important emerging feature of Asia–Pacific operations.

Learning objective 5: Understand the competitive implications of the rise of Asia–Pacific emerging MNEs.

It is hard to underestimate the value of emerging Asia–Pacific economies. The region is home to the two largest emerging economies in the world, one of which, China, appears set to soon become the largest single economy in the world. Recent years have also seen the rise of EMNEs, presenting a competitive challenge in many world markets. Chinese and Indian firms are now strong competitors in a number of industries. The Asia–Pacific region is also home to several countries expected to form part of the next generation of dynamic emerging markets including Vietnam, Cambodia, and Thailand. The diversity and vitality of the Asia–Pacific region means that it is likely to continue to be the world's most dynamic economic grouping in the foreseeable future.

USEFUL WEBSITES

REVISION QUESTIONS

Revision questions

1. What are the distinctive characteristics of Asia–Pacific emerging markets and how do these countries differ from other less dynamic developing economies?
2. Identify, with examples, four key motives for seeking to do business in Asia–Pacific emerging markets. What are the main challenges that international businesses face when they enter such markets and how do the challenges vary with the motive for entry?
3. What do you understand by market failure and institutional weaknesses or voids? How could such failures affect business strategy in Asia–Pacific emerging markets?
4. What are the contributions of GVC analysis in helping us understand contemporary global production systems? What are its weaknesses?
5. Discuss how Asia–Pacific EMNEs can compete in the global economy when they may lack the FSAs that theory argues are fundamental to international business success.

R&D ACTIVITIES

R&D activities

1. Many commentators predict that Vietnam will be the next dynamic Asia–Pacific emerging economy. Research Vietnam's economic and business fundamentals to demonstrate whether it should be classified as an emerging economy. What are likely to be the primary challenges that a foreign firm might expect to face when entering Vietnam?
2. Research and compare the business models of Apple and Samsung in the consumer electronics sector. What distinguishes their business models, and which seems to be more successful in the contemporary global economy?
3. Research a company from your country that operates in China or India. Discuss their motives for entry, the business strategy they have pursued, problems they have faced and the lessons they offer for other firms thinking of entering China or India.

IB MASTERCLASS

Gillette in India

Gillette, which was acquired by Procter & Gamble (P&G) in 2005, looks like a strong innovator. It has used innovation to turn around a market that once seemed lost to BIC disposable razors and electric razors. Through massive investments in R&D and marketing, Gillette has gained a 70 per cent global market share in men's razors, coupled with significant margins.

Gillette, and its parent company, P&G, have recognised the considerable potential of emerging markets, particularly India. For many years both companies followed the traditional approach of Western MNEs tackling emerging markets: selling the same premium products such as Olay moisturiser or Crest toothpaste that were successful in more affluent markets, but which only really appealed to the most affluent consumers in emerging markets. To expand their market reach, in effect to move down the pyramid, P&G adopted a strategy of offering pared-down versions of existing products, such as Downy Single Rinse fabric softener that required less water.

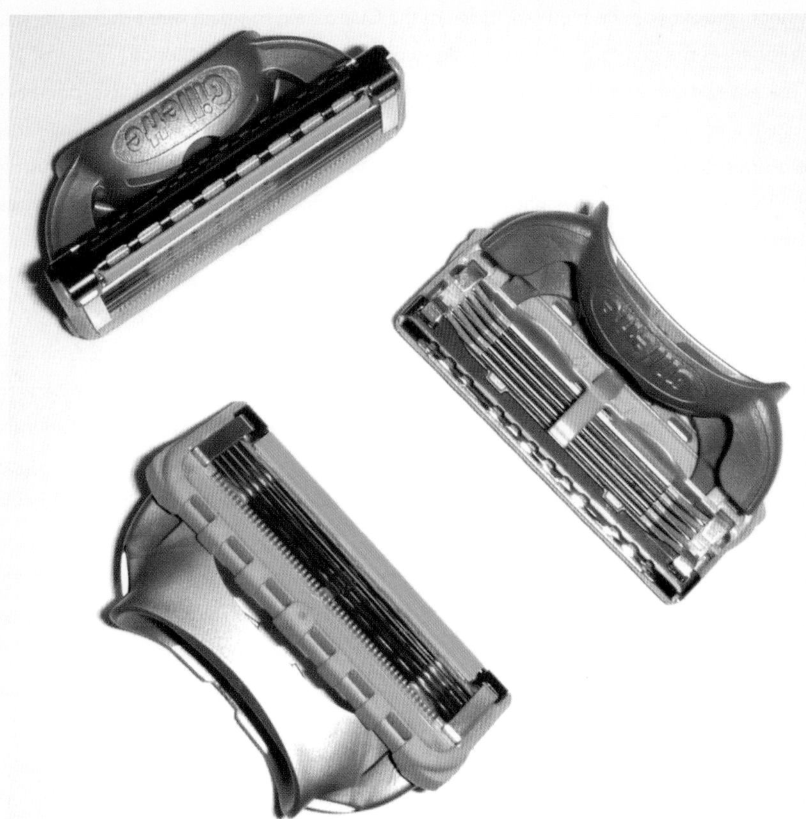

However, to tackle the Indian market for men's shaving products, Gillette took a more radical approach to product and business-model innovation. In 2009, the market for shaving products in India was fragmented with no major competitor holding a market share of more than 15 per cent. Nevertheless, most Indian men, perhaps as many as 400 million, used double-edge blades, a technology more than 100 years old. The attraction of double-edge blades was their low cost. Gillette's global product, the Mach 3 was some 50 times more expensive that the price of a double-edged blade.

To compete at such low-cost levels, Gillette realised that trimming down an existing product would not get them close to the necessary cost structure and would not offer enough value to capture existing double-blade users. The result was a product-development process that started from the bottom up. P&G sent a team to India to undertake ethnographic research and to observe potential customers. This revealed that the typical Indian shaver is quite different from his counterpart in more developed markets. He was much more price sensitive and shaved in a very different way – likely seated on the floor, with a small amount of water in a cup, balancing a handheld mirror in low light, and experiencing frequent nicks and cuts from his double-edged razor.

These observation processes revealed the key priorities of an Indian shaver: hygiene, ease of use and affordability. Considering the priorities, a new razor, termed the Gillette Guard, was developed for the Indian market. Hygiene is certainly an issue as it is difficult to rid a blade of clogged hair and shaving cream using just a cup of water. This was addressed by several features of the new razor, including a comb guard that worked to manage skin bulge and to flatten the face for a safer shave. The blade on the Guard is designed to rinse easily and reduce clogging. In addition, grooves on the blade cartridge of the Guard help to retain water during the shave, which enhances the razor's glide. Double-sided blades have no such provision.

The ease of use was also addressed. The blade cartridge uses a simple two-point docking system and can be secured with a single squeeze, making it much easier to change than a double-sided blade. The handle of the Guard has also been designed to better meet customer needs. The ribbed and lightweight rubber handle facilitates manoeuvrability during shaving. The broader and thicker end of the razor handle enables it to be held vertically when rinsing. In addition, there is a 'hang hole' at the end of the handle that enables it to be hung up to dry after use.

Affordability was a primary consideration for Gillette in launching the Guard. One way of minimising cost was to simplify product design. The Guard uses 80 per cent fewer parts than Gillette's more sophisticated razors as well as just a single blade. Gillette also built an Indian-focused business model. All manufacturing is localised, ensuring strict control over production and distribution costs. The result is a razor that sells for 15 rupees (about US$0.30) and replacement blades for 5 rupees (about US$0.10). To ensure wider distribution and ease of purchase, Gillette built ties with a network of more than 12 million Indian *kiranas* or local shops. Packaging was minimised to lower costs and to facilitate stocking in small retailers. Marketing costs were also contained by using traditional advertising featuring Bollywood actors and soldiers (traditionally regarded as well groomed). This strategy proved to be highly successful, with the Guard capturing more than 50 per cent of the Indian market within just six months of being launched.

This case provides a few lessons for managers seeking to sell in emerging markets. The first is the need for thorough and careful market research. On paper the Indian market for men's shaving products looks compelling: it is the largest market for shaving products, but success requires a fundamental understanding of what the consumer values. Gillette were able to identify these as hygiene, ease of use and affordability. Second, it is apparent that simply paring down older or outdated products from developed markets is unlikely to bring success. Such an approach does not ensure an effective response to market needs, ignores the information available to savvy consumers seeking value for money, and is unlikely to deliver the cost savings required. Consider that blades for the Guard cost 5 rupees – 95 per cent less than the Indian version of Gillette's Mach 3, which sells for around 100 rupees. Third, Gillette carefully aligned all the elements of their business model to maximise the likelihood of success in India. A product design, local manufacturing, and effective distribution and promotion all worked to clarify and reinforce the product offering. Fourth, with the correct product, pricing and positioning, there are considerable profits to be made even when operating towards the bottom of the pyramid.

Sources: Berner et al. 2014; Govindarajan 2012; Reddy & Dula 2013

QUESTIONS

1. Analyse the difficulties of tackling the 'bottom of the pyramid' in an emerging market and how you could research the characteristics of consumers in such a market segment.
2. This case examines an example of vertical brand stretching. How does vertical brand stretching differ from horizontal brand stretching? Discuss the difficulties of a vertical stretching strategy and how it can lead to brand cannibalisation.
3. What advice would you give to Gillette if they were thinking of introducing this product into another emerging market?

References

Amsden, A.H. (1992). *Asia's Next Giant: South Korea and Late Industrialization.* Oxford: Oxford University Press.

Bengsten, P. & Kelly, A. (2016). Vauxhall and BMW among car firms linked to child labour over glittery mica paint. *The Guardian*, 28 July. Retrieved from www.theguardian.com/global-development/2016/jul/28/vauxhall-bmw-car-firms-linked-child-labour-mica

Berner, G., Chang, J., Dunaeva, M. & Scamazzo, L. (2014). Sharp Focus. *Business Today*, April 13.

Bradsher, K. (2017). When solar panels became job killers. *The New York Times*, 8 April. Retrieved from www.nytimes.com/2017/04/08/business/china-trade-solar-panels.html

Buckley, P.J. (2011). International integration and coordination in the global factory. *Management International Review*, 51(2), 269–83.

Buckley, P.J., Clegg, J., Cross, A., Liu, X., Voss, H. & Zheng, P. (2007). The determinants of Chinese outward FDI. *Journal of International Business Studies*, 38(4), 499–518.

Buckley, P.J., Munjal, S., Enderwick, P. & Forsans, N. (2016). Cross-border acquisition by Indian multinationals: Asset exploitation or asset augmentation? *International Business Review*, 25(4), 986–96.

Chamberlain, G. (2013). Sore eyes, bad backs, low pay: the cost of false eyelash glamour. *The Guardian*, 29 December. Retrieved from www.theguardian.com/world/2013/dec/28/false-eyelash-industry-indonesia-low-pay

Chandran, R. (2016). Don't buy mica from child workers, Indian officials tell traders. Reuters, June 22. Retrieved from www.reuters.com/article/us-india-mining-childlabour-idUSKCN0Z7274

Cieply, M. & Barnes, B. (2013). To get movies into China, Hollywood gives censors a preview. *New York Times*, 14 January. Retrieved from www.nytimes.com/2013/01/15/business/media/in-hollywood-movies-for-china-bureaucrats-want-a-say.html

Cohen, W.M. & Levinthal, D.A. (1990). Absorptive capacity: a new perspective on learning and innovation. *Administrative Science Quarterly*, 35(1), 128–52.

Cuervo-Cazurra, A. & Ramamurti, R., eds, (2015). *Understanding Multinationals from Emerging Markets*. Cambridge: Cambridge University Press.

Das, M. & Das, S.K. (2013). *Economic Growth and Income Disparity in BRIC: Theory and Empirical Evidence*. Singapore: World Scientific.

Davies, R. (2016). Uber bows out of China with lots of fight left for dominance elsewhere. *The Guardian,* 7 August. Retrieved from www.theguardian.com/technology/2016/aug/06/uber-chinese-deal-ride-sharing-india-taxis

Dunning, J.H. (1988). The eclectic paradigm of international production – a restatement and some possible extensions. *Journal of International Business Studies*, 19(1), 1–31.

Dunning, J.H. & Narula, R. (1996). *Foreign Direct Investment and Governments: Catalysts for Economic Restructuring.* London: Routledge.

Enderwick, P. (2007). *Understanding Emerging Markets: China and India*. London: Routledge.

——— (2009). Large emerging markets (LEMs) and international strategy. *International Marketing Review*, 26(1), 7–16.

Engardio. P. (2007). *Chindia: How China and India are Revolutionizing Global Business*. New York: McGraw Hill.

Gereffi, G., Humphrey, J. & Sturgeon, T. (2005). The governance of global value chains. *Review of International Political Economy*, 12(1), 78–104.

Gooris, J. & Peeters, C. (2016). Fragmenting global business processes: a protection for proprietary information. *Journal of International Business Studies*, 47(5), 535–62.

Govindarajan, V. (2012). P&G innovates on razor-thin margins. *Harvard Business Review*, 16 April. Retrieved from https://hbr.org/2012/04/how-pg-innovates-on-razor-thin

Govindarajan, V. & Trimble, C. (2012). *Reverse Innovation: Create Far From Home, Win Everywhere*. Boston: Harvard Business School Press.

Graham, E.M. & Wada, E. (2001). Foreign direct investment in China: Effects on growth and economic performance, in P. Drysdale, ed., *Achieving High Growth: Experience of Transitional Economies in East Asia,* Oxford: Oxford University Press.

Hong Kong Trade Development Council (2008). SARFT reiterates film censor criteria. HKTD business alert, 1 April, issue 4. Retrieved from http://info.hktdc.com/alert/cba-e0804c-2 .htm

Johanson, J. & Vahlne, J.E. (1977). The internationalization process of the firm: a model of knowledge development and increasing foreign market commitments.*Journal of International Business Studies*, 8, 23–32.

——— (2009). The Uppsala internationalization process model revisited: from liability of foreignness to liability of outsidership. *Journal of International Business Studies*, 40(9), 1411–31.

Khanna, T. & Palepu, K.G. (2010). *Winning in Emerging Markets: A Road Map for Strategy and Execution*. Boston: Harvard Business School Press.

Luo Y.D. & Tung, R.L. (2007). International expansion of emerging market enterprises: a springboard perspective. *Journal of International Business Studies*, 38(4), 481–98.

Mathews, J.A. (2006). Dragon multinationals: new players in 21st century globalization. *Asia Pacific Journal of Management*, 23(1), 5–27.

McKinsey & Company (2014). India's Economic Geography in 2025: States, Clusters and Cities. Mumbai: McKinsey&Company/Insights India.

Meyer, K.E. (2015). Process perspectives on the growth of emerging economy multinationals, in A. Cuervo-Cazurra & R. Ramamurti, eds, *Understanding Multinationals from Emerging Markets*, Cambridge: Cambridge University Press.

O'Connor, S. & Armstrong, B. (2015). Directed by Hollywood, Edited by China: How China's Censorship and Influence Affect Films Worldwide US–China Economic and Security Review Commission, 28 October. Retrieved from www.uscc.gov/Research/directed-hollywood-edited-china-how-china%E2%80%99s-censorship-and-influence-affect-films-worldwide

Pralahad, C.K & Hart, S.L. (2002). The fortune at the bottom of the pyramid. *strategy+business*, (26), 1–14.

Reddy, S. & Dula, C. (2013). Gillette's shave India movement. *The Financial Times*, 4 November.

Schipke, A. (ed) (2015). *Frontier and Developing Asia: The Next Generation of Emerging Markets*. Washington DC: IMF Publications.

Stuenkel, O. (2015). *The BRICs and the Future of the Global Order*. New York: Lexington Press.

UNCTAD (2013). *World Investment Report 2013: Global Value Chains: Investment and Trade for Development*. Geneva: UNCTAD.

——— (2015). *World Investment Report 2015: Reforming International Investment Governance*. Geneva: UNCTAD.

Urata, S., Yue, C.S. & Kimura, F., eds, (2006). *Multinationals and Economic Growth in East Asia: Foreign Direct Investment, Corporate Strategies and National Economic Development*. London: Routledge International Business in Asia.

Wade, R. (1990). *Governing the Market: Economic Theory and the Role of Government in East Asia*. Princeton: Princeton University Press.

Wang, C.Q., Hong, J.J., Kafouros, M. & Wright, M. (2012). Exploring the role of government involvement in outward FDI from emerging economies. *Journal of International Business Studies*, 43(7), 655–76.

CHAPTER 7

MARKET ENTRY AND DEVELOPMENT STRATEGIES

Learning objectives

In reading this chapter, you will learn to:

1. examine the role foreign distributors play in a firm's international growth process
2. examine the meaning of strategic alliances and their main risks and benefits
3. understand international mergers and acquisitions, and their pitfalls
4. compare and contrast different market entry and development strategies.

IS VIRGIN AUSTRALIA AUSTRALIAN?

The ownership structure of Virgin Australia demonstrates how market entry is an evolving process. Initially, Virgin Australia's major original owners included Air New Zealand (26 per cent), Etihad (25 per cent), Singapore Airlines (23 per cent), and Virgin Group (10 per cent). However, Air New Zealand sold a 20 per cent stake to the Chinese Nanshan Group (the owner of Qingdao Air) in 2016 and the Chinese HNA Group (the owner of Hainan Airlines) acquired 13 per cent of Virgin Australia through the issue of new shares in 2016 (both deals were subject to regulatory approval). Air New Zealand said the sale would allow it 'to focus on its own growth opportunities while … continuing its long-standing alliance with Virgin Australia on the trans-Tasman network' (Anthony 2016). The Chinese buyers were motivated by seeking opportunities for further growth in the Asia–Pacific region. The management of Virgin Australia saw this as an opportunity to grow in the rising Chinese market (Hatch 2016). Examples from Virgin Australia show us how various foreign entry modes, such as alliances and acquisitions, can co-exist. Furthermore, they illustrate how the landscape of Asian–Pacific competition is shaped by and affected by key players from China and beyond.

WEBLINK
VIGNETTE
QUESTION

Introduction

This chapter examines the main foreign market entry and development strategies. It focuses on the role of foreign distributors, international strategic alliances, and cross-border mergers and acquisitions (M&As). Key concepts are first introduced and then seminal ideas are discussed in depth, including Arnold's article 'Seven rules of international distribution', Hamel, Doz and Prahalad's article 'Collaborate with your competitors – and win', and Ghemawat and Ghadar's article 'Dubious logic of global mega-mergers'. These ideas are examined and expanded upon to address contemporary themes such as market entry in emerging markets, entry strategy of Asian–Pacific firms, online distribution and retail channels, and evolving contribution of local partners. Throughout the chapter, dynamics of entry modes and market development are emphasised (market development refers to growing in a market after entering it). In the concluding section, alternative entry strategies are compared. Table 7.1 provides a concept map with the main entry strategies discussed in this chapter conveniently outlined.

TABLE 7.1 Overview of market entry strategies (equity in the purple cells and non-equity in the green cells)

Exporting and channel intermediaries	**International strategic alliances**	**Mergers and acquisitions**	**Alternative market entry strategies**
Agents *Distributors* *Sales representatives*	*Non-equity alliances* *1. R&D contracts* *2. Co-marketing* *3. Networks*	Mergers	Wholly owned greenfield sales subsidiaries
Trading companies	Greenfield joint ventures (JVs)	Full (100%) acquisitions	Greenfield production subsidiaries
Online distribution intermediaries	Partial acquisitions (partial-acquisition JVs)		*Licensing* *Franchising*

Note: equity entry strategies involve an equity investment and ownership stake

The role of foreign distributors

Before covering international alliances, and M&As, which are typically more relevant to large companies, it is important to first introduce one of the least risky and least costly foreign market entry modes in international business: exporting via foreign distributor and other distribution channel intermediaries in international business.

Exporting is the most common entry mode used by small- and medium-sized enterprises (although it is used extensively by large multinationals as well) (Brouthers & Nakos 2004). Exporting can be done through employing staff (abroad or at home) or via distribution channel intermediaries; for example, intermediaries based in the foreign market, intermediaries based in the home country or online intermediaries.

Intermediaries based in the foreign market

International distribution intermediaries are usually based in the foreign market. They function as the exporter's local partner, handling many vital business functions such as market research, arranging local transportation and complying with customs requirements. A foreign distributor distributes and assumes title to the exporter's products or services in a particular territory, and is often responsible for marketing as well. For example, Made4Baby, a New Zealand producer of baby skincare products with over 250 stores in New Zealand, is exporting through distributors in Australia, Korea, Hong Kong and Dubai.

FOREIGN DISTRIBUTOR
an intermediary that works under contract in a foreign market for an exporter, distributes and takes title to the exporter's products or services in a particular territory, and is often responsible for marketing as well.

An agent (also known as broker) may act for either a buyer or seller. The key difference compared to the foreign distributor is that an agent does not assume title or ownership of the goods. Agents operate under contract, with key areas covered in the contract including definition of territory covered, and terms of sale and compensation.

AGENT
an intermediary that buys and sells products or services for a commission.

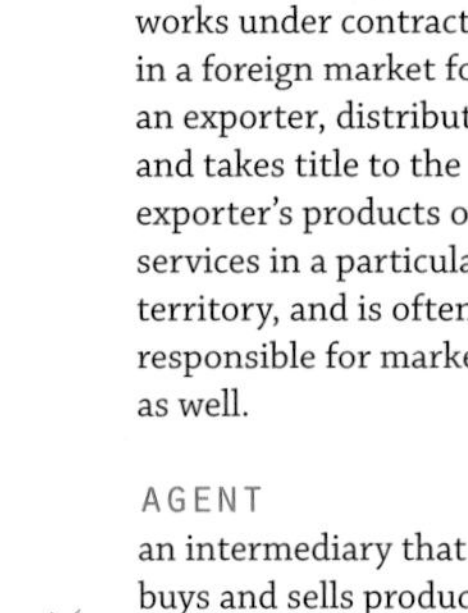

A sales representative, sometimes called a manufacturer's representative or service representative, does not take title to the goods that are represented like foreign distributors do. Like agents, sales representatives have a specified territory and normally, but not always, are compensated by commission, which is unlike foreign distributors who may be compensated by other means. Sales representatives usually do not have marketing capabilities, unlike foreign distributors who do often have these skills. Jobs in this area are challenging, but can lead to high commissions for star performers.

SALES REPRESENTATIVE
a contracted intermediary that represents an exporter and sells its goods in a specified territory.

Intermediaries based in the home country

Some international distribution intermediaries are based in the home market of the exporter. One example of such an intermediary is a trading company, which imports and exports products or services, and undertakes international marketing on behalf of the producer, especially for those with minimal international business knowledge. Characteristically, trading companies have high volumes and low margins. Many Asian countries including Japan, South Korea, China and India have traditionally relied on these types of companies for international trade (Peng & Ilinitch 1998). A number of trading companies – such as Japanese Mitsubishi, Sumitomo and Marubeni – are among the world's largest firms; besides trading, they engage in a range of manufacturing, financial and other services as well.

TRADING COMPANY
a firm that engages in the import and export of a variety of commodities, products or services and assumes the international marketing function on behalf of producers, especially those with limited international business experience.

Another type of domestic-based intermediary is the export management company. Its job is to find export customers, negotiate the terms of sale, and arrange for international transportation and logistics. A disadvantage of this intermediary is that the producer does not have as much control over how its products are marketed overseas. An example of an export management company is

EXPORT MANAGEMENT COMPANY
a firm that acts as an export agent on behalf of producers in return for a commission.

Frederick Export (www.frederickexport.com), which focuses on connecting manufacturers of consumer-branded products with export markets, including North and South Americas, Europe, Asia and Australia.

Online intermediaries

An online intermediary enables buyers and sellers to conduct ecommerce. Key players in this arena, such as Amazon, eBay and Alibaba, are reshaping the global landscape of international distribution. Online retail accounted for 9 per cent of global retail sales in 2016 and is projected to rise to 13 per cent in 2021, according to Euromonitor (Grant 2016). Amazon, Alibaba's Tmall, and eBay's marketplaces accounted for about a third of all internet retailing sales in 2016 (Grant 2016). The main advantage of these third-party marketplaces is that they provide an existing infrastructure that is already trusted by shoppers. This enables several types of retailers and other companies to benefit from the growing ecommerce and m-commerce markets. These online marketplaces are expected to continue accounting for an increasing proportion of total sales. However, according to Euromonitor, global ecommerce sales growth is forecast to drop from around 20 per cent per annum in 2013–15 to around 15 per cent in 2016–18 (Euromonitor International 2016). There are also various challenges facing the online marketplaces like quality control and the fight against counterfeit goods.

ONLINE INTERMEDIARY
a company that facilitates ecommerce by bringing buyers and sellers together on the internet.

In terms of overall online market attractiveness, the US and China were ranked in the top two spots by AT Kearney in its 2015 Global Retail Ecommerce Index (see Table 7.2) (AT Kearney 2015). In regard to industries, electronic goods, apparel, books and services are among the most popular online categories, although these patterns vary between markets. For example, 96 per cent of Chinese consumers bought electronics online in the past three months, compared to just 53 per cent of Japanese consumers. Similarly, 52 per cent of Indians bought groceries online in the past three months, in comparison to a mere 26 per cent in the US. Many global retailers are opening new warehouses and

TABLE 7.2 Global Online Market Attractiveness

Rank	Country	Online market size (40%)	Consumer behaviour (20%)	Growth potential (20%)	Infrastructure (20%)	Online market attractiveness score
1	US	100.0	83.2	22.0	91.5	**79.3**
2	China	100.0	59.4	86.1	43.6	**77.8**
3	UK	87.9	98.6	11.3	86.4	**74.4**
4	Japan	77.6	87.8	10.1	97.7	**70.1**
5	Germany	63.9	92.6	29.5	83.1	**66.6**
6	France	51.9	89.5	21.0	82.1	**59.3**
7	South Korea	44.9	98.4	11.3	95.0	**58.9**
8	Russia	29.6	66.4	51.8	66.2	**48.7**
9	Belgium	8.3	82.0	48.3	81.1	**45.6**
10	Australia	11.9	80.8	28.6	84.8	**43.6**
12	Hong Kong	2.3	93.6	13.0	100.0	**42.2**
14	Singapore	1.3	89.4	15.7	100.0	**41.5**
26	New Zealand	1.7	86.4	25.9	75.4	**38.2**

Note: Scores are rounded. 100 is the highest and 0 is the lowest in each dimension. Top 10 countries (overall score) and Asian–Pacific countries that made it to the top 30 included.

Source: Adapted with permission from AT Kearney 2015

services around the world to improve their position against local retailers and competing platforms; for example, Amazon.com announced that it was entering Australia (Hobday 2017). Amazon is also present in other important Asian–Pacific countries such as India and launched its Prime Now instant delivery service in Singapore in 2017 (Vaswani 2017). Online platforms are also entering the real estate sector, with brands such as Airbnb, Purplebricks and Cubbi (Corderoy 2017).

Google, Facebook and other social networking sites can also be considered online intermediaries, and a myriad of businesses use them to bypass other intermediaries and facilitate their ecommerce (Haucap & Heimeshoff 2014). Google reported revenues from digital advertising of over US$79.4 billion in 2016, while Facebook reported US$26.9 advertising revenues in the same period (Kollewe 2017). According to Zenith, the two companies accounted for almost a fifth of the total global advertising revenue (Gjorgievska 2016). Both Facebook and Google are blocked in China, where Baidu is the leading search engine and Tencent's WeChat and Weibo are the leading social networking platforms. In South-East Asia, Facebook is the most popular social networking platform (Kemp 2017).

Differences between national distribution systems

Countries differ substantially in various facets of their distribution systems. Thus, companies need to take these differences into account in crafting their distribution strategy. The main factors to consider are: (1) retail concentration; (2) channel length; (3) channel exclusivity; and (4) channel quality.

Retail concentration and channel length

Many countries' retail systems are now dominated by a few large retailers, such as Walmart (US), Carrefour (France) and Tesco (UK). Unique challenges are presented when dealing with these mega-distributors which represent a large proportion of a firm's sales (Thomas & Wilkinson 2006). The market power of the mega-distributors has led to continuous downward pressures on prices, and therefore to almost forced offshoring of production to low-cost locations such as China. Unfortunately, such offshoring often serves the profit margins of mega-distributors, not the manufacturers (Thomas & Wilkinson 2006).

Concentration is high, for instance, in Australian grocery retail, where four major players collectively control almost 100 per cent of the market (with Coles and Woolworths controlling over 70 per cent). In the UK, five major retailers control just over 70 per cent of the food retail sector, with the biggest, Tesco, controlling 28 per cent. In the US, the biggest player in food retail is Walmart, with 25 per cent of the market, and in China, the five biggest retailers collectively control 38 per cent (Mortimer 2013). Asia has large retail players with distinct formats, such as 7-Eleven (Japanese convenience stores), Auchan and RT-Mart (Chinese hypermarkets), and Lotte (Korean department stores). In countries such as India, the retail market is more fragmented; in other words, much less concentrated with a plethora of smaller stores and domestic chains. See more on the outlook for retail in the Asia–Pacific in Spotlight 7.1.

CHANNEL LENGTH the number of intermediaries between the producer and the consumer.

Channel length is determined by how many intermediaries there are between the producer and the consumer. The channel is short if the producer sells directly to the consumer. A long channel refers to a large number of intermediaries, such as import agents, wholesalers and retailers. Channel length is related to the retail concentration; fragmented retail systems tend to have longer channels. This is because there tends to be more wholesalers that sell on to the various retailers. This makes it more expensive for a foreign firm in a market like India or Japan to have a relationship with each individual retailer. In Japan, there were traditionally two or three layers of wholesalers between the producer and retail outlets. Large multinational discount superstores (such as Kmart, Carrefour and Tesco) often deal directly with producers and cut out wholesalers.

Channel exclusivity and quality

An exclusive distribution channel shuts out outsiders. For example, many of the large multinational discount superstores such as Kmart or Aldi are unlikely to carry products of small firms, instead preferring established international brands. However, channel exclusivity can also be a problem for multinational producers trying to break in to a market such as Japan. Dominated by domestic retailers with long-term relations between wholesalers and domestic manufacturers, it can be very difficult to form a relationship with these companies. In high-growth emerging markets, such as many of the Asian countries in the Asian–Pacific region, distribution channels are often still malleable, providing manufacturers with the opportunity to shape and mould the way distribution takes place. Firms should deal with distributors in these markets differently than in their domestic concentrated markets, dominated by mega-distributors. In emerging markets, they can attempt to take back control over their products and operations (Thomas & Wilkinson 2005).

EXCLUSIVE DISTRIBUTION CHANNEL
a channel that is difficult for outsiders to access.

Another important consideration is channel quality. This is defined by the capabilities and expertise of established retailers in a nation, as well as their ability to support and sell the products of foreign companies. In emerging markets, channel quality is often low. Multinationals who sell sophisticated products that require significant point-of-sale assistance and after-sales support cannot rely on existing channels. Thus, they need to invest in upgrading the local channel and sometimes even establish their own channel. Apple, the producer of iPhones, iPads and other products, used its Apple retail store concept in several nations including China and Japan. Icebreaker, a New Zealand premium merino wool apparel producer, has used a similar strategy, opening its

CHANNEL QUALITY
the capabilities and expertise of established retailers, and their ability to support and sell the products of domestic and foreign firms.

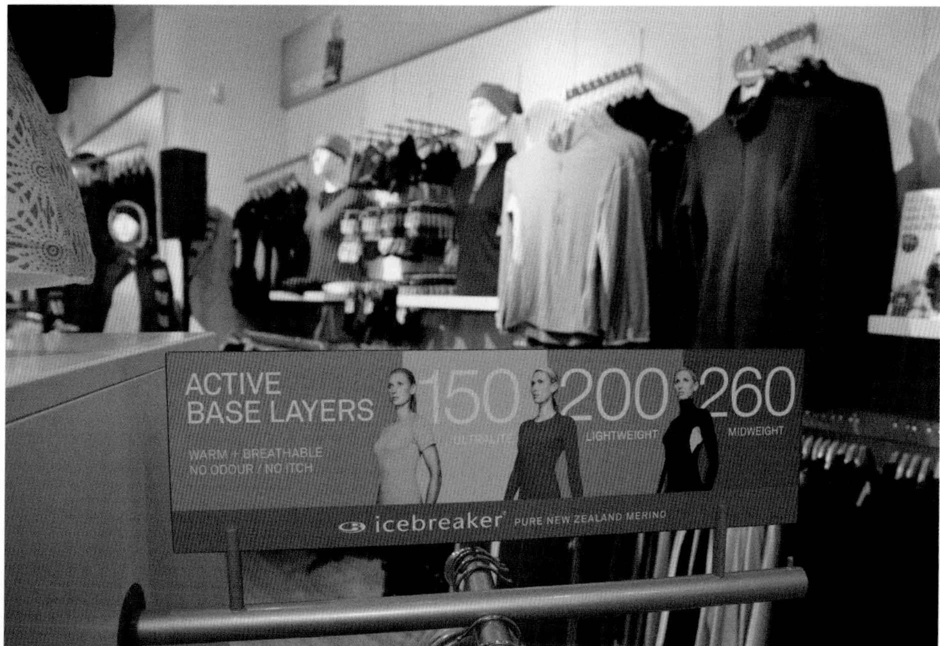

FIGURE 7.1 Icebreaker breaking into foreign markets

Touchlab concepts stores in the US, Canada and Europe. Interestingly, when expanding in Taiwan and Japan, it teamed up with a high-quality local agent in Taiwan and a Japanese sports company called Goldwin. Goldwin will work with Icebreaker to produce clothes in sizes that fit Asian figures (Inside Retail Asia 2012).

SPOTLIGHT 7.1

The Asia–Pacific drives global retail growth

The growth of the global retail industry is expected to be 15 per cent per year from 2016 to 2021, mostly driven by the Asia–Pacific, which is expected to account for 40 per cent of growth in this period (Grant 2016). China earned the top spot in AT Kearney's Global Retail Development Index, which ranks countries according to factors such as market attractiveness, saturation and risk. Mongolia and Malaysia were the other two Asian nations that made it into the top 10. Most other Asian nations saw advances in their rankings, with a continuous inflow of new entrants, and the development of modern retail in Tier 2 and 3 cities (beyond the major cities such as Shanghai). India rose in the rankings to number 15. It benefited from economic stability and regulatory reforms aimed at improving the ease of doing business. However, FDI restrictions on multi-brand retail remain (AT Kearney n.d.). Ecommerce is growing rapidly in the Asian–Pacific region, with AT Kearney reporting that Asia's market size has exceeded North America's. As internet penetration increases and ecommerce offerings improve, Asia's online retail sales could grow as much as 25 per cent annually (Euromonitor). Another major trend shaping the retail landscape in Asia was the launch of the ASEAN Economic Community (AT Kearney n.d.).

QUESTIONS

SPOTLIGHT QUESTIONS

1. Which Asian countries were in the top 20 of AT Kearney's Global Retail Development Index? Which other Asian country (not mentioned in the spotlight) would you expect to be in the top 20 (or would make it there soon)?
2. According to the spotlight, Asia's ecommerce market size exceeds that of North America. Which other major Asian country (other than China) has the most attractive online retail market?

Evolving role of local distributors

In an important *Harvard Business Review* article, David Arnold suggests that, when selling in foreign markets, MNEs should maintain relationships with local distributors over the long term, even after establishing their own local network to handle major clients. In theory, local distributors provide insight into the local market, knowledge of local regulations and business practices, existing major customers at low cost, and the ability to hire appropriate staff and develop relationships with potential new customers. Selecting and managing distributors is difficult though, and Arnold provides a list of seven best practices.

Arnold studied the role of external actors, specifically foreign distributors, in international strategy (2000). He focused on the evolving role of local distributors when MNEs first establish themselves in new markets and then try to grow in these markets. Arnold observes, as does Chapter 2, that many MNEs initially establish relationships with local distributors to reduce costs and minimise risks. In other words, the local distributor's complementary capabilities (such as their local knowledge of business practices, regulations, staff and customers) are substituted for developing new, location-bound FSAs required to access the host-country market in cases where market success is highly uncertain. Unfortunately, however, after enjoying some early market penetration, sales often flatten and may even start declining. Typically, the MNE then responds by calling into question the effectiveness of the local partner, and its ability to make good on performance commitments and expectations. The MNE's reflex may even be to take control of local operations by buying out the distributor or by reacquiring the distribution rights to build a self-owned, dedicated distribution network. The resulting transition period is often difficult, disruptive and costly – problems that could be avoided, according to Arnold, through better strategic planning of distributor selection and governance of the relationships with local distributors.

Arnold's research included a two-year field study of the international distribution strategies of eight MNEs active in the consumer, industrial and service sectors as they entered nearly 250 new host-country markets. Arnold observed, perhaps surprisingly, that MNEs often select new countries for market-seeking purposes in a largely unplanned or reactive way. This approach usually begins with a positive response to unsolicited proposals from local distributors, advertising the location advantages of the host country in which they operate and their own capabilities to help the MNE serve that market.

The MNE then aligns itself with an independent local distributor in order to minimise up-front risk, and to tap existing knowledge about the local market and potential major customers at low cost. Here the distributor is supposed to add complementary capabilities to the MNE's internationally transferable FSAs, which are embodied in the products it wishes to export. Usually the MNE invests little in marketing and business development, as it assumes that the local distributor will take care of these areas critical to foreign market penetration. But in doing so, 'companies cede

control of strategic marketing decisions to the local partners, much more control than they would cede in home markets' (Arnold 2000, p. 132). Arnold calls this minimal, low-risk, low-investment strategy the beachhead strategy. The MNE's attitude is to wait and see what can be achieved with such minimal commitment.

Behind this hands-off 'beachhead' approach may be the MNE's longer-term intent to eventually take direct control of local operations and to integrate these into the MNE's existing international network after some initial market penetration has been achieved. Arnold notes that 'for many multinationals, it's a foregone conclusion that local distributors have merely been vehicles for market entry, temporary partners incapable of sustaining growth in the long term' (2000, p. 132). Observing this past behaviour by MNEs, many local distributors conclude, quite reasonably, that the relationship will only be temporary. In such cases, the local partners may be unwilling to make the significant investments in strategic marketing and business development that are necessary to grow the business over the longer term. Thus, a vicious cycle of increasing challenges in bounded reliability is set in motion: the distributor's expectation of MNE unreliability (to provide adequate long-term support) in turn creates distributor unreliability (to invest for the growth of the business).

If sales growth falters, once the initial low-hanging fruit (selling the MNE's core products to the distributor's existing customer base) has been captured, each side may embark on a path of blaming the other for the disappointing results. Often the MNE laments that the local distributor 'didn't know how to grow the market ... didn't invest in business growth ... [and] just wasn't ambitious enough' (Arnold 2000, p. 133), whereas the local partner counters that the MNE did not provide enough support to match its overly high expectations.

In reality, both parties may share responsibility for the relative failure of the distribution agreement. Arnold's research shows that 'the same themes repeatedly emerge: neither party – the multinational nor the distributor [sic]– invests sufficiently in strategic marketing or in aggressive business development' (2000, p. 133).

However, according to Arnold, senior MNE managers usually deserve the main burden of responsibility, as they should realise that 'distributors are implementers of marketing strategy, rather than marketing departments in the country-market' (2000, p. 137). Arnold's point is that MNEs often relegate too much of their strategic marketing planning activities and the control thereof to local distributors when first entering new markets without providing proper direction and resources. In addition, the local market's life-cycle stage changes after entry, but the MNE often fails to adjust its market strategy or market commitments to reflect the evolution from early penetration to rapid growth. Instead, the MNE sticks with its initial market entry strategy – in other words, the beachhead strategy – for too long.

What is the solution to these common problems between MNEs and their international distributors, especially in developing countries? According to Arnold, 'The key to solving the problems of international distribution in developing countries is to recognize that the phases are predictable and that multinationals can plan for them from the start in a way that is less disruptive and costly than the doomed beachhead strategy' (2000, p. 134).

Interestingly, Arnold finds that companies usually have success when they evolve from a beachhead strategy to a mix of direct distribution by the MNE itself and long-term relationships with local distributors. This mixed strategy often lets the MNE retain control of distribution where feasible, while relying on the complementary capabilities of distributors where necessary:

> It seems probable that some national distributors will become part of a mixed distribution system, in which the multinational corporation will manage major customers directly, while other, independent, distributors will focus on discrete segments of national markets or smaller accounts ... independent local distributors often provide the best means of serving local small and medium accounts (Arnold 2000, p. 133).

In other words, Arnold recommends that MNEs keep their relationships with local partners for the long term even after the MNE has establishing its own local distribution network to provide to its main customers. The key for the MNE is to find the correct balance between three competing objectives: strategic control over important customers, benefits from the local partner's market knowledge and market access, and risk reduction when faced with high-demand uncertainty in the new market.

Arnold's research also contains recommendations for local distributors who want to continue to work with the MNE as it gains market share. Arnold's research shows that, in the cases where distributors successfully maintained their relationship with an MNE over the longer term, these local partners shared a number of characteristics: they did not distribute competing product lines from rivals, they shared market information with the MNE, they initiated new projects and they collaborated with other distributors in adjacent markets. They also invested in areas such as training, ICT and promotion to grow the business (Arnold 2000, p. 133).

Arnold's seven rules of international distribution

Arnold's article concludes by offering a list of seven guidelines for MNEs when dealing with local distributors. These guidelines should help MNEs avoid the commonly observed pattern of local market underperformance as a result of underinvestment and over-reliance on distributors, followed by an over-correction in the form of complete internalisation of all distribution activities.

1. Proactively select locations and only then suitable distributors. The MNE should identify for itself the countries it wants to enter, in relation to its strategic objectives (and the related country-level location advantages), and then suitable partners in those countries, rather than expanding internationally to particular locations in response to unsolicited proposals from local distributors (for example, in the context of trade fairs). The best partners are not necessarily the largest distributors, as the latter may already have contracts with (competing) MNEs for similar product lines, and may thus have an interest in dividing the existing local market among MNE rivals, rather than rapidly building the market for one firm.
2. Focus on distributors' market development capabilities. It is critical to find the best company fit in terms of strategy, culture, willingness to invest and to train staff, and so on, rather than merely a market fit, with those distributors already serving key target customers with related products.
3. Manage distributors as long-term partners. This approach, which may include incentives related to actual sales performance, will make distributors willing to invest more in strategic marketing and long-term development. Using distributors for short-term market penetration purposes only, and making this clear through distribution rights buy-back clauses in the contract, takes away the incentive for distributor investment in market development and may even increase bounded reliability problems. For example, if the buy-back price depends on sales volumes, irrespective of profit margins achieved, the

distributor may attempt to position the MNE's product as a commodity, rather than extract the highest possible price from customers. The distributor may thereby harm the product's future positioning in the local market.

4. Provide resources (managerial, financial and knowledge-based) to support distributors for market development purposes. Arnold's research indicates that MNEs rarely withdraw fully from a new export market. Committing more resources earlier may therefore foster better relationships with local partners as well as higher performance. The resources provided may include skilled support staff, minority equity participations (for example, to co-fund investments) and knowledge sharing (to augment simple equipment selling with related service provision to customers, for instance).
5. Do not delegate marketing strategy to distributors. While distributors should be able to adapt the MNE's strategy to the needs of local markets, it is up to the MNE to provide clear leadership in terms of the choice of products to be marketed, the positioning of these products and the size and use of marketing budgets.
6. Secure shared access to the distributors' critical market and financial intelligence. In many cases, local distribution partners may be the only economic actors holding such valuable information in the host country, and their willingness to share this information signals their commitment to becoming a solid, long-term partner. At the same time, the distributors reduce the MNE's bounded rationality problems by improving its limited understanding of the idiosyncrasies of the local market.
7. Link national distributors with each other, especially at the regional level (spanning several countries). Such linkages, in the form of regional headquarters to coordinate distribution efforts, or autonomous distributor councils, may lead to the diffusion of best practices inside the distributors' network, and act as an internal monitoring mechanism, stimulating more consistent strategy implementation throughout the region.

Arnold's seven rules of international distribution are in line with a key theme in international business thinking, namely that companies may benefit from strengthening their international linkages with external parties that command complementary FSAs, rather than trying to develop such FSAs within the company, especially if those FSAs would take a long time to develop internally and cannot be simply purchased in the host-country market.

Thomas and Wilkinson (2006) provide a complementary perspective on international distribution, suggesting that MNEs may also face a critical distribution challenge at home, with implications for international strategy. They argue that many US manufacturing MNEs, especially those active in consumer goods industries, have made an important strategic mistake in managing their domestic distribution system, and should try to avoid a similar mistake abroad. They observe that, since the early 1970s, many large manufacturing firms have focused on their so-called core competencies and have adopted total quality control systems in production, thereby largely neglecting the distribution and sales side of their business.

The dual outcome has been increased efficiency in production, where allegedly (according to business gurus and consultants) the firm's core competencies are located, and outsourcing of distribution if often given to non-dedicated distributors. Unfortunately, a problem may then arise when these non-dedicated, downstream partners include mega-distributors such as Walmart and The Home Depot – partners that represent a substantial portion of the firm's total sales

volume. For many US manufacturers this has meant the evolution from 'having a global network of loyal and faithful dealers and strong brand loyalty to becoming the manufacturer of a commodity that could be purchased at an ever-growing number of outlets for a lower price' (Thomas & Wilkinson 2006, p. 12).

International strategic alliances

While defining strategic alliance differs among authors, most agree that these alliances stand somewhere between market transactions, such as an agreement with foreign distributors and M&As (Contractor & Lorange 2002). These collaborative market entry modes are also distinct from wholly owned subsidiaries abroad. Licensing and franchising contain elements of market transactions and alliances. While multi-party alliances, such as those in the airline industry, usually come to mind first, these are actually special cases of alliances that are sometimes called alliance constellations (Gomes-Casseres 2003). Often a broader term like 'strategic networks' is used to encompass strategic alliances, joint ventures and long-term supplier-buyer relationships (Gulati et al. 2000).

STRATEGIC ALLIANCE a term encompassing a diverse array of voluntary cooperative agreements between two or more organisations.

Strategic alliances and partnerships are on the rise (Rinaudo & Uhlaner 2014). A PricewaterhouseCoopers 2015 survey of over 1300 CEOs in 77 countries found that 51 per cent of them said their firms would enter into new alliances within the next year, up from 46 per cent in 2010 (PwC 2015). The top motivations for alliances were access to new or emerging technologies, customers, markets and capabilities. For example, Theo Spierings, CEO of New Zealand's dairy giant Fonterra, said, 'We follow that guiding principle of focusing on our own strengths and growing those hard and fast, and then partnering in areas where we are possibly not that good' (PwC 2015, p. 24). Partnerships are also becoming increasingly diverse. While alliances were often traditionally defined as collaborations between competitors, the most attractive partnerships, according to PwC, are with suppliers, customers, business networks, clusters and trade organisations (see Figure 7.2).

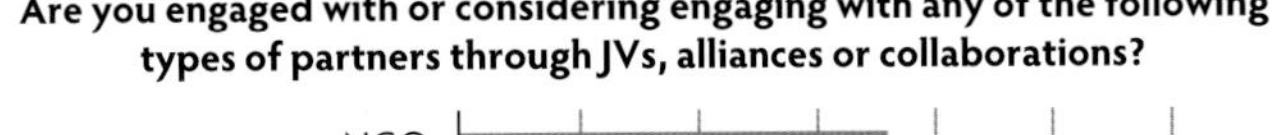

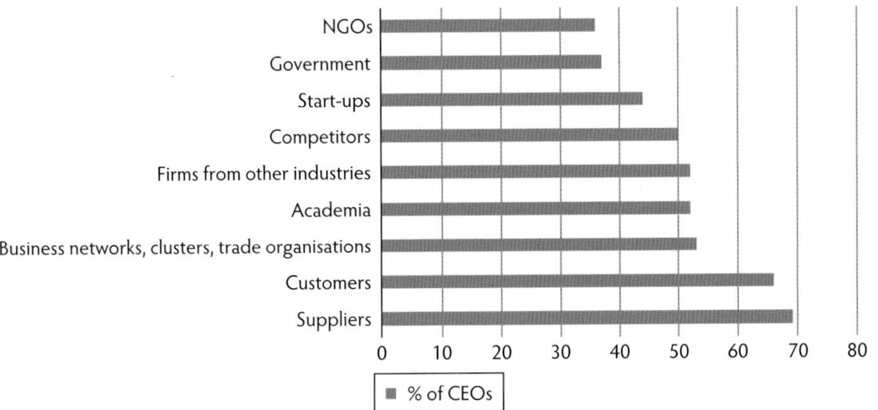

FIGURE 7.2 Most attractive alliance partners
Source: Adapted from PwC 2015

Equity versus non-equity alliances

EQUITY-BASED ALLIANCE
a strategic partnership that involves the use of equity; that is, ownership participation such as joint ventures.

The most common example of an equity-based alliance is an equity joint venture. Equity joint ventures can be greenfield joint ventures where a new, legally independent firm's equity is provided by two or more partners, such as the joint venture between the British Marks & Spencer and the Indian Reliance Industries. Alternatively, minority-acquisition joint ventures are when one firm acquires a stake of up to 50 per cent in another firm (for example, Fonterra's purchase of a 43 per cent stake in the Chinese Sanlu dairy firm – see the IB masterclass case study). Other examples of equity-based alliances are strategic investment where one partner invests in another, such as Air New Zealand's initial purchase of a stake in Virgin Australia, and cross-shareholdings where both partners invest in each other, which is common in Japan and South Korea (Fukase 2015).

NON-EQUITY-BASED ALLIANCE
a strategic partnership that does not involve the sharing of ownership.

The most common non-equity-based alliance is based on a contract and is often a project-based collaboration. Examples include cooperation agreements, co-marketing, co-production or buyback, R&D contracts and consortia, turnkey projects, strategic supplier relationships and strategic distributors; some authors include licensing and franchising in this category as well. R&D consortia between multiple parties are sources of many of today's innovations, as companies need to pool resources to create breakthrough products in the era of blurred industry boundaries and disruption (Porter & Heppelmann 2014). For example, Sony's PlayStation 3 was created in partnership with IBM and Toshiba because it was necessary to develop a super-fast chip for graphics in intensive gaming. Increasingly, the parties for collaboration come from different industries, such as in Cisco Hyperinnovation Living Lab (CHILL), who's membership includes Airbus, DHL and Caterpillar (Furr et al. 2016). Another example of recent cross-industry R&D collaboration is that of car makers such as Honda innovating jointly with Silicon Valley giants like Google on autonomous self-driving vehicles (Burke 2016; Ohnsman 2017). Non-equity technology alliances have been rapidly growing in importance over the past 30 years compared to equity technology alliances, which have been declining (Narula & Martínez-Noya 2014).

International joint ventures

International JVs are formed by partners from two or more countries. They usually indicate that no one party possesses all of the resources and capabilities needed to exploit an available opportunity. A lot of Western companies have been using this entry mode to gain access to markets in Asia. The Asian JV partner provides the local marketing expertise, the means to overcome trade barriers and the contacts with their local government. For example, US Walmart has partnered with Indian Bharti Enterprises to enter the retail market in India for the reasons mentioned above. Emerging multinationals, such as China's Alibaba, are often using similar methods to penetrate markets in Asia. Alibaba's Ant Financial has recently launched JVs in markets such as Indonesia, contributing its established mobile payment platform and technology while seeking local market expertise from their Indonesian partner (Cadell 2017).

SPOTLIGHT 7.2

Rise of strategic alliances in Asia

International joint ventures and alliances are an increasingly popular avenue for growth, especially for non-Asian companies aiming to grow in Asia (Roos et al. 2014). According to the Boston Consulting Group report, 78 per cent of survey respondents said they planned to maintain or increase their JV activity in Asia compared with 63 per cent outside Asia. The consulting company's worldwide survey of over 70 companies in 10 industries found JVs and alliances are often more attractive than M&As. A key reason for this is that M&As typically involve some degree of takeover or control, which can lead to negative publicity. Also, many parts of Asia have regulatory constraints. In China, for example, regulatory restrictions on foreign ownership make JVs the most viable option for gaining access. Twenty per cent of all FDI in China came from JVs in 2011, and 26 per cent of foreign companies operating in China have JVs there (Roos et al. 2014). Other countries, such as India and Indonesia, are too complex for most foreign investors to navigate alone, making a strong local partner crucial. The importance of JVs in emerging markets is partly related to the ownership structures there. Family-owned conglomerates and state-owned enterprises – which generate 10 to 40 per cent of GDP in Asian countries – are often easier to partner with rather than acquire (Roos et al. 2014).

QUESTIONS

1. Why are JVs more popular than M&As as an entry mode in Asia?
2. Name a prominent example of an international M&A and a JV involving firms from the Asia–Pacific.

SPOTLIGHT QUESTIONS

Advantages and disadvantages of alliances

Strategic alliances have advantages and disadvantages to other entry modes, such as exports and M&As. Table 7.3 highlights the main pros and cons of strategic alliances overall compared to other non-cooperative entry modes. It also highlights the relative advantages and disadvantages of equity versus non-equity strategic alliances. The main advantages and disadvantages can be placed within the framework of firm-specific and location advantages introduced in Chapter 2. Most of the advantages relate to the need to exploit firm-specific advantages and also access or combine with foreign resources, capabilities and organisational routines. Some of the advantages, such as the facilitation to market entry, and disadvantages, such as more exposure to political risk, of international alliances relate to the location advantages of the host countries.

TABLE 7.3 The main pros and cons of strategic alliances

Alliance	Advantages	Disadvantages
Both equity and non-equity	Facilitate market entry	Risk of choosing a wrong partner
	Cost and risk-sharing	Risk of partner 'stealing' key IP
	Access to complementary resources and capabilities	Risk of creating a new competitor
	Learning opportunities	Negotiation or coordination costs
	Routes to acquisitions	
	Creating global standards	
Equity strategic alliances	Greater control or influence	Complex management structure
	Better know-how transfer	Higher costs of coordination
	Facilitate common goals	More exposure to political risk
Non-equity alliances	Easy or cheaper to establish	More difficult know-how transfer
	Easier to adjust or modify	No or less equity can mean less trust
	Easier to terminate	Conflicts may be harder to resolve

MULTIPLE-CHOICE QUESTION

Management and performance of international strategic alliances

Strategic alliances and JVs pose substantial management challenges because of the multiple, potentially diverse, partners involved. Indeed, the Boston Consulting Group found that 19 per cent of companies surveyed were dissatisfied with their JV value creation experience and 73 per cent said it could be better, while 54 per cent of respondents said they get less than what they give to the alliance (Roos et al. 2014). To achieve desired alliance performance, companies must skilfully design and manage them. Design happens in the pre-alliance formation stage. It includes clarifying the strategic purpose of the alliance, partner selection, such as analysis, negotiation and decision making, and alliance structuring, including the exact organisational and legal form. Alliance management mostly refers to the post-alliance processes such as coordination, integration and adaptation (Kale & Singh 2009). It is also important to understand that alliances are most often not marriages formed for life but have a life cycle and an expected life span. In each of the phases (pre-deal, post-deal and break-up) there are unique challenges. (See Figure 7.3 for an overview of the major phases and steps of alliance management process.)

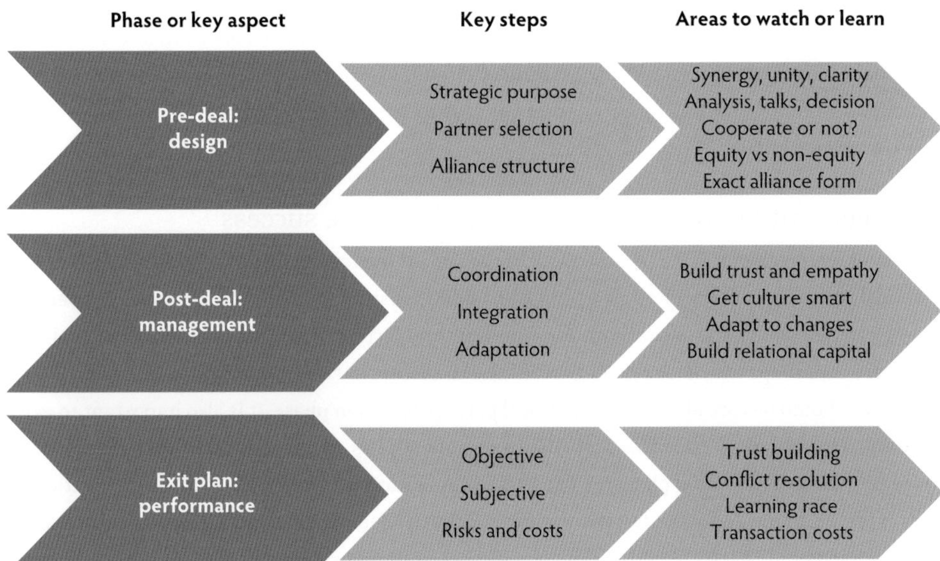

FIGURE 7.3 Roadmap to understanding alliance design, management and performance

Partner selection and alliance structure

Alliance formation follows a process from:

1. the initial decision on whether to cooperate at all or choose a different entry mode, in particular exporting, M&As or wholly owned subsidiaries
2. the choice of a specific partner
3. the choice between equity and non-equity structure
4. the choice of a specific type of partnership within the broad equity and non-equity groups.

As in any relationship, partner selection is crucial and should be approached with utmost care, with a formal process including analysis, negotiation and decision making.

The key characteristics of a good ally are related to synergy, unity and clarity. These were highlighted by alliance expert Ben Gomes-Casseres as underlying what he dubbed the three rules of business combinations (Gomes-Casseres 2015). Synergy refers to the potential to create more value together than the parties could create on their own, with the ideal partner having resources and capabilities that the firm lacks (1+1=3). Unity refers to a shared vision for the strategic purpose of the alliance (1+1=1). Clarity refers to the strategic objectives of the alliance being clear to both parties. There also needs to be a clear agreement regarding the division of contributions and gains from the alliance (say, 1+1 = 1.5+1.5 for equal contributions and gains by both alliance partners), and perhaps clear rules for exiting or termination of the deal as well.

Clarity about the strategic objectives for the alliance is a crucial foundation for its existence, as the partnership's purpose will significantly influence partner choice and alliance structure. For example, if market entry is the strategic objective – for instance entering an attractive market such as China, or an attractive market segment missing from a firm's current portfolio such as super-rich consumers in an emerging Asian market – typical partners will be competitors and other companies that are already in the target market. When the purpose is related more to accessing capabilities a firm is lacking, the typical partner is a competitor or supplier. When business development is driving

the alliance formation, distributors and customers can be potential partners as well. For example, China-based Zhengzhou Coal Mining Machinery Group, the world's leading provider of hydraulic roof supports for the mining industry, forms JVs with customers throughout China, and becomes their exclusive supplier (Roos et al. 2014).

Management lessons for international alliance success

Successful management of international alliances should overcome obstacles both in pre-deal and post-deal operations. First of all, it is crucial to build trust, empathy and reciprocity between or among partners, and to be aware of informal and cultural factors (Khanna et al. 1998). Poor cultural chemistry is perhaps the most significant obstacle to success in cross-border JVs (Roos et al. 2014). While this should be considered in the pre-deal partner selection phase, it is also important to work on cross-cultural issues after the deal. The same rule applies to the definition and alignment of strategic goals and business plans for the alliance. Adaptation is key, with inadequate reaction to both external changes and JV life-cycle evolution being frequently cited by managers as obstacles to success (Roos et al. 2014). Coordination, governance and integration are also important elements of post-deal management (Reuer et al. 2011). Parent companies should strive to focus their active participation on the JV's management board to areas that are directly related to the alliance's performance, such as capital allocation, risk management and performance management (Bamford et al. 2004).

Measuring and evaluating alliance performance

Strategic goals for an alliance can vary, but most of them involve an element of performance measurement and evaluation (Kaplan et al. 2010). It is important to distinguish between the performance of the actual alliance or a JV itself and the implications for the performance of parent firms. Furthermore, there are objective measures of alliance performance such as financial performance, market share, and alliance stability, and subjective measures such as managerial satisfaction, assessment of goal attainment and learning (Christoffersen 2013). There are many factors and determinants of international alliance and JV performance (Reus & Rottig 2009). However, the most important ones seem to be related to: (1) bargaining power, control and commitment; (2) trust, compatibility and justice; (3) culture distance and conflict; and (4) cooperation, relational capabilities and conflict-resolution mechanisms (see Figure 7.4) (Ren et al. 2009).

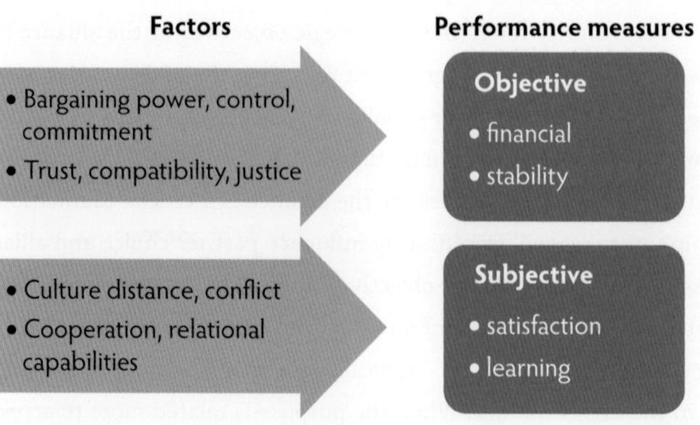

FIGURE 7.4 Framework for understanding factors behind international alliance performance

While partner commitment is positively related to alliance performance, it is not always necessary to have one dominant partner in control. In fact, 50–50 JVs can often outperform majority or wholly owned subsidiaries (Gomes-Casseres, Jenkins & Zámborský 2019). The national and even sub-national context is also important for understanding international JV performance (Li et al. 2018). Studies have shown that international JVs in China have unique characteristics. For example, the effects of partner conflict on international JV performance is less harmful for JVs in China than in other countries (Reus & Rottig 2009). Cultural distance and conflict between partners can be resolved with trust-building and conflict-resolution mechanisms. However, this is not always easy. Danone's high-profile JVs with Chinese Wahaha, for example, failed because of disputes over intellectual property (trademarked brands) and perceived unequal commitments of to the parties to JVs.

Many alliances and JVs don't last very long and it is important to have a clear exit strategy for both parties in the initial agreement. As with divorces in marital relationships, things can get ugly and lawyers can become involved, like it did with the Danone–Wahaha JV. However, there are also ways to engage in a reasonably peaceful dissolution such as through reconciliation and mediation (Peng & Shenkar 2002).

Managing risk in international alliances

International alliances are collaborative organisational forms that involve substantial risks and costs. The dark side of alliances are dependence, exploitation and abuse (Anderson & Jap 2005). The risks can be generally classified as relational risk and performance risk. These risks need to be managed in all stages of the alliance management process, including partner selection, structuring, operations and performance evaluation (Das & Teng 1999).

Strategic alliances in emerging markets

The risks and costs of strategic alliances are even more complex in emerging markets because of the emerging market's underdeveloped institutional environment. There tends to be more erratic regulations, lower political stability or efficacy, and a weaker enforcement of contracts and intellectual property rights (Luo 2007). International JVs in India (especially in the 1990s) were a good example of this. However, with ongoing liberalisation, the incentive to form alliances with a local Indian partner, in many cases, has disappeared, except in special cases of strong resource complementarity. In such cases, where there remained an incentive to form an alliance, the Western MNEs usually appeared to be much better equipped to win the learning race against the Indian partner, which created instability in the JV (Kale & Anand 2006).

Innovation alliances have traditionally been pursued by firms in developed nations. However, there is an increasing recognition of the potential for innovation collaboration with entities in emerging markets, especially in the Asia–Pacific region. For example, the US life-sciences giant Johnson & Johnson recently opened an innovation centre in Shanghai, and now has satellite centres across the Asia–Pacific in Singapore, Australia and Japan. Jesse Wu, Chairman of Johnson & Johnson China, said the Shanghai centre supports the group's larger goals of addressing China's specific healthcare needs, investing in local capabilities and increasing their external collaborations (Janssen 2014).

However, differences in cultural and business practices between China and other countries, as well as a lack of trust between local and foreign firms, can make it more difficult for both sides of a partnership to absorb and integrate their complementary knowledge bases, especially in high-tech strategic alliances (Fang 2011). Further, weak legal and regulatory environments pose a major risk

for strategic alliances in emerging markets. Expropriation risks negatively moderate the effect that complementary knowledge can have, namely the stimulation of product innovation (Fang 2011).

Challenges of close relationships

This section examines Hamel, Doz and Prahalad's idea that, when pursuing strategic alliances with partners who are also rivals, firms should try to learn as much as possible from their partners while giving away as few of their FSAs as possible. In theory, strategic alliances have three main benefits: they allow firms to share risks and costs (particularly R&D costs), they allow firms to benefit from their partner's complementary resources, and they allow the quicker development of capabilities to deliver products and services valued by the output market. Hamel and his colleague's provide other advice on carrying out strategic alliances, including the advice to keep developing FSAs independently and to avoid a vicious cycle of dependency on the partner. These ideas will be examined using the framework presented in Chapter 1.

In 1989, Gary Hamel, Yves Doz and C. K. Prahalad wrote an influential *Harvard Business Review* article on the dynamics of international strategic alliances. They focused on the phenomenon whereby large MNEs form strategic alliances with equally large foreign firms that are also rivals in the international marketplace.

Such competitive collaboration occurs because MNEs find it increasingly difficult to bear enormous R&D costs alone and to single-handedly gain easy access to the scarce resources required in order to launch new products. These problems are amplified in the context of the compressed time frames necessary to stay ahead of rivals. Hamel, Doz and Prahalad attempt to explain why some MNEs benefit greatly from these partnerships, in terms of new FSA development, while others do not.

Their methodology involved a five-year study of 15 international strategic alliances at various levels within the organisations involved, covering industries such as automotive manufacturing, semiconductors, computers and electronics. The sampling reflected a triad-based approach with a mix of cross-region alliances including: seven US–Japanese cases, four US–European ones, two European–Japanese ones and two intra-European ones. Wherever possible, both partners in the alliance were carefully investigated to uncover the role of strategic alliances in corporate strategy and competitive positioning, as well as the factors affecting the company either gaining or losing relative advantage by collaborating with a rival.

The benchmark adopted for evaluating alliance success was not how long the alliance lasted, which the authors claim is a commonly used but a misguided performance parameter. Rather, they focused on the change in each partner's competitive strength: 'We focused on how companies use competitive collaboration to enhance their internal skills and technologies while they guard against transferring competitive advantages to ambitious partners' (Hamel et al. 1989). The authors focused on how to win the so-called 'learning race'; in other words,, how to learn more from your partner than your partner learns from you.

Collaborate with your competitors – and win

The authors identified four key principles that successful companies adhere to when forming strategic alliances:

1. Collaboration is competition in a different form.
2. Harmony is not the most important measure of success.
3. Cooperation has limits. Companies must defend against competitive compromise.
4. Learning from partners is paramount. (Hamel et al. 1989, p. 134).

Their study revealed that overall, Japanese MNEs and Asian firms more generally, benefited the most from their strategic alliances with MNEs from other areas of the world. Hamel, Doz and Prahalad provided four reasons why Asian MNEs tended to win the learning race. First, Asian firms tended to be intrinsically more receptive and more willing to put effort into learning from their alliance partners. This aspect is rooted in cultural and historical differences; the authors suggest that 'Western companies won't realize the full benefits of competitive collaboration until they overcome an arrogance born of decades of leadership' (Hamel et al. 1989, p. 138).

Second, the Asian MNEs viewed alliances as an opportunity to develop new FSAs, and not primarily as a convenient tool to reduce investment costs and risks, (usually) on the upstream, technology development and manufacturing side, in contrast to several Western firms.

Third, Asian MNEs usually defined clear learning objectives regarding what they wanted to achieve from a partnership, and focused their efforts on acquiring new knowledge and observing their partners' practices to support such learning.

Fourth, the Asian MNEs' contribution to alliances often involved complex, tacit process knowledge that is not easily imitated or transferable, whereas the Western partners' contribution often involved easily transferable, codified product and marketing knowledge.

While some companies gain competitive strength from alliances, others fall behind as their FSAs are transferred to and absorbed by the alliance partner. For example, the authors noted that Western companies in particular often fall behind when they form alliances with Asian MNEs that are largely outsourcing arrangements, whereby manufacturing and technology development become the responsibility of the Asian partners, who essentially act as an original equipment manufacturer (OEM). This can cause a dangerous ratchet effect, since outsourcing to an OEM leads to lower investments in R&D, and in product and process design, by the Western firm until eventually not only manufacturing but all the upstream, FSA-developing activities have been transferred to the Asian partner. The risk is that the Asian partner firm can then enter markets on its own and compete outside the realm of the alliance agreement because of what it has learned inside the alliance.

The authors also observed that companies positioned as 'troubled laggards' often pair up with 'surging latecomers' to the market (Hamel et al. 1989, p. 135). The lagging companies are trying to find a quick fix for their own deficiencies, especially in terms of their inadequate innovation capabilities; for example, their lack of 'manufacturing excellence' routines like appropriate total quality control systems. Newcomers, however, are seeking to fill specific capability gaps, often in the realm of standalone knowledge, such as product or market knowledge, that can more easily be absorbed. With this starting position, the weaker firms, which in practice is usually the troubled laggards, may become trapped in a dependency spiral. Here, their attention may shift from continuously reassessing the merits of the alliance vis-à-vis strategic alternatives (such as a wholly owned subsidiary or market-based contracting), towards trying to keep the present partner satisfied with the relationship, which may become increasingly critical to the survival of the dependent company.

When outsourcing, senior MNE managers should respect four principles in order to avoid a vicious cycle of increasing dependency on a partner, and to maintain a focus on developing the FSAs required for competing in the international marketplace. First, outsourcing to provide a competitive product cannot replace the need to build FSAs over the long term. Second, senior managers should consider the negative consequences of outsourcing in terms of capability losses, and not just the short-run beneficial cost effects of de-internalising key value-creating activities. Third, senior managers should be aware of the cumulative effects that individual outsourcing decisions can have, especially in terms of creating a vicious cycle of deepening dependence on outside actors. Fourth,

if FSAs do dissipate towards a partner in an outsourcing relationship, they must be rejuvenated and strengthened as quickly as possible (Hamel et al. 1989, p. 137). Hamel, Doz and Prahlad note that, while ending up with a winner and a loser in an alliance is a common scenario, it is nonetheless possible for both MNEs to benefit from working together. The key condition here is each MNE's willingness and ability to learn from its partner, so as to allow new capability development, while avoiding excessive transfer and diffusion of its own proprietary knowledge. Moreover, the new knowledge obtained from the external partners must be effectively disseminated internally: 'Knowledge acquired from a competitor-partner is only valuable after it is diffused through the organization' (Hamel et al. 1989, p. 139)

In order for both MNEs to benefit from the alliance, each must share some, but not all of its knowledge and skills. Each partner must acquire new knowledge and skills, and foster new FSAs without transferring its proprietary strengths.

> The challenge is to share enough skills to create advantage vis-à-vis companies outside the alliance while preventing a wholesale transfer of core skills to the partner. This is a very thin line to walk. Companies must carefully select what skills and technologies they pass to their partners. They must develop safeguards against unintended, informal transfers of information. The goal is to limit the transparency of their operations (Hamel et al. 1989, pp. 135–6).

The nature of the FSAs contributed by an MNE to an international alliance affects how easily these FSAs will diffuse to a partner. One important variable here is called 'mobility'. Mobility refers to the ease of moving the complete physical instructions of how to duplicate an FSA. For example, if FSAs in the realm of technical knowledge can be represented in their entirety in easily understandable technical drawings and manuals, these FSAs are highly mobile. The more mobile the FSA, the more easily it may diffuse. A second relevant variable is called 'embeddedness'. An FSA is embedded if it cannot easily be shared through communication with actors outside the firm, without problems of interpretation or absorption across cultures. For example, standalone knowledge is usually less embedded than integrated skills or processes. The more embedded the FSA, the less easily it may diffuse.

Hamel, Doz and Prahalad advise companies to take steps to limit the easy replicability and unintended diffusion of FSAs to their alliance partners. Such steps might include limiting the formal scope of the alliance to a well-defined learning area. They might also include carefully considering where the alliance should be physically located, with a preference for a location away from the MNE headquarters, so as to avoid providing the alliance partner with a window on all the MNE's key FSAs, like critical technologies, even those unrelated to the alliance's scope of activity.

Still another step may entail establishing incremental, performance-related checkpoints, whereby specific knowledge bundles valuable to alliance functioning are shared only within the alliance context, and only when the alliance has achieved some pre-set performance benchmarks.

A last step consists of empowering company gatekeepers to control and moderate informal information transfers at lower operational levels to the partner. Here, easy access to key people and facilities must be prohibited, employee discipline and loyalty must be stimulated, and cultural differences that affect information flows must be carefully assessed. For example, as regards the last point on cultural differences, Western engineers often like to share information on their technical achievements, driven by their enthusiasm and professional pride. Their Japanese counterparts, on the other hand, are generally more likely to keep their company's proprietary knowledge confidential.

SPOTLIGHT 7.3

The Global Hotel Alliance seeking growth in the East

Boutique hotel chains from the Asia–Pacific region, including Rydges and Anantara, joined forces with other luxury hotels and formed the Global Hotel Alliance (GHA). The GHA represents over 34 brands with over 500 hotels and resorts operating in more than 76 countries. The alliance moved its headquarters from Geneva, Switzerland, to Dubai, United Arab Emirates in 2014. Thus, it positioned itself for growth in the East rather than focusing on Europe and America, where its competitors hailed from; competitors include another alliance, Leading Hotels of the World, and other luxury brands such as Sofitel and Marriott's Ritz-Carlton. Thirty-three per cent of GHA's hotels are located in the Asia–Pacific region, closely behind Europe (34 per cent) and ahead of the Middle East and Africa (20 per cent). GHA banked on increased tourism traffic in the Asia–Pacific region (6 per cent annual growth rate between 1995 and 2014) and the Middle East and African region (6.2 per cent p.a.) to achieve superior growth. The alliance established an award-winning loyalty program called Discovery, focusing on unique localised experiences to its hotels' clients. Furthermore, it invested heavily in technology solutions for the whole network of hotels to increase efficiency and customer experience. However, there was some degree of competition within the alliance itself. Hotels had to think about the best way to manage their presence in the alliance (Zámborský & Kruesi 2018).

QUESTIONS

1. Why did GHA move its headquarters to Dubai?
2. Which of the lessons from Hamel, Doz and Prahalad's article applies most to GHA?

VIDEO SPOTLIGHT QUESTIONS

International M&As

MERGER
a new legal entity that results from the combination of two firms to form a new, 'merged' firm.

ACQUISITION
a purchase or transfer of control of one company (a 'target') by another (the 'acquirer'); the acquired company becomes a unit of the buyer.

While the term M&As seems to conflate mergers and acquisitions, it is important to understand the distinction between the two as a vast majority of M&As are in fact acquisitions. A merger is a combination of two firms to form a new, merged firm that is a new legal entity. On the other hand, an acquisition is a purchase or transfer of control of one company to another; in other words, one company is a target for another acquiring company and the target company becomes a part of the acquirer company. The distinction is sometimes subtle and companies and some authors often prefer the term combination (Gomes-Casseres 2003).

M&As are important foreign market entry strategies, especially for larger companies. They are an alternative to exporting and international strategic alliances, as well as greenfield investment and other entry strategies such as franchising. Cross-border M&As accounted for 42 per cent of global foreign direct investment inflows in 2014–16, compared to 51 per cent in 2005–07 (UNCTAD 2017). Most M&As are deals within one market, such as Facebook's acquisition of WhatsApp. However, cross-border M&As are on the rise (Summerfield 2014). The capital expended on M&As reached $869 billion in 2016 compared to $428 billion in 2014, and the $729 billion pre-global financial crisis average in 2005–07 (UNCTAD 2017). A prominent recent cross-border merger was the 2017 combination of beer and beverages giants Anheuser-Busch InBev and SABMiller, which combined assets of what were originally US, Belgian, Brazilian and South African companies.

The Asia–Pacific region accounted for about a quarter of global M&A volume and Asian–Pacific acquirers accounted for about a quarter of cross-border M&A deals overall (see Figure 7.5) (UNCTAD 2017). The role of APEC in developing economies in cross-border M&As has been increasing, especially since the late 1990s (Chen & Findlay, 2003). According to Dealogic, China has recently overtaken the US as the largest buyer in the M&A market, including domestic deals made (Xueqing 2016). Examples of cross-border mega-deals involving firms from the Asia–Pacific include Chinese ChemChina buying Swiss Syngenta for US$43 billion, Indian Shire buying American Baxalta for US$32 billion and Japanese SoftBank buying British Arm Holdings for US$32 billion, all of which occurred in 2016. The Australian and New Zealand M&A market is also quite active although deals are usually not as large (Herbert Smith Freehills 2017). For example, Japanese Kirin bought a controlling stake in the Australasian Lion Nathan brewery for AUD$3.3 billion.

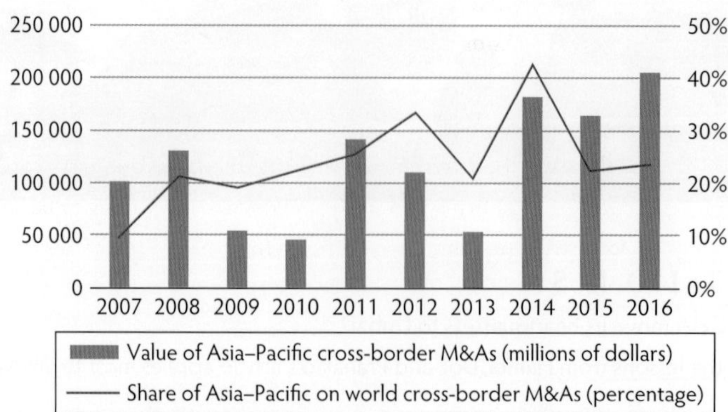

FIGURE 7.5 Share of Asian–Pacific buyers on total world cross-border M&As
Source: Calculated from data in UNCTAD 2017

M&A strategies

What motives drive cross-border M&As such as Kirin's purchase of Lion Nathan, Haier's acquisitions of Fisher & Paykel appliances or the merger of Nissan and Renault? Broadly speaking, M&As are driven by the three main motives for FDI (Dunning, 1993):

1. market seeking (M&A to facilitate access to foreign markets); for example: both Kirin's merger and Haier's deal were partly driven by the desire to grow in Australasia
2. efficiency seeking (acquiring or merging with foreign firms with the aim of having more efficient operations); for example: the Nissan–Renault merger improved efficiency, creating the world's largest car maker
3. resource seeking (acquiring a company which will give access to natural and other resources); for example: Haier was also motivated by access to Fisher & Paykel's design and R&D capabilities.

Cross-border M&As can be understood from three perspectives linked to various motives:

1. mode of entry in a foreign market
2. value-creating strategy
3. dynamic learning process from a foreign culture (Shimizu et al. 2004).

Synergy (1+1=3) is stressed as the main motive by many authors, but this is difficult to achieve (Chen 2008). Numerous authors and studies report that over half of M&As are often abysmal failures (Martin 2016). This may be because many of the motives for M&As are value decreasing (Nguyen, Yung & Sun 2012). They include managerial hubris or a managers' overconfidence in their capabilities, herd behaviour such as following norms and chasing the fads of M&As, and self-interested motives such as empire-building. While both parties of an M&A are hoping to successfully integrate their asset and resource bundles, and to increase in value, the FSAs of the acquired firm, the dominated partner, often shrink due to conflicts when attempting to integrate the dominating firm's routines and capabilities.

One of the main strategic decisions regarding M&As is whether to use them instead of an alternative foreign market entry mode such as alliances and greenfield FDI. M&As are one of the quickest ways to enter foreign markets and are particularly popular with Chinese companies, who tend to acquire strategic assets during international expansion (Deng 2009). However, due to many integration pitfalls and often an inflated price tag they need to be treated with caution. Alliances are often a less risky alternative, and both M&As and alliances should not be treated in isolation as they often are (Yin & Shanley 2008). McKinsey consultants suggest treating both alliances and M&As as portfolios of partnerships or as inorganic-growth initiatives. Furthermore, they emphasise the rising popularity of alliances (Rinaudo & Uhlaner 2014).

When deciding to engage in M&As or a greenfield operation, the choice between the two most popular FDI entry modes depends on a number of factors. In general, M&As are preferable to greenfield entry if a firm is seeking to grow quickly into a market with well-established local enterprises. It is also preferable when global competitors are also considering to establish a presence. On the other hand, when there are no attractive local firms to acquire, or they are not willing to be sold or require too high a price such as an acquisition premium, a greenfield entry may be the better option. A greenfield entry is also the better option if the firm's competitive advantage is based on its own capabilities and routines that would be difficult to transplant into a foreign acquired firm. It is also important to note that firms often first expand using one entry mode, such as a greenfield investment, and then use their subsidiaries to scout for potential acquisition targets. Pernod Ricard, the world's second-largest spirits and wine firm with an extensive presence around the world (including in the Australian and New Zealand wine industry), has often expanded in this way (Jensen & Zámborský 2018).

FIGURE 7.6 Iconic Australian wine brand Jacobs Creek was acquired by the French brand Pernod Ricard

Performance of M&As

M&As have advantages and disadvantages that affect their performance (see Table 7.4). Many, indeed most of them, don't create value. Both consulting companies and academic studies have pointed to the dismal performances of cross-border M&As. For example, McKinsey & Company estimated that around 70 per cent of M&As failed to achieve expected revenue synergies (Christofferson et al. 2004). On average, the acquirer's performance does not improve after takeovers and is often negatively affected. Although, the shareholders of the acquired firm tend to experience an increase in their stock value during the period of the transaction, known as the acquisition premium (King et al. 2004). Target firms, after being acquired, often perform worse than before the acquisition (Kapoor & Lim 2007).

TABLE 7.4 Pros and cons of M&As pre- and post-acquisition

Pros	Cons
Pre-acquisition	
Speed of execution Example: Pernod Ricard's purchase of Jacobs Creek quicker than greenfield development of own vineyards	**Incomplete information** (about what you are buying) Example: especially when under time pressure abroad (inadequate pre-deal screening)
Pre-empting competition Example: in telcos, where often limited licenses are given, getting in a foreign market first can prevent competitor's entry	**Overpaying for acquisitions** Example: acquisition premium in many M&As, Microsoft and Skype, Facebook and WhatsApp

Pros	Cons
Pre-acquisition	
First-mover advantage Example: Foreign firms entering first into risky markets such as Africa or Myanmar	**Poor strategic fit** Example: New Corp's acquisition of MySpace
Market growth Example: Japanese acquisitions in faster growing markets to escape slow growth at home	**Few good targets** Example: in some emerging markets, there are no targets for quality production of wine etc.
Market share Example: Anheuser Bush InBev merger with SABMiller	**Nationalistic concerns** Example: Chinese acquisitions facing protectionism in the US
Post-acquisition	
Reduced risk (acquiring existing productive assets with an established revenue stream rather than building new ones from scratch) Example: Rio Tinto buying Alcan	**Organisational or national culture clash** Example: DaimlerChrysler, two strong national and organisational cultures that were not very compatible
Synergy or complementarity (acquiring something the company couldn't create itself) Example: Amazon buying Wholefoods	**Tricky integration** Example: Haier's acquisition of Fisher & Paykel took some time to integrate Fisher & Paykel into Haier's system
Revenue stream Example: acquiring profitable business, say the purchase of Brancott Estate	**Liability of foreignness** (lack of familiarity with foreign culture, institutions and so on) Example: Geely–Volvo
Resource or brand acquisition Example: Lenovo's acquisition of IBM's PC business	**Nationalistic concerns** Example: BP in Russia faced changing ownership rules
Diversification Example: Fonterra's acquisitions beyond Asia (for instance, in Latin America and Europe) to reduce risk of over-exposure to China	**Stakeholder concerns** Example: managers in acquired companies fearing loss of influence; for instance, in Fisher & Paykel after the deal with Haier

However, this rather negative view of M&As perhaps hinges on how performance is measured and which time frame is used. Fisher & Paykel Appliances, a New Zealand white-goods maker acquired by Chinese Haier in 2012, increased its revenues, operating profit and R&D staff numbers between 2012 and 2014 (Zámborský & Turner 2017). Both companies seemed to have benefited from the acquisition, with Haier gaining exposure to up-market brands and design capabilities, while Fisher & Paykel benefiting from Haier's financial clout and global presence (Zámborský & Turner 2017). A comprehensive study of 367 cross-border acquisitions by Chinese firms found that on average, cross-border transactions created value for the acquirer's shareholders, but cultural distance, between China and the target's country, was negatively related to the extent of that value creation (Li et al. 2016). Firms were advised to invest in their capacity to overcome cultural differences as to increase their chances of positive outcomes in cross-border M&As. Asian M&As are prone to many of the challenges previous research found to hinder M&A performance, but also exhibit many unique features, such as the fragmented nature of Asian countries, markets and customers (Chakravarty & Chua 2012). In mining and metals, the Asia–Pacific was the world's most targeted region for M&As in 2015, with big deals including Barrick Gold's divestments in Australia and Papua New Guinea, and is likely to continue to offer significant M&A opportunities in the future (EYGM 2016). When managed well, M&As have a potential to deliver significant value (Haspeslagh & Jemison 1991).

Managing M&As

The pre-merger management phase is crucial in ensuring success. Consulting companies such as Deloitte stress the importance of finding the right target and executing the right transaction (Jamrozinski n.d.). It is important for companies to choose M&A targets that are a good strategic, capability, organisational and culture fit. Firms need to conduct thorough target screening, focused due diligence and detailed integration planning. Companies also need to thoroughly understand the new host country's laws, regulations, political environment and culture. According to Deloitte, pre-deal, the companies need to tackle these key three issues about the potential acquisition (Jamrozinski n.d.).

- *Strategic fit*: how does the deal add value? What are the specific opportunities and how can we capture them? Have we developed concrete strategies to do so?
- *Potential synergies*: what are the expected benefits of new markets, synergies and cost-savings? What is the sustainability of earnings and business practices abroad?
- *Risk analysis*: are we overpaying for this acquisition? Have we considered all risks and challenges (related to synergies, structure, people, project management and so on)?

Acquisitions can underperform if managers incorrectly match company targets to the strategic purpose of the deal. It is crucial to differentiate between acquisitions that might enhance current operations and those that could significantly transform the firm's growth prospects (Christensen et al. 2011). Companies thus need to consider crafting strategies for M&As where the goal is to reinvent their company's business. To reinvent their company's business, they'll need a new business model to complement, extend, or replace their own (Christensen et al. 2011). In these cases, a firm should plug its best resources into the new company, including the technology and capital it needs to grow. To heavily invest may pay off: successful new business models make a lot of money (Christensen et al. 2011).

One of the main reasons for M&A failure is that too many of them are approached with a 'take' mentality. Merely acquiring a company to enter an attractive new market you do not understand is not sufficient (Martin 2016). Microsoft's acquisition of Nokia's handset business and Google's acquisition of Motorola's handset business may fall into this take category. Successful M&As are typically those where the acquirer has something to 'give' to the target to make it competitive (Martin 2016). The acquirer can increase the target's competitiveness in four ways (Martin 2016):

- being a smarter provider of growth capital; for example, TATA's acquisitions in India
- providing better management oversight; for example, Berkshire Hathaway's acquisitions of Heinz
- transferring valuable skills; for example, Google's purchase of Android Inc.
- sharing valuable capabilities; for example, Procter & Gamble's acquisition of SpinBrush).

KEY STICKING POINTS AND LESSONS FOR SUCCESSFUL POST-MERGER M&A MANAGEMENT

- address the concerns of multiple stakeholders (investors, management, employees and so on)
- try to keep the best talents and key personnel in the acquired company
- deal with roadblocks thrown by people in the target company who may lose power or jobs
- develop capabilities that facilitate successful post-merger integration
- understand the unique target country's national environment (politics, institutions and culture).

Challenges for international operations

As highlighted in the previous section, cross-border M&As involve a number of challenges linked to the potential synergies, structure, people and project management. All of these become more pronounced in an international context. For example, people issues are compounded by cultural differences. Also, the ability to achieve cost synergies can be substantially compromised by national governments and interest groups opposed to the extent and direction of downsizing advocated by purely economic logic. Project management, involving a turnaround and integration of a foreign operation, is also much more difficult in a cross-country context.

Cross-border acquisitions of targets in emerging economies also often involve ethical challenges. Many of the deals have to be approved or won by winning favours with officials of countries with ambiguous records of transparency. For example, Rio Tinto, a major Anglo-Australian mining firm, has been embroiled in a number of corruption allegations over its acquisitions in Guinea and Mozambique (Staff and Reuters 2017). Four of its employees were also found guilty of engaging in corrupt practices (taking bribes and stealing commercial secrets) in China, with jail sentences of 7–14 years (Hornby & Shen 2010). Some analysts suggested the prosecution of Rio Tinto in China could be seen as 'punishment' for walking away from a high-profile M&A deal with Chinalco, the Chinese state-owned mining firm (Waldmeir & MacNamara 2010).

Asian-Pacific firms have been involved in many iconic cross-border acquisitions, including Lenovo's takeover of IBM's PC division and Tata Group's acquisition of Britain's iconic car maker Jaguar Land Rover. M&As in and out of emerging markets are becoming an important phenomenon and deserve special attention since there are significant differences between institutional environments, corporate governance practices, and markets in developed and emerging economies (Lebedev et al. 2015). According to the UNCTAD, emerging-market firms accounted for over a third of global cross-border M&As in 2013 (Lebedev et al. 2015).

The unique motives for M&As by firms from emerging economies relate to their countries' institutions, their latecomer advantages and national pride (Lebedev et al. 2015). For example, Tata's acquisition of Jaguar was arguably motivated partly by national pride; a firm from a former colony acquiring an icon of the colonial master, the UK. In terms of performance of M&As, the unique drivers of M&As in and out of emerging economies are linked to institutional development, quality of corporate governance, and government involvement (Lebedev et al. 2015). China is the major

FIGURE 7.7 Jaguar Land Rover is now in Indian hands

emerging economy which is active in cross-border M&As. A large proportion of Chinese acquisitions abroad are by firms with majority state ownership (Chen & Young 2010). It may be that the Chinese government pushes through such deals even though they are not in the best interest of minority shareholders. Thus, investors are sceptical of cross-border M&As when the government is the majority owner (Chen & Young 2010).

Dubious logic of global mega-mergers

This section is an in-depth examination of Ghemawat and Ghadar's idea that global M&A transactions usually do not make economic sense. The authors note several management biases that lead to inefficient M&As, and they recommend several alternative strategies as superior to global M&As.

Pankaj Ghemawat and Fariborz Ghadar wrote a classic *Harvard Business Review* article in 2000, criticising the observed trend towards international M&As, especially those among large MNEs from different regions of the world (the so-called global mega-mergers). Such M&As typically aim to create a company with a much wider geographic reach than that commanded by each partner individually (Ghemawat & Ghadar 2000).

Ghemawat and Ghadar ask whether such large-scale M&A transactions between MNEs, attempting to create firms with interregional or even worldwide market coverage, make economic sense. According to the authors, a general belief persists in many industries that increasing internationalisation, in the sense of growing interdependence of markets in the world economy, will ultimately lead to industry consolidations whereby only a few large firms, commanding impressive scale economies, will survive. The obvious implication for senior managers is to get big to survive. This view is exemplified by the main strategy rule introduced at General Electric by former CEO Jack Welch. This rule, which still prevails in this highly diversified, US-based MNE, states that the firm should be active only in businesses where it can be the number one or two in the world in terms of size, and should divest businesses in which it cannot achieve that goal.

Ghemawat and Ghadar argue that this approach is inappropriate, since the underlying conceptual rationale for it is weak, and the predicted consolidation is, in many industries, simply not happening (2000). Their empirical research reveals that several industries characterised by increasing internationalisation have actually also witnessed decreasing levels of market share concentration over the past half-century. In light of this observation, they argue that MNEs should contemplate alternatives to strategies of increased geographic reach through large-scale, international M&As.

Their *Harvard Business Review* article starts by briefly discussing some of the economic theories underlying the perceived link between internationalisation and industry concentration. The conventional theory of comparative advantage argues that specific production activities will become concentrated in those countries that possess advantages relative to other countries. But, as the authors correctly point out, this theory 'simply predicts the geographic concentration of production, not concentration of the number of companies in an industry' (Ghemawat & Ghadar 2000, p. 66).

While the conventional theory of comparative advantage does not account for economies of scale, which is a key factor in the trend towards global consolidation, other mainstream economic models, such as the theory of monopolistic competition, do. However, application of the latter models usually does not lead to the conclusion that increased internationalisation triggers extreme consolidation. The exception consists of some rare (mainly theoretical) cases of industries characterised by very large R&D expenditures, whereby a few firms are expected to win the learning race and drive out their less successful rivals (as occurred in the 1960s with US-based Kodak and Japan-based Fuji, who won the innovation race in colour photo technology).

Ghemawat and Ghadar's methodology involved examining data relating to the worldwide market share of companies in over 20 industries, going back more than 40 years to the 1950s. From this work, they computed a so-called 'modified Herfindahl index' for each industry, based on data from the 10 largest companies in each industry (rather than including all the companies in each industry). A Herfindahl index is a measure of market share concentration. The index is smaller than, or equal to, the number 1.00. In this particular case, a modified Herfindahl index was calculated for each industry, as the sum of the squares of the market share of the 10 largest companies. A higher number reflects a higher degree of market share consolidation (the extreme case being the hypothetical scenario of one firm commanding 100 per cent market share, meaning the index would take the value 1.00), while a lower number implies a lower level of concentration. If there were only 10 competitors, each with an identical market share, the index would be 0.1. If there were many more competitors, again with the largest firm or firms holding 10 per cent of the market, but the smallest of the 10 firms included in the index commanding much less than 10 per cent market share, the index could be substantially lower than 0.1.

The article presents a sample of the results by industry. For example, calculations for oil production and refining show an increasing number of companies and decreasing market concentration since the 1950s, rather than a consolidation of companies into a few global energy giants, as is commonly perceived. The only exception to the trend is the observation, in the late 1990s, of a number of mega-M&As that created some of today's largest oil majors (for example, BP Amoco, now BP, formed in 1998 by UK-based British Petroleum and US-based Amoco). The modified Herfindahl index calculated for the oil industry in 1997 stood below 0.05, implying the equivalent of more than 20 significant rivals in terms of market share. Such industry structure is far removed from a conventional monopoly or oligopoly with a small number of dominant firms.

Other natural resource industries such as zinc, bauxite, copper and aluminium also showed a similar increase in the number of international competitors and a decrease in market concentration over the same time period. The automobile industry displayed a trend similar to that of oil with decreasing market concentration for decades, with the exception of the years characterised by a few mega-M&A consolidations in the 1990s (for example, the now defunct merger of Daimler-Benz of Germany with US-based Chrysler Corporation to form DaimlerChrysler in 1998).

Even in high-tech industries, the examples of computer hardware, software and telephony also suggest a decrease in the market share of the largest firms during the 1990s.

As an aside, the authors do concede that their concentration measure does not include other forms of inter-company concentration such as strategic alliances, but they argue that such partnerships often fail or otherwise dissolve over the long term, and are therefore not indicative of a sustained consolidation trend.

Of course, not all industries exhibit this decrease in concentration. In those industries, Ghemawat and Ghadar argue that even if some level of consolidation is observed, and this results mainly from M&As rather than from organic growth, there is not necessarily a sound economic rationale for it. Ultimately, the aim of consolidation must always be to create value. 'To profit from dominating in a concentrating industry, a company needs to extract value by pushing certain economic levers – for example, reducing production costs, reducing risk, or increasing volume' (Ghemawat & Ghadar 2000, p. 68).

Creating value through consolidation, however, is often harder to accomplish successfully than might be expected by senior managers contemplating an M&A. In fact, consolidation often *reduces* value because of the pre-integration (negotiation) challenges, purchase price premiums and post-integration barriers associated with M&As.

Having reached these anti-M&A conclusions, Ghemawat and Ghadar then attempt to discover why some industries have an ineffective and inefficient tendency to consolidate through international M&As:

> [W]hy are cross-border consolidations pursued even when they destroy economic value? It seems there is often a pathology involved. Management appears to suffer from one or more of several motivational and cognitive biases toward mega-mergers, which can lead to irrational decision making and large-scale destruction of value (2000, p. 69).

Management biases and alternatives to mega-mergers

The authors provide a list of six senior management biases, which can all be interpreted as reflections of bounded rationality and, in some cases, also bounded reliability (Ghemawat & Ghadar 2000, pp. 69–70):

1. *Top-line obsession.* This occurs when senior managers focus too much on growing revenues, the top line of an accounting statement, rather than profits, the bottom line of an accounting statement, because corporate goals for growth are formulated in terms of revenue, and performance incentives are tied to achieving such top-line goals. The bounded reliability problem is that, given these ill-conceived incentives, managers neither pursue shareholder interests, nor the interests of consumers or workers, but solely their own interests.
2. *Stock price exploitation.* Senior managers are likely to engage in M&A activity if the firm has an overvalued stock price that makes it more affordable to engage in large M&A

transactions, or if the managers are looking to maintain an elevated share price based on the promise of operational (cost-reducing) synergies, even if few of these synergies will actually materialise over time. To the extent that senior managers know that the promise of substantial synergies is unlikely to occur and provide false information to relevant stakeholders, there is again a problem of bounded reliability, in this case akin to opportunistic behaviour.

3. *Grooved thinking*. Senior managers will often follow the traditional mindset within an industry even if it has become obsolete (for example, the focus of conventional telcos on maximising the number of telephone lines under their control, even in the age of the new communication possibilities provided by the internet).
4. *Herd behaviour*. Senior managers tend to follow and imitate the actions of their main competitors, especially in oligopolistic industries (for example, M&A activity in the European banking industry). Herd behaviour can also reduce managers' individual risk of underperforming rival firms. This is another example of bounded reliability; whereby senior managers engage primarily in self-serving behaviour.
5. *Personal commitments*. Individual senior managers may hold fast to their own personal views in favour of M&As even in the face of evidence that M&As in their industry systematically lead to underperformance.
6. *Trust in interested parties*. Outside parties such as investment bankers and consultants can influence companies to engage in M&As, thereby furthering their own interests in earning commissions and fees. Here, the source of bounded reliability problems resides with the external parties to the transaction; these parties have an incentive to further their own interests, rather than act in the best interest of the firm that hired them.

As an alternative to pursuing international M&A deals, the authors offer a host of alternative strategies that senior managers can pursue. As a general point, they caution that companies must remain focused on developing and profitably exploiting FSAs, rather than on attaining a particular scale as measured by revenues (Ghemawat & Ghadar 2000, p. 72):

1. *Pick up the scraps*. Spin-offs and divestments that arise from the mega-M&As of other companies can offer profitable growth opportunities for the firms that refrained from engaging in large-scale M&As themselves, if the assets are complementary to the buyer.
2. *Stay home*. Many companies have ample opportunity to improve their competitive position locally or in their home region, rather than pursuing large-scale, interregional M&As to expand their geographic reach.
3. *Keep your eye on the ball*. Companies can improve their competitive position by remaining focused on developing and exploiting their key FSAs, while their competitors become consumed with pursuing M&A deals and struggle with post-M&A integration.
4. *Make friends*. Strategic alliances offer an alternative expansion trajectory, often with less resistance internally and from external parties such as government regulators.
5. *Appeal to the referee*. Assuming a company cannot, or will not, pursue a mega-M&A itself, it may be able to slow those of its competitors by calling on regulators to review antitrust implications.
6. *Stalk your target*. In industries where first-mover advantages associated with international market expansion, especially outside the home region, are dubious, it may be best to wait

MULTIPLE-CHOICE QUESTION

and observe as others test the waters, rather than trying quickly to increase the MNE's geographic reach through M&As.

7. *Sell out.* If consolidation is economically justified, it may prove more profitable to be the seller rather than the buyer, given purchase price premiums, integration difficulties and so on.

Alternative entry strategies

This chapter has focused on foreign distribution, international strategic alliances and M&As as three of the main entry strategies used in international business. However, there are other market entry strategies. One of the most prominent alternatives is a greenfield investment. Fletcher Building's establishment of its wholly owned steel roof tile plants in Malaysia and Hungary are examples of wholly owned greenfields (Zámborský 2011). A wholly owned subsidiary contrasts with jointly owned ventures. Both greenfield investment, equity JVs and M&As are called equity entry modes, involving capital investment. Foreign direct investment entails some degree of management control and is distinct from portfolio investment, where firms hold less than a 10 per cent share in the foreign entity.

GREENFIELD INVESTMENT
an entry strategy that involves the establishment of a new operation abroad from scratch.

WHOLLY OWNED SUBSIDIARY
a subsidiary entirely owned by the MNE.

Non-equity entry modes do not entail direct investment or ownership of equity. Examples from the discussion earlier in this chapter include exporting through agents, distributors, sales representatives, trading companies, online channels, non-equity alliances such as R&D contracts, co-marketing, constellations and networks such as airline alliances. Licensing and franchising are also considered to be non-equity modes of entry. ZORB, a New Zealand adventure tourism company that invented the sport of globe riding – rolling down a hill in a patented transparent sphere – initially licensed its patented product, ZORB globes, and brand to foreign operators (Zámborský 2014).

LICENSING
an agreement where one firm gives the right to use its proprietary technology or trademark for a royalty fee to another firm.

Franchising is a similar agreement to licensing, although it is typically used in service industries and tends to involve longer-term commitments than licensing. The franchisee often must abide by strict rules regarding how it operates on an ongoing basis. The hotel industry uses franchising, as well as other non-equity entry modes such as management contracts, extensively in their international growth strategies, including international hotel organisations expanding in New Zealand (Kruesi & Zámborský 2016). The non-equity entry modes are becoming more popular than equity entry modes for many hotel firms, such as Accor (Kruesi & Zámborský 2016, p. 340).

FRANCHISING
an agreement where one firm gives the right to use its proprietary technology or trademark for a royalty fee to another firm, typically used in service industries and involving longer-term commitments than licensing.

Summary

Learning objective 1: Examine the role foreign distributors play in a firm's international growth process.

Foreign distributors are one of the many possible distribution channel intermediaries that facilitate exporting, one of the most common market entry modes in international business. These intermediaries can be based in a foreign market but also in the home country or online. Exporting firms should view their relationships with foreign distributors as long-term and evolving, maintaining ties with them even after establishing their own local network.

Learning objective 2: Examine the meaning of strategic alliances and their main risks and benefits.

Strategic alliances are a broad term including agreements of inter-organisational cooperation. They can be either equity based, such as JVs, or non-equity based, such as strategic networks. International alliances offer a number of benefits including cost and risk-sharing, as well as learning opportunities. However, they also carry substantial risks (for example, losing intellectual property and negotiation or coordination costs), and need to be designed and managed effectively to create value.

Learning objective 3: Understand international M&As, and their pitfalls.

International M&As refer to the combination of two or more firms through equity. They constitute close to a half of all cross-border FDI and have several advantages, such as speed of execution and an immediate revenue stream. However, the disadvantages of M&As are substantial, including overpaying and poor strategic fit. Many analysts criticise the dubious logic of global mega-mergers, which have extremely high failure rates.

Learning objective 4: Compare and contrast the different market entry and development strategies.

While this chapter focused on foreign distributors, alliances and M&As as the main entry modes, there are other important equity market entry modes, such as greenfield investment, and non-equity modes, such as licensing and franchising. The boundaries between various entry modes are sometimes blurred. For example, minority-acquisitions are both M&As and JVs.

Revision questions

REVISION QUESTIONS

1. Does Arnold's article 'Seven rules of international distribution' (2000) recommend that companies delegate marketing strategy to foreign distributors? Explain.
2. What are the four key principles that successful companies adhere to when forming strategic alliances with their competitors, according to Hamel, Doz and Prahalad's article entitled 'Collaborate with your competitors – and win' (1989)?
3. Name and briefly define at least three of the management biases of which Ghemawat and Ghadar consider the 'dubious logic of global mega-mergers' (2000).

4. What is the difference between licensing and franchising?
5. What are the four key ways in which the acquirer in an acquisition can increase the target's competitiveness?

R&D ACTIVITIES

R&D activities

1. How is Amazon's arrival in Australia and other countries around the globe a game changer for local retailers and other businesses? Look up some recent news and information about Amazon's presence and operations in your own country. Select one company, such as a prominent local retailer, and consider how should they respond to Amazon's entry. Provide three concrete recommendations for the company you chose.
2. Work in small groups. Choose a firm that interests you. Research its website and other sources and try to find out whether it is engaged in JVs, alliances or collaborations with particular types of partners such as suppliers, customers and competitors (see Figure 7.2 for a list of typical alliance partners). Report back on the specific partnerships to the class. Does the firm you chose have any alliances or partnerships in the Asia–Pacific region? Recommend one concrete new alliance in the Asia–Pacific that might help the firm to grow there.
3. Consider the global mega-merger between brewing and beverages giants Anheuser-Busch InBev and SABMiller. Research press releases, news articles, analyst reports and other information about the business combination. Critically assess whether it suffers from one of the six management biases suggested in Ghemawat and Ghadar's article 'The dubious logic of global mega-mergers' (2000).

IB MASTERCLASS

Fonterra's affairs in China

Fonterra, the world's leading dairy trader, moved on from the 2008 tainted milk scandal at its Chinese partner Sanlu and teamed up with Beingmate, another Chinese dairy company to grow in the booming Chinese market. What was the strategic logic behind this move and is it going to end up as a success story or another case of soured milk?

The New Zealand dairy giant's first foray into the Chinese market ended up being a headache. They acquired a NZ$150 million (43 per cent) stake in the Chinese baby formula maker Sanlu in 2005, subsequently pouring around NZ$200 million into the venture. Only three years after the partial acquisition the Chinese firm found itself embroiled in a shocking scandal that involved its formula milk being tainted by melamine, an industrial chemical, resulting in six deaths and hundreds of babies falling ill (NZPA 2009). Fonterra had to write off most of its Sanlu investment as the Chinese brand could not be reconstructed (NZPA 2009). Sanlu's general manager was given a life sentence after the scandal (Branigan 2009). Fonterra treaded very cautiously in China for a while.

In their next phase of involvement in China, Fonterra opted for wholly owned subsidiaries and greenfield investment in its own farms. They had already established a farm in Chinese

Hebei province in 2007 and by 2013 they had invested over NZ$350 million in two hubs with seven farms in China. They were pushing their own brand Anmum in a market growing exponentially, forecast to double between 2014 and 2017 to NZ$31 billion (Tajitsu 2014). Its competitors were moving even more aggressively into China. French Danone paid US$665 million to increase its stake in the Chinese Mengniu Dairy. Fonterra felt compelled to act faster and move beyond its tainted Sanlu past.

In late 2014, Fonterra announced it would purchase a 19 per cent stake in Beingmate, China's largest baby formula company, for a total of NZ$755 million. This was 25 per cent over Beingmate's stock price value at the time. Theo Spierings, Fonterra CEO, said Fonterra was moving on from the 2008 Sanlu scandal. 'China is a completely different environment now, Beingmate is a completely different partner ... and we are completely different from where we were six years ago (Tajitsu 2014).' China was a crucial market for Fonterra as it imports about one-quarter of New Zealand's total dairy exports, feeding a growing demand for quality dairy and milk formula (Adams 2016).

Fonterra was strategic about its investment in China, striving for long-term success. One part of its partnership with Beingmate involved building a JV production plant in Darnum, Australia, to produce Beingmate branded products for the Chinese market (Fonterra 2015). Fonterra also became a leader in cheese exports to China, topping more than half the pizzas made in China with New Zealand-made cheese and planning to open a new factory for export of mozzarella from Australia to China (Fonterra, 2017). It appointed a Chinese national, a former McKinsey consultant with an MBA from Columbia University, to head its Chinese operations from Shanghai. One of Fonterra's top management team is a former head of Greater China and India operations (Fonterra, n.d.). However, troubles resurfaced. In 2015, Fonterra CEO Theo Spierings admitted they were putting a halt on the greenfield expansion of Chinese farms after the farms posted a NZ$44 million annual loss (Fulton 2015).

In 2016, Fonterra's Chinese partner Beingmate got embroiled in a scandal where its formula cans were filled with cheaper, lower-quality baby formula by scammers. Beingmate posted a NZ$158 million loss in 2016. In 2016, its shares traded at a 25 per cent discount on the 18 RMB per share paid by Fonterra in early 2015, after peaking at nearly 30 RMB midway through 2015. In 2017, a number of Beingmate's senior executives (including the director, vice president and CFO) left the firm (Hutching 2017). Fonterra commented that its partnership with Beingmate was a 'long-term, strategic investment to grow in the Chinese infant formula market. We remain confident in our overall integrated China strategy' (Hutching 2017). What is Fonterra's future in China and what can it do to be a success there?

Timeline of Fonterra in China

2005: Acquiring 43 per cent of Sanlu for NZ$150 million
2006–07: Investing over NZ$200 million into Sanlu
2007: Fonterra's first greenfield farm in China
2008–09: Sanlu scandal costing Fonterra over NZ$300 million
2010–13: Fonterra's new Chinese farms, worth NZ$350 million
2014: a purchase of 19 per cent stake in Beingmate for NZ$755 million
2015: Fonterra's Chinese farms posted NZ$44 million annual loss

2016: Beingmate in a scandal, posted NZ$166 million annual loss

2017: Three key Beingmate executives left, stock down 25 per cent

QUESTIONS

1. Which entry modes has Fonterra used in China? Which of them were most effective?
2. Do you agree with Fonterra CEO's statement that 'China is a completely different environment now [in 2014], Beingmate is a completely different partner [than Sanlu] ... and we are completely different from where we were six years ago'? Explain your position.
3. How would you characterise Fonterra's market entry and development strategy in China? What would your recommendations be for the firm as to achieving long-term profitability in the market?

References

Adams, C. (2016). Fonterra's Chinese baby steps. *NZ Herald*, 17 June. Retrieved from www.nzherald.co.nz/the-country/news/article.cfm?c_id=16&objectid=11658222

Anderson, E. & Jap, S.D. (2005). The dark side of close relationships. *MIT Sloan Management Review*, 46(3), 75.

Anthony, J. (2016). Air New Zealand sells 20 per cent of Virgin Australia to Chinese firm. Stuff, 10 June. Retrieved from www.stuff.co.nz/business/industries/80925380/Air-New-Zealand-sells-20-per-cent-of-Virgin-Australia-to-Chinese-firm

Arnold, D. (2000). Seven rules of international distribution. *Harvard Business Review*, 78, 131–7.

AT Kearney (n.d.) Lifting the Barriers to E-Commerce in ASEAN. Retrieved from https://web.archive.org/web/20150315004327/https://www.atkearney.com/consumer-products-retail/ideas-insights/lifting-the-barriers-to-e-commerce-in-asean

——— (2015). Global retail e-commerce keeps on clicking: The 2015 global retail e-commerce index. Retrieved from www.atkearney.com/consumer-goods/article?/a/global-retail-e-commerce-keeps-on-clicking

Bamford, J., Ernst, D. & Fubini, D.G. (2004). Launching a world-class joint venture. *Harvard Business Review*, 82(2), 90–100.

Branigan, T. (2009). China executes two for tainted milk scandal. *The Guardian*, 25 November. Retrieved from www.theguardian.com/world/2009/nov/24/china-executes-milk-scandal-pair

Brouthers, K.D. & Nakos, G. (2004). SME entry mode choice and performance: A transaction cost perspective. *Entrepreneurship Theory and Practice*, 28(3), 229–47.

Burke, K. (2016). Honda, Google's Waymo consider self-driving car partnership: Honda could soon join Chrysler in providing vehicles to Waymo. Autoweek, 23 December. Retrieved from http://autoweek.com/article/autonomous-cars/honda-googles-waymo-chat-self-driving-collaboration

Cadell, C. (2017). China's Ant Financial extends mobile payments empire to Indonesia. CNBC, 12 April. Retrieved from www.cnbc.com/2017/04/12/reuters-america-chinas-ant-financial-extends-mobile-payments-empire-to-indonesia.html

Chakravarty, V. & Chua, S.G. (2012). *Asian Mergers and Acquisitions: Riding the Wave*. John Wiley & Sons.

Chen, C. & Findlay, C. (2003). A Review of Cross-border Mergers and Acquisitions in APEC. *Asian-Pacific Economic Literature*, 17(2), 14–38.

Chen, S.F.S. (2008). The motives for international acquisitions: Capability procurements, strategic considerations, and the role of ownership structures. *Journal of International Business Studies*, 39(3), 454–71.

Chen, Y.Y. & Young, M.N. (2010). Cross-border mergers and acquisitions by Chinese listed companies: A principal–principal perspective. *Asia Pacific Journal of Management*, *27*(3), 523–39.

Christensen, C.M., Alton, R., Rising, C. & Waldeck, A. (2011). The big idea: The new M&A playbook. *Harvard Business Review*, 89(3), 48–57.

Christoffersen, J. (2013). A review of antecedents of international strategic alliance performance: synthesized evidence and new directions for core constructs. *International Journal of Management Reviews*, 15(1), 66–85.

Christofferson, S.A., McNish, R.S. & Sias, D.L. (2004). Where mergers go wrong. *McKinsey Quarterly*, (2), 92–9.

Contractor, F. & Lorange, P. (2002). *Cooperative Strategies and Alliances*. Oxford: Elsevier Science

Corderoy, J. (2017). Online real estate platforms are taking off and claim to make property managers redundant. News.com.au, 5 April. Retrieved from www.news.com.au/finance/real-estate/buying/online-real-estate-platforms-are-taking-off-and-claim-to-make-property-managers-redundant/news-story/764c460776f034500e031fb3743668bd

Das, T.K. & Teng, B.S. (1999). Managing risks in strategic alliances. *The Academy of Management Executive*, 13(4), 50–62.

Deng, P. (2009). Why do Chinese firms tend to acquire strategic assets in international expansion?. *Journal of World Business*, 44(1), 74–84.

Dunning, J.H. (1993). *Multinational Enterprises and the Global Economy*. Wokingham: Addison-Wesley.

Euromonitor International (2016). What's new in retail: Emerging global concepts in 2016. Retrieved from http://go.euromonitor.com/white-paper-2016-New-Concepts-Retailing.html

EYGM (2016). A new normal, or the bottom of the cycle? Mergers, acquisition and capital raising mining and metals – 2015 trends and 2016 outlook. Retrieved from www.ey.com/Publication/vwLUAssets/EY-a-new-normal-or-the-bottom-of-the-cycle/%24FILE/EY-a-new-normal-or-the-bottom-of-the-cycle.pdf

Fang, E. (2011). The effect of strategic alliance knowledge complementarity on new product innovativeness in China. *Organization Science*, 22(1), 158–72.

Fonterra (n.d.). Our management team. Retrieved from www.fonterra.com/nz/en/about-us/CorporateGovernance/Ourmanagementteam.html

——— (2015). Fonterra welcomes next step in global partnership with Beingmate. 29 October. Retrieved from www.fonterra.com/nz/en/our-stories/media/fonterra-welcomes-next-step-in-global-partnership-with-beingmate.html

——— (2017). Australian mozzarella to take a bigger slice of China's pizza boom. Retrieved from www.fonterra.com/au/en/news-and-media/announcements/australian-mozzarella-to-take-a-bigger-slice-of-chinas-boom.html

Fukase, A. (2015). Asian Firms Scramble to Unravel Cross-Shareholding Structures: Corporate-governance push in region impels companies to loosen grips on control. *The Wall Street Journal*, 16 June. Retrieved from www.wsj.com/articles/japan-banks-target-cross-shareholdings-1434428677

Fulton, T. (2015). Loss-making Fonterra division wants 'partnerships' for network of Chinese farms. Stuff, 25 September. Retrieved from www.stuff.co.nz/business/farming/dairy/72379246/lossmaking-fonterra-division-wants-partnerships-for-network-of-chinese-farms

Furr, N., O'Keeffe, K. & Dryer, J.H. (2016). Cross-industry innovation that actually works. *Harvard Business Review*, November, 76–83.

Ghemawat, P. & Ghadar, F. (2000). The dubious logic of global megamergers. *Harvard Business Review*, 78(4), 64–74.

Gjorgievska, A. (2016). Google and Facebook Lead Digital Ad Industry to Revenue Record. Bloomberg, 22 April. Retrieved from www.bloomberg.com/news/articles/2016–04-22/google-and-facebook-lead-digital-ad-industry-to-revenue-record

Gomes-Casseres, B. (2003). Competitive advantage in alliance constellations. *Strategic Organization*, 1(3), 327–35.

——— (2015). *Remix Strategy: The Three Laws of Business Combinations*. Harvard Business Press.

Gomes-Casseres, B., Jenkins, M. & Zámborský, P. (2019). Profitability of joint ventures abroad: Explaining a new empirical puzzle, in F.J. Contractor & J.J. Reuer (eds), *Frontiers of Strategic Alliance Research: Negotiating, Structuring and Governing Partnerships*, Cambridge: Cambridge University Press.

Grant, M. (2016). New Retailing Research 2017 Edition: Key Trends for the Industry to 2021 [Web blog post]. Euromonitor International, 23 November. Retrieved from https://blog.euromonitor.com/2016/11/new-retailing-research-key-trends-2017.html

Gulati, R., Nohria, N. & Zaheer, A. (2000). Strategic networks. *Strategic Management Journal*, 203–15.

Hamel, G., Doz, Y.L. & Prahalad, C.K. (1989). Collaborate with your competitors and win. *Harvard Business Review*, 67(1), 133–9.

Haspeslagh, P.C. & Jemison, D.B. (1991). *Managing Acquisitions: Creating Value Through Corporate Renewal*. New York: Free Press.

Hatch, P. (2016). Virgin Australia wants to get more out of China, signs deal with HNA Aviation. Stuff, 31 May. Retrieved from www.stuff.co.nz/business/world/80574581/virgin-australia-wants-to-get-more-out-of-china-signs-deal-with-hna-aviation

Haucap, J. & Heimeshoff, U. (2014). Google, Facebook, Amazon, eBay: Is the internet driving competition or market monopolization?. *International Economics and Economic Policy*, 11(1–2), 49–61.

Herbert Smith Freehills (2017). Asia Pacific M&A Review 2017. Retrieved from www.herbertsmithfreehills.com/sites/contenthub_mothership/files/Asia-Pacific-MA-Review-2017.PDF

Hobday, L. (2017). Amazon to launch in Australia, local retailers vow to fight multinational threat. *ABC News*, 22 March. Retrieved from www.abc.net.au/news/2017–03-22/amazon-to-launch-in-australia-as-local-retailers-vow-to-fight/8376936

Hornby, L. & Shen, R. (2010). China jails Rio Tinto staff for 7–14 years. Reuters, 29 March. Retrieved from www.reuters.com/article/us-china-rio-verdict/china-jails-rio-tinto-staff-for-7-14-years-idUSTRE62S0R020100329

Hutching, G. (2017). Fonterra Chinese partner Beingmate's shares fall as asset sale imminent. Stuff, 13 July. Retrieved from www.stuff.co.nz/business/farming/94708137/fonterra-chinese-partner-beingmates-shares-fall-as-asset-sale-imminent

Inside Retail Asia (2012). Icebreaker expands Asia presence. Inside Retail Asia, 24 January. Retrieved from https://insideretail.asia/2012/01/24/icebreaker-expands-asia-presence

Jamrozinski, M. (n.d.). Planning successful cross-border mergers and acquisitions. Deloitte. Retrieved from www2.deloitte.com/ca/en/pages/mergers-and-acquisitions/articles/planning-successful-cross-border-mergers-and-acquisitions.html

Janssen (2014). Johnson & Johnson Innovation Launches Asia Pacific Innovation Center and Announces New Alliances. Janssen-Cilag Pty Limited, 29 October. Retrieved from www.janssen.com/australia/our-news/jnj-asia-pacific-innovation-center

Jensen, C. & Zámborský, P. (2018). Conviviality evaluated: Market entry and expansion strategy at the Pernod Ricard Groupe. *SAGE Business Cases*. doi:10.4135/9781526437068

Kale, P. & Anand, J. (2006). The decline of emerging economy joint ventures: The case of India. *California Management Review*, 48(3), 62–76.

Kale, P. & Singh, H. (2009). Managing strategic alliances: What do we know now, and where do we go from here? *The Academy of Management Perspectives*, 23(3), 45–62.

Kaplan, R.S., Norton, D.P. & Rugelsjoen, B. (2010). Managing alliances with the balanced scorecard. *Harvard Business Review*, 88(1), 114–20.

Kapoor, R. & Lim, K. (2007). The impact of acquisitions on the productivity of inventors at semiconductor firms: A synthesis of knowledge-based and incentive-based perspectives. *Academy of Management Journal*, 50(5), 1133–55.

Kemp, S. (2017). Digital in Southeast Asia in 2017 [Web blog post]. We Are Social, 15 February. Retrieved from https://wearesocial.com/sg/blog/2017/02/digital-south, ast-asia-2017

Khanna, T., Gulati, R. & Nohria, N. (1998). The dynamics of learning alliances: Competition, cooperation, and relative scope. *Strategic Management Journal*, 19(3), 193–210.

King, D.R., Dalton, D.R., Daily, C.M. & Covin, J.G. (2004). Meta-analyses of post-acquisition performance: Indications of unidentified moderators. *Strategic Management Journal*, 25(2), 187.

Kollewe, J. (2017). Google and Facebook bring in one-fifth of global ad revenue. *The Guardian,* 2 May. Retrieved from www.theguardian.com/media/2017/may/02/google-and-facebook-bring-in-one-fifth-of-global-ad-revenue

Kruesi, M.A. & Zámborský, P. (2016). The non-equity entry mode choices of international hotel organizations in New Zealand. *International Journal of Hospitality & Tourism Administration*, 17(3), 316–46.

Lebedev, S., Peng, M.W., Xie, E. & Stevens, C.E. (2015). Mergers and acquisitions in and out of emerging economies. *Journal of World Business*, 50(4), 651–62.

Li, A., Burmester, B. & Zámborský, P. (2019). Subnational differences and entry mode performance: Multinationals in East and West China. *Journal of Management & Organization*. Forthcoming in 2019. doi:10.1017/jmo.2017.59

Li, J., Li, P. & Wang, B. (2016). Do cross-border acquisitions create value? Evidence from overseas acquisitions by Chinese firms. *International Business Review*, 25(2), 471–83.

Luo, Y. (2007). Are joint venture partners more opportunistic in a more volatile environment? *Strategic Management Journal*, 28(1), 39–60.

Martin, R.L. (2016). M&A: The one thing you need to get right. *Harvard Business Review*, 94(6), 42–8.

Mortimer. G. (2013). FactCheck: is our grocery market one of the most concentrated in the world? The Conversation, 12 August. Retrieved from http://theconversation.com/factcheck-is-our-grocery-market-one-of-the-most-concentrated-in-the-world-16520

Narula, R. & Martínez-Noya, A. (2014). International R&D alliances by firms: Origins and development. John H Dunning Centre for International Business Discussion Papers jhd-dp2014-06, Henley Business School, Reading University. Retrieved from https://s3-eu-west 1.amazonaws.com/assets.henley.ac.uk/legacyUploads/JHD-2014–06-Narula-and-Martinez-Noya.pdf

Nguyen, H.T., Yung, K. & Sun, Q. (2012). Motives for mergers and acquisitions: Ex-post market evidence from the US. *Journal of Business Finance & Accounting*, 39(9/10), 1357–75.

NZPA (2009). Fonterra's Sanlu told to import melamine detection gear. Stuff, 31 January. Retrieved from www.stuff.co.nz/national/662893/Fonterras-Sanlu-told-to-import-melamine-detection-gear

Ohnsman, A. (2017). Honda is turning its Silicon Valley lab into a global hub for tech collaboration. Forbes, 13 April. Retrieved from www.forbes.com/sites/alanohnsman/2017/04/13/honda-upgrades-silicon-valley-lab-to-global-tech-collaboration-company/#4bc8b2c01b8d

Peng, M.W. & Ilinitch, A.Y. (1998). Export intermediary firms: A note on export development research. *Journal of International Business Studies*, 29(3), 609–20.

Peng, M.W. & Shenkar, O. (2002). Joint venture dissolution as corporate divorce. *The Academy of Management Executive*, 16(2), 92–105.

Porter, M.E. & Heppelmann, J.E. (2014). How smart, connected products are transforming competition. *Harvard Business Review*, 92(11), 64–88.

PwC (2015). PwC eighteenth annual global CEO Survey. Retrieved from www.pwc.com/gx/en/ceo-survey/2015/assets/pwc-18th-annual-global-ceo-survey-jan-2015.pdf

Ren, H., Gray, B. & Kim, K. (2009). Performance of international joint ventures: What factors really make a difference and how? *Journal of management*, 35(3), 805–32.

Reuer, J.J., Klijn, E., van den Bosch, F.A. & Volberda, H.W. (2011). Bringing corporate governance to international joint ventures. *Global Strategy Journal*, 1(1–2), 54–66.

Reus, T.H. & Rottig, D. (2009). Meta-analyses of international joint venture performance determinants: evidence for theory, methodological artefacts and the unique context of China. *Management International Review*, 49(5), 607–40.

Rinaudo, E.K. & Uhlaner, R. (2014). Joint ventures on the rise. *McKinsey & Company*, November. Retrieved from www.mckinsey.com/business-functions/strategy-and-corporate-finance/our-insights/joint-ventures-on-the-rise

Roos, A., Khanna, D., Verma, S., Lang, N., Dolya, A., Nath, G. & Hammoud, T. (2014). Getting more value from joint ventures. BCG Perspectives, 17 December. Retrieved from www .bcgperspectives.com/content/articles/alliances_joint_ventures_globalization_getting_ more_value_joint_ventures

Shimizu, K., Hitt, M.A., Vaidyanath, D. & Pisano, V. (2004). Theoretical foundations of cross-border mergers and acquisitions: A review of current research and recommendations for the future. *Journal of International Management*, 10(3), 307–53.

Staff and Reuters (2017). SFO says it is investigating Rio Tinto over Guinea operations. *The Guardian*, 25 July. Retrieved from www.theguardian.com/business/2017/jul/24/rio-tinto-sfo-investigation-guinea-suspected-corruption

Summerfield, R. (2014). Cross-border M&A boom. *Financier Worldwide*, December. Retrieved from www.financierworldwide.com/cross-border-ma-boom/#.W2fN0Y7i6Bu

Tajitsu, N. (2014). Moving on from the milk scandal, Fonterra ties up with China's Beingmate. Reuters, 27 August. Retrieved from www.reuters.com/article/us-fonterra-strategy-idUSKBN0GR0LX20140827

Thomas, A.R. & Wilkinson, T.J. (2005). It's the distribution, stupid! *Business Horizons*, 48(2), 125–34. https://doi.org/10.1016/j.bushor.2004.10.008

——— (2006). The outsourcing compulsion. *MIT Sloan Management Review*, 48(1), 10–14.

United Nations Conference on Trade and Development (UNCTAD) (2017). *World Investment Report 2017: Investment and the Digital Economy*. Retrieved from http://unctad.org/en/PublicationsLibrary/wir2017_en.pdf

Vaswani, K. (2017). Amazon and Alibaba battle it out in Asia. *BBC News*, 3 August. Retrieved from www.bbc.com/news/business-40813092

Waldmeir, P. & MacNamara, W. (2010). Rio Tinto case highlights risks in China. *The Financial Times*, 6 April. Retrieved from www.ft.com/content/fdd1e036-40d4-11df-94c2-00144feabdc0

Xueqing, J. (2016). Chinese companies surpass US as largest buyer of cross-border M&As. *China Daily*, 17 December. Retrieved from www.chinadaily.com.cn/business/2016–12/17/content_27699081.htm

Yin, X. & Shanley, M. (2008). Industry determinants of the "merger versus alliance" decision. *Academy of Management Review*, 33(2), 473–91.

Zámborský, P. (2011). AHI Roofing: from the Pacific Rim to Europe. In G. Suder, ed., *Doing Business in Europe*. Thousand Oaks: Sage.

——— (2014). Globe-riding goes global. In J. Scott-Kennel & M. Akoorie, eds, *Cases in International Business Strategy: A New Zealand Perspective*. Hamilton: MI Publishing.

Zámborský, P. & Kruesi, M.A. (2018). Global hotel alliance: Strategy discovery for the East. *SAGE Business Cases*. doi:10.4135/9781526440044.

Zámborský, P. & Turner, P. (2017). Fisher & Paykel Appliances: Fitting in to Haier's global innovation system. *SAGE Business Cases.* Retrieved from http://sk.sagepub.com/cases/fisher-paykel-appliances-fitting-in-to-haiers-innovation-system. doi:10.4135/9781526404800.

CHAPTER 8

INTERNATIONAL BUSINESS RESEARCH

Learning objectives

In reading this chapter, you will learn to:

1. understand the international business research process
2. characterise secondary sources of information in international markets
3. examine approaches to undertaking primary market research
4. appreciate the challenges and issues associated with conducting international business research
5. outline research reporting methods to ensure effective communication of research results.

INTERNATIONAL BUSINESS RESEARCH: IT'S ABOUT UNDERSTANDING DEMAND

In 2015, Jamaica Blue, an Australian café franchise, wanted to expand its brand in mainland China. Starbucks was the first café chain to enter the Chinese market and it had already achieved overwhelming success with its brand offering. Jamaica Blue knew that the key to understanding how to expand its own café franchise in this competitive market was to conduct research to identify and profile consumers for insights. The study the company undertook was qualitative and quantitative, using secondary and primary research methods.

In the initial phase, Jamaica Blue conducted secondary research to overview the café sector (the competitive landscape). They did this to uncover existing knowledge regarding consumers, including socio-demographic trends and their implications on café usage. The research provided Jamaica Blue with an understanding of the current purchasing behaviours of café patrons in China. The researchers utilised trade journals, empirical studies and publications from industry organisations, and government institutions.

In the second phase, an in-market study was conducted in Shanghai, China, with a focus group employed to gain a deeper understanding of the consumer's choice of café, purchasing preferences related to coffee and menu selections, and attitudes towards local versus international café brands operating in China. The overarching objective was to profile the Chinese café patron. The interaction between consumer behavioural changes, a transforming retail food environment and relevant government regulations played a significant role in shaping the characteristics of the Chinese café market.

The study revealed three key insights critical to defining the profile of the Chinese café patron. First, Chinese consumers are purchasing luxury goods and brands at an increasing rate as a symbol of modern sophistication and to convey status, with coffee being an everyday affordable indulgence. As more Chinese people are exposed to and embrace a Western lifestyle, café and coffee culture is quickly building momentum despite the traditional consumption of tea. Second, the study highlighted the need to ensure a balance between innovative or exotic menu items, and traditional food choices and tastes. An increasing number of Chinese consumers are influenced positively by global tastes and therefore are seeking greater variety from café menus. Finally, the social environment provided by a café plays a significant role in shaping consumers' experiences. The study found that delivering a strong balance of function and aesthetics to create an inviting social space was essential.

The results of the overall study supported the need for Jamaica Blue to continue to acquire and maintain a detailed understanding of food and beverage consumption trends at cafés in China to compete successfully in its dynamic marketplace.

VIGNETTE QUESTIONS

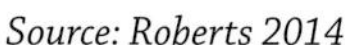

Source: Roberts 2014

Introduction

This chapter begins by outlining the critical role research plays in international business and then examines the international business research process through highlighting the importance of clearly defining the research problem. The discussion describes why international business research is conducted, studies the key types of international business research, and provides discussion around secondary and primary information sources, and the associated benefits and challenges of each. Strategies to help overcome the key issues that complicate cross-country research are also considered, and the challenges associated with conducting international business research are explored. In the international context, the key issues faced by researchers include political, economic, legal and cultural differences. The benefits of engaging a professional research agency, rather than relying on in-house services, are discussed. The chapter concludes by outlining the methods associated with reporting international business research studies.

Understanding the international business research process

Why conduct research? Business research is an essential element in the development of a company's international strategy. Being fully informed about the business-operating environment, the customers and consumers, is key to entering a market successfully and achieving profitability. Many companies fail to undertake appropriate and enough research before entering a foreign market. Their international research often lacks rigour, formality and a quantitative nature in comparison to their domestic research activities.

There are several reasons firms fail to undertake enough research, such as a lack of sensitivity to different cultures, a lack of recognition that not all markets are the same, resource restrictions and hasty decision making in reaction to an opportunity. In some cases, the excitement of the opportunity to expand internationally overshadows the need for rigorous business research. Differences in distribution systems, labour rules and media regulations are examples of market characteristics that must be fully understood in a foreign market. Additionally, a company may fail to understand that specialist and experienced management is needed to interpret international business conditions and real market data, rather than relying solely on internet-based information. Companies that have been exporting and engaged in international business over considerable time, may feel their experience is adequate and a suitable substitute for organised business research.

Appropriate business research is needed at the pre-entry stage and at various stages throughout the international business life cycle. International competition is dynamic and aggressive in the current business-operating environment. The emergence of electronic business and online commerce, intensifying levels of globalisation, technological innovation and the convergence of industries, create a marketplace in a constant state of change. International businesses must have a well-developed understanding of their competitive landscape to hold a sustainable position in their international markets. The role of business research remains pivotal for companies to understand the drivers of their evolving consumer, competition, supply chain and macro dynamics. In 2016, the global revenue of business research reached US$44.51 billion, an increase of almost 42 per cent over the previous five years (Statista 2018).

International markets are complex. A robust research strategy is central to international business decision-making processes. Neglecting the research phase may prove to be a costly mistake and result in missed opportunities.

Planning the research process

Research is vital to inform the evaluation and development of a comprehensive market entry strategy. Pre-market entry research is the first step to evaluate potential new markets. Failing to undertake due-diligence research can result in reduced sales, unforeseen complications and costs. This research generally begins with an analysis of primary variables for a country, including GDP, market size and growth, socio-demographics and competitor analysis. It is also important not to underestimate principal demographic factors, including per capita income, mortality rates, education attainment levels and population figures, as well as the business-operating and economic environments, relevant import regulations and how they may impact the proposed market potential. Each of these factors enables companies to evaluate if successful market entry is achievable. For example, premium consumer products may not succeed in many developing countries as their price may exceed customers' annual salary, or the consumer value of the product may be held differently when compared to the home market. The next step is to focus on product or service specific aspects. This entails a supply-and-demand assessment including relevant regulations and standards within the sector. Finally, a full competitive assessment, to understand current offerings and market gaps for potential products, is required. A systematic and logical approach to analysing these characteristics helps to shortlist potential markets. Business decisions informed by research are more likely to be supported by local subsidiaries.

The six-step international research process

Tools, techniques and approaches used in international business research are like those employed for domestic research activities. They share the same purpose of gathering and analysing information for input into key business planning and decisions. Most research techniques can be applied in the international marketplace, pending available infrastructure. There are six steps to follow when conducting international business research:

1. Define the research problem.
2. Determine the information needs and output requirements.
3. Develop the research design.
4. Capture and collect the data (secondary research and primary research).
5. Analyse the data and document the information.
6. Report and present the findings.

At each of these steps, researchers may confront challenges when the activities take place in a foreign market. The major issues to address include:

- complex research design to accommodate environmental and cultural constraints, including language translation, literacy rates and gender issues
- availability of research infrastructure to implement the study
- access to accurate and up-to-date secondary information
- time and cost requirements for primary research
- coordination of multi-country research and data collection
- establishing comparability and equivalence across multi-country studies
- differences in cultural norms concerning sharing opinions with strangers.

Research should be scheduled as an ongoing requirement within the business environment. Business operations in many countries change rapidly; for example, policy and regulatory changes, and consumer reactions to local and international events can cause transformations. Regularly

RESEARCH DESIGN
a detailed outline of how a research study will be undertaken, including the set of methods and procedures for the collection of data, and the measurement and analysis of the variables specified in a research problem.

SECONDARY RESEARCH
the collection and analysis of data previously collected for another purpose.

PRIMARY RESEARCH
the collection and analysis of data for a specific research purpose through interviews, focus groups, observations, surveys or experiments.

scheduled research enables timely data capture, which links to market indicators and provides insights and feedback that is needed to monitor, evaluate and anticipate business impacts to minimise risks. An ongoing research program allows an international business to anticipate and respond appropriately to local and global competition. For example, the Indian mobile phone company, Bharti Airtel with international business subsidiaries in 17 African nations, sought to expand its business presence through a standardised market entry approach, with a supporting communications campaign across the continent. However, the organisation underestimated the cultural diversity across the African continent. They used South African actors, images of the Savannah and local coins when many African nations use paper money. The company's lack of research and informed market understanding resulted in a significant failure of its international business expansion strategy, which has taken several years for it to recover from (*The Economic Times* 2017).

Business research plays a key role at each stage of the internationalisation process. Once the initial pre-market entry information has been established, companies then require ongoing information to assess market entry modes, opportunities and risks. This research informs operating strategies and determines which elements will be standardised, and which, if any, require adaptation for the new market. As companies continue to expand and obtain more data about their international markets, they amass information and establish global knowledge systems to efficiently manage the allocation of organisational resources.

Identifying the research problem

Clearly defining the research problem or problems is the critical first step in the research process. A research problem, or phenomenon, is an area of concern or opportunity where there is a gap in the knowledge base required to move forward. Failure to clearly define the research problem can lead researchers in a direction that does not solve the root cause of the relevant business concern. This may result in lost time, frustration or, worse, create a bigger issue.

The identification and definition of the problem is not solely a statement of the problem. It may also include the known limiting conditions as well as the overarching objective of the research study. A precise classification will result in a better understanding of the problem to be solved and how to use resource efforts effectively. Even the most elaborate data analysis tools will not compensate for incorrect problem definitions. In many cases, preliminary research is employed to assist in creating a precise description of the research problem. Once the research problem is clarified, it then needs to be translated into specific research questions. The scope of the research questions should be broad-based, with the ability to tackle both strategic-level and tactical-based market operating decisions. In the international business context, research problem formulation can be hindered by three factors:

- self-reference criterion (SRC)
- ethnocentrism
- unfamiliarity with the foreign environment.

SRC was first described in 1966 by the researcher James Lee. His research defined SRC as the unconscious reference to a person's own cultural values, experiences and knowledge as a foundation for decision making (Lee 1966). When confronted by a problem or situation in another culture, the tendency is to react instinctively and refer to one's own SRC rather than using rational thinking.

Closely connected to SRC is ethnocentrism, which is the tendency to view one's culture as superior to others. Both SRC and ethnocentrism reduce the ability to assess a foreign market in real terms, which can lead to serious mistakes and consequences, such as narrow or incorrect problem

definitions. In larger multi-country research projects, SRC contributes to disagreements and disengagement between head office and local subsidiaries. Researchers must try to view the research problem from the cultural perspective of the foreign participants, and isolate the SRC influence to mitigate risk. A consultative approach should be taken with each local subsidiary engaged in the research process.

The third major issue in formulating the research problem is unfamiliarity with the foreign environment. This leads to false assumptions, incorrectly defined research problems and, ultimately, misleading or ill-informed conclusions upon which key business decisions are based.

Once the research problem has been clearly articulated, the next step is to determine the information and output requirements, and develop the research design that will best deliver them. Some pieces of information will already be available from within the organisation or from sources that are publicly available through secondary data. Information that does not exist will need to be collected by the firm in primary research for the specific purpose of the study. In the international context, both secondary and primary data collection may present as challenges for researchers. The following section examines the role of secondary information as an important first step in the research process.

Secondary sources of information in international markets

When conducting international business research, companies require a range of macro and micro data related to the operating sector. Macro-level information includes a country's political, economic, socio-cultural and technological position; while micro-level information relates to customers, consumers, competitors and suppliers. This type of information is obtained by accessing secondary resources. In the preliminary phase of a study, researchers use secondary data as a screening process to inform base-level understanding. The operational outlays of this phase are generally cost effective and time efficient, prior to moving on to primary in-market research.

Secondary information is usually second hand, as a government institution, research agency or trade organisation gathered the data for a purpose other than the specific research project at hand. In this first phase, secondary information assists decision making by:

- evaluating a range of markets for market entry consideration
- estimating demand for products or services in a given market
- assessing the market interconnectedness to guide resource distribution between regions or across international markets.

Secondary data is routinely captured by public and private sector organisations in developed countries, and is readily accessible by businesses. In developing and emerging economies, equivalent databases have not always been available or are difficult to access. The Global Data Lab, based in the Netherlands, provides an online forum that brings together datasets from over 100 countries on a range of topics. The group undertakes analysis and monitoring of large-scale demographic, socio-economic, behavioural, political, cultural, health, institutional and environmental changes occurring in developing countries. The website of UNdata and the WB are also reliable sources of secondary information, covering global trends and statistics. While the online environment offers a range of websites, researchers should be mindful that the quality and quantity of documents might vary depending on the country of study and the level of resources dedicated to the data collection.

International researchers can also access the information resources available within their own organisations. Many large organisations maintain their own libraries and build significant databases that capture historical activities of their operations.

Using the internet for secondary research

A starting point for data search is generally in the worldwide web, where an abundance of international business resources is easily accessible. Computerised database services such as Lexis Nexis provide real-time access to news, legal and business information, captured globally and accessed via keyword searches. Other common sources of secondary data and information include: country census reports, government databases with official statistics, organisational records, annual reports and reviews, technical reports, scholarly journals, trade journals, literature review articles and reference books. Of the resources outlined above, government and professional bodies' websites provide more accuracy and reliability and offer a greater breadth of information. As an example, the globalEDGE an online resource tool, created and maintained by the University of Michigan, is a valuable resource that provides links to information and insights to inform global business research.

Many countries have internal networks of government agencies and industry-supported institutions that maintain databases of key information relevant for international business development; for example, Industry Export Associations or Trade Organisations. These agencies generate market-specific information and insights for their members, since their core purpose is to advise and support domestic companies seeking to trade abroad. The Australian Trade and Investment Commission, known as Austrade, is an example of this type of agency. A wide selection of secondary data resources are available to international businesses (see Table 8.1).

Global information databases, such as those held by the WB or the ADB, provide broad country profiles which are useful in the preliminary phase of a study. These sites offer economic information and statistics, such as GDP and lifestyle data, which cover literacy rates, expected lifespan, and other societal indicators in addition to macroeconomic country data. Examples of global data holders include the UN, the WB, the OECD and the Virtual International Business and Economic Sources (VIBES). These international entities capture large amounts of data in structured sets to allow individual analysis for a given study or specific purpose. A significant number of these sets report information for multiple years, providing a context to examine trends within socio-economic indicators for an individual country, and to compare between countries.

Secondary data challenges

The efficacy of secondary information is underpinned by the quality of the data. This may present several challenges for the international researcher. The process of interpretation and analysis must be rigorous, and a review of the data sources and criteria should be evaluated in the first instance, including qualification, accuracy, reliability and comparability, to ensure the validity for its use. Data discrepancies, in terms of accuracy or equivalence, may arise for several reasons, such as the way a measurement unit is defined, the frequency with which data has been captured, and the level of national industrialisation and taxation structures. In some cases, market-specific data may be missing or does not exist. Where data variables and values are not available, the researcher needs to infer data by using proxy variables or values from previous periods or sources. Interpretation of secondary data also requires a level of creative thinking by the researcher. For example, a researcher for a cruise line may need to forecast the potential demand for a cruise operation in a new seaport from

TABLE 8.1 Sources of secondary information

Country Information
• UN Yearbook of Industrial Statistics
• UN Statistical Yearbook
• OECD Economic Survey
• The Economist Intelligence Unit Country Reports
• UN Demographic Yearbook
• ADB, statistics
• Food and Agriculture Organization of the United Nations (FAOSTAT)
• Global Edge
• Country Watch
• Centre for International Development (CID)
• DFAT
• Ministry of Foreign Affairs of Japan
• Ministry of Commerce, People's Republic of China
• Gov HK, market information and statistics, Hong Kong
Foreign Industry Directories
• *Forbes*, Asia's fab 50 companies
• Companies House, international directory of importers: Europe (Interdata)
• Companies House, mailing lists of worldwide importing firms (Interdata)
• Moody's International
• *Financial Times*, markets data
International Marketing
• Michigan State University, International Business Centre
• Euromonitor International, economics marketing data and statistics
• Global Data Lab, Database Developing World
• Euromonitor International, Asia advertising marketing and media data
• National Library of Australia, Virtual International Business and Economics Sources (VIBES)
International Trade
• UN International Trade Statistics Yearbook
• World Chambers Network
• International Chamber of Commerce
• International Trade Centre
• Hong Kong Trade Development Council
• European Trade Study Group
• Austrade
• ADB
• WB
• WTO

complimentary and comparable city and tourism statistics. This requires creative thinking, but the process of interpretation and analysis should still be thorough.

Qualification

A rigorous process of data qualification is essential in any research study. A lack of appropriate data qualification is arguably one of the major causes of project failures. The aim of data qualification is to clarify and thoroughly document the meaning of the data. The validity of a research study can be called into question where poor quality data has been used or gaps exist. Several documents may report on income measures for a country, but the researcher must ensure all indicators are utilised and reported consistently. For example, what currency is the applicable measure in each report, are gross or net income figures cited? The gap between what is presented, and any erroneous assumptions made by the researcher could completely invalidate the entire analysis. Globally, the definitions used for a range of indicators, such as GDP, often differ between countries, creating a qualification challenge for the researcher.

Accuracy

The accuracy of secondary information may raise questions for few reasons. At the core, the purpose for which the data was collected originally could affect the accuracy and relevance for the study. For example, the original data may have been manipulated or reorganised to meet another purpose unknown to the researcher. Additionally, the components of timeliness and age of data can affect the accuracy. Due to the time required for global data collection, many sources of secondary information, particularly those that are in print, are often outdated by the time of publication.

The researcher must ensure the data aligns with the time that governs the analysis. For example, if the current study is focused on current sales issues, comparing income levels from the previous decade will not provide an appropriate analysis. Many countries collect information relating to their economic activities and conduct their national census on different or infrequent schedules. China, India and the US undertake national census studies once every decade, whereas in Australia a national census is undertaken every five years. In contrast, in some emerging economies, a census seldom occurs or never takes place. The quality of information may also be compromised because of the processes followed in collecting, organising and analysing the original data. Developed countries use sophisticated and well-established procedures to capture national data. However, due to a lack of resources, skills and experience, many developing countries have to rely on inexperienced or unreliable mechanisms (Kotabe & Helsen 2010).

Official data sources often group or aggregate statistics for certain variables into broad categories, and this can negatively impact the usefulness and interpretation of such data. Therefore, inspecting what has been included in a relevant data set to ensure accuracy of reporting is required. Conversely, missing data can cause challenges; for example, cross-border and counter-trading are often not reflected in country-level trade statistics. These transactions, in some instances, are more significant in value and volume than legitimate trade, and therefore the true value of some industries may be grossly underestimated.

Reliability

Despite the ease of access to high volumes of online data, the level of reliability and comparability of the information must be checked to ensure appropriateness for purpose. It should be noted that internet search engines encompass only a portion of international sources and remain heavily biased towards English-based publications. As a result, sole reliance on readily available electronic sources may result in the researcher missing valuable information.

To study trends, the researcher needs to understand the degree to which data has been measured consistently over time. It is not uncommon for the definition of key economic indicators to change swiftly. This is especially likely for variables that have political ramifications, such as unemployment and inflation statistics (Kotabe & Helsen 2010). While not unique to them, less-developed countries are prone to underestimate or overestimate official statistics to seek advantage or reflect national sentiment. Many organisations review historical patterns of variables to identify underlying trends that highlight market entry opportunities opening or to identify a market reaching maturity. Researchers should be aware of such practices that can adversely affect data reliability and, if necessary, make appropriate corrections.

Comparability

Comparability of data maybe a problematic issue in the analysis phase. Cross-country analysis often requires a comparison of indicators across culturally and linguistically diverse countries. Accessing information on a given item from a variety of sources frequently produces contradictory information. The challenge is to reconcile such differences to achieve comparability. Triangulation is one method of managing contradictory information. In this process, information on the same item is obtained from at least three different sources, followed by speculation on potential reasons for any data variances (Kotabe & Helsen 2010). For instance, consider the collection of information on the import penetration of mangoes as a percentage of total consumption in a range of Asia–Pacific countries. Triangulation may highlight that some statistics are based on value, while others are based on volume, and some sources include both fresh and dried mango and others do not.

TRIANGULATION
a commonly used strategy when multiple methods or sources of data are applied to address the same question.

Comparability may be undermined by a lack of functional equivalence. Functional equivalence refers to the degree to which similar activities or products in different countries fulfil similar functions (Kotabe & Helsen 2010). Many products perform a different function in different markets. For example, in Australia and New Zealand, bicycles are primarily used as a social activity, while in countries such as Vietnam and China, they are a major means of transportation. In Vietnam, however, as the middle class becomes more affluent, bicycles are increasingly being used for recreation, while electric motorbikes are becoming more prevalent for transportation.

The process for secondary research: evaluate, validate and rank

Secondary data provides valuable information which can shape and influence international business decisions. However, this data must be evaluated for accuracy and its reliability validated, other wise any analyses may prove to be flawed and detrimental to effective business decision making. In today's global environment, the online environment provides an extensive range of information and information sources, including materials published or posted by institutions, journalists and individuals. Consequently, the challenge is to identify the qualification of the information source. Given the challenges and issues posed by secondary data, six questions should be asked when evaluating it.

1. What was the purpose for the original data captured?
2. Who collected the data?
3. When was the data collected and over what period?

4. How was the data captured?
5. Is the data consistent with data from other sources?
6. Have the variables been redefined or have they remained constant over time?

Asking and answering these questions will help with the process of data validation and determine which sources provide the greatest level of accuracy to guide the analysis. Researchers and managers should always be mindful of the potential value of secondary data or its associated issues.

Using primary research in international business

Secondary information alone will rarely prove enough for a comprehensive market study when a company is seeking to internationalise. Although many studies begin by examining a market through a lens of secondary research sources, the findings are usually followed up and confirmed with in-market primary research. International business research, incorporating this information, is needed for a range of reasons at different points of the internationalisation process. At the beginning, firms require information to assess appropriate market entry and identify opportunities and risks. Given the complexity and volatility of the international business environment, fundamental research is needed to inform judicious business decisions. Moreover, companies can gain support from potential local subsidiaries by engaging in primary research in prospective markets.

A key advantage of primary research is that it is tailored to the unique and specific business objectives, thereby delivering timely and relevant information to guide business decisions. Primary research may be qualitative or quantitative. Qualitative research is predominantly exploratory research conducted on a small scale using a specific target audience sample. It is used to gain an understanding of underlying reasons, opinions and motivations. Qualitative outputs are narrative descriptions which provide insights into relevant business or consumer issues and are used to develop hypotheses for potential quantitative research. Common collection methods of qualitative research data include focus groups, individual interviews and observation studies. Quantitative research is used to measure attitudes, opinions, behaviours and other defined variables. This type of research assigns a number to represent a variable that can then be analysed statistically to formulate specifics and uncover patterns. Data collection methods are much more structured than those employed in qualitative research, and include various forms of survey instruments such as online and paper surveys, phone interviews and online polls. The two most common approaches to undertake primary research are focus groups to elicit thematic information, and survey methods to capture qualitative and quantitative measures.

QUALITATIVE RESEARCH the inductive approaches to building knowledge and meaning, which describe attitudes, opinions, behaviours and motivations of research participants, and provide insights into a research problem.

QUANTITATIVE RESEARCH data collected in numerical order to identify statistical significance or trends.

Focus groups

Prior to commencing a large-scale quantitative market research project, many organisations will undertake exploratory research that is qualitative. The focus group is one of the most popular research techniques for this purpose. Focus groups involve loosely structured discussions among a target group of eight to twelve participants, where qualitative data is generated through opinions expressed in the group. This form of qualitative research is used extensively within Western populations and is an increasingly useful method for engaging with culturally and linguistically diverse populations.

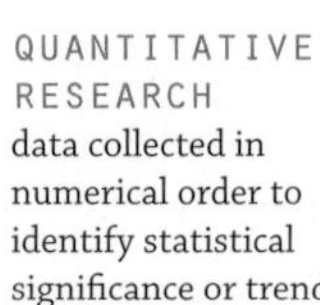

FOCUS GROUP RESEARCH a research method where representatives of a target audience contribute by participating in an unstructured but directed discussion.

Focus groups are used for many different business research applications: to generate a hypothesis to guide quantitative research projects, to reveal new product and service opportunities, and to test new product and advertising concepts. Advances in technology have led to an increasing use of online focus groups, with participating individuals able to connect from anywhere in the world. Once considered an inferior substitute for physical groups, virtual groups are proving to have unique advantages without geographical constraints.

The rules for designing and running focus groups in a domestic setting apply equally in an international context. However, the global environment places extra demands on the researcher, notably:

- the importance of a skilled moderator
- the level of engagement between the moderator and the group
- the levels of literacy amongst group participants.

Firms undertaking focus groups in international settings require the use of an experienced moderator. The role of the moderator is to direct the session, discuss and probe feedback, and provide comments to stimulate thematic information that enriches a profile of the area under investigation. Success in an international context is highly dependent upon the cultural competence of the moderator. Local language familiarity, understanding of social interaction patterns and cultural sensitivity are all critical when conducting focus groups. Many countries in Asia have highly collectivist societies. The Geert Hofstede model, dimensions of culture, identifies the role of individualism versus collectivism as a cultural dimension that most characterises differences among people (see Chapter 4). People from a highly collectivist society tend to be more hesitant about criticising ideas or concepts or sharing their views when compared with people from individualistic societies. In some cultures, gender issues are significant and there may be difficulties with conducting focus groups with women. As a result, constructing the desired group dynamics for focus group research within such societies is often very challenging and requires thorough preparation.

To engage group discussion in an international setting, the following tips are recommended.

- Hire experienced moderators with strong skills in developing group dynamics quickly and with the ability to identify and challenge consensus.
- Ensure the recruitment phase delivers group homogeneity to enable ease of group bonding.
- Be alert to group participants' non-verbal cues, including body language, gestures and intonation. This form of communication can add emphasis relating to the discussion topic or demonstrate opinion in a manner that cannot be picked up by the recording.

When planning focus groups, an incentive may be desirable for participants to encourage their attendance at the session. In some cases, a fee may be payable, or, in some countries, a meal should be offered at the beginning of the session to allow participants to get to know each other and to encourage a relaxed interaction among the group. Once the session is underway, it is important for the moderator to assist the attendees to feel at ease, and to encourage open and frank discussions related to the topics. The moderator also has a key role to ensure that the opinions of one or a few do not influence the entire group. The use of an experienced local or indigenous moderator ensures group interactions are courteous and discussions are not misread.

The levels of literacy and education of each participant are very important considerations for focus groups. If participants cannot understand what is being asked of them, then they cannot provide answers that accurately reflect their opinion on the topic at hand. Research outcomes can be skewed significantly or misinformed if group understanding is limited.

The output of a focus group is generally recorded as a full transcript. The participants are de-identified, and the information is aggregated. Technology applications are often used to analyse and present the themes from the group's discussions. An example of this is NVivo, a software which

supports qualitative and mixed-methods research, that is designed to organise, analyse and identify insights in unstructured or qualitative data, such as focus groups and interviews.

Surveys

SURVEY
a quantitative research instrument where a relatively large number of people are asked a standard set of questions, posed in the same way each time, to extract specific data from a particular target group.

Focus groups are the most popular method for gathering qualitative data, but surveys are the most common method for gathering quantitative data in market research. Survey research uses a cross-sectional approach to study specific characteristics, such as the opinions, behaviours, attitudes, motivations and beliefs of a sample population at a point in time. Surveys are conducted by phone, mail, online and face to face.

The design and development of an appropriate questionnaire is the first step in constructing survey research. In the second step, the target population for the study is defined and selected, ensuring that a major representative sample is taken. Once these two steps are completed, the process of data gathering by questionnaire can commence. Data is acquired, aggregated, analysed and interpreted, forming the body of material from which the results are concluded, and the findings are reported.

Surveys are a powerful tool for keeping up to date with individual market trends and changes. Accurate survey research can lead the company to success while poorly planned research will deliver inferior information. Surveys require the direct engagement of individuals. Individuals differ by culture, education level and attitudes, therefore the choice of survey approach and its instrument needs to be designed for the given international market. Three critical factors must be considered in developing a survey instrument:

- instrument design
- construct equivalence
- measurement equivalence.

Instrument design

RESEARCH INSTRUMENT
a measurement tool designed to gather data to answer the research question.

The selection of the research instrument depends on the research design, applicability and cost. The most popular survey instrument for gathering primary data is the questionnaire. As in domestic marketing, the wording and sequencing of questions in an international research questionnaire are critical. Further, there are significant challenges that must be addressed when designing and implementing multi-country research projects to ensure comparability of survey-based results across multiple languages, cultures and contexts. A cross-national survey instrument is influenced by cultural and political sensitivities. In some countries, surveys related to consumer behaviour studies omit questions relating to national government and leadership, as these subjects are inviting undue scrutiny from authorities and not helpful to directly understand consumer buying behaviours.

In cross-national research, measurement and comparability issues centre around the question: are the phenomena in countries A and B measured in the same way? Likewise, the equivalence or comparability of data collected across countries is a key issue when making inter-country comparisons. For informed analysis to occur, data should have the same meaning across all countries being studied. Biased information or disparate information leads to ambiguous or even flawed conclusions. Therefore, construct equivalence and measurement equivalence is considered.

Construct equivalence

Construct equivalence relates to whether an object, concept or behaviour serves the same purpose and achieves the same salience in all contexts and cultures being studied (Hult et al. 2008, p. 1030).

Ensuring construct comparability is a pre-requisite for testing multi-country differences. Neglecting to establish data equivalence in cross-cultural studies can create bias in the empirical results and any inferences that are made. A failure to acknowledge and correct for construct discrepancies often leads to unfounded results. There are three aspects of construct equivalence recommended in the international research process: functional, conceptual and category equivalence.

Functional, conceptual and category equivalence

Functional equivalence refers to the extent that objects and behaviour take the same role or function across cultures. For example, is a bicycle a mode of transport or a recreational vehicle in the country under study?

Conceptual equivalence refers to the extent to which the attitudes towards the concept or behaviours are the same across cultures. For example, is the ownership of a refrigerator a symbol of status or just a necessity?

Category equivalence refers to the extent to which the same classification scheme can be used for the same concept and behaviour across cultures (Hult et al. 2008, p. 1030). Socio-demographic characteristics and classifications may differ from country to country; for example, the term 'nuclear family' includes parents and children in one society but in another culture the classification includes extended family as well.

Measurement equivalence

In multi-country research it is necessary to ensure measurement equivalence. Measurement equivalence addresses the comparability across different populations of the operationalisation of the constructs, such as the wording, scaling and scoring of measures (Hult et al. 2008, p. 1035). To establish the reliability and validity of items used to measure theoretical constructs, there are three critical components of measurement equivalence that need to be addressed: calibration equivalence, translation equivalence and scalar or metric equivalence.

Calibration, translation and scalar equivalence

The establishment of calibration equivalence is needed to ensure that units of measure are converted correctly between cultures in the research survey. Calibration equivalence reflects equality between physical and perceptual measures across cultures (Hult et al. 2008, p. 1035). Typical calibration equivalence problems relate to monetary units, exchange rates, units of weight, distance and volume measurements. For example, Australians use the metric system for measuring distance in kilometres and liquid volumes in litres. In the US, however, the standard system used measures distance in miles and liquid volumes in gallons. Calibration is required to identify and agree a standard unit of measure for the study.

The next focus should be ensuring translation equivalence by confirming the research instrument and stimuli items are translated appropriately from one language into another. This ensures that items are aligned to the same constructs in different populations. Translation equivalence reflects the conveyance of identical meaning from culture to culture (Hult et al. 2008, p. 1035). While high-quality translations are sometimes difficult to obtain, careless translations can lead to fundamental errors. Two key methods exist to minimise translation errors in international research: forward-and-back translation and parallel translation.

Forward-and-back translation is the most commonly used method for the establishment of translation equivalence. This two-phase process enables researchers to check language, and more

FORWARD-AND-BACK TRANSLATION
the procedure in which a document is first translated from one language to another, then translated back into the original language to confirm reliability and accuracy of the translation.

importantly, to assess compatibility of concepts between cultures. As an example, in an Australia–China study, the questionnaire initially is translated from English to Mandarin, by an accredited English-to-Mandarin translator, whose native language is Mandarin, the target language. In the second phase, an accredited Mandarin-to-English translator, whose native language is English, translates the Mandarin version back to English. This version is then compared with the original survey to uncover any translation errors. Some caution should be taken in focusing on semantics, as literal translations of the measurements have the ability to become stilted and lack the naturalness required for concept understanding (Hult et al. 2008. p. 1035). This two-step process is repeated until an acceptable degree of convergence is achieved.

PARALLEL TRANSLATION the procedure in which multiple interpreters are employed to independently translate the same questionnaire and the results are reviewed for consistency.

Parallel translation employs multiple interpreters to independently translate the same questionnaire. A committee of translators compares each version and the identified differences are then reconciled for the survey instruments. The parallel translation process is considered costlier than the forward-and-back translation process.

To achieve scalar equivalence, survey respondents must understand the measurement of scales in the same way. In cross-national research, pre-planning prevents errors resulting from inadequate scalar equivalence. First, respondents in some countries may not be as familiar with various scaling or scoring formats as those in other countries. Many surveys typically have questions for 'agree/disagree' or 'likely/unlikely' statements using a Likert scale to record responses. In Australia, it is common to use a five- or seven-point scale, while a 10 or 20-point scale is common in other countries. Comparing results from surveys using different scales requires the application of equivalence. Likewise, researchers need to ensure that the responses to questions by respondents from different countries have the same meaning and interpretation. Cultural or social values and experiences may influence the way a target group record their responses, and researchers should note that significant scores in one country are not necessarily significant scores in another country.

International researchers need to take steps to ensure that any differences found between cultures are considered when constructing the survey instrument. This is so participants' responses truly reflect the phenomena of interest and are not simply a reflection of culturally influenced values or a misunderstanding of the scaling measure. When employing a semantic differential scale or a Likert scale, international researchers must test the significance and appropriateness of the scale anchors, in terms of the intended respondents, and adjust it as necessary. In some countries, '1' on a scale of 1 to 5 is perceived to be the best or top score and '5' to be worst or lowest, while the opposite is true in other countries. In an Australia–China study, a pre-test phase identified that Chinese managers did not adequately understand the scale anchors 'agree/disagree'. As a result, the anchors were changed to 'definitely true', 'somewhat true', and 'not at all true'.

Understanding and planning for the features of each research instrument is critical to achieving equivalence. If researchers can demonstrate that the measures used are calibrated consistently across groups and that the meanings taken from the items are equivalent, the results of the study have greater validity (Hult et al. 2008, p. 1036). Pre-testing a survey is often the best solution to remove any issues. While the pre-testing process takes time and speed is often critical when collecting data, commencing a survey in the field without undertaking this step is highly undesirable.

Survey samples and sampling

Once the survey instrument is complete and equivalence has been achieved, the researcher must develop a sampling plan. The ultimate validity of research outcomes or findings is greatly impacted by the efficacy of the sampling plan. The sampling strategy must be comprehensive in its construct and thorough in its implementation to prevent inaccurate or incomplete findings. Techniques to achieve effective sampling are applicable in both the domestic and international contexts, however, the international environment requires researchers to take additional elements into account, including balancing the similarities and differences among selected countries with the representativeness of cohorts from within individual countries. The validity of research results is highly contingent upon the effectiveness of the sampling plan and the rigour with which it is implemented.

At all times, survey research requires due consideration and appropriate balancing of data reliability, costs and timeliness of process. In multi-country research, organisations need to determine which countries should be studied. Ideally, research should be conducted in all countries and contexts relevant to proposed operations. However, due to high costs, researchers may consider the use of findings from one country as a proxy for another. One approach to determining the countries to include in a study is to first employ a large-scale exploratory project utilising an omnibus survey, which covers several or many countries. An alternative approach is to choose just a few countries on which to focus. To identify which countries to include, an organisation may group countries using socio-cultural indicators, then choose one or two countries as representative from each cluster. This process can be repeated to include other countries of interest as required.

OMNIBUS SURVEY
a quantitative research instrument where companies purchase one or more questions and associated responses from a commercial research agency with access to a large-scale target market database.

There are three core elements to a sampling plan:

- *sampling unit*: the target population being surveyed
- *sample size*: the number of respondents being surveyed
- *sampling procedure*: the method for recruiting the survey respondents.

Sampling unit

A sampling unit needs to be created from the target population; this means the researcher must define the sample. The researcher constructs a set of criteria to be measured and then identifies the minimum level of the population that corresponds to those criteria and thereby creates the research sample unit. For example, a research study on customer satisfaction with a restaurant chain would utilise a person who patronised that food outlet. After defining the sample unit, the next step is to obtain a sampling frame, which is a comprehensive list of the population the sample will be chosen from. Examples of sampling frames include purchased lists, website groups and telephone directories. However, in many situations, particularly in emerging markets, such listings do not exist or are incomplete, inaccurate or lack currency, which can create a level of sampling-frame error. The term 'incidence rate' is used by researchers to signify the percentage of individuals who are genuine members of the targeted population. As the incidence rate increases, the chance that an error has occurred in the sampling frame decreases. Developing accurate samples in different countries requires researchers to employ a level of flexibility with the research methods they use.

Sample size

Identifying the sample size needed is the next step in the process. The accuracy of research findings is directly related to and affected by the sample size. The validity and representativeness of findings will improve as a sample size increases, but larger sample sizes naturally incur greater costs. Determining the desired sample size in cross-country research often involves a level of plausible guesswork and the requirement may vary across cultures. Typically, heterogeneous cultures such as India require larger samples than homogenous cultures like Thailand and South Korea. Diverse cultures tend to exhibit more variance in the traits to be measured than homogenous markets (Kotabe & Helsen 2010). A sample is often characterised as a small-sized representation, rather like a snapshot or model, of the broader population. In basic terms, the aim of sampling is to employ small units to represent the larger group. Drawing an appropriate sample for a survey is undertaken through two methods: probability and non-probability sampling.

Probability sampling, also called random sampling, refers to the methods that ensure the likelihood of a member of the population being chosen can be calculated. Almost every person in the targeted population is qualified with a known and non-zero chance of being chosen for the sample; therefore, researchers can make statistical inferences about the collected data. Because of this, most researchers prefer some form of probabilistic sampling. In contrast, non-probability methods are more subjective and are constructed to remove or reduce selection probability. An example of non-probability sampling is constantly using the same group of respondents, regardless of the subject matter. Consequently, there is much greater concern regarding the validity of results from non-probability sampling. In China, there are many well-organised research companies that conduct target market research studies with appropriately structured groups based on probability sampling. In other countries, however, the absence of sampling frames makes a non-probabilistic sampling procedure the only alternative.

Sampling procedure

The final step in the sampling plan is to establish how to contact prospective respondents to complete the survey. Surveys may be conducted in person, online or over the phone. The factors of cost and available infrastructure in a country can be major determinants in the research approach. Cultural considerations may also impact the preferred recruitment process. In business-to-business projects, for example, Chinese professionals are often reluctant to complete survey research over the phone so in these cases, undertaking the survey research face to face would yield significantly better results.

Data collection

Once the sampling plan is complete and implemented, the in-field data collection process can commence. There are a range of challenges which may impact the collection of primary data. These can relate to both the respondents and the investigator.

Respondent-related issues

The first challenge that may be encountered with respondents is simply non-response. This can result from reluctance of consumers to speak with strangers, from concerns around confidentiality and a backlash from their responses or from other cultural biases. One way to address non-response is to increase sample sizes in certain countries where this issue is anticipated. In China, research projects sanctioned by the local authorities will generally result in greater participation rates.

Two other respondent-related factors that can impact the data collection process are courtesy bias and attempts to reflect a certain social status. The courtesy bias is common in Asia and the Middle East, and refers to a desire to be polite to others. Responses may not be a true or entirely true reflection of the respondents' opinions or behaviours as they aim to please the interviewer. Some individual populations and cultures are more likely than others to provide socially desirable answers.

People from more influential groups in society, or from more affluent countries, tend not to exhibit courtesy or a social desirability bias. While there are no specific measures to avoid such biases, pre-testing the survey as well as utilising a well-trained investigator will assist in minimising their incidence. It may also be worthwhile to incorporate questions that measure personal tendencies such as social desirability (Kotabe & Helsen 2010).

Investigator-related issues

Engaging a skilled and experienced investigator is crucial as unmanaged biases or misunderstandings on the part of respondents will impact in-person survey results. The availability of skilled researchers can be a major problem in cross-national research, particularly in developing countries. A lack of supervision or inadequate remuneration may lead to cutting corners or reduced integrity. An example of this could be investigators completing surveys themselves to reduce their workload or ignoring the project sampling procedure. The following actions can be taken to decrease investigator-related biases in cross-cultural survey research.

- Match investigators with respondents in terms of cultural background as this may assist in reducing misunderstandings.
- Ensure solid recruitment, training and supervision of investigators.
- Build redundancy into the questionnaire, such as asking the same question in different ways and in different parts of the questionnaire to enable researchers to cross-check the validity of responses.

Online environment

Increasingly, organisations are employing non-traditional data collection methods by entering the digital environment instead. While traditional methods of research (focus group and survey) continue to be useful, researchers need to reconceptualise what constitutes relevant connections, and be open minded in employing new technologies to complement existing ones in the data collection process. With the rapid advancement of the use of digital in international markets, researchers need to recognise that the consumer interactive environment is now inclusive of their online activity. It is increasingly apparent that digital platforms will be valuable in delivering insights about the physical and social interactions of various groups.

Surveys are commonly administered online through a range of access points, emails, websites and panel surveys. Email surveys are self-administered questionnaires sent as an attachment or embedded within the email, to be completed by the addressee. In website surveys, members of the website are asked to fill out a questionnaire. If they accept, they are directed to a webpage where the survey is located. A variation of this is the pop-up survey which appears in a new window while the user is browsing the website. These are useful for projects seeking to understand a broad target audience. In panel surveys, respondents are members of an online group where their socio-demographic and behavioural preferences are known to the website owner. When eligible for a survey, panel members are contacted via email and are asked to complete a password-protected survey (Kotabe & Helsen 2010).

Survey methods

Table 8.2 highlights the advantages and disadvantages of the various survey methods available to researchers.

TABLE 8.2 Advantages and disadvantages of survey methods

Survey type	Advantage	Disadvantages
Personal survey	• Very high response rate • Most flexible • Visual aids • Immediate clarification • Data quality control • Most effective in developing countries	• Cost intensive • Interviewer bias (gender issues or misinterpretation)
Telephone survey	• Economical • High response rate • Ability to call back to seek clarification	• Short interview only • Interviewer bias • Requires very simple questions • No visual aids
Mail survey	• Inexpensive • (no fieldwork costs)	• Survey cost may be high to achieve the desired response rate
Online survey	• Short response time • Inexpensive to manage (apart from start-up costs) • Use of visual aids • Higher degree of sophistication • Increased flexibility • Error reduction (human) • High-quality response (compared to mail)	• Representativeness may be low • Sampling error • Increased likelihood of • Non-response bias

SPOTLIGHT 8.1

Shipping Australian seafood to Asia: CMG Australia

The Craig Mostyn Group (CMG) is one of Australia's leading food and agribusiness companies. Turnover in its seafood division has doubled in the last six years, largely due to thriving demand for two products: the southern rock lobster and the trademarked Jade Tiger Abalone. These products are prized delicacies, especially in the Chinese luxury wedding market where they signify elegance and prosperity. CMG is targeting this luxury market and is seeking to understand end-user behaviours in Shanghai's competitive wedding sector. To successfully research this market, the company has engaged Chinese firms to develop a market profile and identify expansion opportunities.

CMG's Chief Executive Officer, Mark Wray, believes that seafood export success is about understanding the market, and ensuring processes enable consistent delivery of the quality and freshness expected of a luxury product. Current achievements result not only from having highly desired products, but also from building business structures to identify and meet customer needs. Their diverse team incorporates key skills in specialised seafood business practices, language and culture, and supply-chain expertise to develop crucial distribution partnerships.

With 806 million active accounts for WeChat alone, social networking in China is the primary forum for consumers to recommend products and brands to others. CMG is acutely aware that all supply-chain partners need to understand the brand and their products to communicate with their customers. Going forward, the company is committed to developing partnerships and undertaking ongoing market research to achieve their goal of becoming the largest exporter of luxury Australian seafood.

Source: NAB 2016

QUESTIONS

SPOTLIGHT QUESTIONS

1. What types of social and digital research could CMG undertake to gain more knowledge and build their understanding of the seafood market segments in mainland China?
2. Consider the research process to assess 'buyer trust points'. Why might this be important for CMG to undertake?

Challenges and issues in international business research

Conducting international market research requires a detailed approach to planning new market entry, and to identifying the opportunities and issues for a firm. Research is a central activity for businesses managing the uncertainties and dynamic changes occurring in the global environment. When a firm expands domestic business operations into a foreign market, the uncertainties become more prominent and decisive action is often required.

Understanding the set of actions required, and the appropriate reactions to key challenges and issues is often connected to a time imperative for managers. International business managers experi ence cultural, political and legal differences when operating in foreign countries. Consequently, business research in cross-national settings involves additional considerations when compared to domestic business research. A priority for researchers is to reveal how such inter-country differences translate into different consumer habits, preferences and behaviours. As a result, such research underpins effective decision making when organisations start to internationalise.

Coordinating international research

Cross-national research projects demand careful coordination and planning to validate the research efforts. Coordination of research activities delivers benefits in terms of timeliness, cost management, centralisation of communication and quality control. Two main issues central to the success of an international study are the timely coordination and planning of the research. The first relates to who will coordinate the research and the extent to which research is centralised or decentralised within an organisation. The second relates to the decision to engage either professional external research services or utilise in-house research resources. If the decision is to employ an external research company, the preparation of selection criteria is required to guide the choice of either a large international research firm or select a locally operated one.

The choice of a centralised or decentralised strategy is influenced by the research focus in terms of who will use and who will be impacted by the research outputs. This consideration speaks to those located in head office and those in local subsidiaries within the countries under investigation. The head office for a firm usually favours standardised data collection, sampling procedures and survey instruments. Local user groups within subsidiaries prefer country-customised research designs that recognise the nuances of their local environment (Kotabe & Helsen 2010). Cross-cultural researchers are faced with a choice between emic and etic research approaches.

The emic approach to research focuses on the uniqueness of each country, and emphasises the importance of studying its individualities and characteristics. Attitudinal phenomena and values may vary from country to country and must be identified through culture-specific measures. However, country-specific studies with inferences made about cross-national similarities and differences are generally subjective in nature. An international researcher may consider tailoring the research approach in various countries to suit the national culture and more accurately represent the findings in each nation. This may be at the expense of comparing results across multiple countries. For example, a recent mango field study, conducted in Australia and Vietnam, used on-farm interviews and observations to understand the farming culture and the tasks involved in a typical day on the farm in each country. In Australia, on-farm interviews were conducted, and farmers were asked to go about their normal activities. In Vietnam, this approach was not possible without disrupting the standard household order. In the Mekong region, the researcher was treated as a visiting guest and the whole family was involved in the study. A further issue to resolve was that the local culture where females and children are viewed as inferior to male family members, notwithstanding that the women and children complete most of the farm work. To capture accurate observations, the researcher needed access to the women. To enable this, the researcher gave the males a role to play in the project; they were issued with video cameras in advance and asked to record the on-farm interviews with the women to capture the completion of the daily responsibilities.

The etic approach is primarily concerned with recognising universal attitudes and behaviours across cultures and nations. According to this model, thoughts derived in one nation are potentially universal and may be applicable to other nations. If this assumption is legitimate, such measures make comparisons across nations feasible and objective. Proponents of this school of thought include Geert Hofstede, the prominent cultural researcher, and many psychologists and international marketing professionals.

To gauge such phenomena requires culturally unbiased measures. For instance, there appears to be a convergence in consumer preferences across cultures for many goods and services (Kotabe & Helsen 2010). Therefore, consumer preferences could be studied from an etic viewpoint. The buying motivations behind those preferences, however, often differ substantially across cultures. Hence, a cross-country project that examines buying motivations may demand an emic approach. There are strengths and weaknesses associated with either approach and the researcher should be mindful when planning the research design.

The terms emic and etic were introduced into anthropology in the 1960s by linguist Kenneth Pike (1967). He argued they should not be perceived as opposite approaches, rather they describe the problem of cross-national comparability from two different perspectives. Table 8.3 outlines each approach's strengths and challenges.

TABLE 8.3 Strengths and weaknesses of emic and etic research approaches

Emic approach	
Strengths	**Weaknesses**
• Permits an understanding of the way in which a specific nation or culture is constructed. • Assists the researcher to understand how individuals behave and why they behave in the way they do.	• Subject to systematic bias, which occurs when individuals represent or misinterpret their own behaviour. • Subject to arbitrariness, which refers to the subjective status of scientific knowledge.
Etic approach	
Strengths	**Weaknesses**
• Provides a broad perspective about different events around the world to ensure cultural differences and similarities can be recognised. • Techniques for recording differing phenomena are available. • The only point of entry for research, since all analysis must start with a rough, tentative etic description. • A comparison of selected cultures which allows the researcher to meet practical demands, such as financial or time limitations.	• Easy to overlook the differential aspects of cultural impact. • The definition of the phenomena variables being studied may itself be culture-bound.

With increasing globalisation, the need for comparison and generalisation across nationalities is a core focus in most business research studies. Multi-country studies have therefore tended more heavily towards the etic approach, with an emphasis on similarities and parallels, but they have sought to alleviate the problems of comparability by establishing cross-cultural equivalence, as discussed earlier in this chapter. Nonetheless, to make the research study relevant and acceptable to local users, organisations need to recognise the individualities of local cultures. Ideally, survey instruments developed for cross-country market research projects should encompass both the emic and etic approaches (Kotabe & Helsen 2010). Strategies used to balance these conflicting demands include:

- involvement of all relevant parties, such as from head office and local subsidiaries, from the initial planning stages of the research
- a contribution by all parties in the funding of the research
- ensuring hypotheses and objectives are agreed to by all involved
- collecting data in two stages by initially capturing it from a country-specific pool of psychographic statements, followed by using a standardised-survey instrument, which contains measures that have been country customised from the stage 1 research.

In some cases, coordination is implemented by the research agency that is hired to run the project. When markets differ greatly, or when researchers vary from country to country, the organisation will often prefer to coordinate the project (Kotabe & Helsen 2010).

Key issues in international business research

Researchers must be aware of the presence of biases that may impact the validity of research findings, whether through survey or experimental research methods. One of the most recurrent sources of bias in this context is the concept of social desirability. In simple terms, social desirability bias refers to the tendency of participants to respond to research questions in a manner that will be viewed favourably by others or will portray them in a certain social status, rather than choosing responses that are reflective of their true feelings. This bias often comes to the forefront in studies involving sensitive social or personal matters such as religion, politics, current affairs, personal relationships, drugs and alcohol.

SOCIAL DESIRABILITY BIAS
the tendency of a research respondent to answer questions in a manner viewed as more acceptable by peers rather than as reflective of their real feelings.

While there are no guaranteed ways to eliminate such biases, the following measures are usually employed to minimise their impact

- incorporating a socially desirable scale in a survey instrument wherever possible
- careful wording and use of more indirect questioning in interviews
- thorough pre-testing of the survey instrument
- use of an experienced interviewer to examine and probe issues to confirm the participants' responses
- collection of data through methods that do not require the presence or involvement of an interviewer
- repeating the same or similar questions in a survey or interview at different places to cross-check responses.

In some cases, it might be worthwhile to incorporate questions that measure social desirability tendencies.

Cultural nuances

There is a range of cultural barriers encountered when undertaking business research in an international context. The challenges are particularly apparent in developing and emerging nations. Language is a significant challenge in cross-country research studies. In regions like South Africa, where there are over 1000 languages, it would be cost prohibitive for researchers to translate questionnaires for diverse populations. In some places, it is unacceptable for women to conduct personal interviews with men, or vice versa. In other countries, during religious holidays or events, research activities must be suspended until the period has passed. Cultural taboos in conversations, either business or personal, such as revealing your personal wealth to another person, can inhibit the data gathering process and undermine the validity of the research outcomes.

Historically, researchers have assumed that the prepared discussion guide for a focus group or in-depth interview should be the same in each country under study, to ensure they are comparing like with like. However, in many cases, discussion guides need to be modified to obtain the same information. For example, Pacific-Island focus-group participants require more warm-up time and do not feel comfortable moving directly into specific research questions; and more time is required reassuring Thailand participants about privacy issues versus New Zealand participants. In certain regions, it is advantageous to match the ethnicity of the interviewer with the group being interviewed.

Political influences

In some countries, the law requires the research firm to register and purchase a permit to perform a research study; in a few cases, the government may also require a copy of the research instrument to ensure the study's alignment with its policy and purposes prior to giving approval. This can slow the process so time to obtain the relevant permits and needs to be factored into a project's timeline. Further, administrative corruption is a common feature in developing countries. Researchers may be faced with illegal searches and the confiscation of their study materials if the commissioned research firm does not obtain the appropriate approvals. In some instances, where low socio-economic communities are present, the market research can be highly dangerous due to the presence of criminal gangs threatening researchers with violence or extortion. Civil war and political unrest in certain parts of the world can also present issues for research teams.

Engaging an international research agency

Enlisting the services of experienced research professionals is often essential in foreign markets since skilled experts will have a great capacity to deliver research objectives. Therefore, appointing a reliable and trustworthy local research partner in each country involved in the study is often crucial to the success of the research. Access to expert local market knowledge can mitigate many of the challenges involved in conducting research internationally. Local research firms possess a high level of local market understanding, such as knowledge of optimal research participation rates, local customs and technical expertise. Occasionally, engaging with local research firms is necessary, such as in China, to gain access to the market and navigate government bureaucracy. Timely, focused and unique consumer data is critical to a business seeking to understand a foreign market. Obtaining appropriately qualified research information can facilitate market entry and expansion opportunities, whereas an ill-informed choice of a research agency, inadequate information and poorly interpreted data can seriously damage a business' goals and strategies. A company's selection of an agency should be based on scrutiny and the screening of possible candidates.

The key advantage of using a professional research agency relates to governance and quality. A professionally accredited research agency will ensure research is undertaken ethically and complies with the legislation of the country under investigation. They will ensure that the respondent feedback received and the conclusions drawn are fully objective. International research firms, with different organisational structures, include:

- local agencies in the market under investigation
- national agencies with overseas offices or associated firms

- national agencies that subcontract field work to an agency in the market under investigation
- national agencies with experienced foreign staff
- global organisations with multiple international offices.

Integrity, credibility and experience are three important criteria in selecting a research agency. Integrity is measured by reputation within the research community, and adherence to professional research codes of conduct. Credentials, or suitability of the research firm, relates to the agency's current standing in the market. The agency should demonstrate up-to-date knowledge of the relevant sector or superior technical experience and capability related to the collection of data. Finally, the level of experience speaks to the number of years in business, qualifications of staff, ability to provide client testimonials or referrals to validate their experience, and the scope of previous research problems undertaken.

Cost is a crucial factor in the selection process. Generally, international research is more expensive than domestic research. Infrastructure in developing nations is lacking, making the cost of gathering data more expensive. Other costs need to be factored into an international study, such as the cost of multiple translations, coordination across multiple countries and long-distance project management. However, managers should be cautious about using cost as the sole means of judging the merits of competing research agencies. Seeking to reduce costs by such means as the use of inappropriately small sample sizes or inexpensive research methods only increases the potential for inaccurate and unusable findings. It is more critical for firms to review potential research agencies in terms of their understanding of and experience with the firm's business or at least the relevant wider industry, and their proven capacity to deliver the appropriate information. National and local trade associations and business or market networks often act as valuable sources of referrals in relation to selecting research groups or agencies; for example, a national market research society or a chartered institute of marketing exist in many counties and are reliable sources. Online directories also provide contact details and business synopses for a range of relevant research agencies.

On completion of the research, the agency should provide a comprehensive report on the findings and arrange a meeting to present the research results. The findings should be reported in a way that clearly addresses the research objectives and explores all the areas under investigation agreed at the outset. Opportunity should also be given for the firm to ask questions about the research, raise any questions and ask for clarification on the results presented.

New market information technologies

Traditional methods of surveys and interviewing to perform market research deliver credible results. The emergence of new market information technologies is improving the capacity of researchers to build more robust research platforms that capture more detailed data. In a highly competitive age, there is an ever-pressing need to do more with less, to deliver quickly and better than other firms. Technology provides the opportunity to capture larger sample numbers and to provide analysis that breaks down data into meaningful pieces of information so that informed decisions can be made.

The internet and mobile technology platforms provide an increased access to customer and consumer insights. In some respects, technology has made the job of market researchers a little easier. With the ability to reach target markets at multiple touchpoints and with timely feedback, it is understandable why the online environment has achieved a dominance in data collection. Researchers are adapting to this new, data-rich environment and transforming traditional methodologies with new technologies and techniques.

As the world becomes more globalised, societies are becoming more connected and technological innovations are transforming the way we communicate. However, just as the increased connections reveal our similarities, they also throw our differences into prominence. Increasingly, researchers need to be aware of how to navigate in this complex multicultural world. A dynamic shift is taking place in the international business research sector. Previously, clipboard surveys and focus groups were customary, and the research methodology was time-consuming and arduous. Specific technological changes are utilising computerised modes of data capture, the internet for information access, and data collection software to link information via intranets for business. At a national level, improvements in basic communication infrastructures are impacting both consumers and firms, and providing new opportunities to undertake business research. Despite all the advances in market research over the past two decades, the objectives remain the same: capture insights from customers and consumers, and respond in a manner that will manage market entry risk, increase sales and grow market share. Ultimately, the research is about profiling the market, the customers and the consumers better. Continuing developments in technology underpin these processes.

RESEARCH METHODOLOGY
the process used to collect information and data in a research study.

Consumer panel data

Consumer panels capture large data sets that continually record consumer purchases in long-term studies. GfK, Taylor Nelson Sofres and Nielsen are examples of marketing research organisations that provide this type of panel data. Panellists remain in these studies if they continue to meet the criteria of the research agency that hosts the panel. One approach to the collection of household level data that requires panellists to present an identification card at the checkout ensuring information is captured each time the household member shops. An alternative approach is to place in-home scanners to record purchases when panellists return home from a shopping trip. More detailed information including intended use, as well as when and where they make purchases, is also captured.

Single-source data

Single-source data is continuous data that measures various characteristics of an individual consumer based on information from many sources. The advances in technology has created the ability to ease the research process by shifting data collection online. Attention is now being turned towards further technological development and the need to produce a standardised approach to create a single-data collection platform. For example, the approach could be the measure of media and marketing exposure, and purchase behaviour over time for the same individual or household. Researchers and those collecting information across businesses have traditionally utilised several online survey tools independently to gather data and generate insights. This results in data that is siloed within and across departments, and presented in a range of formats. For example, feedback from an individual customer could be in more than 10 different places. When different parts of the same business rely on different data sources, this can inhibit collaboration, result in errors, and impact information needed to facilitate new market introduction of products and services. Unless this information is readily accessible and open to sharing and assessment, it loses much of its strategic intent.

To fully optimise the impact that corporate data provides, firms often develop a single business-wide collection platform. Setting up and standardising a single-insight repository allows managers within the business to access information for a specific business purpose. For example, the procurement division will be focused on product packaging and format, whereas the R&D team

will require information captured from consumer feedback regarding taste. A central business-wide research platform enables all stakeholders engaged in the strategic business units to be informed and it provides a common platform where information is accessible to the broader business operations.

Online data and social media

Twitter, Facebook, LinkedIn, Instagram and blogging websites such as Tumblr have expanded the landscape in which research is conducted (see Table 8.4). Social media is transforming market research in stimulating new ways. These platforms create environments that yield unfiltered feedback, yet they are considered a validated source for examining business reputation and brand awareness. Researchers can take advantage of the advanced capabilities inherent in social media metrics. Learning to master social media for market research will provide salient information and enhance the knowledge obtained about a potential target market.

TABLE 8.4 Leading global social media platforms, as at April 2018

Social media platforms	Active users (billion/million)
Facebook	2.23 b
YouTube	1.50 b
WhatsApp	1.50 b
Facebook Messenger	1.30 b
WeChat	980 m
Instagram	813 m
Tumblr	794 m
QQ	783 m
QZone	563 m
Sina Weibo	392 m
Twitter	330 m
Baidu Tieba	300 m
Viber	260 m
Snapchat	255 m
Line	203 m
Pinterest	200 m

Source: Adapted with permission from Statista 2018

Social media analytics have experienced a sweeping paradigm shift from humble beginnings nearly a decade ago to a major research source. This segment has taken an active approach by using sophisticated technology to provide actionable insights with the unsolicited data collected. The trend will become more aggressive and methodologically innovative as time goes on. Technology that enables the capture and analysis of what consumers are saying online will continue to be a focus. Social media, with user generated content, are predicted to gain in relevance, and the ability to harness this voluntary feedback will be an important element for international businesses to stay competitive, and deliver products and services that meet market demand.

Ethics in international business research

International businesses must consider the planned interactions between the multiple business stakeholders in the research process. Ethical considerations are paramount at all stages of the research process and must be respected within each country. The issue of respect is considered an overarching responsibility; it relates to the requirement that firms researching should conduct their market research in a socially responsible way and in accordance with international research standards. By doing so, more trustworthy information is generated for managers. Since stakeholders have a specific role in the research process, but a different investment in the outcome, ethical considerations in international research can be challenging. The specific areas of focus relate to the four main parties involved in the research process: the respondent, the interviewer, the research supplier, and the firm.

Research strategies should reflect the nature of the information required, and the privacy and confidentiality of primary data should be safeguarded unconditionally. This is often a legal requirement, which may differ between countries. Therefore, particular attention must be given to the legal consequences in the planning, collection and reporting of data. It is unethical to misrepresent in any way the nature of a research study, the information requested or the content of the results. Further the sharing of sensitive information for commercial gain, such as revealing third-party information from a study, is regulated in a few countries. Researchers are required to safeguard the confidentiality of all information captured, to use information only for prescribed purposes and to ensure the destruction of data on completion of the study.

SPOTLIGHT 8.2

Working in an international R&D team

Multidisciplinary and cross-institutional project teams feature specialist technical researchers working together to share experiences, information and skills to deliver study outcomes. A major outcome for agribusiness is to achieve strategic benefit from investment in research projects. This involves developing key partnerships, and a more coordinated approach to targeting priority areas of research in conjunction with institutions and overseas partners and agencies.The challenge for this type of teamwork is the balance of multiple elements, comprising technical skills, the international environment, languages, private and public sector organisations and structures, and individual relationships. Based on the 2013 research of Nancarrow and her colleagues, there are eight key competencies for an international research team that contribute to an effective, high performing multidisciplinary team.

1. a leader who establishes clear direction and vision for the team, while listening and providing support
2. a documented set of team values, which provide direction
3. a team culture where contributions are valued and consensus is fostered
4. appropriate processes and communication channels in place to deliver the outcomes
5. quality research design informed by internal and external feedback
6. recruitment of researchers who demonstrate multidisciplinary competencies, including team functioning, collaborative leadership, well-developed communication skills, and professional knowledge and experience

7. promotion of research autonomy while respecting individual roles and integration of research activities
8. promotion of personal development through appropriate training, recognition and opportunities for career advancement.

Agribusiness research, industry development and technical capacity remain a high priority for the Australian federal and state governments.

Source: Nancarrow et al. 2013

SPOTLIGHT QUESTIONS

QUESTIONS

1. A new research project is just starting. eBay would like to understand the current Australian consumer journey with their brand over a 12-month period starting in two months. You are the leader and are required to design and recommend the top line areas to be investigated. List the research areas and what types of research methods may be suitable.
2. Consider the same research project above. Now you are required to recruit specialist researchers and form a team for your research project. What types of specialists are required in your team?

Reporting and communicating research results

The objective of business research is to deliver a finding, or a set of findings related to solving a business challenge or issue, and then to convey that information to stakeholders for making informed business decisions. Regardless of the research outcome, if the final report assists the parties involved to formulate appropriate business strategies, the research can then be judged beneficial.

To achieve the full potential of the study, the report must speak to all stakeholders in the target audience, not only to a few interested parties. It is important to keep in mind that different audiences will have different interests and levels of understanding when evaluating the research outputs. Some audiences will have a solid background in the evaluation and will want to know specific elements related to the findings. Other stakeholders will be more interested in the snapshot report, which provides an overview of the key findings, rather than the specifics. A researcher needs to determine if each audience member is interested in the detailed hard facts or a more anecdotal narrative of the evaluation findings at a higher level.

When reporting research, several key points must be covered. First, the background, aim and scope of the study should be clear to the reviewer. This should identify why the research was conducted, what the questions the research is seeking to answer were and what the research outcomes will be used to inform. Then, the methodology should be described. What type of research was undertaken, what instrument was used and what was the sample size; for example, a focus group with 10 people or a larger-scale survey with a sample of 500 consumers. The detail in the methodology will help reviewers in their assessment of the research outputs.

Next is the statement of the actual research results in either a richly themed format or a mix of quantitative and qualitative information. This section should be clear, factual and comprehensive. The research report should then include an analysis, interpretation of findings and discussion relating to the implications of the findings. The research results section should not simply reiterate the results, rather it should provide critical reflection upon the results and the processes of data collection, especially in relation to the research questions.

Finally, the report should provide a conclusion, including how the study met the research questions, describing any challenges encountered in the study, and then stating clear, objective and actionable recommendations. Misleading or inaccurate reporting of information can create unrealistic expectations, and can put businesses at risk of unnecessary commercial harm. Follow-up procedures are an important component of all research studies and are generally undertaken to increase the overall effectiveness of the research effort. They can be conducted for several reasons:

- to review any new developments
- to further explore gaps identified in the current project
- to fulfil research promises
- to ensure compliance with institutional and government protocols
- to ensure milestones are being met
- to thank participants for their time
- to debrief stakeholders.

Follow-up studies may be conducted when time and cost are constraining factors that make ongoing longitudinal studies unfeasible. In some cases, follow-up may be conducted after the original research; this would be to ascertain if an intervention has had the desired result and to gauge the level of impact the change has generated. Follow-up research activities are often necessary and in some cases ongoing in international business operations. To ensure the reviewers have the appropriate information, the suggested research and time frame can be proposed in the recommendations section.

 SPOTLIGHT 8.3

Fresh produce innovation in export markets: challenges and opportunities

Australian broccoli growers wanted to enter the Japanese market. First, they needed to understand and profile Japanese purchasing behaviours relating to vegetable and broccoli consumption, and then collect recommendations for the export of Australian broccoli to Japan. Desktop research was conducted to provide an overview of the current market, food sufficiency and consumer landscape in Japan, with data captured from a range of sources including trade journals, empirical studies, publications from Japanese government departments and Australia government informants. A quantitative in-market study was also used to gain an understanding of consumers' vegetable habits, to examine key purchasing preferences related to consumption and to profile the Japanese broccoli consumer.

The exploratory study first involved computer assisted telephone interviews (CATI) of respondents and then employed an online questionnaire to investigate who purchased broccoli, establish the frequency of purchases and to profile the consumers' socio-demographics. The survey instrument was developed in English, translated to Japanese and then back translated to English for confirmation. It was found that the dynamics of changing consumer behaviours, transformations in the retail trade environment and government interventions all play significant roles in shaping the characteristics of the Japanese market.

Four key insights into understanding the Japanese consumer of vegetables and broccoli were identified in the study. The study had six recommendations to build an understanding of Japanese consumer attitudes and motivations towards broccoli purchasing, and to advance the

competitive position for Australia's successful market entry into Japan. The analysis of the data captured from the in-market study enabled the Japanese broccoli consumer to be defined. Through this research phase, it was reasonable to propose that, with further research and collaboration with a supermarket chain, Australian broccoli would have an entry platform on which to build consumer acceptance and a sustainable market uptake in Japan.

Source: Adapted from RIMS No. 44665 Understanding Vegetable and Broccoli Consumption in Japan. Reproduced with permission of Griffith University.

QUESTIONS

SPOTLIGHT QUESTIONS

1. What research insights would be most helpful to increase the uptake by consumers in Japan of Australian broccoli?
2. This was a new market for Australian broccoli exports. What secondary information would be available online to assist exporters to understand the Japanese market more broadly for fresh vegetables?

Summary

Learning objective 1: Understand the international business research process.

Many companies do little research before entering a foreign market so that often their market entry and expansion decisions are made only after a cursory assessment. International research is usually more formal and in-depth than domestic studies; six steps were highlighted as important when undertaking international research. The first step is defining the research problem, which is essential because a properly formulated research problem will underpin meaningful and actionable research results. The next five steps are: determining the information needs and output requirements; developing the research design; collecting the data; analysing and reporting; and presenting the findings. While not dissimilar to the domestic market research process, there are unique challenges in the international context, including: structuring the appropriate research design, availability of infrastructure and accurate data; time and cost implications; coordination of multi-country studies; establishing comparability; and managing language and cultural nuances.

Learning objective 2: Characterise secondary sources of information in international markets.

The collection of consistent information can be difficult in a multi-country environment. Attention was paid to locating appropriate secondary information. The internet provides a rich source of secondary data gathered by government, research and private agencies. However, importance should be placed on information quality, including the reliability, validity, timeliness and comparability of such data, as it was not collected to answer the researcher's current question. Various types of secondary data are considered in: selecting foreign markets for entry, estimating demand for products and services, and assessing the interconnectedness between a home market and foreign markets.

Learning objective 3: Examine approaches to undertaking primary market research.

Primary data collection in an international environment is fraught with difficulties. The importance of research instrument pre-testing and ensuring equivalence across countries was highlighted. The discussion outlined that primary research can be both qualitative and quantitative in nature, with focus groups and surveys the most common techniques for each type of research respectively. Technological advances are increasingly allowing greater access to more consumers online; it is facilitating and expediting research across the globe.

Learning objective 4: Appreciate the challenges and issues associated with conducting international business research.

In the international context, the key challenges faced by researchers include political, economic, legal and cultural differences. To make cross-country comparisons meaningful, firms need to adequately manage and coordinate their market research projects with an international lens. Engaging local research firms makes it easier to implement changes based on the results, and can also uncover country-specific individualities that cannot be discounted with over-standardised measurement instruments. Engaging a professional research agency in a foreign market, rather than relying on in-house services can significantly improve the quality and validity of the research outcomes.

Learning objective 5: Outline reporting methods to ensure effective communication of research results.

A research study is only meaningful if the results can be communicated clearly with the level of detail relevant to each stakeholder. The chapter concluded by providing an overview of the critical elements of research reporting. These include presenting the results in a concise and factual manner, providing an interpretation and discussion around the results in relation to the research problem, delivering a core set of insights and actionable recommendations, as well as key areas of follow up activities.

USEFUL WEBSITES

Revision questions

REVISION QUESTIONS

1. Describe and explain the six steps in the international research process.
2. Researchers encounter a few challenges when collecting secondary data. Describe at least three of these challenges.
3. An Australian business is wanting to launch a new bike internationally. Provide step-by-step advice as to what issues they need to consider and the steps they should take in designing a primary research activity for a foreign market.
4. What are the key advantages and disadvantages to the emic and etic approaches in cross-cultural research.
5. Follow-up procedures are an important component of all international business research and are generally undertaken to increase the overall effectiveness of the research effort. Outline at least five reasons why this is conducted.

R&D activities

R&D ACTIVITIES

1. You are the marketing director for an Australian manufacturer of beer and wine. Your executive board has asked for a preliminary market scan to consider internationalising the firm. How would you go about quantifying the opportunity?
2. Airbnb is often portrayed as a game changer for the hotel industry. Describe the use of research and its role in their success. What recommendations would you make for further research activity? Explain your reasons.
3. Research and describe the role of the Asia Pacific Research Committee (APRC) and how this institution links with global networks (www.aprc-research.com).

IB MASTERCLASS

Vietnam exports to mainland China and Hong Kong

This study presents a strategic analysis of China and Hong Kong as import markets for fresh mangoes to provide a better understanding of prospects for horticultural trade between Vietnam and China. The principal objectives are to understand import patterns and trends, assess key factors driving import trade, identify market growth opportunities, and assess the current competitive position of Vietnam.

China is a potentially lucrative and large market for Vietnamese mangoes. Hong Kong is one of the main import markets for mangoes and serves as an important gateway to China. While Hong Kong is a well-established market, there is limited knowledge regarding China's mango market and its related import trends. By examining these issues, this study provides an informed perspective on the challenges and opportunities facing Vietnamese mango exporters in accessing the Chinese market.

Methodology

The study employed a two-phase research approach. The first phase comprised a detailed review of trade research, and country statistics provided government statistical information for China and its special administrative region of Hong Kong. Official international data on mangoes is captured by government agencies under a common harmonised code (HS 08045030), and represents an aggregation of fresh and dried mango statistics.

The second phase consisted of in-market business interviews with company executives engaged in the mango trade. Interviews were conducted onsite and covered issues such as market segments, distribution channels, seasonality of supply, importer opinions and consequential drivers of export opportunities for Vietnamese mangoes. For consistent information capture, a question checklist was developed and used to support interviews.

Mainland China

Despite a population of nearly 1.4 billion people in China, mango import figures in 2013 were equivalent to just 6 per cent of those in the US and less than half in countries such as Canada, the UK, Germany or Saudi Arabia (Tradedata 2015). According to published Chinese government statistics, the country imported 31 621 tonnes of mango in 2013, accounting for 2.1 per cent of global imports.

The official data does not fully reflect actual imports owing to unrecorded product inflows from Hong Kong and Vietnam. For example, Chinese statistics in 2013 for mango imports from Vietnam were recorded at 11 760 kg, but sources suggest mango exports are far higher than documented (Nguyen, Nguyen & Tran 2013; Smith 2014). Moreover, during a 2014 Australian Centre for International Agricultural Research study into Vietnam's tropical fruit sector, several key informants reported that between March and June mangoes are regularly shipped by road from southern Vietnam to China.

Import trends

Official figures for 2008–13 essentially reveal a flat line trend for mango imports into China (see Figure 8.1). Official imports increased sharply in 2009, peaking at 33 000 tonnes, but have since stabilised around the 25 000 tonne mark. In value terms, however, imports continued to grow due to rising prices, reaching about US$12 million in 2013.

In the context of high economic growth in China, it is interesting that mango imports have remained relatively stable. This indicates that demand is not very responsive to income, a finding that is corroborated by consumption data collected in three large cities (Beijing, Shanghai and Chongqing) and three coastal provinces (Guangdong, Fujian, and Shandong) (FAO 2009). According to the data, mango has an income-elasticity of demand of 0.32; meaning a 10 per

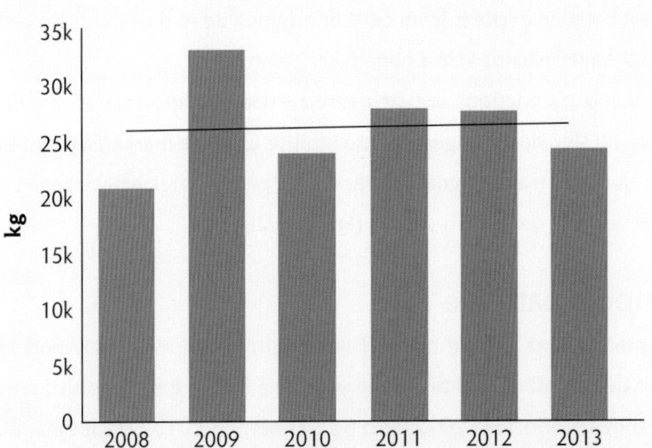

FIGURE 8.1 Total mango imports in mainland China by volume, 2008–13
Note: k = thousand; HS Code 08045030, fresh and dried

cent rise in household income generates an estimated increase in demand of just 3.2 per cent. It is likely that the income-elasticity of demand for the country is even lower.

Recent trends in mango imports are a consequence of demand conditions and supply factors. Mango imports peak during the Chinese harvest season (March to June). At that time, Myanmar has an abundant supply of mangoes that are sold across the border at very competitive prices and there is an unreported cross-border trade in Vietnamese mangoes. Imports from Thailand and the Philippines do not follow a clear seasonal pattern; with both countries supplying small volumes throughout the year. Imports from Taiwan and Australia, in turn, exhibit seasonality like their exports to Hong Kong (see Figure 8.2). Taiwanese mangoes are sourced from May to September, with volumes peaking in July and August. Supplies from Australia are concentrated during the months of December and January, although additional consignments may be sourced in November and February.

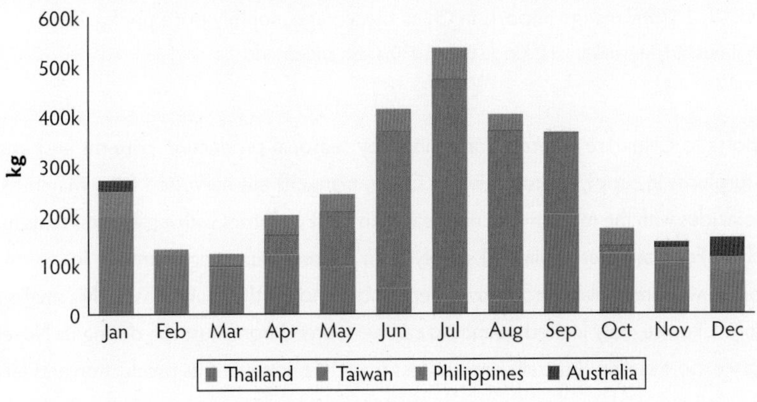

FIGURE 8.2 Top four total mango imports in mainland China, 2013
Note: k = thousand; HS Code 08045030, fresh and dried

Quarantine regulations pose significant challenges for exporters, reducing their willingness or ability to ship mangoes to China. For example, a lack of vapour-heat treatment capacity has limited the ability of the Australian mango industry to increase exports to China (Fruitnet

2010). Infrequent bans on imports from certain origins due to non-compliance with phytosanitary requirements have also impacted negatively on imports.

The way trading transactions are structured exposes exporters to significant price risks, further discouraging significant engagement with the Chinese market. Mango exports to China are typically conducted on a consignment basis, with prices determined when importers sell the fruit, not when an export contract is signed (Fruitnet 2015).

Seasonal import patterns

Mango imports into China have a marked seasonal pattern, with May and June imports far exceeding those during other months of the year (see Figure 8.3). May and June accounted for 79 per cent of annual imports in 2012, and 86 per cent in 2013 (Tradedata, 2015). The figure for these months would be higher if cross-border inflows from Vietnam, which are concentrated during the second quarter of the year, were recorded. During other times of the year, imports are low, rarely exceeding 400 tonnes per month.

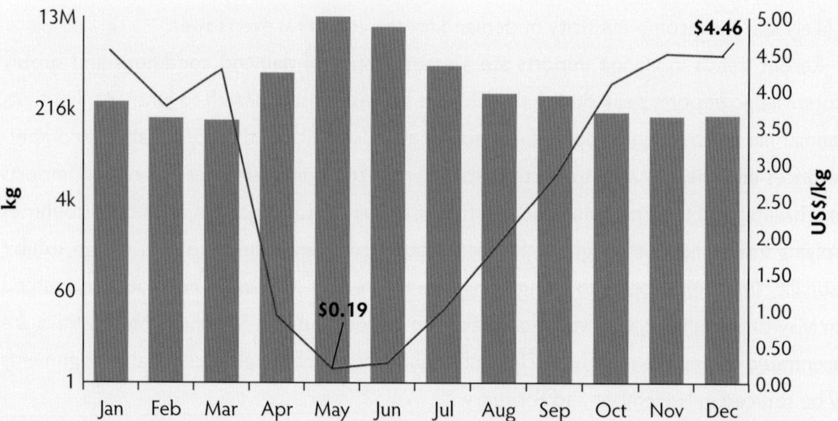

FIGURE 8.3 Total mango imports in China by average monthly price per kg, 2013
Note: k = thousand; M = million; HS Code 08045030, fresh and dried

Exports to China are severely constrained by seasonal production patterns and available export surpluses in supplying countries. In China, mangoes are harvested from March to June, which coincides with the main production season in most countries with legal access to its market. From July to February there is limited supply from regional exporting countries. In-season mangoes from Taiwan are available from July to September, though the country has only a small surplus for export. Likewise, only limited quantities can be sourced from Australia during its November to January export season. Australia exports less than 10 per cent of its production and tends to prioritise markets with low-entry barriers such as Hong Kong, Singapore and New Zealand.

Seasonality in import prices is closely linked to the level and origin of imports (see Figure 8.4). CIF (cost, insurance and freight) import prices are very low in May and June, when significant volumes of cheap mangoes can be sourced from Myanmar. In July and August, the more expensive Taiwanese mangoes gain a significant market share. Prices peak in November or December and remain very high until March. During this period, Thailand is the main origin,

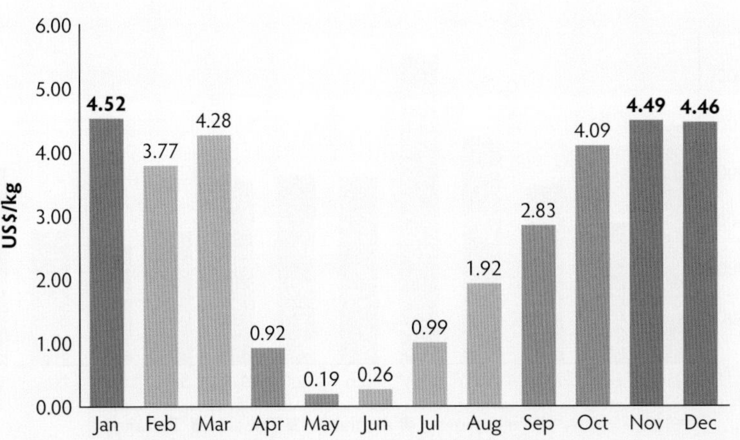

FIGURE 8.4 Total mango imports in China by average monthly CIF price per kg, 2013
Note: HS Code 08045030, fresh and dried

followed by the Philippines and Australia, the three most expensive sources of mango imported into China. The fact that prices are high and imports low during this period is a strong indication that exporters face considerable supply constraints.

Hong Kong

Hong Kong is a free-trade port with an open economy and very few import barriers. No tariffs or taxes are charged on a range of imported foods including mangoes. As an important market access consideration, exporters do not have to comply with expensive phytosanitary regulations, including fruit fly disinfestation treatments. Mango exporters only need to submit a certificate of fitness for human consumption from the department of health of the originating country.

In 2013, Hong Kong imported 23 967 tonnes mangoes, making it the second-largest export market in South-East Asia and the fifth largest in Asia, after Malaysia (58 000 tonnes), Saudi Arabia (49 000 tonnes), the United Arab Emirates (42 000 tonnes) and Yemen (26 000 tonnes). The importance of Hong Kong as an export destination is also linked to its role as a gateway to the Chinese market. A significant share of mango fruit imported into the region is subsequently re-exported to mainland China.

Import trends

Over 85 per cent of mangoes imported into Hong Kong come from three nearby origins, with the more distant and higher-priced source of Australia accounting for most additional supplies (see Figure 8.5). These spatial patterns are not specific to Hong Kong; geographical proximity is a major determinant of access to international mango markets because it enables low-cost transportation by road or sea without major adverse impacts on quality.

Seasonal factors influence import trends. The Philippines accounts for more than two-thirds of mangoes exported to the region, reflecting exporters' ability to deliver minimum volumes throughout the year at competitive prices. Taiwan is the second largest origin country, supplying an affordable source of mangoes from June to September (see Table 8.5). Australia is the third largest supplier of mangoes to Hong Kong. While Australian mangoes are expensive

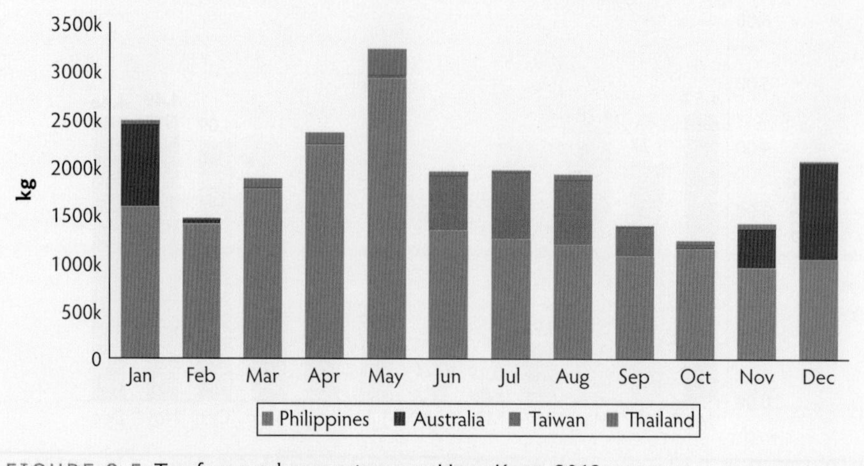

FIGURE 8.5 Top four total mango imports, Hong Kong, 2013

Note: k = thousand; HS Code 08045030, fresh and dried

TABLE 8.5 Vietnam mango exports to Hong Kong (volume & CIF price/kg), 2010–13

	2010	2011	2012	2013
Vietnam mango exports to Hong Kong (kg)	2794	88 973	207 215	175 616
Share of official Vietnam mango exports (%)	3.1	14.1	28.9	26.3
Share of Hong Kong mango imports (%)	0.0	0.4	0.9	0.7
Average CIF price, Hong Kong				
Vietnam (US$/kg)	9.21	2.02	1.56	1.65
Philippines (US$/kg)	1.15	1.20	1.28	1.28
Taiwan (US$/kg)	0.92	1.06	1.36	1.20
Thailand (US$/kg)	1.00	1.12	1.36	1.84
Australia (US$/kg)	3.20	3.70	3.36	3.27

Note: HS Code 08045030, fresh and dried

because of high domestic market prices and distance to market, the country supplies premium quality fruit during the Christmas and Chinese New Year festive periods, two points of relatively high demand in Hong Kong and very limited supply across Asia.

Vietnamese mangoes have a marginal presence in Hong Kong. No mangoes were exported to this market in 2009. Less than three tonnes were exported in 2010 and levels peaked in 2012 at 207 tonnes, valued at US$323 080, but representing only 0.9 per cent of total imports in volume terms. Hong Kong is Vietnam's main official destination market, which underlines the relatively small size of the Vietnamese mango export trade. In 2012, Hong Kong accounted for 29 per cent of official exports of mangoes, 26 per cent in 2013 and 19 per cent in 2014. These figures do not include cross-border flows to China (they do not feature in China or Vietnam's customs data) so the official statistics fall into a grey trade category.

Vietnamese mangoes are slightly more expensive than those from the Philippines and Taiwan, but generally are more affordable than competing fruit from Thailand. Though price is an important determinant of market access, quality considerations should also be factored into any analysis of competitive advantage, alongside end user and consumer preferences, and business linkages between exporters and importers.

Between 2008 and 2013, annual mango imports into Hong Kong varied between 18 500 and 24 500 tonnes, with no significant upward or downward trend, although growth potential should not be discounted (see Figure 8.6). While this market has showed no consistent growth over the last decade, the value of mango imports has been rising due to increased purchases from Australia driving up average annual prices.

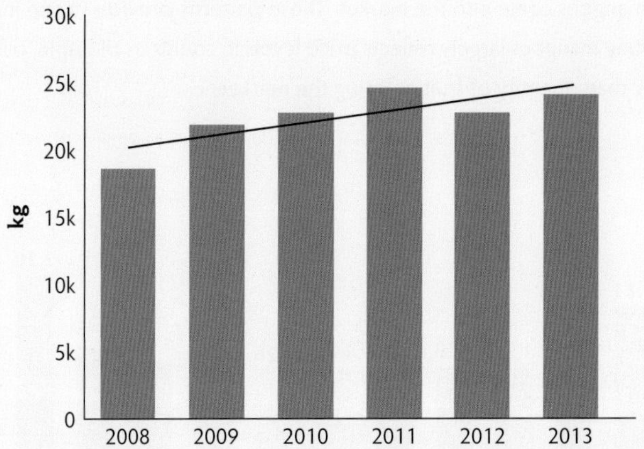

FIGURE 8.6 Total mango imports in Hong Kong by volume, 2008–13
Note: k = thousand; HS Code 08045030, fresh and dried

It is possible that a lack of growth in Hong Kong's imported mango market may be due to either a stagnation of mango as a fruit of choice by consumers or a tightening of controls around the re-export trade to mainland China. Perhaps it is a combination of both.

Seasonal import patterns

Mango import trade in Hong Kong peaks from March to June, with a second, smaller peak in December and January (see Figure 8.7). These seasonal patterns partly mimic peak harvest time in Luzon, the main mango production area in the Philippines (Briones et al. 2013). As this

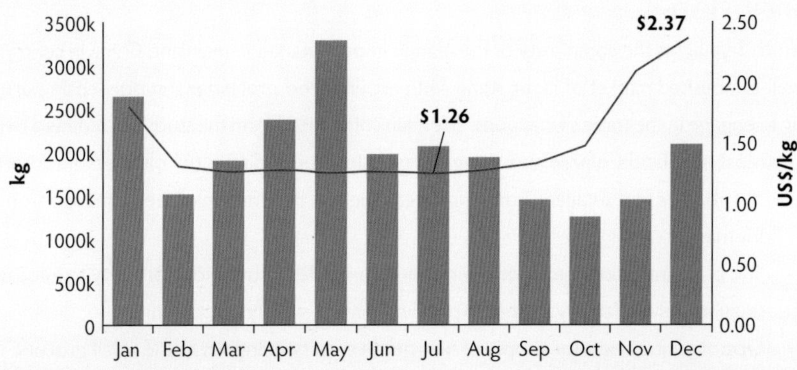

FIGURE 8.7 Total mango imports in Hong Kong by average monthly price per kg, 2013
Note: k = thousand; HS Code 08045030, fresh and dried

source dwindles, Taiwanese mangoes from June to September and Australian mangoes from November to January assist in stabilising supply.

Demand factors also play a key role. Despite high prices, there is a significant increase in imports in December and January due to strong consumer demand during Christmas and Chinese New Year festive periods, when Hong Kong importers rely largely on off-season consignments from the Philippines and much costlier supplies from Australia.

Despite considerable monthly variations in supply, CIF import prices are fairly stable between February and October (see Figure 8.8). There is a significant increase in prices only when Australian mangoes come into the market. These patterns provide strong indication that the cost of importing mangoes largely reflects price levels in countries of origin, particularly the Philippines, rather than quantity of fruit entering the market.

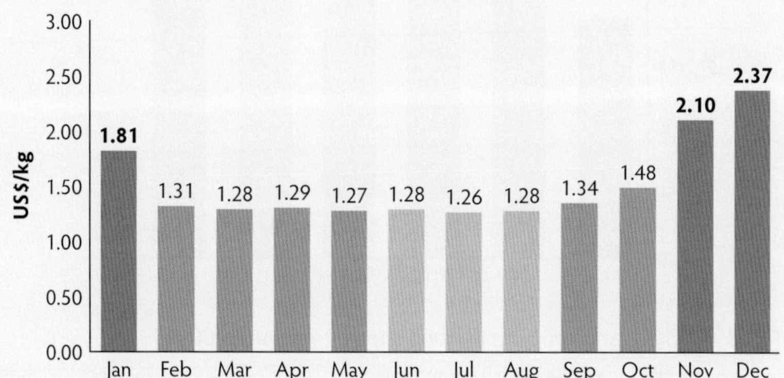

FIGURE 8.8 Total mango imports in Hong Kong by average monthly CIF price per kg, 2013

Note: HS Code 08045030, fresh and dried

In any given month, Hong Kong has a undiversified portfolio of supplying countries, importing mango from one or two main origins. Hong Kong relies largely on the Philippines to meet its consumption needs at different times of the year, with Taiwan and Australia providing additional supplies during their respective export windows, June to September and November to January.

Conclusion

This study highlights the complexity of the mango import market in mainland China in contrast to the well-established market of Hong Kong, with experienced professional supply-chain partners willing to engage in the trade of mangoes. The main conclusions from the study are outlined below.

- Most mainland Chinese and Hong Kong chain intermediaries (wholesalers, importers, distributors and retailers) could not recall the last time they had seen a mango from Vietnam.
- The buoyant Chinese market environment provides a strong opportunity to increase smallholder welfare by further expanding mango supply opportunities.
- Opportunities exist for supply of first-grade quality mangoes to the retail grocery sector, and for second-grade mangoes to the food service and processing sector.

- Regional cross-border markets near Vietnam may provide an opportunity for an increased trade of Vietnam mangoes.
- A planned program to extend the production season will provide a larger window for seasonal opportunities to supply lucrative markets.
- In recent years, Vietnamese mango exports to Hong Kong have peaked during the September to December months, not during the April to June main harvesting season, further supporting the need to evaluate extended season production R&D.

Source: Adapted from RIMS No. 46530 Vietnam Mango Exports to mainland China and Hong Kong. Reproduced with permission of the University of Adelaide, ACIAR and Griffith University.

QUESTIONS

1. What are some of the key factors that may influence import trends of mangoes to mainland China and Hong Kong?
2. Despite Hong Kong's liberal import environment and proximity, mango exports from Vietnam to Hong Kong and China are low. Discuss what factors may be causing this situation.
3. What could Vietnamese mango exporters do to better access these markets?

References

Briones, R.M., Turingan, P.S. & Rakotoarisoa, M.A. (2013). *Market structure and distribution of benefits from agricultural exports: the case of the Philippine mango industry*. FAO Commodity and Trade Policy Research Working Paper No. 42. Rome: Food and Agriculture Organization of the United Nations.

The Economic Times (2017). Airtel's rushed Africa entry was a mistake that took many years to fix, admits Sunil Mittal. *The Economic Times*, 16 December. Retrieved from https://economictimes.indiatimes.com/news/company/corporate-trends/we-should-have-not-taken-decision-to-venture-into-africa-sunil-mittal/articleshow/62087923.cms

FAO (2009). *Demand responses to prices, income and other factors in the Chinese banana and selected tropical fruits markets*. Committee on Commodity Problems, joint meeting of the fourth session of the sub-group on tropical fruits, 9–11 December. Rome: Food and Agricultural Organization of the United Nations.

Fruitnet (2010). Australian mango growers want VHT facility. Asia Fruit website, Fruitnet, 13 July. Retrieved from www.fruitnet.com/asiafruit/article/7452/australian-mango-growers-want-vht-facility

——— (2015). New tax system to be trialled in Shanghai. Asia Fruit website, Fruitnet, 23 September. Retrieved from www.fruitnet.com/asiafruit/article/166542/new-tax-system-to-be-trialled-in-shanghai

Hult, G.T.M., Ketchen Jr, D.J., Griffith, D.A., Finnergan, C.A., Gonzalez-Padron, T., Harmancioglu, N., Huang, Y., Talay, M.B. & Cavusgil, S.T. (2008). Data equivalence in cross-cultural international business research: assessment and guidelines. *Journal of International Business Studies*, 39(6), 1027–44. doi:10.1057/palgrave.jibs.8400396.

Kotabe, M. & Helsen, K. (2010). *Global Marketing Management*, 5th edn, International Student Version. New Jersey: Wiley.

Lee, J.A. (1966). Cultural analysis in overseas operations. *Harvard Business Review*, March–April. https://doi.org/10.1002/tie.5060080303

Nancarrow, S., Booth, A., Ariss, S., Smith, T., Enderby, P. & Roots, A. (2013). Ten principles of good interdisciplinary team work. *Human Resources for Health*, 11, 1–19.

National Australia Bank (NAB) (2016). Shipping Australian sea treasures to Asia. National Australia Bank, 16 November. Retrieved from http://business.nab.com.au/shipping-australian-sea-treasures-to-asia-19361/#.WH7wcptLCok

Nguyen, T.K.D., Nguyen, M.H. & Tran, T.H. (2013). Impacts of China on poverty reduction in Vietnam. In: H. Jalilian, ed., *Assessing China's Impact on Poverty in the Greater Mekong Subregion*. Singapore: Institute of Southeast Asian Studies.

Pike, K. (1967). *Language in Relation to a Unified Theory of the Structure of Human Behavior*. The Hague: Mouton.

Roberts, R.E. (2014). Australian franchise expansion into Asia: Understanding the role of the consumer in product adaptation. Research project. Griffith University.

Smith, W. (2014). *Business engagement in smallholder agriculture: Developing the mango sector in Dong Thap province*. ODI Report.

Statista (2018). Most popular social networks worldwide as of April 2018, ranked by number of active users (in millions). Statista, July. Retrieved from www.statista.com/statistics/272014/global-social-networks-ranked-by-number-of-users

Tradedata (2015). China Trade Statistics. Prepared by Tradedata International.

PART THREE

FUNCTIONAL ISSUES

CHAPTER 9

FOREIGN CURRENCY AND INTERNATIONAL FINANCIAL MANAGEMENT

Learning objectives

In reading this chapter, you will learn to:

1. explain how international financial managers establish their firms' capital structure
2. understand how firms manage their working capital and cash flow
3. outline the nature of foreign exchange markets and the exchange risks faced by MNEs
4. understand how MNEs manage currency risk exposures
5. understand complex international accounting and taxation issues.

THE BITCOIN ROLLERCOASTER RIDE

In the late 1990s, the East-Asian economies exposed themselves to a financial crisis due to poor corporate governance, insider trading and corruption (Radelet et al. 1998). In an address to a WB seminar in 1997, the then Malaysian Prime Minister, Dr Mohamad Mahathir, blamed currency speculators for his country's problems (BBC News 1997).

In 2009, bitcoin started as a cryptocurrency and payment system. Currently, 1100 cryptocurrencies exist, such as Ethereum and Ripple, with a market capitalisation of over US$150 billion. More and more people are investing in virtual currencies, but the market is not stable and comes with highs and lows, crashes and recoveries, and is therefore seen as a speculative currency. In 2017, bitcoin prices surged to record highs as traders prepared for the launch of the first cryptocurrency futures contracts.

The contracts expired on 18 January 2018, resulting in trading volatility and the price fell by as much as 10 per cent. It was expected that prices would increase again, but they only became worse. From a high of US$13 412, bitcoin has fallen to US$6358 in November 2018 (Official Data Foundation 2018).

There have been several attempts by governments, especially in Asian countries such as South Korea and China, to tighten controls over cryptocurrency trading. The People's Bank of China has suggested a ban on centralised trading of cryptocurrencies due to the anonymity of its transactions.

Many analysts see a grim future ahead for cryptocurrencies due to the rapid rise of transaction fees, driven by the limited number of transactions that can be processed per second. Others believe the price could go 10 times higher, with a market crash potentially causing a crisis since 40 per cent of global bitcoin is owned by 1000 people, which gives them the power to get their money out first. 'The fact that this is our first global mania will make this the single most speculative bubble of our lifetime', stated Mike Novogratz, a billionaire with 30 per cent of his wealth in cryptocurrency in January 2018.

Comparisons have been made between the dotcom bubble of the late 1990s and cryptocurrency. The dotcom bubble was driven by a fear of missing out, with many investors acting without really understanding what they were doing. Are cryptocurrencies just a speculative investment with investors following the crowd without understanding the intricacies of how cryptocurrencies work and why they exist? Have the world's financial markets really changed since the Asian crisis of 1997?

VIDEOS

VIGNETTE QUESTIONS

Sources: Bird & Hunter 2018; Silverman, Murphy & Authers 2017

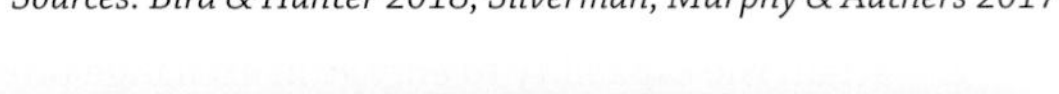

FIGURE 9.1 Bitcoin is a digital currency without a central bank that can be sent from user to user without the need of financial intermediaries

Introduction

Financial management for an MNE refers to the acquisition and use of funds to support its business operations in diverse environments and foreign currencies. International financial management differs from domestic financial management as MNEs must consider the different currencies, the various political situations, the unique ways that markets operate, and the varied opportunities available in the countries they operate. Capital is required by an MNE to finance its investment in new projects, expand existing ventures, and support its current local and international projects. The requirements of each country must be considered together with the overall financial management of the MNE.

International financial management

Economic exposure, also known as operating exposure, is the impact of changes in real exchange rates relative to the MNE's competitors; that is, the effect on the net present value of the MNE's future income streams. To minimise this impact, Lessard and Lightstone (1986) recommend that senior managers strive to:

1. have a flexible sourcing structure (in other words, be able to shift production from one country to another quickly and efficiently)
2. attain the capability to engage in exchange rate pass through (that is, the capability to raise prices in response to exchange rate fluctuations without losing sales volume).

To obtain this second capability, senior managers should try to obtain a market leadership position with highly differentiated products. Senior managers at MNEs need to take economic exposure into account when determining their international business strategy. This means that they will need to consider the likelihood of negative currency fluctuation when assessing location advantages.

Capital structure and sources of finance

Capital is necessary for MNEs to invest in new ventures, expand existing ones and support projects that are currently underway. The capital structure of a company determines the cost of capital and the profitability of its projects, and therefore impacts the value of the firm.

CAPITAL STRUCTURE
also referred to as the debt-equity structure; reflects how the company finances its assets. It shows the proportion of assets financed by debt relative to equity.

The capital structure is made up of the debt and equity finance used by the company to support its operations. A company's ability to remain in business, expand and grow depends largely on its ability to access additional capital. Although companies generate profits that are partly reinvested into the business operations, these are generally insufficient to fund expansion. The debt-equity structure of the firm indicates its risk profile, and influences the company's cash flows and its ability to raise finance.

Equity financing

EQUITY FINANCING
funds a company raises by issuing capital or ownership rights through ordinary and preference shares.

Equity financing refers to the sale of ownership rights to other investors generally in the form of ordinary shares. Ordinary shares have an initial issue price paid to the company itself, and any subsequent transactions are made on a secondary exchange such as, for example, the Singapore Stock Exchange (SGX). An ordinary share provides equity in a company and the return on that investment is the dividend that the company pays per share. The profit of the company is accumulated as retained earnings. Retained earnings may be retained by the company to finance expansion or returned to shareholders as dividends. Generally, it is a combination of the two. The benefit of equity financing is that the company obtains access to capital without the requirement to repay funds at a specific time. If shareholders wish to dispose of their shares they can do so on the relevant stock market. Additionally, dividends paid to shareholders are at the discretion of the company. The primary disadvantage is the dilution of shareholding each time an equity raising is undertaken. Further, a shareholder may take a controlling stake in the company resulting in the existing management losing its control over decisions.

Traditionally, shares have been traded on stock exchanges in the shareholders' own country. Currently, there is an important trend of shares being traded on foreign exchanges, which is supported largely by the growth of institutional investment. MNEs' are increasingly issuing new shares in global markets and listing stocks on foreign stock exchanges. The global integration of capital markets resulted from the effects of international trade and was necessary for several reasons, including the desire to gain access to a larger investor base and the consequence of technological advancements, such as the internet and information tools that facilitated efficient and fair trading. Further, listing shares on a foreign stock exchange, referred to as cross-listing, creates a recognition of a company in a foreign country and provides a company profile to support its further capital raising.

In addition to ordinary shares, equity finance can be raised through using preference shares, rights and options, and private equity placements.

Debt financing

Debt financing occurs when a company borrows funds from a lender, with the borrower required to repay the principal at a specified time alongside the interest charge, which is the cost of the borrowing. The benefit of debt financing is that there is no loss of ownership of the company, but the disadvantage is that the borrowing must be repaid at a specified time. Businesses require short-term financing or working capital and long-term financing from institutions and financial markets. Long-term financing is provided through loans, bonds, debentures and unsecured notes.

DEBT FINANCING the funds borrowed by a company for specified maturities, repayment structures, interest rates and currency denominations.

BONDS represent a major form of debt financing, where the debt is contracted directly with investors. They are generally only available to entities with strong credit ratings.

A company can raise long-term finance in its domestic market or in a foreign market, with the loan denominated in the domestic currency or another foreign currency as required. Borrowing funds from financial institutions provides companies with access to funds and establishes a relationship with the institution that can then give the company access to other financial services, such as lines of credit, foreign exchange and funds management expertise. This can be very useful for foreign subsidiaries who benefit from a business banking relationship in their local country, and receive a loan and interest rate in their local currency. Loans are made with specified terms and conditions, including repayment dates, interest rates and debt restrictions (such as a specified debt or an equity ratio). A bond is a formal debt instrument that enables the issuer (the borrower) to raise funds by promising to repay the principal plus interest at a specified time (at its maturity) (Cavusgil et al. 2015).

Corporate bonds are unsecured and so are reliant on agency credit ratings for their credibility. If the company issuing bonds is deemed high risk, then it is less likely that the company will be able to repay the bond at maturity. Bonds are traded through an international marketplace called the global bond market. A bond offering can be made in the domestic market and denominated in the domestic currency, or a company can sell bonds outside of the bond issuer's country and the bonds can be denominated in multiple currencies. Foreign bonds denominated in the domestic market's currency are generally issued by foreign firms conducting a large amount of business in a domestic

market; these usually involve significant currency, political and repayment risks. Recent examples of large MNEs issuing bonds in foreign markets include Apple's issue of US$6.5 billion in US domestic bonds, Coca-Cola's issue of about €8.5 billion euro-denominated bonds, and the Irish pharmaceutical company, Allergan, issuing euro-denominated bonds as an economic hedge of the company's rising euro revenues.

Intra-corporate financing

In addition to external funding of capital through debt and equity raising, an MNE can also obtain funding from within its own group of subsidiaries and related entities. If some companies within the group are cash-rich, cash-poor companies within the group can tap into their capital through loans, equity raising or other credit terms. Although there are many advantages for intra-corporate financing, it is important that the arms-length principle is applied as taxation authorities have increased their focus on these kinds of arrangements (Price, Rahman & Yohana 2012). The advantages include the tax-deductibility of the loan interest to the lender, reduced transaction costs and the lack of impact on the financial statements of the group through the consolidation process. These transactions are subject to transfer pricing arrangements, discussed later in the chapter.

INTRA-CORPORATE FINANCING the funds provided by sources within the company group, such as from parent companies, subsidiaries and associates, which includes financing through equity, debt and credit in the ordinary course of business.

SPOTLIGHT 9.1

Britain's exit from the EU

On 23 June 2016, the British people voted to leave the EU, which impacted many areas of the British economy. Although Britain kept the British pound during its time with the EU, the exit from this union had consequences for its exchange rate. Broadbent (2017) advised that there was a big drop in the

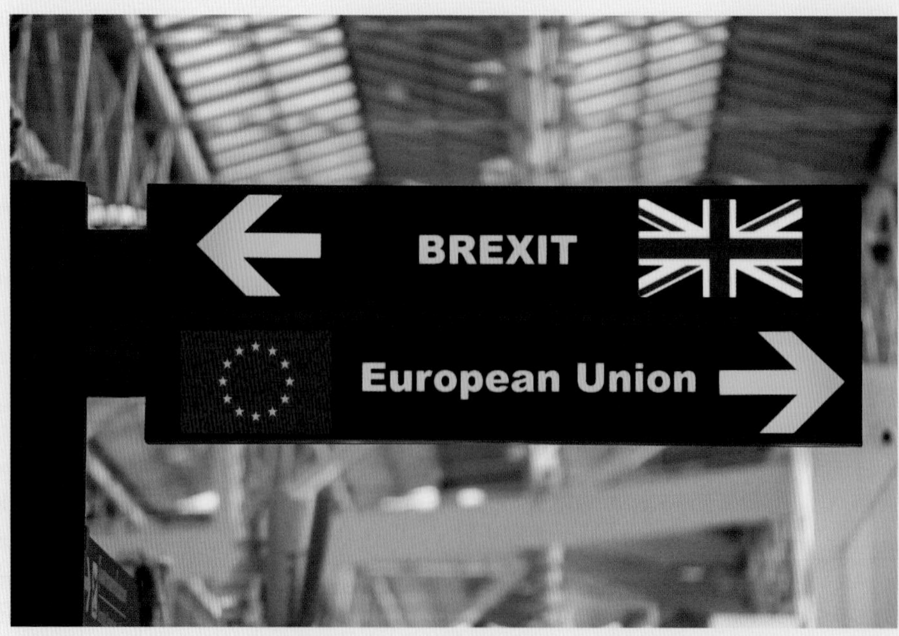

exchange rate after the vote, decreasing household's real income as a result of the increase in import prices and an increase in export prices of approximately 12 per cent in pounds sterling. Britain's decision to exit the EU impacted financial markets and affected London's financial district; Xavier Rolet was reported to comment at the time that over 200 000 jobs could be lost (Rodiowove 2017). Part of a financial district's operations is to act as a clearing house for large multinational capital flows. The current EU regime was not developed to have a major central counterparty operating outside the EU to clear capital flows (Cœuré 2017). This caused problems for the economy and the British exchange rate, and there was a decrease in capital flows. However, Broadbent (2017) believes that, shortly after Britain's exit from the EU, the government's goal for an ambitious free trade agreement will open trade with non-EU countries and result in a rebound in the exchange rate. As the 2018 Brexit negotiations have shown, undoing 43 years of treaties is proving to be a complex and difficult task.

REAL INCOME
the income of an individual or country after adjusting for inflation.

QUESTIONS

SPOTLIGHT QUESTIONS

1. What is the current position of the Brexit deal?
2. How did the vote on leaving the EU affect the British pound and household's real income:
   a. at the time of the Brexit referendum in 2016?
   b. at the current time?
3. What was the effect on businesses that export:
   a. at the time of the Brexit referendum in 2016?
   b. at the current time?

Working capital and cash flow management

Liquidity is essential for the long-term survival of any company. It is the measure of a company's ability to convert an asset into cash to ensure that its debts can be paid on time. Working capital is defined as the difference between current assets and current liabilities; it represents the amount of available current assets after paying the company's debts. Current assets are the things that a company owns that can be converted to cash within 12 months such as cash, debtors or receivables, and inventories. Current liabilities refers to the amount due to be paid within the next 12 months and include creditors or accounts payable, taxes and employee benefits due.

WORKING CAPITAL
the residual amount after deducting current liabilities from current assets.

Cash flow management is required to ensure that companies can maximise their profitability. If a company cannot pay its debts, either in the short or long term, it must source alternative sources of finance to finance the company's day-to-day business as well as its long-term expansion. Debt finance is associated with the expenses of paying interest and debt covenants that are put in place by the lender. In MNEs, there is the added risk of changes in foreign exchange rates, which needs to be managed.

FOREIGN EXCHANGE
all forms of money that are traded internationally.

Foreign exchange and currency risk

Foreign exchange risk refers to the risk that the value of an investment, asset or transaction will change due to variations in currency exchange rates. The risk is created by volatile exchange rates and is useful in discussing aspects of international finance as part of the strategies of MNEs. Lessard and Livingstone wrote a *Harvard Business Review* article (1986) more than 30 years ago, which has become a classic reference for multinational strategic management today; they provide recommendations on how MNEs should deal with economic exposure. In essence, Lessard and Livingstone's

ECONOMIC EXPOSURE
the changes in expected future cashflows and therefore the present value of the company resulting from unexpected changes in exchange rates. Also called operating exposure and strategic exposure.

study notes that fluctuations in foreign exchange rates create the risk of net present value reduction of the firm's future income streams. This potential value reduction is called economic exposure. It is different from the more conventional transaction exposure (reflecting the risk of financial losses resulting from outstanding but unfulfilled contractual commitments, such as sales contracts in a foreign currency to be fulfilled at a later date; here, the relevant income streams are known, and can often be secured fully in the home-country currency through simple hedging instruments) and translation exposure (reflecting the risk of losses resulting from the translation of accounting statements expressed in foreign currencies into the home-country currency at consolidation date).

Economic exposure

In strategy terms, economic exposure refers to the possible negative effects of largely unexpected changes in exchange rates on a firm's competitiveness relative to rivals. A firm's economic exposure is affected by the geographic configuration of its input and output markets: 'The measurement of [economic] exposure requires an understanding of the structure of the markets in which the company and its competitors obtain labour and materials and sell their products, and also of the degree of their flexibility to change markets, product mix, sourcing and technology' (Lessard & Lightstone 1986, p. 111).

Therefore, MNEs need to understand how fluctuating foreign exchange rates directly affect a company's income stream through immediate price changes, as well as gain insights into the longer-term relative impacts of those fluctuations on the income streams of the various firms competing in the industry.

If two firms have the same structure in terms of sourcing production inputs from a foreign country and command a similar position in the market in terms of market share, product differentiation, flexibility to shift production and so on, then any changes in the corresponding exchange rates will impact both firms equally and advantage neither firm relative to the other. If, however, one of these firms or a third competitor sources its inputs from a different country, or is very differently positioned in terms of market share, product differentiation, flexibility to shift production and so on, then fluctuating exchange rates will affect the firms differently. Here, the firm with the strongest market position, most differentiated products and the greatest flexibility to shift production will incur the lowest negative impact on the net present value of its future income stream. It is important to note that even purely domestic firms, without foreign operations or production imports, can incur economic exposure if their market rivals include MNEs that have a competitive position which are positively affected by exchange rates for internationally sourced inputs.

Nominal and real exchange rates

When assessing economic exposure, it is important to distinguish between real versus nominal exchange rates. Nominal rates refer to the direct exchange ratio between currencies – such as how many euros or yen one US dollar will buy – while real exchange rates refer to changes in the nominal exchange rate minus the difference in inflation rates between two countries. So, for example, a nominal rate change of four per cent with an inflation difference of 3 per cent implies a 1 per cent change in the real exchange rate. Here, the country faced with the higher inflation should experience an equivalent drop in the value of its currency, mirroring the fact that a unit of this currency can now only purchase a lower volume of goods and services (Lessard & Lightstone 1986, p. 108).

The distinction between changes in nominal and real exchange rates is significant, as it is changes in real exchange rates that affect the level of economic exposure for firms. If, in the very long run, purchasing power parity holds, then (starting from an equilibrium situation) differences in inflation rates and resulting price levels between countries should be precisely offset by corresponding changes in their nominal exchange rates. In that case, changes in real exchange rates would be negligible or close to zero. However, casual empiricism teaches that differences do persist in the medium term, sometimes spanning several years, and it is these real exchange rate fluctuations that create economic exposure risk for companies: 'In the short run of six months to several years, however, exchange rates are volatile and greatly influence the competitiveness of companies selling to the same market but getting materials and labour from different countries' (Lessard & Lightstone 1986, p. 107). For example, an Australian manufacturer of durable consumer goods that sources, sells and finances its operations entirely domestically, would not be considered exposed to contractual foreign exchange risk in the form of transaction exposure or to translation exposure. However, if its main competitors in the market are Korean, centralised exporters sourcing from Asia, the company is exposed to economic risk through the Australian dollar to Korean won exchange rate. While the Korean firms' price and sell their products in Australian dollars, their underlying competitiveness may be largely dependent on won-based costs. As a result, if the Australian dollar depreciates against the won in real terms, then the Australian manufacturer will enjoy an improved competitive position vis-à-vis its Korean competitors. But if the dollar's real exchange rate increases, the company's position will be weakened through higher relative costs, and its economic exposure will become visible in the form of a negative impact on its income streams.

Only in cases (again starting from an equilibrium situation) whereby the nominal exchange rate changes between the dollar and yen correspond exactly with differences in inflation rates between the Australia and Korea, is purchasing power parity maintained. In this unlikely scenario, the companies do not experience any change in their competitive positions due to exchange rate changes, since the real exchange rate does not change and no negative impact on the income stream occurs during that period.

There are three elements of economic exposure that are important to consider.

1. Economic exposure should be viewed as a parameter that adds uncertainty to the value of a firm's location advantages. It implies that even unfettered, privileged access to location advantages in a desirable geographic area may not lead to long-run competitive advantage if the economic value attributed to these location advantages depends on the evolution of macro-level parameters such as currency exchange rates.
2. The concept of economic exposure also implies that the location advantages benefiting an MNE should be considered, not solely in a positive sense, and on a country-by-country basis, but also as a portfolio of potential risks for future cash flows.
3. MNEs can choose to develop specific FSAs allowing risk mitigation in the foreign currency area by 'immunising' their products to economic exposure, thereby enabling MNEs to bypass the effects of fluctuations in exchange rates.

Companies occupying a market leadership position with highly differentiated products will generally be best positioned to engage in what's referred to as 'exchange rate pass through', which means that they can adjust their pricing if necessary to offset any increased costs arising from economic exposure without incurring a loss in sales volume. For such firms, economic exposure is minimal. In the case of an MNE with a geographically dispersed subsidiary network, each subsidiary may face a unique level of economic exposure depending on the industry and geographic market in which it operates, its sourcing policies and the market power it commands.

Figure 9.2, inspired by the Lessard and Lightstone article, describes the situation faced by each MNE unit in terms of two parameters.

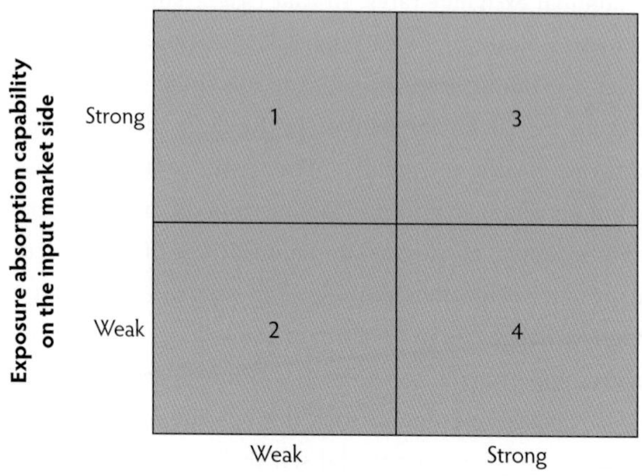

FIGURE 9.2 A classification of operating exposure at the subsidiary level

First, there is each MNE unit's capability relative to rivals to adjust its sourcing structure, and thus its cost position, to a potential new exchange rate reality. This is weak or strong exposure absorption capability on the input market side, measured on the vertical axis. It is important to realise that the value of the unit's exposure absorption capability needs to be assessed relative to competitors; even if the unit's sourcing structure is relatively inflexible, its absorption capability would still be 'strong' if its rivals are faced with the same situation of having to import materials from the same input markets, characterised by real exchange rate increases.

Second, there is each unit's capability to 'pass through' changes in real exchange rates; is the subsidiary in a position to pass any price changes on to its customers, without a loss of volume and thus income? This is weak or strong exchange rate pass-through capability on the output market side, measured on the horizontal axis.

Quadrant 3 describes the most desirable situation, where economic exposure effects are absent. The MNE unit can make the necessary adjustments on the input market side relative to rivals to reduce the effect of real exchange rate changes. At the same time, its market position is sufficiently strong that any cost increases can be translated into price increases for customers without a loss of business.

Quadrant 2 is clearly the least favourable (1 and 4 being intermediate cases), since the MNE unit lacks any exposure reduction capability in its supply chain. MNEs in this quadrant typically sell commodity-type products, the sales of which can be greatly affected by even a small price increase; that is, there is high price elasticity of demand. This is typical for subsidiaries that import products from the parent company home base, such as in retail, and that lack a strong market position in the host country, for instance if the subsidiary is faced with other, larger providers of similar product. If the home country real exchange rate increases and the subsidiary is fully dependent on supplies from the home-country, whereas rivals in the host country source domestically, then economic exposure may substantially affect the subsidiary's profit ability and growth, since any price increase imposed on customers will lead to a substantial drop in sales volume. Hence, the subsidiary will need to engage in a difficult trade-off between reduced profitability and lower sales.

This is illustrated in the aviation industry as airline carriers incur revenues and expenses in a few different currencies, and some of these cash flows require conversion to a different currency, giving rise to foreign exchange risk. In addition, exchange rate changes can also impact airlines through their capital structure, depending on the currencies they have borrowed and hold investments in. Foreign exchange risk affects an airline through three main channels as shown in Figure 9.3.

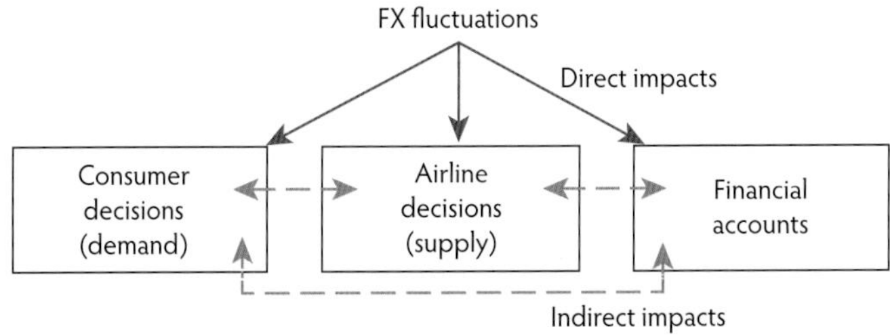

FIGURE 9.3 Impacts of foreign exchange fluctuations on airlines
Source: IATA 2015, © International Air Transport Association 2015, all rights reserved

On international routes, airlines from one country compete directly with airlines from other countries. For example, the Australian Qantas competes with Singapore Airlines, Malaysia Airlines, Cathay Pacific and Etihad Airways. Forsyth and Dwyer (2007) describe Qantas as hiring staff in Australia and overseas, buying its fuel in Singapore and purchasing its aircraft in the US. They note that as 'exchange rates change, the relative prices of these inputs will change. If the [Australian dollar] rises relative to other currencies, the input costs of Qantas will rise relative to other airlines' costs' (Forsyth & Dwyer 2010, p. 13). This means that the cost of Australian-purchased inputs will increase for other currencies, and costs will fall for Australian currency, 'but those of its competitors, which purchase (nearly) all their inputs outside Australia, will fall by more. A rise in the exchange rate will unambiguously lessen the competitiveness of the home country airlines' (Forsyth & Dwyer 2007, p. 13).

Strategy implications

So, what are the implications for MNE strategy, apart from the rather simple observation that differentiated products are more likely to allow exchange rate pass through, and thus immunisation against economic exposure? Lessard and Lightstone advise that for the long-term, 'managers should consider [economic] exposure when setting strategy and worldwide product planning' (1986, p. 107). Companies that hedge their transaction exposure but fail to take economic exposure into account may be raising their total exposure (Lessard & Lightstone 1986, p. 108).

From their research, Lessard and Lightstone suggest that companies typically manage economic exposure through one of three approaches. These tend to be more strategic in nature than the more administratively oriented, currency hedging instruments available for managing contractual exposure. Their recommended approaches are outlined below.

1. Each business unit is assessed individually, and each unit therefore configures its own operations in such a way as to reduce its specific economic exposure. This strategy entails a trade-off between increased production costs and lowered risks (for example, a higher number of operating plants can be established in various countries or regions at the expense of gaining economies of scale).
2. The company takes a company-wide perspective, whereby a portfolio of businesses and operational structures is selected with offsetting exposures, which balance each other (like investment management principles underlying the creation of diversified mutual funds).

The result of such diversification is a lower total rate of exposure across the company, even though individual units may continue to have higher levels of risk on their own.

3. The company incorporates flexibility in its operational planning and exploits fluctuating exchange rates by switching production between factories. Here again, a trade-off is necessary between the increased costs of carrying excess capacity (to allow production transfers) on the one hand, and reduced economic exposure risks on the other.

At the time Lessard and Lightstone's article (1986) was written, floating exchange rates were becoming more volatile than they had been in previous decades when many currencies in developing countries were pegged to benchmarks such as the US dollar. There was currency instability in Latin America and Asia, and several countries – including Mexico, Argentina and Thailand – experienced acute financial crises and sudden devaluations of their currencies.

The demise of the Soviet empire in the early 1990s also brought new volatility to the currencies of Eastern Europe and Central Asia, which had previously been pegged to the Russian rouble under a centrally planned communist system. Lessard and Lightstone also observed that countries were increasingly following divergent monetary policies in managing their own domestic economies. One significant exception to this trend emerged in the decade following the publication of their article, when several member states of the EU decided to link their currencies and national monetary policies more closely together through the European Monetary Union and the introduction of the euro, though this currency itself has been under fire from 2011, thereby increasing the volatility of European financial markets.

There has also been a move away from American hegemony, and the rise of triad power: 'The US no longer has a 70 per cent or 80 per cent world market share in key industries but shares markets more equally with Europe and Japan' (Lessard & Lightstone 1986, p. 107) This statement is still valid now. In the present, triad-based regional system with large MNEs from Asia, Europe and North America competing internationally in the same industries, fluctuations in the currencies of both traditional powerhouse economies and newly emerging low-cost production regions, continue to impact the operating profits and exposure risks of MNEs around the globe.

A complementary perspective on the issue of international financial management and global cash management is in the following example. BMW was founded in Germany in 1916 but, by 2016, motor vehicles were produced in 31 facilities in 14 countries, including China, Brazil, South Korea and Mexico. China has become a key market for BMW, with sales growth of 11.3 per cent in 2016 (IATA 2015). BMW noted that despite rising sales revenue, profits were often eroded by the negative effect of foreign exchange rates. When Porsche had passed on exchange rate costs to customers, their sales plunged due to price increases and BMW did not want to follow this path.

BMW approached this issue in two ways. First, they engaged in a natural hedge strategy by establishing production and assembly facilities in the countries where their products are sold. Second, they engaged in a strategy of making purchases in the currency denomination of their main markets. This strategy resulted in increased employment in the countries where the facilities were established (paid in the local currency), and the shortening of the supply chain between Germany and the country of sale. This is evidenced by a JV entered between BMW and Brilliance Auto Group in Shenyang, China, where about half of the BMWs sold in China are now produced. The purchasing department for the facility was set up locally to source competitive supply contracts in China. By having a local facility, customer service was improved and the supply-chain risk was diversified. The Chinese regional treasury reviews its exchange rate exposure on a weekly basis and reports these to the group treasurer to consolidate as global exchange rate risk figures. Foreign exchange risk can thereby be mitigated (Bin & Ying 2012).

MNEs can develop FSAs in functional areas such as international financial management, and these FSAs can have important implications for MNE strategy beyond the functional area itself. In the case of BMW, the new FSA of improved coordination with suppliers led to a higher level strategic collaboration with those suppliers.

Management insights

Lessard and Lightstone's analysis is more than the study of one specific, functional area in international business. Rather, the research sheds additional light on the nature of location advantages; any configuration of location advantages, whether in input or output markets, carries risks, in this case the risk of unexpected exchange rate fluctuations affecting future cash flows. In response, MNEs should aim to develop, as an FSA, a central routine that integrates economic-exposure information into the capital budgeting evaluation of large investment projects. This is especially relevant in the context of large-scale foreign expansion. The development of this type of FSA reflects the MNE's ability to transfer the advantage internationally without adaptation (see Figure 9.4). However, especially for large subsidiaries, it may be useful to combine this internationally transferable knowledge with local capabilities in the affiliates; in other words, the internationally transferable FSA is developed at home, but to exploit its profitably in host countries, location-bound knowledge from the host country is added to make it more effective. Obviously, especially in the absence of a central economic-exposure policy, one would also expect location-bound FSAs developed in each host country the MNE operates, whereby individual affiliates learn how to protect themselves against the hazards of economic exposure.

Limitations with Lessard and Lightstone's approach to economic exposure

There are some limitations with Lessard and Lightstone's classic research study in the *Harvard Business Review*.

First, in relation to FSAs that are developed in the host country, Lessard and Lightstone suggest that operations managers who are not responsible for setting economic-exposure policy should not be held accountable for performance differentials resulting from such exposure. The problem is that many large MNE subsidiaries, operating without strict firm-wide economic-exposure policies or guidelines, have substantial autonomy in their supply-chain management processes and targeting of markets – in other words, actions that create economic exposure. Why should the managers of such subsidiaries be exempted from the risks resulting from economic exposure? How is this different from any other type of external risk facing the entrepreneurial MNE subsidiary, such as unexpected new restrictions on business imposed by government agencies, or technological changes making existing product lines obsolete? The reality is that subsidiary managers who can influence the supply-chain management of their own operations, as well as the geographic markets where they will operate, should be held responsible for the economic exposure they have created. The key managerial challenge is not to exempt individuals who have somehow been forced to accept the economic-exposure policies of the MNE corporate headquarters from being accountable for the consequences thereof. On the contrary, the much more common challenge, arising in the absence of a strictly imposed firm-level economic-exposure policy, is to make subsidiary managers responsible

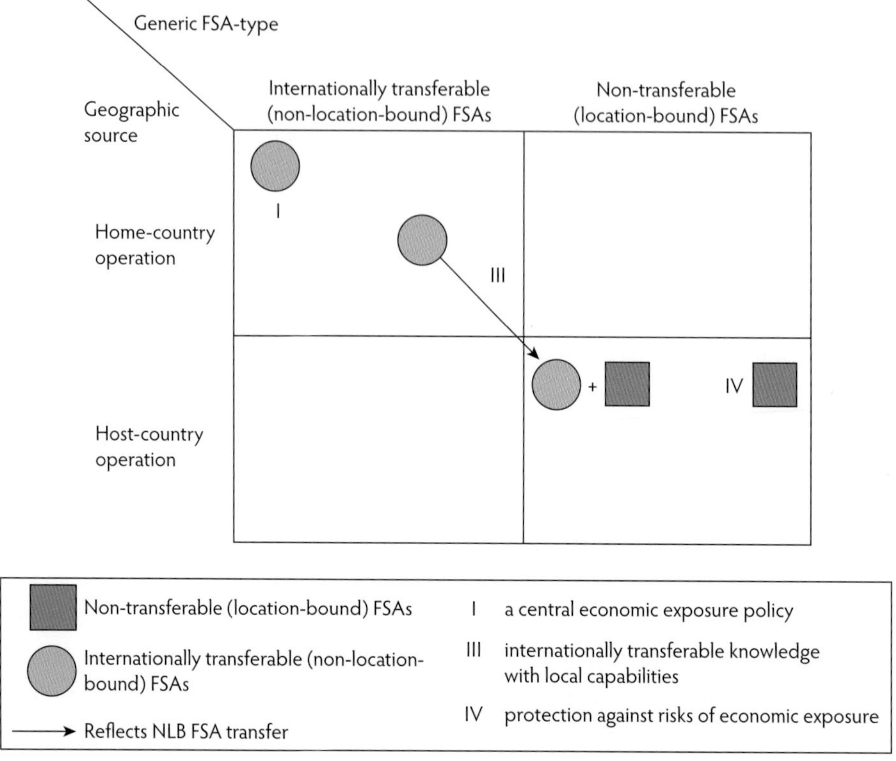

FIGURE 9.4 Patterns of FSA development from managing operating exposure in MNEs

for the economic exposure they create themselves through their own decision making at the affiliate level. This averts a bounded-reliability problem, whereby these subsidiary managers could argue that poor results are the outcome of unfortunate external circumstances.

A second limitation of Lessard and Lightstone's research is that the way to address economic exposure and how to link it with strategy will depend critically on the MNE's administrative heritage. Here, the nature of the MNE's FSAs, its internal organisation, and its historical trajectory of location decisions will largely determine the content and process of international financial management decisions.

Economic exposure and the centralised exporter

In the case of a *centralised exporter* (for example, a Japanese firm exporting to the US), shown in Figure 9.5, the main economic exposure at the firm level results from all of production occurring in the home country. Two questions then arise. The first (on the input market side): is the firm's supply chain, often managed primarily through contracting with external parties, sufficiently flexible that the firm can change suppliers rapidly and effectively in case of high economic exposure? This is usually not the case if the main part of the cost structure is incurred at home, in the home-country currency. The second and usually more important question (on the output market side): are the exchange rate pass-through problems (caused by a high price elasticity of demand) sufficiently threatening to support moving production into a host country, thereby creating a more decentralised production system?

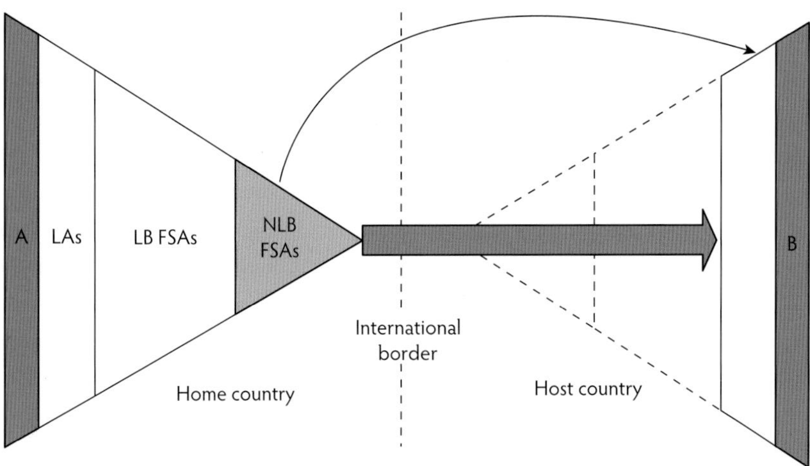

The thin, curved arrow out of the home-country triangle, pointing to the host country's LAs, means that the firm's NLB FSAs allow for a strong exchange rate pass-through capability in the output market: unfavourable changes in exchange rates, leading to price increases in the host country's currency, are simply passed on to host-country customers without loss in exported sales volume. The areas A and B reflect macro-level location characteristics affecting the real exchange rate between the currencies of countries A and B.

FIGURE 9.5 Centralised exporter: operating exposure from changes in the real exchange rate between the currencies of countries A and B

Note: LAs = local advantages; LB FSAs = non-transferable (or location-bound) FSAs; NLB FSAs = internationally transferable (or non-location bound) FSAs

For example, consider that in 2013–14 foreign activity on nine feature films made wholly or partially in Australia accounted for AUD$197 million, which equates to 24 per cent of Australian TV production. The upsurge was partly driven by the spend on several high-profile feature films, including Angelina Jolie's *Unbroken* and Dwayne Johnson's *San Andreas*, but largely the foreign activity was because of a downturn in the Australian dollar. In 2011, when the Australian dollar was on par with the US dollar, foreign film production was AUD$1 million – a fraction of later figures. There has also been a growth in foreign investment in film with over 50 per cent of funding being from overseas (Quinn 2014).

In 2017, the Australian dollar strengthened, which made it seem overvalued at around AUD$0.80 to US$1 and Australian exports, such as film production, looked expensive in the eyes of foreign investors (Stanford 2017). The more the Australian dollar rises, the less competitive film production becomes, not because of quality or efficiency but because the exchange rate is making it too expensive to produce in Australia.

An alternative effect of exchanges rates on the movie business relates to the European distribution of Hollywood films. Since the international movie business is almost exclusively priced in US dollars, the rise in the value of the US dollar can make US movies too expensive for European distributors. As a result, US producers have sometimes found it hard to pre-sell the foreign rights of films. In response to this issue, US producers and European distributors have looked for ways to deal with exchange rate fluctuations. European distributors have sought creative financing, such as stretching out payments or setting a floor price with additional payments for future currency appreciation; US producers have talked about lowering prices or switching to contracts in euros for their foreign rights (Goldsmith 2000).

Economic exposure and the multi-centred MNE

In the case of a *multi-centred MNE*, shown in Figure 9.6, the economic exposure challenge is really the opposite of the one characterising the *centralised exporter*: here, the firm's overall economic exposure results from the individual exposures of all the foreign affiliates. In a conventional firm of this type, there is no powerful, centralised treasury function because all host-country subsidiaries have substantial autonomy. Here, economic-exposure challenges will usually be addressed at the subsidiary level, and solutions are more likely to involve changing international suppliers on the input market side, rather than making changes on the output market side. A change in this decentralised approach is likely to occur only as one ingredient of a much larger move towards more balance between the centre and the subsidiaries. Here, location-bound FSAs become increasingly complemented by an infusion of non-location-bound capabilities where useful; a centralised exposure management tool may be part of such a move.

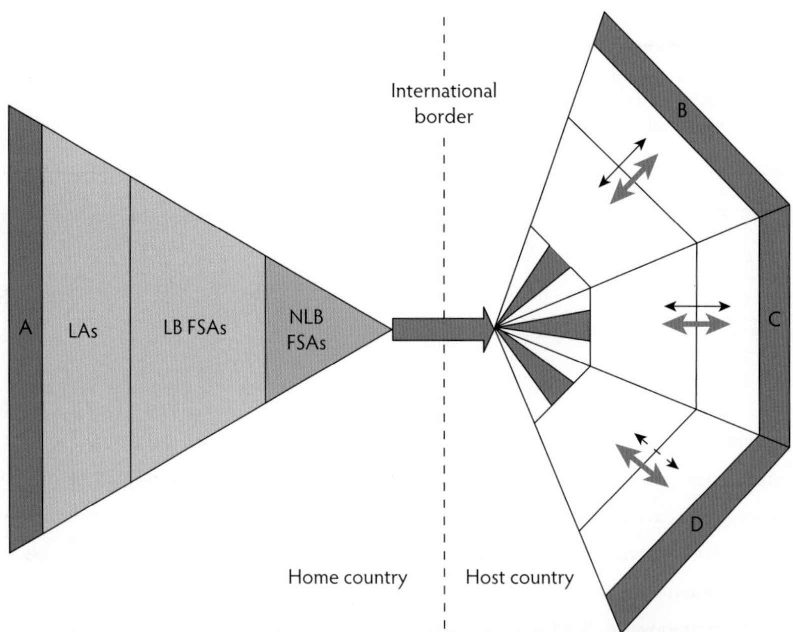

Each subsidiary commands its own exchange rate pass-through capability (weak or strong) when serving its host-country market, as shown by the three thin, double-headed arrows. The dotted arrow for country D suggests a weak exchange rate pass-through capability in that country. A and B, A and C, and A and D reflect macro-level location characteristics affecting the real exchange rates between the currencies of countries A and B, A and C, and A and D, respectively.

FIGURE 9.6 Multi-centred MNE: overall exposure from the individual exposures of all foreign affiliates
Note: LAs = local advantages; LB FSAs = non-transferable (or location-bound) FSAs; NLB FSAs = internationally transferable (or non-location bound) FSAs

Lafarge is a typical multi-centred MNE. It is one of the world's largest manufacturers of building materials, and manages exposure using its central treasury department and its subsidiaries. Due to the local nature of its business, in most cases operating costs and revenues are in the same currency. When purchase and sale transactions are performed in currencies other than this prevailing functional currency (usually the domestic currency) at the subsidiary level, the subsidiary managers themselves address the economic exposure. Lafarge also expects each subsidiary to borrow and invest excess cash in its functional currency. At the same time, the corporate treasury department attempts to reduce the overall exposure by netting purchases and sales in each currency on a global basis when possible (Lafarge 2004).

Economic exposure and the international projector

The growth of *international projectors* (shown in Figure 9.7) can produce substantial new economic-exposure problems. This occurs when new subsidiaries replicate not only home-country production patterns, but also home-country supply-chain strategies (with contracts in foreign currencies from the perspective of the host country-subsidiary). This may create economic-exposure challenges if the subsidiaries' exchange rate pass-through capabilities are much weaker than those in the home country, especially if the subsidiaries' market position is much weaker than in the home country. The upshot is that it may be much easier to introduce a centralised economic-exposure management system in these companies than in multi-centred MNEs.

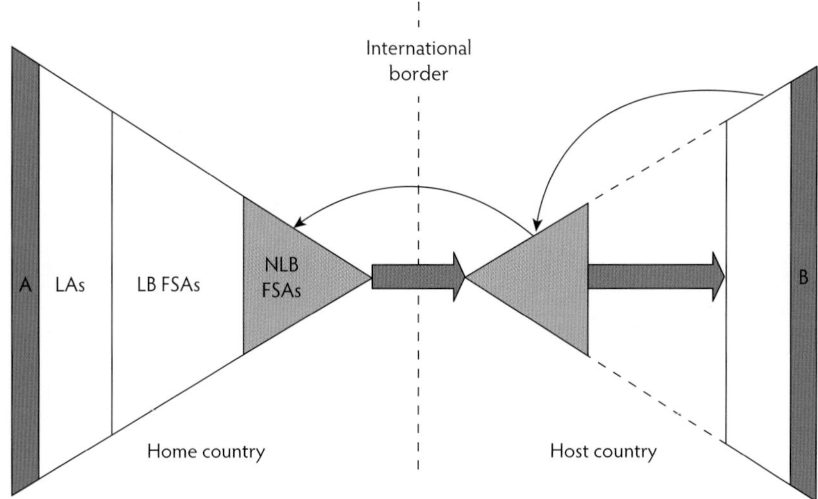

The firm operates a centralised exposure management system, meant to reduce overall operating exposure risks faced by the firm, but the unique currency exposure position of each subsidiary co-determines the functioning of this central system (shown by the thin, curved double-headed arrow connecting home and host country). The exchange rate pass-through capability of each subsidiary depends on the specific inputs it is mandated to access in the host country and/or on the specific outputs it must sell in the host country (shown by the second double-headed arrow). A and B reflect macro-level location characteristics affecting the real exchange rate between the currencies of countries A and B.

FIGURE 9.7 International projector: centralised exposure management

Note: LAs = local advantages; LB FSAs = non-transferable (or location-bound) FSAs; NLB FSAs = internationally transferable (or non-location bound) FSAs

Before 1994, Goodyear mostly imported supplies for its Mexican plant and then sold the plant's output to local Mexican customers. However, in December 1994, the crash of the peso dramatically decreased the domestic demand for Goodyear tyres by more than 20 per cent, or 3500 units a day. Goodyear managers had only two options: to downsize or to look for new export markets. The headquarters and the Mexican subsidiary managers worked together to export the Mexican production, mostly to the US but also to Europe and South America (Moffett, Stonehill & Eiteman 2008, p. 244).

Economic exposure and the international coordinator

Finally, for *international coordinators*, shown in Figure 9.8, managing economic exposure is usually completely integrated into their overall strategy. This MNE type's main strength is precisely the coordination of internationally dispersed operations, with substantial product and knowledge flows that may be traded internally and externally in a variety of currencies, and may be exposed to a broad spectrum of external risks. In the case of commodities, as in many resource-based industries, the main protection against economic exposure is to add value that makes the products more differentiated (a common strategy in the petrochemical and chemical industries), to improve the firm's exchange rate pass-through capabilities. Of course, if no such value is added and the products remain commodities (in the extreme case with a single, world market price), then there is no issue of exposure pass-through capability. The firm must accept the world price, and its only defence against economic exposure (assuming its cost structure is not incurred in the same currency as the world price) is the use of financial instruments such as currency swap agreements.

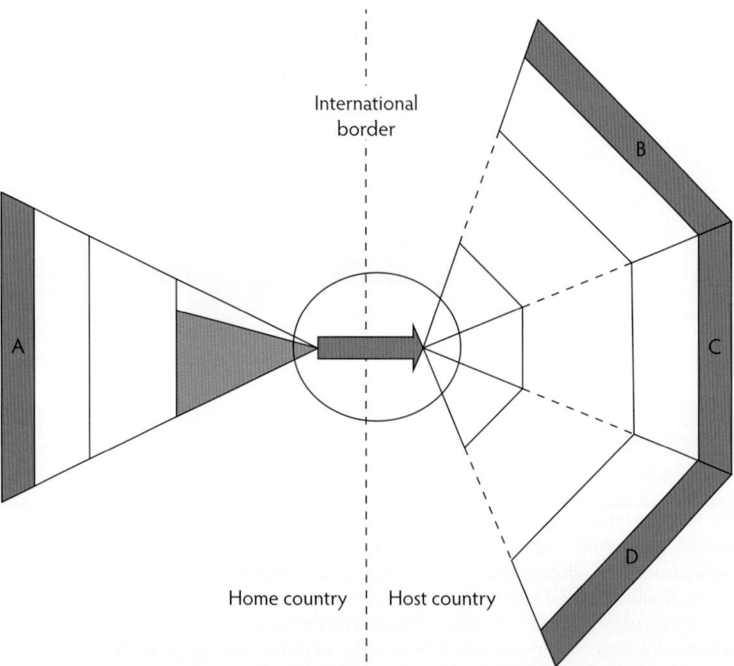

The firm's centralised exposure management system acts as an FSA to optimise results for the network as a whole (shown by the circle). Impacts of this central system on individual subsidiaries are considered secondary. A, B, C and D reflect macro-level characteristics affecting real exchange rates, and can influence the complex network linkages that exist among subsidiaries in countries A, B, C and D.

FIGURE 9.8 International coordinator: network optimisation

This is illustrated through Statoil, a Norwegian company and one of the largest oil firms in the world, does business in all the vertical industries associated with petroleum and petrochemical products, such as exploration, production, processing, transport, sales and trading of crude oil, natural gas and refined products.

Statoil's petroleum and petroleum products are priced on world markets primarily in US dollars. However, costs and cash disbursements are to a large extent denominated in Norwegian kroner. Thus, fluctuations in exchange rates could have significant effects on the operating results of Statoil. To manage its exchange risk, Statoil utilises different types of foreign exchange contracts such as hedges, forward foreign exchange contracts and non-functional currency swaps. At the same time, Statoil also enters into commodity-based derivative contracts (for example, futures, over-the-counter forward contracts and market swaps) (Statoil 2005).

A third limitation of Lessard and Lightstone's research is that Lessard and Lightstone detail the benefits of a flexible sourcing structure without also addressing its costs. They are correct that a flexible sourcing structure (the capability to quickly shift production from one country to another) yields a strong exposure-absorption capability on the input market side, with all the benefits they discuss.

However, exposure-absorption capability is not the only legitimate goal of international business strategy. As we shall see in Chapter 11, Ferdows would strenuously object to Lessard and Lightstone's view, pointing out that at least some factories should be considered long-term investments. A factory that is no longer the low-cost producer due to exchange-rate fluctuations can still make contributions in other ways. For example, it can be the company specialist in a knowledge area, develop best practices in a product area, innovate or develop new FSAs. Realising these benefits typically requires long-term commitment. Thus, there is a trade-off between the benefits of a flexible sourcing structure and the benefits of long-term commitment. This trade-off must be assessed for each plant in the MNE network.

The foreign exchange market

The foreign exchange (FX) market provides the market place that enables the exchange of one currency for another and determines the exchange rate. This may be for immediate exchange (spot rates) or future exchange (forward rates). This was once a physical exchange of money, however, the sheer volume of foreign currency trading in today's market, in terms of the number of trades and the value of the transactions, has resulted in the development of an efficient computerised system of trade instead. According to the Bank for International Settlements, volumes in 1995 averaged US$1.2 trillion daily, and by 2016 the average daily volume was approximately $5.1 trillion (BIS 2018). The foreign exchange market has undergone significant growth in the last 20 years. The market is currently experiencing a period of change, resulting from increased bank regulation, the slowdown in world growth and trade, and the decline in growth in emerging and developing markets.

FOREIGN EXCHANGE (FX) MARKET the international marketplace enabling the conversion of one currency into another, foreign trade financing, trading in foreign currency options and contracts, currency swaps and other foreign currency related transactions.

Managing exposure to currency risk

When foreign exchange rates change, companies are vulnerable to accounting and economic exposures. From an accounting perspective, exposure to movements in exchange rates occurs because transactions and financial reports are denominated in foreign currency, and must be translated to the functional currency. Economic or operating exposure, as discussed earlier, is the change in the value of the firm because of the effect on cash flows of movements in foreign exchange rates.

Accounting exposure incorporates transaction and translation exposure. Transaction exposure measures changes in cash flows resulting from existing contractual obligations due to be settled after the exchange rate change. Translation exposure comes from the translation of financial statements of a foreign subsidiary denominated in a foreign currency into the functional currency of the parent company as part of accounting consolidation. Consolidated financial statements present the financial performance and financial position for the parent company and the companies it controls (subsidiaries and associates) as a single economic entity.

The three types of currency exposure (transaction, translation and economic) result in positive and negative effects for an MNE. International money managers focus on the negative effects because they produce undesirable outcomes. The creation of the EU, with its single currency, the euro, eliminates the currency risk for countries trading within that zone; it will be interesting to follow the foreign currency risk implications for the UK now that it has left the EU, and the potential risks for other countries that are scheduled to leave in 2019.

Currency exposure and risks

Currency risk arises because consumers globally prefer to conduct business and engage in transactions in their own currency. Therefore, foreign buyers must monitor and manage the currency exchange, and minimise their exposure to foreign exchange risk. Currency risk is the change in cash flows expected from transactions because of unexpected changes in foreign exchange rates. Dealers in foreign currency markets quote prices for which they will buy and sell currency in terms of spot rates and forward rates. A spot rate refers to the rate of exchange for a current transaction with immediate delivery. For example, this applies to over-the-counter transactions at a bank or money exchange bureau. A forward rate is an exchange rate quoted today for settlement of a transaction at some time in the future. A forward contract has a specific maturity date and is based on a rate of exchange at which two currencies will be purchased and sold.

SPOT RATE
the exchange rate for the almost immediate purchase or sale of foreign exchange.

Hedging

HEDGING
a financial instrument used to reduce exposure to currency risk.

Hedging is the most common method used to manage exposure to risks, such as changes in exchange rates, interest rates and commodity prices. Hedging involves setting the value ('the taking of a position') by acquiring an asset, a cash flow or a financial contract that will rise or fall in value and will offset the fall or rise in the value of the existing exposure. In this way, hedging protects the owner by limiting losses through the reduction or elimination of exposure to the risk; it establishes a balanced or near-balanced position where assets exposed to risk equal exposed liabilities. It should be noted that hedging does limit the gains that could be made from an increase in the value of the asset hedged. The most common hedging instruments are forward contracts, futures contracts, currency options and currency swaps. Natural hedging describes the arrangement of currency inflows and outflows to occur at about the same time and in the same amounts, thereby offsetting foreign currency cash flows. This requires significant financial management expertise to achieve.

MULTIPLE-CHOICE QUESTION

SPOTLIGHT 9.2

Managing exchange rate risk

When dealing in multinational markets, investors face constant foreign exchange movements caused by interest rate differentials and changes in economic growth (Radatz & Sirak 2014). When looking at the correlation in values of currencies and the US dollar, Radatz and Sirak (2014) found that the British pound had a correlation of 0.42, the Australian dollar was 0.01 and the Japanese yen was 0.58.

An example of the effect of this can be seen in Flight Centre 2017 Annual Report, which advised profits in its UK operations were up 9 per cent, but in Australian dollars they were down by 10 per cent. The impact of Britain's exit from the EU is described in Spotlight 9.1. However, the effects of exchange rate fluctuations can be very serious on MNE profits (Flight Centre 2017).

To help mitigate this risk, MNEs use different types of derivatives, including swaps, futures, forwards and options. MNEs can also use a natural hedge by matching foreign currency receipts with payments in that currency. Using derivatives is not always advisable and can be viewed with scepticism; Buffet, for example, has advised to 'view them as time bombs, both for the parties that deal in them and the economic system' (Buffet 2002). Others believe that these instruments have their place and although the Australian dollars suffers from wild fluctuations, the economy has stayed resilient partly due to their use (Becker & Fabbro 2006).

QUESTIONS

SPOTLIGHT QUESTIONS

1. What are the names of the derivatives that are used to hedge foreign exchange movements?
2. What is a natural hedge?

International accounting and taxation issues

Business today is complex and more integrated because there are an increasing number of global transactions taking place. These transactions include foreign investments and trade relations with many different countries. The complexities of running a global business are mirrored in changing accounting and financial requirements, and new financial reporting regulations that have been introduced. International accounting refers to the accounting for international transactions by different countries, and encompasses management accounting, auditing, taxation and financial reporting.

Management accounting focuses on the provision of information for users (managers) within an organisation and is largely unregulated. Financial reporting, as well as auditing and taxation, are subject to extensive regulations and scrutinised by external stakeholders (investors, creditors, shareholders and government bodies). The discussion will focus on international accounting issues in financial reporting.

International financial reporting practices

For accounting periods beginning on or after 1 January 2005, Australia adopted the accounting standards issued by the International Accounting Standards Board (IASB). This was a major change in the Australian accounting standards regime, and resulting in the removal of differences between Australian Accounting Standards (AAS) and International Financial Reporting Standards (IFRS). The benefits of harmonisation were promoted by the Financial Reporting Council (FRC) as an increased ability for investors of companies to access funds from international sources, which would enable investors to compare the results of Australian companies with foreign companies. The main benefit has been that the financial reports for global companies have been prepared using IFRS, rather than prepared based on the standards applicable in each country's jurisdiction. Although differences remain between practices and principals adopted in some countries, convergence to IFRS has progressed. The main variances remain in the convergence of IASB with the US' Financial Accounting Standards Boards (FASB).

INTERNATIONAL FINANCIAL REPORTING STANDARDS (IFRS) a set of accounting standards developed to ensure that transparent and comparable financial reporting is adopted across countries.

The IASB Conceptual Framework, paragraph OB2, states the objective of general-purpose financial reporting as:

> to provide financial information about the reporting entity that is useful to present and potential equity investors, lenders and other creditors in making decisions about providing resources to the entity. Those decisions involve buying, selling or holding equity and debt instruments, and providing or settling loans and other forms of credit (IASPlus 2018a).

International accounting relates to the accounting processes required by global businesses to account for and report on transactions, such as foreign currency transactions, foreign investments, and the consolidation of parent and foreign subsidiaries. As accounting practices and principals may differ among countries, these processes should be understood when comparing company financial reports, and the standards' impact should be considered by MNEs that are investing in foreign countries by FDI, expanding their operations or comparing performance. The diversity of practices may be due to variations in accounting regulations or due to environmental, cultural and religious factors.

In terms of accounting practice, there are several differences in accounting for property plant and equipment in Australia (IAS 16) and the US (US GAAP). For example, US GAAP does not allow revaluation of assets, whereas IAS 16 permits revaluation as an accounting policy election for an entire class of asset and it requires revaluation to fair value on a regular basis. Additionally, US GAAP does not include exchange rate differences in eligible borrowing costs and it does not allow for the offset of interest costs in the period, whereas IAS16 includes exchange rate differences in eligible borrowing costs, and allows the offset of borrowing costs and investment income earned (IASPlus 2018b). From 2007, SEC no longer requires companies listed on the New York Stock Exchange (NYSE) that prepare accounts in accordance with IFRS to reconcile those accounts to US GAAP, which has resulted in a decrease in preparation costs for financial statements (Ernst & Young 2011).

International accounting practice is also influenced by the environment in which the company operates, including economic, political, legal and social factors. The taxation system has a major influence on accounting practice where financial reports are used to calculate tax liability, like in France and Japan. Other countries have different expenses allowed for deduction for tax, such as in Australia where depreciation rates may differ for accounting and taxation purposes. In Indonesia, certain types of income are subject to a final income tax that is different for different income types as a specified rate of the gross amount of income, without regard to attributable expenses; for example, the rent from land and buildings is calculated at 10 per cent, whereas income from lottery prizes is calculated at 25 per cent. The company stakeholders will also influence the financial reporting system. Where financing comes from equity or share issues through the stock exchange, shareholders will demand certain levels of information disclosure when compared with debt finance from banks and lending institutions. Additionally, the political system influences the ownership of companies so that in some countries state ownership or family-controlled businesses are the norm.

With the growth in global business, there is an increasing awareness of the impact of culture on business relationships and on accounting practices. Societal values have been found to explain and predict international differences in accounting systems (Gray 1988). The values of conservatism and secrecy were found to be the most influential. It is perhaps not surprising that in cultures where uncertainty exists have a cautious approach and are more conservative in their measurement of financial statement amounts. Secrecy relates to the disclosure of information; therefore, where countries prefer a closed and secretive approach, the disclosure of financial and accounting information will be less. Religion forms part of societal values and can play an influential part in accounting practices. For example, Islamic law sets business ethics, and economic and financial principles, through regulations that prohibit the charging of interest and the lending of money at an unreasonably high cost. Despite this, the Malaysian Accounting Standards Board has begun the process of bringing Malaysia, a largely Islamic country, to full convergence with IFRS, to take advantage of the increased globalisation of the capital markets.

Foreign currency translation for reporting purposes

Foreign currency translation is required for accounting and subsequent reporting in two areas: individual business transactions conducted in a foreign currency and financial reporting for MNEs with foreign subsidiaries.

FOREIGN CURRENCY TRANSLATION the translation of transactions and reports denominated in foreign currencies into the company's functional currency.

First, international trade is often conducted in a currency other than that of the home currency, giving rise to the need to convert the foreign currency transactions into the home currency. This is also the case where debts, receivables and other monetary items are denominated in currencies other than the home currency. This is necessary to prepare meaningful financial statements in one single currency for the company accounting for the transactions. If amounts were reported in the foreign currency of the transaction, the financial statements would add different currencies together, such as the US dollar, the Hong Kong dollar, the Vietnamese dong and the Chinese renminbi, which would create a meaningless total.

Second, where a multinational parent company has foreign subsidiaries, accounting standards require these to be incorporated into the accounts of the parent to form group consolidated accounts. In most cases, the financial statements of the foreign subsidiary will be prepared in the currency of that country. To enable the accounts of the foreign subsidiary to be included in the consolidated accounts, they must be translated to the currency used by the parent company for its reporting.

For financial reporting purposes, the issues relating to translation of the financial statements of a foreign subsidiary from its local currency to a functional currency and then to a specific presentation currency are addressed in IAS 21, *The effects of changes in foreign exchange rates*. There are, therefore, two different translation processes to be considered. Local currency is as it sounds, the currency of the country where the foreign subsidiary is based, whereas the presentation currency is defined in IAS21, paragraph 8, as 'the currency in which the financial statements are presented'. The objective of the translation process is to 'provide information that is generally compatible with the expected economic effects of an exchange rate change on an entity's cash flows and equity' (IAS 21/AASB 121) and to reflect the financial results and relationships in the consolidated financial statements. As the parent entity has invested in a foreign subsidiary, they are exposed to the effect of changing exchange rates on the value of those assets and this must be reflected in the translation process.

An example of how the translation process occurs will assist in understanding the application of IAS 21. Parent Ltd is an Australian company with a subsidiary, FS Ltd, which is based in Hong Kong. FS Ltd is a food-and-beverage processing business that sources products from the ASEAN region, particularly Vietnam. FC Ltd would most likely prepare its accounts using Hong Kong dollars (the local currency), while the functional currency could reflect the operations in Vietnam (the Vietnamese dong). As the parent company is in Australia, the consolidated financial statements would be presented in the presentation currency, which would be the Australian dollar. Therefore, the accounts of FS Ltd would first be translated from the local currency of Hong Kong dollars to the functional currency of the Vietnamese dong and finally translated to the presentation currency of the Australian dollar.

SPOTLIGHT 9.3

International taxation issues

MNEs, by the nature of their operations, are impacted by accounting, taxation, legal and reporting requirements, and environmental factors of the different countries in which they operate. In addition, MNEs have a potentially large number of transactions using different currencies. Taxation systems vary widely across countries, with many countries offering incentives to attract foreign investors and business operations. Recent public debates have focused on tax avoidance by MNEs, with some countries seeking to ensure that MNEs pay their fair share of tax, based on the profits that MNEs earn, in their jurisdictions.

International taxation

MNEs or international investors must work within the tax jurisdiction established by the country in which they invest or do business. There are two types of tax jurisdictions: the worldwide or residential and the territorial or source. In practice, most countries combine the two methods and have an established mechanism to prevent double taxation. The worldwide method taxes national residents of the country based on their worldwide income, irrespective of where the income is earned. Therefore, a parent company with foreign subsidiaries would be taxed in its home country on income earned by both the parent and subsidiaries, irrespective of where the income is earned. The issue of double taxation arises where the subsidiary is also taxed on the income earned in the country in which it was earned. The second method is the territorial method where all income within the country by any taxpayer is taxed at its source. That is, any income earned within that territory, regardless of whether it is earned by a domestic or foreign taxpayer, is taxed by that country.

To avoid the issue of double taxation, two approaches may be considered. First, a country will not tax the foreign source income of its residents on which tax has already been paid. Second, is the establishment of a system where a non-refundable tax credit is given for income taxes paid to a foreign government; this is the same as for taxes paid to foreign tax authorities on foreign source income, and some profits and gains. A limit generally applies to foreign tax credits, which is calculated as the amount of tax due on foreign source income as if it had been calculated using the tax rates in the home country. Countries that have a tax treaty with Australia include China, Indonesia, Korea, Malaysia, Vietnam, the US and the UK (ATO 2016). The tax credit system gives rise to cash flow considerations for companies because the foreign income tax may be paid in an earlier or later year than the home country allows the tax credit to be recognised.

Taxes imposed by governments fall into two categories: direct and indirect taxes. A direct tax (the most common form is corporate income tax) is levied directly on the income derived by a taxpayer. The income may include business profits, capital gains and losses, royalties, interest and dividends. An indirect tax applies to purchase prices, royalty or interest payments in the form of a sales tax, goods and services tax (GST) or value added tax (VAT). Sales tax is levied as a flat percentage on the value of goods and service sold and paid by the ultimate consumer. GST and VAT operate similarly, and are calculated by adding a percentage of tax at each stage in the supply chain of a good or service. Periodically businesses calculate the difference between tax collected and tax paid, and remit this to the tax authority. In Australia, GST and personal or corporate income tax are both used as sources of revenue, as opposed to the EU where VAT is the primary revenue source.

Tax havens

Tax havens are countries where taxation is levied at a low rate in a politically and economically stable environment typically sharing little information with foreign taxation authorities. Tax havens are attractive to MNEs because they offer a place to funnel or invest funds where tax payments are minimised.

TAX HAVEN
a country that has a low corporate tax rate and low withholding tax rates on passive income.

They will continue to exist because tax systems vary greatly around the world and, while substantial differences continue in tax rates around the world, foreign investors and MNEs will seek the most attractive tax arrangements. Tax haven countries include the Channel Islands, Hong Kong, Cayman Islands, Monaco and the Cook Islands.

Cook Islands: a surprising tax haven

The Cook Islands are a protectorate of New Zealand. This spotlight examines how the Cook Islands are now a Pacific haven for tax evaders and why the financial institutions registered on this island are under scrutiny. The IMF (2004) reported that in 2000 the Cook Islands were placed on the Financial Action Task Force (FATF) list of non-cooperative countries for the lack of adequate supervision to prevent money laundering. Wayne (2013) reports that hundreds of wealthy people have been using the Cook Islands to hide their assets, including business partners, soon to be separated couples, professional people who could be sued as well as a lawbreaker who ran a US$7 billion Ponzi scheme. The Cook Islands have also been named in a US congressional research service paper as a tax haven. The Cook Islands has its own currency which can be used on the island, although New Zealand dollars can also be used, which the island currency is pegged to. An increase in currency issuance and rising government deficits caused the currency to have a crisis of confidence in 1994, and the Cook Islands lost its ability to have an independent monetary policy in 1995 (Burdekin 2008). Due to the work done by the FATF, an OECD (2015) report advised that the Cook Islands were largely compliant in the second phase of its 'Implantation of the standards in practice in the global forum on transparency and exchange of information for tax purposes'.

SPOTLIGHT QUESTIONS

QUESTIONS

1. What is a reason for a sharp currency decrease?
2. Name an international institution which polices money laundering activities.

Transfer pricing

TRANSFER PRICING the practice of pricing products sold, transferred and exchanged between subsidiaries and associates of the same company.

MULTIPLE-CHOICE QUESTION

A transfer price is the price for which a business transfers its goods and services to another business or subsidiary within the company group. Although each business is run as a separate entity, and must account for inputs and outputs, they are essentially all part of one group of companies. Therefore, the transfer price impacts the profit of each party to the transaction. For example, if a product is sold at a high transfer price from Division A to Division C, Division A will record a high sales price and profit while Division C will record high expenses and a lower profit. For an MNE, transfer pricing potentially allows the company to move profits from high-tax jurisdictions to low-tax jurisdictions and so is of great interest to taxation authorities. Regulations consequently exist to ensure the fairness and accuracy of transfer pricing, and to ensure that companies establish pricing structures based on the option of an arm's length transaction. That is, transfer prices reflect the price in the market place as if the company was purchasing from or selling to a non-associated company. Transfer pricing is closely scrutinised by regulatory authorities and has strict documentation requirements.

Summary

Learning objective 1: Explain how international financial managers establish their firms' capital structure.

The capital structure of a firm refers to the proportion of debt and equity used to finance the firm. As debt financing grows, a firm is perceived as being a riskier investment and its cost of finance will also increase. This affects the firm's profitability and cash flows, and hence its ability to raise capital for its expansion.

Learning objective 2: Understand how firms manage their working capital and cash flow.

Working capital refers to a firm's ability to pay their debts in the short term. Liquidity is required to ensure that the business can continue to operate on a day-to-day basis without raising additional short-term debt finance. Short-term debt finance is generally expensive and will affect the profitability and cash flows of the firm.

Learning objective 3: Outline the nature of foreign exchange markets and the exchange risks faced by MNEs.

The foreign exchange market provides the market place that enables the exchange of one currency for another and determines the exchange rate. When foreign exchange rates change, companies are vulnerable to exposure from an accounting perspective (translation and transaction exposure) and from an economic perspective (economic or operational exposure). Managers should be aware of these risks, and ensure that potential detrimental effects on profits and cash flows of the firm are minimised.

Learning objective 4: Understand how MNEs manage currency risk exposures.

Currency risk arises because all consumers prefer to conduct business and engage in transactions in their own currency. Foreign buyers therefore must monitor and manage the currency exchange, and minimise their exposure to foreign exchange risk. Hedging is the most common method used to manage exposure to risks such as changes in exchange rates, interest rates and commodity prices

Learning objective 5: Understand complex international accounting and taxation issues.

The complexities of running a global business are reflected in the changing taxation, accounting and financial requirements being introduced globally. International accounting refers to the accounting for international transactions by different countries, and encompasses management accounting, auditing, taxation and financial reporting. Many MNEs now produce financial reports prepared using IFRS, rather than preparing accounts based on the standards applicable only in each country's jurisdiction. This allows for ease of reporting, understandability and comparability of financial information. Taxation systems vary widely, with many countries offering incentives to attract foreign investors and business operations. Recent debate has focused on MNEs that avoid paying tax; some countries want MNEs to pay tax on the profits they earn in their jurisdictions.

REVISION QUESTIONS

Revision questions

1. What is the difference between translation and transaction exposure?
2. What is the difference between real and nominal exchange rates?
3. What are the three classic approaches to managing economic exposure outlined by Lessard and Lightstone?
4. What are the three sources of finance that an MNE has and how can it use these sources to decrease exchange rates risk?
5. What are the five actions that management can take away from Lessard and Lightstone's discussion of foreign exchange and currency risk?

R&D ACTIVITIES

R&D activities

TRANSFER PRICING

Background

Transfer pricing is the leading edge of what is wrong with international tax
Lee Sheppard, Tax Analysts, August 2012

Transfer pricing is one of the most important issues in international tax. It happens when two companies that are part of the same multinational group trade with each other; for example, when a US-based subsidiary of Coca-Cola buys something from a French-based subsidiary of Coca-Cola. When the parties establish a price for the transaction, this is transfer pricing.

Transfer pricing is not illegal or necessarily abusive. What is illegal or abusive is transfer mispricing, also known as transfer pricing manipulation or abusive transfer pricing. (Transfer mispricing is a form of a more general phenomenon known as trade mispricing, which includes trade between unrelated or apparently unrelated parties – an example is reinvoicing.)

It is estimated that about 60 per cent of international trade happens within, rather than between, MNEs; that is, across national boundaries but within the same corporate group. Global Financial Integrity in Washington estimates the amount lost due to mispricing at several hundred billion US dollars annually. A March 2009 Christian Aid report estimated $1.1 trillion in bilateral trade mispricing into the EU and the US alone from non-EU countries from 2005 to 2007.

Source: Tax Justice Network n.d.

1. Read the extract above and investigate the mechanisms that MNEs can use for transfer pricing. Why do you think the article claims that transfer pricing is one of the most important issues in international taxation?
2. Research an MNE and discuss its foreign exposure.
3. Look up General Electric (GE) and discuss whether it has exchange rate risk.
4. How does a currency crisis affect a country's economy?

IB MASTERCLASS

Avon: dancing with volatile exchange rates

Famous for selling cosmetics door to door through 'Avon ladies' sales representatives, Avon is the world's largest direct seller of beauty products, with more than US$11 billion in annual revenues from over 100 domestic and foreign markets (Avon 2012).

Avon was founded as the California Perfume Company by David McConnell in 1886 and named Avon in 1939. In 1914, it opened its first international office in Montreal, Canada. By 1986, more than a third of its US$3 billion sales came from abroad (Avon 2006). By the end of 2011, the foreign share of its total consolidated revenue from outside North America had risen to 81 per cent (Avon 2011, p. 29).

Extensive cross-border activities expose Avon to all kinds of effects brought about by volatile exchange rates. For example, in the mid-1980s, the dollar reached a peak in 1985. As the dollar rose to its 1985 peak, converting foreign earnings from weakening currencies into dollars reduced Avon's profits. However, as the dollar fell between 1985 and 1987, conversion from strengthening currencies increased the profits from foreign markets. During the Asian crisis of 1997–98 and the Latin American currency crisis in the 1990s, sharp devaluations of currencies, such as the baht (Thailand), the peso (Mexico) and the real (Brazil), also hit Avon.

Such volatile exchange rates forced Avon to introduce effective tools to reduce the risk of losses resulting from changes in the values of currencies. However, with Avon's key markets being located outside of the US, the firm continues to face challenges when attempting to mitigate foreign exchange risk.

Sources of operating exposure

The market position of Avon vis-à-vis its competitors, including the geographic sourcing of its inputs, the geographic dispersion of its outputs and its comparative flexibility at switching locations, largely determines the company's operating exposure.

Because of its market position, Avon has sometimes outperformed the competition during currency crises. For example, during the Mexican peso crisis in 1994, when the peso was devalued, Avon's main competitors in Mexico faced much more expensive imports when expressed in pesos, leading their prices to almost double. Unlike its main rivals, however, Avon relied mainly on domestic producers in Mexico for its supplies. As a result, Avon was able to raise its prices higher than required by inflation rates, but still lower than its competitors.

Managing exposure

Besides using financial options to reduce its transaction exposure risk, Avon has configured its international business activities to reduce the potentially negative effects of volatile exchange rates. More importantly, Avon's senior financial managers communicate extensively with operating managers and help them to understand the possible impacts of operating exposure.

Financial options

When the dollar declined against the yen in late 1987, John E. Donaldson Jr, then Avon's treasurer, reduced the transaction risk of losses by using various tools, including purchasing forward contracts from foreign exchange brokers, buying options contracts from brokers and applying stop-loss orders.

To effectively manage the financial risk arising from its international business activities, Avon now utilises a combination of tools such as forward contracts, swaps and options. These financial instruments help to reduce Avon's 'exposure to fluctuations in cash flows associated with changes in interest rates and foreign exchange rates' (Avon 2011, p. 42).

Although Avon has successfully managed its foreign exchange exposure in the past, the firm has faced many challenges in recent years. Avon's operations in Latin America underperformed as compared to expected sales projections, despite being a key market for the company. The situation was exacerbated when Venezuela devalued its currency after a prolonged period of high inflation, which negatively affected Avon's net profits in 2010 and 2011 (Avon 2010, p. 10).

In 2011, the bulk of the company's foreign exchange exposure was to 'the Argentine peso, Brazilian real, British pound, Canadian dollar, Chinese renminbi, Colombian peso, the euro, Mexican peso, Philippine peso, Polish zloty, Russian rouble, Turkish lira, Ukrainian hryvnia and the Venezuelan bolivar' (Avon 2010).

Configuring manufacturing activities

Prior to 2007, most of Avon's cosmetics were manufactured within the country where they were sold. When viable, Avon would try to source materials from local suppliers, but the company has recently moved to take greater advantage of economies of scale. The company's strategy is to move towards a 'globally coordinated' approach to sourcing, rather than one that is locally oriented (Avon 2010, p. 6). This Strategic Sourcing Initiative (SSI) was implemented in 2007 and had provided a cumulated value of US$300 million by 2010. The initiative allowed Avon to decrease the costs of materials and to select suppliers with complementary capabilities. The SSI and price increases on selected products helped to mitigate the foreign exchange effects faced by Avon in 2010 (Avon 2010, p. 28).

Avon has also shifted production in response to fluctuating exchange rates. For example, during the Asian crisis, Avon replaced its European lace supplier with a Thai company, to reduce the negative impact of having to pay for inputs in a strong European currency.

Continuing communication between finance officers and operating managers

In 1997, Avon treasurer Dennis Ling was in daily contact with Jose Ferreira Jr, head of the Asia–Pacific region for Avon. Together, the two chose financial options and other reconfiguring activities to manage potential risks. Such communication with finance specialists helped operating managers to understand the threats and opportunities brought by currency volatility.

Transferring knowledge to manage exposure

In countries throughout Latin America, such as Brazil, Venezuela, Mexico and Argentina, senior managers have developed specific knowledge to cope with economic crisis, political crisis and hyperinflation. Avon has used this knowledge to develop a set of responses to deal with volatility. Further, Avon can also move these experienced managers to help Avon managers in other countries in crisis. For example, when Russia experienced a currency crisis in 1998, Avon called in Miguel Salbitano and Richard Foggio to give a hand. The former was the head of the Central America region, and the latter spent eight years in Latin America. Similarly, a team of Latin American executives was taken to visit Avon's Asian units country by country to help them out in 1997 during the Asian financial crisis.

Outlook

With the impact of the 2008 recession still felt across the globe, Avon has had a difficult time trying to turn around its operating performance since 2009 (Thomson Reuters 2012). Avon's strong presence in emerging markets continues to be a key driver in its success, which opens the company up to significant operating exposure (Gottfried 2011). Avon must continue to manage its foreign exchange risks to ensure these markets continue to contribute to their growth.

Avon has faced an uphill battle since 2008 with allegations regarding its participation in bribery in China. Numerous executives were fired and an investigation by the SEC was imposed for many of Avon's international operations, costing the firm millions of dollars. In 2012, Avon's debt rating has also been downgraded from a triple-B-plus to a triple-B by Standard and Poor's. Weak operating results and bribery allegations have negatively affected the firm (Glazer, Chon & Das 2012).

In December 2011, the company announced that its current CEO, Andrea Jung, would be stepping down to take on the sole position of executive chairman. This move created significant debate among employees, ex-employees and the public. Past CEOs made public statements disagreeing with Mrs Jung staying on as executive chairman as they felt a new direction needed to be taken (Lubin & Glazer 2012). Former executives indicated whom they felt should have been appointed, signalling to the public that dissatisfaction had existed with the internal functioning of the firm (Lublin & Glazer 2012). After a five-month search, Avon announced that

Sherilyn McCoy, a former executive of Johnson & Johnson, would replace Jung as CEO, effective 23 April 2012 (Goudreau 2012).

On 2 April 2012 Avon was presented a buyout offer from Coty Inc. for US$10 billion (Coty Inc. 2012). The offer was priced at a 20 per cent premium from the closing price on 30 March 2012. However, Avon rejected the offer stating that the company was undervalued. Avon hopes the appointment of a new CEO will help to revive and realign the struggling firm (Wahba 2012).

Unfortunately, Avon closed its operations in Australia and New Zealand in 2018. The decision to exit these markets is based on poor performance and potential for growth.

Sources: Bleakley 1997, p. 1; Hayes 1987, D.1; Whitford 1999, pp. 229–35

QUESTIONS

1. How do volatile exchange rates affect Avon's operations? What are the major risks and benefits?
2. Explain Avon's position in Mexico as described in the case. Explain the effects of Mexican inflation and the peso devaluation on Avon Mexico and its competitors, who rely on imports to service the Mexican market. (Note: to answer this question, you must know the inflation rates in Mexico and the US, and the exchange rate between the peso and the dollar.)
3. Can you provide an update on Avon's management of its operating exposure, using materials available online?

References

Australian Tax Office (2016). Attachment A: Countries that have a tax treaty with Australia. Retrieved from www.ato.gov.au/Forms/Guide-to-foreign-income-tax-offset-rules-2016/?page=6#Attachment_A__Countries_that_have_a_tax_treaty_with_Australia

Avon (2006). Company information. Retrieved from www.annualreports.com/Company/avon-products-inc

——— (2010). Annual report. Retrieved from www.annualreports.com/Company/avon-products-inc

——— (2011). Annual report. Retrieved from www.annualreports.com/Company/avon-products-inc

——— (2012). Company information. Retrieved from www.annualreports.com/Company/avon-products-inc

BBC News (1997). Asian tigers lost pride. *BBC News*, 28 January. Retrieved from http://news.bbc.co.uk/1/hi/special_report/1997/asian_economic_woes/34395.stm

Becker, C. & Fabbro, D. (2006). *Limiting Foreign Exchange Exposure through Hedging: the Australian Experience*. Research Discussion Paper RDP 2006–2009. Reserve Bank Australia economic publications, Melbourne. Retrieved from www.rba.gov.au/publications/rdp/2006/pdf/rdp2006-09.pdf

Bin, X. & Ying, L. (2012). The case study: How BMW dealt with exchange rate risk. *Financial Times*, 30 October. Retrieved from www.ft.com/content/f21b3a92-f907-11e1-8d92-00144feabdc0

Bird, M. & Hunter, G.S. (2018). Another plunge on the bitcoin rollercoaster ride. *The Australian*, 18 January.

BIS (2018). Triennial central bank survey of foreign exchange and OTC derivatives markets in 2016. Retrieved from www.bis.org/publ/rpfx16.htm

Bleakley, F.R. (1997). How US firm copes with Asia crisis – Avon moves to protect against volatile currencies. *Wall Street Journal*, A2, A4, 26 January.

Broadbent, B. (2017). *Brexit and the pound*. Imperial college. Retrieved from www.bankofengland.co.uk/publications/Documents/speeches/2017/speech969.pdf

Buffet, W. (2002). Letter to shareholders. Berkshire Hathaway. Retrieved from www.berkshirehathaway.com/letters/2002pdf.pdf

Burdekin, R.C.K. (2008). Currency boards vs dollarization: Lessons from the Cook Islands. *Cato Journal*, 28(1,Winter). Retrieved from https://object.cato.org/sites/cato.org/files/serials/files/cato-journal/2008/1/cj28n1-7.pdf

Cavusgil, S.T., Knight, G., Riesenberger, J.R., Rammal, H.G. & Rose, E.L. (2015). *International business*. Melbourne: Pearson.

Cœuré, B. (2017). European CCPs after Brexit. Speech by Mr Benoît Cœuré, Member of the Executive Board of the European Central Bank, at the Global Financial Markets Association, 20 June. Retrieved from www.bis.org/review/r170706b.htm

Coty Inc. (2012). About Coty. Retrieved from www.coty.com

Ernst & Young (2011). *US GAAP versus IFRS: the basics*. London: Ernst & Young Retrieved from www.ey.com/Publication/vwLUAssets/US_GAAP_v_IFRS:_The_Basics/$FILE/US%20GAAP%20v%20IFRS%20Dec%202011.pdf

Flight Centre (2017). FY17 results. Flight Centre Travel Group annual result presentation. Retrieved from www.fctgl.com/wp-content/uploads/2017/08/04-FLT-FY17-FULL-YEAR-RESULTS-PRESENTATION.pdf

Forsyth, P. & Dwyer, L. (2010). Exchange rate changes and the cost competitiveness of international airlines: The aviation trade weighted index. *Research in Transportation Economics*, 26(1), 12–17. https://doi.org/10.1016/j.retrec.2009.10.003

Glazer, E., Chon, G. & Das, A. (2012,). Scarred Avon is takeover target. *Wall Street Journal*, 3 April. Retrieved from www.wsj.com/articles/SB1000142405270230402350457731926094323798

Goldsmith, C. (2000). Moguls rewrite script at Cannes as euro tanks. *Wall Street Journal*, (Eastern edition), B.1, 19 May.

Gottfried, M. (2011). Avon needs more than lipstick. Barron's, 19 December. Retrieved from www.barrons.com/articles/SB50001424052748703856804577098621608626372

Goudreau, J. (2012). Avon names Sherilyn McCoy as new CEO. *Forbes*, 9 April. Retrieved from www.forbes.com/sites/jennagoudreau/2012/04/09/avon-names-sherilyn-mccoy-as-new-ceo/#182f44314685

Gray, S.J. (1988). Towards a theory of cultural influence on the development of accounting systems internationally. *ABACUS*, 24(1), 1–15. doi.org/10.1111/j.1467–6281.1988.tb00200.x

Hayes, T.C. (1987). Puzzling out foreign profits. *New York Times*, D.1

IASPlus (2018a). Conceptual framework for financial reporting 2018. Deloitte website. Retrieved from www.iasplus.com/en/standards/other/framework.

——— (2018b). IAS 16 – Property, plant and equipment. Deloitte website. Retrieved from www.iasplus.com/en/standards/ias/ias16.

International Air Transport Association (IATA) (2015). Exchange rates and aviation: examining the links, IATA, p. 1. Retrieved from www.iata.org/publications/economic-briefings/FX%20 impacts%20on%20airlines%20(Dec%202015).pdf

International Monetary Fund (2004). Cook Islands: Assessment of the Supervision and Regulation of the Financial Sector Volume II – Detailed Assessment of Observance of Standards and Codes. IMF country report No 04/414, 20 December. Retrieved from www.imf.org/en/Publications/CR/Issues/2016/12/31/Cook-Islands-Assessment-of-the-Supervision-and-Regulation-of-the-Financial-Sector-Volume-I-17935

Lafarge (2004). 20-F Report. LafargeHolcim website, 26 March. Retrieved from www.lafargeholcim.com

Lessard D.R. & Lightstone, J.B. (1986). Volatile exchange rates can put operations at risk. *Harvard Business Review*, 64, 107–14.

Lublin, J.S. & Glazer, E. (2012). Corporate news: Avon ex-CEOs push alumnus for post. *Wall Street Journal* (Eastern Edition), B.4, 30 March.

Moffett, M.H., Stonehill, A.I. & Eiteman, K. (2008). *Fundamentals of Multinational Finance*. Boston: Pearson Education.

OECD (2015). *Global Forum on Transparency and Exchange of Information for Tax Purposes Peer reviews: Cook Islands 2015. Phase 2: Implementation of the standard in practice*. Paris: OECD. Retrieved from www.oecd.org/tax/global-forum-on-transparency-and-exchange-of-information-for-tax-purposes-peer-reviews-cook-islands-2015–9789264231450-en.htm

Official Data Foundation (2018). Bitcoin historical prices. Retrieved from www.in2013dollars.com/bitcoin-price

Price, R., Rahman, N. & Yohana, B. (2012). Intra-group financing: transfer pricing and intra-group financing. International Tax Review, July 9. Retrieved from www.internationaltaxreview.com/Article/3057688/Intra-group-financing-Transfer-pricing-and-intra-group-financing.html

Quinn, K. (2014). A cinema ticket in Australia can cost up to $40: Here's why. *The Sydney Morning Herald*, 10 July.

Radatz, E. & Sirak, A. (2014). Efficiently managing foreign exchange risk in the portfolio context. *Deutsche Asset and Wealth Management*, September. Retrieved from https://institutional.deutscheam.com/content/_media/Deutsche_AWM_Foreign_exchange_risk_0914.pdf

Radelet, S., Sachs, J.D., Cooper, R.N. & Bosworth, B.P. (1998). The East Asian financial crisis: Diagnosis remedies, prospects. *Brookings Papers on Economic Activity*, (1), 1–90. Retrieved from www.earth.columbia.edu/sitefiles/file/about/director/documents/BPEA19981withRadelet-TheEastAsianFinancialCrisis.pdf

Rodiowove, Z. (2017). Brexit: London financial hub could lose more than 200 000 jobs amid uncertainty, LSE boss warns. *Independent*, 10 January. Retrieved from www.independent.co.uk/news/business/news/brexit-latest-news-london-city-jobs-losses-lse-boss-warning-uk-eu-a7519396.html

Silverman, G., Murphy, H. & Authers, J. (2017). Bitcoin: an investment mania for the fake news era. *Financial Times*, 1 December. Retrieved from www.ft.com/content/c84caffc-d683-11e7-a303-9060cb1e5f44.

Stanford, J. (2017). The soaring Aussie dollar will short-change Australia's export industries. *HuffPost*, 31 July. Retrieved from www.huffingtonpost.com.au/jim-stanford/the-soaring-aussie-dollar-will-short-change-australias-export-i_a_23054997

Statoil (2005). Annual report. Retrieved from www.equinor.com

Tax Justice Network (n.d.). Transfer pricing. Tax Justice website. Retrieved from www.taxjustice.net/topics/corporate-tax/transfer-pricing

Thomson Reuters (2012). S&P cuts Avon Products Inc. Thomson Reuters, 3 April. Retrieved from www.reuters.com/article/idUSWNA412520120402

Wahba, P. (2012). Wanted: one makeover; Avon ladies looking for a new look amid executive changes, bribery probes. *National Post*, FP.5, 19 March.

Wayne, L. (2013). Cook Islands, a paradise of untouchable assets. *The New York Times*, 14 December. Retrieved from www.nytimes.com/2013/12/15/business/international/paradise-of-untouchable-assets.html?mcubz=0

Whitford, D. (1999). A currency drowns – can you stay afloat?. *Fortune*, 139, 229–35.

CHAPTER 10

INTERNATIONAL MARKETING

Learning objectives

In reading this chapter, you will learn to:

1. recognise the key elements in international marketing decisions
2. recognise the drivers of international business pricing
3. understand international distribution and networks
4. appreciate promotional issues and challenges in international markets
5. realise the benefits of evaluating marketing measurement metrics.

THE RISE OF SOCIAL MARKETING

The practice of marketing is considered to be a social process, composed of human behaviour patterns related to the exchange of resources, behaviours or values. It is no longer a mere function used to increase business profits. Social marketing plays a significant role in driving personal behaviour and social change around the world.

From 2010, the attention of public-sector agencies, non-government organisations and the private sector is focused increasingly on the potential power, application and impact of social marketing beyond the traditional challenges of health and safety concerns, such as obesity and chronic disease. Social marketing is extending to environmental, economic and educational fields, and addresses global issues such as climate change, environmental destruction, natural resource shortages, fast population growth, hunger and poverty, as well as insufficient social services (Beall et al. 2011). There is an impetus to evolve the science and art of social marketing to reflect strong standards of practice and evaluation, while encouraging creativity and innovation.

The ADB is at the forefront of social marketing initiatives. Poverty reduction has been a core objective since the bank's establishment. Rapid economic growth in the Asia–Pacific region, and significant shifts in the international aid, development and financial landscape have generated a need and an opportunity for ADB to set a new strategic course (ADB 2008). Robust regional economic growth is a key driver in poverty reduction, but also is contributing to the depletion of natural resources, accelerating environmental degradation and impacting climate change. Reducing poverty requires more people to become economically productive, but only environmentally sustainable growth can eliminate poverty, given many of the poor depend on natural resources for their livelihoods (ADB 2008, p. 12). Poverty reduction can be 'accelerated when neighbouring economies work within larger and freer markets and when governments achieve common interests through common efforts' (ADB 2008, p. 11).

Under Strategy 2020, ADB is committed to making substantive contributions by 'focusing its support on three distinct but complementary development agendas of the region: inclusive economic growth, environmentally sustainable growth and contribution to harmonious regional growth' (ADB 2008, p.11). ADB actively supports the use of environmentally friendly technologies and environmental-safeguard measures, establishing institutional capacities to strengthen their enforcement (ADB 2008, p. 12).

VIDEO VIGNETTE QUESTIONS

Dragonfly bikes for transport is a project of ADB to promote community sharing, green transport and physical health with the cooperation of Bonifacio Global City (BGC) in the Philippines.

Introduction

This chapter starts by examining the elements of international marketing decisions made by managers seeking to enter new markets, particularly regarding advances in technology, distribution developments such as omni-channels and social marketing. The drivers linked to international pricing decisions are discussed and issues linked to anti-dumping behaviours are considered. The challenges associated with international distribution are explored by reviewing the desired elements to establish a good distribution network and to select a supply-chain partner. The role of promoting products in international markets, and the elements of advertising, sales promotion and public relations are then examined. The chapter concludes by outlining the importance of evaluating marketing performance metrics.

Key elements in international marketing decisions

Expanding internationally can be a profitable way for an organisation to expand their business and reduce dependence on domestic markets. With an increasingly globalised world, organisations can no longer expect to survive and thrive on domestic market sales alone.

The Australian Trade and Investment Commission, known as Austrade, contends that, on average, exporting companies are more profitable than their non-exporting counterparts (Austrade 2017a). Broadening into international markets exposes organisations to novel ideas, management practices, marketing techniques and ways of competing that trading only in a home market cannot bring. This approach improves an organisation's ability to compete in the domestic market; expanding abroad acts to improve efficiency and productivity within a business. Exporting companies generally have better growth prospects, with highly skilled and highly productive staff members who tend to adapt to technology and best practice techniques at a faster pace (Austrade 2017a).

Even with a limited domestic market, exporting can deliver growth to a business. In the past, many companies found their size and resources limited their ability to adopt international marketing strategies. Today, the development and augmentation of technology in international business operations, and the ability to identify niche markets have enabled expansion for all businesses, large and small, not just well-established firms and large MNEs. Approximately a quarter of new exporters are 'born globals' and have emerged from small domestic companies from rural and regional areas (Austrade 2017b). Organisations must, however, understand the global nature of their relevant industry, target markets and the desired product offering, and then formulate strategies which allow the establishment of the organisation in the new market.

The changing landscape

Over the last two decades, the world has been undergoing digital transformations, where no sector is immune. With technology developing at an unprecedented pace and consumer expectations constantly evolving, international business survival is dependent on understanding and adapting products and services in this changing landscape. These shifts in consumer behaviour, expectations and experiences provide incredible opportunities for business growth. Since the industrial revolution, change is continuous and companies are operating in an environment that is constantly altering over time; the pace of progressive upheavals over the last several decades is especially fast and encompasses enormous transformations. These shifts occur in societies, in the use of our technology and the way we live our lives (Frampton 2017; NAB 2017).

Information technology and the internet are transforming international business by allowing firms to conduct ecommerce online, as well as to integrate ebusiness capabilities for activities such as sourcing and managing customer relations. The modern firm, small or large, manages geographical distance and time zones using modern technology. As barriers to trade and investment continue to decline, globalisation of markets is increasing, creating further impetus for organisations to adopt international marketing strategies.

Emerging international marketing advances

Rapid internationalisation for organisations of all sizes has emerged as a critical area to understand. Three trends which are at the forefront of change in international marketing today relate to technology advancements, omni-channels and social marketing.

Technology advancements

Approaches to marketing are changing as customers and consumers spend more time engaging with technology as a part of their daily lives. The use of smart phones, tablets and laptops has become integrated as a lifestyle norm. The challenge for organisations is to connect with their target audiences through these devices in real time, and to develop communication strategies and create campaigns that work across multiple platforms including ecommerce, social media and advertising.

A primary focus for international marketers is to understand people's motivations, and then utilise those insights to develop clear messages that promote their company's products and services. It is a creative and often intuitive process which technology can support. The use of software, such as Oracle CX Solutions, tracks the customer journey and provides predictive analysis to forecast future buying behaviour; the use of sophisticated instore and online technology, which employs touchpoints to track customer and consumer engagement with products, are producing significant volumes of data. These types of technologies provide real-time, critical business information which the organisation can use to make judicious decisions to develop their international business strategies. Advancements in marketing technology have led to the development and widening of the channels companies can utilise to reach multiple target markets to grow their businesses.

Distribution developments: the rise of omni-channels

The omni-channel is a marketing concept that refers to the cross-use of multiple channels of distribution to harvest benefits from synergies. It is gaining increasing significance in many Asia–Pacific markets. The top 500 retail companies implement strategies that integrate their multiple retail channels. For example, in Japan, 'bricks and clicks' retailers, those who have a store and online offering, are increasing their presence in a wider range of channels. Ryohin Keikaku Company, a household and consumer goods retailer which owns the brand Muji, is one such organisation. Ryohin Keikaku employs the use of innovative technologies to create a more convenient and extensive retail offering, seamlessly integrating online and offline channels together. The buying behaviours of consumers shopping instore and online have significantly changed in the last decade. The chief factors contributing to organisations adopting an omni-channel strategy for their business relate to:

- *High online and internet engagement*: in 2015, 43.8 per cent of internet users were from the Asia–Pacific region (Statista 2018a).
- *Rising ecommerce offerings*: retail ecommerce sales in Asia amounted to US$1.36 trillion in 2017, an increase of 29.6 per cent when compared with 2016. Annual double digital sales growth is expected to endure as the uptake of ecommerce continues (Frampton 2017).
- *A growing middle class*: estimates indicate that by 2020, there will be 740 million new middle-class consumers in the Asia–Pacific region, representing 85 per cent of major markets (WTO 2017).
- *Strong demographics*: the earning population in the Asia–Pacific is at its peak, with the majority of the population aged between 15 and 64 years (ESCAP 2015).

- *Hyper-connectivity of consumers*: about 37 per cent of consumers in the Asia–Pacific are more likely to purchase goods and services through mobile devices as compared to the global average of 26 per cent (Euromonitor International 2015). In India, the expectation is for mobile internet retailing to experience significant growth, shifting from desktop platforms to operating through mobile applications.

In a competitive environment, organisations must increasingly provide a seamless shopping experience for consumers. Whether at home or work, online or instore, the successful transaction causally relates to a successful experience. The strategy to build a coherent, aligned experience across multiple platforms requires companies to interact with multiple departments within their organisation including marketing, operations, distribution, customer service and IT.

The Walt Disney Company is an MNE leading the way in the omni-channel approach. It provides a vast range of experiences and multiple touchpoints for consumers to engage with their products; it has seven theme parks to coalesce consumer engagements (Hubspot 2017). The Disney experience starts by planning the journey, with the consumer engaging with the business through a My Disney MagicBand; the MagicBand is wearable technology that plans, records and tracks activities to ensure the consumer's interaction is maintained. The MagicBand wristband activates on arrival at a Disney theme park, and allows admission to the parks and accommodation, signals attractions, enables purchases and allows the consumer to see the images they have taken during the visit. Technology monitors the consumers' movements and provides a guide for the parks, while communicating information about the consumers' activities to the Disney organisation. These insights contribute to the company's customer improvement program, which aims to ensure ongoing enhancement of the Disney experience for visitors.

Social marketing

SOCIAL MARKETING the design, implementation, and control of programs created to induce attitudinal and behavioural changes in a target audience to achieve a social goal.

International businesses are altering the way they plan and operate their businesses through the principles and techniques of social marketing. Social marketing emerged in the 1970s, and is now a subdiscipline of marketing. Social marketing is a management practice grounded in a marketing viewpoint; it incorporates marketing tools and techniques to affect behavioural change in target audiences to improve personal and community welfare in a society.

Key areas where social marketing methodologies have been engaged include individual health, road safety and physical activities. The rational of social marketing is that public change is best brought about by persuading the individual to change their current behaviour to a new behaviour with a greater social outcome (Dann & Dann 2014, p. 15). The key defining principle of social marketing is, therefore, an emphasis on customer-driven solutions, meaning the individual must want to change their behaviour; for example, a person no longer wants to drive after the consumption of alcohol or drugs, whereas before the person did not give the action much thought.

CUSTOMER ATTITUDES a composite of a consumer's beliefs and feelings about and behavioural intentions towards a product or service.

Social marketing focuses on identifying customer attitudes; that is, what target adopters know and how they feel about an issue before developing a campaign designed to modify their attitudes or behaviours. To reach the point of sustained behavioural change, the 'product' offered by the social marketing needs to be communicated and positioned in such a way as to make it more attractive to the target market than the current behaviours, or any other behavioural alternative, including those which are equally as damaging' (Dann & Dann 2014, pp. 10–11). In November 2017, Uber Singapore left giant tissue packets in several parking spaces in Singapore, a parody on the uniquely Singaporean behaviour of using tissue packets to reserve seats, known as *chope*. The company engaged bloggers and influencers to post pictures of the parking spaces on social media, which sparked discussions on parking issues in Singapore. The *chope* campaign is part of a broader mission to reduce traffic in Asia's most congested cities, including Ho Chi Minh City, Jakarta and Bangkok (*The Drum* 2017).

Research shows that the positive outcomes of adopting these practices go past CSR and positive public appearances. They have a positive effect on industry accomplishments while helping to address persistent social issues. Papakosmas, Noble and Glynn. state that 'if the potential to improve performance alone were not sufficient incentive for organisations to adopt and manage sustainable business practices, governments in many countries are [now] legislating to force businesses to do so' (2012), p. 88). Social marketers characterise such government interventions as an example of upstream social marketing. An example of this is Australia's *National Greenhouse and Energy Reporting Act 2007*, which requires corporations to report on energy production and consumption, and greenhouse gas emissions. Successful social marketing campaigns are based on the application of strategic approaches usually aligned to government policies to address a social problem (Mintz 2016). Examples of essential components in social marketing include:

- a consumer emphasis to realise managerial goals
- prominence on the voluntary interactions of goods and services between suppliers and consumers
- recognising target audiences through analysis and segmentation studies
- an analysis of circulation and communication channels
- employment by stakeholders in the intervention planning and implementation phases
- a tracking system with both amalgamating and regulating functions
- an organisational process that involves problem identification, planning, implementation and feedback functions.

Products and services

Products or services form the core of any organisation's international operations. Success ultimately depends on customer satisfaction; that is, how well products or services satisfy consumers' needs and wants in a given market, and how well the product is positioned when compared to the competition. Organisations operating in foreign situations need to make decisions on the product offering they make in overseas markets. Some or all the following factors may influence a company's decision to alter a product:

CUSTOMER SATISFACTION a measure of how products or services supplied by a company meet or surpass a consumer's expectations, and can be expressed by the number of repeated consumptions.

- compliance and regulations
- government policies
- consumer attitudes and behaviours
- physical environment
- competitive landscape
- economic position of markets
- environmental events and trends.

Typically, the market environment mandates most product amendments. However, the strictest requirements often result from regulations imposed by governments. Some may serve no direct marketing purpose but are for political and governance reasons, such as responses to political pressures and protection of a domestic industry. Due to the sovereignty of nations, individual companies must comply with these regulations. Organisations seeking to enter a new market may choose to lobby directly to a government or through an industry association to have issues raised during

trade negotiations. One such institution informing, connecting and advocating trade matters is the China–Australia Chamber of Commerce (AustCham), which has its head office in Beijing. AustCham provides important trade networking links, as well as support for lobbying and trade negotiations. The core mission of AustCham is to lead and facilitate Australian business growth in China.

An international business must ensure that its products do not contain ingredients that violate legal regulations, or religious or social customs. Keeping well informed of changes in such requirements is critical. For example, the Japanese Ministry of Health, Labour and Welfare banned 19 types of ingredients from use in medicated soaps in late 2016 (Spencer 2016). A selection of products under a variety of brands commonly uses two of the disqualified ingredients throughout the Asia–Pacific region and the rest of the world. In 2017, South Korea adopted a ban on domestic and imported cosmetics that undergo animal testing or contain animal-tested ingredients. Manufacturers had a year to remove any banned ingredients or products, with non-compliant organisations facing hefty fines. The Philippines, too, are clamping down and making changes in this area.

International businesses face several market entry challenges relating to products, including minimum product standards, approval procedures, market entry protocols and certification. As an example, all food items imported into China are subject to inspections by the China Entry-Exit Inspection and Quarantine Bureau. Businesses wanted to enter China need to manage the required documentation, associated costs and time requirements involved to enter this market. Keeping up to date on market entry protocols including labelling, minimum chemical-residues levels, approved ingredients and packaging requirements is a formidable task. Engaging a specialist consulting firm to act as an agent can facilitate and manage organisational risk in international environments. Businesses operating globally have strategies in place, either dedicated personnel internally or consultant firms externally, to manage the dynamic nature of import markets.

Local behaviour, tastes, attitudes and traditions influence the product decisions of manufacturers and traders since these factors can all reflect customer endorsement. A knowledge of cultural and attitudinal differences is often the key to business success. Nowhere is this more apparent than in the offering and acceptance of national food preferences and habits. Food is highly culturally sensitive. Across most of the world, the Nestlé brand Maggi is known best for its soups and sauces. In India, Maggi has become the generic word for instant noodles. Maggi was introduced there in 1982 with masala flavouring and over the next 25 years the flavour maintained a leading number one position (Knowledge@Wharton 2009). Nestlé continued to launch noodle flavours to appeal to local and regional tastes, but none achieved the popularity of the masala variety. Differences in regional infrastructure also result in a need for product modifications in different markets. One of the most common examples of product localisation is with Indian consumer appliances in the home. White goods firms in India must adjust their washing machines to manage the frequent power outages and uncertainty of fresh water supply related to the use of that type of product. Whirlpool India developed a series of semi-automatic washing machines that require less water and feature an engineering design that prompts the machine to restart automatically after a power failure to address this regional challenge. Other examples of modified products include fridges that aim to keep food cold four to five hours without power, after an electrical black out. Regional challenges are common with white goods, and continue to require organisations to modify regional market offerings. For instance, after intensive consumer research, LG Electronics in East Asia launched refrigerators in a range of different, darker colours. Research revealed that the generous use of oil and strong spices, such as turmeric, in the regional cooking styles stained pastel-coloured appliances, which created the need for darker shades of kitchen and laundry appliances.

The rate of product diffusion is much greater today than it was a decade ago. International businesses face the risk of international or domestic competitors copying product ideas and advancing into existing or completely new markets. The monitoring of competitive landscape in each market is a necessary task for an international manager. With an understanding of the competition, managers can determine product changes and actions required to maintain market presence in a timely manner. Further, understanding competitive offerings provides a manager with a baseline to measure the firm's internal operations. For example, competitive knowledge assists with understanding market supply and demand drivers. In these operational environments, businesses formulate judicious decisions to standardise or adapt their product to meet the needs of the target market. Recognising the need for a strategic approach from all parts of the business is necessary.

Standardising and customising for international markets

Once the international market or markets is identified and confirmed, the operational planning commences. The first step is to consider the product offering and the marketing mix for the new market. A critical issue for managers to consider is the extent the firm should standardise the marketing elements of product, price, place and promotion, and the extended elements of people and processes. At the same time, managers also need to consider whether the internationalisation process requires an alternative, tailored approach to deliver optimal results. There are three approaches to planning an international marketing mix. The

- The standardisation approach: make no distinctive product changes, but identify potential target markets and choose uniform products or services that can easily be marketed with little or no alterations.
- The multi-domestic approach: identify cross-border differences, and adapt products to suit local market conditions and consumer needs in each individual country or region.
- The globalisation approach: incorporate differences into a regional and global strategy that makes allowances for local differences in implementation.

STANDARDISATION APPROACH elements of the marketing mix that are the same or have minimal changes for an international market.

MULTI-DOMESTIC APPROACH some or all elements of the marketing mix are tailored to suit local consumer needs and wants for each market entered.

GLOBALISATION APPROACH a universal marketing mix strategy implemented in all markets.

Today, standardisation frequently relates to cross-national strategies rather than the policy of viewing a foreign market as inferior and consequently not important enough to adapt products for local requirements. The business manager should assess the intended market on its own merits, while considering the firm's global position, and put this information in context before deciding whether to adapt or standardise in the local target market. There are three elements to consider in forming the decision to standardise or adapt: the intended market, the product's features and benefits, and the organisation, including its assets and strategy.

There are several organisations that deliver standardised characteristics with a localised offering. Yum! Brands, the parent company of KFC, Pizza Hut and a range of other fast-food brands, is a multi-domestic corporation. The company generally uses the same brand names for its stores globally, but adjusts the menu offering to meet local food preferences. For example, in Japan, KFC offers tempura-coated food options and, in China, KFC offers sweet-corn soup varieties as menu options to meet consumer expectations.

The multi-domestic approach requires firms to customise and adapt products for individual markets but with an overarching aim to deliver consistent brand messages. The electrical sector frequently encounters this type of challenge. The Australian firm, Cisco Systems, takes a multi-domestic approach to marketing electrical switching and routing equipment in their operating markets. The multi-domestic approach is typically costlier to implement, and takes more time to research the explicit needs and interests for each separate market. The product is adapted but the design of the brand message is consistent and then modified as required for each country. Multi-domestic marketing is challenging for firms seeking to achieve economies of scale from business operations including marketing.

A globalisation approach capitalises on the commonalities in customer and consumer needs within and across countries. The overarching aim is to minimise costs internally with the potential to deliver cost savings to the end consumer through lower end pricing. Seven factors encourage product standardisation or favour product adaptation for a firm in foreign markets:

- common consumer needs
- global customers
- economies of scale
- speed to market
- degree of standardisation
- company considerations
- counterfeiting, imitations and piracy risk.

Common consumer needs

For many product groups, consumer needs are alike in distinctive markets. Consumers generally use the product for the same purposes or the benefits from using the product are frequently similar. For example, Coca-Cola launched Coke No Sugar in Japan in 2015, in Mexico in 2016, and then in the markets of Australia and New Zealand in 2017. As a global trend, consumer preferences have shifted towards beverages with lower sugar levels. Coke No Sugar appeals to consumers who are seeking to reduce or replace their sugar intake but still seek the traditional Coca-Cola taste. Many food and beverage brands want to access this trend, and develop single-identity products to launch in multiple markets.

Global customers

Shoppers in developing markets are gradually becoming aware of international products and universal standards but they are unable to pay premium pricing. Despite demand for the same product characteristics, some modification of the marketing elements is often required to reflect differences in product usage, price sensitivity, and promotion and distribution channels. A business may remove avoidable luxuries from a product to lower its price, while maintaining its product's functional performance. In this form of market, packaging, for example, is strengthened to mitigate delivery challenges – such as poor road conditions and dirty air – to ensure the smooth management and delivery of the product, and its working order. Promotional mixes, choice of advertising, and selling techniques may need to be adapted to meet local tastes and preferences in individual markets. As developing markets experience increasing levels of economic affluence, companies are taking note of these emerging target markets.

Consumers from diverse backgrounds and countries are beginning to share similar lifestyles, economic conditions, educational attainments and income levels so their consumption needs are converging, which has given rise to the notion of global consumers. The global consumer provides the motivation for businesses to develop global products and standardised marketing approaches between countries. The service and product sectors have many examples of global brands appealing to global consumers: Coca-Cola, Microsoft, Apple, Qantas and McDonald's, to name just a few. Nike has developed its global brand by marketing an image of quality, versatility and status since its inception in 1964. The slogan 'Just do it' and Nike's logo, containing the 'swoosh', have delivered a globally consistent message since 1988. International awareness and the ease of recollecting a product or brand increases its value, and translates to its engagement with global consumers.

Economies of scale

Economies of scale in manufacturing and distribution of internationally traded products are frequently key drivers behind standardisation strategies. MNEs that source productivities or reduce R&D costs often produce investments, which are then passed on to consumers through low pricing. Economies of scale offer firms a significant competitive advantage over regional competitors. However, in several evolving industries this rationale has been lost.

Speed to market

Operational procedures such as adaptable processing and just-in-time (JIT) manufacturing have moved the attention from volume to timeliness. Innovation is not enough to be competitive today. Companies must also seek ways to reduce their delivery times to produce new products to market. Centralising research and consolidating new product development efforts on fewer projects is a way to achieve this. This approach was a key pillar for Steve Jobs when he was at the helm of Apple's product development. Apple concentrated on a handful of projects expected to 'bear successful fruit', rather than overextending itself by working on a larger number of projects with lesser chances of success.

Degree of standardisation

The chief obstacle to operationalising an international marketing strategy is that not all products and messages suit every market. Products sometimes have changeable uses, which require distinctive value propositions. For instance, people wash their laundry washing differently around the world, which makes international marketing a challenge for household cleaning manufacturers. The cultural context in this example also plays a part, as do gender roles, responsibilities and methods of undertaking laundry activities. Identifying the cultural norms, behaviours and values in individual markets, and managing them with respect and sensitivity when developing and implementing a global marketing strategy, is necessary to shape the message and product.

Company considerations

'Is it worth it?' is a commonly asked question by many organisations when assessing a proposal to standardise or adapt a product. A detailed analysis of the market that encompasses formal market research and product testing should support this decision. From a financial point of view, an organisation needs confidence in its ability to control costs, accurately forecast market size potential,

MARKET SIZE
the quantifiable value of the potential number of buyers or potential sales volume of a product or service.

stimulate growth and deliver profitability for the firm. Some companies have specific return on investment (ROI) targets to meet before considering whether to adapt. Others let the requirement vary as a function of the market considered and the time in the market. For example, profitability may initially be compromised to achieve market penetration quickly, gain market share and ensure long-term presence in a given market. Beyond cultural, political and economic differences, organisational realities may weaken the ability for a firm to pursue truly global marketing strategies. A balance between the necessity for greater international integration and the need to exploit existing resources more effectively is essential. Many firms explore the use of regional and single country strategies.

MARKET PENETRATION
the percentage of target consumers reached at least once in a given period.

MARKET SHARE
a measure of company or product sales over a given period, relative to the total sales of the industry or market in which the company operates.

Counterfeiting, imitation and piracy risk

Firms annually lose a considerable amount of domestic and export revenue because of product counterfeiting, and trademark and patent infringement of consumer and industrial products. Clothing and accessories, pharmaceutical, software and entertainment industries are typically the most vulnerable to counterfeit activity. Counterfeit products are any items bearing an unauthorised trademark, patented invention or copyrighted work that is legally protected in the county where it is marketed. Asia–Pacific governments continue their efforts to curb counterfeiting, imitation and piracy. In the Philippines, for example, the Intellectual Property Office (IPOPHIL) has developed extensive programs aimed at providing appropriate and efficient ways to enforce trademark rights. They have enacted many initiatives to pursue legal reforms to create stronger intellectual property rights, and to build an administration that values and respects intellectual property. Recently India has become a frontline for intellectual property litigation. However, the problem persists because a substantial number of consumers engaged in this behaviour do not understand the concept. Many small businesses and consumers are unfamiliar with the notion of intellectual property rights as it is largely a concept developed by the Western economy.

A more recent and concerning trend is the growing use of websites and social media to market infringed products to a global audience (Plane & Livingston 2017). According to Plane and Livingston, these sales channels represent a significant new risk for rights holders, and are a sharp contrast to infringed goods that are largely available through domestic sales, and traditional brick-and-mortar outlets and local markets. The online problem is 'exacerbated by China's sophisticated manufacturing base, which allows counterfeiters to quickly manufacture knock-off products at low cost for domestic and international distribution'(Plane & Livingston 2017). The growth of online organisations such as Amazon and eBay has unknowingly facilitated the increased sales of counterfeit goods. Expensive watch brands such as Rolex, Cartier and Bvlgari are frequently found online. In 2016, counterfeit watches and jewellery with a retail value worth US$653.6 million were seized in China. The challenges faced in China make the inclusion of an intellectual property strategy a necessary element (Plane & Livingston 2017).

One of the largest threats posed by counterfeit goods is consumer safety. Replica medicine, for example, often contains the wrong dosage of a pharmaceutical ingredients or lacks a key ingredient altogether. It is not just counterfeit pharmaceuticals that pose a serious risk to consumers, any product that does not meet the national government safety standards or is manufactured with low-quality materials can present a danger.

In today's environment, companies are taking more aggressive steps to protect themselves. High-end luxury brands such as Chanel, Gucci and Fendi are some of the most copied products in the Asia–Pacific region. These firms control their own distribution channels to prevent the circulation of copied products. Louis Vuitton (LVMH group), for example, controls every step of the distribution channel by developing a global network of company-owned manufacturers, distributors and retailers. In addition to the normal measures of registering trademarks and patents, companies are utilising innovative technologies to prevent the copying of their brands. New authentication materials in labelling and packaging are protecting products, and making identification easier for store representatives. Victimised companies are losing not only sales but brand equity in the longer term. The impact of consumers believing they are receiving the real product, when they are receiving an inferior 'copy' product, is significant.

SPOTLIGHT 10.1

A rising star from China: the Haier Group

After facing bankruptcy in 1984, The Qingdao General Refrigerator Factory, better known as the Haier Group, is now a leading consumer electronics and home appliances manufacturer in over 100 countries. In 2016, Haier's sales reached almost US$9.97 billion (Statista 2017). Haier represents an international marketing success story of an exemplary MNE from an emerging economy that has achieved a global brand status.

Haier faced many challenges, principally poor reputation and low-quality standards. The priority was to improve core business quality and implement a brand-building strategy. Through strategic JVs and partnerships with foreign companies, Haier amassed advanced technological knowledge and updated its product offering. The company then diversified by acquiring related businesses and integrating numerous local enterprises. Haier continuously increased its product offerings worldwide, established more foreign sales offices and negotiated with JV partners in

various countries. By 2010, Haier shifted its strategic direction from a production-focused company to a marketing service-focused company that emphasised customisation; Haier won the 2011 Industry Forum Communication Design Award

Today, Haier has transformed from being a conventional manufacturer to an entrepreneurial company. The company is extending its focus on the ecosystem to social networks and community economies, while enhancing the user value of Haier products and services.

Source: Haier n.d.

SPOTLIGHT QUESTIONS

QUESTIONS

1. Many manufacturing companies move to China to gain advantage of cheap labour. However, Haier – a Chinese company – opened production plants around the world. Why?
2. Which market entry strategy did Haier choose for its various international markets?

Drivers of international business pricing

International businesses confront a range of challenges when planning pricing targets for foreign markets. Price is the only element of the marketing mix that delivers revenue for a company; all the other elements require expenditure to deliver their part. Therefore, the focus on price is central to operational planning – all other elements merge into the company's approaches to price planning. A range of factors impacts international pricing including organisational goals, consumer demand, the competitive environment, government policies, managing price escalation and handling anti-dumping pricing measures. These are explored in the following sections.

Planning international pricing

Product pricing strategies can make or break an organisation's export efforts. One of the biggest challenges for firms to overcome is how to set and maintain pricing across different countries. Pricing in an international environment is considerably more complicated than in a domestic market. There are a range of factors to consider when setting prices for the same product in different countries, including government regulations, the consumers' willingness and ability to pay, and the additional costs involved in operating abroad. When determining pricing strategy in international markets, it is critical to understand the price floor (the amount of expenditure incurred to purchase the product or to manufacture the product) and the market price (the amount the market pays for the product). International pricing situations are considered through three approaches: export pricing, foreign market pricing and intra-company or transfer pricing.

STANDARD GLOBAL PRICING
a pricing strategy based on the average unit cost of fixed-, variable- and export-related costs applied in all markets.

DUAL PRICING
the practice of setting prices for the same product or service at a different level in foreign markets versus the domestic market.

MARKET-DIFFERENTIATED PRICING
a pricing method in which prices are determined for each individual market based on consumer demand rather than cost.

Export pricing

There are three broad models to export price-setting: standard global pricing, dual pricing and market-differentiated pricing.

Both standard global and dual pricing are cost-oriented methods that are relatively simple to establish, easy to understand and cover all necessary costs. Standard global pricing uses the average of all fixed, variable and export costs to establish a single unit price. In dual pricing, domestic and export prices are different. These two approaches are generally used in a cost-plus or marginal-cost based strategy. The cost-plus pricing method uses actual expenditures, including the full sharing of domestic and international costs incurred to the product. While this ensures goals are met, the final price may put the product outside consumers' reach in the target markets. The marginal-cost pricing method takes into account the direct costs of manufacturing and retailing for export as the base or floor below which prices cannot be set. Fixed costs for plant, R&D, domestic outgoings and marketing are ignored, allowing the export price to be more competitive and not exceed the market price consumers are prepared to pay for the product or service.

COST-PLUS PRICING
a pricing method in which the full domestic and foreign costs of making the product are allocated to the product's price along with a profit margin.

MARGINAL-COST PRICING
a pricing method which considers the direct costs of manufacturing and retailing for export as the base or floor below which prices cannot be set.

Market-differentiated pricing is the most difficult approach to undertake. This model is the most consistent with the marketing notion as it is based on consumer demand and considers external competitive forces. The main challenge with this strategy is linked to a lack of information and so, in many situations, marginal costs provide the foundation for competitive assessments to determine the export price.

Influences which may determine pricing in export markets relate to: organisational goals, consumer demand, the competitive environment and government policies. These influences differ from country to country, as do the internal pricing policies of organisations.

Organisational goals and costs

When setting prices in foreign markets, an organisation first determines what it is seeking to accomplish through its international pricing strategy. The firm's goals will vary and change over time, but generally include meeting objectives that maximise its profits, penetrate markets, maintain or achieve improved market share and reinforce the brand image. When first entering a new market, business may set a competitive price point compared to other markets to assist with the implementation of the entry strategy. Once established, the price points may increase to align with or exceed the competition, and to bring the pricing into line with the internal organisational pricing targets.

Consumer demand

The consumers' willingness to pay for a product in a target market sets a benchmark for its price. Consumer demand is a utility of buying power, and integrates taste, attitude, preferences, cultural norms and product substitutes. This manifests as the value that customers place on a given product, which changes from market to market.

Buying power is a key consideration in pricing decisions. Markets in under-developed countries with low per capita incomes are generally far more price sensitive than those in developed economies. To overcome this challenge, businesses target and make their products appeal to a larger volume of consumers; they also make product adjustments to reduce overall prices. To reach a more accessible price point, product modifications include altering the product quality or downsizing the product (producing a smaller volume or fewer units per package). A penetration pricing strategy, where a lower price is set during the early stage, may be useful when a business needs to encourage product trials in a new country to stimulate consumer demand. After the establishment of repeat buying behaviour and brand loyalty, price will play less of a role in the purchase decision.

An organisation's ongoing success depends on its ability to differentiate its products from those of the competition. For example, Australian business KeepCup manufactures reusable environmentally friendly coffee cups (KeepCup n.d.). The managers of KeepCup realised that their distributors in China were selling their products in the Chinese market for three times the Australian retail price. After the initial product launch and promotional offer, the Chinese distributors felt the product

was undervalued and needed to be sold at a premium price point. The lower price point was dissuading the Chinese consumer from purchasing as they felt the product must be of lower quality. Product quality perceptions are of high importance to the target market of specialist coffee drinkers in China. The product with a higher price point commands an improved competitive position and continues to maintain market share in this market segment in China. Another strategy is to develop niche products suitable for underdeveloped markets, by targeting a more affluent consumer and charging a price point that is like the offering in a developed market. Australian and New Zealand wine producers often use this model for wine exports (for example, see www.yellowtailwine.com). A third option is to design a portfolio of branded products which delivers the product to different income levels. Multi-branded portfolios are challenging but play a significant role in delivering profitability in international markets. One example is the international brand Sephora. Sephora is a retail chain of cosmetic stores offering company and international branded cosmetic products for men and women. The store has a portfolio of branded products with different pricing for the range of markets in which they operate (see www.sephora.com).

Competitive environment

Competing in international markets is more challenging compared to domestic markets. Variances in the competitive environment between countries typically lead to inter-regional price disparities for a range of motives. The number of competitors differs from place to place, and in some markets there can be many competitors while in others, the firms enjoy monopoly positions. The nature of the competition varies as well, which means there are global firms that manufacture under different regulations versus the local operators, and private corporations compete against state-owned entities. Additionally, competing in developed countries can be more challenging due to the established advantages held by local companies. While local organisations are not state-owned, they are national advocates and managed appropriately by their native governments. This status brings subsidies or other benefits which enable price reductions that confront the international competition. Finally, businesses may have to compete with counterfeit products in some markets. The presence of these copies may force a business to lower their price.

If the competitive environment in a given market is price sensitive, an organisation may have to absorb the cost of currency appreciation by accepting lower margins to maintain a competitive pricing strategy, despite the product or service being unique. To tackle this situation the organisation must understand how the end user values and evaluates the offering against substitute products.

Government policies

In many nations, government policies direct how prices may be set in that country; these regulations must be adhered to. Governments can control the price directly by setting price floors or price ceilings. International businesses must familiarise themselves with the required import regulations and taxes, and take these into consideration when costing and determining the purchase price they expect consumers to pay for their products. RTAs are a prominent feature of the international environment, and can support and facilitate the market entry pricing. For example, ChAFTA, which came into effect in December 2015, resulted in a sliding scale of tariff reductions on various consumer food products, producing greater opportunities for Australian fresh and processed food manufactures to prosper in the Chinese market (Austrade 2017a). A further example is the GST in the Australian and New Zealand markets. Most goods and services have this tax at each level of transaction through the distribution chain. This tax is payable on all imported items in addition to those produced locally. Some goods and service sectors are exempt from this tax though, so a regulations and policies need to be carefully analysed to check whether payment is necessary.

Managing price escalation

To cover the incremental costs involved in international trade, retail prices in international markets are often much higher than those in the domestic market. This is known as price escalation. Management must determine whether the product offering will be competitive in the foreign market after the consequence of price escalation as compared to the rival product offering. Elements that may impact the price escalation for trade in the foreign market include:

- fluctuations in international currency
- tariffs and changes in FTAs and RTAs
- logistics and distribution costs
- facilitation in-market to manage credit risk, including method of payment
- price controls and local laws.

If the desired international markets are hesitant or not willing to pay the price for the firm's product or service, there are two broad options to mitigating price escalation: identify ways to reduce the export price, or adopt a premium product positioning.

Common tactics to reduce export pricing include modifying components of products, reducing or removing packaging materials, seeking better pricing for input materials from suppliers, shortening credit terms, quoting prices in stable currencies and pursuing strategies which enact prompt inventory turnovers. Areas where organisations may find opportunities to reduce costs to counter price escalation include:

- *rearrange the supply chains:* supply chains and channels are often largely responsible for price escalation, either because of their length (number of intermediaries from production to consumer) or because of excessive margins applied at each point in the chain. Shortening the supply chain is one solution. Alternatively, firms rearrange a channel distribution to deliver cost savings and become more price-competitive. As an example, trading with importers and distributors in a market for your product will encounter price escalation; supermarkets in Asian countries often trade directly with Australian and New Zealand agricultural producers because it makes the landed price of the produce acceptable in the foreign market.

INTERMEDIARY
also known as the middleman; an individual or business that facilitate the sales process between the manufacturer and end user.

- *eliminate costly features:* many organisations manage price escalation by eliminating or making features optional; for example, by offering a no-frills version of the product, or retailers can purchase the core product and then offer a user-pays service for extra optional features rather than having to buy an entire bundle. To reduce the price in the export market, European car manufacturers, such as Peugeot, modify the motor vehicles sold in China by reducing the size of the vehicle's boot while maintaining the product and brand integrity.
- *downsize products:* by offering a smaller version or a lesser amount; for instance, different package sizing or pricing may be arranged. Convenience and shopping goods sold in supermarkets, where consumers are unaware of product differences between countries, often use this approach to reduce costs. As an example, the Cadbury Chocolate brand offers their product range in several Asia–Pacific countries in a variety of sizes. Often in Chinese, South Korean and Japanese markets, the product has smaller size packages, whereas Australian and New Zealand markets demand larger 'family-sized' offerings.

- *manufacture or assemble in a foreign market:* outsourcing the manufacture or assembly of a product line in a foreign market is often the choice for many international businesses. The lower cost of production inputs (such as labour or sources of supply) and the delivery of an improved speed to market often have the effect of lowering the export price. The Zara fashion brand, for example, has retail stores all over the world. When supplying the European market, the brand sources the core inputs for their product lines from the lowest cost providers in Asia and then assembles the final product in an EU country such as Spain. This allows Zara to take advantage of a 'no tariff' fee for product made in the EU and conforms to the ROO (the criteria used to determine where the final product is made) for goods and products.

There have been instances where businesses may decide to withdraw from a foreign market when inflation or pricing regulations are too expensive for the business. However, if a company can improve the management of these challenges, they will gain a competitive advantage by operating at its best terms in the face of existing and new competitors in the long-term.

Anti-dumping and international pricing

In the international trade environment, dumping occurs when a product is sold to a foreign country at a price lower than the accepted normal rate. The normal rate is the comparable domestic price of the good or the cost of production plus a reasonable addition for selling outlays and profit. It is the unfair price discrepancy between markets.

If an organisation sets the product price too aggressively, this may instigate anti-dumping measures including a protectionist tariff that will damage their competitive position. An example of dumping is shipping an excess supply of a product below its manufacturing cost, often to clear a discontinued line. In other cases, the government of the exporter's country may provide a variety of support measures to the exporting firm which lowers the export price of the product. These include direct subsidies, company tax reductions related to the exported product, low interest loans, and free advice and services provided by the exporting nation's overseas offices. Export subsidies and export financial assistance are contentious issues in many countries. They assist exporters to counteract competition, protect against monopolies and increase international trade. For this reason, many countries develop anti-dumping measures. It is important for international businesses to recognise and be aware of anti-dumping laws when determining international pricing strategies.

With increases in FTAs, tariffs have been declining globally over the last 20 to 30 years. This has caused many economies to switch from relying on tariffs to non-tariff barriers, such as anti-dumping laws, to safeguard and provide protections for product pricing. Anti-dumping is one of the few protectionist measures permitted under WTO rules. Before any action is taken against dumped or subsidised goods, the domestic industry involved must demonstrate not only that dumping has occurred but that a financial disadvantage has resulted. A dumping duty is the tax imposed on imported goods to offset the consequences of dumping. An alternative solution to imposing a dumping duty is for the government customs department to accept a price from the exporter that future trade will be at or above a minimum export price point. The Australian Government, at the behest of Australian firms, has a reputation for using anti-dumping laws very rigorously. This takes the form of non-tariff barriers.

Organisations with international businesses follow a range of strategies to minimise exposure to and the risk of having an anti-dumping action taken out against the firm. These include:

- *trading up*: moving away from low-value products by offering higher value items instead through product differentiation.

- *service enhancement*: adding support services to a product or product line to move the focus away from competing solely on price.
- *communication strategies*: developing communication strategies which focus on less price-sensitive products and away from vulnerable products in the company portfolio.
- *strategic alliances*: establishing communication channels with in-market distributors and developing cooperative distribution arrangements.

Ascertaining the optimum pricing strategy for international markets is challenging. The principal argument to pursuing an international pricing strategy is that a standardised approach for all markets may not work in all countries. Some markets have specific desires or are more value focused than others. Additionally, a firm's products generally may be more accepted in a market than another market. Determining in which market a product will be popular is the first challenge, followed by focusing on pricing that will allow the product to gain consumer acceptance and achieve a sustainable market position.

MULTIPLE-CHOICE QUESTION

Understanding networks and international distribution

Distribution and supply-chain networks provide the essential links that connect sellers with buyers. When international businesses commence trading across borders, the sourcing, shipping, and supply of raw materials and components among a range of manufacturing sites needs to occur economically and at reliable rates. Simultaneously, the companies need to ensure timely shipping, and the supply of fully completed goods to businesses and consumers in multiple markets around the world. Today, shorter product life cycles, sophisticated international mergers and acquisitions, and the development of special economic zones, and FTAs makes the actual movement of products key to successfully planning international sourcing and distribution strategies.

Distribution refers to the movement of a business' products to its customers. The main activities associated with this undertaking are channel selection and physical distribution, including inventory control, warehousing, materials handling, logistics, transportation and customer service. This section examines international distribution channels and the issues that surround them, the change of retail market focus, the choice of distribution partners, and the management of relationships and networks.

Distribution channels

The consumer and industrial products that MNEs trade across and in markets are all subject to some form of distribution process. For an organisation to realise its business objectives, the products must be accessible to the target markets at a viable and reasonable price. An organisation cannot do this if the distribution structures are rigid, uneconomical and arduous. Designing dependable and well-organised worldwide supply channels can be one of the most problematics tasks for a firm to face. Channel design refers to the length and width of the channel; in the Asia–Pacific region, where local customers, language and level of modernity are remarkably diverse, channels tend to be wide and lengthy. Access to local distributors who understand a company's product and can navigate the often fragmented, underdeveloped and disorganised supply lines and networks is consequently essential.

CHANNEL DESIGN the length and width of a distribution channel.

Although the functions of physical supply are common, the business environment influences the nature of distribution systems in a market. Channel design is impacted in each country by

factors such as tradition, culture, economic infrastructure, land ownership, topography, tariffs and transport costs. Organisations have two broad options to configure their international distribution system when entering a foreign market.

- Supply direct to the customer in a foreign market by investing directly or co-investing in a local sales and distribution entity, which provides bricks-and-mortar stores and supplies via the internet.
- Engage, via contracts or agreements, appropriate in-country independent intermediaries at the local level to act as agents for the organisation.

There is no standard or one-size-fits-all approach to channel design. An organisation may have a different channel design for different markets. Regardless of the method used, before engaging channel members, international expansion tactics need to consider the 10 Cs: consumers, culture of the market, competitors, company objectives, capital available, costs, coverage of the market, control of the supply chain, continuity of supply chains and communication methods.

Consumers

The demographic, geographic and physiographic features of the target market are key influencers in forming the channel design. Understanding the composition of the target audience, why they purchase product, and how, when and where they purchase is essential. The same product could have two different channels of distribution because of consumers' buying behaviours. For example, in China, retailers purchase imported fresh fruit in a traditional supply channel, online auction sites such as Tmall and WeChat trade imported fruit, and it can be purchased directly by consumers and delivered to their homes or places of work as well.

Culture of the market

The structure of existing channels and the distribution culture in each market varies significantly and so an MNE needs to analyse and understand the networks thoroughly. Legislation differs widely in overseas markets and forms an essential component of some distribution centres. Some countries require market agents of fully imported products to be registered and there may be quotas for the number of agents allowed within a given sector. Language translation and in-market interpretation challenges require a planned process; engaging agents to deal with the issues in the chain is common.

Competitors

Often, the main trading competitors only use one channel to distribute through the supply chain in a country or region. This situation is prevalent in the Asia–Pacific region. In this case, the international business must assess and consider supply structure to be effective and efficient. An alternative strategy for the MNE, is to use a completely different distribution method to create competitive advantage. For example, Walmart's operations in Asia required retailers to vertically integrate their supply chains and, in some situations, develop collaborative relationships with intermediaries to shore up distribution.

Company objectives

The corporate goals of the organisation can sometimes conflict with the optimal channel design required for a market. The company must strike a balance between the ability to meet the corporate economic goals and creating a channel that delivers stability and control, and can be realistically managed. For example, the café franchise Gloria Jean's Coffees attempted to enter the Chinese market by opening many stores to achieve timely profitability but the company failed. This type of market entry strategy must be tempered with the reality of controlling large volumes, and the logistics of implementing a product offering which involves systems, people and food products.

Capital available

An organisation's financial position often determines the type and basis of its channel relationships. An organisation with strong financials can usually affect the control in channels or even own them outright. Other factors influencing the chosen approach include the type of intermediaries to be engaged in a channel, inventory management, loans and credit, selling on consignment and required training.

Costs

Costs relate to the expenditure incurred to maintain the channel from its outset; costs encompass trading margins, sales mark-ups and payments to agents, which may inflate the sale price in an overseas market. Direct distribution by an organisation can allow complete control over all elements in the channel and assist in maintaining costs. Distribution costs will naturally change over the life cycle of the product.

Coverage of the market

Market coverage is the number of market segments or geographic areas where products are traded. Although market dominance may be an organisation's objective in a foreign market, it is not always possible or desirable. In several countries in the Asia–Pacific region, only a few cities in the country may contain the most affluent consumers and sustainable market segments. A company may need several intermediates in a range of channels to achieve a full representation in the market.

Control of the supply chain

Engaging intermediaries inevitably leads to the loss of some control over the distribution of a company's products. A longer channel, involving more intermediaries, further engenders a greater loss of control, particularly in relation to end price, type of retail outlets, required inventory levels and associated promotional activities. If the organisation seeks to maintain control, then developing its own controlled distribution system is necessary.

Continuity of supply chains

Designing a channel with a long-term view in mind is paramount. Many international businesses have made the mistake of having a short-sighted view of trading in foreign markets. Continuity of supply requires businesses to adopt a proactive rather than a reactive perspective, develop rapport with market agents and nurture longer term relationships with supply-chain intermediaries.

Communication methods

Two-way communication is the key to successful business dealings. This includes sharing the organisation's objectives with distributors and negotiating conflict resolution quickly when required. Overall, open, transparent and regular communication supports the successful accomplishment of a distribution strategy.

One element does not dominate another when configuring a global distribution channel strategy. A channel with the appropriate coverage and within minimal costs is the desired consequence; however, balance and comprise is usually needed. The focus for channel choice is on the design that will deliver the greatest returns, complement the organisation's objectives and provide an operational model that performs.

The face of product distribution that consumers interact with the most is the retail store, whether it is bricks and mortar or online. International retailers are now some of the largest organisations and, in terms of global reach, often rival or exceed the size of those that are solely manufacturing businesses. Retailing involves well-established, in-house activities such as store inventory administration (procurement and supply), product ranging and promotional events, and customer service management including relationship-building programs. Historically, retailers used a push strategy to encourage consumer purchasing and store engagement. Today, consumers drive retail decisions and this approach is known as a pull strategy.

In its 2017 annual report, the Global Retail Development Index (GRDI) identified the top 10 regions that offer long term opportunities for retailing (AT Kearney 2017). Five of the top 10 countries were from Asia: India, China, Malaysia, Vietnam and Indonesia (see Table 10.1).

TABLE 10.1 Global Retail Development Index, 2017

2017 Rank	Country	GRDI score	Population (millions)	GDP per capita (PPP)	National retail sales (US$ billion)
1	India	71.7	1329	6658	1071
2	China	70.4	1378	15424	3128
3	Malaysia	60.9	31	27234	92
4	Turkey	59.8	80	21147	241
5	United Arab Emirates	59.4	9	67696	73
6	Vietnam	56.1	93	6422	90
7	Morocco	56.1	35	8360	40
8	Indonesia	55.9	259	11699	350
9	Peru	54.0	32	13019	61
10	Columbia	53.6	49	14162	90

Source: Adapted with permission from AT Kearney 2017

The GRDI reveals, in terms of mass and sheer market force, the Asian region is driving the momentum in retail development and the expansion of branded food and beverage products, personal care goods, and fashion and luxury items. Telecommunications is one category changing the face of retailing. Mobile phones increased globally in 2017 by 121 per cent in India, 192 per cent in China and 151 per cent in Vietnam (AT Kearney 2017). In most markets, telecommunications and online shopping are altering the way international businesses address market entry decisions, channel design, retail marketing and connection with consumers.

Selecting partners and managing relationships and networks

Once the design of the channel has been determined, the MNE needs to search for and engage intermediaries with defined roles. The company's options are linked to its desired business objectives, and overall philosophy towards distributors and agents; the organisation will align its planned approach to its new direct or indirect foreign market accordingly, and may choose to work with one or more agents or merchandise intermediaries.

The difference between an agent and a merchandise intermediary relates to the ownership of goods. A representative does not take title over the goods, but rather supplies the goods on behalf of the exporting organisation in exchange for a fee or percentage of the transaction value. Traders or agents hold title over the products and usually operate as independent, fully registered businesses in the foreign country. Both agents and merchandisers represent the interests of an organisation in a foreign market. Since they are the in-market 'face' of the organisation, it is critical that the MNE chooses an intermediary in a formal way, like the engagement of its staff and contractors in the home country.

Most government agencies and in-country embassies have support services to assist organisations in identifying suitable and bona fide representatives in a foreign market. Globaltrade.net is one example of a private company that supplies trade service information. The types of services offered are access to sales agents, freight forwarders, sourcing services, market research, market entry, distributors, customs brokers, trade compliance and accounting.

The selection and appointment of an intermediary is often challenging. To ensure the decision is accurate and objective, MNEs should apply screening criteria to assess potential agents on a market-by-market basis. Three screening questions to review potential agents used by a range of organisations include:

1. customer relationship experience
   a. What is the businesses' local market share relative to others?
   b. How well positioned are they to reach the firm's market entry objectives?
   c. What growth has the business demonstrated over the last 5- and 10-year periods?
2. product and category knowledge
   a. Is the business seen by local customers as a leader in the category?
   b. Is the business able to show expert technical knowledge for current and potential future product category offerings?
3. sales and trade capabilities
   a. Have the current contractors with the agent or distributor realised significant sales growth in the market in recent years?
   b. Does the business have the capacity to provide the desired levels of customer reach and relationship management that the company wants?

After identifying the right partners, the organisation must collaboratively develop appropriate incentives that encourage the agents to focus on their products, customers, regions and consumers to achieve success. Agents are like a company's employees and customers in that they represent the company's brand and market their items. Ensuring open and transparent communication and operating methods is the key to achieving successful partnerships. Differences in expectations can lead to channel conflicts. To avoid this negative behaviour, organisations must decisively manage the relationship with the intention of creating harmonious relations underpinned by cooperation, open communication and trust to earn the loyalty of the partner.

The profit margin agreed to by the organisation and the agent is the crucial factor in the relationship. Once a reasonable margin has been determined, the parties can negotiate and settle their partnership arrangement. Improvements to partnership arrangements include:

- *a joint organisational vision, aims and objectives*; this sharing creates a link, provides a common goal and keeps the interest of agents in the partnership.
- *sharing of culture and traditions by both partners*; by maintaining a genuine interest in the agent and the foreign market, organisations can avoid cultural misunderstandings, appreciate nuances and minimise disagreements.
- *a focus on capacity building*; many agents manage several product lines, often across a range of in-country regions. In some cases, they may not have in-depth experience, but capacity building improves knowledge and capabilities in the foreign market, and creates mutual benefit.
- *dedicated support materials (internal and external use)*; organisations should develop a range of support materials such as frequently asked questions (FAQs), product brochures, marketing collateral, sales training videos and podcasts, all accessible in local languages and available online where possible.
- *developing a customer or consumer feedback system*; this activity is vital to create a win-win situation for the partnership. The MNE's understanding from the customer or consumer perspective is vital to improving existing products and developing an innovation pipeline for new products and services.

Organisations that have committed arrangements with their agents have greater market intelligence, which rewards and supports their business growth. Therefore, garnering greater agent assistance, often through product launches and end-buyer loyalties, reduces an agent's interest in engaging with competitor brands. Agents in a committed partnership will tend to seek out opportunities to expand the current product line and deliver an elevated level of performance by working with the organisation, rather than operating independently or at disinterested levels.

Identifying a foreign agent takes time and resources, but an efficient foreign agent brings faster revenue in a more secure manner. Building a long-term relationship is also critical to ensure the distribution of the organisation's product offering to the market. The most prosperous international businesses will always consider the goal of the partnership; that is, the outcomes sought, who to partner with and how the arrangement can benefit both parties.

MULTIPLE-CHOICE QUESTION

SPOTLIGHT 10.2

International franchising expansion: Australian retailers venturing abroad

Franchising is an established, sophisticated industry in Australia. The economic impact of franchising is substantial and growing. It is hard to think of take-away food, petrol stations and stores in shopping centres without thinking of a known franchise. The Franchise Council of Australia estimates there are over 1160 franchise brands and over 79 000 franchise units in Australia. Increasing numbers of Australian franchises are successfully taking their systems overseas through international service channels. Fast-food and café chains dominate this group. The Coffee Club has over 400 stores across Australia, New Zealand, Thailand, Malaysia, Indonesia, the Maldives, Dubai and Abu Dhabi. Foodco, owner of franchises Muffin Break, Dreamy Donuts and Jamaica Blue, has set up Jamaica Blue operations extensively in South-East Asia, and Muffin Break outlets across New Zealand, UK and India. Food

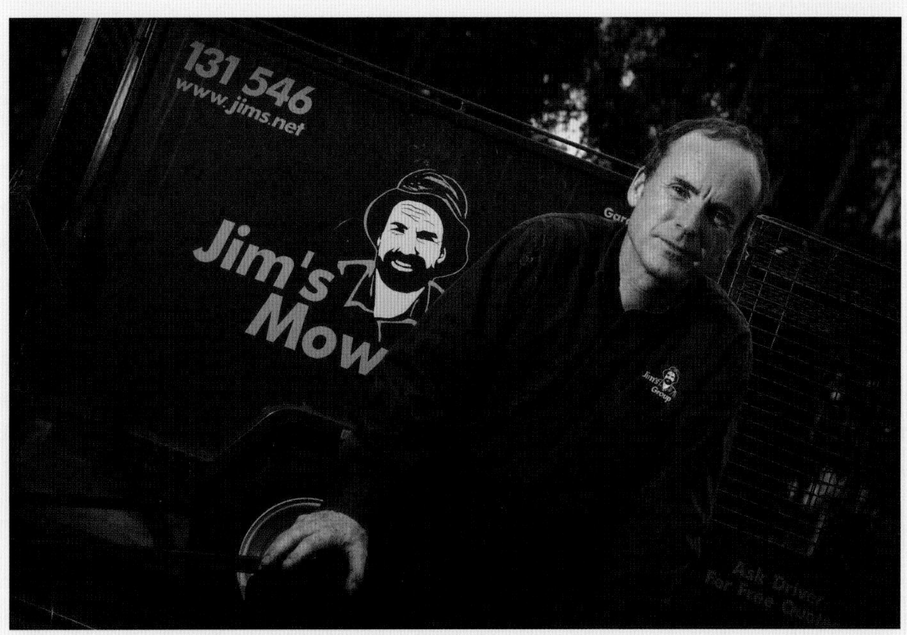

FIGURE 10.1 Jim Penman, owner of Jim's Group

chain, Guzman y Gomez, launched in Sydney in 2006, has 92 stores across Australia; the chain launched in Japan in 2015 and recently in Singapore.

Two prime examples of Australian home-maintenance franchise brands expanding into overseas markets are Poolwerx, a pool cleaning franchise, and Gutter-Vac, a gutter cleaning service. Utilising retail stores and mobile service vans, Poolwerx has plans to launch in the Sun Belt region of the US. Gutter-Vac is looking to the deciduous climates of Europe and the UK to tap into the high demand for gutter cleaning services that are there.

Sources: ANZ Business Chief 2016; Franchise Council of Australia 2018

QUESTIONS

1. Explain why franchising would be an attractive business model for people seeking to own a small business.
2. What type of information should the prospective buyer ask for when buying an international franchise?

SPOTLIGHT QUESTIONS

Promoting products in international markets

Communicating in international markets requires considerable prior planning. Determining the appropriate combination of promotional tools for each market is vital. The promotional mix may include advertising, product promotions and personal selling, social media and public relations or a combination of diverse options. The purpose of the promotional strategy is to reach the desired target market and convey the 'brand story'; this helps to connect with existing customers and attract new consumers to the product or service. The method of approach by a business will depend on the target audience, the product, the access to and availability of in-market resources, and the organisation's own objectives.

Advertising

Organisations selling the same product in multiple markets will choose between standardising or adapting advertising content to connect with target audiences. Standardising refers to one or more of the advertising elements and media campaign being kept the same. Whether to standardise or adapt can create heated discussions between firms and their advertising agencies. A truly global advertising campaign is uniform in nature. That means the message and the visuals are consistent and, if necessary, only minor changes are made in the content to conform to local policies or to make the advertising more engaging to target audiences; for example, a campaign has its spoken commentary in local accents.

There are many instances of standardisation failing. This results from international campaigns not being sensitive to social structures, failing to recognise national and regional cultures, misunderstanding communication styles, lacking media availability and access, misjudging legal constraints, and miscalculating production costs.

Media strategies

The choice of media in a new or existing foreign market is critical for an MNE. The organisation formulates a media strategy, selects a choice of mediums and prepares a timetable known as a media schedule.

Media spend globally is vast. In 2018, US$557 billion was predicted to be spent on advertising, including television, transit advertising (taxis, buses, trains and airlines), outdoors (bus stops, highway and transit billboards), commercial leasing buildings (toilets and lifts), and online (Statista 2018b). The top five corporate advertising brands in 2016 were Procter & Gamble, Samsung, Nestlé, Unilever and L'Oréal (AdBrands 2016).

The advertising spend in the Asia–Pacific is forecast to hold 33.4 per cent of global spend by 2019, compared to 32.1 per cent realised in 2016 (Yu 2017). The region will remain central to global advertising spending, contributing an estimated 43 per cent of expected growth. China and Japan are the second and third highest global spenders for advertising after the US (Statista 2018b).

In several markets, decisions made about media content are more important than other creative aspects of the advertising strategy. For example, in Japan, the strength in media buying is fundamental, given there is a scarce supply of advertising space in the country. International media planners need to overcome a wide range of issues. The media landscape can vary radically between countries or in some cases been regions within the one country. For instance, differences in media infrastructure may exist within a country in terms of media availability, accessibility, costing, literacy levels, and media engagement habits (PWC 2014). The media landscape is dynamic. The emergence of the digital age and the advancement of technology have meant that the nature and function of media in our society continues to change (Kaul 2012). Barriers to entry have been lowered, distribution has broadened the audience width and media production has been democratised in some countries. This new environment provides extra competition for media mediums such as television, radio, news publishing, and film and video production.

Typically, in broadcast media, advertising relies heavily on international or regional media networks. Truly global campaigns are uncommon as complete uniformity is difficult to achieve. For example, language and cultural nuances across markets, variances in media infrastructure and availability, and legal differences between countries, do not support a complete uniformity in content and delivery across markets.

Over the past five years, digital media use has grown at more than one-third, year on year. The US$40 billion paid for digital advertising in China in 2016, represented 40 per cent of its total media spend. In 2017, digital media accounted for the largest share, with 42.3 per cent of advertising budgets in the Asia–Pacific region, ahead of television with 32.5 per cent share (Statista 2018b). For the first time since measurements have been collected, digital media has surpassed mainstream television sales to become the number one category for advertising revenues, passing the US$200 billion level. According to Magna Global projections, television advertising budgets will continue to lose share to digital choices through to 2021 (Yu 2017). In addition to personal computers, mobile phones and interactive television content also continue to increase in relevance. Apps dominated Asia, with mobile advertising spending at over US$54 billion; the region now leads the global advertising spend growth. In the digital sector, the majority of advertising sales (54 per cent) are generated by impressions and clicks on mobile devices (eMarketer 2017). By 2021, the mobile market is anticipated to grow to a 77 per cent share of digital, with a 37 per cent share of total media advertising investment (eMarketer 2017).

Media regulations vary from country to country. While the Asia–Pacific region certainly shares many similarities with other regions, there are also some evident differences. The requirements for separation between programs and advertisements is almost a universal requirement. Local regulations include the submission of advertisements for approval as well as conformity with local content guidelines and requirements. For example, the Chinese government exercises strict control over television and radio content, and its industry. The Chinese regulator, SARFT, has placed a total ban of advertising on several products including tobacco items, prescription drugs, chat-room services, and milk products that contain the words 'breast milk substitute'. In China, there are strict guidelines on the amount and scheduling of advertising for alcohol, and in Malaysia alcohol advertising is highly regulated. In Indonesia, regulation stipulates that, where possible, media agencies must only use domestic actors and locations for filming and the preparation of television and radio advertisements. In South Korea, the Communications Standards Commission (KOCSC) implements rigid guidelines and prohibits the broadcast of advertisements in a number of categories, including bars with female entertainment, dating services, gambling, fortified milk and milk powder, baby bottles and teats, fundraising, and unregistered consumer financial services (Baker & McKenzie 2012).

International media agencies provide a variety of services, domestically and internationally, and typically offer expertise in strategic planning, media research, client servicing, media negotiations, media buying and performance tracking. These agencies collaborate with the lead organisation, the in-market agents and local agencies undertaking promotional activities for the product.

Promoting and selling

Several organisations have internal capacity to perform a full range of promotional activities in their home market. In most cases, however, firms rely on the outside expertise of advertising and media agencies and promotions-related companies to assist in international markets. Large international media agencies, such as Ogilvy and MRM//McCann, have regional offices offering local knowledge as a useful resource. Alternatively, in-country agencies may be more advantageous due to their expertise in the local market, understanding of the local regulatory situation and cultural nuances.

Promotions that do not involve advertising or publicity are known as sales promotions. Consumer-oriented sales promotions include instore merchandising efforts through sampling methods, product premiums, competitions, consumer education and demonstration activities, product coupons and discounts and direct mail. Sales promotions directed at intermediaries or in-market agents are known as trade promotions, and include activities such as trade shows and exhibits, trade discounts, cooperative promotions and incentives. These are inherently less global in nature and tailored more to a specific market to achieve a specific outcome, such as an increased movement of product, greater market share or an introduction of a new product offering. There are occasions where firms develop a global focus for promotional activities and collaborate with several agents to achieve an international reach; examples of this might include sporting events such as the FIFA World Cup and the Olympic Games; product placement in mainstream movies like Disney and Pixar animations; cause marketing such as Earth Hour; and support for music, entertainment and other touring groups.

One type of promotional activity is product placement, which involves placing branded products into the action or an element of a movie, video or television program. The notion is to align the product and brand with the content in the production. The target audience then sees the product use and the brand profile from an engagement perspective. This is especially applicable for young and impressionable target market segments. There are numerous high-profile examples which showcase this type of promotional activity. For example, in a 2012 James Bond movie, the script broke with tradition and instead of Bond consuming his usual Martini, 'shaken not stirred', he opted for a Heineken beer. The US movie franchise, *Transformers*, has attracted a few brands seeking to showcase their products. For example, Bumblebee, a transforming 1976 and 2006 Chevrolet Camaro, is a walking, talking advertisement for General Motors. Product placement can connect with consumers, increase product recall, and improve brand salience (consumer's ability to recall a brand). Furthermore, research reveals that product placement affects viewers on both a conscious level and a subconscious level. However, businesses need guidance to ensure the product placement is appropriate and aligned to the brand image. If the placement is too obvious or is inconsistent with the 'brand story', a negative consumer connection with the product and the brand can result. For the same reasons, many luxury goods companies offer clothing, shoes, and accessories for actors and style icons to wear during awards and other high-profile events to highlight their brand. Media outlets providing content for online and in-print publications circulate the images to garner consumer support and encourage purchase.

Promoting and selling in Asia is dynamic. There are several proven suggestions for promoting in these market, such as:

- identifying a key opinion leader as an endorser for the product or brand
- creating availability of detailed product information with ease of access, for example QR codes
- generating genuine consumer reviews to start consumer dialog, and to build peer support and trust for the product and brand
- identifying the markets where consumers are willing to pay a price premium for a quality international product because of high concern for safety or product choice
- acknowledging the markets where price competitiveness is critical and consumers are not willing to pay a price premium
- knowing the local terminology for the product when designing the promotion; for example, in the UK, 'trousers' is used for the same item of clothing known as 'pants' in the US and Australia

- understanding consumer expectations related to product delivery. Consumers in Asia have myriad choices of online and traditional suppliers, with a range of promotional offers for product delivery and payment terms to deliver products on time.

Promotions and selling are a key part of the first stage of market entry efforts; in many cases promotion activities involve direct selling. In the preliminary stages of internationalisation, businesses often rely heavily on personal contact. In some cases, chiefly with high-priced and premium items such as industrial goods and medical equipment, the best interest for the company lies in establishing a solid base of dealerships staffed by local people. Direct selling has been particularly successful in Asia–Pacific countries partly because of the culture of business relationships. With the advancement of methods of communication and digital technology, MNEs are implementing direct selling more easily than ever before. The initial stages to assess and review a new market opportunity are completed online and, when approved, the business can travel to the destination to confirm and finalise arrangements with in-market partners.

Public relations

The importance of corporate communications in an interconnected world is a fundamental consideration for organisations trading in international and domestic markets. Public relations and social media activities involve organisations focusing on approaches to influence their stakeholders externally (such as agents, customers and consumers) and internally (like staff, suppliers and consultants). MNEs do this via traditional public relations efforts, publicity and attracting the attention of governments through newsworthy stories. Seeking to influence government policy is known as lobbying.

Internal communication is fundamental, especially in large international organisations where creating and sharing company messages form a foundation for the corporate culture. Gumtree, the Australian online trading organisation, has a teamwork culture and strives to achieve workplace balance for young technology specialists and marketers. The company provides a fun environment while working with modern agile technology systems, and offers the benefits of share ownership in the parent company, eBay, for its employees. Externally, the firm is highly corporate with the use of brands, symbols, colours and customer relationship programs, consistently delivered through their online presence.

A substantial part of public relations is to assist global organisations that are criticised for business activities ranging from offshore production to establishing manufacturing sites in developing countries. Whether the business operation is desirable or undesirable is debated in the media by anti-globalisation campaigners, researchers, academics and government officials. Organisations are accountable and obliged to respond, which requires their preparation of an appropriate response. In Asia, for example, in several countries Shell has developed community programs such as the collaboration with Earthwatch to offer employees the opportunity to contribute to conservation efforts around the globe. At Coca-Cola, the company is committed to giving back 1.0 per cent of the yearly operating income. This commitment is made through the Coca-Cola Foundation providing more than US$115 million each year to directly benefit nearly over 250 organisations in more than 60 countries (see www.coca-colacompany.com).

In general, a firm requires public relations to anticipate, respond to and counteract criticisms against the organisation. The complaints may be against the organisation or about the products and services that the business offers. Criticisms can also be directed towards a business' operations in a given country or region. For example, the detaining and jailing of Crown Hotel and its casino staff from Australia and Hong Kong for promoting gambling in mainland China was a public relations challenge for the organisation. The legal position by the Chinese government was clear: the promotion of gambling is not permitted. Nineteen Crown employees pleaded guilty and although the defence contended that the employees were promoting hotel packages, the Chinese court did not accept this position and ruled that the employees were promoting gambling and should face the penalty of jail time.

Some cases have been about ethical and trading conduct. In Australia, the franchise convenience store chain company, 7-Eleven, used exploitative and illegal work practices to decrease instore workforce costs. Employees were paid less than half the national legal minimum wage. Students and international workers were especially targeted. The 7-Eleven Chairman, Russ Withers, and the CEO, Warren Wilmot, resigned based on the legal review of the company.

Misrepresenting product quality, such as in the case of Volkswagen, is unethical and potentially illegal, and creates a public relations challenge. In late 2015, German car manufacturer, Volkswagen, was brought to trial over the installation of software in its cars that falsely guaranteed vehicles passed emission tests. Over a seven-year period this involved 11 million cars. The CEO, Martin Winterkorn, was forced to resign over the matter and is now facing possible criminal charges.

Marketing performance metrics

Entering and maintaining business operations in foreign markets requires a sizeable investment for an organisation. Therefore, MNEs rely on market performance measurements to evaluate the success of their planned activities. The marketing metrics are systematically planned, and tied to the goals and objectives of the firm (Wyner 2014). Organisations use various methods to evaluate market performance. Early measurements, when entering a foreign market, will assist the organisation through evaluation, control and ongoing monitoring. Some of the most common metrics captured in the early internationalisation phase include: early market traction, conversion rates, competitive account wins, top-line results incorporating revenue, bookings, capital efficiency, and partner and channel performance.

Marketing performance goals should be at the centre of strategy development, resource allocation and execution of key operational initiatives. The development of performance metrics requires careful consideration. The operational goals should be both measurable and applicable to business performance. MNEs need to systematically review a range of potential measures and place focus on those that have a demonstrated relationship to business performance goals. Businesses use several different methodologies to measure marketing performance and to monitor commercial performance.

Marketing metrics provide insight to monitor and improve several operational elements: net sales, sales volume and value; number bookings or registrations; advertising reach and frequency; online hits, page turns and click throughs; and level of brand awareness. The benefits to the organisation accrued through monitoring and evaluation metrics include:

- providing the operational team with accurate market information to evaluate marketing assets (such as brand equity and the level of effectiveness among target audiences)
- offering an understanding of operational progress linked to annual goals and allowing for change if required

- validating how market revenues generate and contribute to organisational goals
- establishing a regular process to review and reflect, based on new insights to foster a pattern of continuous improvement
- determining what areas of the marketing mix need modification or improvement to increase business performance
- gaining executive support and positive reinforcement for continued growth
- building competitive intelligence and ability to anticipate target market reactions to fresh marketing strategies.

The resources required to build and maintain an organisational measurement infrastructure are often some of the largest line items in a marketing budget. As new media produces new measurement options for elements such as brand buzz from online discussions, and eye-tracking captured from online social media and mobile application apps, it becomes highly likely that the structure itself must be adapted to stay relevant to organisations. It is especially difficult to draw accurate comparisons over time while the nature of the measures themselves may change. There is a reasonable need to assess the reliability and validity of new measures as they emerge, and the extent to which they are related to established measures such as brand equity and sales. There is little value in tracking buzz ratings unless there is a viable link to business performance. MNEs should consider marketing performance measures from the end-buyer perspective and link the information to their marketing operations. Selecting the right measures focuses management's attention on what operational goals should be the highest priority.

After an MNE's key performance measures are developed, consistency within the instruments is crucial for the information to be valuable and reliable. Researchers may develop a common scale to evaluate performance metrics to ensure business activities have appropriate evaluations among brands and over different time periods. These different measurements, which evaluate communications, competitors and markets, can present challenges for direct assessments. Businesses generally want to see where their marketing plans are performing well and where operational adjustments are required so they use formalised methodologies, and regular capturing and monitoring of this type of information. Long-term observations and studies provide valid insights, and highlight critical control points in the firm's marketing operations. Without the capability to measure how marketing investments contribute to overall organisational value, managers are unable to make the critical trade-offs, re-allocations and investment decisions required to remain competitive in today's dynamic and rapidly changing international markets.

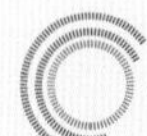

SPOTLIGHT 10.3

Measuring for success: how does Google Analytics work?

Measurement is critical to international marketing success. Without measurement of performance, improvement is impossible, so an organisation's website should encompass this kind of evaluation. Google Analytics (GA) has become the world's most popular web analytics tool. Installed on over 10 million websites, it has quickly become the industry standard for web analytics (Astek 2017). GA's popularity is not only because it is simple to set up, but also because it is a free and powerful platform

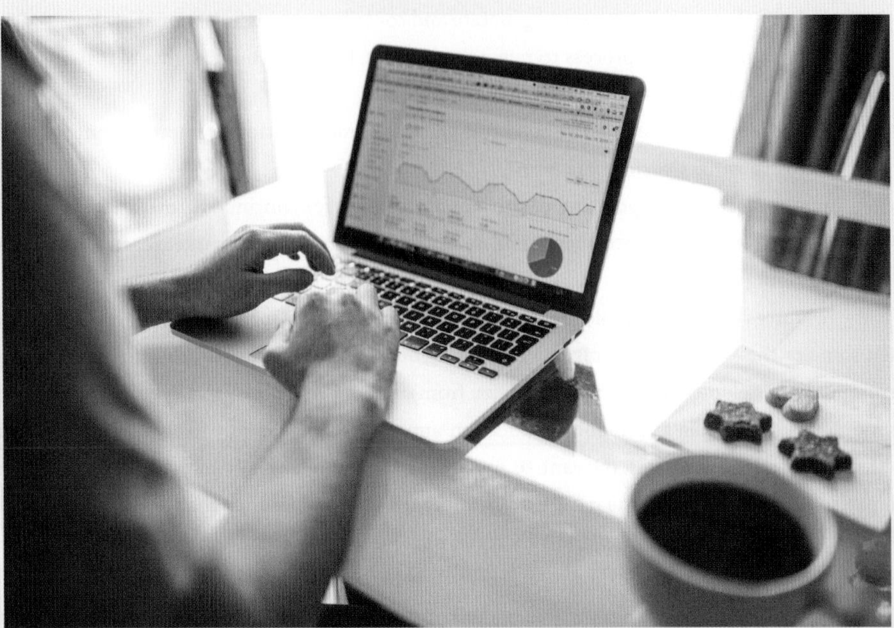

FIGURE 10.2 Real-time Google Analytics

which provides the tools to measure site traffic, conversions, advertising performance and how people interact with an organisation's website. GA constructs a complete picture of an organisation's audience and their needs, at any point of the purchase pathway, through providing the necessary insights that lead to a website's success.

With over 130 reports, and an additional 100 custom reports available for delivery on a daily, weekly or monthly basis, GA can provide measurement solutions across areas that include revenues and costs, traffic sources, campaign performances, conversion rates, click-through rates as well as specific tactic performance. The dashboard interface is easy to access, share and print, and allows a single view of individual reports in graph and chart form, enabling marketers to focus on the work rather than reviewing the analytics.

SPOTLIGHT QUESTIONS

QUESTIONS

1. How can Google Analytics assist with improvements in online content?
2. What are the three ABCs Google Analytics can categorise your data into?

Summary

Learning objective 1: Recognise the key elements in international marketing decisions.

Once the organisation identifies and confirms the market or markets, its operational planning commences. The first step an MNE considers is its product offering and marketing mix. A recurring issue for international business managers is the extent that a business should standardise its marketing elements, product, price, distribution approach and promotion, including advertising, personal selling, and public relations. An international business manager also needs to consider if a tailored approach is necessary in a market to deliver optimal results in the internationalisation process. The final aspect for the manager to scrutinise is the monitoring and evaluation of the international marketing strategies devised.

Learning objective 2: Recognise the drivers of international business pricing.

Product pricing strategies can make or break an organisation's export efforts. One of the biggest obstacles for firms to overcome is how to set and maintain pricing across different countries. Pricing in an international environment is considerably more complicated than in a domestic market. A range of factors are considered when setting prices for the same product in different countries, including government regulations, the consumers' willingness to pay, and the additional costs involved in operating abroad. When determining the pricing strategy in international markets, it is critical to understand the price floor (the amount of expenditure incurred to purchase that product or to manufacture the product) and the market price (the amount the good is bought or purchased for by the market).

Learning objective 3: Understand international distribution and networks.

Distribution and supply-chain networks provide the essential links that connect sellers with buyers. When international businesses commence trading across borders, the sourcing, shipping and supply of raw materials and components, among a range of manufacturing sites, needs to occur economically and at reliable rates. Simultaneously, the timely shipping and supply of finished goods to customers and consumers in multiple markets around the world is required. Distribution refers to the movement of a business's products to its customers. The main activities associated with this undertaking is channel selection and the physical distribution including inventory control, warehousing, materials handling, logistics, transportation and customer service.

Learning objective 4: Appreciate promotional issues and challenges in international markets.

Communicating in international markets requires considerable planning. Determining the appropriate combination of promotional tools for each market is vital. The promotional mix may include advertising, product promotions and personal selling and public relations, or a combination of all options. The purpose of the promotional strategy is to reach the desired target market and convey the 'brand story' with a view to connecting with existing customers and attracting new consumers to the product or service. The method of approach will depend on the target audience, the product, the access to and availability of in-market resources, and the organisation's own objectives.

Learning objective 5: Realise the benefits of evaluating marketing performance metrics.
Entering and maintaining business operations in foreign markets requires a sizeable investment from an organisation. A business needs market performance measurements to evaluate the success of its planned activities. Organisations use various methods to evaluate market performance. Early measurements when entering a foreign market will assist the organisation through evaluation, control and ongoing monitoring. Some of the most common metrics captured in the early internationalisation phase include early market traction, conversion rates, competitive account wins, top-line results incorporating revenue, bookings, capital efficiency, and partner and channel performance.

USEFUL WEBSITES

Revision questions

REVISION QUESTIONS

1. What elements of the marketing mix does an MNE need to consider when planning an international marketing strategy and why?
2. Organisations that want to enter foreign markets follow a range of strategies to minimise exposure and risk to anti-dumping actions being taken out against them. Explain two of these strategies.
3. Define and explain the concept of distribution in a marketing channel.
4. Describe sales promotion and list four types of its activities.
5. What is the value of marketing metrics for an international organisation? Provide some examples.

R&D activities

R&D ACTIVITIES

1. Japan's domestic food-sufficiency supplies are low and the situation is complex. Put simply, Japan is unable to produce enough food domestically to supply their people. Consider how trade agreements are assisting Australia to export fresh and packaged food products to Japan. What examples of international marketing opportunities are there and how are these supported by government interventions?
2. AT Kearney prepares the annual GRDI as discussed in this chapter. Review the latest report and identify the current global retail trends. Which sectors are growing in demand and which are falling? Prepare an analysis and presentation showing the current global retail situation.
3. The opening vignette highlights the role of social marketing in ADB's strategy in helping developing markets. Visit the ADB website (www.adb.org) and identify the main elements of its strategies. Discuss and provide examples of how these strategies might assist developing economies.

IB MASTERCLASS

The dual-system model: Dell's distribution strategy in China

A US-college student, Michael Dell, founded Dell in 1984. It is famous for its direct sale to end-user model, which operates in contrast to the traditional supply chain of manufacturer to dealer, or distributor to end user. Dell aimed to deal directly with the end user via telephone or fax, and later online, to reduce costs, understand consumer needs and manage inventory closely to provide personal computers (PCs) specifically designed for end-user requirements. The success of Dell's direct sales model was phenomenal, as the company's annual sales amounted to US$60 million by the end of 1986, just two years after its inception.

The issue for Dell was whether its famous direct sales model would achieve similar levels of success in an international context, particularly with the company's planned entry into China in the early 1990s. Despite Dell's corporate philosophy of rejecting the traditional indirect sales model, given the complexities of navigating and functioning in the Chinese market environment, Dell began initial operations using an indirect sales model. However, Dell was able to adapt its premier supply-chain method into a dual-system model that offered both direct sales methods and supply through a chain of distributors. Dell's willingness to adapt and evolve its preferred sales methods has been fundamental to the company's success in the Chinese market despite periods of achievement and setbacks.

Characteristics of mainland China's PC market

Based on its population size and continued economic growth, China presents as a potentially lucrative large-size market for international companies. The PC market in China, not surprisingly, expanded considerably during the mid-1990s: sales increased from RMB ¥7.6 billion in 1990 to RMB ¥66.2 billion in 1996 (Buchel & Raub 1999, p. 51). By 1998, China was the fifth-largest PC market in the world, behind only the US, Japan, Germany and the UK.

In comparison to other international markets targeted by Dell, including the UK, Australia, New Zealand, Singapore, Malaysia and Taiwan, China was a different profile in two ways (Chowdhury 1999). First, retail buyers were still new to the PC market, comprising only about 10 per cent of total sales. A PC was a significant purchase as costs were equivalent to almost two years of a Chinese average-income savings level. Chinese retail consumers were characterised by a desire for in-person purchasing experiences, where it was possible to examine the PC, see how it worked and ask questions of the dealer or retailer. Second, the use of credit cards was not common with most Chinese consumers at the time; those kinds of financial options were usually the preserve of corporations or individuals with a high social rank. Consequently, Dell focused on the corporate market, including MNEs and government agencies. Information technology personnel in these organisations were usually technologically aware, prepared specific requirements and were comfortable dealing over the telephone or via other non-personal means.

Entering the China market: pre-1998

Despite Dell's commitment to the direct sales model as a core business strategy, the company possessed the business acumen to assess international markets for individual requirements. Dell recognised that successful market entry would be contingent upon any necessary adaptation or alteration to the sales model after evaluating the entire value chain of a market. Four questions were posed. First, to what extent would end users accept direct sales from Dell? If end users were unfamiliar with Dell computers, it would be difficult to convince customers to buy via telephone. Second, to what extent would Dell be able to recruit a skilled sales force for direct sales? Third, were capable suppliers and carriers available to meet JIT management? Fourth, was the market size large enough?

Based on its assessment of the market, Dell opted for an indirect sales model to support its first entry into China. Dell began exporting PCs to China in 1993 using Star Advertising Corporation as its sole agent and setting up a network of four resellers (*Wall Street Journal* 1993, B.4). The cooperation lasted less than a year. Dell re-entered mainland China in 1995 and, until late 1998, imported computers from other countries and then sold Dell PCs through distributors. The distribution system included four first-tier distributors located in metropolitan areas, including Beijing, Shanghai, Guangzhou and Xi'an, as well as second- and third-tier resellers. Dell's representative office in China decided on the sales plan, designed promotion strategies such as sales rebates and coordinated relationships among distributors. However, Dell's performance was not impressive. By 1996, Dell had sold only 20 000 computers in China, equalling a 1 per cent market share and placing it tenth among PC vendors (Arnold 1997, B.16.B). These poor results largely reflected the country's still relatively small-size PC market, and the lack of effort from both Dell and its distributors. Dell was looking for the right time to apply its direct sales model, with no intention of maintaining a long-term relationship with distributors. Similarly, distributors did not want to invest much in market development, anticipating a switch by Dell to its well-known direct model.

Operating the dual-system model in China: 1998–2004

From 1998, Dell operated a dual-system model of sales in China: a modified direct sales method incorporating online and in-person contact, and an indirect sales method utilising a network of authorised distributors known as system integrators.

Dell established a China Customer Centre (CCC) in Xiamen to manufacture and sell PCs as well as provide service and technical support. The company assessed that its direct sales model would best suit the corporate segment in China. The business put the corporate customer base into three groups: relationship companies (companies with more than 3000 employees), mid-sized companies (companies with 500–3000 employees), and small-sized companies and family customers (companies with less than 500 employees and individual customers). Dell considered the first two segments as primary focus for their sales efforts.

To connect with target markets, Dell adapted its direct sales model at two key points to meet distinctive local characteristics. First, to address the issue of preference for personal contact, Dell utilised door-to-door sales and telephone sales as well as online sales. Second, to address the issue of payment, besides the usual online credit card option, Dell signed agreements with several banks to facilitate payments, and Dell's delivery men could also collect cash or transfer money through mobile wireless debit card machines. Dell's direct sales efforts resulted in a much-improved market penetration (Chowdhury 1999). In 1999, Dell was ranked seventh among the top PC manufacturers in China, with a market share of 2.3 per cent. By 2004, Dell had become the leading company in sales of servers and commercial computers.

In terms of the retail market, Dell implemented an indirect sales method through its network of authorised dealers. These system integrators referred customers' orders to Dell, sold Dell computer products, and provided technical support and product advice to retail buyers, particularly small-sized businesses and family customers. Reported figures indicate the dual system worked very well initially. Between 2000 and 2002, Dell's share in the retail market rose from 0.2 per cent to 4.7 per cent, most of which came from system integrators, as Dell itself focused on large and mid-sized companies.

While the use of system integrators provided Dell with a strategy to maintain and expand its market in China, Dell was never completely comfortable with the indirect sales method. System integrators diverted sales volume away from the direct channel owing to their ability to bundle orders from several retail buyers into a single order and obtain better per-unit prices than those available through online purchasing. When Dell identified an unacceptable business practice on the part of some system integrators, that of placing large orders with Dell to obtain below-retail prices and then on-selling PCs to agents or resellers rather than end users, Dell took legal action. In 2003, Dell engaged in a widely reported lawsuit against the Shanghai Zhiqi Corp for this practice (Li 2003). The lawsuit ended with a private settlement between the two parties. However, the legal case signalled to Dell that its dual system model no longer suited changing market conditions. A sales model may work well for a certain market for a certain period, but changes in the market can impact the efficacy of that model. In the case of China, from 2004, the rise of the retail market changed variables in the equation.

Retail market growth and impacts on the dual system model: after 2004

The mainland Chinese PC market continued to expand in the early 2000s, with significant growth in the retail market, not the corporate market, and in areas outside major urban centres. The growth rate of PC demand in urban centres such as Beijing and Shanghai fell to an annual rate of 2 to 3 per cent in 2004, while the growth rate in mid-sized cities and small towns increased to around 40 per cent. Consumers in these areas desired in-person contact with retailers prior to making purchase decisions and also expected post-sales technical support (Dickie & Morrison 2005, p. 13). Commentators noted that businesses also required services that Dell did not traditionally supply: 'demand is emerging elsewhere – in hundreds of smaller cities … where even some business customers want to see products before they buy' (Lee, Burrows & Einhorn 2005, p. 46).

In China, Dell's performance started to fall after 2004. From being second in 2003, it fell to fourth in 2004 with a market share of 7.2 per cent, even though PC shipments rose by 29 per cent. In 2004, Dell exited the low-end PC market, because that market expected in-person contact with distributors. In 2005 and 2006, the presidents of Dell China and Dell Asia–Pacific, and four other top executives, left Dell to join Lenovo, citing disagreement with Dell over the lack of focus on distributors and resellers. In 2007, Dell attempted to re-engage with low-end consumers by offering a new computer priced and styled to meet the needs of novice users in the emerging market (Fairclough & Spencer 2007, B.3). However, the ongoing problem for the company remained, as summed up by one consultant, '"Dell needs to establish more of a presence on the street" either through kiosks or retailers' (Lee, Burrows & Einhorn 2005, p. 46).

In April 2007, Michael Dell indicated that Dell would pursue new models of manufacturing and distributing computers. 'The direct model has been a revolution, but is not a religion … We will continue to improve our business model, and go beyond it, to give our customers what they need' (Lawton 2007, A.6). With its experience in China, Dell recognised that while the direct model was effective in mature markets, there was an evident need to open other distribution channels in emerging markets (Hoffman 2008). From 2007, Dell partnered with retail chains in various countries including the UK, Japan, and China.

Ongoing adaptation: redesigning the dual-sales model in China

Capturing market share in China required Dell to compete in a similar retail fashion to its main competitors, Lenovo and Hewlett-Packard. Selecting the right retailer was imperative for Dell as it intended to pursue a selective strategy. In 2007, Dell partnered with Gome, a large electronics retailer, to provide the face-to-face contact that the Chinese consumers' desired. Gome is found extensively throughout China, with over 1000 stores in 168 cities (McSherry 2007). To target commercial clients, Dell developed its service capabilities to compete more effectively with market rivals. In 2010, Dell started to see its efforts pay off with record growth in China that has been unmatched by any other country. In the first quarter, Dell experienced 81 per cent growth over the previous year's results (Chao 2010, B.8).

To continue growing, Dell is targeting the rural market in China where vast numbers of potential customers are attracting attention from many PC manufacturers. Accessing this segment requires Dell to display its technology and educate residents on the benefits of using a Dell PC. By tapping into new customer segments, increasing service capabilities and improving distribution tactics, Dell aims to improve its position as the second largest PC manufacturer in China (Raghuvanshi 2012).

QUESTIONS

1. What were the advantages that Dell identified that would spur on growth for the company in the China market?
2. What type of market entry assessments did Dell undertake?
3. Consider and explain how Dell captured market share in China.

References

Adbrands (2016). Worldwide advertisers. Adbrands website. Retrieved from www.adbrands.net/top-global-advertisers.htm

ANZ Business Chief (2016). Top 10 Australian franchises. Business Chief, 10 June. Retrieved from http://anz.businesschief.com/top10/2050/Top-10-Australian-Franchises

Arnold, W. (1997). Dell feels the heat in computer dispute with Chinese buyer. *Wall Street Journal*, (Eastern edition), 18 April.

Asian Development Bank (ADB) (2008). *Strategy 2020: The Long-Term Strategic Framework of the Asian Development Bank 2008–2020*. Philippines: Asia Development Bank. Retrieved from www.adb.org/sites/default/files/institutional-document/32121/strategy2020-print.pdf

Astek (2017). What is Google Analytics and how does it work? Astek. Retrieved from www.astekweb.com/web-analytics/what-is-google-analytics-how-does-it-work

AT Kearney (2017). The 2017 Global Retail Development Index. AT Kearney. Retrieved from www.atkearney.com/global-retail-development-index/article?/a/the-age-of-focus-2017-full-study

Austrade (2017a). Food and beverage to China. Austrade. Retrieved from www.austrade.gov.au/Australian/Export/Export-markets/Countries/China/Industries/Food-and-beverage

——— (2017b). The state of world trade – an IMF perspective. Austrade, 26 March. Retrieved from www.austrade.gov.au/News/Economics-at-Austrade/the-state-of-world-trade-an-imf-perspective

Baker & McKenzie (2012). *Guide to Media and Content Regulation in Asia Pacific*. Illinois: Baker & McKenzie. Retrieved from www.commsalliance.com.au/__data/assets/pdf_file/0016/42136/Guide-to-Media-and-Content-Regulation-in-Asia-Pacific.pdf

Beall, T., Wayman, J., D'Agostino, H., Liang, A. & Perellis, C. (2011). Social marketing at a critical turning point. *Journal of Social Marketing*, 2(2),103–117. Retrieved from www.emeraldinsight.com/doi/abs/10.1108/20426761211243946

Buchel, B. & Raub, S. (1999). Legend Group and the Chinese Computer Industry. *Asian Case Research Journal*, 3(5), 51.

Chao, L. (2010). Dell intends to extend services unit in China. *Wall Street Journal* (Eastern edition), March 25.

Chowdhury, N. (1999). Dell cracks China. *Fortune*, 139(6), 120–4.

Dann, S. & Dann, S. (2014) *Insight and Overview of Social Marketing*. Brisbane: Queensland Government. Retrieved from www.parliament.qld.gov.au/Documents/TableOffice/TabledPapers/2014/5414T4842.pdf

Dickie, M. & Morrison, S. (2005). In China the agent enters the equation. *Financial Times*, 26 August.

The Drum (2017). The best social media campaigns in Asia Pacific in 2017. *The Drum*, 21 December. Retrieved from www.thedrum.com/opinion/2017/12/21/the-best-social-media-campaigns-asia-pacific-2017

eMarketer (2017). Worldwide ad spending: The eMarketer forecast for 2017. eMarketer, 12 April. Retrieved from www.emarketer.com/Report/Worldwide-Ad-Spending-eMarketer-Forecast-2017/2002019

ESCAP (2015). *Population and Development Indicators for Asia and the Pacific, 2015*. Bangkok: United Nations Economic and Social Commission for Asia and the Pacific. Retrieved from www.unescap.org/sites/default/files/SPPS%20PS%20data%20sheet%202015%20final%20online.pdf

Euromonitor International (2015). Omni-presence a key strategy for retailers to succeed in India. Euromonitor, 15 May. Retrieved from https://blog.euromonitor.com/2016/05/omni-presence-a-key-strategy-for-retailers-to-succeed-in-india.html

Fairclough, G. & Spencer, J. (2007). Dell's PC for China marks developing-market rush. *Wall Street Journal* (Eastern edition), March 22.

Frampton, J. (2017). Growth in a changing world. Interbrand. Retrieved from http://interbrand.com/best-brands/best-global-brands/2017/articles/growth-in-a-changing-world

Franchise Council of Australia (2018). Franchising: An introduction. Franchise Council of Australia. Retrieved from www.franchise.org.au/franchising–an-introduction.html

Haier (n.d.). Haier website. Retrieved from www.haier.net

Hoffman, W. (2008). Redirecting Dell. *Traffic World*, 21 April.

Hubspot (2017). 7 Inspiring Examples of Omni-Channel User Experiences. Hubspot. Retrieved from http://blog.hubspot.com/marketing/omni-channel-user-experience-examples

Kaul, V. (2012). Changing paradigms of media landscape in the digital age. *Journal of Mass Communication and Journalism*, 2(110). Retrieved from www.omicsonline.org/open-access/changing-paradigms-of-media-landscape-in-the-digital-age-2165–7912.1000110.php?aid=4210&view=mobile

KeepCup (n.d.). The KeepCup story. Retrieved from www.keepcup.com.au/about-us/our-story

Knowledge@Wharton (2009). Made for India: Succeeding in a market where one size won't fit all. Wharton, University of Pennsylvania, 12 March. Retrieved from http://knowledge.wharton.upenn.edu/article/made-for-india-succeeding-in-a-market-where-one-size-wont-fit-all

Lawton, C. (2007). Dell could go beyond its direct-sales model in bid to bolster growth. *Wall Street Journal* (Eastern edition), 28 April.

Lee, L., Burrows, P. & Einhorn, B. (2005). Dell may have to reboot in China. *Business Week*, 7 November.

Li, M. (2003). What is hidden under the direct model. *21 Century Economic Report*, 5 June.

McSherry, M. (2007). Dell to sell computers through China's Gome. *Wall Street Journal*, 23 September.

Mintz, J. (2016). Importance of upstream social marketing. Centre of Excellence for Public Sector Marketing, 2 February. Retrieved from https://cepsm.ca/blog/importance-of-upstream-social-marketing

NAB (2017). The future of retail. National Australia Bank, September. Retrieved from https://business.nab.com.au/wp-content/uploads/2017/09/The-future-of-retail-September-2017.pdf

Papakosmas, M.F., Noble, G. & Glynn, J. (2012). Organization-based social marketing: An alternative approach for organizations adopting sustainable business practices. *Social Marketing Quarterly*, 18(2),87–97.

Plane, D. & Livingston, S. (2017). Procedures and strategies for anti-counterfeiting: China. World Trademark Review, 24 May. Retrieved from www.worldtrademarkreview.com/Intelligence/Anti-counterfeiting/2017/Country-chapters/China

PWC (2014). *Developing Infrastructure in Asia Pacific: Outlook, Challenges and Solutions*. Singapore: PricewaterhouseCoopers. Retrieved from www.pwc.com/sg/en/capital-projects-infrastructure/assets/cpi-develop-infrastructure-in-ap-201405.pdf

Raghuvanshi, G. (2012). Dell counts on local leaders. *Wall Street Journal*, 5 April. Retrieved from www.wsj.com/public/page/archive-2012–4-4.html

Spencer, N. (2016) Japan bans 19 ingredients used in medicated soaps. Cosmetic Design-Asia, 19 October. Retrieved from www.cosmeticsdesign-asia.com/Article/2016/10/20/Japan-bans-19-ingredients-used-in-soap

Statista (2017). Revenue of Haier Electronics Group from 2009 to 2016. Statista. Retrieved from www.statista.com/statistics/232840/revenue-of-haier-electronics-group/

——— (2018a). Distribution of worldwide internet users as of May 2015, by region. Statista. Retrieved from www.statista.com/statistics/271401/regional-distribution-of-internet-users-worldwide

——— (2018b). Global advertising spending from 2010 to 2018 (in billion US dollars). Statista. Retrieved from www.statista.com/statistics/236943/global-advertising-spending

Wall Street Journal (1993). Business briefs. *Wall Street Journal*, 7 October.

World Trade Organization (WTO) (2017). World trade and GDP growth in 2016 and early 2017. *World Trade Statistical Review 2017*. Geneva: World Trade Organization, pp. 16–27. Retrieved from www.wto.org/english/res_e/statis_e/wts2017_e/WTO_Chapter_03_e.pdf

Wyner, G. (2014). Performance evaluation. *American Marketing Association Marketing Insights 2014*, January–February. Retrieved from www.ama.org/publications/MarketingInsights/Pages/Performance-Evaluation.aspx

Yu, E. (2017). APAC leads global ad spend growth; digital to consume largest share of APAC ad budget. Exchange Wire, 21 June. Retrieved from www.exchangewire.com/blog/2017/06/21/apac-leads-global-ad-spend-growth-digital-consume-largest-share-apac-ad-budget

CHAPTER 11

INTERNATIONAL SOURCING AND PRODUCTION

Learning objectives

In reading this chapter, you will learn to:

1. appreciate changes in the international business environment that lead to new trends in global sourcing and production
2. understand the key parameters that fundamentally define the roles of foreign production plants
3. recognise the benefits of production planning tools such as flexible manufacturing systems, just-in-time and total quality management
4. appreciate the difficulties associated with transferring production knowledge in multinational firms
5. know the limitations and risks of a global sourcing and production strategy.

THE DOWNFALL OF THE AUSTRALIAN CAR INDUSTRY

Global competition produces winners and losers; not even national icons are safe. After almost a century of car making in Australia, all three major car makers present in the market – Ford, Toyota and General Motors (GM) – have announced closures (Dowling 2017). Ford shut its Broadmeadows and Geelong factories in October 2016 after 91 years of operation. Toyota, who had manufacturing operations in Australia since 1963, announced it was closing its Camry factory in Altona in 2017. GM confirmed it was closing its Australian Holden production in 2017 as well (Dowling 2017). The Holden Commodore, which had been assembled in Elizabeth, Southern Australia, will be replaced by a German made-model, produced by GM's former Opel division, which was sold to the French car manufacturer Groupe PSA in 2017.

What were the reasons for the downfall of Australian car manufacturing? One factor was the trade agreements made with Asian nations such as Japan, South Korea and Thailand, which are the major sources of motor vehicles in Australia; Thailand, for example, has a Toyota Camry factory. Lower costs of labour and increased manufacturing productivity in these nations, and other major car-producing nations such as Germany, the US and Mexico, have outpaced Australia's capability (Sirkin et al. 2014).

VIDEO VIGNETTE QUESTION

Introduction

This chapter examines the role of sourcing and production in international business. It focuses on the role of foreign production plants, flexible manufacturing systems (FMS), global supply chains, transferring production knowledge across borders and risks in international sourcing and production. Key concepts are introduced and then formative ideas are discussed in depth. This includes Kasra Ferdows's article 'Making the most of foreign factories' (1997) as well as articles on the new dynamics of global manufacturing site location, and transferring core manufacturing technologies in high-tech firms. These ideas are examined then expanded upon to address contemporary themes, such as the role of the Asia–Pacific in global production and the rise of services. Throughout the chapter, dynamics of international sourcing and production are emphasised. Figure 11.1 provides a conceptual map for this chapter, highlighting key decisions, activities, and issues in international sourcing and production.

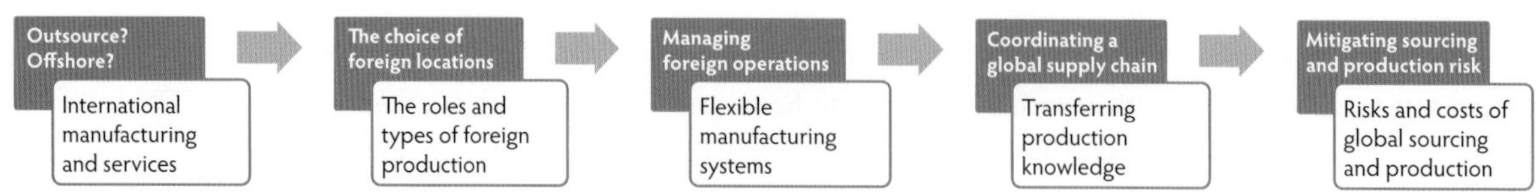

FIGURE 11.1 Key decisions, activities, and issues in international sourcing and production

Overview and key trends

As we saw in the opening story, companies often produce outside of their home country. The Toyota Camry, for example, is produced not only in Japan, but also in the US, Russia, Thailand, China, Taiwan and Vietnam. Inputs and parts for production are also routinely sourced from suppliers around the world. Companies must make strategic decisions around the share of sourcing they do from outside their own production locations. For example, the US Camry sources about 25 per cent of the value of its parts from outside of the US. In comparison, the US BMW plant, producing X4, X5 and X6 models, derives only 25 per cent of its value from domestic content made in the US (Kogod School of Business 2016; Walsworth 2016).

INTERNATIONAL SOURCING the purchasing of goods, services or business processes from abroad; also known as international procurement.

International sourcing, also called international procurement, often has a dedicated department in major organisations, as cost competitiveness and profitability are significantly affected by purchasing decisions (Bain Insights 2014). Procurement represents as much as 80 per cent of costs in many industries (Tang et al. 2013). According to a study by Bain consultancy, while the Asia–Pacific is a key region for global sourcing, relatively few firms in this region described their procurement as world class (Tang et al. 2013). International sourcing can be from independent suppliers or firm-owned subsidiaries (in other words, from in-house). It applies to manufacturing and services, and includes subcontracting the performance of specific processes, such as payroll, customer service and technical support.

Production and international production are best seen as parts of the value chain, consisting of value-creating activities such as R&D, design, production, logistics, information technology, human resource management, marketing and customer support. In the international context, the global value chain encompasses the value-creation activities dispersed across different countries (Gereffi & Fernandez-Stark 2016; OECD n.d.). International production is typically associated with the manufacturing of physical goods, but it also applies to intangible activities, such as the delivery of services in the hotel or financial industries. For example, European luxury hotel operators such as Kempinski Hotels can operate facilities in Asia instead of attracting Asian tourists to their European locations (Zámborský & Kruesi 2018).

INTERNATIONAL PRODUCTION the activities involved in creating a product or service abroad.

There are four key drivers behind the internationalisation of production. The first is cost efficiency. This stems from a motivation to lower costs by moving production to countries with lower business costs, such as labour, energy and taxes. For example, most of world's apparel products are produced in low-cost nations, with a recent retreat from China to even cheaper Asian nations such as Bangladesh, Vietnam and India (Berg & Hedrick 2014). The second driver is improved productivity. A favourable combination of high productivity and low costs can deliver superior performance compared to the home location. While manufacturing productivity rose 50 per cent in some countries such as Mexico, India and South Korea in 2004–14, it declined in others such as Japan and Italy (Sirkin et al. 2014). The third driver is related to the desire to add value by better serving customer

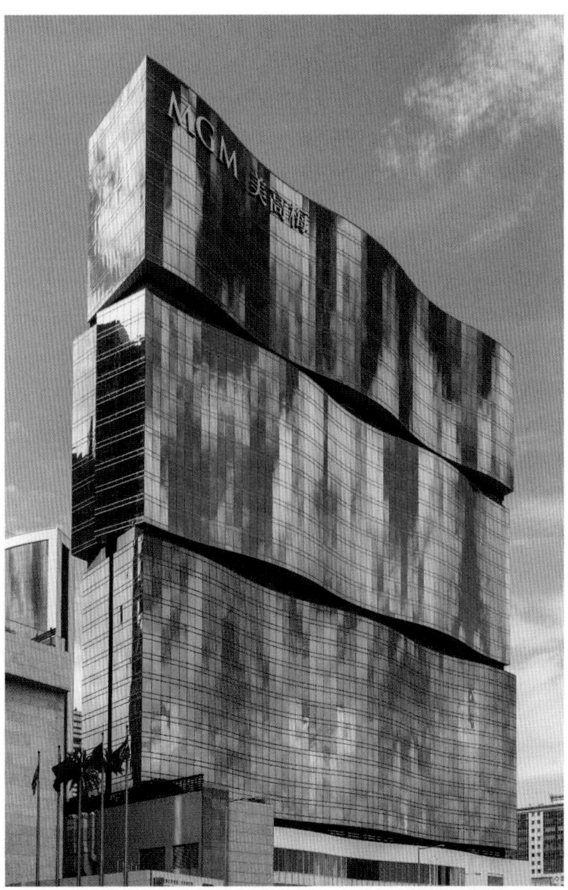

FIGURE 11.2 MGM Macau Casino is 50 per cent owned by the US MGM Resorts International

needs. Being closer to the foreign consumer is a crucial factor in determining the overall quality of a product or service. The last driver is the exchange rate, with some locations offering cost and diversification advantages because of the low value of their currencies. Singapore, Taiwan and South Korea have the most undervalued currencies in Asia, and are trying to keep their currencies from appreciating, according to Peterson Institute (Harding 2017).

Manufacturing and services

The first major wave of international production and sourcing related mostly to the manufacturing of physical goods, with a shift from developed to emerging economies. Countries in Asia, Latin America and Eastern Europe have attracted numerous manufacturing plants due to their lower labour costs. By the early 2000s, China had emerged as the world's dominant 'production workshop' for a plethora of goods ranging from toys to cell phones. Other low-cost countries around the world, including Mexico and Poland, got a piece of the manufacturing pie as well. Developed nations generally retained the higher value-added functions such as R&D, design and marketing. According to the Boston Consulting Group, when it came to total value generated by manufacturing, the US retained its leadership spot in 2010, followed by China, Japan and Germany (Harding 2017).

SPOTLIGHT 11.1

Factory Asia

Asia now manufactures almost half of the world's merchandise goods (*The Economist* 2015). China's share of global manufacturing value rose from 3 per cent in 1990 to nearly 25 per cent by 2015 (*The Economist* 2015). According to *The Economist*, there are four reasons why China and Asia will continue to dominate global manufacturing. First, China is clinging on to low-cost manufacturing, even as it invests in developing more sophisticated and high value-added activities, such as R&D and robotics. Large pools of low-cost and highly qualified labour allow for both of these strategies. Excellent infrastructure and the presence of most suppliers at home also bolster China's position. Second, with wages rising in China, the country outsources some of its production to countries in South-East Asia with low wages and large populations, such as Malaysia, Philippines and Myanmar. This reinforces China's central position in the supply chains it has created. The third advantage of China and Asia is that the region is becoming a key source of global demand. As the spending and sophistication of Chinese and other Asian consumers grow, the region is attracting higher-margin marketing and customer service. Lastly, trade policy initiatives such as ASEAN have encouraged development of manufacturing in South-East Asian nations. Thailand's strength in vehicle production is a case in point.

VIDEO SPOTLIGHT QUESTIONS

QUESTIONS

1. What are the main reasons for Thailand's strength in vehicle production?
2. Can you think of a major threat to Asia's dominance in manufacturing?

Manufacturing accounts for less than 20 per cent of global output and employment but for about 70 per cent of global trade as well as over 75 per cent of global R&D (Sirkin et al. 2014). Manufacturing is still important both for advanced and emerging economies as it contributes to over a third of global productivity growth (Sirkin et al. 2014). In Asia, manufacturing was the largest sector in Taiwan, South Korea and China, about 30 per cent of total value added, and it accounted for around a quarter or more of value added in Thailand and Malaysia in 2016, according to Asian Productivity Association (APO 2016). However, the distinction between manufacturing and services is becoming blurred. Close to half of manufacturing jobs are in service-type activities, such as R&D, procurement, distribution, sales and marketing, post-sales service, back-office support and management (APO 2016). This is especially true in industries focusing on global technologies and innovation, such as computers and office machinery, and global innovation for local markets, such as motor vehicles and appliances. These industries, along with labour-intensive tradable goods such as apparel and toys, also have the highest international trade intensity (APO 2016).

Services, a major employer and contributor to global output, are increasingly sourced and produced globally as well. India has become a leader in the global sourcing of business services. India has hundreds of thousands of people employed performing tasks ranging from customer support to IT services for companies based in advanced economies. Other business processes that are often sourced from abroad are back-office activities such as payroll and billing, and front-office activities such as marketing and technical support. The trend spans industries ranging from finance to IT and healthcare. India may have been the first country to embrace this trend, and has produced world-leading providers such as Wipro and Infosys. However, other emerging economies in Asia, especially China, Malaysia and Indonesia, and around the world, such as Brazil, are catching up and gaining a foothold in this market. See Spotlight 11.2 for more insights and analysis of global services offshoring.

Outsourcing

Outsourcing does not necessarily have to come from abroad, which distinguishes it from international sourcing. The term outsourcing relates to one of the main decisions firms have to make to either keep activities in-house (internal to the company) or source them from other parties, In business, these are often known as make-or-buy decisions (Parmigiani 2007). In particular, companies have to think hard about which parts of the value chain constitute their core competencies, which are the activities that are the key source of their competitive advantage (Quinn & Hilmer 1994). These are often proprietary and involve intellectual property that the companies want to prevent from leaking to competitors. For example, many world-leading companies such as Apple and Canon keep their R&D and design in-house, while they are willing to outsource what they consider non-core activities, such as production and after-sales customer support (Narula 2001).

OUTSOURCING the contracting out of a business process to an independent party. It can involve the sourcing of parts, value-adding activities or an entire product from independent suppliers.

Both make and buy options have their relative advantages. Given bounded reliability of a partner, keeping activities in-house is the best guarantee of protecting proprietary technology or valuable signature capabilities from being expropriated and imitated. The make option is also attractive when firms need to invest in specialised assets, contingent on a particular relationship (with a supplier) persisting. Firms may be hesitant to invest in such assets and be dependent on the supplier. They instead may opt to make these components themselves so as to not be vulnerable to the other party's actions, intentions or competency (Poppo et al. 2008).

Reasons to make your own components are also linked to FSAs. They are:

1. potentially lower costs – if the firm is more efficient in making the part or activity than its potential suppliers and partners
2. build dynamic capabilities – skills crucial to a company's success that become more valuable over time through learning
3. improve production coordination – having a larger part of the value chain in-house makes it easier to plan and schedule processes for timely, efficient delivery.

The buy option offers the benefit of flexibility. Namely, it makes it easier to switch from one external supplier to another compared to owning the value creation and having to change or divest it. In international business companies often source from a range of countries so they have some flexibility to re-shuffle production. This can be invaluable when there are serious changes regarding factors such as political risk and exchange rates. However, suppliers may not remain committed if their partner is too opportunistic in the relationship. The other main advantage of the buy option is that in many cases it is more efficient to let a supplier or partner conduct an activity for you. Again, in the context of international business, having your product manufactured in Asia may be much cheaper; you may lack the expertise or willingness to own and engage in Asian production though your own operations. For example, the fashion retailer H&M outsources a huge portion of their production to specialised partners abroad, leaving them to focus on marketing and management. This contrasts with Zara, who keep a large part of their production in-house (Ghemawat et al. 2003). These two examples show that both approaches can work, but fit different strategies. H&M has a more cost-focused, mid-market approach, versus Zara's fast fashion, up-market approach.

CONTRACT MANUFACTURING
an outsourcing arrangement in which a firm contracts with an independent supplier to manufacture its products according to predefined specifications.

Contract manufacturing is a common arrangement in industries ranging from apparel to aerospace. The Taiwanese firm Foxconn is a major player in this arena. They work under contract for well-known brands such as Apple and Sony, with production facilities worldwide that employ over a million workers. According to *Fortune* magazine, it was the world's fifth-largest private employer in 2017. Another major player in the contract manufacturing sector is Flex, formerly called Flextronics, from Singapore (portrayed in the IB masterclass case study). With 150 000 staff, it is in the top 500 global firms by sales.

Offshoring

OFFSHORING
the relocation of a value-adding activity (including production, business processes and tasks) to a different country.

Offshoring and outsourcing together create a gamut of four options for a firm's locus and location of activity. These are inside or outside of firm and inside or outside of its home country (see Table 11.1). A multinational firm's activities can be conceptualised by slicing the firm's value chain into distinct value-adding activities, followed by decisions on how each slice should be allocated organisationally (such as outsourcing) and geographically (such as offshoring) (Contractor et al. 2010).

TABLE 11.1 Types of outsourcing and offshoring

Location of activity	Inside the home country	Outside of home country
Inside the firm	Domestic in-house sourcing	In-house offshoring (captive sourcing)
Outside the firm	Domestic outsourcing	Outsourced offshoring (offshore outsourcing)

Note: varied terms are used, we thus included 'captive sourcing' and 'offshore outsourcing'.

Source: Adapted from Contractor et al. 2010

In the last 15 years, outsourcing and offshoring have been frequently used and researched within the context of service industries. There are three types of service tasks typically associated with outsourcing and offshoring:

1. call contact centres; for example, help desk and technical support
2. shared services centres; for example, claims and data processing
3. IT services centres; for example, software development and applications design (Doh, Bunyaratavej & Hahn 2009).

The location of outsourced operations for each of these depend on a variety of factors including wage levels, language proficiency, education, country risk and infrastructure (see Spotlight 11.2 for details) (Doh, Bunyaratavej & Hahn 2009). Indian firms Tata Consultancy Services, Wipro and Infosys were among the world's top 10 IT outsourcing service firms in 2017, according to *CIO* magazine, with the US Accenture, Cognizant and IBM topping the list (Overby 2018).

SPOTLIGHT 11.2

Asia dominates global services offshoring

According to AT Kearney's Global Services Location Index, Asian countries are well positioned to benefit from offshoring opportunities in the service industry (Gott & Sethi 2017). There are four Asian countries in the top 5. India leads the index, which measures countries' financial attractiveness, people skills, labour availability and business environment. Offshoring investment in India's service industry goes beyond the scope of traditional call centres opened by Western multinationals. For example, Chinese telco giant Huawei, has 2700 R&D engineers in Bangalore and wants to increase this to 5000. China is in the number 2 spot, with gains in educational skills and cultural adaptability, but

still weak in IP protection and pollution problems. Malaysia is the world's third most attractive destination for offshored services, with a solid performance across the board; Tech Mahindra, an Indian IT company, has its centre of excellence based there. Indonesia is at the number 5 spot after Brazil. With a large Chinese-speaking community, Indonesia is a target for offshoring from China. The Philippines, ranked number 7, is a global leader in offshored voice services. While Asia's current position is strong, the current models of offshoring are threatened by new technologically driven offerings. This includes robotic process automation and so-called 'business process as a service', or, in other words, standardised interface and process across multiple customers. A number of innovators from countries that range from Israel to Germany are creating solutions such as artificial intelligence chatbots and big data analytics that may threaten some of the existing offerings of Asian offshoring players.

VIDEO SPOTLIGHT QUESTIONS

QUESTIONS

1. Do you think Asian countries are well positioned to remain leaders in offshore services? What types of offshoring are the Asian region best positioned to lead in?
2. How does the rise of robotic process automation constitute a threat and an opportunity regarding offshoring for Asia?

NEARSHORING locating the offshored activity to a country geographically or culturally close to the client country's company.

RE-SHORING bringing the offshore production back to the home country.

NO-SHORING a trend of replacing value-adding activities performed by humans by automated robotic processes.

More recent trends in offshoring relate to four phenomena. The first one is nearshoring, which moves an offshore activity to a country closer geographically or culturally to the client country's company. For instance, Indian offshoring providers such as Infosys and Tata Consulting Services have established operations in the Czech Republic and Hungary to be closer to their European customers. Another trend is re-shoring, which brings production based offshore back to the home country. Political backlash has partly driven this in countries such as the US and the UK against offshoring. For example, both Infosys and Foxconn recently announced large investments into the US. No-shoring is replacing value-adding activities performed by humans by automated robotic processes. According to McKinsey, digital sourcing is significantly different from sourcing in non-digital contexts. Some of these differences include a larger focus on talent, ever-changing scopes of projects and there being small niche providers dominating in the digital sector. These factors tend to favour outsourced as opposed to in-house digital solutions.

The role of foreign production plants

Chapter 2 has described how MNEs can tap their foreign subsidiaries as sources of competitive advantage by selectively giving certain subsidiaries increased control and decision-making power. For example, foreign R&D centres can develop new knowledge that exploits or even augments the knowledge developed in the home country. This section will extend this analysis further, looking at how MNEs can tap their foreign factories.

Making the most of foreign factories

In 1997, Kasra Ferdows wrote an article for *Harvard Business Review* entitled 'Making the most of foreign factories'. In the article, Ferdows provides a detailed argument in support of the market seeking and strategic resource seeking arguments for FDI in the context of international manufacturing.

Ferdows bases his research on a wide variety of sources including: his own consulting work with a dozen large manufacturing MNEs; a four-year study conducted with 10 large MNEs (Apple, Digital Equipment, Electrolux, Ford, HP, Hydro Aluminium, IBM, Olivetti, Philips and Sony); industry surveys of companies (pharmaceuticals, food processing and paper machinery); and the Global Manufacturing Futures Surveys project, which studied the practices of nearly 600 manufacturers operating in the triad regions of North America, Europe and Japan.

Ferdows (1997) attempts to answer one key question: How can a factory located outside of a company's home country be used as a competitive weapon not only in the market that it directly serves but also in every market served by the company? The answer depends largely on the mindset of home country senior managers: what do they think is the proper role of foreign factories? Senior managers who view their factories merely as sources of efficient, low-cost production typically don't allocate their factories many resources, and these managers get only what they expect: efficient, low-cost production. In contrast, senior managers with higher performance expectations from their foreign factories require innovation and customer service as well; these managers 'generally expect their foreign factories to be highly productive and innovative, to achieve low costs, and to provide exemplary service to customers throughout the world' (Ferdows 1997, p. 108). They therefore allocate their factories more resources and get more in return.

In his study, Ferdows observes that the most successful manufacturing MNEs view their foreign factories as sources of FSAs beyond the ability to save costs as with conventional offshoring plants. Ferdows therefore concludes that, beyond the traditional motives such as 'tariff and trade concessions, cheap labour, capital subsidies, and reduced logistics costs', MNEs should leverage their foreign factories 'to get closer to ... customers and suppliers, to attract skilled and talented employees, and to create centres of expertise for the entire company' (1997, p. 73).

Ferdows describes three changes in the international business environment driving the assignment of these new foreign factory roles. First, international trade tariffs declined substantially in the second half of the twentieth century, reducing the need to establish foreign plants merely to overcome trade barriers. Second, modern manufacturing is increasingly technologically sophisticated, meaning capital-intensive, and has complex supply-chain requirements. As a result, MNEs seldom select manufacturing locations based simply on the lowest possible wages. Rather, the emphasis is on the overall productivity level, which is determined by several factors, including the available levels of infrastructure, technology, worker education and skills. Third, the time frame available to move from development to actual manufacturing and marketing has become shorter. As a result, MNEs increasingly co-locate development and manufacturing activities in highly specialised plants, which then receive broad geographic mandates within their areas of expertise.

These changes are consistent with the argument that the successful penetration of foreign markets requires more than merely transferring non-location-bound knowledge from the home country to the host country. MNEs are increasingly attempting to augment conventional, host-country production with at least some local R&D activities, rather than centralising such activities in the home country and then deploying this non-location-bound knowledge to host countries as the basis of foreign manufacturing. A subsidiary located in a specialised foreign knowledge cluster must become the company specialist for those knowledge areas in which the cluster has core strengths. In other words, the subsidiary must develop, in its own right, internationally transferable FSAs, building upon the location advantages of the host-country cluster.

Types of foreign manufacturing facilities

The article distinguishes among six possible roles for foreign manufacturing facilities, based upon two parameters. The first parameter is the strategic purpose of the plant, which is intimately related to the host-country location advantages the MNE wants to access; for example, proximity to market, access to low-cost production, and access to knowledge and skills.

The second parameter is the level of distinct FSAs held by the plant, whether they are weak or strong. Here, the level of distinct FSAs refers to the additional strengths added by the plant itself, augmenting the FSAs transferred from the home country. Note also that this includes the plant's higher-order FSAs, such as the ability to generate new knowledge and new FSAs.

As regards purpose, the first parameter, a distinction should be made between the subsidiary's role in accessing host-country input markets, such as for skilled labour, versus output markets, such as selling the company's products. Ferdows makes a similar distinction in the context of manufacturing activities. His 'proximity to market' purpose reflects the importance of output markets for selling the MNE's products (output market seeking investments). His second purpose, 'access to low-cost production', reflects the factory's need to access input markets. Finally, his third purpose, 'access to knowledge and skills', is often closely tied to both input and output markets. It encompasses some need to tap into input markets, especially for sophisticated production factors, but in many cases the ultimate goal is to serve (output) markets with innovative products.

The two parameters outlined allow Ferdows to distinguish among the six specific factory roles (see Figure 11.3):

1. *Offshore factory*: this factory's primary purpose is simply to access low-cost production factors as an implementer on the input side. The plant's manufacturing output, typically predetermined by senior management in the home country, is then exported. This factory type typically does not develop new FSAs and receives minimum autonomy.
2. *Server factory*: this factory's primary purpose is to manufacture goods and to supply a predefined, proximate national or regional output market. Market imperfections, such as trade barriers, logistics costs and foreign exchange exposure, usually explain the establishment of such factories in specific host countries. A server factory may engage in some FSA development, but it ultimately has a narrow charter with relatively little autonomy or specialised capabilities.
3. *Outpost factory*: the primary purpose of this factory is to gather valuable information from advanced host-country clusters, mainly on the input side. On the actual manufacturing side, this role is usually combined with that of an offshore (input market driven) or server (output market driven) factory.
4. *Source factory*: this factory's primary purpose is to gain access to low-cost production factors on the input side, similar to an offshore factory. However, it also receives resources to engage in resource recombination and to develop FSAs that will turn it into a best practice plant in the MNE's network for the assigned product range. It therefore has more autonomy in terms of logistics, product customisation, redesign and so on. The MNE sets up source factories in locations with good infrastructure and a skilled workforce. This type of factory may be a strategic leader on the input side of the value chain, but nonetheless has a narrow charter.
5. *Contributor factory*: this factory type is oriented primarily towards the host-country or host-region output market, similar to a server factory, but it commands stronger capabilities than a server factory. More at the upstream end of the value chain, it is responsible for

resource recombination in the form of process improvements, new product development, customisations, and so on.

6. *Lead factory*: this factory type is the most important one in terms of resource recombination and new FSA development. It accesses valuable inputs from the local cluster where it is embedded and plays a key role in localised manufacturing innovation. It is also connected with both the key players on the input side (such as research labs) and the end users on the output side.

Strategic purpose of the plant \ Level of distinct FSAs held by the plant	Weak	Strong
Access to knowledge and skills	Outpost	Leader
Proximity to market	Server	Contributor
Access to low cost production	Offshore	Source

FIGURE 11.3 Six roles of foreign manufacturing plants

Overall, says Ferdows, the MNE should aim to upgrade its offshore, server and outpost factories so that they gain the ability to develop FSAs as source, contributor and lead factories. However, this upgrading process requires a high level of commitment, as it 'entails a substantial investment of time and resources, as well as changes in a factory's culture and management style' (Ferdows 1997 p. 86).

Upgrading, according to Ferdows, involves substantial resource recombination spread over three stages:

1. enhancing internal performance: for example, through employee training and education, self-managed teams and adopting just-in-time (JIT) manufacturing

JUST-IN-TIME (JIT)
inventory management that allows an immediate response to specific customer demands and largely eliminates the need to hold inventories

2. accessing and developing external resources: for example, strengthening the plant's supplier network and improving the logistics integration with distributors
3. developing new knowledge that can benefit the overall MNE network.

As the MNE guides its foreign factories towards taking on upgraded, FSA-developing roles, it tends to place greater emphasis on intangible internal strengths and location advantages, rather

than tangible ones such as lower costs, taxes or the benefit of avoiding trade barriers. Intangible strengths include the factories' recombination capabilities, especially their capacity to absorb host-country knowledge, to learn from customers, suppliers and rivals, and to attract new talent. The end result of the upgrading process is a 'robust network' of factories with FSA-developing roles, able to adapt swiftly to changes in the marketplace (Ferdows 1997, p. 86).

According to Ferdows, such a network is conducive to stability and security of internal MNE functioning over the long term, even if many plants are in so-called high-cost locations. This robust network view of the MNE is in sharp contrast with the popular view that many MNEs should operate a 'footloose' set of plants. Footloose operations imply low exit barriers, as well as the capability to relocate manufacturing operations and redeploy resources across geographic space rapidly in response to changing cost conditions.

Ferdows contends that MNE strategic manufacturing planning should focus on specialising foreign factories, with each plant taking on a leadership role in a specific area, and avoiding the duplication of R&D efforts: 'the solution lies in specialisation. Whenever feasible, a foreign factory's ultimate mission should include developing a world-class specialty' (1997, p. 87).

A number of examples illustrate this point. In the late 1970s, the US-based technology company NCR (set up in 1884 as the National Cash Register Company, acquired by AT&T in 1991 and re-established as a separate company in 1996) had closed down five factories in the area of Dundee, Scotland, and had one remaining, a server factory that was fighting for its survival. Building upon a structural change inside NCR that included a new focus on business units, the subsidiary management decided to refocus this factory, specialising in automated teller machines (ATMs) for the banking industry. The upgrading efforts included improving performance and speeding up product development cycle times. 'By 1990, Dundee had become NCR's lead plant for ATMs, with primary responsibility for developing and manufacturing the products that the billion-dollar business needed' (Ferdows 1997, p. 83).

During the same period, Sony built a new plant in Wales (UK), initially intended as a server factory to overcome European trade barriers against outsiders. Over 15 years, however, the factory pioneered new quality-control processes, both internally and with local suppliers, and eventually took on responsibility for R&D to customise television product designs for the European market. 'Since 1988, the plant has designed and developed most of the products it has produced ... It continues to be a strong and valuable contributor plant in Sony's global network' (Ferdows 1997, p. 84).

In closing, Ferdows cautions managers about four common obstacles that may prevent the upgrading of foreign factories:

1. fear of relying on foreign operations for critical skills
2. treating overseas factories like cash cows and neglecting long-term investment
3. creating instability by shifting production in reaction to fluctuating exchange rates and costs
4. the enticement of government relocation incentives to move factories to new locations that possess minimal potential for upgrading.

Achievement of strategic goals

At the time that Ferdows' article was published, 1997, it had become necessary for many firms to improve linkages between host-country manufacturing and knowledge development activities, so as to command the required location-bound FSAs to function effectively in host-country environments. In addition, senior MNE managers perceived the need to gain access to geographically dispersed innovation clusters as the basis for new resource recombinations, culminating in new, internationally transferable FSAs. For these two reasons, many MNEs created R&D labs in host countries, often in conjunction with host-country factories.

The potential of host-country subsidiaries as a source of both location-bound and internationally transferable knowledge provided the impetus for companies to review their international operations. Freer trade in the form of lower tariffs and non-tariff barriers alike resulting from institutions and agreements such as GATT, NAFTA and the EU had dramatically changed the landscape of international business. Companies were no longer forced to establish factories in local areas simply to overcome unnatural market imperfections imposed by governments. At the same time, fiscal instability, dramatic devaluations of currencies and political uncertainty in developing countries in Latin America, Asia and Eastern Europe, created new bounded rationality problems for MNEs trying to reconfigure their dispersed subsidiary networks. The latter part of the 1990s also saw a halt in the seemingly endless boom of several Far East economies, as Japan and the developing Asian tigers became mired in a prolonged recession. Senior MNE managers were thus forced to rethink the bigger picture when planning the location of their factory networks to achieve optimal efficiency and effectiveness. As Ferdows suggests, companies were beginning to realise that across-the-board relocation of activities to low-wage, offshore production areas was not necessarily the panacea to achieve higher overall productivity, lower manufacturing costs and better access to customers (Ferdows 1997).

Ferdows' analysis has three main limitations. First, Ferdows ultimately believes that senior managers should try to upgrade *all* their factories rather than giving subsidiaries different roles. Ferdows most definitely does not view the MNE as a portfolio of operations, with some of these acting as implementers indefinitely. Even though he is correct that an internal MNE network of plants is a dynamic system, and that plants' roles can change, it would be somewhat naïve to assume, especially for large manufacturing firms, that all plants should be candidates for upgrading in the sense of becoming specialised centres of excellence with a distinct knowledge base inside the MNE. Here, the economies of scale and scope resulting from an approach with little plant upgrading obviously need to be weighed against the benefits of allowing plants to become increasingly embedded in host locations, and to deviate substantially from adopting and applying the MNE's key routines. This trade-off must be assessed for each plant in the MNE network, and there is no guarantee that every single plant should be upgraded. In fact, most large MNEs operate with a number of strategic leader plants, positioned on the upper part of Figure 11.3, but usually also have many implementer plants, consistent with the various roles described by Ferdows on the lower part of Figure 11.3.

A second limitation is that Ferdows' article does not discuss the changing nature of production in terms of outsourcing and the increased use of long-term, relational contracting with external suppliers. Especially within the sampled industries of technology-based companies, many of the market leaders such as Nortel, Lucent and Cisco have long pursued an outsourcing strategy. For these companies, manufacturing generally occurs in host country, emerging economies by dedicated contract manufacturers or OEMs such as Flextronics, Solectron and Sanmina-SCI, in exchange for long-term, exclusive contracts to manufacture products designed by the MNE. These large MNEs focus instead on the control of R&D on the upstream side and investments in branding on the downstream side.

A significant driver of outsourcing is the use of information communications technology (ICT) to monitor and coordinate with outside suppliers. Here, the MNE can easily and inexpensively identify poor quality, cost inefficiencies, delays in the logistics chain and so on. The result is increasingly blurred organisational boundaries between in-house product development, and manufacturing and

similar activities performed by manufacturing partners. This new division of labour may give the MNE full access to attractive production factors, including knowledge and skills in host environments, without the need to upgrade its own manufacturing facilities. The possibility of long-run, relational contracting adds a new trade-off to be considered when reflecting upon the upgrading of factories abroad: a robust network may include robust relationships with external contracting parties, rather than solely a set of upgraded factories.

The third limitation of Ferdows' analysis is that he underestimates the value of having low-cost, highly efficient factories in host countries, especially emerging markets that simply adopt and exploit both standalone technological knowledge from the parent as well as its key routines. On the one hand, this allows MNEs to improve their margins in their home country and other highly developed economies; these are markets where large and powerful distributors may try to squeeze the manufacturers' prices, and there may be strong competition and low growth rates. On the other hand, low-cost, highly efficient production may in some cases be the most practical tool to penetrate emerging, host countries because these markets are characterised by lower income levels and local low-cost manufacturers, with lesser quality products.

Cost efficiency and emerging markets

Cost efficiency due to the lower labour and operating costs associated with emerging markets remain a principal factor underlying international production and sourcing decisions. Indeed, scholars such as Pankaj Ghemawat have noted that arbitrage – benefiting from economic, political, geographic and cultural differences among nations – is an important and often 'forgotten strategy' (Ghemawat 2003). Differences in labour, energy and other costs between developed countries, such as Australia and emerging economies, such as Thailand can be vast. These factors are playing a significant role in the MNEs' decisions around closing or expanding their production plants. For example, Thai workers in the car industry can earn as little as AUD$1.12 per hour (Drill 2012).

In a report by the Boston Consulting Group, Australia has been ranked as the least cost competitive exporting nation in manufacturing; in 2014, Australia was 30 per cent more expensive than the US and only about 9 per cent more expensive than the US in 2002 (Sirkin et al. 2014). This calculation took into consideration labour costs (adjusted for productivity) and other operating costs, including energy costs, such as electricity and natural gas. Manufacturing wages rose 48 per cent between 2004 and 2014 in Australia, while productivity remained flat. Energy costs also increased (Sirkin et al. 2014). According to the 2014 Manufacturing Cost Index Indonesia, India, Thailand and Mexico were ranked as the world's most cost competitive nations in manufacturing.

After the global financial crisis of 2008–09, the pressure for cost effectiveness increased. This resulted in multinational firms (especially export-oriented ones) concentrating their production capacities. They did this in an attempt to exploit the benefits of higher capacity utilisation and to leverage the superior relation between variable and fixed costs in their existing locations (Kinkel 2012). German multinational manufacturers found this resulted in more efficient far-shore destinations in Asia gaining in attractiveness over the increasingly costly near-shore locations in Eastern Europe (Kinkel 2012). Interestingly, while overall relocation of production activities abroad declined significantly for German manufacturers after the global financial crisis, the amount of re-shoring back to Germany remained stable (Kinkel 2012).

MULTIPLE-CHOICE QUESTION

Flexible manufacturing systems and global supply chains

International production and logistics have dual goals of reducing costs while increasing quality and reliability. Cost efficiencies can be achieved by locating in countries with high productivity as well as low operating and transport costs and. However, they can also introduce efficient production techniques. These include flexible manufacturing systems (FMS), which 'integrate computer-controlled tools and material handling systems with a centralized monitoring and scheduling function' (MacCormack et al. 1994). They are an efficient response to the reduction of product life cycles and the need to adapt products to satisfy idiosyncratic customer needs. JIT inventory management enable an instant response to specific customer demands and mostly removes the necessity of holding inventories. Finally, total quality management (TQM) focuses on continuous improvement whereby 'heavy emphasis is placed on understanding and incorporating customer requirements into daily job routines at every level' (MacCormack et al. 1994).

FLEXIBLE MANUFACTURING SYSTEMS (FMS) systems that bring together computer-controlled tools and material handling systems, and have a central monitoring and scheduling function.

TOTAL QUALITY MANAGEMENT (TQM) concentrates on continuous improvement across every level in daily job routines; it emphasises understanding and integrating customer requirements into this high standard.

TQM, Six Sigma and ISO 9000

The total quality management and Six Sigma quality improvement methodologies are important tools that allow multinationals to increase the reliability of their product offerings. The TQM philosophy suggests that mistakes, defects, and materials of poor quality should be eliminated through management practices that encourage employees to spend time on quality-related issues. Standards should be defined not just in terms of quantity but with a focus on defect-free output and continuous improvement. This philosophy was widely adopted by Japanese and US companies in the 1980s and 1990s. Later it was modified into a more recent Six Sigma philosophy that strives to decrease flaws, increase productivity, eradicate waste and cut overall costs. Companies ranging from major multinationals (such as Motorola and GE) to SMEs and service sector organisations have embraced this philosophy to boost their product quality and productivity (Aboelmaged 2010).

SIX SIGMA production philosophy that aims to reduce defects, boost productivity, eliminate waste and cut overall costs.

When considering regulations and certifications, international quality standards, such as the ISO 9000, are also focusing companies' attention towards quality. They can often provide useful information when deciding which business partner you should source from or cooperate with. However, it may not be sufficient to merely comply with these standards. For example, some Australian companies sought quality certification because of externally-imposed reasons. Namely, the necessity to obtain a certificate. In contrast, other companies sought quality certification because of an internally driven desire to improve organisational performance. These internally driven companies derived more beneficial outcomes than their externally driven counterparts (Jones et al. 1997).

Flexible manufacturing and mass customisation

The goal of production efficiency does not mean that products must be standardised and produced on a massive scale. FMS have challenged this notion with production techniques that can deliver both low cost and high levels of product customisation. They are related to the concept of lean management, which advocates continuous improvement and systematically seeks to achieve small, incremental changes in processes to improve efficiency and quality. More specifically, flexible manufacturing and lean management aim to reduce set up times for complex equipment, increase the utilisation of individual machines through better scheduling and improve quality control at all stages of the production process (Krafcik 1988). Toyota is one of the most famous examples of how to successfully implement flexible manufacturing technology (Ohno 1988). However, in some of its

LEAN MANAGEMENT a long-term oriented approach to running an organisation that supports the concepts of continuous improvement, systematically seeking to achieve small, incremental changes in processes to improve efficiency and quality.

factories, it has modified its flexible body line system to what it calls a 'global body line' to produce Camry and other models even more efficiently across multiple nations, including Vietnam, Japan and the US (Visnic 2002).

MASS CUSTOMISATION the capability of providing individually designed products and services to all customers through having a highly flexible and integrated process.

Mass customisation relates to the ability to provide individually designed products and services to every customer through high process flexibility and integration (Da Silveira et al. 2001). For example, customers buying from Opel Adam can customise a large number of the interior and exterior features on the car company's website before they order and purchase the car. One of the advantages of mass customisation is that it makes high value-added products and services possible through the premium profits inherently derivable from customised products (Jiao et al. 2003). This strength is particularly attractive to OEM-based industries (Jiao et al. 2003). The key to mass-customising effectively can be to postpone differentiating a product for a specific customer until the latest possible point in the supply chain (Feitzinger & Lee 1997). For example, HP decided to customise its DeskJet printers for the European market in its German distribution centre, rather than in its Singapore manufacturing facility, where they were produced (Feitzinger & Lee 1997). Mass customisation is making inroads into major Asian economies including China, where it can be potentially a game changer. According to McKinsey, a typical manufacturer in China, even with enormous online sales, knows relatively little about their customer. Mass customisation can change this (Orr 2014). A typical Chinese consumer will want to show off their customisation to friends and beyond. This can be on the manufacturer's site and on social media (Orr 2014). Ultimately, we may be heading for 'the experience economy', an era in which businesses will have to orchestrate memorable events and experiences, and not just products, for customers (Orr 2014).

The new dynamics of global manufacturing site location

Consultants Alan MacCormack, Lawrence Newman and Donald Rosenfield, in a *Sloan Management Review* article entitled 'The new dynamics of global manufacturing site location', argue that senior MNE managers in capital-intensive, mature industries should not neglect qualitative parameters when locating manufacturing plants (1994). Senior managers, facing severe bounded rationality constraints, tend to favour easily quantifiable variables such as factor cost advantages, thereby neglecting what may be much more important in the longer run: the knowledge and skills held by the local workforce. It is this workforce's quality that ultimately determines the effectiveness of MNE subsidiaries in implementing skill-based process technologies.

The authors identify a trend towards regionalisation, with many firms attempting to seek a manufacturing presence in each of the triad regions of North America, Europe and Asia to mitigate a variety of political risks (such as non-tariff barriers) and economic risks (such as foreign currency exposure) typically associated with the strategy of 'international projectors'. The question then arises where to locate manufacturing plants in host regions. The authors observe a critical manufacturing trend.

The emergence of manufacturing technologies and methodologies such as FMS, JIT manufacturing and TQM have reduced scale, increased the importance of worker education and skill, and placed demands on local infrastructure (MacCormack et al. 1994, p. 72).

The key point in the international context is that FMS, JIT and TQM all place significant demands on the host-country workforce, which is viewed as an important location advantage, supposed to implement and perhaps improve these systems. For example, in MNEs that use these systems, engineers typically 'outnumber production workers three to one' (MacCormack et al. 1994,

p. 73). In this context, the authors suggest human resources requirements be imposed on potential site locations.

> All employees must be highly flexible and multiskilled. For FMS, an ability to understand complex machinery and computers is essential. Successful JIT manufacturing requires that employees perform preventive maintenance, repairs, and complex planning activities. TQM ... improvement tools make extensive use of mathematics and statistics. Softer skills such as team dynamics and proactive problem-solving techniques are also important (MacCormack et al. 1994, p. 73).

If these high-quality requirements are imposed on the workforce, then manufacturing plants will benefit from being located in places with sophisticated labour markets, an extensive educational infrastructure, and substantial experience with advanced manufacturing, including experience embedded in component suppliers, logistics services providers and so on. A critical point here is that an excellent site location must provide resources that can be combined with the MNE's extant set of FSAs. These resources can usually only be found in high-cost locations, which will thus still be attractive in the future. In turn, the MNE's recombination capabilities are crucial to access, exploit and augment such advanced human resources available in the highly developed sites selected for manufacturing operations.

Managing a global supply chain

The process of managing the global supply chain is often referred to as logistics. Its key objectives are to achieve the lowest possible cost in a way that best serves customer needs. Supply chain is different from the value chain in its focus on the collection of logistics, specialists and activities that provide inputs to manufacturers or retailers. Examples of independent global providers of logistics services are DHL and FedEx. One way to reduce costs and better serve customer needs through supply-chain management is by using a JIT inventory system. Its key advantage is that it reduces inventory costs on delivering materials and other inputs at the manufacturing JIT to enter the production process and not before then. Another advantage is that defective inputs can be spotted right away and the supplier is informed about this quicker than under a traditional warehoused inventory system.

GLOBAL SUPPLY CHAIN
the firm's worldwide network of sourcing, production and distribution.

LOGISTICS
the process of managing the supply chain.

Logistics more broadly includes transportation, information, inventory, warehousing, materials handling and other activities related to the delivery of inputs, parts, components and finished products. Costs associated with delivering a product to an export market can account for close to half of the total cost (while material costs often account for most of the costs). A reduction in costs associated with sourcing and delivering the product to the market can have an enormous impact on profitability. While logistics and transport are often outsourced to third-party logistics providers, firms need to be aware of various choices related to international transportation modes such as land, ocean or air transport. The main factors affecting the choice are time, cost and reliability. Air transport is fast and reliable, but very costly. The cost of ocean freight is much lower, often accounting for less than 1 per cent of the final price, but it is slower and less reliable. Land transport is usually more expensive than ocean transport but cheaper than air freight. Logistics is a big business with a number of important players challenging the global heavyweights. New Zealand's Mainfreight, for example, offers freight transport and logistics services through its offices in Australia, China, Europe and the US.

Information technology is transforming the world of logistics and supply-chain management. Electronic data interchange (EDI) is becoming widespread, with electronic coordination of the flow of inputs into manufacturing and to the end user. Overseas buyers are increasingly demanding implementation of EDI tracking by their Asian and other suppliers to optimise supply-chain management, inventory management and responsiveness to customer needs (EDI Asia n.d.). Factors such as perceived benefits, government support and management support were found to be significant determinants of EDI adoption in SMEs in a study of 50 SMEs from Brunei (Seyal et al. 2007).

Transferring production knowledge across borders

Craig Galbraith provides a perspective on the transfer of core manufacturing technologies in high-technology firms (Galbraith 1990). He observes many firms locked into a situation of 'profitless prosperity', whereby continuous investment in innovation – combined with fierce international competition and short product cycles – brings little if any financial rewards. One way to escape from this situation, according to Galbraith, is to move towards a system of flexible, smaller manufacturing plants that can easily adapt to changes on both the demand and supply sides. For example, in terms of supply conditions, smaller plants can be set up to take advantage of lower input costs for simple value chain activities, such as the final stages of assembly and testing, or to be closer to places of technology creation. As regards demand, a decentralised manufacturing network facilitates region-specific production (for instance, geared specifically towards the EU countries) and also allows the MNE to easily expand, contract or refocus plants in response to changes in demand.

In the context of this chapter's discussion of factories' ability to generate transferable FSAs, the question then arises: can manufacturing technologies be easily transferred, deployed and exploited across factories in a firm's network? Galbraith found, after investigating a sample of domestic and international 32 manufacturing technology transfers, that these transfers were accompanied by substantial resource costs as well as productivity and know-how losses. Resource costs include pre-transfer planning and engineering costs, as well as post-transfer management and control costs. The productivity and know-how losses reflect the need for a start-up phase at the plant receiving the manufacturing knowledge, during which experiential knowledge from the source facility must be relearned at the recipient plant. There is a trade-off between the two above cost categories: higher resource costs (better planning and execution) should in principle reduce the productivity and know-how losses.

Even though Galbraith did not consider explicitly the complex issue of knowledge recombination, he observed that standalone and routine-type manufacturing knowledge faced substantial transfer difficulties. Even though the transfers were all intra-firm and limited to proven technologies, initial productivity losses averaged 34 per cent, with some recipient facilities never achieving pre-transfer productivity levels, and most taking several months to attain the levels prevailing at the donor facility. Galbraith observed an important bounded rationality problem: more pre-transfer training did not reduce productivity losses. The two main reasons for the disappointing effects of training were:

1. the training team often lacked operational responsibility and on-the-floor operational experience
2. insufficient attention was paid to production support activities, such as ordering and inventory control procedures, and the redefinition of personnel requirements and job responsibilities.

Galbraith also observed a bounded reliability problem; in several technology relocation cases, donor facility personnel refused to provide long-term support to the recipient facility. Such a lack of cooperation, obviously increasing productivity losses, occurred when manufacturing relocation was viewed as unfairly removing commercially viable production from the donor facility.

Offshoring high value-added activities

Offshoring has evolved from the global sourcing of low-value added activities such as product assembly and call centres, to moving high value-added activities such as R&D and design offshore. R&D offshoring and outsourcing still tend to only be utilised in relatively early phases of development. However, many companies from developed and emerging economies look for locations abroad where they could benefit from factors such as proximity to market, government support and local knowledge (Zámborský & Jacobs 2016). Key factors to consider when choosing the location of offshore R&D activities are: R&D labour costs, knowledge infrastructure, the science and engineering talent pool size, and political risk (Demirbag & Glaister 2010). At the firm level, experience of overseas R&D projects and prior experience in the host country are also important location determinants (Demirbag & Glaister 2010).

The Asia–Pacific region is an increasingly attractive location for FDI in R&D, accounting for almost half of the total global cross-border R&D investment in 2003–2012 (Hervás et al. 2014). For example, there are over 1500 foreign R&D centres in China and each year there are more being set up in there than anywhere else in the world (Yip 2014). General Electric has three R&D and three regional innovation centres in China. Other companies conducting R&D in China include Oracle, Daimler, Boston Scientific and Toyota. In 2016, even Apple, known for keeping their R&D and design concentrated in California, established a US$45 million R&D centre in Beijing and plans a second one in Shenzhen (Jennings 2016). The R&D offshoring goes both ways however; Asian–Pacific firms are

FIGURE 11.4 The Asia–Pacific is an increasingly attractive R&D location

also investing in R&D abroad. Chinese firms are important investors in European R&D (Di Minin et al. 2012). Australian and New Zealand firms also establish innovation-intensive activities in Europe and elsewhere (Zámborský & Ingršt 2016). For example, an Australian financial services provider Macquarie has its innovation hubs located in London, New York and Hong Kong. Rakon, a New Zealand high-tech manufacturer, has innovative subsidiaries in France and the UK.

While China has emerged as an important destination for R&D offshoring, India is also a key player. Tech giants including Microsoft, Intel and Cisco have invested billions of dollars in R&D and IT services in India. Indian offshoring providers have also matured from providers of lower value-added activities (such as call centres and back-office functions). Now they also provide higher value-added activities such as consulting, both from India and their foreign bases. In line with this strategy, Infosys recently announced it was planning to add about 10 000 new jobs in the US (Weise 2017). Indian IT service offshoring firms also employ thousands of workers in their bases located throughout Europe. One of the most recent trends is innovation-intensive investment by emerging multinationals in emerging economies (Zámborský & Ingršt 2017). Although still in its infancy, it is gaining momentum (Chaminade & Gómez 2016).

Regional learning and centres of excellence

Foreign sites with strategic roles involving high value-added activities often serve as conduits for the development of products to fit the specific needs of regions where they are located. For example, Hewlett-Packard's printer design centre in Singapore serves as a hub for products tailored to the needs of the Asian–Pacific market. This strategy implies that MNEs engage in regional learning from people, firms, and the innovation systems of countries and regions in which they are located. Subsidiaries in specific countries can have mandates to develop products for their country, group of countries, or region, or have a global mandate.

CENTRE OF EXCELLENCE
a business unit that exemplifies the capabilities recognised by the organisation as a significant source of value creation, with the aim for these capabilities be leveraged and disseminated across the other units of the firm.

Some companies use the term centre of excellence to describe a particularly proficient subsidiary. This is defined as an 'organizational unit that embodies a set of capabilities that has been explicitly recognized by the [parent] firm as an important source of value creation, with the intention that these capabilities be leveraged by and/or disseminated to other parts of the firm' (Frost et al. 2002). These centres of excellence often have regional mandates. For example, the US firm Honeywell announced an industrial cybersecurity centre of excellence for the Asia–Pacific in Singapore in 2017. Honeywell stated that the centre would provide an innovation platform for securing the industrial Internet of Things within the region (Ross, 2017). A multinational's capability of coordinating multiple, often regional, centres of excellence can be a decisive competitive advantage that is at the heart of a global learning process (Reger 2004).

Global and regional learning between multinationals' subsidiaries, centres of excellence and headquarters do not come without tensions though. The headquarters often have superior technological capabilities, which present a paradox (Song & Shin, 2008). On the one hand, they enhance the headquarters' learning capabilities. On the other hand, they reduce the headquarters' motivations to outsource knowledge from host countries. There are multiple factors that influence the extent to which a multinational corporation's headquarters sources knowledge from the host countries of its R&D labs. It is important to consider both relative and absolute levels of technological capabilities. The relative levels of technological capabilities can influence headquarters' motivations to source knowledge from host countries (Song & Shin, 2008). As the relative gap between the headquarters' technological capabilities and capabilities of regional centres of excellence shrinks, the motivation for the headquarters to learn increases. The recent rise of Asian centres of excellence from Singapore to Shanghai and Bangalore reflects the shrinking gap in relative technological capabilities and infrastructure in Asia versus the West.

Alliances with suppliers and customers

The previous discussion around transferring core manufacturing technologies and offshoring of high value-added work such as R&D mostly assumed that companies were keeping these activities within the firm. However, firms can also find external partners abroad to perform these core activities for them. As discussed in Chapter 7, one of the most popular partners for such alliances are suppliers. Even the largest multinationals realise that there is enormous potential for innovation and other high value-added work outside of their firm. For example, Procter & Gamble calculated that there were over 50 000 R&D staff in their supply network and that it would be beneficial to tap into that brainpower to diversify and complement its own R&D (Huston & Sakkab 2006).

Japanese and South Korean firms are excellent examples of multinationals that invested into long-term relationships with their suppliers. Toyota and other Japanese car makers have strategic alliances with their suppliers that go back decades, often involving minority equity stakes to signal commitment and trust. In these long-term partnerships, the car makers and their suppliers collaborate on ways to increase value additions by cooperating in the design of component parts to improve quality, or by implementing JIT delivery. These relationships often persist when companies establish operations abroad. For example, Korean car makers brought their suppliers with them to distant countries such as Slovakia when they established their outposts in the European Union (Zámborský 2012b). The Toyota Yaris is produced in a close network and collaboration with over 100 suppliers throughout Europe.

VIDEO

Alliances with customers are an alternative to strategic alliances with suppliers. A study of over 200 companies representing different manufacturing industries in Malaysia found that the key differences between the two are: the relationship between the business environment factors and alliance motives is stronger for alliances with suppliers than for alliances with customers; and the relationship between perception of opportunistic behaviour and interdependence in the alliance is significant for alliance with suppliers (Loke et al. 2013). A related study compares US and East Asian companies' strategies to integrated operations with suppliers and customers in the supply chain (Zailani & Rajagopal 2005). It found that East Asian companies differ from US companies in their approaches to information sharing, and to internal and external integration and control in the supply chain. It concludes that the potential benefits of integrated supply chain are substantial. However, this will only be realised if the interrelationships among various parts of the supply chain, including suppliers and customers, are recognised and proper alignment is ensured between the design and execution of the firm's strategy (Zailani & Rajagopal 2005).

MULTIPLE-CHOICE QUESTION

Risks in international production and sourcing

While international production and sourcing has many benefits, there are caveats. These include potentially higher employee turnover in foreign countries and possibly lower product quality and productivity. This may sometimes result in firms moving production or sourcing back to the home country (BCG 2015). The Boston Consulting Group found that US manufacturers were more likely to add production capacity in the US than in China in 2015–2020 (2015). Factors such as logistics, inventory costs, ease of doing business, and the risks of operating extended supply chains are influencing executives' decisions to bring manufacturing back to the US. Over 75 per cent of respondents reported that a primary reason for re-shoring production of goods sold in the US was to 'shorten our supply chain', while 70 per cent cited reduced shipping costs and 64 per cent said 'to be closer to customers' (BCG 2015).

It is important to consider the dynamic nature of cost drivers, including labour, transportation, energy and environmental costs, such as carbon offsets. The cost elements in global sourcing can be static, dynamic or hidden. Hence, companies need to carefully evaluate them in a comprehensive framework of benefit, cost and risk assessment (Holweg et al. 2011). A high share of global sourcing does not necessarily improve a firm's competitiveness. There are limits to global sourcing if the firm is unable to become a preferred customer of its strategic suppliers (Steinle & Schiele 2008). Achieving preferred customer status is more realistic for firms located in the same region or nation than it is for foreign firms attempting to access a remote supplier (Steinle & Schiele 2008). Furthermore, the instability of exchange rates has also led to increased costs and risks of global sourcing (Kotabe & Murray 2004).

SPOTLIGHT 11.3

Fletcher Building: challenges in constructing global success

Fletcher Building, one of the largest companies in New Zealand and Australia, operates in more than 40 countries, manufacturing and sourcing globally. Its key international businesses are the Formica Group (with production in Asia, Europe and North America) and the Roof Tile Group (with pro-

duction in New Zealand, Malaysia, Hungary and the US). Global production and sourcing are at the centre of the company's success. One of the key challenges for the firm was the location of its new manufacturing plants, shifting from a focus on the US and Europe to Asia. Formica manufacturing's operations now include plants in Thailand, Taiwan, China and India. To reflect the importance of international business to Fletcher Building, the company has a dedicated international division, about NZ$2.1 billion in revenue and over 5000 people, alongside its other major divisions such as building products, about NZ$2.5 billion in revenue, construction, about NZ$1.7 billion in revenue, and distribution, about NZ$3.2 billion in revenue (Fletcher Building n.d.). Key businesses of the international division include Formica (laminates used for decorative surfaces such as kitchen benchtops), Homapal (laminates with special surfaces of metal), Laminex (laminates and surface solutions for interior spaces), Decra and Gerard (steel roof tiles), Dimond (metal roofing, cladding, rain water, flooring and structural solutions). These businesses source many of their inputs, such as steel, globally. Fletcher aims to further source from low-cost countries (Fletcher Building 2016). However, the sourcing of steel from China came under controversy due to irregular and possibly fake quality certification (Edmunds 2017; Pennington 2016). One alternative to sourcing steel from China is New Zealand Steel Ltd.

QUESTIONS

1. Is there a rationale for bringing some of Fletcher Building's foreign production back to New Zealand or Australia?
2. How should Fletcher Building respond to emerging problems regarding sourcing steel from China and abroad?

WEBLINK

SPOTLIGHT QUESTIONS

Political, social and ethical issues in global sourcing

International production and sourcing are often not popular with workers in home countries. Even in countries that receive the offshored production or other work, there are often concerns about the impact on local firms and the overall benefits to the host country (Zámborský 2012a). On the other hand, consumers tend to benefit from the lower prices of imported goods. Furthermore, companies that produce and source internationally benefit from improved overall efficiency. People around the world, such as Donald Trump's voters in the US and Britain's Brexit voters, made it clear that they fear excessive globalisation of production but also migration. Politicians and companies need to be sensitive to the popular backlash against globalisation. While an increasing array of jobs can now be offshored, the openness of the world economy also constitutes an opportunity for specialised sectors and people in home economies to be internationally competitive. The best response to fear is to change and prepare for the future. For example, while the rise of Asian competitiveness in manufacturing and services is a threat to many Australian and New Zealand jobs, the rise of Asia is also creating a massive new opportunity for Australia and New Zealand in the services sector. A report entitled 'Australia's jobs future: the rise of Asia and the services opportunity' demonstrated that by 2030, services can become Australia's number 1 export to Asia in terms of total value added. Furthermore, this could support over a million Australian jobs (PwC Australia, ANZ Banking Group & Asialink Business 2015). These jobs can be generated through increasing the exports of services from Australia, expansion of offshore operations by Australian services businesses, and service

industries supporting the growth of Australian goods exports (PwC Australia, ANZ Banking Group & Asialink Business 2015).

Finance, transport, information technology and engineering services businesses can expand the supply of specialised capabilities to Australian export-oriented firms. The urbanisation and modernisation of Asian economies will also create opportunities for Australian businesses supplying services from Australia (for example, in financial services, education, business services, transport and healthcare industries) (PwC Australia, ANZ Banking Group & Asialink Business 2015). Inbound tourism has been an important industry for Australia and will continue to grow. New Zealand can capture similar opportunities in service sectors ranging from hospitality to transport and education.

Global sourcing also has social and ethical implications. Sourcing and manufacturing around the globe raises concerns related to the multinationals' role in improving working conditions and labour practices, promoting human rights and protecting our natural environment. Incidents, such as the 2013 collapse of the Rana Plaza factory in Bangladesh where over 1000 workers died in a facility producing clothing for brands such Benetton and Primark, have raised the risk for companies that source their products from low-cost countries with potentially unsafe working conditions. While some of the multinational companies' responses were only reactive, such as compensating the victims of this tragedy, many also recognised their response to these types of issues had to be more proactive and vowed 'never again'.

The new governance arrangements created by Western clothing companies reflects a corporation-led model, rather than government-led one, for governing the apparel industry supply chains (Hira & Benson-Rea 2017). Western brands put together two agreements to incorporate safety and human rights into their supply chains. The agreements legally bind companies to invest into improving garment factory conditions. One area for improvement is to conduct more due diligence

FIGURE 11.5 Activists protest H&M clothing production labour conditions

regarding the suppliers of raw materials, rather than just the suppliers at the final stage of production. Moving to higher value-added activities is critical for supplier firms, but it does not necessarily lead to better work conditions within supplier firms (Khattak et al. 2017). The combination of economic and social upgrading is positively associated with suppliers manufacturing high value-added goods and operating in relational (not captive) networks (Khattak et al. 2017).

Strategies for minimising risk in international sourcing

Table 11.2 summarises the major costs and risks of international sourcing and production, including cross-cultural, compliance, quality, competitive and ethical risks. Other risks include low productivity or skill of foreign workers, negative impact on home staff morale, over-dependency on suppliers, exchange rate risk and a weak legal environment. Companies need to devise strategies to mitigate these risks. However, many companies do not have a structured supply-chain risk management and mitigation system; instead, they only use informal approaches to cope with risk (Christopher et al. 2011). A multidisciplinary approach is required when dealing with global sourcing risks. This starts with the classification of risks into different categories. These can include: supply risk, process and control risks, environmental and sustainability risks, and demand risks (Christopher et al. 2011).

TABLE 11.2 Major global sourcing costs, risks and strategies for their mitigation

Cost or risk	Example from the Asia–Pacific	Mitigation strategies
Cross-cultural	Yellow Pages New Zealand offshored call centres to the Philippines to find out that local staff misunderstood Kiwi colloquialisms	Select right country Cross-cultural training Build relationship
Compliance	Coca-Cola's bottling factory in India had to be put on hold due to concerns about impact on ground water and local farmers	Foresee local opposition Coopt local stakeholders Regulatory vigilance
Quality	Fake quality certificates for steel imported from China hurt Fletcher Building's reputation for quality products	Independent certification Total quality control Captive offshoring
Competitive	Samsung and HTC used to be contract suppliers, then created their own branded products to compete with former clients	Don't share core IP Be a preferred supplier Don't become dependent
Ethical	Collapse of Rana Plaza supplier factory in Bangladesh, killing over 1000 people, hurt reputation of Primark, Benetton and other brands	Regular producer audit Supplier due diligence Proactive support

Strategies for minimising risk in international sourcing and production should start with a careful evaluation of the actual long-term strategic reasons for this venture beyond just cost cutting. How the strategy coalesces with the company's value proposition and core competencies must also be clarified. Employees and other key stakeholders at home and in relevant locations have to be coopted. This is so that international sourcing does not hurt the morale of staff in locations which are vital to company's long-term success. Careful decisions need to be made about whether to make or buy and some activities may be offshored to captive subsidiaries, perhaps with the help of expatriate managers from home or core bases. Transparent communication and the exchange of information with suppliers is also essential so that ambiguity doesn't lead to misunderstanding (Craig & Willmott 2005). Communication should also lead to collaboration and, when appropriate, joint initiatives such as co-development and co-design like what exists between Toyota and its suppliers. Lastly, the firm needs to protect itself from losing its key intellectual property and prevent suppliers from becoming potential competitors. For example, Giant, the world's largest bike manufacturer from Taiwan, was previously a supplier to US bike makers.

While these strategies mostly consider the perspective of a large Western multinational, local suppliers in East Asia are rightly striving to move up the value chain. In the World Bank book *Global Production Networking and Technological Change in East Asia* (Sturgeon & Lester 2004), the authors argue that the region's firms need to develop their ability to harness the potential of global production networks and build their own innovative capability.

According to the book, East Asian firms must not only achieve greater efficiency, but also become more innovative, offering differentiated products in order to vie with other first-tier MNE suppliers (Sturgeon & Lester 2004). Firms in the region will also need to develop a technological edge if they are to compete with multinationals from the developed countries and form their own global production networks. A strategy linked to technological advance will be necessary to foster the growth of innovative Asian firms that can remain competitive in global markets (Sturgeon & Lester 2004). In the last 10 years, many Asian firms have followed this advice and, in some cases, bargaining power shifted from lead (Western) firms in GVCs to large suppliers in developing countries, particularly in East Asia (Gereffi 2014).

Summary

Learning objective 1: Appreciate changes in the international business environment that lead to new trends in global sourcing and production.

Sourcing and production of goods, services and business processes has become global. While manufacturing has been a sector significantly exposed to this trend over the last few decades, services such as technical support or engineering design are emerging as an important sector. Service tasks are offshored to different countries and often outsourced to independent providers. Politics and technology are reshaping these trends though, with developments such as re-shoring back to home countries, as well as robotic automation replacing humans through no-shoring.

Learning objective 2: Understand the key parameters that fundamentally define the roles of foreign production plants.

Foreign production plants can have different and evolving roles based upon two parameters. First, the strategic purpose of the plant, which is related to the host-country location advantages the MNE wants to access; for example, its proximity to the market, low costs or high skills. Second, the amount of firm specific advantage a company can gain from its subsidiary. This hinges upon a comparison between the parent and subsidiary's potential capabilities. Cost efficiency is an important, but not the only, strategic goal driving the uptake of foreign plants.

Learning objective 3: Recognise the benefits of production planning tools such as FMS, JIT and TQM.

Efficient production techniques contribute to the dual goal of reducing costs and increasing quality and reliability. FMS integrate computer-controlled tools and material handling systems with centralised monitoring and scheduling functionalities. JIT inventory management allows for an immediate response to specific customer demands and reduces the need to hold inventories. TQM focuses on continuous improvement, placing a strong emphasis on customer requirements in daily worker routines.

Learning objective 4: Appreciate the difficulties associated with transferring production knowledge in multinational firms.

Transferring production knowledge in manufacturing firms entails numerous challenges and can often lead to resource costs, as well as productivity and know-how losses. An example of when this can occur is when donor facility personnel refuse to provide long-term support to the recipient facility. Despite there being difficulties surrounding the management of transferring sophisticated technological knowledge, offshoring has evolved from global sourcing of low-value added activities, such as product assembly, to locating high value-added activities, such as R&D and design, abroad.

Learning objective 5: Know the limitations and risks of a global sourcing and production strategy.

While global production and sourcing have many benefits, they also have their risks. Some companies are re-assessing excessive offshoring, opting to bring production and sourcing closer to home. They cite reasons like, shortening their supply chain, reducing shipping costs and becoming closer to

USEFUL WEBSITES

customers. Political, social and ethical issues also affect global sourcing. Multinationals increasingly engage in thorough supplier audit and community involvement in developing countries, where their goods are often produced in unsafe conditions by poorly paid workers.

REVISION QUESTIONS

Revision questions

1. What is the difference between offshoring and outsourcing?
2. What are the six key roles of foreign production plants, according to Kasra Ferdows?
3. What human resource requirements are relevant for foreign plants using FMS, JIT and TQM techniques?
4. What is a centre of excellence and how does it relate to the concept of regional learning?
5. Name and briefly describe a couple of strategies for minimising risk in global sourcing.

R&D ACTIVITIES

R&D activities

1. Consider a product you are familiar with, such as a Dell laptop or a Samsung smartphone. Research the company's website and learn about where each of the main value-creation activities of the company's or the product's value chain is located in the world. Create a video presentation explaining how globalised the value chain of the product is.
2. H&M, the second-largest fashion retailer in the world, has about four-fifths of its production in Asia, far more than Inditex (owner of Zara, the world's largest fashion retailer), which sources around half of its products from countries close to its main markets. Should H&M move to sourcing less of its production from Asia? Why? Explain your reasoning.
3. Read about H&M's and Zara's supply chain on their websites. Describe a concrete initiative that one of these companies put in place to respond to ethical concerns about worker safety, compensation and other work conditions at its suppliers. Suggest one other concrete initiative that the company may consider and present your proposal to class.

IB MASTERCLASS

Defining the roles of manufacturing plants at Flex

As an electronics manufacturing services (EMS) company, Singapore's Flex initially managed from its headquarters in San Jose, California. Called Flextronics until 2015, Flex may be an unfamiliar name to many, but it produces and delivers printers for Hewlett-Packard, mobile phones for Motorola and Xboxes for Microsoft, just to name a few of its customers. Its net sales in the fiscal year 2017 reached US$23.9 billion, with 36 per cent from the Americas, 18 per cent from Europe and 46 per cent from Asia. Its manufacturing facilities are dispersed in about 30 countries in Asia, Europe and the Americas (Flex n.d.).

Originally founded by Joe McKenzie and his wife in California in 1969, Flex initially soldered components into printed circuit boards (PCBs) for electronics firms, commonly referred to as OEMs, in Silicon Valley. In 1980, the McKenzies sold Flex to a group of private investors, who expanded the firm's business from a mere 'stuffer' to a contract manufacturer. When Flex was just a stuffer, OEM customers shipped PCBs and components to Flex, which soldered components into the PCBs and then shipped the finished PCBs back to the OEM customers for further assembly. In contrast, when Flex became a contract manufacturer, OEM customers provided only the PCB design, and Flex took on the responsibility of purchasing the components and manufacturing the board.

In the 1980s, Flex expanded internationally. Setting up a facility in Singapore in 1981, it became one of the first US manufacturers to move offshore. By 1989, Flex's sales had reached US$202 million, with several operations in Asia and the US. However, the Silicon Valley downturn in the early 1990s seriously reduced the demand for Flex's services. A complex buyout privatised the firm in 1990, and the new owners moved the formal home base to Singapore and shut down US operations. Flex went public again in 1994.

Acquiring a global presence

Michael Marks became Flex's Chairman in 1993 and its CEO in 1994. He decided to rebuild the international presence of Flex through an aggressive strategy. Flex acquired manufacturing assets from OEMs and then used these assets to provide electronics manufacturing services, often to the very same OEMs. For example, Flex acquired manufacturing assets in Canada, Brazil, Malaysia and Mexico from Xerox, and then used these assets to manufacture copiers for Xerox. Flex moved aggressively, acquiring 53 operations between 1993 and 2001. Major acquisitions included the printed circuit board assemblies (PCBAs) business from the Astron Group Ltd in Hong Kong in 1996, the assembly for industrial automation from ABB in 1999 and the systems assembly for GSM mobile phones from Bosch Telecom in Denmark in 2000 (Flextronics 1996–2006).

The considerable number of acquisitions led to a global network of manufacturing plants. In 1999, Flex started to report its facilities using a classification that included industrial parks, regional manufacturing facilities, product introduction centres, and manufacturing and technology centres. After 2002, Flex changed its reporting, classifying its facilities into three types: industrial parks, regional manufacturing facilities and product introduction centres.

Industrial parks are located in low-cost areas close to major electronics markets. With facilities ranging between 270 000 square feet and more than 1.9 million square feet, these industrial parks contain both Flex's manufacturing and distribution operations, and a number of its major suppliers, thereby reducing transportation costs and turnaround times in the manufacturing process. These parks were designed for fully integrated, large-volume manufacturing. In 2012, Flex had nine industrial parks located on three continents, with one in Poland, two in Hungary, two in Mexico, one in Brazil, one in India and two in China.

Regional manufacturing facilities engage in medium- and high-volume manufacturing in locations close to strategic markets.

Product introduction centres provide low-volume manufacturing services and a broad range of engineering services.

Finally, a fourth category, regional manufacturing and technology centres, are a combination of regional manufacturing facilities and product introduction centres. Regional manufacturing and technology centres were set up to launch new products, transform new products to mass production, and conduct medium- and high-volume manufacturing. Such regional centres include product introduction centres with advanced technological competencies, see below.

Industrial parks in focus

Industrial parks have been a major driver for the fast growth at Flex; former CEO Marks even commented, over 20 years, ago that 'the future is big locations like these' (Dolan 2002).

Since 2001, the company consolidated more of its production into its industrial parks. Only a year after its inception, 30 per cent of Flex's business was performed through the parks (Dolan 2002). Flex's approach was to purchase extra land adjacent to its manufacturing facilities, and then attract suppliers and distributors to set up facilities in the park, where the supply of water, electricity and other services was readily available. Flex sometimes even took responsibility for government relations or put up buildings and leased them to the suppliers. Such services were crucial to its suppliers, many of whom were small US firms lacking Flex's recombination abilities.

While some industrial parks faced internal competition, others did not. For example, the Chennai industrial park in India was built to be Flex's only industrial park for India. It served the Indian market exclusively for many years, although it has now become part of Flex's global supply network and India now boasts several manufacturing centres (Babu & Sachitanand 2005; Flex n.d.). In contrast, other parks experienced internal competition when they were first set up. The Guadalajara industrial park in Mexico and the Hungarian industrial parks, for example, mainly targeted the North American market and European market respectively, due to their proximity to these markets. They now are part of Flex's global supply chain. However, back in the early 2000s, some of the jobs completed at the industrial parks in Mexican and Hungarian parks were moved to the Doumen industrial park in China.

The Doumen industrial park quickly moved from making simple mobile phone chargers, to advanced miniature printed boards, to Microsoft's sophisticated Xbox and beyond. Today, the park is involved in making 'high-end smartphones, module devices dedicated to the Internet of Things, communications equipment, cloud data network switches, smart homes, intelligent robots, and precision machinery among other high-end products' (China Daily 2018). Tony Capretta, who was Flex's resident General Manager in the early 2000s and today is the Vice President of Flex's Customer 360, acknowledged the technical capability and experience of the plant's workforce back in the early 2000s: 'We can do anything here that we make anywhere else … The learning curve is a fast ramp' (Wonacott 2002).

During the early 2000s, the Doumen industrial park enjoyed the proximity of a dense local supplier network, as almost all materials the firm needed were available from thousands of suppliers that were within a two-hour drive of the park. In contrast, many materials and components needed by the Guadalajara industrial park in Mexico and the Hungarian industrial parks had to be sourced from the Far East. So, the Doumen industrial park boasted lower labour costs, strong local suppliers and rising technological capabilities, which made it very competitive within Flex.

In 2018, Doumen industrial park has become Flex's 'global flagship' and is the company's 'exemplary park'; over the next four years, the park is set 'to make production systems up to 30 per cent faster and 25 per cent more efficient, and elevate mass customization to new levels' (China Daily 2018).

However, not all production was moved to China back in the early 2000s. In a comment on the disruption of its supply chain (including maritime shipping) in China caused by the SARS virus, former CEO Marks said, 'Some companies are moving stuff to China that really doesn't belong there. It makes sense to make cell phones in China because they are inexpensive to air freight. But personal computers don't travel well. If you start to air-freight PCs because of a supply disruption, your cost-savings disappear instantly (Business Week 2003).' In the case of Xbox game consoles, Flex initially centralised production for the European market in Hungary and production for the US market in Mexico, but soon shifted all its production to China. After the shutdown of the Xbox production line in Hungary, however, Flex ramped up other production lines at its Hungarian industrial parks, hiring personnel to make other products such as TVs for France's Schneider Electric (Smith 2003).

Restructuring the global network of plants

The many acquisitions made by Flex over 20 years resulted in a wide variety of plants spread around the globe. With a booming EMS business in the 1990s, such a huge, internationally dispersed network met demand very well. However, the slow growth period of the US economy after 2001 and the duplication of manufacturing triggered restructuring efforts from the company.

Flex consolidated its production by closing (or exiting from) some duplicate plants and concentrating its similar activities into fewer locations. In mid-2001, Flex laid off 11 168 employees (Flextronics 2001). At the same time, it shut down around 20 per cent of its factory space (Dolan 2002). In Singapore, it shut down its manufacturing plants and changed the Singaporean operation into a competency centre in design (Serant 2001b).

However, the restructuring did not mean simply moving all manufacturing to low-cost countries. The CEO at the time, Marks, commented:

> it's a great simplification – and a lot of people fall into this trap – to say that all manufacturing is going to get done in Mexico, Hungary, and China. Consumer products will be made there. But the infrastructure products – technically complex value-added products – are easy to manufacture in developed countries. That's why we also have big operations in the US, Germany, France, and Sweden, where you have high capabilities in engineering. The OEMs like us to be everywhere (Bilinsky 2000).

As noted by Marks, Flex still operated plants in some high-cost locations, either to stay close to key customers or to gain advanced technological capabilities. For example, although the firm shut down 26 of its 40 regional plants in electronics enclosures, it kept 14 regional plants to be close to customers and to offer specific value-added activities, such as focusing on new product introduction and design (Serant 2001a).

Gaining technological competencies was the other reason to stay in some high-cost locations. This is reflected in Flex's revised acquisition strategy, whereby acquisition activities focused primarily on companies that had the recombination capabilities to offer technological solutions customised to customer needs. One example of this new strategy was the acquisition of US-based Instrumentation Engineering, Inc. (IE, based in Oakland, New Jersey) in 2001, a systems test equipment developer and manufacturer. IE had experience in designing and building customised test systems for optical and wireless network equipment, which would enhance Flex's capacity and capabilities in the functional test market. IE's president took on a global role within Flex's test operations worldwide (Shedd 2001).

After the recession in 2008, Flex took on another round of restructuring to cope with the impact of lower demand faced by its customers. This time, the restructuring focused on cost cutting and improving operational efficiencies. Flex aimed to save around US$230–260 million by shifting operations to more efficiently run locations and laying-off some of its workforce (Flextronics 2009). The company also consolidated its suppliers to leverage its economies of scale and develop more strategic relationships. Flex now makes 90 per cent of its purchases with just 10 per cent of its suppliers (Carbone 2009).

Flex in Asia

Asia continues to be a stronghold for Flex's operations with an estimated 60 per cent of production being performed there (Supply Chain Asia Magazine 2012). Production locations can be found throughout China, India, Japan, Malaysia, Singapore and Taiwan. Each location has developed specific strengths derived from the environment it operates in. For example, in Singapore, where the country is known for its advances in healthcare, Flex, as it was then known, established a medical manufacturing facility to help benefit the firm from innovative medical technologies. In China, the future largest auto market in the world, it operated a product design centre to assist automotive clients with product development.

China, in particular, remains an important market for Flex. In 2012, it had an estimated 600 000 employees across 17 locations (Supply Chain Asia Magazine 2012). Given the scale of the firm's operations in China, it was important for the company to develop specific skills to succeed in its various markets. Target markets in China often consist of smaller, locally based customers, as opposed to the large multinational corporations that make up the majority of customers in Western markets. To meet the needs of these smaller customers, the firm developed the Flex supplier portal, which allowed customers to effectively track supplies to better meet end user needs. Further, Flex developed human resource practices aimed at retaining local workers in an industry that typically experiences high turnover after the Chinese New Year. By responding to local pressures in China, Flex were able to develop successful practices that could be transferred across Asia.

Conclusion

After its change of name in 2015, the firm aimed to continue its successful growth in Asia; however, it also wanted to focus on diversifying globally (Supply Chain Asia Magazine 2012). Asia's share on its net sales fell from 52 per cent in 2011 to 46 per cent in 2017, with the Americas' share rising from 29 per cent in 2011 to 36 per cent (Flex 2017, p. 33). China, Mexico, the US and Malaysia were the key countries with over 10 per cent shares on sales, which were 30 per cent, 17 per cent, 11 per cent and 10 per cent respectively (Flex 2017, p. 96).

In 2012, Flex operated regional manufacturing and technology centres in over 20 countries, distributed across both high-cost and low-cost manufacturing locations in Europe, the Americas and Asia. Roughly 74 per cent of production in 2011 was completed in low-cost manufacturing locations to provide customers with competitive prices (Flextronics 2011, p. 10). By 2017, the company's emphasis had shifted from assembly and manufacturing operations, which still generates the majority of its revenues, to innovation services, and design and engineering services (Flex 2017, p. 6).

QUESTIONS

1. Define the strategic roles of the following plants mentioned in the case: the Chennai industrial park in India, the Guadalajara industrial park in Mexico, the Doumen industrial park in China, regional manufacturing and technology centres, and the plants acquired from IE.
2. Why does Flex still have manufacturing activities in some high-cost regions?
3. What changes happened at the Singapore operations? What changes happened at the Doumen industrial park in China? What was expected for the Chennai industrial park in India?

References

Aboelmaged, M.G. (2010). Six Sigma quality: a structured review and implications for future research. *International Journal of Quality & Reliability Management*, 27(3), 268–317.

Asian Productivity Organization (APO) (2016). *APO Productivity Databook 2016*. Retrieved from www.apo-tokyo.org/publications/wp-content/uploads/sites/5/APO-Productivity-Databook-2016.pdf

Babu, V. & Sachitanand, R. (2005). Heralding a hardware boom. *Business Today*, 6 November, p. 98.

Bain Insights (2014). Saving to grow: Using procurement to win in Asia. *Forbes*, 23 January. Retrieved from www.forbes.com/sites/baininsights/2014/01/23/saving-to-grow-using-procurement-to-win-in-asia/#1bbfecfa416a

Berg, A. & Hedrick, S. (2014). What's next in apparel sourcing? McKinsey&Company, May. Retrieved from www.mckinsey.com/industries/retail/our-insights/whats-next-in-apparel-sourcing

Boston Consulting Group (BCG) (2015). Reshoring of Manufacturing to the US Gains Momentum. 10 December. Retrieved from www.bcg.com/publications/2015/reshoring-of-manufacturing-to-the-us-gains-momentum.aspx

Business Week (2003). Weathering the tech storm: How Michael Marks boosted efficiency at contract manufacturer Flextronics. *Business Week*, 5 May, p. 24B.

Bilinsky, G. (2000). Heroes of U.S. manufacturing. *Fortune* 141, 20 March, p. 192A.

Carbone, J. (2009). Flextronics focuses more spend with fewer suppliers. *Purchasing*, 17 December, p. 30.

Chaminade, C. & Gómez, L. (2016). Technology-Driven Foreign Direct Investment within the Global South, in WIPO (ed.), *The Global Innovation Index 2016*, Geneva: WIPO, pp. 81–90. Available at: www.wipo.int/edocs/pubdocs/en/wipo_pub_gii_2016-chapter3.pdf

China Daily (2018). Doumen stands behind Flex with its 50 000 workers. China Daily, 12 June. Retrieved from http://subsites.chinadaily.com.cn/zhuhai/2018-06/12/c_241646.htm

Christopher, M., Mena, C., Khan, O. & Yurt, O. (2011). Approaches to managing global sourcing risk. *Supply Chain Management: An International Journal*, 16(2), 67–81.

Contractor, F.J., Kumar, V., Kundu, S.K. & Pedersen, T. (2010). Reconceptualizing the firm in a world of outsourcing and offshoring: The organizational and geographical relocation of high-value company functions. *Journal of Management Studies*, 47(8), 1417–33.

Craig, D. & Willmott, P. (2005). Outsourcing grows up. *The McKinsey Quarterly*, 1, 13–26.

Da Silveira, G., Borenstein, D. & Fogliatto, F.S. (2001). Mass customization: Literature review and research directions. *International Journal of Production Economics*, 72(1), 1–13.

Demirbag, M. & Glaister, K. (2010). Factors determining offshore location choice for R&D projects: A comparative study of developed and emerging regions. *Journal of Management Studies*, 47(8), 1534–60.

Di Minin, A., Zhang, J. & Gammeltoft, P. (2012). Chinese foreign direct investment in R&D in Europe: A new model of R&D internationalization?. *European Management Journal*, 30(3), 189–203.

Doh, J.P., Bunyaratavej, K. & Hahn, E.D. (2009). Separable but not equal: The location determinants of discrete services offshoring activities. *Journal of International Business Studies*, 40(6), 926–43.

Dolan, K.A. (2002) The detour economy. *Forbes*, 169, 52.

Dowling. J. (2017). Why Australian car manufacturing died and what it means for our motoring future. *The Advertiser*, 4 February.

Drill, S. (2012). Thai auto workers will get a $1.12 an hour to replace Aussie jobs. *The Courier Mail*, 7 August. Retrieved from www.couriermail.com.au/news/national/thai-auto-workers-will-get-112-an-hour-to-replace-aussie-jobs/news-story/42fa9b3e6b6cd741787b3fd04af1b668?sv=6506d60a5bf40d2b2ee77202b180fe85

The Economist (2015). Made in China? *The Economist*, 12 March. Retrieved from www.economist.com/leaders/2015/03/12/made-in-china

EDI Asia (n.d.) REDI-to-Wear. Retrieved from www.edi.asia/reditowear/index.asp

Edmunds, S. (2017). Fletcher's steel product in spotlight after Commerce Commission complaint. Stuff, 9 May. Retrieved from www.stuff.co.nz/business/92382986/fletchers-steel-product-in-spotlight-after-commerce-commission-complaint

Feitzinger, E. & Lee, H.L. (1997). Mass customization at Hewlett-Packard: the power of postponement. *Harvard Business Review*, 75, 116–23.

Ferdows, K. (1997). Making the most of foreign factories. *Harvard Business Review*, 75, 73–91. Retrieved from https://hbr.org/1997/03/making-the-most-of-foreign-factories

Fletcher Building (n.d.). Our business. Retrieved from https://fletcherbuilding.com/our-business

——— (2016). Fletcher Building annual report 2016. Retrieved from https://fletcherbuilding.com/assets/4-investor-centre/annual-reports/annual-report-2016-final-website-version-1.pdf

Flex (n.d.). About. Retrieved from https://flex.com/about

——— (2017). 2017 Annual report: Igniting intelligence. Retrieved from https://s21.q4cdn.com/490720384/files/doc_financials/annual_reports/2017/2017-AR-Flex.pdf

Flextronics (1996–2006). Annual reports.

——— (2001). *Third Quarter report*.

——— (2009). Flextronics announces restructuring plans [Press release] 10 March. Retrieved from http://news.flextronics.com/phoenix.zhtml?c=235792&p=irol-newsArticle&ID=1469515&highlight=

——— (2011). Annual report.

Frost, T.S., Birkinshaw, J.M. & Ensign, P.C. (2002). Centers of excellence in multinational corporations. *Strategic Management Journal*, 23(11), 997–1018.

Galbraith, C.S. (1990). Transferring core manufacturing technologies in high-technology firms. *California Management Review*, 32(4), 56–70.

Gereffi, G. (2014). Global value chains in a post-Washington consensus world. *Review of International Political Economy*, 21(1), 9-37.

Gereffi, G. & Fernandez-Stark, K. (2016). *Global Value Chain Analysis: A Primer*, 2nd edition. Retrieved from http://hdl.handle.net/10161/12488.

Ghemawat, P. (2003). The forgotten strategy. *Harvard Business Review*, November. Retrieved from https://hbr.org/2003/11/the-forgotten-strategy

Ghemawat, P., Nueno, J.L. & Dailey, M. (2003). *ZARA: Fast Fashion*, Vol. 1. Boston, MA: Harvard Business School.

Gott, J. & Sethi, A. (2017). The widening impact of automation: Global services location index. AT Kearney. Retrieved from www.atkearney.com/digital-transformation/gsli

Harding, R. (2017). Donald Trump's anger at Asian currency manipulators misses target. *Financial Times,* 13 February. Retrieved from www.ft.com/content/d2aeb4bc-ef71-11e6-930f-061b01e23655

Hervás, F., Siedschlag, I. & Tübke, A. (2014). Boosting the EU's attractiveness to international R&D investments: What matters? What works? *JRC Policy Brief, European Commission*. Available at: https://ideas.repec.org/p/ipt/iptwpa/jrc92084.html

Hira, A. & Benson-Rea, M. (2017). *Governing Corporate Social Responsibility in the Apparel Industry after Rana Plaza*. Palgrave Macmillan.

Holweg, M., Reichhart, A. & Hong, E. (2011). On risk and cost in global sourcing. *International Journal of Production Economics*, 131(1), 333–41.

Huston, L. & Sakkab, N. (2006). Connect and develop. *Harvard Business Review*, 84(3), 58–66.

Jennings, R. (2016). Apple turns again to a savvy China for new ideas and a new image. Forbes, 1 November. Retrieved from www.forbes.com/sites/ralphjennings/2016/11/01/apple-turns-again-to-china-in-search-for-new-ideas-and-new-image/#5ce8730656c6

Jiao, J., Ma, Q. & Tseng, M.M. (2003). Towards high value-added products and services: mass customization and beyond. *Technovation*, 23(10), 809–21.

Jones, R., Arndt, G. & Kustin, R. (1997). ISO 9000 among Australian companies: impact of time and reasons for seeking certification on perceptions of benefits received. *International Journal of Quality & Reliability Management*, 14(7), 650–60.

Khattak, A., Haworth, N., Stringer, C.A. & Benson-Rea, M. (2017). Is social upgrading occurring in South Asia's apparel industry? *Critical Perspectives on International Business*, 13(3), 226–43.

Kinkel, S. (2012). Trends in production relocation and backshoring activities: Changing patterns in the course of the global economic crisis. *International Journal of Operations & Production Management*, 32(6), 696–720.

Kogod School of Business (2016). 2016 Kogod Made in America Auto Index. Kogod School of Business, American University. Retrieved from http://kogodbusiness.com/auto-index/

Kotabe, M. & Murray, J.Y. (2004). Global sourcing strategy and sustainable competitive advantage. *Industrial Marketing Management*, 33(1), 7–14.

Krafcik, J.F. (1988). Triumph of the lean production system. *MIT Sloan Management Review*, 30(1), 41–52.

Loke, S., Downe, A.G. & Sambasivan, M. (2013). Strategic alliances with suppliers and customers in a manufacturing supply chain: From a manufacturer's perspective. *Asia–Pacific Journal of Business Administration*, 5(3), 192–214.

MacCormack, A.D., Newman, L.J. & Rosenfield, D.B. (1994). The new dynamics of global manufacturing site location. *Sloan Management Review*, 35(4), 69–81.

Narula, R. (2001). Choosing between internal and non-internal R&D activities: some technological and economic factors. *Technology Analysis & Strategic Management*, 13(3), 365–87.

Ohno, T. (1988). *Toyota Production System: Beyond Large-scale Production*. Portland, Or: CRC Press.

Organization for Economic Co-operation and Development (OECD) (n.d.). Global Value Chains (GVCs). Retrieved from www.oecd.org/sti/ind/global-value-chains.htm

Orr, G. (2014). Mass customization comes to China [Web blog post]. McKinsey&Company China, 4 February. Retrieved from http://mckinseychina, February 4.com/mass-customization-comes-to-china/

Overby, S. (2018). The top 10 IT outsourcing service provides of the year – and the top 10 challengers. CIO, 15 March. Retrieved from www.cio.com/article/3030989/outsourcing/the-top-10-it-outsourcing-service-providers-of-the-year.html

Parmigiani, A. (2007). Why do firms both make and buy? *Strategic Management Journal*, 29(3), 285–303.

Pennington, P. (2016). Steel supplier has issued fake quality certs. *Radio New Zealand*, 1 July. Retrieved from www.radionz.co.nz/news/national/307694/steel-supplier-has-issued-fake-quality-certs

Poppo, L., Zhou, K.Z. & Zenger, T.R. (2008). Examining the conditional limits of relational governance: Specialized assets, performance ambiguity, and long-standing ties. *Journal of Management Studies*, 45(7), 1195–216.

PwC Australia, ANZ Banking Group & Asialink Business (2015). *Australia's jobs future: The rise of Asia and the services opportunity*. Retrieved from www.pwc.com.au/asia-practice/assets/anz-pwc-asialink-apr15.pdf

Quinn, J.B. & Hilmer, F.G. (1994). Strategic outsourcing. *Sloan Management Review*, 35(4), 43–55.

Reger, G. (2004). Coordinating globally dispersed research centres of excellence – the case of Philips Electronics. *Journal of International Management*, 10(1), 51–76.

Ross, K. (2017). Honeywell opens Asia Pacific cybersecurity centre. Power Engineering International, 13 June. Retrieved from www.powerengineeringint.com/articles/2017/06/honeywell-opens-asia-pacific-cybersecurity-centre.html

Serant, C. (2001a). Flextronics consolidates EMS empire. *EBN*, 1.

——— (2001b). Singapore no longer an EMS magnet – Mainstay Flextronics latest to look for lower cost destination. *EBN*, 3.

Seyal, A.H., A Rahman, M.N. & Awg Yussof Hj Awg Mohammad, H. (2007). A quantitative analysis of factors contributing electronic data interchange adoption among Bruneian SMEs: A pilot study. *Business Process Management Journal*, 13(5), 728–46.

Shedd, J. (2001). Flextronics to acquire Telcom, expands business unit. *Circuits Assembly* 12, 16.

Sirkin, H.L., Zinser, M. & Rose, J. (2014). The shifting economics of global manufacturing: How cost competitiveness is changing worldwide. *Boston Consulting Group*, 19 August. Retrieved from www.bcg.com/publications/2014/lean-manufacturing-globalization-shifting-economics-global-manufacturing.aspx

Smith, G. (2003). Wasting away despite SARS, Mexico is still losing export ground to China. *Business Week,* 2 June, 42.

Song, J. & Shin, J. (2008). The paradox of technological capabilities: a study of knowledge sourcing from host countries of overseas R&D operations. *Journal of International Business Studies*, 39(2), 291–303.

Steinle, C. & Schiele, H. (2008). Limits to global sourcing? Strategic consequences of dependency on international suppliers: Cluster theory, resource-based view and case studies. *Journal of Purchasing and Supply Management*, 14(1), 3–14.

Sturgeon, T. & Lester, R.K. (2004). The new global supply-base: new challenges for local suppliers in East Asia. *Global production networking and technological change in East Asia*, 35–87.

Supply Chain Asia Magazine (2012). The Flextronics effect. *Supply Chain Asia Magazine*, 19 March.

Tang, R., Sinha, A. & Mattios, G. (2013). Winning with procurement in Asia [Bain brief]. Bain & Company, 11 December. Retrieved from www.bain.com/publications/articles/winning-with-procurement-in-asia.aspx

Visnic, B. (2002). Toyota adopts vew flexible assembly system. *Wards Auto*, 1 November. Retrieved from www.wardsauto.com/news-analysis/toyota-adopts-new-flexible-assembly-system

Walsworth, J. (2016). Toyota Camry returns to No. 1 on 'most American' list. Automotive News, 28 June. Retrieved from www.autonews.com/article/20160628/OEM01/160629860/toyota-camry-returns-to-no.-1-on-most-american-list

Weise, E. (2017). In major shift, Indian outsourcer Infosys will hire 10, 000 US workers. *USA Today*, 2 May Retrieved from www.usatoday.com/story/tech/news/2017/05/02/outsourcer-infosys-add-2000-us-jobs-indiana/101177986

Wonacott, P. (2002). Talent pool – China's secret weapon: smart, cheap labor for high-tech goods – beyond toys and garments, country raises the bar again in manufacturing – view from Mr. Li's balcony. *Wall Street Journal*, 14 March, A.1.

Yip, G. (2014). Can multinationals innovate in China? *Forbes*, 17 December. Retrieved from www.forbes.com/sites/ceibs/2014/12/17/can-multinationals-innovate-in-china/#3464caa2edf4

Zailani, S. & Rajagopal, P. (2005). Supply chain integration and performance: US versus East Asian companies. *Supply Chain Management: An International Journal*, 10(5), 379–93.

Zámborský, P. (2012a). Competitiveness gap and host country effects of FDI in the new OECD. *International Journal of Trade and Global Markets*, 5(3–4), 336–354.

——— (2012b). Emergence of transnational clusters: Evidence from the Slovak automotive industry. *Journal for East European Management Studies*, 17(4), 464–79.

Zámborský, P. & Ingršt, I. (2016). Australian and New Zealand innovation in Europe: motives and knowledge flows. Ashridge Conference on Global Disruption and Organisational Innovation.

——— (2017). Emerging multinationals innovating in emerging markets. Paper presented at the Emerging Markets and Global Strategy Conference, Northeastern University, Boston, MA.

Zámborský, P. & Jacobs, E.J. (2016). Reverse productivity spillovers in the OECD: The contrasting roles of R&D and capital. *Global Economy Journal*, 16(1), 113–33.

Zámborský, P. & Kruesi, M. (2018). Global hotel alliance: Strategy discovery for the East. *SAGE Business Cases*. Doi: 10.4135/9781526440044

CHAPTER 12

MANAGING MANAGERS IN AN ASIA–PACIFIC ENVIRONMENT

Learning objectives

In reading this chapter, you will learn to:

1. recognise the challenges and issues with international staffing policies
2. appreciate the process for selecting managers for international assignments
3. understand the reward-and-remuneration structures in overseas postings
4. outline the issues and constraints with the role of labour in Asia–Pacific markets.

THE DEVELOPMENT OF UNIQUE ORGANISATIONAL CULTURES IN MULTICULTURAL MANAGEMENT TEAMS

Brett, Behfar and Kern note that 'multicultural teams offer a number of advantages including deep knowledge of different product markets, culturally sensitive customer service, and 24-hour work rotations' (2006). However, issues relating to cultural differences may reduce the effectiveness of a team. Research has shown that the most successful teams and managers deal with multicultural challenges in one of four ways: *adaptation* (acknowledging cultural gaps openly and working around them), *structural intervention* (changing the shape or makeup of the team), *managerial intervention* (setting norms early or bringing in a higher level manager), and *exit* (removing a team member when other options have failed) (Brett, Behfar & Kern 2006). The appropriate strategy to use is one that best aligns with the particular circumstances.

Given the worldwide changes in recent times, talent management and succession planning are critical to ensuring that the competitive advantage of a firm is maintained. In particular, increased globalisation has raised issues for MNEs in the management of human resources in their Asian subsidiaries where training requirements differ from the home country (Zheng, Hyland & Soosay 2007). The Asian financial services sector, for instance, is moving from a large physical presence in Asia to embrace digital solutions to serve their clients; the move includes sovereign funds, companies and individual investors. As clients grow more comfortable with online and digital platforms, digital tools can complement human-delivered services, thereby changing the makeup of the delivery team to include tech-savvy talent located anywhere in the world.

Several economies in the Asia–Pacific region, including China, Singapore, Thailand, Hong Kong and Thailand, are characterised by talent shortages but have unused potential in the female side of the workforce. Cultural barriers and resistance to change in many Asian subsidiaries has resulted in senior leaders failing to fully utilise the talent pool available. This contrasts with the US, where anti-discrimination laws have encouraged positive discrimination towards women and disadvantaged groups. Similarly, in Europe, quotas ensure that women are on corporate boards.

WEBLINK
VIGNETTE QUESTIONS

Source: Brett, Behfar & Kern 2006

Introduction

People, often described as a labour force, are the key to an organisation's success and generally its greatest expense. Human resource management (HRM) is therefore critical to the organisation, both at the home- and host-country levels, and it is essential for the working of the organisation that management of people is done well. The HRM requirements for an MNE are rapidly changing as technology improves, travel times reduce and the ability for managers to undertake business globally from anywhere in the world becomes realistic. This chapter will examine international HRM (IHRM) from a traditional perspective as this foundational knowledge is essential to understanding human resource issues in global contexts, alongside their differing workplace practices and legal requirements.

International staffing policies

INTERNATIONAL HUMAN RESOURCE MANAGEMENT (IHRM)
the management of human resources in an international context, including planning, recruitment, training and performance appraisal.

PERFORMANCE APPRAISAL
the evaluation of an employee's performance based on mutually agreed criteria set at the start of the appraisal period.

CULTURAL INTELLIGENCE
the capability to relate to and work effectively across cultures in other countries.

International human resource management (IHRM) has several functions in common with domestic HRM including job analysis, human resource planning, and training and development. However, IHRM must extend these to adapt to international requirements as the global dimension to an MNE's business complicates its activities and processes. IHRM must consider crucial issues such as pre-departure training, compensation policies and differences in performance appraisal systems across countries, equal employment legislation, labour union functions, cultural intelligence dimensions and repatriation.

MNEs must develop managers with a broad mental map covering the entirety of the MNE's geographically dispersed operations. This is critical to the MNE's long-term profitability and growth, especially in an era when foreign markets are becoming increasingly important contributors to innovation and cost reduction at the upstream end of the value chain, as well as to overall sales performance at the downstream end. This concept of reverse diffusion is sometimes overlooked by managers in the home country due to a lack appreciating that local subsidiaries can make a significant contribution to global effectiveness. In fact, managers commanding deep knowledge of internal MNE functioning – including the challenges of simultaneously addressing legitimate business objectives and interests at multiple geographic levels within the firm – represent the MNE's key resource to facilitate international expansion and to coordinate geographically dispersed, established operations. These managers are best able to:

- engage in the international transfer of non-location-bound FSAs from the home nation
- identify the need for new FSA development in host countries and facilitate such development
- meld location-bound and non-location-bound FSAs.

These managers are especially valuable when transferring the MNE's routines across borders if those routines include a substantial tacit component.

International staffing performs several key functions for the MNE. It fills positions in developing countries with qualified personnel from abroad and facilitates knowledge transfers across MNE units. International staffing policies, therefore, expose qualified personnel to diverse cultural environments and develops them as global managers. Such personnel are able to transmit the company culture to the host country's subsidiaries. One of the biggest factors influencing an MNE's international staffing policy is turnover costs resulting from difficulties in staff members' adapting to their new positions.

Research has found that a firm's global staffing policy can follow four main approaches, which can operate together or individually. Staffing can be ethnocentric, polycentric, geocentric and regiocentric.

Ethnocentric staffing

An ethnocentric staffing policy is primarily a home-country orientation. Managers from the home country fill the key management positions of the offices in other countries. In these organisations, the home-based policy, practice and personnel are generally viewed as superior to local employees. There are limited opportunities for promotion among local employees to key positions or outside of the local subsidiary operations since the main positions are filled by home-country employees and controlled through the parent company. The ethnocentric approach has been extremely popular in the past and is still used; for example, Procter & Gamble (P&G), Philips, Samsung and Panasonic have all followed this policy. P&G have traditionally appointed staff to key management positions in foreign subsidiaries following many years of employment in their US operations. Nearly all senior executives in Japanese MNEs and their international subsidiaries are Japanese, with international experience viewed as non-essential and even a negative to advancement, which results in a Japanese-culture and language focus that makes it difficult for foreigners to succeed in Japanese businesses.

Ethnocentric staffing policy is most appropriate at the initial stages of setting up a foreign subsidiary when the need for control is greatest. There are, however, a few other sound business reasons for pursuing this policy. First, there may be a perceived lack of host-country nationals qualified to fill senior management positions, particularly in less-developed countries. Second, there may be a need to maintain effective communication, co-ordination and control links with the parent company or head office. This is especially important in terms of corporate culture as an ethnocentric staffing policy allows for the development of a common basis of cultural understanding, incorporating country-specific cultural idiosyncrasies. The disadvantages of this policy are that advancement opportunities are limited for local employees, which can stifle their motivation, and cause resentment and tension among workers. Talent skills transfer is essentially one way – from parent personnel to local country. This can lead to negative implications for management and marketing when the parent country fails to understand the local country culture or does not incorporate cultural considerations in its planning.

CORPORATE CULTURE
the ideas, customs, and social behaviours that are learned and shared within a company by employees.

Polycentric staffing

A polycentric staffing policy is where the MNE treats each subsidiary as a distinct national entity with some decision-making autonomy. MNEs recruit senior managers from the host country and they are rarely transferred to a foreign subsidiary. As a result, parent-country personnel do not impact other countries and subsidiaries because talent-acquisition policies and training are unique to each country. For example, Hindustan Unilever Limited, the Indian subsidiary of the US transnational, Unilever, has locals employed in key executive management positions (Hindustan Unilever Ltd 2016).

There are several advantages of a polycentric policy. Employing host-country nationals eliminates language barriers, avoids the problems of adjustment experienced by expatriate managers and their families, and reduces cultural awareness challenges. As a result, managing local politics and government administration and employee negotiations should be easier. Generally, employment of host-country nationals is less expensive and MNEs can avoid the turnover of key managers repatriated to their home country.

EXPATRIATE
an employee from one country that is appointed to an employment position in another country for an extended period.

There are, however, a few disadvantages with this staffing approach. The main drawback is the gap between host-country managers and parent-country managers due to language barriers, cultural differences and loyalty of staff to their home country. In addition, host-country managers have limited opportunities to gain exposure to and experience outside of their own subsidiaries, and hence cannot progress beyond their positions in the host country. Further, it becomes difficult to embed the original culture of the MNE into the subsidiary because of the lack of involvement of the parent company. Polycentric staffing of an organisation is difficult to change. For example, in the case of Unilever, a 'little kingdom' developed in a host country that opposed attempts by the parent company to limit its autonomy and control it centrally. Similarly, Philips had to deal with fiercely independent national management teams.

Geocentric staffing

GLOBAL TEAM
a team of managers across countries who work together to achieve a common outcome.

Adopting a geocentric staffing policy means that the best people are selected for key positions throughout the organisation, without the consideration of nationality. This occurs when the MNE takes a global team approach to its operations and recognises that each part of the organisation makes a unique contribution with its unique competence. The MNE develops core competencies by recruiting the best talents for the core team. This approach allows an MNE to develop an international executive team that has a global perspective, promotes resource sharing and is comfortable working across a few cultures. As a result, employees can circulate throughout the global organisation, deploying their talent and skills where needed to meet the MNE's goals while achieving the host country's requirements. Talent-acquisition policies will consequently maximise the strength of the global organisation. An example of geocentric staffing is the appointment of Howard Stringer as the chief executive officer of Sony Corporation. It is believed that Mr Stringer is the first foreign-born (British) CEO of a major Japanese corporation (Zinzaro 2009).

MNEs need to study costs when they implement the geocentric staffing policy. Host countries generally require a high number of their citizens employed, and impose visa requirements and extensive documentation. In the Australian context, immigration policies entail the selection of local talent before other nationals will be considered for work in the country. This can be an expensive investment in the training and development of the employee. Benchmarking of salary with the international compensation package must also be well thought out since this is generally higher than the salary given to the employee in their home country.

Regiocentric staffing

In regiocentric staffing, the organisation selects the best people for key positions on a regional basis, with transfers generally being within regions. This differs from geocentric, where the focus is on international selection rather than on regional selection. Subsidiaries within a region may have a relatively large degree of autonomy, with corporate policies and communication generally conveyed through the regional headquarters (Collings & Scullion 2012).

This strategy has become more popular in recent years with many MNEs choosing to organise operations regionally. This approach reduces the need for costly duplication of support services when an organisation has a significant presence in a region. For example, an MNE may have a regional human resource services centre, which is in a central location, and where all questions related to human resources are handled. The approach promotes localisation of policy as host-country employees generally fill key positions in subsidiaries and have a reasonable knowledge of the host context. In 2009, Nike, the world's largest athletic shoe maker announced that it was re-organising its brand into regions, including North America, Western Europe, Eastern and Central Europe, greater China, Japan and emerging markets (Korea, Australia, Brazil, India and South-East Asian countries).

The disadvantage of the regiocentric approach is that it limits the MNE in developing a truly global mindset as staff transfers and management know-how is generally restricted to a regional level. This also limits career opportunities for key personnel to regional structures, with restricted opportunity for development beyond the area.

The second best practice involves selecting appropriate candidates whose 'technical skills are matched or exceeded by their cross-cultural abilities' (Black & Gregersen 1999, p. 53). Cross-cultural abilities are often overlooked, as companies tend to send people who are 'capable but culturally illiterate' (Black & Gregersen 1999, p. 58). In other words, effective resource recombination requires a mix of technical and social skills.

The third best practice involves devoting substantial attention to reintegrating expatriates into their home country after their assignment. Here, successful MNEs 'end expatriate assignments with a deliberate repatriation process' (Black & Gregersen 1999, p. 54). Such a process allows effective absorption of the former expatriate into the home country's professional and personal environment.

REPATRIATION the return of expatriates to their home or original country of employment after an extended period of employment in a foreign country.

Honda of America Manufacturing is cited as 'perhaps one of the best examples of a company that implements all three practices' (Black & Gregersen 1999, p. 62). Its expatriation approach systematically includes clearly stated expatriate assignment objectives, personal strengths or weaknesses surveys completed by the individuals selected for expatriate assignments, a repatriation job-matching program triggered six months before the end of the assignment, and a debriefing interview after the expatriate's return to capture the learnings from the expatriate's experience. Honda's approach has resulted in consistently successful assignments that meet or surpass objectives and expectations, with a turnover rate of less than 5 per cent.

In addition to outlining the appropriate way to manage expatriate employees, the required personal characteristics for employees to be high-potential expatriate prospects include: a drive to communicate, broad-based sociability, cultural flexibility, a cosmopolitan orientation and a collaborative negotiation style (Black & Gregersen 1999, p. 58). For example, LG Group, a large South Korean conglomerate (set up in 1947 as Lucky Goldstar), employs a much more formal approach. The firm uses an extensive survey early in the employee's career to assess individual preparedness for expatriate assignments. It then organises discussions between potential candidates and senior managers to identify how personalised development and training plans might contribute further to honing the individual's strengths and shoring up weaknesses. This long-term approach to developing individuals ready for expatriation is costly and time intensive, but has led to a 97 per cent success rate in overseas assignments.

Colgate-Palmolive, a US-based company established in 1928 as the result of a merger between Colgate and Palmolive-Peet, looks for prior international experience in new hires, thereby leveraging the investments and training in international management provided by previous employers. Colgate-Palmolive then sends prospects for expatriation on short-term, foreign training assignments (6 to 18 months). These training assignments are devoid of the costly perks and compensation packages normally provided to expatriates. Only after completion of such assignments are prospects given longer-term expatriate positions.

Any MNE's expatriate selection process entails a trade-off between accuracy and cost. Here, a thorough assessment process in the form of carefully crafted routines – like those used by LG Group and Colgate-Palmolive – is costly upfront but also fully accurate in terms of selecting the right individuals for expatriation. This approach reduces the risk of subsequent costs resulting from failed expatriate assignments. In the end, 'the key to success is having a systematic way of assessing the cross-cultural aptitudes of people you may want to send abroad' (Black & Gregersen 1999, p. 60). The stress associated with the perceived and actual security risks of travelling and living abroad for expatriates (and more generally in many developing countries) must also be well thought out.

Selecting managers for international assignments

The selection process for a global manager is a critical and difficult one that must take into consideration several international selection criteria. The relative importance of each may vary depending on the position requirements, the experience of the MNE and cultural considerations. After identifying potential candidates that may be suitable for the position description, candidates must be screened and evaluated to enable a decision to be made as to the best person for the job.

It is important for IHRM to carefully design the job description of the international manager from the view of the MNE and then to match this with the most suitable applicant. The job description should consider:

- the company strategy and purpose of the role to achieve the strategy
- the duties, purpose, responsibilities, scope, and working conditions of the position
- the skills, behaviours and experience considered necessary
- if the position is suited for an internal or external applicant
- the training required to make the applicant ready for the internal posting
- the key performance indicators to assess the manager's performance
- any gender and cultural background contexts that will assist the incumbent in the role.

For organisations to survive in the international arena, their perspective must be wide and consider transnational skills and perspectives as an integral part of the MNE's success. Given the growing costs of international assignments for many international organisations, the first issue for international recruitment and selection is whether an international manager is needed. There may be other options to sourcing an international manager, such as using a local national manager to manage subsidiary operations.

Not all managers want an overseas posting or assignment, and those who do are not always suitable for the position. There are three main criteria for selecting managers for global assignments: competence, adaptability and personal characteristics. The following attributes reflect these criteria.

- Technical knowledge, which refers to the managerial and technical capabilities that a manager requires to fulfil the company's goals and objectives in a foreign country subsidiary.
- Leadership ability is the ability of the manager to influence people to act in a way. If a person has demonstrated effective leadership in their home country, and possesses characteristics such as maturity, emotional stability, independence, initiative, creativity and can communicate well, then the person will probably also do well in a foreign country.
- Language skill is an area of recognised weakness in preparing managers for foreign country employment. Knowledge of the relevant foreign language is vital, although fluency is generally not necessary. International business is generally conducted using English and most expatriates use English for communication, however, there is a disadvantage for managers where business is conducted in a non-English language.
- Age, experience, gender and education are significant factors when considering a manager for an overseas placement. Younger employees are generally more eager for placements in foreign countries and although they may be more attuned culturally than older employees, they are the least developed in terms of real-world experience.
- Cultural knowledge is essential for an overseas placement as it essential that managers can adapt to change and withstand cultural shock. Managers are generally excited by the challenge of their overseas posting for the first few months, but after a few months they become frustrated and confused by the unfamiliar environment. There are several

characteristics signifying the ability to adapt well to foreign cultures including: previous overseas travel and work experience, cultural empathy, diplomacy and a positive attitude to managing operations in stressful situations. In most developed countries, equal opportunities exist for men and women, but in some countries women's work roles and legal rights are restricted.

- Interpersonal skills are essential for the manager to ensure that they can build and maintain relationships with a wide variety of people, including employees from the foreign country subsidiary as well as home office employees, colleagues and government officials.
- Good physical health and an elevated level of emotional intelligence are critical for managers living in a foreign country. Culture shock is often experienced and general medical care is often of a lower standard than in their home country. It is crucial that the manager has resilience and a network of family or peers, that can support them to cope in the new international environment.

MULTIPLE-CHOICE QUESTION

Management of international staff

EXPATRIATE FAILURE
the failure of the expatriate employee to adapt to the new country or company of employment.

Expatriate failure is an issue in international staffing that is attributed largely to the selection of people that are not 'right' (Perera, Chew & Nielsen 2017). The costs of expatriate failure include both direct costs (such as salary, training costs, travel and relocation expenses) and indirect costs (such as damaged relations with host-country organisations, loss of market share and requests for the replacement of parent-country nationals with host-country nationals). Some researchers in this area have argued that the damage to the MNE's reputation in key strategic foreign markets or regions caused by the request for the replacement of a manager is the biggest risk faced by MNEs and could severely damage the prospects of successfully developing the company's international business (Shay & Tracey 1997; Graham & Cascio 2018; Mulkeen 2017).

Role specification and resourcing strategies are different for every organisation, and selection and assessment criteria are firm specific. Success or failure for expatriates is often defined by whether the expatriate returns prematurely before the assignment is complete. However, expatriates can remain in assignments while experiencing issues such as not being prepared for the assignment, which results in an inability to adjust to local conditions and to work with local nationals. In addition, the assignment may not be what the expatriate expected with a focus on, for example, technical skills rather than the managerial and other selection criteria (Scullion & Collings 2006).

The main cause of expatriate failure is culture shock. Culture shock refers to feelings of anxiety and uncertainty that expatriates may experience when they move to live in a country that they are not familiar with for any period. In culture shock, positive and negative feelings take turns so that expatriate managers feel like they are on an emotional rollercoaster ride. This may be dependent on the managers themselves or their family members, and arises due to the difficulties in adapting to their unfamiliar environment. International assignment failure rates depend on the country and challenges presented to the manager, nevertheless, managers assigned to developed countries have a failure rate of approximately 25 per cent but when assigned to underdeveloped countries this increases to around 70 per cent (ShieldGeo 2018).

A manager who has been appropriately trained and prepared for an international assignment prior to leaving is likely to have a significant reduction in the probability of culture shock. For an international assignment, training must include three main components.

1. Knowledge of the country that the manager is going to, including economic, political, geographical and historical.
2. Cultural awareness of the host country, including language, customs, cultural sensitivities and other knowledge required to ensure that the manager can interact appropriately with people associated with doing business in the host country.
3. General information about living in a country, including housing, education, transportation, healthcare, shopping and telecommunications.

Managers must also be prepared for repatriation to their home country. Expatriates may experience problems readjusting to their home environments; financial difficulties such as cuts in pay, having a perceived 'lesser' job position and finding their international experiences are not used or valued can take their toll. Organisations must be aware of these difficulties and provide support for returning managers to ensure they do not resign and take their valuable experience away with them.

SPOTLIGHT 12.2

Expatriate performance management: Nokia

Nokia is an international technology company that operates in 11 countries. The organisation transfers its managers between countries to support the spread of ideas, initiatives and knowledge.

HMD Global, based in Finland, make Nokia's phones. Senior executives, together with the HRM at Nokia, continually identify engineers, designers and managers that display leadership characteristics to put into development teams. Nokia uses these ad-hoc teams rather than having a central R&D function. The initiatives from these teams in inventing new products has been extraordinarily successful. The teams are together for up to two years and bring together entrepreneurial

personnel from Nokia's widespread international operations. This effective approach is shown by the success of the Nokia 6 and Nokia 8 models, launched in India in 2016.

Source: Spence 2017

QUESTIONS

1. What is the significance of creating teams that last for up to two years? What advantage does Nokia expect to gain?
2. Nokia's culture emphasises the speed and flexibility of decision making in a networked organisation. Discuss Nokia's approach to R&D and how this might impact its employee management strategy.

Performance management

The major challenges presented by global expansion are related to how people are sourced, developed and managed. In other words, human resource decisions are what determines who executes an MNE's business strategy, leads and manages innovation, and serves an MNE's customers in different markets. Global performance management is the evaluation and continual improvement of individuals and team performances within an international staffing context.

Performance can be defined in terms of task factors and contextual factors. Task factors are the technical competencies of the organisation, while contextual performance relates to personal characteristics such as perseverance, conscientiousness, adaptability and interpersonal skills. Although task performance is essential in an international assignment, it is generally the contextual performance that has the greatest influence on an MNE's success.

Managing your people

The way that labour is organised in the local workplace and the surrounding legislation differs among countries. Therefore, MNEs generally play an advisory role and set the overall tone of international employment agreements. Executing a global human capital strategy requires coordination and management of talent, leadership, culture and organisational structures. Many MNEs put their head office managers in global operations because they are familiar and have confidence in those employees. However, this approach comes with the business risks associated with differing attitudes and presumptions between the emerging market and the management practices of the home-country leadership team, and vice versa. For example, leadership teams from Australia, the UK and the US that are managing their markets' growth in Indonesia, Vietnam and China have the same issues as a leadership team from China or India moving into more developed Western markets.

In a global environment, the MNE needs to manage expatriates from the home country, host-country nationals and other nationals that may come from any other country. It is difficult to implement a standardised policy of grade-scales and terms of employments due to the multifaceted workforce, however, unless a policy is developed and communicated in a clear, fair and well-understood manner issues may arise among personnel from different countries undertaking similar work. In addition, in developing countries, both skilled and unskilled labour is readily available at

low cost, which gives rise to issues of employee sourcing and development or political intervention to limit foreign workers. Demotions for sub-par performance are common as a motivational policy in some Asian cultures. Although this policy is not seen in the same light in other countries and would not translate well as a broad HRM practice.

Most MNEs nowadays use a people management policy that combines a globally consistent management structure with a regional or local focus. Considering the individual needs of the growth market ensures that there are structures in place to put the right people in the right places, and to make the most of opportunities anywhere in the world as they arise. Anticipating cultural differences is essential as labour laws may differ greatly between countries, and leadership styles that are successful in a home-country business may be inappropriate in other countries. As HR policies and strategies are critical to the success of global growth, MNEs must develop them to include several competencies and activities. This includes attracting and managing skilled workers, fashioning a culture that is consistent with the home country but reflects the host country's practices, creating a stable labour force in the new market while motivating it to increase productivity, and adopting a neutral global perspective where no country's role dominates.

Measuring your people

Employees of a company work individually and together in teams to achieve the goals set by an organisation. This is illustrated through the saying 'companies don't succeed, people do'; that is, at the level of the individual, the people who work for the company must understand the tasks that are important in achieving the organisation's overall goals. It is a necessary part of the assessment and improvement process to evaluate and appraise the performance of managers. A performance appraisal assesses how well a manager did their job compared with a benchmark, such as the employee's previous achievements, the budget of an individual, team, area or company, or a comparison with a competitor. Therefore, the definition of key performance indicators for a manager is essential and provides a key motivational tool for a manager's job satisfaction, the firm's performance and, in many cases, financial rewards.

A principal component of a company's performance appraisal system is its control systems. The MNE's management uses internal controls, comprised of policies and procedures, to ensure the effectiveness and efficiency of the MNE's operations, as well as the company's compliance with a country's laws and regulations. The management of a company has the responsibility to maintain an adequate system of controls that include:

- ensuring the enterprise is run competently
- establishing clear lines of responsibility
- maintaining effective records
- safeguarding company assets
- adequately paying and motivating employees.

The controls reduce uncertainty, increase predictability and ensure that employees' behaviour is consistent with company goals. They emphasise behaviour that is compatible with the company's corporate values and culture, despite physical, cultural and temporal and social distances. In appraising a manager's performance, the employee's performance is compared with the MNE's expected outcomes. In a global business, geographic and cultural issues make the appraisal process more complex. Performance may be measured using both quantitative and qualitative tools.

Quantitative measures are numeric in nature and relate to the budget and planning systems. Budgets are simply the operationalisation of the entity's plans and assist in decision making in a variety of ways. Some quantitative measures a company may use are:

- operationalising the strategic plans of the company
- setting targets for managers
- identifying resource constraints
- assisting with short-term planning decisions such as staffing and production requirements
- providing financial data such sales and profit forecasts.

Qualitative or non-financial performance measures are generally more operational in nature; for example:

- customer satisfaction
  - customer response time
  - number of customer complaints
  - customer survey
- delivery and throughput
  - production and delivery lead time
  - on-time delivery
  - set-up times
- stock or inventory
  - stock turnover
  - warehouse space utilisation
- employee performance measures
  - employee morale: absenteeism, staff turnover
  - health and safety.

The use of quantitative measures alone is insufficient to appraise the performance of a manager – qualitative measures are also necessary. Consideration should be given to the multiple measures that provide a full picture of the employee's performance, including the operating market and employee measures as well as financial indicators. The performance-appraisal process can be subject to unintentional bias, making it difficult to evaluate the performance of global managers objectively.

Geographic distances between the home and host country may result in misunderstandings about expectations and goals. The host-country culture provides an important contextual variable in the appraisal process. The key to reducing unintentional bias lies is determining who conducts the appraisal and how it is conducted. A manager's performance appraisal should be conducted at the host- and home-country level. Appraisals may be particularly valid where they are undertaken by a manager of the same nationality as this will reduce cultural bias. In this case, the home-country management generally receives the host-country manager's performance appraisal for evaluation. It is necessary for performance evaluations to be undertaken by a manager who has cultural awareness of the host country. For example, in the past, Australian expatriates working in Hong Kong felt that they were unfairly evaluated as the skills and experience they brought to that culture were not considered.

Rewarding your people

Compensation packages for international postings vary from country to country. Some factors that impact rewards for work include:

- mandated benefits of the host country
- costs of living of the host country
- costs to allow managers to maintain their usual standard of living
- an incentive payment to live and work in the host country
- family needs such as a partner's career or inability to work
- costs associated with repatriation.

Therefore, MNEs often must pay a premium to incentivise managers to take up international assignments. Costs of living vary greatly depending on the country the expatriate goes; for example, capital cities such as Sydney, Auckland, Hong Kong, Tokyo, Seoul and Shanghai usually have higher standard-of-living costs. In some countries, family members may be unable to work in their current employment area, so in those cases the MNE compensates for the family members' loss of income.

There are two main categories of compensation: base remuneration, and benefits, allowances and incentives. A base salary is the salary that the manager would receive for a similar role in the home country. To ensure that managers can maintain their living standards in the host country, a cost-of-living allowance may be offered to support the higher cost of their living in the host country. In addition, the manager may be paid a range of benefits including health insurance, relocation allowances, additional annual leave, and a trip allowance to visit their home country. Hardship allowances and other incentives are often paid to managers to provide an incentive for them to undertake an international assignment, particularly when they are relocating to a less desirable location where there may be political and economic instability. Tax equalisation is often an issue as managers may be subject to tax payments in both the home and host country or at higher rates in the host country. The salary, allowances and benefits may be paid by the home office, the host office or both, as negotiated with the manager.

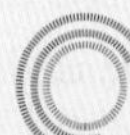

MULTIPLE-CHOICE QUESTION

In addition to their compensation package, as part of the individual performance-measurement process, an executive performance compensation scheme is sometimes put in place. Generally, an executive salary package consists of a mix of a base salary, other benefits (as noted above) and long- and short-term incentives that are dependent on achieving specified measurement targets. Short-term incentives include rewards like cash bonuses, and long-term incentives include motivations like shares and options. The executive performance package also includes quantitative and qualitative measures that are aligned with the company's goals.

SPOTLIGHT 12.3

Spotlight on locals and Asian-outbound assignees

Mercer consultant Olivier Meier (2016), provides the following assessment of the role of assignees:

> Locals and Asian outbound assignees are playing an increasingly vital role in the mobile workforce, especially as the greatest planned increase of assignments lie in those from and within Asia. A talent shortage means that competition is fierce for the best and brightest, and there is a premium on international experience and managerial skills.

Key career and reward drivers for Asian employees vary according to location. In performance-driven China, for instance, employees expect prompt salary and career progression and aren't afraid to leave if disappointed. A more traditional structure still prevails in Japan and Korea: age, service, and a level drive career structure and pay, but job grades are strictly defined and very much the gift of the employer. Singapore plots a middling course: it is partly Westernised in its philosophy – compensation structures are comparable to the US and Europe, and employees take responsibility for their career progression – but it also respects the local need for hierarchy. Competition for talent is fierce in India, where variable pay plays a critical role in managing performance and cost.

QUESTIONS

1. Discuss the effect of global mobility on MNEs' retention of talent in Asia.
2. In the past, expatriates generally moved from developed countries to subsidiaries in developing countries. This is changing as talent is increasingly found within local economies. Discuss the impact of this change on local talent and international mobility.

Managing a workforce in Asia–Pacific markets

A major asset of a global company is its people – the talent and skills of a company's labour force is its strength, but it can also be problematic to manage. MNEs need to consider the cultural context of their workers when they manage their workforces into the future.

In the Asia–Pacific region, work prospects are positive due to the flow of goods and services within the area, integration with the global economy, price stability and the rule of law (Packard & van Nguyen 2014). Although growth has slowed in the region, it has resulted in an increase in living standards and middle-class prosperity.

Employment in the Asia–Pacific region has been characterised by a move from registered, regulated work to unregulated and informal contracts, from full-time to part-time work, and from jobs in the cities to farm work in rural areas. Following the global financial crisis in 2008, demand from the external economic environment, especially in high-income countries, has been slow and the region is turning to service and domestic consumption to sustain its growth. For example, in 2013, domestic consumption and services replaced investment and manufacturing as the lead economic drivers in China (Packard & van Nguyen 2014, p. 6). In addition, the rising cost of labour in many Asia–Pacific countries has resulted in moving garment production to lower-cost countries such as Bangladesh and Mexico.

Further, Australia and New Zealand also receive many migrant workers from the Asia–Pacific. In 2017, the Temporary Skill Shortage Visa was introduced for employers to sponsor skilled overseas workers to work in Australia in the short or medium term. Temporary migrants have typically been noted as international students and fruit-pickers; however, in addition, there are many highly skilled workers that come to Australia to work in a professional capacity, including doctors, engineers and managers. It is therefore essential that HRM considers these regional developments when managing human resource issues in the Asia–Pacific.

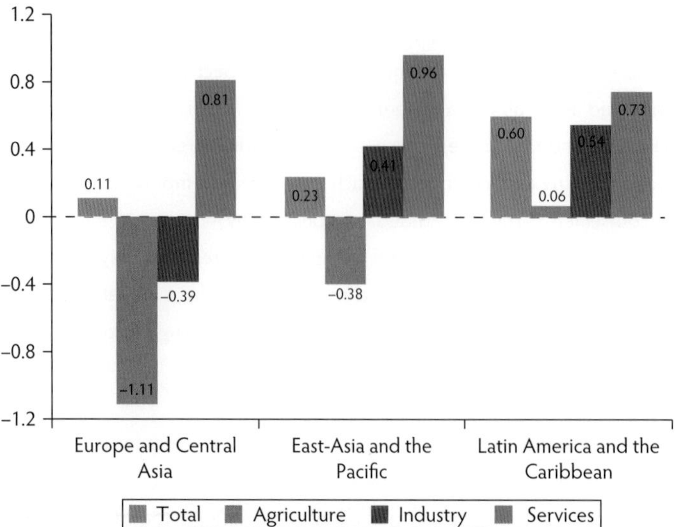

FIGURE 12.1 Growth creates more employment in services than in other sectors: the elasticity of employment to economic growth, by country groups, 1990–2010

Note: Data are disaggregated by sector for all regions with at least 17 observations out of the 21 years of data; that is, comparison with other regions are not possible given the limited number of observations.

Source: Packard & van Nguyen 2014, p. 11, licensed by CC BY 3.0 IGO, https://creativecommons.org/licenses/by/3.0/igo

Labour participation in organisations

As in most parts of the world, the private sector accounts for the majority of employment in the Asia–Pacific region. Small firms are an important segment, particularly in the agricultural sector. The labour force is characterised by many women, access to education, and labour mobility within and between countries. The demand for and supply of labour for the workforce are the result of economic growth, changes in technology, productive assets, the investment climate and the governments labour policy in each country. Opportunities for work with an MNE in the Asia–Pacific region continue, with companies requiring specialised knowledge in the form of language and culture, as well as business practice and management.

Governments in the many Asia–Pacific countries have demonstrated foresight in their consideration of the supply and demand of labour, and the wellbeing that people derive from their work. Policymakers are concerned not only with the quantity of work available but also the quality of that work. Countries such as Indonesia, the Philippines, Vietnam and Malaysia are working to raise productivity and improve the skills of the workforce. Many countries, especially in regional and geographically isolated areas, are also concerned about the large numbers of youth in their populations and the high level of unemployment they are experiencing.

The management of labour relations

Labour market policies in the Asia–Pacific region are characterised by high flexibility and a low level of worker protection. Policies are put in place by governments in each country to ensure that market imperfections are addressed. Market imperfections include such things as uneven power between employees and employers, and a lack of information and inadequate protection for workers to limit the effects of employment risks, including health and safety measures. Regulations in many

Asia–Pacific countries is of a higher level than the OECD minimum; they have strict regulations for minimum wages and the dismissal of workers, especially in Indonesia, China, the Philippines and Cambodia. However, many MNEs are finding the labour codes to be onerous and restrictive, and consequently they are becoming uncompetitive as their smaller competitors can evade the regulations.

On the other hand, countries such as Singapore and Malaysia are the least restrictive in employment regulations. Following the trend set by many developed countries, reforms in income protection in these countries have included extending the length of fixed-term contracts, promoting the hire of employees from temporary work agencies and shortening the necessary period to give an employee notice that they are no longer required to work.

Maintaining a global–local balance in the MNE

The goal of HRM is to build a capability for an MNE that can facilitate its business and take advantage of opportunities as they arise anywhere in the world. Global companies must carefully balance the MNE's need for standardised operations across their operations with the needs of specific markets. To do this, HRM develop tools and processes to support agile human resource operating platforms, balanced leadership, and consistent technologies and system across the countries the MNE operates.

Human resource structures that can utilise shared services platforms can assist a company in finding a balance between being globally efficient while being locally responsible. An example of this in operation is Diageo, a global leader in alcohol beverages, which has a presence in 180 countries across five regions. Diageo's ambition is to be 'one of the best performing, most trusted and respected consumer companies in the world' (Diageo 2018). Diageo has been innovative in becoming competitively global, creating a workforce that is agile, innovative and responsible to the needs of the business. It has created human resource services with standardised processes and consolidated transaction processing that is flexible in accommodating business expansion, while also creating operating models that suit the different regions and markets.

Leadership is an essential component of a global company and governance structures should enable decisions to be made locally. Leaders should be selected from local areas where expansion is being undertaken, with decision making encouraged at the local level. Leadership structures should reflect the company's global focus and pay due attention to developing the talents of the next generation of leaders. The Shell group is a global energy and petrochemical company that uses short-term assignments for managers to meet the demands of different regions, and to develop the knowledge and experience of their workforce.

The growth in the use of technology and information systems has made it an essential part of doing business globally. The creation of global human resource systems provides a means of consistency for human resource information and processing, and allows for a streamlined system with local innovations.

MULTIPLE-CHOICE QUESTION

Summary

Learning objective 1: Recognise the challenges and issues with international staffing policies.

IHRM has many commonalities with domestic HRM such as role analysis, planning for human resources, and developing and training staff. However, IHRM functions extend to cover the international requirements of a company, and this global dimension is often complicated to manage. IHRM must consider crucial worldwide issues such as the differences across countries in compensation policies and performance appraisal systems, differences in legislation for equal employment, differences in labour union functions, and the diversity of cultures more generally. In addition, MNEs must develop managers that have a broad understanding and territorial map of the company's geographically dispersed activities.

Learning objective 2: Appreciate the process for selecting managers for international assignments.

The selection process for a global manager is a critical, difficult and must follow specific criteria. The IHRM must carefully design the job description from the MNE's perspective and match its requirements with the most suitable applicant. An MNE needs a global perspective if it is to survive in the international arena. Therefore, given the growing costs of international assignments for many global organisations, the MNE must carefully weigh appropriate options for procuring an effective international manager.

Learning objective 3: Understand the reward-and-remuneration structures in overseas postings.

Executive salary packages are usually a combination of a base salary, benefits and incentives which motivate the manager to perform in alignment with the MNE's organisational objectives. The package may include quantitative and qualitative measures, and comprise short-term bonuses and long-term gains like shares and options. International postings are performance managed through staff evaluations and measurements of improvement across individual and team levels.

Learning objective 4: Outline the issues and constraints with the role of labour in Asia–Pacific markets.

Work prospects are positive in the Asia–Pacific region because of the flow of goods and services, integration with the global economy, price stability and rule of law. High growth has resulted in increased living standards and middle-class prosperity, and IHRM should manage the workforce of this region by ensuring their practices and processes reflect this cultural background. The goal of IHRM is to facilitate the business capitalising on opportunities worldwide and as they arise. MNEs need to balance their need for worldwide company standardisation with specific market needs, and they need to develop human resource tools to support this endeavour. Agile human resource operating platforms, balanced leadership, and consistent technologies and systems are paramount to effective IHRM governance.

USEFUL WEBSITES

Revision questions

REVISION QUESTIONS

1. Discuss why recruiting the right people with the right talents has become so difficult for MNEs.
2. How does a firm's administrative heritage affect the purposes and forms of expatriation in an MNE?
3. Kotter's model (1996) provides a step-by-step approach to assist managers to lead and implement change in their company. Research and discuss the eight steps in the implementation process that Kotter suggests for the fine-tuning of an MNE's organisational context.
4. What can an MNE do to improve its international assignment strategies?
5. Discuss the use of technology and information systems in human resource systems in the Asia–Pacific region.

R&D activities

1. Select an MNE with operations or subsidiaries in Asia. What is the current approach to the management of international staff assignments at the MNE? How can they improve their management approach to take advantage of opportunities as they arise?
2. Assume you currently hold a management position with an MNE. The company has offered you a similar position to work in their Shanghai office for two years. You believe that this position will provide you with international experience and will be beneficial for your future career prospects.
   - What aspects of this experience do you need to consider in your decision? Investigate and quantify these.
   - Considering your findings, how will these impact on the salary and allowances you negotiate?
   - What happens at the end of the two years? Does this need to be part of your negotiation?
3. As companies implement a growth strategy based on global expansion, their ability to design and implement a human resource strategy and capability becomes increasingly important to their success. Investigate the human resource issues faced by Huawei Technologies Co. as part of its global expansion. What did they do to overcome these?
4. Explore the Shell Australia website careers page. What type of international staffing policy is used? Select a position from the list to examine it in more detail, click on 'apply for this opportunity for a more detailed position description'. Does it support the staffing policy as you expected? Is the job described in enough detail to understand what is required? Is it a permanent position or a contract? What support do Shell provide for the employee in moving to a new country?

IB MASTERCLASS

Managing expatriates at Louis Vuitton Moët Hennessy

Think for a moment about the brand names of high-end fashion and leather goods. Names such as Louis Vuitton, Donna Karan, Fendi, Loewe, Céline, Marc Jacobs, Berluti, Rossimoda and StefanoBi might spring to mind. What do these brands have in common with alcoholic beverage brand names such as Moët et Chandon, Hennessy and Dom Pérignon? Or perfume brands like Christian Dior, Guerlain, Givenchy and Kenzo? Or even watch brands such as TAG Heuer, Zenith

and OMAS? The answer is that they are brands in the world's largest luxury goods group, the French-based Moët Hennessy Louis Vuitton (LVMH).

LVMH was created in 1987 as the result of a merger between Moët Hennessy and Louis Vuitton. As of 2016, the company was a highly internationalised conglomerate with annual revenue of €37.6 billion and an international retail network of more than 3860 stores (LVMH 2018). Geographically, 10 per cent of its revenues came from France, 18 per cent from the rest of Europe, 27 per cent from the US, 7 per cent from Japan, 26 per cent from the rest of Asia and 12 per cent from other markets, which makes the MNE one of the world's few truly global companies in terms of geographic sales dispersion.

With a presence in 72 countries and 80 per cent of its 134 000 worldwide employees based outside of its French home base, LVMH has had to carefully design its IHRM. A crucial component of IHRM at LVMH is the management of international assignments, with expatriates occupying key strategic positions. Such assignments are often a stepping towards even more important jobs at the company in the future.

In 2001, LVMH had 260 expatriates, and the number of its expatriates is rising. In 2011, one-fifth of all transfers within the LVMH group were to a different country. Additionally, 1500 executives were transferred to various brands across the LVMH portfolio (LVMH 2012, p. 24).

QUESTIONS

1. What is the current approach to expatriate management at LVMH?
2. What is the administrative heritage of LVMH? How does the practice of international assignments reflect this heritage? What roles do expatriates play in LVMH's organisation?
3. Does LVMH pay much attention to cross-cultural differences in its international assignments? What should it do to better prepare its expatriates for adjustment in the host country they are sent to?

References

Black, J.S. & Gregersen, H.B. (1999). The right way to manage expats. *Harvard Business Review*, 77, 52–63.

Brett, J., Behfar, K. & Kern, M (2006). Managing multicultural teams. *Harvard Business Review*, November. Retrieved from https://hbr.org/2006/11/managing-multicultural-teams

Collings, D.G. & Scullion, H. (2012). Global staffing: a critical review. In G.K. Stahl & I. Borkman, eds, *Handbook of Research in International Human Resource Management*, 2nd edn. Cheltenham: Edward Elgar Publishing.

Dalai, R. (2015). Expat: does Asia need Western expats, or perma-pats? *Wall Street Journal* (Eastern edition). New York.

Diageo (2018). Our Business. Retrieved from www.diageo.com/en/our-business

Graham, B.Z. & Cascio, W.F. (2018). The employer-branding journey: Its relationship with cross-cultural branding, brand reputation, and brand repair. *Management Research: Journal of the Iberoamerican Academy of Management*, 16(4), 363–79.

Haslberger, A., Brewster, C. & Hippler, T. (2013). The dimensions of expatriate adjustment. *Human Resource Management*, 52(3), 333–51.

Hindustan Unilever Ltd (2016). HUL is the no. 1 employer of choice in India. Hindustan Unilever Limited. Retrieved from www.hul.co.in/news/press-releases/2016/hul-is-the-no-1-employer-of-hoice-in-india-for-fifth-successive-year.html

Kotter, J.P. (1996). *Leading Change*. Boston: Harvard Business School Press.

LVMH (2012). Annual Report 2011. Retrieved from https://en.calameo.com/read/000046992e4b4b9ec54b1

——— (2018). Investors. LVMH. Retrieved from www.lvmh.com/investors

Meier, O. (2016). Expatriate management in Asia. Mercer. Retrieved from https://mobilityexchange.mercer.com/Insights/article/Expatriate-Management-in-Asia

Mulkeen, D. (2017) How to reduce the risk of international assignment failure. *Communicaid*, 20 February. Retrieved from https://www.communicaid.com/cross-cultural-training/blog/reducing-risk-international-assignment-failure/

Packard, T.G. & van Nguyen, T. (2014). *East Asia Pacific At Work: Employment, Enterprise, and Well-being*. Washington DC: World Bank. doi:10.1596/978-1-4648-0004-7

Perera, H.K., Chew, E.Y.T. & Nielsen, I. (2017). A psychological contract perspective of expatriate failure. *Human Resource Management*, 56, 479–99. doi:10.1002/hrm.21788

Scullion, H. & Collings, D.G., eds, (2006). *Global Staffing*. London: Routledge.

Shay, J. & Tracey, J.B. (1997). Expatriate managers: Reasons for failure and implications for training. *Cornell Hotel and Restaurant Administration Quarterly*, 38(1), 30–5.

ShieldGeo (2018). International assignment failure and tracking methods. ShieldGeo. Retrieved from http://shieldgeo.com/international-assignment-failure-and-tracking-methods/

Spence, E. (2017). Nokia 6 tastes a single minute of success. *Forbes*, 24 August. Retrieved from www.forbes.com/sites/ewanspence/2017/08/24/nokia6-android-sales-leak-rumor-new/#4ea4a6037c8c

Zheng, C., Hyland, P. & Soosay, C. (2007). Training practices of multinational companies in Asia. *Journal of European Industrial Training*, 31(6), 472–94, https://doi.org/10.1108/03090590710772659.

Zinzaro, F. (2009). The geocentric human resource policy. Ezine Articles, 19 December. Retrieved from http://ezinearticles.com/?The-Geocentric-Human-Resource-Policy&id=3407520

CHAPTER 13

ONGOING CHALLENGES FOR INTERNATIONAL BUSINESS IN THE ASIA–PACIFIC

Learning objectives

In reading this chapter, you will learn to:

1. appreciate the breadth of information needed to assess international business entry into emerging markets
2. recognise the growth and development of ecommerce in the Asia–Pacific region
3. explain the multifaceted challenges that the security agenda plays in the Asia–Pacific for international business operations
4. appreciate what international business careers may look like in the future, and understand the career prospects and job roles in international business.

THE EMPLOYEE IS THE NEW CONSUMER

Investing in employees to increase their productivity and deliver organisational growth is fundamental for many international businesses. Therefore, central to an MNE's success is the understanding of its workforce and the wellbeing of its employees. Companies need to developing strategies that meet the changing needs of their staff and advance their employees' work experiences as these factors influence their choice of employer.

International firms can look to successful consumer-focused companies for direction when planning their hiring strategies. There are many similarities between a consumer and an employee role.

As with profiling consumers, better employee profiling improves commitment and retention, and enhances their performance to achieve overall business improvements. Employee ideals are often like those of target consumers; for example, personalised experiences such as exercise facilities and financial planning are sometimes offered to employees. Just like with consumers, employees want confirmation of their contribution; they want their interests and desires understood, not only within the work environment but on a personal level as well. Firms capture data on employees but sometimes fail to ask the questions directly to employees. An MNE's understanding of its employees – the goals and aspirations that its staff have – provides a holistic picture of the workforce and enables the MNE to align personnel assignments with the company's operational intent and ambitions.

The employees that experience prominent levels of workplace satisfaction characteristically produce greater productivity and an improved bottom line for an international business. Thus, organisations that offer greater flexibility to their employees through agile work environments will have the competitive advantage.

VIDEO VIGNETTE QUESTION

Introduction

This chapter captures the essential elements of international business to develop a market entry evaluation framework so that the future opportunities in emerging markets can be assessed. A market entry survey, with over 50 questions, provides a platform to capture in-depth information, and creates the foundational knowledge necessary for understanding the establishment of a potential new market. A discussion concerning the rise of regional ecommerce platforms, the leading Asian online firms and their main characteristics is presented. The chapter discusses the multifaceted challenges related to security in the Asia–Pacific region; specifically reviewed are threats to sovereignty and nation states, political interactions, biodiversity and the environment, and energy resources. The future and design of the international business workforce and workplace are also examined, which leads to a presentation on how to plan for this new era by changing business cultures and adapting to changing expectations. Finally, the chapter concludes by outlining careers in international business and describing the types of international business job roles graduates may consider.

Future international business growth in emerging markets

Many international businesses have kept away from emerging markets in the Asia–Pacific region when they could have engaged with them more closely. Since the early 2000s, the region has consistently been delivering growth for most products and services. Proactive promotion by governments has provided pathways to access markets. They have done this by streamlining regulatory requirements to set up manufacturing operations, establishing special trade zones with trans-shipment points, and creating networking groups and associations to aid the 'open for business' platforms, which provide information about low-cost resource inputs such as labour, raw material and land.

Dedicated government departments and the promotion of collaborative programs are contributing to the expansion in the region. The growth of international business into emerging markets is often stalled by intermediaries that are not as effective as they could be, underdeveloped logistics and distribution providers, and non-existent or unskilled market research firms that are incapable of providing timely market information. Governments know the benefits to be gained by developing their systems, processes and people in this area. Therefore, they open dialogues with international businesses and look for joint-development strategies, sometimes implementing novel methods.

SPOTLIGHT 13.1

International business meetings

Preparing for your first international business meeting requires attention to detail. The planning process is just the same as for home-market meetings. Customise your preparation and employ the use of a briefing document and include the aims and purpose of the meeting. The document should contain who you will be meeting, their title, role in the organisation and where they are based. List the key pieces of information that will help inform you about this firm and the context of the discussion. Pre-meeting preparation should include:

- *Research*: undertake a study to obtain company and relevant personnel information.
- *Time*: allow plenty of time in case of delays; arrive early and stay a little later.
- *Plan the conversation*: focus on the higher purpose of the meeting in early emails and again in the first stages of the meeting.

- *Be professional*: formality shows professionalism and courtesy.
- *Start the meeting with small talk*: open the discussion with general conversation; know your counterpart's country, as well as their customs, history and current popular cultural figures.
- *Formal documents*: prepare a 'memorandum of understanding' (MOU). Often in Asian countries, especially with government institutions, this document is required before formally working with foreign entities.
- *Humour*: is culturally specific, therefore, be aware of differences between cultures. Attempting to be humorous during business meetings is not advised.
- *Flexibility*: in Asia, businesspeople are extremely comfortable with constant interruptions and dispensing with agendas in service of important relationships. Be mindful that other cultures have diverse ways of working and flexibility is required during meetings.

Be prepared for meetings by developing the brief, undertaking the pre-meeting planning and address each meeting separately.

QUESTIONS

SPOTLIGHT QUESTIONS

1. Describe the tasks that should be undertaken before an international business meeting.
2. Describe the issues that need to be considered on the day of the meeting.

Holistic framework to screen new markets

DEGREE OF OPENNESS
the degree to which imports and exports take place in a country and affect the size and growth of a national economy. Sometimes known as economic openness.

By tailoring market entry strategies to each different market, an international business can take advantage of a country's opportunities. In the first instance, an MNE's examination of a country by studying the elements of governance and social systems, degree of openness, the market for the product or service, and labour and finance markets will provide the company with valuable information to adapt its business models to the market. After capturing the new market data, the company can take a comparative analysis of the information against existing operational models to evaluate the new market opportunity and identify any additional costs that may be incurred in its entry. Some market entry studies have over 100 questions to probe and examine the potential new market. The following is a proposed list of questions for five key subgroups. The example questions have been adapted from a classic article called 'Strategies that fit emerging markets' written by Khanna, Palepu and Sinha and published by *Harvard Business Review* (2005).

The chapters in this textbook provide a foundation to holistically review market entry opportunities. Using this knowledge, international business managers can seek a clear understanding of new markets by asking the following questions in the following five areas.

Governance and social systems:

- To whom are the politicians accountable?
- Do elections take place regularly?
- Are the roles of the legislative executive and judiciary (the courts) clearly defined?
- Does the government go beyond their power to regulate business and does it interfere with the running of organisations?
- What are government office holders' incentives and career trajectories? What level of education have they attained or are required to hold?
- Are the officers of the courts independent? Do the courts adjudicate disputes and enforce international and local business contracts in a timely manner?

Degree of openness:

- Is the country's government, businesses and people receptive to foreign trade and investment?
- Are there negative sentiments towards any foreign countries?
- Do the people trust brands, products and businesses from other parts of the world?
- What restrictions does the government place on foreign products or investment? What is the purpose of the restrictions?
- Can international businesses make greenfield and brownfield investments? Can a foreign business acquire local companies or only by JVs?
- Does the country allow the presence of foreign intermediaries to develop market understanding; for example, market research, advertising and media, banking and finance, venture capital, auditing and management consulting companies?
- How complex are the government procedures for launching a wholly foreign-owned business?
- Are there restrictions on portfolio investments or on dividend repatriation by international businesses?
- Does the market drive exchange rates or does the government control them?
- What would be the impact of tariffs and quarantine protocols on international products and raw material imports?
- Can an international business set up its operations anywhere in the country?
- Has the country signed an FTA with the home country for the international business? Or any other countries?
- Does the government allow foreign executives to enter and leave the country freely?
- Is it challenging to organise work permits for managers and technical employees?

Product markets:

- Can international businesses easily obtain reliable data on customer and consumer preferences and purchase behaviours?
- Are there any cultural barriers to undertaking market research?
- Can consumers easily obtain unbiased information on the quality of goods and services they are seeking to buy?
- Is access to raw materials and other inputs of decent quality readily available?
- Can contracts with suppliers be legally enforced?
- How well-developed are the distribution and logistics services in the country?
- Is modern retailing established? What is the national coverage for retailing?
- What types of distribution channels are operating – direct to consumer, ecommerce platforms, bricks-and-mortar discount retail channels?
- Has a formal finance and trading structure been established between international businesses and local retailers?
- Do consumers use credit cards or online payment mechanisms?
- What mechanisms exist for consumers to make claims against poor or false products?
- How do companies deliver after sales services in the business-to-business (B2B) channel and the business-to-consumer (B2C) channel?
- What are the product related environment and safety regulations in place? How do authorities enforce these?

ECOMMERCE
national and international commercial transactions conducted electronically using the internet.

BUSINESS-TO-BUSINESS (B2B)
represents the trade conducted between businesses to other businesses.

BUSINESS-TO-CONSUMER (B2C)
represents the trade conducted between businesses and consumers.

Labour markets

- How well developed is the country's education infrastructure – its tertiary, technical and management education?
- What is the quality of elementary and secondary schooling systems?
- Do people study in English or a mainly a local language?
- Is data available to review the country's educational institutions?
- Can employees move easily from one company to another and from one geographical region to another?
- What are the major post-recruitment training needs of the people that could be hired by the firm?
- Is pay for performance a standard or is there another system in place?
- Are employment contracts enforceable?
- Can the firm stop employees taking or stealing trade secrets and intellectual property?
- Does the local culture accept foreign managers?
- Is there a different employment structure when a local firm and international business are operating a JV?
- How are the rights of workers protected?
- Do the laws regulate how a firm may restructure, downsize or shutdown?

Financial markets

- How effective are the country's banks and insurance companies at collecting savings and directing them into investments?
- Are financial institutions managed well? Are their decision-making processes transparent and open for review?

- Can businesses raise substantial amounts of equity capital in the stock market?
- Does a venture capital industry exist?
- How reliable are sources of information on company performance?
- Do independent financial analysts and rating agencies offer unbiased information on companies?
- Do corporate governance standards exist?
- Are corporate boards independent and empowered?
- Are regulators effective at monitoring the banking sector and stock market?
- How well do the courts deal with fraud?
- Do laws permit companies to engage in hostile takeovers?
- Is there a structured and orderly bankruptcy process?

The responses to these questions are the foundational knowledge for understanding the potential market and can be used by the MNE to align the market's opportunities to its own operating model. It is generally accepted that if an international business has to move too far from its existing business propositions it may lose its advantages from global scale and branding (Khanna, Palepu & Sinha 2005).

Ongoing rise of ecommerce platforms

In the Asia–Pacific region, ecommerce is expanding and escalating at an unprecedented rate (AT Kearney 2015). Four chief elements are driving its growth. First, the region has large populations and markets that are mostly untapped. Second, advancements in technology have provided fast internet speeds, and improvements in service and communication platforms are pushing ecommerce development. Third, in many markets, ecommerce spending, mobile phone uptake and internet usage rates continue to climb. Finally, the region is now the global centre for manufacturing and distribution, which has propelled the expansion of ecommerce in the B2C and B2B channels (AT Kearney 2015; Thirwell 2018). The region is set to become the largest digital retail market in the world, offering opportunities for local and global online retailers. Retailers such as TMall Global (China), Snapdeal (India), Coupang (South Korea) and Lazada (Indonesia, Malaysia, Singapore, the Philippines, Thailand and Vietnam) are leading the market.

TMALL GLOBAL

Formerly a spin off from Taobao, this online market is owned by the Alibaba Group, which has substantial market power in mainland China (TMall Global 2018). TMall Global was originally set up to provide access for Chinese consumers to purchase Western brands. The online retailer's close association with Alibaba means an important level of consumer trust and distribution to all Chinese cities across the country. The sales platform is integrated, and this means suppliers ship to dedicated warehouses and the internal supply chain does the rest. Leading global brands such as Disney, Zara and Burberry trade on this B2C site. TMall Global's main characteristics are:

- over 20 countries have an online presence in the platform
- it offers bonded warehousing and storage services for international businesses
- it has sales analytics and reporting which are provided daily.

SNAPDEAL

Snapdeal commenced in 2010 and is now one of India's largest online marketplaces (Snapdeal 2017). The platform is backed by eBay, and has over 40 000 online buyers and over 300 000 sellers. The company has developed through strategic purchases of competitor online businesses, and by promoting its value to sellers through its geographical reach and accessibility to Indian consumers. The company promises consumers the best priced deal on branded products, and provides trading terms that are friendly to both buyer and seller. Snapdeal's main characteristics are:

- it delivers to over 5000 cities in India
- it trains and supports sellers by offering help with visual merchandising and marketing free of charge
- it aims to have a target market of 20 million daily visitors by 2020.

COUPANG

Coupang is the largest online and ecommerce website in South Korea and the seventh largest retail ecommerce market globally (Coupang 2018). In 2010, the company started from humble beginnings as a daily deals website. Coupang is believed to be one of the fastest growing online retailers with over US$2 billion in sales in 2017. It is estimated that about two out of five South Korean shoppers are using the platform. It is interesting to note that Coupang has succeeded in in the South Korean market when others, like Amazon, have tried and failed. Coupang's strategy appears to be connecting with its local consumers so it can meet their tastes and needs. The business has invested in mobile optimisation and same-day delivery as value propositions for the brand. Coupang's main characteristics are:

- the main traffic and revenue is derived from mobile technology placed orders
- its bespoke logistics and delivery systems, RocketPay, to ensure a same-day delivery service
- its discounted pricing is a prominent feature on the site.

LAZADA GROUP

Lazada is the largest ecommerce site in South-East Asia (Lazada Group 2017). International businesses that want to connect with consumers in Singapore, Indonesia, Malaysia, the Philippines, Thailand and Vietnam market their products on Lazada. The platform is easy to use and provides exposure to over 50 million visitors a month. The online site gives customising options for sellers to build their own online shopfront. The company also offers fulfilment services, making the supply-and-purchase process easy to manage. They have an extensive offering from consumer electronics to fashion and household items. Lazada's main characteristics are:

- its service reaches over 550 million customers across six South-East Asian countries
- it has an investment of US$500 million in the business by Alibaba
- there are no monthly or listing fees for sellers.

The online retail marketplace in Asia will continue to grow. By 2020, half of all Chinese online shoppers, or approximately a quarter of the population, will have purchased an item from a cross-border ecommerce platform (AT Kearney 2015; Thirwell 2018).

In the Asia–Pacific region, technology continues to develop and push the transformation between the interaction of businesses and customers (NAB 2017). The space is increasing between businesses that deliver superior service and those who do not. The customer expectation of timely payment and delivery of goods is growing. Conventionally, the fastest and simplest way to shop was via traditional bricks-and-mortar retail stores. However, shopping behaviours compelled by technology, mobile-focused consumers, social media, the latest business prototypes and international information has profoundly changed present-day consumer beliefs.

A South Korean government initiative recently converted old truck depots and delivery complexes into high-tech centres (JLL Real Views 2017). These centres are known as eLogis Towns; they already have well-established transport structures and provide an entry to regional cities, including Seoul. Reports argue that eLogis Town could reduce delivery times and further drive growth in the online sales channels in South Korea.

While ecommerce platforms continue to thrive, there are still several challenges facing the channel, particularly for emerging markets. These are listed below.

- Brands entering into the region's highly fragmented online markets need to recognise different languages, religions and shopping cultures.
- Traditional business and management styles are slowing down technological advancements in ecommerce.
- Varying degrees of infrastructure and technological acceptance exist.
- Current business technologies are generally used for internal purposes only, and they are not yet fully understood or planned for external use.
- The majority of small- and medium-sized businesses are lagging international competition due to insufficient technology, innovation diffusion, awareness and education.
- Many emerging markets operate in a 'cash culture'.
- Suspicion exists around online payment security, especially among the older demographic.

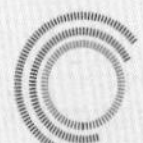

SPOTLIGHT 13.2

Ecommerce mania: queue … Beardbrand

Beardbrand, created by Eric Bandholz, was founded in 2012. The brand started with YouTube videos and progressed into a phenomenally successful ecommerce business. The founder identified a gap in the market, and created content online about beard care, male grooming and beard culture. In the next phase, the purpose of the brand was identified in its mission statement: To foster confidence through grooming. From this point, the business only developed products that were directly aligned to its purpose. On Beardbrand's website, the focus is directed to 'beardsmen' to encourage them to feel proud of their beards and take pride in their appearance. This term was coined by the owner and refers to men with facial hair.

Ecommerce businesses must understand how consumers value their product. What is the brand proposition? Having a real mission behind your product that connects consumers with your brand will establish and maintain an ongoing relationship.

Source: Beardbrand 2018

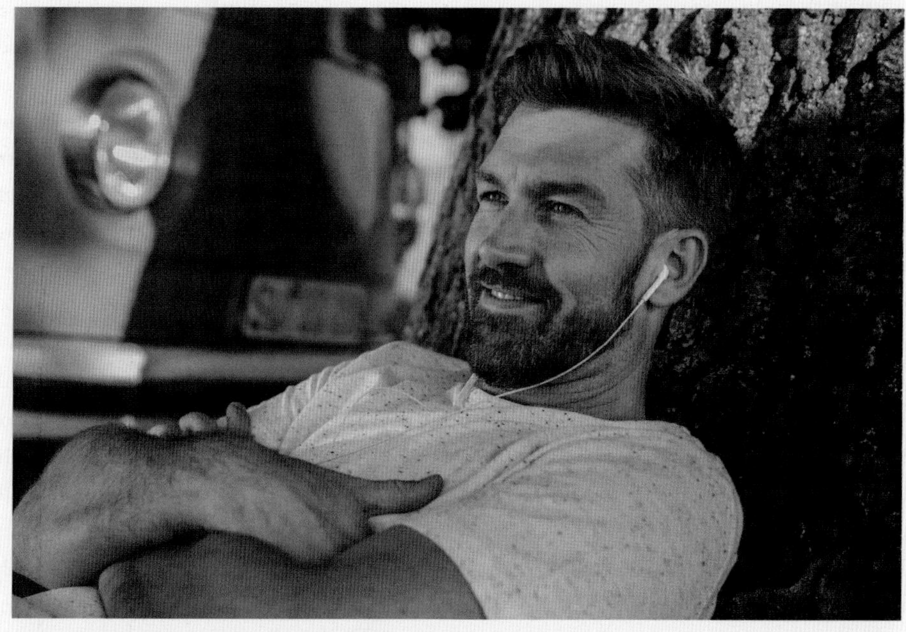

QUESTIONS

SPOTLIGHT QUESTIONS

1. What contributes to the success of ecommerce innovation?
2. What was the second phase of the ecommerce development for Beardbrand?

Nonetheless, despite this backdrop of challenges, the Asia–Pacific region still represents significant opportunities for companies within and outside the region to invest in and further develop ecommerce capabilities. Foreign distributors fear their services will become obsolete within the global market. However, despite the sales function being performed online, promotion and delivery services continue to stay offline, and local distribution partners will continue to play a role in this area.

The post-1990s generations are emerging as a robust instrument of consumption for online sales, against contemporary trends in Asian consumer purchasing. For example, evidence that Chinese consumers are confident online shoppers is in the commercially created event 'Singles Day', held on 11 November each year. This day has moved from being a day dedicated to lonesome single people to the largest ecommerce day in the Chinese calendar. In 2017, Singles Day amassed over 1 billion transactions per hour and was hailed to be larger than the combined marketing promotions of Black Friday and Cyber Monday in the US (Baan, Luan, Poh and Zipser 2017). Singles Day outcomes reinforce the notion that Chinese consumers are now earning higher levels of incomes, and are purchasing a broader range of premium-priced and higher quality products.

Research undertaken in 2017 on 10 000 Chinese consumers aged between 18 and 65 across 44 cities and seven rural towns, revealed consumers' first-hand, attitudes, behaviours and trends towards purchasing (Baan, Luan, Poh and Zipser 2017). Chinese consumers are in-the-moment shoppers, and not necessarily mindful of possible adverse future events. The rising cost of healthcare, and the cost and burden of caring for elderly family members are of concern, as is the rising cost of real estate, especially in tier one cities. However, Chinese consumer confidence is still optimistic and spending on discretionary items continues to rise. Consumers continue to be health conscious and seek healthy alternatives to lifestyle choices, including diet, exercise, and their living environment. The results of this research reveal over 65 per cent of respondents are seeking ways to lead a healthier lifestyle. Chinese consumers define health differently and analysis reveals five groups: those interested in back to basics, exercise enthusiasts, balance seekers, driven workaholics and those that are indifferent. The purpose of understanding the detail of these consumers is to provide international businesses with target market knowledge to offer the right products and services, and to craft appropriate and thoughtful messaging through the ecommerce platforms.

MULTIPLE-CHOICE QUESTION

Regional security, a multifaceted challenge

Observations of the key international security threats facing the Asia–Pacific region differ widely on a subregional level, depending on whether the focus is about the northern or southern areas of the Pacific (Reilly 2002). In North Asia, the security concerns are related to 'power politics', specifically the rivalry between China and the US. Dialogues and analyst reports tend to focus on the problems that surround the Korean Peninsula, the Taiwan Strait and South China Sea debates. Conversely, when the discussions turn to the southern regions of the Pacific, especially in South-East Asia and the South Pacific, the tone of the conversation alters noticeably. It is not the threat of war between nations but the increasing number of intra-state conflicts (civil wars, communal violence and secessionist activities) threating political stability and national security in many countries. This section examines the external and internal security challenges in the Asia–Pacific region, including threats to sovereignty and to nation states, political interactions, environmental concerns and energy resources, and the implications of these for international business in this area.

NATION STATE
a sovereign state of which most of the population are united by factors that define a nation, such as language or common background.

Threats to sovereignty and nation states

The central issue in the region is the weakness of many national structures in the face of resurgent regional, religious and indigenous identities (Reilly 2002). The escalation of internal conflicts is partly due to the disconnect often created when traditional societies confront emerging modern state structures. Internal conflicts are becoming difficult to resolve using orthodox mediation methods.

The concept of a 'strong state' is highly valued in most Asia–Pacific nations (Reilly 2002). Countries such as Cambodia and Thailand have long histories and claim to be nation states. Some South-East Asian and South Pacific economies are artificial formations from the twentieth century in the post-colonial era, rather than nation states. For instance, Indonesia is the amalgamation of sultanates and states created by Dutch colonialism. Burma, now known as Myanmar, was established from territorial manifestations. Malaysia was formed from the peninsular and eastern territories as a product of British colonialism (Reilly 2002). In Papua New Guinea and other Melanesian nations, the notion of a state is even more simulated. In this setting, a number of small, stateless traditional societies were combined, for reasons of international 'statehood', into fragile and disadvantaged modern states, some of which lack the capacity to deliver basic national responsibilities such as education, healthcare and housing (Reilly 2002). This makes these economies prone to developing safe haven opportunities for international businesses that may otherwise be rejected in developed economies.

In 1991, the Cold War came to an end, and global and regional security was redefined. The characterisation of global security threats fundamentally changed to transcend individual countries and military threats to include climate change, mass involuntary migration and global crimes (Stothart 2014). The notion of security speaks to the economic, social and political needs of individuals and nations. This concept of security acknowledges the links between environmental degradation, population growth, ethnic or religious conflicts, human rights violations, income inequalities, gender issues and migration.

The geopolitical region of the Asia–Pacific embodies a varied range of people, cultures, religions, languages, histories, and political structures, and is now host to a plethora of international businesses. Today's interactions among nations and international businesses are conducted within a context of former hostilities and competition (US Dept. of Defence 2018). The Asia–Pacific region has experienced a reasonable degree of political stability since the end of the Vietnam War in 1975. However, conflicts continue to exist between and within some nations and these have led to concerns that regional security problems will escalate.

Nations in the Asia–Pacific region have tended to think of security in far-reaching terms (Stothart 2014). There are three possible conflicts in particular in the region that could impact international business operations: the ongoing hostilities between North and South Korea, with involvement from the US; the historical issues between mainland China and Taiwan; and the disagreement among six nations over the ownership of the Spratly Islands in the South China Sea. These specific areas of political conflict are the largest threats to the region and represent destabilising factors for international business advancements.

The Korean Peninsula

The involvement of the US in the Asia–Pacific is based in the ashes of Hiroshima and Nagasaki, and its leadership as the first nation with atomic power. From this point in time, nuclear weapons have defined geopolitics in the Asia–Pacific region. The Korean Peninsula has a strong hold in nuclear technology, which is set to the shift the power balance in the region. The 2018 North Korea–United States Summit between the US President, Donald Trump, and the North Korean leader, Kim Jong-un, delivered a cautious outcome. Predictions have been made that the unravelling of North Korea's nuclear capability may well be the trigger that removes the need for the US to take the strategic leadership position in Asia.

The next questions to be answered concern the future roles of the US and China. In the Cold War period, this question was easily answered for the US as it was committed to confronting and defeating communism globally. This was the aim behind the US development of a network of alliances, business engagements and military bases in the Asia–Pacific region (Ravenhill 2013). However, after European communism collapsed in early 1989, the US found a new strategic purpose in the wake of the terrorist attacks on 11 September 2001. While the battle against fundamentalist terrorism was not the overarching reason behind US regional agreements in the Asia–Pacific, these agreements continue to provide the US with strategic advantages. In China, the US now has a competitor in Asia. By 2030, China's economy could be valued at US$42.4 trillion when compared to US$24 trillion for the US economy. China has not signalled an intention to have a military standing in the region (Lantis 2015; Ravenhill 2013). The Chinese President, Xi Jinping, has clearly voiced that his nation aims to be a global model of governance and development to rival the US and Europe. The US needs to determine if it wants to maintain its leadership position in the Asia–Pacific region and how much it is prepared to do to defend the position.

It is interesting to consider these geopolitical events from the view point of international business expansion and trading arrangements. With the US considering its leadership position in Asia, the security and risk position for international businesses seems unclear. From an outside position looking at the evidence, China presents no direct threat to US interests or societal values. The challenge is from an economic leadership viewpoint. Therefore, considering the next stages in the Asia–Pacific future, North Korea is too small to be a core security concern, and China is too large and too significant an economic trading partner for the US. MNEs wanting to gain a foothold in the region will need to monitor and evaluate geopolitical behaviours and actions.

China and Taiwan

There is still concern regarding the conflict between China and Taiwan. From 1995 to 1996, during the Taiwan Strait Crisis, China undertook a series of missile tests in the waters of the Taiwan Strait. The first missiles, fired in late 1995, were reportedly sent as a strong signal to Taiwan under the leadership of Lee Teng Hui. The second set of missiles was fired in early 1996, with the aim of influencing the Taiwanese people in the lead up to the 1996 presidential election. While the anxiety of the time has since reduced, relations between China and Taiwan are still tense. Expectations as to what actions China may be willing to take are unknown. It is predicted low-level military exercises against Taiwan by China will continue. Consequently, trading constraints relating to Taiwanese firms and JV business partners seeking to expand into China and across the region, will continue to face obstacles over the longer term. Taiwan will continue to be a source of international business and trading challenges.

The South China Sea

The third source of conflict in the Asia–Pacific region, which may influence international business operations, has received a considerable amount of attention. The focus is the South China Sea, particularly the Spratly Islands. Six national governments, Brunei, Malaysia, China, the Philippines, Taiwan and Vietnam have all made claims on all or parts of the region (Lantis 2015). The region and the islands are considered important for security reasons relating to shipping, aquaculture, and hydrocarbons (petroleum and natural gas). Hydrocarbons are an important source of energy security for these economies.

The intense competition in this region has led to several occupations in the islands and low-level military confrontations. Forecasters argue this situation is likely to become heated and is predicted not to be resolved quickly. Other than the vested interest in hydrocarbons, the region is the major shipping channel that connects the Pacific Ocean with the Indian Ocean. The control of the Spratly Islands by one nation would see a significant shift in the balance of power in the region. It is unknown to what extent this control issue would generate challenges for international businesses operating along this trading route.

Political interactions

Many countries in the Asia–Pacific region are undergoing significant political, economic and social change, transitioning from traditional cultures to modern societies with a capitalist emphasis, and from an authoritarian rule to a more democratic political structure (Lantis 2015).

This process by its very nature creates conflicts. While some researchers have argued that traditional societies will willingly embrace modern values, this has not always been the case (Lantis 2015;

Ravenhill 2013). In fact, the strengthening of cultural identities, languages and religious beliefs has been evidenced instead. In political sectors, different ethnicities have demonstrated they are a powerful means of marshalling populations to support a common cause. This has been seen when competing for or protecting natural resources in a country. The challenge with modernisation is that it is not a panacea for peace. It is true that, in the long term, large societies with democratisation will have lower levels of conflict, but countries undergoing the process of democratisation will experience higher levels of internal conflict in the earlier stages of the process. One of the challenges for individual groups is the loss of self-determination and the sense that independence has been taken away. Historically several ethnic minorities have experienced this situation and felt the need to take up arms, as in the case of Bougainvilleans in Papua New Guinea, the Moros in the Philippines and the Kashmiris in India.

In the Asia–Pacific over the last decade, a few authoritarian governments have shown a documented trend towards democracy and good governance as identified by ASEAN, including Thailand, the Philippines and Indonesia. This change provides altered prospects for international businesses seeking to trade, form networks and establish joint ventures within the region.

Biodiversity and the environment

The Asia–Pacific region is acknowledged as a globally significant biodiverse area that is under threat (Hughes 2017). The area is unique and ecologically complex, and home to the highest diversity of mammals, birds and amphibians. On the other hand, the region is also the largest and fastest growing trading region internationally. Has the desire for trade over taken the need to protect our environment? The region has been frequently overlooked and international discussions have mainly featured trade and deforestation issues. Other issues infrequently mentioned encompass hunting and trade, mining, reservoir construction, fire, pollution, disease, species endangerment and climate change. These issues are not simple but rather need to be considered in the context of international business and trading operations. Organisations and societies must be mindful of environmental impacts and consider them in international business planning.

Ecosystems and plant or animal species are highly vulnerable to ecological threats. Many environments such as forests, mangroves and rivers are likely to suffer degradation due to the impact of business development and the growth in demand for palm oil, rubber, timber, cement and development of dams. Protected areas are being reduced in size, and are not immune from climate change or the ravages of natural disasters, such as fire, tsunami and earthquakes. Trade is a complicated issue to manage especially in high-value timbers and high-value animals targeted by both legal and illegal activities.

Technologies and platforms now exist to detect and report environmental concerns of all types. It is the dissemination of this information that requires improvement to aid early detection and warning. Increasing levels of policy and legislation are making changes through sanctions, international treaties, protocols and agreements, to ensure that protection and enforcement is on the agenda for government and international business. The projection for much of the Asia–Pacific region's biodiversity is poor, and sustainable mandates are needed to share information and develop best practice (Hughes 2017). The monitoring of plant and animal trade will continue to improve with government intervention and international business support through better licensing, which will prevent the spread of disease and protect endangered species.

BIODIVERSITY the variety of living things such as plants, animals and micro-organisms on earth or in a particular ecosystem.

SPOTLIGHT 13.3

Regional security: the fight for survival in Kiribati

Kiribati is an island republic in the Central Pacific and home to an estimated 100 000 people. There is only one road on the island and all activities are undertaken using this road. Children travel to school, the sick travel to hospital, food and water is transported, workers, transport mini-buses, private vehicles, motorbikes and taxis all use the one road. Australian aid has supported the ongoing development of infrastructure including road maintenance and upgrades for several decades. However, Kiribati is facing a far greater challenge that cannot be controlled: rising sea levels.

The citizens of this tiny island nation are struggling to manage storm damage and diminishing agricultural land as they cope with rising sea waters threatening to shrink the island. Ultimately, the effects of climate change is likely to displace the people of this island nation long before it submerges.

SPOTLIGHT QUESTIONS

QUESTIONS

1. How could international business in collaboration with international aid agencies assist Kiribati in their plight?
2. What is the main environmental challenge Kiribati is facing?

Energy resources and supply

The risks related to energy supply have been present for developed economies for more than 50 years and are linked to the changes in global foreign policy. The vulnerability of energy supply is solely due to a dependence on a small number of energy sources, where substitution is problematic or impossible, and suppliers and locations are restricted (Cronshaw & Grafton 2013). Historically, the world's largest energy disruption occurred in 1973 during the Yom Kippur War between Egypt, Syria and Israel, and the member countries of the Organization of Petroleum Exporting Countries (OPEC). This disruption resulted in a global economic change that saw increased unemployment, inflation and lower levels of economic growth. Energy supply risks are not exclusively related to petroleum supply and international conflicts. Issues such as 'cascading blackouts' resulting from interruptions to electricity generating networks have disastrous effects. Natural catastrophes, for example, the Great Sendai Earthquake in north-eastern Japan in 2011 and the ensuing aftermath, resulted in a complete closure of the country's nuclear electricity generation capacity.

ORGANIZATION OF PETROLEUM EXPORTING COUNTRIES (OPEC) an organisation coordinating petroleum and oil policies to protect the exporting interests of its 15 member countries.

Many countries in the Asia–Pacific region, in particular Japan and South Korea, depend on energy imports and this makes the region vulnerable when disruption to an energy supply occurs (Cronshaw & Grafton 2013). More recently, evidence reveals a collaboration or reliance on the major energy producing economies to manage this risk. Economies such as China and India have significant levels of coal and oil imports. Further, it is proposed that China will be become the world's largest oil importer by 2020 (International Energy Agency 2012). Energy imports into India could rival and may overtake China by 2025.

With respect to oil supplies in the region, Japan and South Korea have proactively expanded their energy supply sources. Both countries are active in developing energy efficiency measures in areas such as transport, motor vehicle requirements, business manufacturing and infrastructure, and consumer appliances for homes. China is the world's largest consumer of primary energy; the power sector is overwhelmingly coal dependent with a projected dependence increase by two-thirds by 2020 (Cronshaw & Grafton 2013). China's primary focus has been to develop fuel efficiency and alternative mechanisms to reduce its reliance on oil and coal; this focus has included electric motor vehicles, mass transit and railway systems, and innovative street lighting. Significant investment in new developments of gas, hydro and other renewable energy sources has also been a priority in China, with a view to reducing coal consumption for the long term. Australia has developed energy-intensive industries to address its physical distance to markets and to take advantage of local resource endowments. By 2020, Australian is expected to become the global leader in liquefied natural gas (LNG) exports (BREE 2013).

Countries within in the Asia–Pacific region vary greatly in their energy endowments, and in their economic and cultural backgrounds. International businesses need access to a secure, reliable and competitive energy supply that minimalises environmental impact. Current policy formulations are directed at maintaining energy security, and improving societal and environmental reliance and impacts. Examples include the focus on motor vehicle efficiencies through reduced tariffs on hybrid and fully electric vehicles, transport incentives for international firms using transport in cost-effective operations, and the use of low carbon, nuclear and other renewable energy sources in manufacturing and distribution processes. International businesses need an advanced understanding of energy input mechanisms when planning business operations in new markets. Identifying ways to lower energy inputs while maximising economic value is essential for an MNE. Otherwise, logistic, legal and other related challenges will arise in international operations and supply chains.

What will an international business career look like?

Many international businesses want to attract the future workforce to join their companies. Today, businesses require a global community of employees dedicated to the organisation's mission. MNEs that are genuinely putting their consumers and employees first are at the forefront of growth and sustainability. In many Asia–Pacific organisations, the structure is still hierarchical and very authoritarian. Changing organisational culture and management processes is taking time.

Evidence that this change is occurring, however, can be seen in the case of Unilever India. The organisation aligns employment strategies with business strategies. They start by looking at long- and short-term planning to construct a vision of what they think the business will look like in five years' time. Then they identify what considerations will move the business forward, including employees and workforce requirements. This is in the form of a needs analysis and it identifies the quantity of employees necessary and the qualities the roles will require. The analysis is conducted yearly by the organisation and links activities to corporate strategic plans. The human resource team then documents the top 50 'hot jobs' and 'hot people' by size, scale, strategic business risk and future within Unilever India. Hot people are those who, regardless of what role they are performing, deliver value to the organisation. They have an exceptional quality and will progress rapidly through the organisation. Generally, they are identified as future company leaders. The hot jobs are reviewed and analysed to ensure a pipeline has been developed to recruit the right people for the right roles. The Unilever India recruitment strategy and workforce planning fully mirrors the company's business strategy.

The future of work: adapt or be left behind

No matter what the size of the organisation is, the job roles performed by employees will be far different in 2025 than today, and even more so in 2030. This constant change has consequences for international business operations, engaging with consumers and managing enabling technologies. Asia–Pacific companies are reluctant to mechanise to augment job roles and effectiveness. In the service sector, job roles that were largely immune are now at risk because of advances in robotics and high-end engineering. For instance, the Thai restaurant Hajime, located in the capital city of Bangkok, exclusively uses robot waiters to take orders and deliver food to consumers.

Employees must acquire and continually update their technical skills to stay competitive, in addition to working longer hours to deliver their value to the organisation. This business culture sentiment is present in many Asian organisations, with the pervading idea that if an employee is not spending long hours at work (>10 hours) then that individual is not productive and not delivering value. The belief is that by spending more hours at work, an employee can be visible to management and considered to be of value to the organisation. Spending fewer hours in the workplace is perceived as underperforming and lacking in commitment. By contrast, in several international firms, the focus for person's choice of employer continues to be on career advancement, equal opportunity, work–life balance, mentoring and networking. Strategies to allow employees, both men and women, to manage family commitments and careers, provide a strong impetus for many international business workers. This is championed by a few organisations with programs for parental leave, workplace re-entry, equity scholarships or programs, flexible working options and childcare services. Organisations that have dedicated internal or external mentoring or networking programs want to support their employees' transition into leadership positions. This may include taking advantage of role models and linking employees to broader networks. One such program is the international

Athena Network that focuses exclusively on female executives. The network provides a platform for members to share knowledge and experiences across a diverse range of industry sectors; it provides international collaboration opportunities where businesswomen can interact, share information, and develop skills and business contacts. Programs like this enable career and personal advancement through international networking opportunities.

Careers in international business

An international business career offers travel around the world, interaction with global firms and opportunities to contribute to organisational outcomes. It is a career that requires practitioners to engage in complex cross-cultural issues, be part of innovation and advancements in international trade, and to position themselves as truly global professionals. The industries that offer international business opportunities are broad and may include:

- agribusiness
- asset management
- banking and capital markets
- construction and transport
- defence and military
- education
- energy
- entertainment and media
- financial services
- government
- healthcare
- insurance
- mining
- non-profit organisations
- power and utilities.

Many organisations expand strategically and establish a few international satellite offices, which offer a range of positions such as economists and analysists, marketing and business development professionals, human resource and training officers, and operational roles engaged in logistics and distribution. Through their tertiary studies, international business and management students can prepare for a global future.

International business job roles

Studying international business exposes students to a range of disciplines. Most positions in organisations, either in the public or private sector, engage in cross-institutional work in multidisciplinary teams. Having a well-developed understanding of the vast range of the fundamentals in international business sets graduates up and opens more employment opportunities. Examples of job roles and duties are presented below.

International business analyst

International business analysists, also known as consultants in some disciplines, develop new and improved ways to deliver efficiency within and across international business operations. They recommend strategies to a company's management to improve organisational performance by solving issues and taking advantage of opportunities. Graduates work with organisations on assignments across a range of business operations, including finance, market research, market entry and development, and information technology and business strategy. Specifically, international business analysts assist organisations to find solutions to challenges in global markets. The responsibilities for an international business analysist may include:

- designing research to capture and analyse internal data, such as income, expenditure, and employment within and across international divisions
- identifying how to reduce overheads including financial expenditure, staffing levels and input supply costs
- engaging with the internal management in foreign offices to identify the best method and resources required to resolve issues on a global scale
- recommending new systems, practices and business changes to be implemented across company offices
- developing relationship models to ensure that changes and continuous improvement occur effectively.

The largest international business consultancies, such as Deloitte, Ernst & Young, KPMG and PricewaterhouseCoopers, employ a prominent level of international business graduates. The focus of consultants is to deep dive into problems and issues from a range of perspectives, understand the root causes and provide solutions for the organisation. Employees require the ability to build relationships and to engage in continual self-improvement.

Economist

Economists in international businesses analyse the production and movement of resources and products by analysing data, developing models and evaluating economic issues. Specifically, economists in international firms look to global issues, such as supply and demand for specific products, with a view to increase an organisation's profits. Many economists work in the public and private sectors analysing economies, markets, employment, pricing, productivity, wages and environmental data. Responsibilities for an economist may include:

- examining international data, from primary surveys or databases, using statistical analysis, and developing mathematical models to assess organisational performance
- reviewing and forecasting international market trends and changes
- presenting investigations and research findings in the form of reports, tables and graphs
- developing policies and recommending solutions to economic issues.

Economist roles may be found in institutes such as FAOSTAT, the IMF or the WB. The focus of these type of roles is to solve challenges for developed and developing economies, through better understanding of productivity, employment and livelihood data. Given the impact of economists' research, their findings are often published in journal articles, government publications and newspapers.

International marketing manager

International marketing encompasses creative work alongside business strategy that is grounded on facts. Often these roles require attention to detail on the analysis of country data, consumer research and market trends. The working environment involves engagement with creative directors, sales teams, product developers, procurement managers and public relations managers. The overarching aim for international marketing managers is to increase international sales for the organisation. Responsibilities for an international marketing manager may include:

- analysing sales (value and volume) and understanding purchasing behaviours in business and consumer markets
- developing budgets, organising contracts, and implementing marketing plans including advertising and public relations with internal teams or external agencies
- developing and planning multicountry marketing campaigns to reach existing and new markets with either standardised or customised programs.

The key to an international marketing role is having a well-developed understanding of the business' operations and the overarching business objectives. For instance, is the company seeking a truly global brand presence or just seeking markets to trade excess production? Examples of truly global firms with dedicated international business programs include: Amazon, Apple, General Electric, L'Oréal, Louis Vuitton Moët Hennessy (LVMH) and Nestlé. Additionally, government agencies seeking to hire international business graduates to perform international marketing roles include: Austrade (based within the Australian Trade and Investment Commission), and the New Zealand Foreign Affairs and Trade Department.

Human resource manager

Human resource managers recruit and hire employees aligned to the goals and objectives set by their executive teams. They serve as a liaison between the executive managers and the employees. International HR personnel manage workforce diversity, legal requirements, and the training and development of the country teams. They align legal compliance with labour and taxation laws for each country in which the organisation operates. Responsibilities for an international HR manager may include:

- aligning employees with management to support the organisational objectives, staff development and building the corporate culture
- managing staff issues, including disciplinary actions, performance reviews, training, compliance, payroll and outsourcing
- coordinating and directing employee benefit packages in the foreign subsidiaries
- working with the management team on sensitive HR issues in accordance with national and international regulations such as equal opportunity provisions
- supervising international contractors, host-country staff and employees
- overseeing company retention initiatives and working towards a supportive collaborative company culture.

The chief role of the human resource manager is to enhance the organisation's efficiency by identifying ways to retain skilled employees and recruit the organisation's future workforce.

Policy analyst

Policy analysts study multifaceted problems and recommend resolutions for an extensive range of policy issues. They study and examine legal systems, political issues and regulatory requirements with a view to inform public policy. The focus generally is related to international business, trade relations, economics and laws. The typical sectors of employment include healthcare, environment, trade and defence. Responsibilities for a policy analyst may include:

- assessing and evaluating proposed new or existing regulations, legislation or resourcing

- observing and monitoring international events and policy decisions
- developing and modelling statistical methods
- capturing information either from primary research studies or databases
- identifying changes and trends related to international business and government policies.

These types of roles require policy analysts to have well-developed oral skills, strong written communication skills and superior interpersonal skills. Many roles are with government institutions, agencies and MNEs, which require exacting standards of work outputs to deliver presentations to government officials and senior management.

Summary

Learning objective 1: Appreciate the breadth of information needed to assess international business entry into emergent markets.

Many international businesses have not engaged closely with emerging markets in the Asia–Pacific region but the area has consistently delivered market growth for most products and services since the early 2000s. An MNE can take advantage of a country's opportunities by tailoring a market entry strategy to its market. First, collecting information to adapt to the MNE's business model is necessary; this involves studying the country's: governance and social systems, degree of openness, the market for the product or service, and labour and finance markets. After capturing the market information, the MNE can make a comparative analysis and identify shortfalls within existing operational models and the potential additional costs in entering the market.

Learning objective 2: Recognise the growth and development of ecommerce in the Asia–Pacific region.

Ecommerce in the Asia–Pacific region is expanding and escalating at an unparalleled rate. Four chief elements drive this growth: the region has very large populations and markets that are mostly untapped; technological advances are providing faster internet speeds, and there are improvements in service and communication platforms; spending, mobile phone uptake and internet usage rates continue to climb; and the region is now the global centre for manufacturing and distribution, propelling the expansion of ecommerce in B2C and B2B channels. The region is set to become the largest digital retail market in the world; it offers opportunities for local and global online retailers, with TMall Global, Snapdeal, Coupang and Lazada Group leading the market.

Learning objective 3: Explain the multifaceted challenges that the security agenda plays in the Asia–Pacific for international business operations.

The key international security threats facing the Asia–Pacific region differ widely on a subregional level. In North Asia, the security concerns relate to power politics between China and the US. There are also problems that surround the Korean Peninsula, the Taiwan Strait and South China Sea. In the southern region of the Pacific, especially in South-East Asia and the South Pacific, the problem is not the threat of war between countries but the increasing number of intra-state conflicts that threaten the national security and political stability of nations.

Learning objective 4: Appreciate what international business careers may look like in the future, and understand the career prospects and job roles in international business.

Businesses today need a global community of employees loyal to their company's objectives. MNEs that put their consumers and employees first are leading growth and sustainability. The structure of many Asia–Pacific companies is still hierarchical and authoritarian. Future employment depends on changing business culture and matching it to employee goals; work–life balance is now a prominent consideration. Studying international business creates opportunities in many disciplines. Positions can be in the private or public sector and often engage in cross-institutional work in multidisciplinary teams. Having a well-developed understanding of international business fundamentals facilitates greater employment opportunities. Some examples of job roles are international business analyst, economist, international marketing manager, human resource manager and policy analyst.

REVISION QUESTIONS

Revision questions

1. Why is it important for an international business to assess and undertake in-depth market screening prior to entry?
2. Explain the four chief elements that are driving ecommerce growth in the Asia–Pacific region.
3. Describe the different historical developments of nation states in the Asia–Pacific region.
4. What elements are employees seeking in a balanced working environment?
5. What kinds of responsibilities does an international business analyst have?

R&D ACTIVITIES

R&D activities

1. Craft a curriculum vitae (CV) or personal profile document and an application letter presenting yourself to an international business for a graduate position. Research the firm, understand their values and organisational mission, and prepare your documents accordingly. Remember to highlight the value you would bring to the organisation.
2. Global institutions such as the IMF, WTO, OPEC, APEC and WB have a considerable influence on the international trading system. Research and document, using information captured from the institutional websites, the purpose or goal for each institution and how they deliver benefits to international businesses. Conclude your study with a discussion about the latest activities for the institution.
3. What is democracy and how does this help international businesses?
4. Planning for your future international business career requires evaluating your employment environment. Research and analyse an MNE, and prepare a paper or presentation to profile the current employment opportunities there. Select one of the following firms or find an alternative organisation to use for your study.
   - KPMG Australia
   - L'Oréal
   - Louis Vuitton Moët Hennessy
   - WB.

   Provide the answers to the following questions in your paper or presentation.
   a. What attributes is the organisation looking for in a graduate?
   b. How does the organisation show they are training and motivating their employees?
   c. How do they increase their global talent pool? Is it through engaging home- or host-country employees?
   d. Develop a checklist of must-haves for your ideal organisation and explain the purpose to your audience.
   e. Does this organisation meet your brief as a graduate?

References

AT Kearney (2015). Global retail ecommerce keeps on clicking. AT Kearney, 25 June 2018. Retrieved from www.atkearney.com/consumer-goods/article?/a/global-retail-e-commerce-keeps-on-clicking

Baan, W., Luan, L., Poh, F. & Zipser, D. (2017). Double-clicking on the Chinese consumer. McKinsey&Company, November. Retrieved from www.mckinsey.com/featured-insights/china/double-clicking-on-the-chinese-consumer

Beardbrand (2018). Beardbrand website. Retrieved from www.beardbrand.com

Bureau of Resources and Energy Economics (BREE) (2013). Resources and energy quarterly: March 2013. Department of Industry, Innovation and Science. Retrieved from https://industry.gov.au/Office-of-the-Chief-Economist/Publications/Pages/Resources-and-energy-quarterly.aspx#

Coupang (2018). Coupang website. Forward Ventures. L.L.C, 25 June. Retrieved from www.coupang.com

Cronshaw, I. & Grafton, Q. (2013). Reflections on energy security in the Asia Pacific. *Asia & The Pacific Policy Studies*, 1(1), 127–43. doi: 10.1002/app5.4

Hughes, A. (2017). Understanding the drivers of Southeast Asian biodiversity loss. *Ecosphere*, 8(1), e01624. doi: 10.1002/ecs2.1624

International Energy Agency. (2012). *World Energy Outlook, 2012*. IEA, Paris.

JLL Real Views. (2017). Asia Pacific's warehouses adapt to the ecommerce effect. Real Views, 14 November. Retrieved from www.jllrealviews.com/industries/logistics/how-asia-pacifics-warehouses-are-adapting-to-the-e-commerce-effect

Khanna, T., Palepu, K.G. & Sinha, J. (2005). Strategies that fit emerging markets. *Harvard Business Review*, 83, 63–76. Retrieved from http://search.proquest.com.libraryproxy.griffith.edu.au/docview/227815214?accountid=14543

Lantis, J. (2015). *Strategic Cultures and Security Policies in the Asia–Pacific*. London: Routledge.

Lazada Group (2017). Lazada website. Lazada Group, 25 June. Retrieved from www.lazada.com

National Australia Bank (NAB) (2017). The future of retail. National Australia Bank, 20 September. Retrieved from https://business.nab.com.au/the-future-of-retail-2-26386/

Ravenhill, J. (2013). Economics and security in the Asia–Pacific region. *The Pacific Review*, 26(1), 1–15. doi: 10.1080/09512748.2013.755363

Reilly, B. (2002). Internal conflict and regional security in Asia and the Pacific. *Pacifica Review: Peace, Security & Global Change*, 14(1), 7–21. doi: 10.1080/13239100120114345.

Snapdeal (2017). Snapdeal website. Jasper Infotech Private Limited, 25 June. Retrieved from www.snapdeal.com

Stothart, W. (2014). *Nation-States, Separatist Movements and Autonomy Arrangements: Between War and Independence – What Options Does the Nation-State Have?* Centre for Defence and Strategic Studies. Canberra: Commonwealth of Australia.

Thirwell, M. (2018). Ecommerce and Australian business. Austrade, 25 June. Retrieved from www.austrade.gov.au/News/Economic-analysis/e-commerce-and-australian-business

TMall Global (2018). TMall website. Alibaba Group. Retrieved from www.tmall.com

US Department of Defence (2018). Transnational security threats in Asia. Conference report. In *Sub-Regional Perspectives on Transnational Security Threats*. Honolulu, Hawaii, 25 June. Retrieved from https://apcss.org/college/workshops/past-conferences/transnational-security-threats-in-asia/

APPENDIX: IB SKILL BUILDERS

Communicating business outputs

'Well-developed communication skills are essential for this position' is a standard criterion shown in advertised job roles and organisational position description documents. Communication refers to spoken, written and visual communication, and can be individual or in a group or team setting. The context of the communication may be in intercultural, inter-gender, public or corporate, online or in-print, and verbal or non-verbal. The challenge for business professionals is to acquire an understanding of what is considered effective communication skills early in their career and to continuously develop their communication capabilities.

Effective communication in international business settings ensures a message is understood; it contributes greatly to the operational success of an individual and a team. In international business roles, you may be required to write a range of different reports or deliver specific types of presentations to explain research outputs, technical studies or strategic plans.

Developing written and verbal communication skills

Effective communication can influence the success of international business activities. Avoiding communication mistakes and misunderstandings requires practice and personal development. It can be embarrassing to make communication mistakes. To present information that hasn't been fact-checked and later realise your presentation contained an error, leaves the presenter looking careless and unprofessional. Other communication mistakes may have more serious results. Poor communication can upset clients, ruin or tarnish a reputation and may lead to the loss of clients or damaged relationships. Some of the common mistakes made are:

- *not being assertive*. Asking questions, and qualifying the purpose and target audience for a communication is necessary. Assertiveness is about being prepared to ask questions to address your communication needs. Clearly understanding the task will lead to better communication outcomes.
- *not preparing thoroughly*. Poorly prepared reports and presentations can irritate your colleagues and the audience. Over time your value to the firm and reputation can be eroded. To overcome this situation, plan to consider the time needed to complete the task. Leave time to review your work, check the layout, find the appropriate images needed and rehearse the presentation to ensure your timing is on point.
- *not editing your work*. Editing is an area that is often left to last and either completed quickly or not completed at all. Inaccurate grammar, poor spelling or an inappropriate tone of communication can make work look unprofessional. Consider asking a colleague or friend to review your work or present your work to a family member. It is essential to check all the elements in your communication because together they will form a lasting view that the audience has of your work.
- *assuming your communication has been fully understood*. Building in a mechanism that tests your audiences' understanding of the content is essential. Consider time for the audience to reply with some questions or comments. Set up a specific time to review your work and, in the case of presentations, allow a period at the end of the presentation

to discuss your main points. Contemplate using a moderator or facilitator to support a question-and-answer (Q&A) session.

This appendix has two skill builders. They have been prepared to assist you with: the development process for writing a business report; and delivering an international business presentation.

The skill builders includes a framework to plan, prepare, develop and deliver the information you need to communicate. Take care that you understand the desired outcome necessary for the report or presentation.

Further reading

Eunson, B. (2016). *Communicating in the 21st Century*, 4th edn. Milton: Wiley.

Ledden, E. (2017). *The Presentation Book: How to Create it, Shape it and Deliver it!* 2nd edn. London: Pearson.

International business reports

One of the most useful skills you can acquire as a business student is the ability to write professional, corporate-style reports. A business professional who can write good reports, can describe and offer a detailed analysis of a circumstance, and can summarise and provide realistic action-based recommendations to solve a problem. Business reports may be research based, analytical in nature or a combination of both. The audience for a business report is generally directed internally to decision makers, process monitors and staff in an organisation, or externally to regulators, shareholders, stakeholders and clients.

There is a range of reporting formats that you may encounter. These include periodic reports, progress reports, short memorandums or snapshot reports, justification reports, accountability reports, incident or accident accounts, funding proposals, annual reports and research or analytical reports.

Business reports, technical reports, and research or analytical reports all have the same basic structure. You should always check the exact requirements desired by the organisation with your manager or supervisor. Effective business reports:

- are usually longer (1500+ words)
- involve extensive research (including written analysis and discussions that provide an accurate presentation of information)
- present objective judgements
- clearly describe the research method if the output is based on primary research
- are clear, concise and goal directed
- have a structured document with numbered subheadings
- provide a conclusion
- include practical and actionable recommendations.

There are many types of reports but in this section, we will focus on research or analytical business reporting. The main function of this type of report is to give a detailed analysis of a given situation such as entering a new market. The target audience is predominantly for an internal decision maker. Research reports may be as short as 1500 words; they involve technical research and analytical discussions. The structure and format is usually predetermined and can follow an organisational format. In most cases there is a conclusion and set of actionable recommendations required. References to statistical information is required and proof of the research approach may also be necessary.

Structure of a business report

There are generally three main sections to a research report. The content may include the following types of items: *preliminary section* (title page, executive summary, table of contents, list of tables and figures, abbreviations and acronyms, a preface or acknowledgements and a copyright statement supporting the rights of the preparing organisation), *body of the report* (introduction, scope, limitation of analysis, research analysis, discussion, conclusion and recommendations), and the *supplementary material* (references and appendix).

The preliminary section includes all the initial information required before the report discussion commences. Next is the body of the report where the main discussion is shown. The body starts from the introduction and ends after the recommendations. The introduction may cover a background to the topic under investigation, the aims, objectives, purpose and scope of the research. A research methodology section may be required if data was collected from an external source, such as field research or use of a database. In some reports a section highlighting the limitations and delimitations of the analysis is included here too. Finally, any additional information that supports the discussion and is referred to in the body of the report is included as supplementary material in the last section such as a reference list, bibliography or appendix.

TABLE A.1 Report content formats

Preliminary section	• title page • executive summary • copyright statement • table of contents • list of figures • list of tables • abbreviations • acronyms • preface • acknowledgements
Body of the report	• literature review or background to the issue • research methodology (if required) • analysis* • discussion* • conclusion • recommendations
Supplementary material	• references • bibliography • appendix

*in some cases, these two sections maybe combined

Planning your business report

The key to achieving positive outcomes with report writing is to have a plan and develop a checklist. There are three steps to planning and writing your report, with several phases to guide your preparation of the content.

Use the tables in this appendix as a checklist and plan the time you need to complete each step. Depending on the size of the task and the required report, the amount of time necessary will vary. The one element that is known from experience is the 5Ps saying, 'prior planning prevents poor performance'.

Step 1: plan and organise

The first step to preparing your business report is to plan and organise its research, contents and timelines. An effective business report is an accurate presentation of information, with an objective that is clear, concise and goal directed. Before you write, plan, and organise the materials and content you will need to complete the report.

Phase 1: planning

To start your plan, list and formulate the answers to the questions in the following table.

Objectives	Who wants the report? What is required to be presented? What have I been asked to present? Requests may include: • Secondary research studies such as a review of existing knowledge from a database, websites or specific industry sector. • Primary research studies where specific pre-planned research has been undertaken such as surveys, in-depth interviews or focus groups.
Scope and limits	Why do they want it? What needs to be and should be included? (i.e. the content)
Audience	Who will read the report? Who will see the report?
Time line	When do they want it? Is a preliminary summary required or a full report?
Method	How will I complete the task? What information will I use? Where will I collect information from? Will the report be presented in hard or soft copy or both?
Review criteria	Am I aware of the purpose and/or the criteria for the report?

Phase 2: gathering and analysing the information

To help you gather and analyse the information you collect, use the following table to make notes, create your checklists and plan your time.

Gathering	**Primary research** The information may be sourced from field research, if so what was the research design? Describe the steps taken to undertake the field research and present this in the research methods section. **Secondary research** What secondary sources will be needed to identify the information in the report? Consider the credibility of the sources (fact or opinion based? Research reports vs news articles?) Sources may include: industry reports, government papers, academic articles, research reports and websites
Organising	Keep the information organised, referenced and focused to the required elements.
Combining	Prepare summaries, market profiles, concepts and strategies as required and keep the content in separate groups for ease of access.

Analysing	How will the information be interpreted? What concepts and strategies can be used? Prepare charts, tables, figures and summaries in a separate electronic file linked to the data set.
Evidence	Using evidence adds credibility. Ensure the supporting evidence is relevant and timely. Prepare the references properly. Be aware of referencing formats and organisational requirements. Insert tables and graphs in text or the appendix (number, label and cite the references or sources for the information). If images are required ensure permission has been granted for use of the images and appropriate sourcing or acknowledgement has been authorised.

Phase 3: decision making

The following table contains questions that will assist you in your research analysis and help you to make decisions about your findings.

Findings	What do they reveal?
Relevance	Which are most relevant to your report?
Audience	Where do they lead your thinking?
Outcomes	What are your recommendations or future directions that your findings suggest? What do you now understand about the topic concepts? What is your interpretation of the requirements? What do the report findings indicate?

Phase 4: develop and refine your plan

Use the following table to develop and refine your plan, and pull the structure and content of your research material together.

Identify	Identify the section headings, subject topics and issues to be covered.
Decide	Decide on a logical order.
Clarify	Clarify main ideas, link supporting evidence and references.
Compare	Compare the draft with the terms of reference for the report. Check the task criteria.
Consider	What kind of tone is appropriate to use for this style of writing?
Review	Review the criteria or purpose for the report again. Reconfirm that the correct table of contents has been prepared. Have the task objectives been addressed and presented in the report?

Step 2 Structuring, drafting and writing the report

The second step to planning and writing your business report is to structure, draft and write the report's content. The following tables outline what each section of the report contains.

Phase 1: Preliminary section

The outline below provides an overview of what is in the preliminary pages of the report.

Letter of transmittal	Letter of transmittal or internal memorandum (if required)
Title page	This part of the report showcases the report's content. Include a title page and acknowledgements (if required)
Executive summary	Briefly sums up the document and condenses the document. Use the four-key paragraph method to overview your report to the reader (topic, supporting evidence, analysis, conclusion).
Table of contents	This provides a clear structure of the report and shows the logical approach and analysis in the report. Sections must be numbered and match the page numbers in the document.

Phase 2: Body of the report

The contents in the body of the report are shown in this next table.

Introduction	Capture the reader's attention. State the background, aims, scope and any limitations or assumptions in relation to your report.
Analysis and discussion	Subdivide sections as necessary; the use of figures and tables is recommended to enhance the readers understanding of the content
Conclusion	This is a summary of the key points from your discussion. No new information should be introduced in this section.
Recommendations	Describe a clear course of action. Recommendations should be practical, realistic and actionable.

Phase 3: Supplementary material

The supplementary material common to a report is outlined below.

References or Bibliography	All sources that have been referred to in the report must be acknowledged in the report in the references. A bibliography is a selected list of the literature in the subject area that you consulted to prepare your report. Remember to check the referencing style requested for your institution or organisation.
Appendix	Any additional graphical, statistical or other supplementary material that will help the reader to understand your report fully is placed here. Each item should be clearly labelled (e.g. 'Appendix A') and cited in the body of the report.

Step 3 Editing and presenting the report

The third step to planning and writing your business report is to edit the content you have created. The following table provides advice on how to best to hone and present your content.

Phase 1: Editing and polishing the presentation of your report

Revisit	Return to step 1 and review the report plan and the evaluation criteria.
Flow	Make sure your issues are in sequential order. Do they tell a story? Does your information flow?
Check	Supporting evidence and reference style Does your executive summary, introduction, body content, conclusion and recommendations all link together to tell the story? Do the recommendations flow logically from the conclusions? (these may be written in bullet form) Finally, review the criteria for the report against the final report.

A sample international business report

The following is an example to guide your preparation of a report. There are ten sections shown; the supporting content is presented in the margin of each section to guide the preparation of the report.

	LETTER OF TRANSMITTAL
Author's details	Susan Smith Research Manager Griffith Agribusiness Griffith University 170 Kessels Road Nathan QLD 4111
Date	1 April 2018
Details of the person requesting the report	Robyn Black Operations Manager Airline Alliance Consortium Star Alliance 500 Sims Street Brisbane QLD 4000
Opening statement	Dear Ms Black As requested, the Research Unit has prepared a report examining the strategic alliances with the global airline industry. The purpose of this report is to present the findings of the research and provide recommendations for future opportunities.
Closing statement	The findings of the report show that despite the current global challenges it is reasonable to propose that, after reformulating current strategies your organisation can expand its horizons beyond current market share into more lucrative sectors that provide sustainable growth.
	Yours sincerely Susan Smith Research Manager

EXECUTIVE SUMMARY

The purpose of this report is to provide a strategic analysis of the global airlines industry in terms of the prescribed analytical framework and to provide recommendations. The report overviews the global airlines industry and defines the notion of strategic airline alliances as the principal operating environment and succinctly reviews the Star Alliance network as a leading exemplar.

> The ***first*** paragraph is based on the introduction

A literature review was used to gain an understanding of the airlines industry through the structure of strategic airline alliances and to examine key industry characteristics. Porter's Five Forces analysis explores the operating environment to provide an understanding of the industry context. The dynamics of technology, cooperation and chance all play additional roles in shaping the characteristics of the industry. In order to analyse the opportunities that impact on the industry the Value Net framework has been reviewed and applied to industry examples.

> The ***second*** paragraph comes from the body. It is a summary of the key findings or situational analysis

The report reveals that competition within the airline industry stems from the drive to gain a greater advantage over competitors by offering consumers superior value or by providing increased benefits and services in order to ultimately deliver economic profitability for the airline and its shareholders.

> The ***third*** paragraph is a summary of the conclusions

Five key action recommendations illustrate how the airlines industry and major alliances should aim to sustain and advance its competitive position by changing to a customer-centric approach, which will be necessary to meet the challenges of the twenty-first century. In summary, these are:

- creating a basic philosophy platform focusing on customers
- moving the business orientation towards relationship building
- updating the product positioning to meet customer needs
- having an organisational structure with high priorities towards customers
- changing to an external organisational focus.

Despite a recent history of financial losses, the industry is currently experiencing an upturn, which is predicted to continue. It is reasonable to propose that, after reformulating its strategies and adjusting its organisational structure, Star Alliance should expand its horizons beyond current market share into more lucrative sectors of growth.

> The ***final*** paragraph outlines the recommendations This can be completed using a bullet point list

i

Preliminary section
Page numbers in Roman numerals

Headings, sub-headings and minor sub- headings should all be numbered sequentially

Heading

Sub-heading

TABLE OF CONTENTS

ii

TABLES AND FIGURES

TABLES

FIGURES

iii

Be sure to **label** (number) each table and figure, and give it a **title** indicating what it represents. Indicate the relevant **page** number

Note that graphs, illustrations (pictures), photographs and diagrams are all considered to be **figure**s

The main body of the report should begin with the introduction

Note how headings and subheadings are numbered sequentially. It also helps to highlight headings with bold font

Generally, leaving at least 3cm margins and 1.5 spacing is helpful.

Remember to reference

1.0 INTRODUCTION

1.1 BACKGROUND

The end of the twentieth century saw the emergence of a movement from well-defined and individual national markets to a single immense market place; this movement is known as globalisation. Positive support for globalisation argues that it provides connectivity, interdependence and integration into the world economy (Collins 2001). The motivating forces behind globalisation in the airline industry provide the catalyst for strategic airline alliances (Agusdinata and de Klein 2002; Ali 2001). Dynamic factors impacting the airline industry have moved companies away from the informal loose cooperation of the past towards formal contractual strategic alliances specifically designed to maximise their competitive position (Agusdinata and de Klein 2002; Gudmundsson, de Boer and Lechner 2002; Boehmer 2003). It has become increasingly evident that the long-term survivability of international airlines with global ambitions will be determined by their affiliation to alliance groups (Agusdinata and de Klein 2002; Delios et al. 2004).

Increased consumer demand for airline travel means strategic alliances represent significant market opportunity for companies to achieve economies of scale and increase their market share because of operating within an alliance (Delios et al. 2004; Gudmundsson, de Boer and Lechner 2002; IATA 2006; Vowles 2000). Therefore, this strategic analysis of the global airline industry is based on alliances which are the standard for the industry. Moreover, the analysis will further highlight the challenges and opportunities facing the industry which may constrain or limit growth while seeking to deliver value to customers, investors and the world economy.

1.2 AIM

The purpose of this report is to provide a strategic analysis of the global airlines industry ('the industry') in terms of the prescribed analytical framework. The report is structured in five key parts. Firstly the report overviews and describes the airline industry in terms of globalization effects and principal operating characteristics. The next section applies Porter's Five Forces to provide an understanding of the industry context and highlights the role of government. The third section reviews key remaining dynamics that impact on the industry. The fourth section examines the aspects of the industry through the Value Net framework. The report concludes with five key recommendations identified for the airlines industry and major alliances should aim to sustain and advance its competitive position.

1

1.3 SCOPE

To deliver a strategic analysis of the global airlines industry through its major operating environment of strategic alliances, utilising the Star Alliance network as an exemplar owing to its dominant position in the industry and its subsequent need to focus on a global solutions for its customers and shareholders.

1.4 ASSUMPTIONS AND DELIMITATIONS

This report highlights the strategies and business platforms employed by strategic airline alliances in a generalised global environment. The analysis is undertaken by reviewing academic journals and texts, websites and other secondary sources. The amount of information was limited and consequently restricted the explanation and analysis contained within this report. Based on the information available the writer has concluded that International Air Transport Association (IATA) is the peak industry body and that Star Alliance is the leading strategic airline alliance at the time of writing this report. The writer assumes that the Porter's Five Forces and the Value Net frameworks are the appropriate models to analyse the global airlines industry and that the available information relating to Star Alliance's achievement of dominance in the industry reflects valid business practices.

Once the introduction is complete, begin your discussion making sure to continue to use appropriate numbered headings and sub-headings

2

Remember to include page numbers

The **conclusion** should be a summary of your findings. It should attempt to provide a response to key questions you posed in the introduction

Remember: **no new information**

5.0 CONCLUSION

From the academic and industry literature reviewed, it is broadly accepted that is better to collaborate than compete in today's dynamic, global business environment. In a highly competitive industry, such as the airline industry, competitive advantage stems from an advantage over competitors gained by offering customers greater value, either by means of lower prices, increased number of destinations or by providing greater benefits and service whilst attempting to improve the carriers' bottom line.

However, strategic alliances are not all plain sailing. Alliances should be entered into when the capabilities and probabilities of the partners are similar, when the power and management expertise are comparable and when the fusion of these elements produces a mutually beneficial synergy.

The range of identified problems, particularly jet fuel expenditure and non-fuel costs, faced by the industry can be better addressed from within the framework of an alliance structure. The network formed by Star Alliance has given members the ability to gain economies of scale and to increase their market share but they must continue to re-evaluate their strategic plans, amend their organisational structure and maintain the trust and confidence of existing customers whilst expanding their customer base.

Future success for the Star Alliance network will depend on the group's ability to better understand and manage factors within the alliance, foresee new opportunities and influence consumer preferences. Superior customer service, optimal flight schedules, quality control and product consistency will continue to afford Star Alliance advantages over its competitors.

8

6.0 RECOMMENDATIONS

The analysis has revealed the industry and major airlines alliances have a product-centric approach to the way business has been conducted over the last years. The recommendation to change to a customer-centric approach is necessary to meet the challenges of the twenty-first century. The following recommendations target a customer-centric approach (framework adapted Delios et al. 2006):

- *Basic philosophy platform*

  All customers of airlines need to be served; interactions commence with all decisions being focused on customer satisfaction and proactively seeking opportunities for competitive advantage.
- *Business orientation*

  Relationship building with all stakeholders to ensure continued loyalty and industry or alliance.
- *Product positioning*

  Market product and service benefits in terms of meeting individual customer needs.
- *Organisational structure*

  Establish organisational structures that reflect a high priority towards customer relationship management.
- *Organisational focus*

  Shift organisational focus from an internal business operation to an external focus on profitability through customer loyalty enhanced by an employee understanding of customer behaviour and the provision of superior service levels.

9

This section **recommends** specific actions that should or could be taken based on your conclusions

This could be completed using a bullet point list

Remember to list all sources you refer to in-text in a **reference list**

Generally reference lists are not numbered or bulleted

Place all sources in **alphabetical order** according to the author's family name

The format for a reference list will depend on the preferred choice of referencing format by the institution

REFERENCES

Agusdinata, B & de Klein, W 2002, 'Dynamics of airline alliances', *Journal of Air Transport Management*, vol. 8, pp. 201–211.

Ali, A 2001 'Globalization: the great transformation', *Advances in Competitiveness Research*, vol. 9, no. 1, pp. 1–10.

Beamish, P 2000, *Asia–Pacific cases in strategic management*, McGraw-Hill, Boston.

Besanko, D, Dranove, D, Shanley, M & Schaefer, S 2003, *Economics of strategy*, Wiley, New York.

Boehmer, J 2006, 'Airlines finally post profits in Q2', *Business Travel News*, vol. 23, no. 14, p. 3.

Brandenburger, A & Nalebuff, B 1995, 'The right game: use game theory to shape strategy', *Harvard Business Review*, July–August, pp. 51–61.

British Airways 2005, Harmondsworth, viewed 2 October 2006, www.britishairways.org.

Collins, J 2001, *Good to great: why some companies make the leap... and other don't*, Random House, London.

Cravens, D, Merrilees, B & Walker, R 2000, *Strategic marketing management*, McGraw Hill, Sydney.

Delios, A, Inkpen, A, Molloy, A, Doga, G & Ross, J 2004, 'Escalation in international strategic alliances', *Management International Review*, vol. 44, no. 4, pp. 457–479.

Gudmundsson, S, de Boer, E & Lechner, C 2002, 'Integrating frequent flyer programs in multilateral airline alliances', *Journal of Air Transport Management*, vol. 8, pp. 409–417.

IATA 2005, 'Economic results and prospects report', viewed 3 October, 2006, www.iata.org.

IATA 2006, 'New financial forecast', September 2006, viewed 3 October, 2006.

International Air Transport Association 2004, 'Montreal', viewed 2 October 2006, www.iata.org.

Porter, M 1990, *The competitive advantage of nations*, MacMillan, London.

Vowles, R 2000, *Global business alliances: theory and practice*, Cambridge University Press, Melbourne.

10

APPENDICES

Appendix A: Global airlines industry – reporting institutions

A list of organisations and national statisticians that participate, prepare and supply statistical information to form global airlines industry reports:

- African Airlines Association
- Air Transport Association of America
- Air Transport Association of Canada
- Airline Association of Southern Africa
- Airports Council International
- Arab Air Carriers Association
- Arab Civil Aviation Commission
- Association of Asia Pacific Airlines
- Association of European Airlines
- Association of South-East Asian Nations
- Association of South Pacific Airlines
- Civil Aviation Authority of China
- European Association of Aerospace Industries
- European Business Aviation Association
- European Regions Airlines Association
- International Air Transport Association
- International Airline Passengers Association
- International Association of Latin American Transport
- Latin American Civil Aviation Commission
- Organization for Economic Co-operation and Development
- Pacific Asia Travel Association
- United States of America, Department of Transportation
- Universal Federation of Travel Agents' Association

Source: www.iata.org

11

All appendices must be labelled
Each should have a separate title

Appendices usually present additional information that supports the body of the report and that the reader may need to see to understand the discussion

Make sure to place each appendix on a separate page

Oral communication

Sharing your business research

At some point in your business career you will be required to share your research in an oral presentation. In the current business climate, you may be required to present via a virtual platform, rather than the traditional communication of face to face. You also need to be culturally aware of your word choice and delivery style.

Business presentations are delivered to inform, persuade motivate or challenge the audience, who are made up of a range of stakeholders that are interested in or have a need for the information. The two core components of a business presentation are the content and the delivery. Effective oral presentations:

- are usually short (10–15 minutes), but sometimes long (1 hour)
- are planned and structured
- gain and maintain the attention of the audience
- are clear and concise
- end with a result or call to action.

Your business presentation should be planned and structured with a full consideration of your audience. All audience members will be thinking, *What's in it for me?* The commonly used acronym is WIIFM. The following example has been prepared to guide the planning phase and you can use it as a checklist.

Planning your oral presentation

Your business presentation should start with the most important message to gain the audience members' attention. You follow this with the relevant facts, details and general information, all of which is linked to the initial, most important message. You conclude the presentation with a summary of key points and something for the audience to take away or do. Always thank your audience and offer the opportunity for your listeners to ask questions.

Step 1: Planning

An effective business presentation is delivered to inform, persuade, motivate or challenge an audience. Before you prepare your presentation, the message needs to be planned and tailored to your audience to ensure they understand the content.

Purpose	Identify the purpose of your presentation.
Key message	What is the most important message of your presentation?
Goal	What do you want to achieve?
Time	How much time have you been given in total? What portion of that time will you use for questions and discussion?
Introduction	Will you introduce yourself? If you are being introduced, provide information for the introduction.
Venue	Is this a face-to-face or virtual presentation? Ensure you know what resources are available and the alternative options.
Who?	Who is your audience?
What?	Identify what the audience may already know and need to know.
Why?	Why should the audience listen to your presentation?

Step 2: Structuring content

Take the purpose, key message, goal and why from the planning stage and use this to guide the structure of your content.

Introduction	Briefly greet your audience (good morning or afternoon) and introduce yourself.
Content	Consider your audience and prioritise the information. Decide what must be included and what you can leave out. Ensure the included content is relevant. Group the content in to topic areas (a maximum of three).
Topics	Ensure the topic areas lead from one to the next. Structure the relevant content under each topic.
Conclusion	Summarise the key points. Clearly state what the audience can take away or needs to do. Thank the audience and provide an opportunity for questions or discussion.

Step 3: Delivering the presentation

Public speaking can be a challenge for some people, however it is easier if you are prepared. There are many resources available to help you develop the visual aids to support your presentation. Know your content well; the key to this is to rehearse the presentation before its delivery.

Manage stress or anxiety	Consider strategies to manage your stress or anxiety towards delivering your presentation. This may include taking deep breaths or stretching before the presentation.
Non-verbal communication	Keep eye contact when delivering a presentation. Always face the audience and avoid turning your back. Be aware of your gestures and ensure your arms or hands do not distract the audience from your message.
Personal presentation	Consider what you are wearing in conjunction with your message and audience. Is casual attire appropriate for the message or your credibility?
Voice	Speak clearly and concisely. Avoid or explain jargon and terminology to ensure the audience has the same understanding. Vary your pitch, speed and tone to match the message you are presenting.
Audiovisual aids	This can include whiteboard, flipchart, visual slides, props, samples and handouts. Use these to your advantage to help get the message across. Audiovisual aids should support your message. Take care the audience is not distracted by them.
Rehearse	Always practice your presentation before the delivery. Practise aloud so you can hear how it sounds. Whenever possible, practise using the technology and resources that will be used for the presentation.

GLOSSARY

absorptive capacity the ability of a firm to recognise, assimilate and apply new information.

acquisition a purchase or transfer of control of one company (a 'target') by another (the 'acquirer'); the acquired company becomes a unit of the buyer.

agent an intermediary that buys and sells products or services for a commission.

arms-length market transactions business transactions in which the buyer and seller act independently and with no interest in the other's benefit.

Asia–Pacific Economic Cooperation (APEC) a forum established in 1989 that aims to secure free and open trade and investment among 21 member countries in the Asia–Pacific.

Association of Southeast Asian Nations (ASEAN) established in 1967 to promote political and economic cooperation. It includes the countries of Brunei, Cambodia, Indonesia, Laos, Malaysia, Myanmar, the Philippines, Singapore, Thailand and Vietnam.

autarky a strategy of economic independence or self-sufficiency.

balance of payments (BOP) the record of all of a country's economic transactions between one country and the rest of the world for a given period.

big emerging markets (BEMs) the emerging economies expected to drive international trade; these include: Argentina, Brazil, China, India, Indonesia, Mexico, Poland, South Africa, South Korea and Turkey.

bilateral treaty an agreement between two countries.

biodiversity the variety of living things such as plants, animals and micro-organisms on earth or in a particular ecosystem.

bonds represent a major form of debt financing, where debt is contracted directly with investors. They are generally only available to entities with strong credit ratings.

business-to-business (B2B) represents the trade conducted between businesses to other businesses.

business-to-consumer (B2C) represents the trade conducted between businesses and consumers.

capital account the record of all international economic transactions relating to the transfers of financial assets, and the acquisition and disposal of non-financial assets.

capital structure also referred to as the debt-equity structure; reflects how the company finances its assets. It shows the proportion of assets financed by debt relative to equity.

centre of excellence a business unit that exemplifies the capabilities recognised by the organisation as a significant source of value creation, with the aim for these capabilities be leveraged and disseminated across the other units of the firm.

channel design the length and width of a distribution channel.

channel length the number of intermediaries between the producer and the consumer.

channel quality the capabilities and expertise of established retailers, and their ability to support and sell the products of domestic and foreign firms.

common market is a free trade agreement that allows mobility of factors of production, including labour, capital and technology.

contract manufacturing an outsourcing arrangement in which a firm contracts with an independent supplier to manufacture its products according to predefined specifications.

corporate culture the ideas, customs, and social behaviours that are learned and shared within a company by employees.

corporate governance the mechanisms by which corporations are managed, directed and controlled to ensure that management is held accountable for its actions.

corporate social responsibility (CSR) the management and operation of a business' activities is done in a manner that meets or exceeds the ethical, legal, business and societal expectations of their stakeholders. CSR refers to good corporate citizenship.

corruption the exercise of power in a dishonest or fraudulent manner for private or business gain.

cost-plus pricing a pricing method in which the full domestic and foreign costs of making the product are allocated to the product's price along with a profit margin.

cross-subsidisation a strategy of supporting a product using profits generated by another product.

cultural intelligence the capability to relate to and work effectively across cultures in other countries.

culture the ideas, customs, and social behaviours that are learned and shared by a group of people or society.

current account an account in the BOP that records all international economic transactions involving the income or payment for the import and export of goods and services.

customer attitudes a composite of a consumer's beliefs and feelings about and behavioural intentions towards a particular product or service.

customer satisfaction a measure of how products or services supplied by a company meet or surpass a consumer's expectations, and can be expressed by the number of repeated consumptions.

customs union a formal agreement among trading countries where trade barriers are removed for members and a common trade policy is agreed with respect to non-members.

debt financing the funds borrowed by a company for specified maturities, repayment structures, interest rates and currency denominations.

degree of openness the degree to which imports and exports take place in a country and affect the size and growth of a national economy. Sometimes known as economic openness.

developed economies nations that have a highly developed and stable economy, advanced technological infrastructure relative to other less industrialised nations and a very high per capita income.

developing economies nations with an underdeveloped industrial base and a low Human Development Index (HDI) relative to other countries.

double-entry bookkeeping the recording of financial transactions in which every transaction has equal and opposite effects on at least two different accounts. This keeps the accounting equation Assets = Liabilities plus owners' equity in balance.

dual pricing the practice of setting prices for the same product or service at a different level in foreign markets versus the domestic market.

early mover the competitive advantages a business obtains by being the first to bring a product or service to a market.

ecommerce national and international commercial transactions conducted electronically using the internet.

economic exposure the changes in expected future cashflows and therefore the present value of the company resulting from unexpected changes in exchange rates. Also called operating exposure and strategic exposure.

economic institutions institutions in society that support economic activity and security through the provision of market facilitating services.

economic union a union among trading countries that has the characteristics of a common market as well as provisions for the harmonisation of monetary policies, taxation and government spending.

emerging economy a country enjoying an above average economic growth rate and experiencing structural change in progressing towards advanced economic development.

emerging market multinationals (EMNEs) multinational enterprises that originate from emerging markets.

equity-based alliance a strategic partnership that involves the use of equity; that is, ownership participation such as joint ventures.

equity financing funds a company raises by issuing capital or ownership rights through ordinary and preference shares.

ethical dilemma a situation that arises when there is a choice to make between two or more options, but all approaches to resolve the problem do not meet ethical standards.

ethics the standards of conduct based on moral principles and values that govern the behaviour of people and businesses in society.

exclusive distribution channel a channel that is difficult for outsiders to access.

expatriate an employee from one country that is appointed to an employment position in another country for an extended period.

expatriate failure the failure of the expatriate employee to adapt to the new country or company of employment.

export and import trading an import is a product or service brought into one country from another. Imports and exports form the foundation for international trade.

export management company a firm that acts as an export agent on behalf of producers in return for a commission.

externalisation the contracting out of a business process or task to an outside provider.

factor mobility the ability to freely move factors of production across borders.

factors of production all inputs in the production process: capital, labour, land and technology.

financial account the record of all international economic transactions relating to direct investments, portfolio investments and other asset investments.

firm specific advantage (FSA) the distinct resource base available to the firm, critical to achieving its success in the marketplace. FSAs usually comprise of propriety advantages, often related to a firm's intangible assets, that enable it to compete against other firms.

fixed exchange rate an exchange rate regime where the value of a currency is set relative to the value of another single currency, a basket of currencies or another measure of value, such as gold at a specified rate. It is often referred to as a pegged exchange rate.

flexible manufacturing systems (FMS) systems that bring together computer-controlled tools and material handling systems, and have a central monitoring and scheduling function.

floating exchange rate an exchange rate regime where the value of a currency naturally responds to the supply and demand for currencies in the foreign exchange market. The current price is set by the foreign exchange market based on supply and demand for a currency compared with other currencies.

focus group research a research method where representatives of a target audience contribute by participating in an unstructured but directed discussion.

foreign currency translation the translation of transactions and reports denominated in foreign currencies into the companies functional currency.

foreign direct investment (FDI) an establishment or the expansion of company operations in a foreign country. Like all investments, it assumes a transfer of capital.

foreign distributor an intermediary that works under contract in a foreign market for an exporter, distributes and takes title to the exporter's products or services in a particular territory, and is often responsible for marketing as well.

foreign exchange all forms of money that are traded internationally.

foreign exchange (FX) market the international marketplace enabling the conversion of one currency into another, foreign trade financing, trading in foreign currency options and contracts, currency swaps and other foreign currency related transactions.

forward-and-back translation the procedure in which a document is first translated from one language to another, then translated back into the original language to confirm reliability and accuracy of the translation.

Fourth Industrial Revolution a range of new technologies that are blending the physical, digital and biological worlds, impacting all disciplines, economies and industries, and stimulating ideas about what it means to be human.

franchising an agreement where one firm gives the right to use its proprietary technology or trademark for a royalty fee to another firm, typically used in service industries and involving longer-term commitments than licensing.

free trade area a geographic area where all barriers to trade among member countries are removed to allow goods to be landed, stored, handled, manufactured or reconfigured, and re-exported with no taxes for member countries. It is a trade bloc that comprises of member countries who have signed a free trade agreement (FTA).

global supply chain the firm's worldwide network of sourcing, production and distribution.

global team a team of managers across countries who work together to achieve a common outcome.

global value chains (GVCs) include all of the people, processes and activities in different parts of the world that each add value to the production of a good or service.

globalisation an awareness and understanding of, and response to, global developments and links. A shift towards a more integrated and interdependent world economy.

globalisation approach a universal marketing mix strategy implemented in all markets.

greenfield investment an entry strategy that involves the establishment of a new operation abroad from scratch.

gross domestic product (GDP) the total monetary value of goods produced and services provided by a country over a one-year period.

hedging a financial instrument used to reduce exposure to currency risk.

high-context culture a culture where behavioural nuances strongly influence communication of information. Non-verbal messaging is considered important in fostering congenial relationships.

home country the domestic market where the headquarters of a firm are located.

host country the foreign market where a firm may invest or set up operations.

human rights basic rights that belong to each person. They are based on dignity, equality and mutual respect regardless of nationality, religion or beliefs.

institutional failure a situation where market facilitating institutions are either absent, or not functioning effectively, raising transaction costs.

intermediary also known as a middleman; an individual or business that facilitate the sales process between the manufacturer and end user.

internal capital market a capital allocation process whereby funds are collected across a company's various divisions and the dispersion decisions are made by a central authority.

internalise to conduct transactions within the confines of a corporation rather than in the open market.

International Financial Reporting Standards (IFRS) a set of accounting standards developed to ensure that transparent and comparable financial reporting is adopted across countries.

international human resource management (IHRM) the management of human resources in an international context, including planning, recruitment, training and performance appraisal.

International Monetary Fund (IMF) an organisation of 189 countries working to develop global monetary cooperation, secure financial stability and facilitate international trade.

international production the activities involved in creating a product or service abroad.

international relations are concerned with the political and economic relations between two or more nations.

international sourcing the purchasing of goods, services or business processes from abroad; also known as international procurement.

intra-corporate financing the funds provided by sources within the company group, such as from parent companies, subsidiaries and associates, which includes financing through equity, debt and credit in the ordinary course of business.

jugaad innovation a process of innovation that emphasises lower costs through the reduction of complexity.

just-in-time (JIT) inventory management that allows an immediate response to specific customer demands and largely eliminates the need to hold inventories.

lean management a long-term oriented approach to running an organisation that supports the concepts of continuous improvement, systematically seeking to achieve small, incremental changes in processes in order to improve efficiency and quality.

liability of foreignness the challenges a foreign firm faces when compared with local firms, which is possibly reflected in its lower survival rate.

licensing an agreement where one firm gives the right to use its proprietary technology or trademark for a royalty fee to another firm.

lobbying a firm-level strategic action aimed at changing policy proposals to benefit firms and/or industries to further their commercial interests.

logistics the process of managing the supply chain.

low-context culture a culture where verbal communication and clarity of spoken words is important.

marginal-cost pricing a pricing method which considers the direct costs of manufacturing and retailing for export as the base or floor below which prices cannot be set.

market-differentiated pricing a pricing method in which prices are determined for each individual market based on consumer demand rather than cost.

market entry timing the decision as to when to enter a market in comparison to competitors.

market failure a situation where free markets fail to allocate resources efficiently. Such failure may prompt government intervention to remedy the perceived malfunction.

market penetration the percentage of target consumers reached at least once in a given period of time.

market positioning efforts to influence buyer perceptions of the positioning in a market of a product or brand relative to a competitor's

offerings. The objective is to define a unique and competitively advantageous position in the mind of the consumer.

market share a measure of company or product sales over a given period, relative to the total sales of the industry or market in which the company operates.

market size the quantifiable value of the potential number of buyers or potential sales volume of a product or service.

mass customisation the capability of providing individually designed products and services to all customers through having a highly flexible and integrated process.

merger a new legal entity that results from the combination of two firms to form a new, 'merged' firm.

multi-domestic approach some or all elements of the marketing mix are tailored to suit local consumer needs and wants for each market entered.

multilateral agreement an agreement between three or more countries.

multinational enterprise (MNE) a company that has facilities and other assets in at least one country other than their home country; typically an MNE has offices and manufacturing in different countries, usually with a centralised head office.

nation state a sovereign state of which most of the population are united by factors that define a nation, such as language or common background.

national culture the set of norms, behaviours, beliefs and customs that exist within the population of a sovereign nation.

nearshoring locating the offshored activity to a country geographically or culturally close to the client country's company.

net errors and omission account the resulting net credit or net debit balance that results when all actual BOP entries are collated and finalised.

no-shoring a trend of replacing value-adding activities performed by humans by automated robotic processes.

non-equity-based alliance a strategic partnership that does not involve the sharing of ownership.

official reserve account the record of foreign currencies and securities held by the government generally in its central bank. It is a subdivision of the capital account. It is used to balance the payments; that is, it will decrease when there is a net deficit and increase when there is a net surplus on the BOP.

offshoring the relocation of a value-adding activity (including production, business processes and tasks) to a different country.

omnibus survey a quantitative research instrument where companies purchase one or more questions and associated responses from a commercial research agency with access to a large-scale target market database.

online intermediary a company that facilitates ecommerce by bringing buyers and sellers together on the internet.

organisational culture the pattern of shared values and beliefs that govern how employees behave within an organisation.

Organization of Petroleum Exporting Countries (OPEC) an organisation coordinating petroleum and oil policies to protect the exporting interests of its 15 member countries.

outsourcing the contracting out of a business process to an independent party. It can involve the sourcing of parts, value-adding activities or an entire product from independent suppliers.

parallel translation the procedure in which multiple interpreters are employed to independently translate the same questionnaire and the results are reviewed for consistency.

performance appraisal the evaluation of an employee's performance based on mutually agreed criteria set at the start of the appraisal period.

poverty the state of being extremely poor and having little or no money, goods or means of support.

predatory pricing the pricing of goods or services at such a low level that other firms cannot compete and are driven from the market.

primary research the collection and analysis of data for a specific research purpose through interviews, focus groups, observations, surveys or experiments.

private sector the part of an economy that is not under state or national control.

protectionist economic policies government policies that restrict trade with the aim of limiting competition faced by domestic industries.

public sector the part of an economy that is controlled by a state or nation.

qualitative research the inductive approaches to building knowledge and meaning, which describe attitudes, opinions, behaviours and motivations of research participants, and provide insights into a research problem.

quality fade a gradual and deliberate reduction in the quality of a good or service with the intention of increasing profit margins.

quantitative research data collected in numerical order to identify statistical significance or trends.

re-shoring bringing the offshore production back to the home country.

real income the income of an individual or country after adjusting for inflation.

Regional Trade Agreements (RTAs) reciprocal preferential trade agreements between two or more countries created for partners to obtain economic benefit, ensure increased market access, improve bargaining strength and promote regional domestic industries.

repatriation the return of expatriates to their home or original country of employment after an extended period of employment in a foreign country.

research design a detailed outline of how a research study will be undertaken, including the set of methods and procedures for the collection of data, and the measurement and analysis of the variables specified in a research problem.

research instrument a measurement tool designed to gather data to answer the research question.

research methodology the process used to collect information and data in a research study.

reverse innovation also known as trickle-up innovation; describes innovations that are first developed and applied in developing economies, and then transferred to more developed economies.

risk premium the return in excess of the risk-free rate of return an investment is expected to yield.

rules of origin (ROO) a specific criterion related to determining where a product is made and is a main feature of contemporary free trade area agreements.

sales representative a contracted intermediary that represents an exporter and sells its goods in a specified territory.

secondary research the collection and analysis of data previously collected for another purpose.

Six Sigma production philosophy that aims to reduce defects, boost productivity, eliminate waste, and cut overall costs.

small- and medium-sized enterprises (SMEs) small and generally independent firms that employee less than a given number of employees (in the case of Australia, this is usually less than 200 employees).

social desirability bias the tendency of a research respondent to answer questions in a manner viewed as more acceptable by peers rather than as reflective of their real feelings.

social marketing the design, implementation, and control of programs created to induce attitudinal and behavioural changes in a target audience to achieve a social goal.

spot rate the exchange rate for the almost immediate purchase or sale of foreign exchange.

stakeholders the individuals or groups that an organisation impacts or that influence the organisation in the management of its business operations.

standard global pricing a pricing strategy based on the average unit cost of fixed-, variable- and export-related costs applied in all markets.

standardisation approach elements of the marketing mix that are the same or have minimal changes for an international market.

strategic alliance a term encompassing a diverse array of voluntary cooperative agreements between two or more organisations.

survey a quantitative research instrument where a relatively large number of people are asked a standard set of questions, posed in the same way each time, to extract specific data from a particular target group.

sustainability the patterns of development that meet the needs of the present without harming the ability of future generations to meet their needs.

tax haven a country that has a low corporate tax rate and low withholding tax rates on passive income.

tier-one cities (China) the big four cities of Beijing, Shanghai, Guangzhou, and Shenzhen.

tier-three cities (China) primarily the open coastal cities, high income cities, and cities experiencing significant economic development, such as Hangzhou and Chongqing.

total quality management (TQM) concentrates on continuous improvement across every level in daily job routines; it emphasises understanding and integrating customer requirements into this high standard.

trade protectionism a form of government policy that limits unfair competition for domestic industries from foreign industries. Countries use a variety of strategies to protect their domestic industries. One way is to impose tariffs that place high levels of tax on imports to create a competitive advantage for domestic products and services.

trading company a firm that engages in the import and export of a variety of commodities, products or services and assumes the international marketing function on behalf of producers, especially those with limited international business experience.

transaction costs the costs associated with exchange of goods or services; they are incurred in overcoming market imperfections.

transfer pricing the practice of pricing products sold, transferred and exchanged between subsidiaries and associates of the same company.

treaty an agreement of achieving international cooperation on matters of trade politics and security.

triangulation a commonly used strategy when multiple methods or sources of data are applied to address the same question.

values judgements about what is important in life, which form standards for behaviour.

whistleblowing when a member of an organisation discloses to an outside party the organisation's illegal, immoral or illegitimate practices.

wholly owned subsidiary a subsidiary entirely owned by the MNE.

working capital the residual amount after deducting current liabilities from current assets.

World Trade Organization (WTO) facilitates the rules of trade and oversees the flow of trade between nations, with the aim of liberalising trade under rules agreed to by member countries for reciprocal benefits.

INDEX